EBONY
RISING

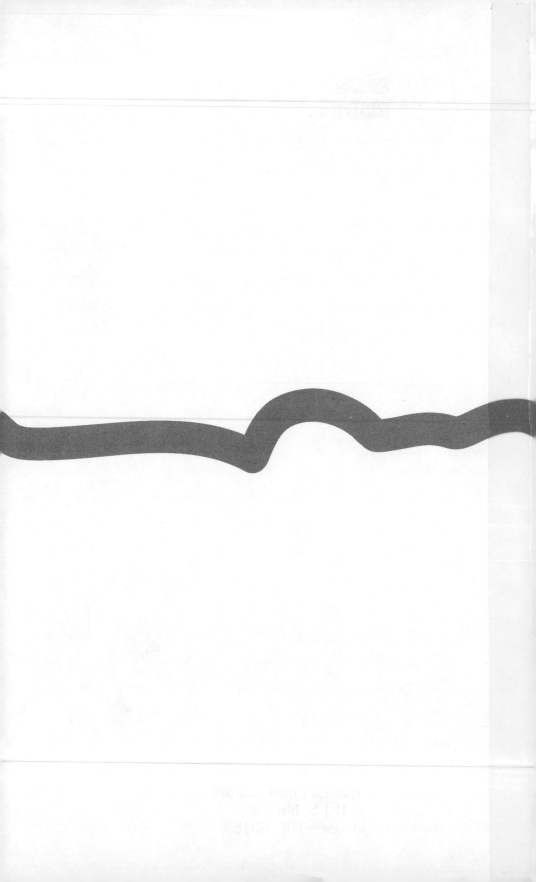

Ebony Rising

SHORT FICTION OF THE GREATER HARLEM RENAISSANCE ERA

Edited by Craig Gable

Indiana University Press
BLOOMINGTON AND INDIANAPOLIS

This book is a publication of

Indiana University Press
601 North Morton Street
Bloomington, IN 47404-3797 USA

http://iupress.indiana.edu

Telephone orders   800-842-6796
Fax orders 812-855-7931
Orders by e-mail   iuporder@indiana.edu

The paper used in this publication meets the minimum requirements
of American National Standard for Information Sciences—Perma-
nence of Paper for Printed Library Materials, ANSI Z39.48-1984.

Manufactured in the United States of America

Library of Congress Cataloging-in-Publication Data

Ebony rising : short fiction of the greater Harlem Renaissance era /
edited by Craig Gable.
      p.   cm.
Includes bibliographical references and index.
ISBN 0-253-34398-4 (alk. paper) — ISBN 0-253-21675-3 (pbk. : alk.
paper)
    1. Short stories, American—African American authors.
    2. American fiction—New York (State)—New York.
    3. American fiction—20th century.
    4. African Americans—Fiction.
    5. Harlem Renaissance.
    I. Gable, Craig, date
PS647.A35E24 2004
813'.010889607307471—dc22   2003015585

1 2 3 4 5 09 08 07 06 05 04

Harlem—one has to like it. And not because it is the "Mecca of the New Negro," rather because it is the "Maker of the New Negro." It is a part of all it has met—Grand Boulevard, Beale Street, St. Antoine Street, Birmingham, Atlanta, Little Rock, London, Paris, and The Islands; social leaders, bums, erudite students, fanatics, rich-man, poor-man, beggar-man, thief. An immense picture in all colors.

—Ira DeAugustine Reid,
"Why I Like Harlem" (1927)

The New Negro is not to me a group of writers centered in Harlem during the second half of the twenties. Most of the writers were not Harlemites; much of the best writing was not about Harlem, which was the show-window, the cashier's till, but no more Negro America than New York is America.

—Sterling A. Brown,
"The New Negro in Literature (1925–1955)"
(1955)

In time I fervently believe that the literature of the United States will be colored to an amazing degree by the exploits of these gallant youngsters, and the way the cards read at present that time is not very far off.

—Eric Walrond,
"The Negro Literati" (1925)

CONTENTS

PREFACE

In the last few decades the Harlem Renaissance has received an unprecedented amount of critical and popular attention. Though its literary legacy languished in relative obscurity from the 1940s up until the mid-1970s, the years that followed witnessed a steady and, of late, rapid growth in the number of Harlem Renaissance literature anthologies populating the shelves of bookstores and libraries. Davis and Peplow's *The New Negro Renaissance* (1975) distinguished itself as the first retrospective collection. The following year came Nathan Irvin Huggins's *Voices from the Harlem Renaissance* (1976). Over a decade later Maureen Honey's *Shadowed Dreams: Women's Poetry of the Harlem Renaissance* (1989) was released. Seemingly intent on making up lost ground from the preceding decades, the 1990s fairly exploded with editorial activity, letting loose with Tony Martin's *African Fundamentalism: A Literary and Cultural Anthology of Garvey's Harlem Renaissance* (1991), Marcy Knopf's *The Sleeper Wakes: Harlem Renaissance Stories by Women* (1993), William L. Andrews's *Classic Fiction of the Harlem Renaissance* (1994), David Levering Lewis's *The Portable Harlem Renaissance Reader* (1994), and Hatch and Hamalian's *Lost Plays of the Harlem Renaissance, 1920–1940* (1996). Soon afterwards Patton and Honey's *Double-Take: A Revisionist Harlem Renaissance Anthology* (2001) welcomed in the new millennium. Additionally, numerous other anthologies include substantial Harlem Renaissance coverage despite not necessarily qualifying as Harlem Renaissance collections per se (e.g., Dianne Johnson-Feelings's *The Best of* The Brownies' Book; Sondra Kathryn Wilson's *The* Opportunity *Reader;* Kathy A. Perkins's *Black Female Playwrights: An Anthology of Plays before 1950*).

That the Harlem Renaissance, an admittedly brief literary period, could generate so much ongoing after-the-fact enthusiasm is not so surprising considering the breadth and depth of literary production from the era and its substantial cast of major and minor contributing talents. Yet despite the several anthologies already produced, an obvious need remains for the creation of comprehensive genre-specific, gender-balanced collections in the areas of poetry, drama, and short fiction. Editors thus far have succeeded in producing anthologies that do one of the following: (1) provide a general overview (Davis and Peplow, Huggins, Lewis, Patton and Honey); (2) focus exclusively on female authorship in one or more genres (Honey, Knopf, Perkins); or (3) sample materials from a given black periodical from the era (Martin, Johnson-Feelings, Wilson). Anthologies falling into these categories serve a genuine purpose in satisfying the needs of readers in a wide range of contexts; however, they do not satisfy the needs of readers wishing to enjoy and/or study a truly broad representative selection of works in a given genre by a balanced number of male and female authors. Indeed, readers wishing to survey a generous sampling of male- *and* female-authored short fiction, for example, are forced to utilize multiple Harlem Renaissance literature anthologies and/or procure copies of individual authors' collections—an obviously inconvenient, time-consuming, and labor-intensive process for those willing and able to see it through.

Ebony Rising: Short Fiction of the Greater Harlem Renaissance Era is the end result of my own dissatisfaction with not having a single comprehensive anthology of Harlem Renaissance short fiction. Two previous collections of fiction already exist: Knopf's *The Sleeper Wakes* (1993) and Andrews's *Classic Fiction of the Harlem Renaissance* (1994). Although Knopf's anthology is a groundbreaking work celebrating women's largely forgotten contributions to Harlem Renaissance short fiction, it contains fewer than thirty stories and is limited by gender. The Andrews anthology, on the other hand, is a mixture of short fiction, full-length novels, and excerpted novels. The work covers only seven authors (five men, two women) and reproduces only eight short stories (three by Zora Neale Hurston), a smaller selection than that which is found in some of the multigenre Harlem Renaissance anthologies. Accordingly, with no truly comprehensive short fiction anthology available, I set out to edit one myself.

In editing this work, I had to determine early on how precisely I would represent the Harlem Renaissance since scholars themselves are often at odds about various aspects of this literary movement. Even the name itself, Harlem Renaissance, has been a subject of much discussion because its self-identification with urban New York is problematic given its suggested favoring of artistic activity at that site over other cities and, more generally, favoring of the urban Northeast over the remainder of the country. Scholars have argued, too, over whether this black arts movement of the 1920s and 1930s (also known as the New Negro Arts Movement and the New Negro Renaissance) actually constitutes a *renaissance*. It is neither my intent nor my goal to resolve such issues herein, but it is accurate to say that I have been mindful of these and other issues during the story selection process.

One key decision for me involved establishing a timeline for the Harlem Renaissance. When did it begin, and when did it end? Early conservative assessments, including those by the participants themselves, restrict the movement to the mid- to late 1920s, whereas more recent liberal assessments identify it as beginning around the end of World War I in 1918 and ceasing around the time of the Harlem race riots in 1935. While I favor the more liberal perspective, I have found it convenient to eschew depending on sociopolitical factors (e.g., wars, social unrest, economic turmoil) in favor of utilizing literary landmarks as milestones for marking the key transitional moments in what I am terming the greater Harlem Renaissance era, 1912–40. The Harlem Renaissance, like all literary movements, can be viewed in three stages: onset (1912–22), flourishing (1923–36), and decline (1937–40). When looked at with respect to the production of literature, particularly fiction, the literary milestones occur as follows:

1912   The first major evidence of a new literary age arrives with James Weldon Johnson's anonymous novel, *The Autobiography of an Ex-Colored Man*. Also, Claude McKay publishes his first two books of poetry and relocates to the United States.

1923   The renaissance begins in earnest with the release of Jean Toomer's *Cane*. The National Urban League's magazine *Opportunity* gets under way.

1925–1929   This five-year span witnesses the publication of many of the most important novels and poetry collections plus groundbreaking anthologies edited by Alain Locke, Charles S. Johnson, and Countee Cullen. Literary magazines such as *Fire!!*, *Harlem*, *Black Opals*, and *Saturday Evening Quill* come into being.

1937   Zora Neale Hurston publishes *Their Eyes Were Watching God*, the "last great renaissance novel." Richard Wright signals the coming of a new aesthetic with his manifesto, "Blueprint for Negro Writing," in *New Challenge*.

1940   The publication of Wright's best-selling novel *Native Son* marks the ascendancy of the new school of African American literary expression.

Having settled on the timeline, the next step was deciding which authors to include and how to arrange the stories.

Authors included in *Ebony Rising* can be divided into three categories: writers whose activity predates the movement but who remained productive during it; writers whose activity begins during the movement; and writers whose activity begins during the latter part or decline of the movement but who are generally classified with the post-renaissance period. The table below categorizes the authors appearing in this anthology. While the authors in the third category are not Harlem Renaissance authors per se, I felt it necessary to include them because, as with the important older transitional literary figures at the movement's onset, these younger figures—Chester Himes, Marian Minus, Ted Poston, J. Saunders Redding, and Richard Wright—represent an equally important third generation of authors whose earliest writings during the latter years of the movement represent a transitioning into the post-renaissance era. (Note:

Despite their association with the post-renaissance era, it's worth remembering that Chester Himes published his first short story in a major periodical in 1928, J. Saunders Redding in 1930, and Richard Wright in 1931.) Yet including these latter transitional figures raises the difficulty of how best to demonstrate their natural segueing into the literary scene in some organic, nonarbitrary fashion rather than giving readers the impression that these figures simply appeared *in the wake of* the Harlem Renaissance instead of *in the midst of* it. Arranging stories alphabetically by author or chronologically by author birthdate fails to achieve this end.

CATEGORY 1	Author activity predates HR, but segues into it.
	W. E. B. Du Bois, Alice Dunbar-Nelson, Angelina Weld Grimké, Georgia Douglas Johnson, Leila Amos Pendleton, Florida Ruffin Ridley, Eloise Bibb Thompson
CATEGORY 2	Author activity begins during HR.
	Gwendolyn B. Bennett, Marita Bonner, Arna Bontemps, Anita Scott Coleman, Marion Vera Cuthbert, Jessie Redmon Fauset, Rudolph Fisher, Mercedes Gilbert, Eugene Gordon, Ottie B. Graham, Langston Hughes, Zora Neale Hurston, S. Miller Johnson, Nella Larsen, John F. Matheus, Claude McKay, May Miller, Richard Bruce Nugent, Maude Irwin Owens, George S. Schuyler, Wallace Thurman, Jean Toomer, Eric Walrond, Dorothy West, Octavia B. Wynbush
CATEGORY 3	Activity begins during latter HR, but author classified with post-HR period.
	Chester Himes, Marian Minus, Ted Poston, J. Saunders Redding, Richard Wright

Of course the only truly organic, nonarbitrary method of arranging the stories is placing them in chronological order according to their original date of publication. A glance at the table of contents is instructive in demonstrating how, for the 1930–40 period, such a scheme succeeds in commingling authors from category 1 (Georgia Douglas Johnson), category 2 (Bonner, Bontemps, Coleman, Cuthbert, Fisher, Gilbert, Hughes, Larsen, McKay, Miller, Nugent, Wynbush), and category 3 (Himes, Minus, Poston, Redding, Wright). But aside from achieving this sought-after blending, the chronological arrangement also reaps other benefits. First, it enables readers to recognize the consistent ongoing production of short fiction during the movement thanks to the provision of at least one story per year for 1919–40. This is intended to encourage readers to think of the movement more in terms of its natural progress and fluidity. Second, this chronological organizing principle also serves to place more emphasis on the (production of) literature than on its authors. Given the historical domination of the movement by a handful of high-profile male authors—chiefly James Weldon Johnson, Langston Hughes, W. E. B. Du Bois, Arna Bontemps, Countee Cullen, Rudolph Fisher, Claude McKay, Alain Locke, Wallace Thurman, Jean Toomer, Walter White, and George S. Schuyler—I deemed it useful to arrange the stories in a way that de-emphasizes authorial identity. Accordingly, since the stories in *Ebony Rising* are arranged by publication date rather than by author, and since arranging the stories in this manner highlights the movement's progression through time rather than spotlighting its participants (as discussed above and immediately hereafter), the *when* of each story, at least to a limited extent, is somewhat more important than the *who*. Lastly, in light of the fact that the Great Depression is believed to have played a significant role in the demise of the Harlem Renaissance, I specifically included stories portraying life during the Depression. Thanks to the chronological arrangement, these stories by Hughes, Himes, Minus, and Bonner appear quite naturally toward the end of the anthology in close proximity to one another (1934–40).

While I have endeavored in the story selection process to make this the best representative collection possible, it is inevitable that some readers already familiar with Harlem Renaissance short fiction will wish I had included stories that, in fact, do not appear here. For example, some of the best-known short stories—Hughes's "The Blues I'm Playing," Dorothy West's "The Typewriter," Marita Bonner's "One Boy's Story," Eric Walrond's "The Wharf Rats," and several choice stories by Zora Neale Hurston—are not included in this anthology. This may puzzle some readers at first, but there are very good reasons for excluding such stories. First and foremost, *Ebony Rising* is not offered as a Harlem Renaissance "greatest hits" collection. Its purpose is not to showcase only the best known (i.e., most frequently anthologized, read, and studied) short stories from the era but rather to delineate through short fiction the full range of talent, style, form, subject matter, and social awareness brought to bear by Harlem Renaissance–era writers. Furthermore, there is great potential harm to the legacy of the movement if anthologies like this one insist on reprinting the same well-known stories time and again, reducing Harlem Renaissance literature to its most common popular denominator. For these reasons I have had to make some admittedly painful choices in determining which stories to select and which to omit. Yet I believe in the end I have struck a satisfactory balance between choosing that which is familiar and that which is less so.

Altogether *Ebony Rising* features fifty-two stories published over twenty-seven years by twenty women and seventeen men. In addition to traditional fiction, there are examples of detective fiction (Fisher's "John Archer's Nose"), science fiction (Du Bois's "The Comet"), political satire (Himes's "A Modern Fable"), and what might be described as "creative journalism" (Schuyler's "Lynching for Profit"). Three of the stories (Hurston's "The Eatonville Anthology," Nugent's "Smoke, Lilies and Jade," and Walrond's "Vignettes of the Dusk") present non-traditional approaches to narrative structure and form. While many of the stories are set in New York (oftentimes in Harlem itself), many are set throughout the United States. Accordingly there are stories set elsewhere in the Northeast as well as in the South, West, and Midwest; stories set in Louisiana, Massachusetts, Georgia, Michigan, Arizona, Florida, Mississippi, and Illinois; stories set in various unidentified rural and urban settings. The stories present myriad issues and topics that, not surprisingly, go beyond questions of race. While it is true that many of the stories are concerned to varying degrees with issues relating to race (e.g., interracial relations, prejudice, lynching, miscegenation, institutional racism, northern migration), many of these same stories are simultaneously concerned with a host of other issues: rape, drug abuse, old age, marital relations, economics, suicide, parenthood, employment, mental and physical health, crime, politics, religion, child abuse, and literacy.

Much could undoubtedly be said about the authors appearing in this anthology. They range from the most famous Harlem Renaissance figures to the most obscure; from those who penned many short stories and published collections to those who dabbled in the genre or published only one or two stories. Authors like Langston Hughes, Zora Neale Hurston, Rudolph Fisher, Dorothy West, Jean Toomer, and Richard Wright are well known for their short fiction, while Eric Walrond, Claude McKay, Alice Dunbar-Nelson, Arna Bontemps, Chester Himes, Marita Bonner, and Ted Poston have garnered considerably less attention (though still far more than the likes of Marion Vera Cuthbert, Eugene Gordon, Maude Irwin Owens, Octavia B. Wynbush, and their fellow forgotten comrades). Yet what is perhaps most instructive about the line-up of authors in *Ebony Rising* is that they hail from places across the United States and even the Caribbean. This is well worth keeping in mind given the popular misconception of the movement's headquartering in Harlem. (Refer to the epigraphs by Ira DeAugustine Reid and Sterling A. Brown for a glimpse into two competing opinions on Harlem's place in the renaissance.) True, some of the authors relocated to New York City, but they grew up first in Florida, Massachusetts, Utah, California, New Mexico, Louisiana, Rhode Island, Delaware, Georgia, Kansas, West Virginia, and Ohio. Furthermore Claude McKay, born and raised in Jamaica, expatriated to Europe and Africa while Eric Walrond, who spent his early years in British Guiana, Barbados, and Panama, expatriated to England. Some of the authors never resided in New York, much less Harlem, and a fair amount of literary activity took place in other urban centers like Chicago, Boston, Philadelphia, and Washington, D.C. Certainly while it cannot be said that Harlem, and more generally New York, did not play a central role in the Harlem Renaissance, Harlem was not the geographical be-all and end-all of this literary movement that bears its name.

Some of the stories in this anthology have already been anthologized several times beforehand, making them familiar favorites of readers. Such stories include Bennett's "Wedding Day," Fisher's "The City of Refuge," Bontemps's "A Summer Tragedy," Fauset's "Mary Elizabeth," Thurman's "Cordelia the Crude," Toomer's "Esther," and Nugent's "Smoke, Lilies and Jade." As for the remainder, several appear to have only been anthologized once before while a select number, insofar as I have been able to determine, have never been anthologized prior to their appearance in *Ebony Rising*. Stories in this latter category include Schuyler's "Lynching for Profit," Matheus's "Anthropoi," Miller's "Door-Stops," Gilbert's "Why Adam Ate the Apple," Redding's "The Needle's Point," Hughes's "Spanish Blood," Fisher's "John Archer's Nose," Nugent's "Pope Pius the Only," Johnson's "Gesture," and Himes's "A Modern Fable." Though all of the stories appearing in this anthology were first published during the greater Harlem Renaissance era, a few stories were subsequently revised for republication after 1940. In such cases, the original versions are reprinted here. A possible exception to this, however, is Hughes's "Spanish Blood." I was unable to locate a copy of the story as it originally appeared in either *Metropolis* (1934) or *Stag* (1937), forcing me to rely instead on the version from his 1952 *Laughing to Keep from Crying* story collection.

In addition to the short fiction, I have included a few resources to aid readers. There is a selected bibliography documenting nearly three hundred relevant books and articles on the Harlem Renaissance, including important primary sources from the period itself. There is also a separate listing of books and periodicals containing other short stories by the authors represented in this work. Since the literary contests sponsored by the NAACP's *Crisis* and National Urban League's *Opportunity* magazines during the 1920s and 1930s were instrumental in fostering literary production by black authors, I have included information pertaining to award-winning short fiction in these same contests. The large selection of stories has prompted me to include a chart identifying primary issues, topics, and plot components shared by these stories. The chart is designed largely as an introductory aid to teachers, students, and reading groups who need to be able to quickly identify basic commonalities without necessarily having an immediate or broad familiarity with the stories. Lastly, in keeping with the chronological arrangement of the stories, I have included historical information for the 1912–40 period in order to give readers a better understanding of the sociohistorical context for the writing. Such information includes key historical events, facts, and statistics relating to the United States and the world.

Naturally, special attention is given to black history. In this regard I have denoted events and achievements in black history and culture, statistics on lynching in the United States, deaths of notable persons, recipients of the NAACP's Spingarn Award for outstanding achievement, publication of black-authored books, and first appearance of black periodicals.

ACKNOWLEDGMENTS

Many thanks to the following for their assistance and support in making this work a reality: Maria Balshaw, Michael Basinski, Steven W. Burks, Amanda Cain, Richard Deming, Darryl Dickson-Carr, Heidi Dodson, Adrienne Furness, Edward Gibson, Adrienne Gosselin, Norma Sue Hanson, Charles Heglar, Stephanie Huthmacher, Nancy Kuhl, Lori Lampert, John Lowe, Mara McFadden, Cathy Lynn Mundale, Karen Munro, Christine Quillen, Jean Rainwater, Lisa Rodwell, Annette Ruiz, Deborah Shedrick, Ryan M. Shepard, Craig Tenney, Michelle Toth, Leida I. Torres, Steven Tracy, Cassandra Vivian, and Thomas Wirth. I extend special thanks to Mary Owens Cooper and Owen A. Cooper for providing me with biographical information about Maude Irwin Owens.

I owe a large debt of gratitude to the staff of Indiana University Press and most especially to my editors, Robert J. Sloan and Kendra Boileau Stokes, both of whom were a great source of continued courtesy, patience, and support during this project.

Finally, it needs be said that this anthology would scarcely be possible without the existence of the great many fine and freely accessible public and academic libraries in the United States and the careful preservation of our country's history and culture that these libraries facilitate. I am immensely grateful to have such institutions at my disposal and am deeply appreciative of the work they do.

INTRODUCTION

Darryl Dickson-Carr

Florida State University

Ebony Rising constitutes a breakthrough for students, scholars, and general aficionados of the "New Negro" or Harlem Renaissance, a movement that never ceases to fascinate anyone interested in studying African American literature and culture. The Harlem Renaissance was the first major African American literary movement, lasting from the years immediately preceding World War I to the cusp of America's entry into World War II. By any measure, it was a prolific and exciting time for African American intellectual and artistic activity as a generation of "New Negroes" rejected the relative timidity of the previous generation of black leaders and artists in favor of modernity, more aggressive civil rights activism, and greater freedom of artistic expression.

The majority of this generation reacted to and was a product of World War I, in which hundreds of thousands of black soldiers served honorably, proving for the umpteenth time that African Americans should have all of the rights and privileges of citizenship that both legal and customary segregation in the South and North had denied them since the end of Reconstruction. When new economic, social, and cultural opportunities arose in the urban, industrialized North, especially in New York's Harlem community during and after World War I, the "Great Migration" of millions of African Americans from the Deep South was sparked, along with increased emigration of black Caribbeans, and more than a few Africans.

The movement was generally called the "New Negro" Renaissance at the time, since it was the embodiment of a spirit that inspired African Americans throughout the nation, not just in the urban North and Harlem. Nevertheless, the most famous destination of these newcomers was indeed black Harlem, where well-built brownstones had but recently opened to black owners and renters, civil rights organizations had opened up offices and headquarters, and opportunity seemed open to all. New York was virtually unrivaled as the nation's cultural center at the time, and the greatest symbol of modernity and progressivism. The presence of a burgeoning black metropolis and a concentration of leading artistic, cultural, and political figures within the most important city in the United States eventually convinced scholars to refer to the movement as the *Harlem* Renaissance, despite the inaccuracy of the term. If the name has stuck, it is because Harlem continues to conjure mythical images in the popular mind, even if it has not always matched past glories.

Nevertheless, the "New Negro" celebrated, supported, and published by such intellectual, political, and social luminaries as Alain Locke, W. E. B. Du Bois, James Weldon Johnson, Jessie Redmon Fauset, and Charles S. Johnson was perhaps equal parts myth and model, constructed to guide black authors and artists toward craftsmanship that would help engender a shift in the ways African Americans participated in American democracy. In addition, the "New Negro" would be the creator of a cultural paradigm that would alter the way the rest of the nation would perceive African Americans. The Harlem Renaissance, as a vehicle for the "New Negro," sought to construct a voluble image for the African American in the "New Negro" that implicitly accepted the importance of full black participation in American institutions while maintaining some degree of cultural difference. Ironically, the goals and standards that the authors of the Harlem Renaissance upheld differed considerably from those of its social leaders. Even though they lived in an era in which vicious racism was commonplace, not every author felt compelled to address "race" problems in his or her poetry and prose. Most writers, however, did choose to examine problems of the color line, since they had been affected by it in innumerable ways. They might have avoided explicitly propagandistic writing, but they resisted critical silence just as often.

It is ironic, then, that previous otherwise excellent Harlem Renaissance short story collections have been unintentionally handicapped by the limits their editors placed upon them, as necessary as those limits might have been, as Craig Gable explains in his preface to this volume. *Ebony Rising* places before us virtually all of the most captivating stories of the period, reflecting ideas, morals, and perspectives that varied and shifted considerably over three fascinating decades. By including stories from almost every year of the movement and from every major author, *Ebony Rising* allows us to see the Harlem Renaissance's continuous artistic and ideological growth. The authors who emerged during the Harlem Renaissance were a mostly young and invariably dynamic cadre of intellectuals and artists. As is true of most artists, they found and explored their identities as artists via continuous practice of their craft. The stories found in this volume represent a qualitative range extending from competent, engaging journeywork, to the finely honed craft of the mature artist, to the avant-garde.

These stories thus represent every level of achievement found within the movement, which has been praised for ushering in the first modern flourish of African American literature almost as often as it has been virtually dismissed as a failure. The latter view is based in no small part on the fact that few authors and even fewer works from the period made a lasting impression upon the general public at the time. As Houston A. Baker, Jr., has noted, though, judgments of the Harlem Renaissance as a failure are based upon excessively high expectations that the movement's intellectuals had for the artists to master their craft and achieve widespread acclaim in a short period of time. One of the movement's critics (and artists), George S. Schuyler, argued that it failed because no major books emerged, but this view is based upon the slightly disingenuous assumption that books are the only true measure of success. In fact, most of the artists reached one of the movement's most important goals: to establish a beachhead for African Americans in the fine arts (Baker 9–11).

The stories found herein—a mere fraction of the movement's output—are conclusive proof that the Harlem Renaissance succeeded on those grounds, and was successful in other ways. Forty-nine black-authored novels were published between 1920 and 1935, considered the peak years of the New Negro Renaissance, and more followed between 1935 and 1940 (Wintz 162), when most scholars agree that the movement was essentially defunct. This might seem an apparently small handful of novels until we consider that only twenty artists produced these books (Wintz 156). Most of these writers produced numerous short stories, essays, and poems before, during, and after their books appeared, to the point that we may easily argue that the true standard for the Harlem Renaissance should be not the novel, but rather the short story or poem.

It is also worth mentioning that nearly all of the period's authors also worked full-time in other occupations and enjoyed few opportunities for assistance via patronage. Such critics of the movement as author Richard Wright and philosopher Alain Locke have argued that the movement consisted, in Wright's words, of "humble novels, poems, and plays, prim and decorous ambassadors who went a-begging to white America" and who "entered the Court of American Public Opinion dressed in the knee-pants of servility, curtsying to show that the Negro was not inferior, that he was human, and that he had a life comparable to that of other people" (Wright 53). Wright's criticism, which was directed primarily toward the Renaissance's artists, has some merit, even if his characterization of his predecessors as servile to white America is both inaccurate and harsh. Wright argued correctly that most of the movement's authors were attempting to assert African Americans' basic humanity, often because that fact was not a common assumption at the time. They did so at the expense of the type of politically charged social realism that Wright demanded and practiced.

Contrary to Wright's opinion, though, most writers did not eschew politics; they simply couched their politics in irony. Most writers simply could not ignore the pervasiveness of racism in both its legal and informal manifestations, as the violent Red Summer of 1919, in which hundreds of African Americans were killed in dozens of "race riots," was still a fresh memory in the 1920s. Millions of African Americans in the nation's agrarian states were trapped in the corrupt systems of sharecropping, tenant farming, and wage slavery. The barbaric practice of lynching was still common enough during the Harlem Renaissance that readers of the *Amsterdam News,* the *Chicago Defender,* the Baltimore

Afro-American, the *Pittsburgh Courier*, and other black newspapers could expect to read or hear of a new incident somewhere in the nation every few weeks, at the very least, while the Dyer Anti-Lynching Bill languished for years in Congress, blocked by Southern politicians. The Ku Klux Klan had been revived in 1915 and by 1924 could boast a membership of up to three million men, women, and children. The nation's leaders, including Presidents Wilson, Harding, Coolidge, Hoover, and, for most of his first term, Franklin Roosevelt, were normally indifferent, if not openly hostile, to African Americans' concerns. While it was possible to ignore the political and economic situation of African Americans at the time, it was certainly unconscionable, and virtually no notable black artists did so. If the American literary landscape was to be conquered, it could not occur solely via the indirection of the past.

Lynching and white hostility seemed so intransigent, in fact, that George S. Schuyler mused sarcastically in his 1927 "Lynching for Profit" that white Southern leaders such as I. M. A. Sapp of fabled Moronville, Georgia, could simply start regulating a cottage industry of lynching, down to selling tickets (which occurred in the case of quite a few lynchings, including one of the most infamous at Waco, Texas, in 1919), thereby raising revenue and giving black civil rights leaders a *raison d'être*. Incidentally, Schuyler would reproduce this idea in his most famous work, *Black No More* (1931), one of the best satires to emerge from the movement. Although more domestic in scope and completely devoid of satire, Marion Vera Cuthbert's "Mob Madness" (1936) is a short but mercilessly succinct morality tale showing how lynching can be as destructive to the lynchers and their families as to the victims. "Mob Madness" could easily be cast among the stories set in the domestic sphere discussed below in its assertion that women have power over the horrors men commit to the extent that they are willing to sacrifice their reproductive abilities, their children, or themselves.

In establishing their beachhead upon the American literary scene, then, Harlem Renaissance artists tended to focus on a number of common themes, some of which the reader may notice quickly, while others are more subtle. In one way or another, the overwhelming majority of these narratives reflect the consciousness of the "New Negro," whose task it was to reject the accommodationist politics of the earlier generation of African American leaders and intellectuals. This agenda was embodied most forcefully in Booker T. Washington, the powerful president of Tuskegee University, whose death in 1915 a few years before the Renaissance arguably opened a space for other, younger leaders and more daring ideas to emerge and find wider exposure and expression.

The ideas these younger intellectuals championed ranged from the fairly conservative to the radically progressive, but all of them reflected a consciousness among the greater populace that modernity, especially as it was expressed through scientific achievements, was here to stay. For African American authors, modernity meant new evidence that made it easier to reject openly the racist opinions of their potential that ruled the nineteenth century. That rejection could take many forms, including the sort of vicarious violence that wove its way into many stories, but became more popular in the latter part of the Renaissance. More often than not, rejection of racism could be much more subtle.

Although it has no apparent racial context, Georgia Douglas Johnson's rare "Gesture" (1936) captures subtly the emphasis on personal dignity that found a safe home among Harlem Renaissance artists. Its publication in *Challenge*, which author Dorothy West founded as a means to revive the spirit of the Harlem Renaissance, is a sign of its artistic aspirations. Rather than focus upon the explicit political content of its successor, *New Challenge*, West's magazine gathered together the movement's artists seeking new artistic vistas. Johnson's protagonist is a drifter who chooses to walk through the Arizona desert alone rather than accept the condescension implicit in a ride from motorists who'd passed him earlier, who offer later only because the protagonist has helped them repair a tire. The ending's ambiguity is poignant: Who is the real "damn fool" in the story, the drifter or the cowboy and his companion? The story's subject, moreover, is somewhat typical of Johnson's work. Unlike most of her peers, Johnson made a conscious effort to tackle subjects in her poetry and short fiction that brought some criticism from her audience. At the very least, though, "Gesture" should be read as a tightly crafted yet open-ended tale that offered its readers—black and white—an example of human dignity and pride.

Johnson's nameless gentleman shares a literary kinship with Bush Winter of John F. Matheus's "Anthropoi" (1928), who suspends his friendship with Greek immigrant and ice cream parlor owner Demetrius Pappaniasus after the latter refuses to serve Winter's family. "Anthropoi" highlights some of the struggles that African Americans had with the immense wave of immigration in the late nineteenth and early twentieth century. To be specific, the swarthy Pappaniasus is naturalized and attempts to assimilate by shortening his name to Pappan, two options either irrelevant or unavailable to his erstwhile friend. This relationship arcs wildly over many years into a type of détente, but the irony of a recent immigrant possessing more power than a native-born American in a nation of immigrants is inescapable.

Winter and Pappaniasus resolve their differences largely because of their sons' simultaneous service in World War I, and the bigotry they both witness as their sons return to their homeland. The postwar situation was not always so kind to returning black veterans, especially in the South, as the nameless narrator of Ottie B. Graham's "Slackened Caprice" (1924) discovers in the story of black composer Jaimeson. We see quite quickly that the war veteran has gone mad due to a number of factors: a poison gas attack during the war; witnessing black children ejected from a segregated park; the color line that prevents a gifted black composer and musician from performing his music before white audiences. His only respites from the toll that madness takes upon his psyche are his music and his caged bird. The latter clearly serves as a metaphor for Jaimeson's condition, but it is also an allusion to African American poet Paul Laurence Dunbar's classic "Sympathy," with its haunting plaint, "I know why the caged bird sings, ah me"; the bird sings out of sorrow and a desire for freedom. As in "Anthropoi," though, a bitter irony underlies "Slackened Caprice," in that the black men who fought the great War for Democracy were routinely denied democratic freedoms before and after the war, regardless of their valor, talents, or skills.

That same irony fed Jean Toomer's concept of America as a nation that spawned a new "race"—the American—out of an admixture of African, Anglo, Indian/ Native American, Gallic, and Spanish influences. Toomer's *Cane* (1923), considered then and now to be among the greatest literary works to emerge from the Harlem Renaissance, embodies this philosophy, being itself an admixture of abstract poetry and prose influenced heavily by Toomer's friend, white writer Waldo Frank. Each of the many vignettes that *Cane* comprises acts as a song in a lyrical cycle musing upon the alternating confluence of and conflict between the ethnicities and identities that make the American. The two stories included here, "Becky" and "Esther," illustrate Toomer's vision in slightly different yet consistent ways. "Becky" tells of a white woman who gives birth to two black sons and is consequently shunned by both the white and black communities in her rural Georgia village, revealing the extent to which the new American is ultimately rejected for crossing the color line. "Esther" repeats the same argument by more nuanced means as young, light-skinned Esther becomes infatuated with the mystical King Barlo, who preaches of a "big an black an powerful" man captured by "white-ant biddies" and taken into a slavery in which "[t]he old coast didnt miss him, an th new coast wasnt free, he left the old-coast brothers, t give birth t you an me." This allegorical description of slavery and its product—Toomer's American—captivates Esther's imagination, as she is an issue of that mythical black man. When she approaches Barlo many years later to bear his progeny and therefore to fulfill the complex promise found within Barlo's sermon, she is as soundly rejected as the black man in the mythical past.

As might be expected, Toomer was himself, like Esther, the descendant of both white and black forebears and had spent time in the white and black worlds. *Cane* is his most accomplished attempt to come to terms with all of the peoples who contributed to his heritage, which he characterized in notes he made for an unpublished biography: "[T]hough I personally had experienced no prejudice or exclusion either from the whites or the colored people, I had seen enough to know that America viewed life as if it were divided into white and black. . . . What was I? I thought about it independently, and, on the basis of fact, concluded I was neither white nor black, but simply an American. I held this view and decided to live according to it."

Celebrating the Folk

If Toomer's *Cane* melds the mythic and the folk, Zora Neale Hurston's early fiction assumes that black folk are already both subjects and creators of myths in the form of folklore. "The Eatonville Anthology," published in *The Messenger* in 1926, draws directly from Hurston's experiences growing up in Eatonville, Florida, one of the first all-black towns to be established after the Civil War. Its vignettes reveal a view of intraracial class struggles that is alternately warm and sympathetic and cynical. Eatonville emerges as a community whose ties depend upon the citizens' abilities to tell stories—myths—and therefore express their creative powers. Equally important, "The Eatonville Anthology" gives us an early glimpse of characters and situations that would be revised more than ten years later as part of Hurston's masterpiece *Their Eyes Were Watching God* (1937). Mercedes Gilbert's "Why Adam Ate the Apple" (1931) also takes an originary folk myth and gives it a hilarious, modern twist, in which Adam eats the forbidden apple to spite Eve. The source of that spite is indeed delicious, and revises the traditional dogmatic interpretation of the myth of the Garden of Eden, in which Eve, as representative of all women, tempts man and causes his downfall, thereby incorporating both feminism and the folk.

Regardless of gender, some young black intellectuals and artists favored the forethoughts of W. E. B. Du Bois, a prominent intellectual mentor and a midwife of the New Negro Renaissance. As the editor of *The Crisis,* the organ of the National Association for the Advancement of Colored People (NAACP), Du Bois was instrumental in publishing and promoting everything from various forms of scientific socialism to literature. Harlem Renaissance writers' consciousness was not simply a product of the simple historical fact that black writers had been repeatedly excluded from the literary marketplace; rather, their awareness was largely the product of attempts to understand what it meant to be African American, often by taking close, sympathetic looks at black folk culture, as philosopher Alain Locke had argued they would need to do in his 1925 essay "The New Negro."

It would be inaccurate, though, to assume that all or even most African American writers became connoisseurs of folk culture. Instead, many were interested in the alliances and tensions that existed between or among the different classes, regions, and subcultures that African American communities comprised. The reader will find that the majority of the stories in this collection attempt to show how African Americans from all classes were affected just as often, if not in precisely the same ways, by everything from racism to the simple vagaries of human existence. The goal was twofold: first, to show that racism, like "Jes Grew" in Ishmael Reed's *Mumbo Jumbo,* is pandemic, not endemic; second, to demonstrate that African Americans are *humans,* first and foremost, who live complex lives with love, loss, triumph, defeat, loneliness, and sorrow. These goals were neither new nor unique to the Harlem Renaissance, but more authors had a chance to pursue them than ever before.

Harlem, the City of Refuge

As discussed above, the leading *auteurs* of the Harlem Renaissance were fully conscious of the cultural significance of their entrée into American letters. This consciousness depended as much upon the simple historical fact that black writers had been repeatedly excluded from the literary marketplace as it did upon their recognition that African American communities, particularly those of Harlem, were undergoing sharp changes in their cultural makeup and economies. These changes swept African Americans and a gaggle of curious white patrons into a new appreciation of the urban environment as a site of freedom that differed significantly from the Deep South whence they or their forebears had come. Harlem itself became the subject of more than a few stories precisely because it and its Renaissance had introduced hundreds of thousands of Southern black migrants to the advantages of the urban, industrialized North as well as its peculiar forms of racism. This theme often combined with the others listed above to add to a story's *pathos.*

A favorite subject of these Harlem/urban life tales was the Southern yokel, recently arrived in the North, who must adjust to the fast pace, highly competitive job market, cultural differences, and comparative decadence of the North, even as he or she enjoys its freedoms. Of the many stories published on this subject, none is more foundational or heavily copied than Rudolph Fisher's "The City of Refuge," published in the *Atlantic Monthly* in 1925, and reprinted shortly thereafter in Alain Locke's *The New Negro.* The events in King Solomon Gillis's life are emblematic: He is fleeing oppression and nearly certain death in the South, which makes Harlem his "city of refuge"; upon his emergence from the New York subway station at 135th Street, then the heart of Harlem, he sees a vast metropolis comprising African Americans of all types and hues, including his first black policeman, who not only possesses the authority to command whites, but also wields it effectively; he is recruited into Harlem's underground economy of street hustlers, which leads to his eventual demise. Save perhaps for the criminal element, Gillis's experience is a metaphor for the overwhelming majority of Harlem's new residents, including the Renaissance's artists. Painter Aaron Douglas, for example, sacrificed a steady job as a high school principal in Kansas City when told that even a dishwasher in Harlem would have more opportunity. Zora Neale Hurston arrived in Harlem with virtually no money, but "a lot of hope," not unlike Pinkie Jones in Hurston's "Muttsy" (1926), who slowly becomes acclimated to Harlem's fast pace, which makes her more susceptible to the rascally Muttsy's charms. As was true of Hurston's "Eatonville Anthology," the characters and situations in "Muttsy" are based in Hurston's personal experience and, in Muttsy's case, were revised for later works, including, again, *Their Eyes Were Watching God*.

Culture Clash

Yet the city of refuge also contained startling cultural differences that were far less pleasant. Valerio Gutierrez in Langston Hughes's "Spanish Blood" (1934) has to deal with the conflicts between his "American" (read: white), black, and Latino bloodlines, which forces him to try to define himself vis-à-vis three identities, two languages, and multiple cultures. Valerio's struggles were multiplied many times in Harlem's mix of cultures and nationalities. Native-born African Americans found themselves fighting Jamaicans, Haitians, Africans, Puerto Ricans, and, of course, white Americans for housing, jobs, power, mates, and virtually everything else, which allowed the uglier stereotypes between the groups to emerge. These tensions were the darker side of the new American "race" that Jean Toomer envisioned, the products of a nation evolving from an isolationist pretender to European heritage to a reluctant international power.

African Americans themselves, as part of this evolution, had to deal with their own prejudices against themselves along color lines. Beyond Toomer's Becky and Esther, who are rejected by African Americans almost as strongly as whites, the subjects of Eric Walrond's "Vignettes of the Dusk" (1924) include light-skinned blacks refused service by whites; native-born blacks who refer to Jamaicans as "monkey-chasers" or "monkeys"; light-skinned black bourgeoisie who have no faith in the experiments of the younger generation; darker-skinned blacks refusing to confrere with "yalla" men; and darker men who refuse to marry black women who are "too white." Walrond's implicit irony, of course, is that all of these subjects (save for the narrator) forget that they are "Negroes" in the eyes of most states and certainly most Americans. Their blindness to their shared heritage may not be the cause of the bigotry they encounter, but it cannot be resolved until they recognize that commonality and transcend their differences. Compare Walrond's "Vignettes" to Wallace Thurman's "Grist in the Mill" (1926), Maude Irwin Owens's "Bathesda of Sinners Run" (1928), or Florida Ruffin Ridley's "He Must Think It Out" (1928). In the former, a gothic satire upon the South's futile obsession with pure bloodlines reminiscent of Edgar Allan Poe, white "Colonel" Summers loses his sanity at the prospect that his miserable life was saved by a blood transfusion from an African American. "Bathesda" is about a young woman whose white paternal heritage "was always politely ignored in strict accordance with the manners and customs of the

South," resulting in her being classified as black. The pain this brings Bathesda compels her to resist learning or using the inherited "conjure" capabilities of her black grandmother Anne until she commits herself to healing, rather than creating conflict and strife. The thought that torments Henry Fitts in Ridley's tale is the possibility of receiving a great inheritance at the price of giving up his purportedly "white" heritage and all the privileges that come with it. These particular selections share a wry irony based upon the same idea expressed in the dedication to George Schuyler's *Black No More*, written for "all Caucasians in the great republic who can trace their ancestry back ten generations and confidently assert that there are no Black leaves, twigs, limbs or branches on their family trees." In other words, the book is dedicated to no one (Schuyler v).

The "New Negroes" on Their Renaissance and Artistic Freedom

Inarguably, one of the most popular and controversial topics among Harlem Renaissance authors was white fascination with Harlem and African American culture. Many authors perceived this attention as a backhanded compliment toward the richness of black music, art, performance, language, and literature. Whites generally saw Harlem as the repository of primitive "darkies" who engaged in endless bacchanalia. The truth, of course, was much more mundane than the fiction, but that did not stop a flood of thrill-seekers from downtown New York and environs from trekking to Harlem and making it their night spot of choice. As Langston Hughes and others noted, though, Harlemites were commonly segregated from whites in these social settings, unless they were "black and tan" parties at which interracial socializing was the norm.

The sometimes awkward situations produced in such settings provided extensive fodder for black fiction, which made the Renaissance itself one of the most popular subjects. Hughes's "Why, You Reckon" modifies the familiar tale of a gullible Harlemite who gets drawn into crime by a seasoned veteran of the streets. In this case, our hapless protagonist helps kidnap and mug one of the ubiquitous white downtowners, who ultimately finds the experience an "exciting" and authentic one. Harlem residents at the time would have found both motifs all too familiar, which would have also given Hughes's yarn greater resonance. The downtowner's reaction also illustrates the stereotype-driven idea of primitivism, or the notion that African Americans, especially Harlemites, somehow contained the key to "real" existence that whites could never find because they (blacks) were supposedly closer to nature. By the time Hughes wrote and published this story in 1934, he had bitterly broken away from the patronage of Charlotte Osgood Mason, a wealthy white dowager who encouraged the artistic ambitions of Hughes and Zora Neale Hurston, but also admonished them when they veered away from the "primitive" in their poetry and fiction.

Alternately, such selections as Ottie B. Graham's "Blue Aloes" (1924) and Octavia B. Wynbush's "The Return of a Modern Prodigal" (1937) use allegory to show that the "primitive" or folk must be cultivated, not ignored. In the former, Melrose rejects her Granna's cultivation of the blue aloe plant as a Southern superstition and moves away, only to find herself cursed and unable to be cured after Granna disappears. Wynbush draws upon the biblical parable of the prodigal son to show that cultivating and maintaining relationships means more than material wealth. Slim Sawyer, consumed by wanderlust, leaves his Southern home and later ends up in prison for almost two decades, never communicating with his parents. By the time he returns to them in a false identity, the father admonishes his supposedly absent son for never making any attempt to contact them and for assuming that material wealth—especially when gained illegally as Slim has done—can supplant human connections, whereas the mother simply wants her son back, regardless of his fate. In both their views, though, family and community should always come first.

Notably, Hughes's "Why, You Reckon" was produced when the nation was deeply ensconced in the Great Depression, under whose effects African Americans undeniably suffered the worst. Even before the Depression, though, Harlem and the urban North had been revealed as falling far short of the paradises they appeared to be to Southern migrants. Renaissance authors were especially fond of showing how the urban environment and modernity could be a corrupting as well as enriching experience throughout the period. Wallace Thurman's "Cordelia the Crude" (1926) and May Miller's "Door-Stops" (1930) both tell of young women who compromise their moral standards to the point of becoming prostitutes. Stephen Crane had popularized this type of reformist narrative in his landmark novella *Maggie, a Girl of the Streets* (1893), and many authors had tried to reproduce his eventual success. Thurman and Miller adopt the form to show how their protagonists Cordelia and Irma, respectively, are placed in an environment in which the pressure to engage in vice is so common, and the opportunities for honest work are so rare, that such circumstances are bound to affect the *naïf*.

Honest work, in fact, often meant submission to humiliating circumstances, as young Carrie discovers when she tries to obtain a nanny's position normally reserved for a white girl in Marian Minus's "Girl, Colored" (1940), written in the midst of the Depression. Buddy Smith of Ted Poston's vignette "A Matter of Record" (1940) is also forced by the desperate circumstances of the Depression to box for prize money despite being half blind. Even if an African American woman or man could get employers to break the color barrier, they were rarely made to feel welcome, and virtually never earned what their white counterparts would. Skeeter Gordon, in Arna Bontemps's "Barrel Staves" (1934), discovers that the chaos and fast pace of Harlem may be physically escaped, but the same difficult labor conditions that are found in the great city within a city extend to other parts of New York. This is especially true if one is both black *and* irresponsible, as Skeeter discovers to his chagrin.

None of this is to say that black workers could not find ways to show their white employers that their assumption of superiority by virtue of their "race" was merely a construction based upon a different perspective. Leila Amos Pendleton's "The Foolish and the Wise: Sallie Runner Is Introduced to Socrates" (1921) offers a satirical tale of folksy maid Sallie Runner's ability to outsmart her highly educated employer, Mrs. Maxwell Thoro (read: Max, or supremely, Thoro[ugh]), whose condescending attempts to teach the hired help about Socrates and Greek culture are transformed into a damnation of Southern arrogance.

The new artistic freedom certainly did not go unnoticed or undocumented within the authors' own works. Wallace Thurman, Rudolph Fisher, Jessie Redmon Fauset, Langston Hughes, Richard Bruce Nugent, Zora Neale Hurston, and Claude McKay each wrote stories, essays, and novels that commented upon the *zeitgeist* of the Harlem Renaissance, especially Harlem's social scene, in which it was nearly impossible to avoid bumping into such white patrons (or, in Hurston's terms, "Negrotarians") as Carl Van Vechten, Gertrude Stein, and Waldo Frank, to say nothing of many different artists. Similarly, modernist experiments with form, content, and theme became more commonplace, and affected every black writer's own ambitions and sense of possibilities.

The sense that African Americans' art was free to explore new vistas extended into the subject matter and genres they chose. Rudolph Fisher became one of the first significant African American writers of detective fiction via his novel *The Conjure-Man Dies* (1932) and one of his finest short stories, "John Archer's Nose" (1935), whose black detectives display extraordinary wit, intelligence, and knowledge of both science and human nature. "John Archer's Nose," a sequel to his pioneering novel, is a finely crafted detective novella, as its dramatic tension scarcely ever ebbs; nor does the wit for which friends such as Langston Hughes celebrated Fisher. Perhaps most important, Fisher's detective fiction cleared a path for Chester Himes, who became a highly successful author in the genre, which in part led to Fisher being overshadowed as the trailblazer he is.

By the same token, Richard Bruce Nugent's "Smoke, Lilies and Jade" (1926), which first appeared in the magazine *Fire!!*, was the first published story by an African American that both openly mentioned and depicted homosexuality and homoerotic acts. It also experimented with rhythm via its complete absence of conventional punctuation. All sentences, clauses, and phrases are bookended by ellipses, simultaneously incorporating the new "stream-of-consciousness" technique and suggesting the syncopation of jazz and blues music as they were currently being reinvented by Louis Armstrong and his compatriots. Today, Nugent's subject matter seems altogether tame, but at the time it inspired the reviewer at the Baltimore *Afro-American* to boast of tossing his copy of *Fire!!* into the fire!

Nugent went on to pen other stories, including "Pope Pius the Only" (1937), most of which is a dream inspired by a strong marijuana high. As with "Smoke, Lilies and Jade," it is far more than a stream-of-consciousness, proto-psychedelic drug trip. Algy's drug-induced hallucinations form a pageant of some of the major historical black figures and events, including Alexander Pushkin, Hannibal, Crispus Attucks, Alexandre Dumas, and Toussaint L'Ouverture, and touchstones of black life, from slavery, to lynching, to "conking" the hair. "Pope Pius the Only" evidences the new attention to "racial" pride, one of the strongest undercurrents of the Renaissance. It bears at least one link to Leila Amos Pendleton's "The Foolish and the Wise: Sanctum 777 N. S. D. C. O. U. Meets Cleopatra" (1922), which at first glance appears to be a satire of the extensive system of black fraternal lodges, yet is truly a vernacular lesson about the essential role that Cleopatra and black Africans in general played in the history of the ancient Mediterranean world. As with Pendleton's first installment in her "Foolish and the Wise" series, "Sanctum 777" obviates the stereotype linking mastery of standard English with intelligence on the one hand, while supporting the efforts of African American historian J. A. Rogers, who published a series of pamphlets in the 1920s and 1930s that compiled facts and theories about blacks' roles in world history.

Nugent's story is ultimately amoral when it comes to the question of drug use, a stark contrast to J. Saunders Redding's earlier "The Needle's Point" (1931), a startling account of heroin addiction and its possible social origins. Although her circumstances are not given the same type of sophisticated treatment as those of Sonny in James Baldwin's "Sonny's Blues" (1957) a quarter of a century later, Peacie's wrenching addiction and relapse are clearly linked to the same lack of opportunity, the same dull existence that confronted her literary descendant.

The younger artists, especially Nugent and Thurman, and more accomplished yet radical voices such as Claude McKay were hardly deterred by negative notices and continued to include explicit references of sexual activity in their works. In most cases, this was not for titillation's sake, although some reviewers felt, as W. E. B. Du Bois did after reading Claude McKay's novel *Home to Harlem* (1928), "distinctly like taking a bath" after reading the more daring material (202). The adventures of Nicey and Primus in Eric Walrond's "City Love" (1927) are noteworthy both for their humor and for their thinly veiled innuendoes as the lovers struggle to gain admittance to a string of rather seedy motels for a rendezvous. Claude McKay was equally capable of writing the relatively explicit "Crazy Mary" (1932) or the semi-autobiographical "Highball" (1927), which depict the complexities of sexual and racial relations (or the lack thereof, in "Crazy" Miss Mary's case), respectively.

The former story is a rather straightforward attack upon sexual, religious, and moral hypocrisy taken from McKay's Jamaican roots, while the latter indicts the unconscious racism and class stratification that could be found among progressive whites and the purportedly liberal downtowners. When black blues artist Nation Roe jettisons his black wife, Ethel, in favor of white Myra Roe, he does so to gain entrée to white society, but he soon finds his wife snubbed by leftist George Lieberman and his cohorts. Lieberman and friends seem more offended by Myra's crudeness and "low-class" behavior than her race, but both Myra and George seem to fear, with some justification, that this crowd found Nation's presence more tolerable due to a condescending affinity for his black wife's "simple charm," whereas Myra abounds only in simple crudity. The best evidence of Myra's qualities, or lack thereof, is the company she keeps, specifically her friend Dinah, whose slur against Nation indicates the ubiquity of casual, unconscious racism.

McKay seems to find levels of racism in progressive whites that range from the unconscious (Lieberman) to the thoughtlessly cruel (Dinah and, to a slightly lesser extent, Myra), but no less offensive. Nor is Nation the innocent victim. His callous rejection of his first wife in order to "marry up," so to speak, is equally repugnant and ironic; his generic name itself signifies, in conjunction with his speech, how "common" he is as well. The story's attention to African Americans' attempts to transcend "race" links it to Gwendolyn B. Bennett's "Wedding Day" (1926), in which African American expatriate Paul Watson discovers that black "wasn't white nowhere," including gay Paris, which held fond memories for black servicemen during World War I. Paul, however, has a different view and occupies a different position. He left the United States for Paris before World War I because of his great hatred for racism's evils and for American whites in particular. He serves in the war, but only because he is pardoned from his jail sentence for aggravated assault, along with thousands of other prisoners, and fights as a Frenchman! When he later falls in love with a white American prostitute, the irony is not lost on Paris's black expatriate community. The moment when Paul makes his discovery about the permanent nature of his black identity offers a devastating, almost mercilessly ironic critique of the pandemic that is American racism.

Even the more patrician participants in the movement, such as W. E. B. Du Bois, could write material as daring as "The Comet" (1920), a satirical story that blends elements of science fiction with the gothic while flirting with sexual themes, including the great taboo of interracial sex. Note, for example, how Julia contemplates the curved shape of the long black mouthpiece on her phone as she considers the likelihood that she and Jim Davis will repopulate the earth. The barely concealed sexual innuendo in the story would be certain to infuriate most of white America, and more than a few black Americans, yet its premise was both simple and commonplace: It is the power and privileges reserved for whites and entrenched racist traditions that keeps African Americans and their white compatriots separate and unequal. When either racism's structure or the presumption of racial superiority is removed, both the absurdity and fictional nature of race will be revealed.

This premise was the philosophical basis of numerous factions within the Harlem Renaissance, among them the editorial boards of such outlets as *The Crisis* (the NAACP's official magazine, which Du Bois edited from its inception until 1934), *Opportunity* (official organ of the National Urban League, edited by Charles S. Johnson), and most African American newspapers. The magazines are of particular concern to us because they made concerted efforts to publish stories that expressed this principle in one way or another. By the same token, progressive editors at *Survey Graphic, The New Republic, The Nation, World Tomorrow, Forum,* and other periodicals embraced the work of new black writers who wished to show how destructive the social myth of race could be by asserting African Americans' basic humanity and pursuit of the American Dream.

In contrast, such politically and artistically radical publications as *The Messenger* and *Fire!!,* respectively, were less concerned with asserting black humanity than they were with assuming it. This meant irreverence toward the integrationist goals of the NAACP and NUL in favor of democratic socialism in the case of *The Messenger,* whose publishers, A. Philip Randolph and Chandler Owen, were card-carrying members of the Socialist Party, and rejection of the middle-class morality of the older generation of black leaders, in the case of *Fire!!* The latter magazine was edited by Wallace Thurman, one of the Harlem Renaissance's central artistic figures, and a writer who took his philosophical cues from Friedrich Nietzsche, which meant that he had little tolerance for what he perceived as the movement's prima donnas, including Du Bois and Alain Locke. In the view of Thurman and many other writers, Victorian morality was the worst sort of sin because it stood in the way of modern ideas, especially new scientific and sociological discoveries that would supposedly liberate humanity from the shortsightedness and prejudices that led to World War I and, for African Americans, to slavery, peonage, and segregation.

Of course, excoriation of Victorian morals certainly could not and would not solve African Americans' extensive problems in and of itself. When the younger artists wrote stories that depicted sexuality and the sensual realities of life for many African Americans, ranging from simple partying, to jazz and the blues—considered "low-down" musical forms by the black bourgeoisie—to drug use, they effectively brought the range of black experiences out of the closet, thereby accentuating African Americans' humanity. Relatively conservative black critics decried such depictions because they wished to present African Americans' best faces to a hostile white public to ease the process of integration, or even assimilation. "We younger Negro artists who create now," Langston Hughes wrote in 1926, "intend to express our individual dark-skinned selves without fear or shame. If white people are pleased we are glad. If they are not, it doesn't matter. We know we are beautiful. And ugly too. The tom-tom cries and the tom-tom laughs. If colored people are pleased we are glad. If they are not, their displeasure doesn't matter either. We build our temples for tomorrow, strong as we know how, and we stand on top of the mountain, free within ourselves" (Hughes, "Negro" 694).

African American Women, the New Feminism, and the Domestic Sphere

For black women authors in particular, modernity was the gateway to women's freedom from sexist oppression in science, education, medicine, and marriage. The stories in *Ebony Rising* that champion modernity are legion, although they have many different ways of working toward that goal. Perhaps the most remarkable legacy of the Harlem Renaissance was the wealth of women authors who published their first—and in a few cases, their only—fiction. This body of work is not remarkable, however, simply because the authors were women. Rather, it is because these women were not trying either to emulate male authors or to avoid representing women's experiences in fairly realistic ways. In fact, many of these stories tended to express overtly feminist agendas, frequently due to the fact that they were published in such outlets as *The Crisis,* whose literary editor, Jessie Redmon Fauset, was as much a feminist as she was a member of the "Talented Tenth" who hoped to lead African Americans to freedom with their skills gained in elite schools. The women of the Harlem Renaissance tended to write what we now might call domestic fiction. Their stories were often focused on the home, marriage, and the family, but not for the sake of extolling these institutions' virtues per se. Rather, they demonstrated repeatedly that for African Americans, each institution was fraught with danger that stemmed directly from racism's effects. In other words, racism has the power to warp African Americans' personal relationships and institutions beyond any form that whites would recognize, inasmuch as whites seldom have to endure these sorts of risks.

In Nella Larsen's "Sanctuary" (1930), for example, mother Annie Poole must choose whether to uphold her promise to hide her son's killer, another black man, from justice. Her promise is made with the assumption that the man will be lynched, but once this possibility is eliminated, she must decide whether to honor a promise made under false pretexts. Such a choice between a mother's love on the one hand and honor and justice on the other turns out to be more wrenching than the reader might expect. Angelina Weld Grimké's "The Closing Door" (1919) revolves around Agnes Milton's decision whether to bring a black male child into a nation and a world that has declared African American men's lives virtually worthless except as laborers. Agnes goes from being a lively, loving wife and mother to a mere shell as the men she loves are lynched and debased. It is not insignificant that this story originally appeared in *Birth Control Review* in 1919, as Agnes's torment and mental deterioration echo the suffering of feminist and birth control advocate Charlotte Perkins Gilman's protagonist in "The Yellow Wall-Paper" (1892), one of the most significant works of nineteenth-century American women's literature.

Alice Dunbar-Nelson's "Hope Deferred" (1914) takes a slightly different tack by focusing upon the ways in which the hopes and educations of the "Talented Tenth" are wasted in an economy that regularly discriminates against African Americans, regardless of their talent and training. Edwards, a young civil engineer, must accept a job as a headwaiter and strikebreaker because no one has faith in the abilities and credentials of an African American, yet he must pay his and his wife's bills. In the story's denouement, Edwards discovers that his skills will always be in question, regardless of his occupation, except by his wife. This story accentuates, as do the others it resembles, two major points, one explicit, the other implicit: (1) The home and hearth may be a refuge for black men and women beset by racism, but it is also a decidedly insecure one; (2) Booker T. Washington's promises that African Americans' white fellows would credit them once they showed they could be thrifty and industrious proved to be false for far too many. Given this last point, it is no surprise that Dunbar-Nelson's story appeared in *The Crisis* in 1914, one year before Washington died, and while his conservative program still dominated black politics.

Although not nearly as explicit in its politics, Anita Scott Coleman's "Cross Crossings Cautiously" (1930) uses the metaphor of a railroad crossing to represent the dangers found when African Americans crossed the color line. Sam Timons, a black welder unemployed and unable to find work because of his race, takes Claudia, a young white girl, to the circus, both as a good deed and out of human affection for the young girl, despite the dangers she represents in a segregated nation. He is mistaken for a kidnapper, however, and Sam and Claudia both discover that good intentions count for little when race colors the vision of her parents' generation.

Crossings of the intraracial color line could be equally perilous, albeit not so visibly traumatic in their effects. Several stories offer searing indictments of African Americans' own obsession with color—or, more accurately, the privileges that blacks and whites grant to or rescind from each other on the basis of their particular hues. The marriages in Marita Bonner's "Hate Is Nothing" (1938) and Dorothy West's "Prologue to a Life" (1929) are both between a light-skinned and a dark-skinned partner, but the outcomes of these marriages are entirely different. In "Hate Is Nothing," lighter-skinned Roger Sands marries the darker, working-class Lee, much to the chagrin of Roger's mother, Mrs. Sands, who harbors destructive, petit bourgeois aspirations. Mrs. Sands believes that selective breeding will eliminate darker influences within the family tree and lead inevitably to greater intelligence and class status for her progeny, a not un-usual belief for a substantial portion of the black bourgeoisie of the time. She stands as a foil to Lee, who learns that true love transcends artificial divisions that Mrs. Sands values via her short but exceedingly stormy first marriage and her encounter with the same sort of working-class African Americans that Mrs. Sands abhors. Just as Lee survived the emotional turmoil of her self-destructive first husband, Annie Mae Smith and Lee Andrew Miller refuse to let the racism of their provincial town destroy their relationship. Why should Mrs. Sands's own intellec-tual provincialism succeed where other circumstances fail? The story focuses on the intersections of class, race, and colorism to reveal how the individual need not be enslaved to them, unlike Lily Bemis in "Prologue to a Life." Lily finds the darker Luke Kane attractive due to her desire to "see her race perpetuated," but she does not love him either; "[m]en were chiefly important as providers," and she "would have married any healthy man with prospects." Predictably, Luke has much greater love for Lily, and provides her with a set of "golden" twins. When they die in a horrible accident, Lily at first becomes an empty shell of her former self. Later, however, the plot takes an unusual turn as West transforms her into a "God" (al-beit an unwilling one) for her ability to perpetuate and create life, specifically the couple's third child, a daughter. West seems to dispense with the issue of colorism for the sake of introducing a feminist argument into her plot. The result is a some-what uneven, if fascinating story.

Eugene Gordon's "Game" (1927), which won half of *Opportunity* magazine's first prize for fiction in 1928, uses the exotic meats—"game"—that Sam Desmond must bring home to his spoiled "yaller" wife Marguerite and her cat Mussolini—definitely a fascist—to symbolize the privileges that African Ameri-can communities customarily accorded lighter-skinned blacks, leading to the destruction of many marital unions. Dorothy West's "Hannah Byde" (1926) follows a similar track, although it is as much concerned with class as with race. The story's namesake, we are told, undervalues both her husband, George, and her own life. Hannah's feelings stem from her obsession with becoming free of the limitations that even the African American middle class must endure. She is light enough ("gloriously golden") to be as demanding as Marguerite of "Game," yet just dark enough that "passing" for white is impossible. She is there-fore denied the white privilege that she believes would satisfy her, a fate ce-mented by a baby that will link her forever to the black world. This drives her to the brink of hysteria, a situation made worse when George attempts to soothe Hannah's nerves by playing jazz. His choice of music parallels his "awkward attempt to walk lightly" around her, as the jazz—black music—filling the room underscores the tragedy her fate. Hannah may seem "self-centered" to her doc-tor, but this oversimplifies her situation. Hannah's psychological outlook may be flawed and self-destructive, but it is shaped at least as much by the artificial limitations placed upon her as by any other element.

Jessie Redmon Fauset's framed narrative (a story-within-a-story) "Mary Elizabeth" (1919), on the other hand, is more hopeful and satisfying. Married couple Roger and Sally learn to appreciate and forgive their minor faults in the wake of their housekeeper Mary Elizabeth's story of her enslaved ancestors, Maggie and Cassius, who reunite many years after being separated during slavery. The object lesson for Roger and Sally's union is clear: Love and marriage are far more than matters of complementarity; they require bonds that enabled African Americans to survive slavery itself.

Eloise Bibb Thompson's "Masks" (1927) and "Mademoiselle 'Tasie" (1925), both set in New Orleans' Creole communities, criticize the pretenses of the color line in marriage and courtship, respectively. Paupet in "Masks" loses his wife Julie in childbirth directly because of her own deeply entrenched prejudice against the African side of her family's heritage, while Mademoiselle 'Tasie learns to accept the social ostracization that follows from falling in love with a "Negre aux grosses orielles" in a New Orleans divided sharply between the French and the "Americains," a category that comprises phenotypically white and black folks to this day.

Strangest of all is S. Miller Johnson's "The Golden Penknife" (1925), which is barely classifiable as domestic fiction. Although it concerns a stormy relationship reminiscent of Claude McKay's "Highball," it spends less time focusing upon race than it does upon ethnicity, except for a shocking denouement reminiscent of O. Henry. When Anna meets a mysterious suitor, Tervanovitch, his ambiguous "race" or ethnicity is the source both of suspicion within the immigrant community and of the motivation for the story's conclusion. It reveals the extent of the American phobia toward even the slightest "racial" taint, as well as the speed with which relatively new immigrants bought into such fears. Contemporary readers would likely have caught the implicit irony of this occurring among the same sort of immigrant communities that were targeted by calls for "100% Americanism" by both the revived Ku Klux Klan and 1920s American immigration policies. With its extensive focus on the lives of immigrants (rather than African Americans), prolonged mystery, and peculiar conclusion, "The Golden Penknife" may be the most singular contribution to this collection. It is easily among the least anthologized, and one worthy of greater notice.

The End of the Renaissance

As some of the stories discussed in the previous section indicate, much of the hope and optimism of the Harlem Renaissance could not withstand the crushing conditions of the Depression. When Richard Wright and Chester Himes began writing in the early 1930s, the labor conditions that concerned so many black writers had grown considerably worse. Wright, Himes, West, Hughes, and many others began to find attractive the program of the Communist Party USA

(CPUSA), which openly recruited African Americans, particularly writers. The CPUSA argued that capitalism was on the wane, and that a state-run economy similar to that of Stalin's Soviet Union was the only hope for the nation, and artistic productions should reflect this argument via social realism. Yet Wright's and Himes's respective interests in that genre were more than mere ideological or artistic choices; they were also calls for the most brutal realities of black laborers' lives to be depicted in art without compromise to the tastes or sensitivities of the reading public, especially those whites within the audience.

One of Himes's earliest published stories, "His Last Day" (1932), delves deeply into the psychology of a condemned man. His resistance both to his own fear and to religion precedes remarkably similar scenes in Wright's *Native Son* (1940) and the existentialism of Albert Camus's *L'étranger* (1942). Himes's later "A Modern Fable" (1939) contains no identifiable African American characters, but its overt condemnation of Senator McDull's political double-dealing at the expense of the Works Progress Administration (WPA), which provided work and relief for millions of poor whites similar to Henry Slaughter and African Americans alike, resonated with black readers nonetheless. Its politics are preachy, but this was hardly unusual in the literature of the Depression's worst years. We find Wright's 1937 story "Silt," which introduces the type of poor black Southern sharecroppers that would dominate much of his early fiction, mining a similar vein. Wright compares the effects of a devastating flood to the eminence of white supremacy, which engulfs poor blacks inexorably and without mercy. Forced to rebuild after the flood, these sharecroppers discover that the white landlord is about as forgiving as the waters or their hunger, which is to say not at all. The only discernible difference is that the waters do recede, but they are as sure to return as sharecropping and peonage are to keep African Americans in virtual slavery. Wright seems to have taken a cue from Arna Bontemps's 1933 "A Summer Tragedy," in which older black sharecroppers Jeff and Jennie find themselves faced with the triple burden of their growing inability to work in the corrupt sharecropping system, the loss of their children, and the fear of an apparently hopeless future. "Silt" incorporates all of the elements that made Wright's reputation when his landmark *Native Son* was published three years later. Wright's fiction and essays of this time consistently reveal his belief that freedom for African Americans has everything to do with their ability to *create* their worlds, to exert the will to power. When institutional racism curtails that ability, the result is invariably death, some form of economic enslavement, or, for Wright's African American males, literal or psychological emasculation. Other stories of the period, such as "Big Boy Leaves Home" (1936) and "The Man Who Was Almost a Man" (1940), play upon this same basic riff.

This scenario was not the exclusive province of males, however, whether as authors or as characters. Marita Bonner's "The Whipping" (1939) is set in the same kitchenettes on the South Side of Chicago that Wright made his haunting literary muse and physical home, the same Chicago of *Native Son* and the autobiographical *Black Boy*. As in the other fictional accounts of African American migration from the South to the urban North included here, Bonner's protagonist Lizabeth finds her faculties for resilience in the face of adversity tested and ultimately conquered by an environment in which blacks, including black women, are assumed to be irresponsible, alcoholic, and violent; in which relief for her destitute family is impossible to obtain from Depression-era agencies; in which she is assumed to be sexually promiscuous, again due to vile stereotypes. In a fairly short space, Bonner creates a portrait of withering urban poverty as devastating as the much longer novels by Wright and one of his artistic ancestors, Upton Sinclair (*The Jungle*, 1906).

Bonner's tale also signifies a change in focus that emerged as the nation began to enter the Great Depression in earnest and, consequently, as many of the artists who had established their reputations during the early days of the Harlem Renaissance found other themes to occupy them. Whereas the earlier stories focused more on asserting black humanity and the need for civil rights, later ones—especially those from the mid-1930s forward—more often hammered home the brutally stark economic conditions that African Americans endured. As Langston Hughes wrote later, he and other artists felt alienated from the African American on the street, which stimulated or strengthened their new faith in leftist groups, particularly the Communist Party. It was in the CPUSA's "front" groups and publications, which included the John Reed Club and *The Negro Worker, Negro Liberator,* and *The New Masses,* that Hughes was to meet and mentor a slightly younger new generation of writers, including Richard Wright, Chester Himes, Ralph Ellison, Marian Minus, and Ted Poston. Throughout the 1930s, these writers would use the lessons learned under the tutelage of Hughes, Fauset, and others to help maintain the steady flow of innovative writing begun the previous decade. In the case of Richard Wright, Chester Himes, and Dorothy West, these writers would come to dominate much of African American fiction in the 1940s.

Perhaps more than any other single author's, Wright's fiction signifies and epitomizes the influence that political radicalism and naturalism had upon African American authors. Artists who had started their careers in earnest in the early days of the movement usually did no more than flirt with naturalism, a literary genre in which humanity is invariably beholden to its base physical needs, psychological desires, and environment. If earlier Harlem Renaissance authors saw the urban North as one that made vice more attractive to the migrant and her or his children, Wright argued that both the urban North and rural South virtually forced African Americans—especially males—into lives of desperation and submission, respectively. Since the height of Wright's influence in the early 1940s, of course, subsequent authors have sharply criticized his naturalistic vision through either their reviews and essays or their own works;

Ralph Ellison's equally important *Invisible Man* is the first, and perhaps the greatest, homage to (and parody of) Wright's premises. Yet for all of his own criticism of his artistic forebears, Wright himself built upon their experiments. His righteous antipathy toward segregation, peonage, and the scourge of lynching had already been explored repeatedly through the same artists he dismisses as servile in "Blueprint for Negro Writing." Wright's realism, references to folk culture, and attention to the struggles of the black laborer, for example, owe extensive debts to the radical poems (especially "Goodbye Christ") and stories (especially those in *The Ways of White Folks*) of his mentor Hughes, as they do to others Wright later condemned, such as Zora Neale Hurston. Even "Blueprint for Negro Writing" is a more radical revision of the hopes for black literary expression found in Alain Locke's anthology *The New Negro* (1925).

In returning to Wright, I wish neither to prop him up as a straw man nor to make it seem as though his view of the Harlem Renaissance is definitive. I would like instead to help correct some of the shortsightedness within Wright's criticisms and add to scholarly efforts that show how rich and diverse the literary offerings of the Harlem Renaissance were. By placing a substantial portion of this diversity in one volume, *Ebony Rising* will help ease this burden. We can see how a rich blend of younger and more established writers created fertile ground for the innovations that have emerged since the 1940s. The fiction of the Harlem Renaissance provided more than sufficient evidence to several generations of African American writers and scholars that it was possible for many vastly different creative voices to assert themselves at once. It also proved that those same artists and intellectuals could be both militant and supremely skilled at their art. Here is to be found some of the twentieth century's first assertions of political radicalism, sexual diversity, and feminism by African American authors. Even if the Harlem Renaissance produced few great *books*, *Ebony Rising* puts to rest, once and for all, the argument that the movement did not produce great literature.

Works Cited

Baker, Houston A., Jr. *Modernism and the Harlem Renaissance.* Chicago: University of Chicago Press, 1987.

Du Bois, W. E. B. "Two Novels." *Crisis* June 1928: 202.

Hughes, Langston. *The Big Sea.* 1940. New York: Hill, 1975.

———. "The Negro Artist and the Racial Mountain." *Nation* 23 June 1926: 692–94.

Schuyler, George. *Black No More.* 1931. Boston: Northeastern University Press, 1989.

Wintz, Cary D. *Black Culture and the Harlem Renaissance.* Houston: Rice University Press, 1988.

Wright, Richard. "Blueprint for Negro Writing," *New Challenge* Fall 1937: 53–65.

EBONY
RISING

1912–1919

- Woodrow Wilson elected president of the United States (1912).
- British luxury liner *Titanic* sinks on its maiden voyage after striking an iceberg (1912).
- W. C. Handy publishes *Memphis Blues,* the first blues composition (1912).
- The Clef Club Orchestra, composed of 125 African American musicians, performs at Carnegie Hall (1912).
- In South Africa, the Natives Land Act grants whites possession of over 90% of all land (1913).
- William Foster establishes the Foster Photoplay Company, making him the first black motion picture producer (1913).
- World War I begins; the United States maintains neutrality (1914).
- The Panama Canal officially opens (1914).
- Spingarn Medal awards for black achievement instituted by Joel E. Spingarn, chairman of the board of directors of the NAACP (1914).
- W. C. Handy publishes *St. Louis Blues* (1914).
- Jamaican Marcus Garvey establishes the Universal Negro Improvement Association (1914).
- U.S. forces invade Haiti (1915).
- The Association for the Study of Negro Life and History is founded by Carter G. Woodson (1915).
- The modern Ku Klux Klan is formed (1915).
- Woodrow Wilson reelected (1916).
- Gen. John Pershing leads all-black 10th Cavalry into Mexico in pursuit of Pancho Villa (1916).
- The United States enters World War I; eventually over 300,000 African Americans serve in the military, including over 1,400 commissioned officers (1917).
- Russian Revolution begins (1917).
- Race riots in East St. Louis, Illinois, and Houston, Texas (1917).

- Approximately 10,000 blacks march in silence down New York City's Fifth Avenue to protest racial violence (1917).
- World War I ends (1918).
- An influenza pandemic begins, ultimately killing over 20 million worldwide (1918).
- Race riots in Philadelphia and Chester, Pennsylvania (1918).
- Indian nationalist leader Mohandas Gandhi initiates a civil disobedience movement in India (1919).
- Father Divine starts his congregation in Sayville, N.Y. (1919).
- Race riots erupt in 25 U.S. cities (1919).
- Oscar Micheaux's company produces its first film, *The Homesteader* (1919).
- Jessie Redmon Fauset becomes literary editor of the NAACP's *Crisis* (1919).
- The Associated Negro Press is formed, becoming the first national news service for African American newspapers (1919).
- The Pan African Congress, organized by W. E. B. Du Bois, meets in Paris (1919).

Lynchings in the United States:

1912—61 blacks, 2 whites	1916—50 blacks, 4 whites
1913—51 blacks, 1 white	1917—35 blacks, 3 whites
1914—49 blacks, 3 whites	1918—60 blacks, 4 whites
1915—54 blacks, 13 whites	1919—76 blacks, 7 whites

Deaths:

Harriet Tubman (10 Mar. 1913)
Booker T. Washington (14 Nov. 1915)
Joseph S. Cotter Jr. (3 Feb. 1919)
Madame C. J. Walker (25 May 1919)

Spingarn Medal:

1915—Ernest E. Just (biologist)
1916—Maj. Charles Young (soldier, statesman)
1917—Harry T. Burleigh (composer, singer)
1918—William Stanley Braithwaite (poet, literary critic)
1919—Archibald H. Grimké (attorney, statesman)

Books:

1912—Joseph S. Cotter, *Negro Tales* (short stories)
1912—James Weldon Johnson [published anon.], *The Autobiography of an Ex-Colored Man* (novel)

1912—Claude McKay, *Constab Ballads* (poetry)
1912—Claude McKay, *Songs of Jamaica* (poetry)
1913—Fenton Johnson, *A Little Dreaming* (poetry)
1913—Oscar Micheaux, *The Conquest* (novel)
1914—Olivia Ward Bush-Banks, *Driftwood* (poetry, short stories, nonfiction)
1914—Alice Dunbar-Nelson (ed.), *Masterpieces of Negro Eloquence* (nonfiction anthology)
1915—F. Grant Gilmore, *The Problem: A Military Novel* (novel)
1915—Fenton Johnson, *Visions of Dusk* (poetry)
1915—Oscar Micheaux, *The Forged Note* (novel)
1916—Fenton Johnson, *Songs of the Soil* (poetry)
1917—Raymond Garfield Dandridge, *Penciled Poems* (poetry)
1917—Henry F. Downing, *The American Cavalryman* (novel)
1917—James Weldon Johnson, *Fifty Years and Other Poems* (poetry)
1917—Oscar Micheaux, *The Homesteader* (novel)
1918—Joseph S. Cotter Jr., *The Band of Gideon and Other Lyrics* (poetry)
1918—Sarah Lee Brown Fleming, *Hope's Highway* (novel)
1918—Georgia Douglas Johnson, *The Heart of a Woman and Other Poems* (poetry)
1919—Herman Dreer, *The Immediate Jewel of His Soul* (novel)
1919—Maggie Shaw Fullilove, *Who Was Responsible?* (novel)
1919—R. Archer Tracy, *The Sword of Nemesis* (novel)

Periodicals:
Half-Century Magazine (1916–25)
Journal of Negro History (1916–current)
Messenger (1917–28)
Negro World (1917–33)
Crusader (1918–22)

1 HOPE DEFERRED

Alice Dunbar-Nelson

From *Crisis*, September 1914

The direct rays of the August sun smote on the pavements of the city and made the soda-water signs in front of the drug stores alluringly suggestive of relief. Women in scant garments, displaying a maximum of form and a minimum of taste, crept along the pavements, their mussy light frocks suggesting a futile disposition on the part of the wearers to keep cool. Traditional looking fat men mopped their faces, and dived frantically into screened doors to emerge redder and more perspiring. The presence of small boys, scantily clad and of dusky hue and languid steps marked the city, if not distinctively southern, at least one on the borderland between the North and the South.

Edwards joined the perspiring mob on the hot streets and mopped his face with the rest. His shoes were dusty, his collar wilted. As he caught a glimpse of himself in a mirror of a shop window, he smiled grimly. "Hardly a man to present himself before one of the Lords of Creation to ask a favor," he muttered to himself.

Edwards was young; so young that he had not outgrown his ideals. Rather than allow that to happen, he had chosen one to share them with him, and the man who can find a woman willing to face poverty for her husband's ideals has a treasure far above rubies, and more precious than one with a thorough understanding of domestic science. But ideals do not always supply the immediate wants of the body, and it was the need of the wholly material that drove Edwards wilted, warm and discouraged into the August sunshine.

The man in the office to which the elevator boy directed him looked up impatiently from his desk. The windows of the room were open on a court-yard where green tree tops waved in a humid breeze; an electric fan whirred, and sent forth flashes of coolness; cool looking leather chairs invited the dusty traveler to sink into their depths.

Edwards was not invited to rest, however. Cold gray eyes in an impassive pallid face fixed him with a sneering stare, and a thin icy voice cut in on his half-spoken words with a curt dismissal in its tone.

"Sorry, Mr.—Er—, but I shan't be able to grant your request."

His "Good Morning" in response to Edwards' reply as he turned out of the room was of the curtest, and left the impression of decided relief at an unpleasant duty discharged.

"Now where?" He had exhausted every avenue, and this last closed the door of hope with a finality that left no doubt in his mind. He dragged himself down the little side street, which led home, instinctively, as a child draws near to its mother in its trouble.

Margaret met him at the door, and their faces lighted up with the glow that always irradiated them in each other's presence. She drew him into the green shade of the little room, and her eyes asked, though her lips did not frame the question.

"No hope," he made reply to her unspoken words.

She sat down suddenly as one grown weak.

"If I could only just stick it out, little girl," he said, "but we need food, clothes, and only money buys them, you know."

"Perhaps it would have been better if we hadn't married—," she suggested timidly. That thought had been uppermost in her mind for some days lately.

"Because you are tired of poverty?" he queried, the smile on his lips belying his words.

She rose and put her arms about his neck. "You know better than that; but because if you did not have me, you could live on less, and thus have a better chance to hold out until they see your worth."

"I'm afraid they never will." He tried to keep his tones even, but in spite of himself a tremor shook his words. "The man I saw to-day is my last hope; he is the chief clerk, and what he says controls the opinions of others. If I could have gotten past his decision, I might have influenced the senior member of the firm, but he is a man who leaves details to his subordinates, and Mr. Hanan was suspicious of me from the first. He isn't sure," he continued with a little laugh, which he tried to make sound spontaneous, "whether I am a stupendous fraud, or an escaped lunatic."

"We can wait; your chance will come," she soothed him with a rare smile.

"But in the meanwhile—," he finished for her and paused himself.

A sheaf of unpaid bills in the afternoon mail, with the curt and wholly unnecessary "Please Remit" in boldly impertinent characters across the bottom of every one drove Edwards out into the wilting sun. He knew the main street from end to end; he could tell how many trolley poles were on its corners; he felt that he almost knew the stones in the buildings, and that the pavements were worn with the constant passing of his feet, so often in the past four months had he walked, at first buoyantly, then hopefully, at last wearily up and down its length.

The usual idle crowd jostled around the baseball bulletins. Edwards joined them mechanically. "I can be a side-walk fan, even if I am impecunious." He smiled to himself as he said the words, and then listened idly to a voice at his side, "We are getting metropolitan, see that!"

The "That" was an item above the baseball score. Edwards looked and the letters burned themselves like white fire into his consciousness.

STRIKE SPREADS TO OUR CITY.
WAITERS AT ADAMS' WALK OUT
AFTER BREAKFAST THIS MORNING.

"Good!" he said aloud. The man at his side smiled appreciatively at him; the home team had scored another run, but unheeding that Edwards walked down the street with a lighter step than he had known for days.

The proprietor of Adams' restaurant belied both his name and his vocation. He should have been rubicund, corpulent, American; instead he was wiry, lank, foreign in appearance. His teeth projected over a full lower lip, his eyes set far back in his head and were concealed by wrinkles that seemed to have been acquired by years of squinting into men's motives.

"Of course I want waiters," he replied to Edwards' question, "any fool knows that." He paused, drew in his lower lip within the safe confines of his long teeth, squinted his eye intently on Edwards. "But do I want colored waiters? Now, do I?"

"It seems to me there's no choice for you in the matter," said Edwards good-humoredly.

The reply seemed to amuse the restaurant keeper immensely; he slapped the younger man on the back with a familiarity that made him wince both physically and spiritually.

"I guess I'll take you for head waiter." He was inclined to be jocular, even in the face of the disaster which the morning's strike had brought him. "Peel off and go to work. Say, stop!" as Edwards looked around to take his bearings, "What's your name?"

"Louis Edwards."

"Uh huh, had any experience?"

"Yes, some years ago, when I was in school."

"Uh huh, then waiting ain't your general work."

"No."

"Uh huh, what do you do for a living?"

"I'm a civil engineer."

One eye-brow of the saturnine Adams shot up, and he withdrew his lower lip entirely under his teeth.

"Well, say man, if you're an engineer, what you want to be strike-breaking here in a waiter's coat for, eh?"

Edwards' face darkened, and he shrugged his shoulders. "They don't need me, I guess," he replied briefly. It was an effort, and the restaurant keeper saw it, but his wonder overcame his sympathy.

"Don't need you with all that going on at the Monarch works? Why, man, I'd a thought every engineer this side o' hell would be needed out there."

"So did I; that's why I came here, but—"

"Say, kid, I'm sorry for you, I surely am; you go on to work."

"And so," narrated Edwards to Margaret, after midnight, when he had gotten in from his first day's work, "I became at once head waiter, first assistant, all the other waiters, chief boss, steward, and high-muck-a-muck, with all the emoluments and perquisites thereof."

Margaret was silent; with her ready sympathy she knew that no words of hers were needed then; they would only add to the burdens he had to bear. Nothing could be more bitter than this apparent blasting of his lifelong hopes, this seeming lowering of his standard. She said nothing, but the pressure of her slim brown hand in his meant more than words to them both.

"It's hard to keep the vision true," he groaned.

If it was hard that night, it grew doubly so within the next few weeks. Not lightly were the deposed waiters to take their own self-dismissal and supplanting. Daily they menaced the restaurant with their surly attentions, ugly and ominous. Adams shot out his lower lip from the confines of his long teeth and swore in a various language that he'd run his own place if he had to get every nigger in Africa to help him. The three of four men whom he was able to induce to stay with him in the face of missiles of every nature, threatened every day to give up the battle. Edwards was the force that held them together. He used every argument from the purely material one of holding on to the job now that they had it, through the negative one of loyalty to the man in his hour of need, to the altruistic one of keeping the place open for colored men for all time. There were none of them of such value as his own personality, and the fact that he stuck through all the turmoil. He wiped the mud from his face, picked up the putrid vegetables that often strewed the floor, barricaded the doors at night, replaced orders that were destroyed by well-aimed stones, and stood by Adams' side when the fight threatened to grow serious.

Adams was appreciative. "Say, kid, I don't know what I'd a done without you, now that's honest. Take it from me, when you need a friend anywhere on earth, and you can send me a wireless, I'm right there with the goods in answer to your S. O. S."

This was on the afternoon when the patrol, lined up in front of the restaurant, gathered in a few of the most disturbing ones, none of whom, by the way, had ever been employed in the place. "Sympathy" had pervaded the town.

The humid August days melted into the sultry ones of September. The self-dismissed waiters had quieted down, and save for an occasional missile, annoyed Adams and his corps of dark-skinned helpers no longer. Edwards had resigned himself to his temporary discomforts. He felt, with the optimism of the idealist, that it was only for a little while; the fact that he had sought work at his profession for nearly a year had not yet discouraged him. He would explain carefully to Margaret when the day's work was over, that it was only for a little while; he would earn enough at this to enable them to get away, and then in some other place he would be able to stand up with the proud consciousness that all his training had not been in vain.

He was revolving all these plans in his mind one Saturday night. It was at the hour when business was dull, and he leaned against the window and sought entertainment from the crowd on the street. Saturday night, with all the blare and glare and garishness dear to the heart of the middle-class provincial of the smaller cities, was holding court on the city streets. The hot September sun had left humidity and closeness in its wake, and the evening mists had scarce had time to cast coolness over the town. Shop windows glared wares through colored lights, and phonographs shrilled popular tunes from open store doors to attract unwary passersby. Half-grown boys and girls, happy in the license of Saturday night on the crowded streets, jostled one another and pushed in long lines, shouted familiar epithets at other pedestrians with all the abandon of the ill-breeding common to the class. One crowd, in particular, attracted Edwards' attention. The girls were brave in semi-decollete waists, scant short skirts and exaggerated heads, built up in fanciful designs; the boys with flamboyant red neckties, striking hat-bands, and white trousers. They made a snake line, boys and girls, hands on each others' shoulders, and rushed shouting through the press of shoppers, scattering the inattentive right and left. Edwards' lip curled, "Now, if those were colored boys and girls—"

His reflections were never finished, for a patron moved towards his table, and the critic of human life became once more the deferential waiter.

He did not move a muscle of his face as he placed the glass of water on the table, handed the menu card, and stood at attention waiting for the order, although he had recognized at first glance the half-sneering face of his old hope— Hanan, of the great concern which had no need of him. To Hanan, the man who brought his order was but one of the horde of menials who satisfied his daily wants and soothed his vanity when the cares of the day had ceased pressing on his shoulders. He had not even looked at the man's face, and for this Edwards was grateful.

A new note had crept into the noise on the streets; there was in it now, not so much mirth and ribaldry as menace and anger. Edwards looked outside in slight alarm; he had grown used to that note in the clamor of the streets, particularly on Saturday nights; it meant that the whole restaurant must be prepared to quell a disturbance. The snake line had changed; there were only flamboyant hat-bands in it now, the decolleté shirt waists and scant skirts had taken refuge on another corner. Something in the shouting attracted Hanan's attention, and he looked up wonderingly.

"What are they saying?" he inquired. Edwards did not answer; he was so familiar with the old cry that he thought it unnecessary.

"Yah! Yah! Old Adams hires niggers! Hires niggers!"

"Why, that is so," Hanan looked up at Edwards' dark face for the first time. "This is quite an innovation for Adams' place. How did it happen?"

"We are strike-breakers," replied the waiter quietly, then he grew hot, for a gleam of recognition came into Hanan's eyes.

"Oh, yes, I see. Aren't you the young man who asked me for employment as an engineer at the Monarch works?"

Edwards bowed, he could not answer; hurt pride surged up within him and made his eyes hot and his hands clammy.

"Well, er—I'm glad you've found a place to work; very sensible of you, I'm sure. I should think, too, that it is work for which you would be more fitted than engineering."

Edwards started to reply, but the hot words were checked on his lips. The shouting had reached a shrillness which boded immediate results, and with the precision of a missile from a warship's gun, a stone hurtled through the glass of the long window. It struck Edwards' hand, glanced through the dishes on the tray which he was in the act of setting on the table, and tipped half its contents over Hanan's knee. He sprang to his feet angrily, striving to brush the dèbris of his dinner from his immaculate clothing, and turned angrily upon Edwards.

"That is criminally careless of you!" he flared, his eyes blazing in his pallid face. "You could have prevented that; you're not even a good waiter, much less an engineer."

And then something snapped in the darker man's head. The long strain of the fruitless summer; the struggle of keeping together the men who worked under him in the restaurant; the heat, and the task of enduring what was to him the humiliation of serving, and this last injustice, all culminated in a blinding flash in his brain. Reason, intelligence, all was obscured, save a man's hatred, and a desire to wreak his wrongs on the man, who, for the time being, represented the author of them. He sprang at the white man's throat and bore him to the floor. They wrestled and fought together, struggling, biting, snarling, like brutes in the dèbris of food and the clutter of overturned chairs and tables.

The telephone rang insistently. Adams wiped his hands on a towel, and carefully moved a paint brush out of the way, as he picked up the receiver.

"Hello!" he called. "Yes, this is Adams, the restaurant keeper. Who? Uh huh. Wants to know if I'll go his bail? Say, that nigger's got softening of the brain. Course not, let him serve his time, making all that row in my place; never had no row here before. No, I don't never want to see him again."

He hung up the receiver with a bang, and went back to his painting. He had almost finished his sign, and he smiled as he ended it with a flourish:

WAITERS WANTED. NONE BUT
WHITE MEN NEED APPLY

Out in the county work-house, Edwards sat on his cot, his head buried in his hands. He wondered what Margaret was doing all this long hot Sunday, if the tears were blinding her sight as they did his; then he started to his feet, as the warden called his name. Margaret stood before him, her arms outstretched, her mouth quivering with tenderness and sympathy, her whole form yearning towards him with a passion of maternal love.

"Margaret! You here, in this place?"

"Aren't you here?" she smiled bravely, and drew his head towards the refuge of her bosom. "Did you think I wouldn't come to see you?"

"To think I should have brought you to this," he moaned.

She stilled his reproaches and heard the story from his lips. Then she murmured with bloodless mouth, "How long will it be?"

"A long time, dearest—and you?"

"I can go home, and work," she answered briefly, "and wait for you, be it ten months or ten years—and then—?"

"And then—," they stared into each other's eyes like frightened children. Suddenly his form straightened up, and the vision of his ideal irradiated his face with hope and happiness.

"And then, Beloved," he cried, "then we will start all over again. Somewhere, I am needed; somewhere in this world there are wanted dark-skinned men like me to dig and blast and build bridges and make straight the roads of the world, and I am going to find that place—with you."

She smiled back trustfully at him. "Only keep true to your ideal, dearest," she whispered, "and you will find the place. Your window faces the south, Louis. Look up and out of it all the while you are here, for it is there, in our own southland, that you will find the realization of your dream."

2 THE CLOSING DOOR
Angelina Weld Grimké

From *Birth Control Review*,
September–October 1919

I was fifteen at the time, diffident and old far beyond my years from much knocking about from pillar to post, a yellow, scrawny, unbeautiful girl, when the big heart of Agnes Milton took pity upon me, loved me and brought me home to live with her in her tiny, sun-filled flat. We were only distantly related, very distantly, in fact, on my dead father's side. You can see, then, there was no binding blood-tie between us, that she was under absolutely no obligation to do what she did. I have wondered time and again how many women would have opened their hearts and their homes, as Agnes Milton did, to a forlorn, unattractive, homeless girl-woman. That one fine, free, generous act of hers alone shows the wonder-quality of her soul.

Just one little word to explain me. After my father had taken one last cup too many and they had carried him, for the last time, out of the house into which he had been carried so often, my mother, being compelled to work again, returned to the rich family with whom she had been a maid before her marriage. She regarded me as seriously, I suppose, as she did anything in this world; but it was impossible to have me with her. I was passed along from one of her relatives to another. When one tired of me, on I went to the next. Well, I can say this for each and all of them, they certainly believed in teaching me how to work! Judging by the number of homes in which I lived until I was fifteen, my mother was rich indeed in one possession—an abundance of relatives.

And then came Agnes Milton.

Have you ever, I wonder, known a happy person? I mean a really happy one? He is as rare as a white blackbird in this sombre-faced world of ours. I have known two and only two. They were Agnes Milton and her husband, Jim. And their happiness did not last. Jim was a brown, good-natured giant with a slow, most attractive smile and gleaming teeth. He spoke always in a deep sad drawl, and you would have thought him the most unhappy person imaginable until you glimpsed his black eyes fairly twinkling under their half-closed lids. He made money—what is called "easy money"—by playing ragtime for dances. He was one of a troupe that are called "social entertainers." As far as Jim was concerned, it would have slipped away in just as easy a manner, if it hadn't been for Agnes. For she, in spite of all her seeming carefree joyousness, was a thrifty soul. As long as Jim could have good food and plenty of it, now and then the theatre, a concert or a dance, and his gold-tipped cigarettes, he didn't care what became of his money.

"Oh, Ag!"

If I close my eyes I can hear his slow sad voice as clearly as though these ten long years had not passed by. I can hear the click of the patent lock as he closed the flat door. I can hear the bang of his hat as he hung it on the rack. I can get the whiff of his cigarette.

"Oh, Ag!"

"That you, Jim?" I can see Agnes' happy eyes and hear her eager, soft voice. And then after a pause, that sad voice:

"No, Ag!"

I can hear her delighted little chuckle. She very seldom laughed outright.

"Where are you, anyway?" It was the plaintive voice again.

"Here!"

And then he'd make believe he couldn't find her and go hunting her all over that tiny flat, searching for her in every room he knew she was not. And he'd stumble over things in pretended excitement and haste and grunt and swear all in that inimitable slow way of his. And she'd stand there, her eyes shining and every once in a while giving that dear little chuckle of hers.

Finally he'd appear in the door panting and disheveled and would look at her in pretended intense surprise for a second, and then he'd say in an aggrieved voice:

"'S not fair, Agnes! 'S not fair!"

She wouldn't say a word, just stand there smiling at him. After a little, slowly, he'd begin to smile too.

That smile of theirs was one of the most beautiful things I have ever seen and each meeting it was the same. Their joy and love seemed to gush up and bubble over through their lips and eyes.

Presently he'd say:

"Catch!"

She'd hold up her little white apron by the corners and he'd put his hand in his pocket and bring out sometimes a big, sometimes a little, wad of greenbacks and toss it to her and she'd catch it, too, I can tell you. And her eyes would beam and dance at him over it. Oh! she didn't love the money for itself but him for trusting her with it.

For fear you may not understand I must tell you no more generous soul ever lived than Agnes Milton. Look at what she did for me. And she was always giving a nickel or a dime to some child, flowers or fruit to a sick woman, money to tide over a friend. No beggar was ever turned away empty, from her flat. But she managed, somehow, to increase her little hoard in the bank against that possible rainy day.

Well, to return. At this juncture, Jim would say oh! so sadly his eyes fairly twinkling:

"Please, m'a'm, do I get paid today too?"

And then she'd screw up her mouth and twist her head to the side and look at him and say in a most judicial manner:

"Well, now, I really can't say as to that. It strikes me you'll have to find that out for yourself."

Oh! they didn't mind me. He would reach her, it seemed, in one stride and would pick her up bodily, apron, money and all. After a space, she'd disentangle herself and say sternly, shaking the while her little forefinger before his delighted eyes:

"Jim Milton, you've overdrawn your wages again."

And then he'd look oh! so contrite and so upset and so shocked at being caught in such a gigantic piece of attempted fraud.

"No?" he'd say. If you only could have heard the mournful drawl of him.

"No? Now, is that so? I'm really at heart an honest, hard-working man. I'll have to pay it back."

He did. I can vouch for it.

Sometimes after this, he'd swing her up onto his shoulder and they'd go dashing and prancing and shrieking and laughing all over the little flat. Once after I had seen scared faces appearing at various windows, at times like these, I used to rush around and shut the windows down tight. Two happy children, that's what they were then—younger even than I.

There was just the merest suspicion of a cloud over their happiness, these days; they had been married five years and had no children.

It was the mother heart of Agnes that had yearned over me, had pity upon me, loved me and brought me to live in the only home I have ever known. I have cared for people. I care for Jim; but Agnes Milton is the only person I have ever really loved. I love her still. And before it was too late, I used to pray that in some way I might change places with her and go into that darkness where though, still living, one forgets sun and moon and stars and flowers and winds—and love itself, and existence means dark, foul-smelling cages, hollow clanging doors, hollow monotonous days. But a month ago when Jim and I went to see her, she had changed—she had receded even from us. She seemed—how can I express it?—blank, empty, a grey automaton, a mere shell. No soul looked out at us through her vacant eyes.

We did not utter a word during our long journey homeward. Jim had unlocked the door before I spoke.

"Jim," I said, "they may still have the poor husk of her cooped up there but her soul, thank God, at least for that, is free at last!"

And Jim, I cannot tell of his face, said never a word but turned away and went heavily down the stairs. And I, I went into Agnes Milton's flat and closed the door. You would never have dreamed it was the same place. For a long time I stood amid all the brightness and mockery of her sun-drenched rooms. And I prayed. Night and day I have prayed since, the same prayer—that God, if he knows any pity at all may soon, soon release the poor spent body of hers.

I wish I might show you Agnes Milton of those far off happy days. She wasn't tall and she wasn't short; she wasn't stout and she wasn't thin. Her back was straight and her head high. She was rather graceful, I thought. In coloring she was Spanish or Italian. Her hair was not very long but it was soft and silky and black. Her features were not too sharp, her eyes clear and dark, a warm leaf brown in fact. Her mouth was really beautiful. This doesn't give her I find. It was the shining beauty and gayety of her soul that lighted up her whole body and somehow made her her. And she was generally smiling or chuckling. Her eyes almost closed when she did so and there were the most delightful crinkles all about them. Under her left eye there was a small scar, a reminder of some childhood escapade, that became, when she smiled, the most adorable of dimples.

One day, I remember, we were standing at the window in the bright sunlight. Some excitement in the street below had drawn us. I turned to her—the reason has gone from me now—and called out suddenly:

"Agnes Milton!"

"Heavens! What is it?"

"Why, you're wrinkling!"

"Wrinkling! Where?" And she began inspecting the smooth freshness of her housedress.

"No, your face," I exclaimed. "Honest! Stand still there in that light. Now! Just look at them all around your eyes."

She chuckled.

"How you ever expect me to see them I don't know, without a glass or anything!"

And her face crinkled up into a smile.

"There! That's it!—That's how you get them."

"How?"

"Smiling too much."

"Oh no! Lucy, child, that's impossible."

"How do you mean impossible? You didn't get them that way? Just wait till I get a glass."

"No, don't," and she stopped me with a detaining hand. "I'm not doubting you. What I mean is—it's absolutely impossible to smile too much."

I felt my eyes stretching with surprise.

"You mean," I said, "you don't mind being wrinkled? You, a woman?"

She shook her head at me many times, smiling and chuckling softly the while.

"Not the very littlest, tiniest bit—not this much," and she showed me just the barest tip of her pink tongue between her white teeth. She smiled, then, and there was the dimple.

"And you only twenty-five?" I exclaimed.

She didn't answer for a moment and when she did she spoke quietly:

"Lucy, child, we've all got to wrinkle sometime, somehow, if we live long enough. I'd much rather know mine were smile ones than frown ones." She waited a second and then looked at me with her beautiful clear eyes and added, "Wouldn't you?"

For reply I leaned forward and kissed them. I loved them from that time on.

Here is another memory of her—perhaps the loveliest of them all and yet, as you will see, tinged with the first sadness. It came near the end of our happy days. It was a May dusk. I had been sewing all the afternoon and was as close to the window as I could get to catch the last of the failing light. I was trying to thread a needle—had been trying for several minutes, in fact, and was just in the very act of succeeding when two soft hands were clapped over my eyes.

"Oh, Agnes!" I said none too pleasantly. It was provoking. "There! You've made me lose my needle."

"Bother your old needle, cross patch!" she said close to my ear. She still held her hands over my eyes.

I waited a moment or so.

"Well," I said, "what's the idea?"

"Please don't be cross," came the soft voice still close to my ear.

"I'm not."

At that she chuckled.

"Well!" I said.

"I'm trying to tell you something. Sh! not so loud."

"Well, go ahead then; and why must I sh!"

"Because you must."

I waited.

"Well!" I said a third time, but in a whisper to humor her. We were alone in the flat; there was no reason I could see for this tremendous secrecy.

"I'm waiting for you to be sweet to me."

"I am. But why I should have to lose my needle and my temper and be blinded and sweet just to hear something—is beyond me."

"Because I don't wish you to see me while I say it."

Her soft lips were kissing my ear.

"Well, I'm very sweet now. What is it?"

There was another little pause and during it her fingers over my eyes trembled a little. She was breathing quicker too.

"Agnes Milton, what *is* it?"

"Wait, I'm just trying to think *how* to tell you. Are you sure you're very sweet?"

"Sure."

I loved the feel of her hands and sat very still.

"Lucy!"

"Yes."

"What do you think would be the loveliest, loveliest thing for you to know was—was—there—close—just under your heart?"

But I waited for no more. I took her hands from my eyes and turned to look at her. The beauty of her face made me catch my breath.

At last I said:

"You mean—" I didn't need to finish.

"Yes! Yes! And I'm so happy, happy, happy! And so is Jim."

"Agnes, Oh my dear, and so am I!" And I kissed her two dear eyes. "But why mustn't I whoop? I've simply got to," I added.

"No! No! No! Oh, sh!" And for the very first time I saw fear in her eyes.

"Agnes," I said, "what is it?"

"I'm—I'm just a little afraid, I believe."

"Afraid!" I had cried out in surprise.

"Sh! Lucy!—Yes."

"But of what?" I spoke in a half whisper too. "You mean you're afraid you may die?"

"Oh, no, not that."

"What, then?"

"Lucy," her answer came slowly a little abstractedly, "there's—such—a thing—as being—*too* happy,—*too* happy."

"Nonsense," I answered.

But she only shook her head at me slowly many times and her great wistful eyes came to mine and seemed to cling to them. It made my heart fairly ache and I turned my head away so that she couldn't see her fears were affecting me. And then quite suddenly I felt a disagreeable little chill run up and down my back.

"Lucy," she said after a little.

"Yes?" I was looking out of the window and not at her.

"Do you remember Kipling's 'Without Benefit of Clergy?'"

I did and I said so. Agnes had Kipling bound in ten beautiful volumes. She loved him. At first that had been enough for me, and then I had come to love him for himself. I had read all of those ten volumes through from cover to cover, poetry and all.

"You haven't forgotten Ameera, then?"

"No."

"Poor Ameera!" She was thoughtful a moment and then went on: "She knew what it was to be too happy. Do you remember what she said once to Holden?"

Again I felt that queer little shiver.

"She said many things, as I remember, Agnes. Which?"

"This was after Tota's death."

"Well!"

"They were on the roof—she and Holden—under the night."

Her eyes suddenly widened and darkened and then she went on:

"She turned to Holden and said: 'We must make no protestations of delight but go softly underneath the stars, lest God find us out.'" She paused. "Do you remember?"

"Yes," I answered; but I couldn't look at her.

"Well," she spoke slowly and quietly, "I have a feeling here, Lucy," and she placed her left hand against her heart, "here, that Jim and you and I must go softly—very softly—underneath the stars."

Again I felt that unpleasant chill up and down my back.

She stood just where she was for a little space, her hand still against her heart and her eyes wide, dark and unseeing, fixed straight ahead of her. Then suddenly and without a sound she turned and went towards the door and opened it.

I started to follow her; but she put up her hand.

"No, Lucy, please—I wish to be alone—for a little."

And with that she went and shut the door very slowly, quite noiselessly behind her. The closing was so slow, so silent, that I could not tell just when it shut. I found myself trembling violently. A sudden and inexplicable terror filled me as that door closed behind her.

We were to become accustomed to it, Jim and I, as much as it was possible to do so, in those terrible days that were to follow. We were to become used to entering a room in search of Agnes, only to find it empty and the door opposite closing, closing, almost imperceptibly, noiselessly—and, yes, at last irrevocably—between us. And each time it happened the terror was as fresh upon me as at the very first.

The days that immediately followed I cannot say were really unhappy ones. More to humor Agnes at first than anything else "we went softly." But as time passed even we became infected. Literally and figuratively we began to go "softly under the stars." We came to feel that each of us moved ever with a finger to his lips. There came to be also a sort of expectancy upon us, a listening, a waiting. Even the neighbors noticed the difference. Jim still played his ragtime and sang, but softly; we laughed and joked, but quietly. We got so we even washed the dishes and pots and pans quietly. Sometimes Jim and I forgot, but as certainly as we did there was Agnes in the door, dark-eyed, a little pale and her, "Oh, Jim!—Oh, Lucy! Sh!"

I haven't spoken of this before because it wasn't necessary. Agnes had a brother called Bob. He was her favorite of all her brothers and sisters. He was younger than she, five years, I think, a handsome, harum-scarum, happy-go-lucky, restless, reckless daredevil, but sweet-tempered and good hearted and lovable withal. I don't believe he knew what fear was. His home was in Mississippi, a small town there. It was the family home, in fact. Agnes had lived there herself until she was seventeen or eighteen. He had visited us two or three times and you can imagine the pandemonium that reigned at such times, for he had come during our happy days. Well, he was very fond of Agnes and, as irresponsible as he seemed, one thing he never failed to do was to write her a letter every single week. Each Tuesday morning, just like clock-work, the very first mail there was his letter. Other mornings Agnes was not so particular; but Tuesday mornings she always went herself to the mailbox in the hall.

It was a Tuesday morning about four months, maybe, after my first experience with the closing door. The bell rang three times, the postman's signal when he had left a letter, Agnes came to her feet, her eyes sparkling:

"My letter from Bob," she said and made for the door.

She came back slowly, I noticed, and her face was a little pale and worried. She had an opened and an unopened letter in her hand.

"Well, what does Bob say?" I asked.

"This—this isn't from Bob," she said slowly. "It's only a bill."

"Well, go ahead and open his letter," I said.

"There—there wasn't any, Lucy."

"What!" I exclaimed. I was surprised.

"No. I don't know what it means."

"It will come probably in the second mail," I said. "It has sometimes."

"Yes," she said, I thought rather listlessly.

It didn't come in the second mail nor in the third.

"Agnes," I said. "There's some good explanation. It's not like Bob to fail you."

"No."

"He's busy or got a girl maybe."

She was a little jealous of him and I hoped this last would rouse her, but it didn't.

"Yes, maybe that's it," she said without any life.

"Well, I hope you're not going to let this interfere with your walk," I said.

"I had thought—," she began, but I cut her off.

"You promised Jim you'd go out every single day," I reminded her.

"All right, Agnes Milton's conscience," she said smiling a little. "I'll go then."

She hadn't been gone fifteen minutes when the electric bell began shrilling continuously throughout the flat.

Somehow I knew it meant trouble. My mind immediately flew to Agnes. It took me a second or so to get myself together and then I went to the tube.

"Well," I called. My voice sounded strange and high.

A boy's voice answered:

"Lady here named Mrs. James Milton?"

"Yes." I managed to say.

"Telegram fo' you'se."

It wasn't Agnes, after all. I drew a deep breath. Nothing else seemed to matter for a minute.

"Say!" the voice called up from below. "Wot's de mattah wid you'se up dere?"

"Bring it up." I said at last. "Third floor, front."

I opened the door and waited.

The boy was taking his time and whistling as he came.

"Here!" I called out as he reached our floor.

It was inside his cap and he had to take it off to give it to me.

I saw him eyeing me rather curiously.

"You Mrs. Milton?" he asked.

"No, but this is her flat. I'll sign for it. She's out. Where do I sign? There? Have you a pencil?"

With the door shut behind me again, I began to think out what I had better do. Jim was not to be home until late that night. Within five minutes I had decided. I tore open the yellow envelope and read the message.

It ran: "Bob died suddenly. Under no circumstances come. Father."

The rest of that day was a nightmare to me. I concealed the telegram in my waist. Agnes came home finally and was so alarmed at my appearance, I pleaded a frightful sick headache and went to bed. When Jim came home late that night Agnes was asleep. I caught him in the hall and gave him the telegram. She had to be told, we decided, because a letter from Mississippi might come at any time. He broke it to her the next morning. We were all hard hit, but Agnes from that time on was a changed woman.

Day after day dragged by and the letter of explanation did not come. It was strange, to say the least.

The Sunday afternoon following, we were all sitting, after dinner, in the little parlor. None of us had been saying much.

Suddenly Agnes said:

"Jim!"

"Yes!"

"Wasn't it strange that father never said how or when Bob died?"

"Would have made the telegram too long and expensive, perhaps," Jim replied.

We were all thinking, in the pause that followed, the same thing, I dare say. Agnes' father was not poor and it did seem he might have done that much.

"And why, do you suppose, I was not to come under any circumstances? And why don't they write?"

Just then the bell rang and there was no chance for a reply.

Jim got up in his leisurely way and went to the tube.

Agnes and I both listened—a little tensely, I remember.

"Yes!" we heard Jim say, and then with spaces in between:

"Joe?—Joe who?—I think you must have made a mistake. No, I can't say that I do know anyone called Joe. What? Milton? Yes, that's my name! What? Oh! Brooks. Joe Brooks?—"

But Agnes waited for no more. She rushed by me into the hall.

"Jim! Jim! It's my brother Joe."

"Look here! Are you Agnes' brother, Joe?" Jim called quickly for him. "Great Jehoshaphat! Man! Come up! What a mess I've made of this."

For the first time I saw Jim move quickly. Within a second he was out of the flat and running down the stairs. Agnes followed to the stairhead and waited there. I went back into the little parlor, for I had followed her into the hall, and sat down and waited.

They all came in presently. Joe was older than Agnes but looked very much like her. He was thin, his face really haggard and his hair quite grey. I found out afterward that he was in his early thirties but he appeared much older. He was smiling, but the smile did not reach his eyes. They were strange aloof eyes. They rested on you and yet seemed to see something beyond. You felt as though they had looked upon something that could never be forgotten. When he was not smiling his face was grim, the chin firm and set. He was a man of very few words, I found.

Agnes and Jim were both talking at once and he answered them now and then in monosyllables. Agnes introduced us. He shook hands, I thought in rather a perfunctory way, without saying anything, and we all sat down.

We steered clear quite deliberately from the thoughts uppermost in all our minds. We spoke of his journey, when he left Mississippi, the length of time it had taken him to come and the weather. Suddenly Agnes jumped up:

"Joe, aren't you famished?"

"Well, I wouldn't mind a little something, Agnes," he answered, and then he added:

"I'm not as starved as I was traveling in the South; but I have kind of a hollow feeling."

"What do you mean?" she asked.

"Jim-Crow cars," he answered laconically.

"I'd forgotten," she said. "I've been away so long."

He made no reply.

"Aren't conditions any better at all?" she asked after a little.

"No, I can't say as they are."

None of us said anything. She stood there a minute or so, pulling away at the frill on her apron. She stopped suddenly, drew a long breath, and said:

"I wish you all could move away, Joe, and come North."

For one second before he lowered his eyes I saw a strange gleam in them. He seemed to be examining his shoes carefully from all angles. His jaw looked grimmer than ever and I saw a flickering of the muscles in his cheeks.

"That would be nice," he said at last and then added, "but we can't, Agnes. I like my coffee strong, please."

"Joe," she said, going to the door. "I'm sorry, I was forgetting."

I rose at that.

"Agnes, let me go. You stay here."

She hesitated, but Joe spoke up:

"No, Agnes, you go. I know your cooking."

You could have heard a pin drop for a minute. Jim looked queer and so did Agnes for a second and then she tried to laugh it off.

"Don't mind Joe. He doesn't mean anything. He always was like that."

And then she left us.

Well, I was hurt. Joe made no attempt to apologize or anything. He even seemed to have forgotten me. Jim looked at me and smiled, his nice smile, but I was really hurt. I came to understand, however, later. Presently Joe said:

"About Agnes! We hadn't been told anything!"

"Didn't she write about it?"

"No."

"Wanted to surprise you, I guess."

"How long?" Joe asked after a little.

"Before?"

"Yes."

"Four months, I should say."

"That complicates matters some."

I got up to leave. I was so evidently in the way.

Joe looked up quietly and said:

"Oh! don't go! It isn't necessary."

I sat down again.

"No, Lucy, stay." Jim added. "What do you mean 'complicates'?"

Joe examined his shoes for several moments and then looked up suddenly.

"Just where is Agnes?"

"In the kitchen, I guess." Jim looked a trifle surprised.

"Where is that?"

"The other end of the flat near the door."

"She can't possibly hear anything, then?"

"No."

"Well, then, listen, Jim, and you, what's your name? Lucy? Well, Lucy, then. Listen carefully, you two, to every single word I am going to say." He frowned a few moments at his shoes and then went on: "Bob went out fishing in the woods near his shack; spent the night there; slept in wet clothes; it had been raining all day; came home; contracted double pneumonia and died in two days time. Have you that?"

We both nodded. "That's the story we are to tell Agnes."

Jim had his mouth open to ask something, when Agnes came in. She had very evidently not heard anything, however, for there was a little color in her face and it was just a little happy again.

"I've been thinking about you, Joe," she said. "What on earth are you getting so grey for?"

"Grey!" he exclaimed. "Am I grey?" There was no doubt about it, his surprise was genuine.

"Didn't you know it?" She chuckled a little. It was the first time in days.

"No, I didn't."

She made him get up, at that, and drew him to the oval glass over the mantel. "Don't you ever look at yourself, Joe?"

"Not much, that's the truth." I could see his face in the mirror from where I sat. His eyes widened a trifle, I saw, and then he turned away abruptly and sat down again. He made no comment. Agnes broke the rather little silence that followed.

"Joe!"

"Yes!"

"You haven't been sick or anything, have you?"

"No, why?"

"You seem so much thinner. When I last saw you you were almost stout."

"That's some years ago, Agnes."

"Yes, but one ought to get stouter not thinner with age."

Again I caught that strange gleam in his eyes before he lowered them. For a moment he sat perfectly still without answering.

"You can put it down to hard work, if you like, Agnes. Isn't that my coffee I smell boiling over?"

"Yes, I believe it is. I just ran in to tell you I'll be ready for you in about ten minutes."

She went out hastily but took time to pull the portière across the door. I thought it strange at the time and looked at Jim. He didn't seem to notice it, however, but waited, I saw, until he had heard Agnes' heel taps going into the kitchen.

"Now," he said, "what do you mean when you say that is the story we are to tell Agnes?"

"Just that."

"You mean—," he paused, "that it isn't true?"

"No, it isn't true."

"Bob didn't die that way?"

"No."

I felt myself stiffening in my chair and my two hands gripping the two arms of my chair tightly. I looked at Jim. I sensed the same tensioning in him. There was a long pause. Joe was examining his shoes again. The flickering in his cheeks I saw was more noticeable.

finally Jim brought out just one word:

"How?"

"There was a little trouble," he began and then paused so long Jim said:

"You mean he was—injured in some way?"

Joe looked up suddenly at Jim, at that, and then down again. But his expression even in that fleeting glance set me to trembling all over. Jim, I saw, had been affected too. He sat stiffly bent forward. He had been in the act of raising his cigarette to his lips and his arm seemed as though frozen in mid-air.

"Yes," he said, "injured." But the way in which he said "injured" made me tremble all the more.

Again there was a pause and again Jim broke it with his one word:

"How?"

"You don't read the papers, I see," Joe said.

"Yes, I read them."

"It was in all the papers."

"I missed it, then."

"Yes."

It was quiet again for a little.

"Have you ever lived in the South?" Joe asked.

"No."

"Nice civilized place, the South," Joe said.

And again I found myself trembling violently. I had to fight with might and main to keep my teeth from chattering. And yet it was not what he had said but his tone again.

"I hadn't so heard it described," Jim said after a little.

"No?—You didn't know, I suppose, that there is an unwritten law in the South that when a colored and a white person meet on the sidewalk, the colored person must get off into the street until the white one passes?"

"No, I hadn't heard of it."

"Well, it's so. That was the little trouble."

"You mean—"

"Bob refused to get off the sidewalk."

"Well?"

"The white man pushed him off. Bob knocked him down. The white man attempted to teach the 'damned nigger' a lesson." Again he paused.

"Well?"

"The lesson didn't end properly. Bob all but killed him."

It was so still in that room that although Jim was sitting across the room I could hear his watch ticking distinctly in his vest pocket. I had been holding my breath and when I was forced to expel it, the sound was so loud they both turned quickly towards me, startled for the second.

"That would have been Bob." It was Jim speaking.

"Yes."

"I suppose it didn't end there?"

"No."

"Go on, Joe." Even Jim's voice sounded strained and strange.

And Joe went on. He never raised his voice, never lowered it. Throughout, his tone was entirely colorless. And yet as though it had been seared into my very soul I remember word for word, everything he said.

"An orderly mob, in an orderly manner, on a Sunday morning—I am quoting the newspapers—broke into the jail, took him out, slung him up to the limb of a tree, riddled his body with bullets, saturated it with coal oil, lighted a fire underneath him, gouged out his eyes with red hot irons, burnt him to a crisp and then sold souvenirs of him, ears, fingers, toes. His teeth brought five dollars each." He ceased for a moment.

"He is still hanging on that tree.—We are not allowed to have even what is left."

There was a roaring in my ears. I seemed to be a long way off. I was sinking into a horrible black vortex that seemed to be sucking me down. I opened my eyes and saw Jim dimly. His nostrils seemed to be two black wide holes. His face was taut, every line set. I saw him draw a great deep breath. The blackness sucked me down still deeper. And then suddenly I found myself on my feet struggling against that hideous darkness and I heard my own voice as from a great distance calling out over and over again, "Oh, my God! Oh, my God! Oh, my God!"

They both came running to me, but I should have fainted for the first and only time in my life but that I heard suddenly above those strange noises in my ears a little choking, strangling sound. It revived me instantly. I broke from them and tried to get to the door.

"Agnes! Agnes!" I called out.

But they were before me. Jim tore the portière aside. They caught her just as she was falling.

She lay unconscious for hours. When she did come to, she found all three of us about her bed. Her bewildered eyes went from Jim's face to mine and then to Joe's. They paused there; she frowned a little. And then we saw the whole thing slowly come back to her. She groaned and closed her eyes. Joe started to leave the room but she opened her eyes quickly and indicated that he was not to go. He came back. Again she closed her eyes.

And then she began to grow restless.

"Agnes!" I asked. "Is there anything you want?"

She quieted a little under my voice.

"No," she said. "No."

Presently she opened her eyes again. They were very bright. She looked at each of us in turn a second time.

Then she said:

"I've had to live all this time to find out."

"Find out what, Agnes?" It was Jim's voice.

"Why I'm here—why I'm here."

"Yes, of course." Jim spoke oh! so gently, humoring her. His hand was smoothing away the damp little curls about her forehead.

"It's no use your making believe you understand, you don't." It was the first time I had ever heard her speak irritably to Jim. She moved her head away from his hand.

His eyes were a little hurt and he took his hand away.

"No." His voice was as gentle as ever. "I don't understand, then."

There was a pause and then she said abruptly:

"I'm an instrument."

No one answered her.

"That's all—an instrument."

We merely watched her.

"One of the many."

And then Jim in his kindly blundering way made his second mistake.

"Yes, Agnes," he said. "Yes."

But at that, she took even me by surprise. She sat up in bed suddenly, her eyes wild and staring and before we could stop her, began beating her breast.

"Agnes," I said. "Don't! Don't!"

"I shall," she said in a strange high voice.

Well, we let her alone. It would have meant a struggle.

And then amid little sobbing breaths, beating her breast the while, she began to cry out: "Yes!—Yes!—I!—I!—An instrument of reproduction!—another of the many!—a colored woman—doomed!—cursed!—put here!—willing or unwilling! For what?—to bring children here—men children—for the sport—the lust—of possible orderly mobs—who go about things—in an orderly manner—on Sunday mornings!"

"Agnes," I cried out. "Agnes! Your child will be born in the North. He need never go South."

She had listened to me at any rate.

"Yes," she said, "in the North. In the North.—And have there been no lynchings in the North?"

I was silenced.

"The North permits it too," she cried. "The North is silent as well as the South."

And then as she sat there her eyes became less wild but more terrible. They became the eyes of a seeress. When she spoke again she spoke loudly, clearly, slowly:

"There is a time coming—and soon—when no colored man—no colored woman—no colored child, born or unborn—will be safe—in this country."

"Oh Agnes," I cried again. "Sh! sh!"

She turned her terrible eyes upon me.

"There is no more need for silence—in this house. God has found us out."

"Oh Agnes." The tears were frankly running down my cheeks. "We must believe that God is very pitiful. We must. He will find a way."

She waited a moment and said simply:

"Will He?"

"Yes, Agnes! Yes!"

"I will believe you, then. I will give Him one more chance. Then, if He is not pitiful, then if He is not pitiful—" But she did not finish. She fell back upon her pillows. She had fainted again.

Agnes did not die, nor did her child. She had kept her body clean and healthy. She was up and around again, but an Agnes that never smiled, never chuckled any more. She was a grey pathetic shadow of herself. She who had loved joy so much, cared more, it seemed, for solitude than anything else in the world. That was why, when Jim or I went looking for her we found so often only the empty room and that imperceptibly closing, slowly closing, opposite door.

Joe went back to Mississippi and not one of us, ever again, mentioned Bob's name.

And Jim, poor Jim! I wish I could tell you of how beautiful he was those days. How he never complained, never was irritable, but was always so gentle, so full of understanding, that at times, I had to go out of the room for fear he might see my tears.

Only once I saw him when he thought himself alone. I had not known he was in his little den and entered it suddenly. I had made no sound, luckily, and he had not heard me. He was sitting leaning far forward, his head between his hands. I stood there five minutes at least, but not once did I see him stir. I silently stole out and left him.

It was a fortunate thing that Agnes had already done most of her sewing for the little expected stranger, for after Joe's visit, she never touched a thing.

"Agnes!" I said one day, not without fear and trepidation it is true. "Isn't there something I can do?"

"Do?" she repeated rather vaguely.

"Yes. Some sewing?"

"Oh! sewing," she said. "No, I think not, Lucy."

"You've—you've finished?" I persisted.

"No."

"Then—," I began.

"I hardly think we shall need any of them." And then she added, "I hope not."

"Agnes!" I cried out.

But she seemed to have forgotten me.

Well, time passed, it always does. And on a Sunday morning early Agnes' child was born. He was a beautiful, very grave baby with her great dark eyes.

As soon as they would let me, I went to her.

She was lying very still and straight, in the quiet, darkened room, her head turned on the pillow towards the wall. Her eyes were closed.

"Agnes!" I said in the barest whisper. "Are you asleep?"

"No," she said. And turned her head towards me and opened her eyes. I looked into her ravaged face. Agnes Milton had been down into Hell and back again.

Neither of us spoke for some time and then she said:

"Is he dead?"

"Your child?"

"Yes."

"I should say not, he's a perfect darling and so good."

No smile came into her face. It remained as expressionless as before. She paled a trifle more, I thought, if such a thing was possible.

"I'm sorry," she said finally.

"Agnes!" I spoke sharply. I couldn't help it.

But she closed her eyes and made no response.

I sat a long time looking at her. She must have felt my gaze, for she slowly lifted her lids and looked at me.

"Well," she said, "what is it, Lucy?"

"Haven't you seen your child, Agnes?"

"No."

"Don't you wish to see it?"

"No."

Again it was wrung out of me:

"Agnes, Agnes, don't tell me you don't love it."

For the first and only time a spasm of pain went over her poor pinched face.

"Ah!" she said. "That's it." And she closed her eyes and her face was as expressionless as ever.

I felt as though my heart were breaking.

Again she opened her eyes.

"Tell me, Lucy," she began.

"What, Agnes?"

"Is he—healthy?"

"Yes."

"Quite strong?"

"Yes."

"You think he will live, then?"

"Yes, Agnes."

She closed her eyes once more. It was very still within the room.

Again she opened her eyes. There was a strange expression in them now.

"Lucy!"

"Yes."

"You were wrong."

"Wrong, Agnes?"

"Yes."

"How?"

"You thought your God was pitiful."

"Agnes, but I do believe it."

After a long silence she said very slowly:

"He—is—not."

This time, when she closed her eyes, she turned her head slowly upon the pillow to the wall. I was dismissed.

And again Agnes did not die. Time passed and again she was up and about the flat. There was a strange, stony stillness upon her, now, I did not like, though. If we only could have understood, Jim and I, what it meant. Her love for solitude, now, had become a passion. And Jim and I knew more and more that empty room and that silently, slowly closing door.

She would have very little to do with her child. For some reason, I saw, she was afraid of it. I was its mother. I did for it, cared for it, loved it.

Twice only during these days I saw that stony stillness of hers broken.

The first time was one night. The baby was fast asleep, and she had stolen in to look at him, when she thought no one would know. I never wish to see such a tortured, hungry face again.

I was in the kitchen, the second time, when I heard strange sounds coming from my room. I rushed to it and there was Agnes, kneeling at the foot of the little crib, her head upon the spread. Great, terrible racking sobs were tearing her. The baby was lying there, all eyes, and beginning to whimper a little.

"Agnes! Oh, my dear! What is it?" The tears were streaming down my cheeks.

"Take him away! Take him away!" she gasped. "He's been cooing, and smiling and holding out his little arms to me. I can't stand it! I can't stand it."

I took him away. That was the only time I ever saw Agnes Milton weep.

The baby slept in my room. Agnes would not have him in hers. He was a restless little sleeper and I had to get up several times during the night to see that he was properly covered.

He was a noisy little sleeper as well. Many a night I have lain awake listening to the sound of his breathing. It is a lovely sound, a beautiful one—the breathing of a little baby in the dark.

This night, I remember, I had been up once and covered him over and had fallen off to sleep for the second time, when, for I had heard absolutely no sound, I awoke suddenly. There was upon me an overwhelming utterly paralyzing feeling not of fear but of horror. I thought, at first, I must have been having a nightmare, but strangely instead of diminishing, the longer I lay awake, the more it seemed to increase.

It was a moonlight night and the light came in through the open window in a broad, white, steady stream.

A coldness seemed to settle all about my heart. What was the matter with me? I made a tremendous effort and sat up. Everything seemed peaceful and quiet enough.

The moonlight cut the room in two. It was dark where I was and dark beyond where the baby was.

One brass knob at the foot of my bed shone brilliantly, I remember, in that bright stream and the door that led into the hall stood out fully revealed. I looked at that door and then my heart suddenly seemed to stop beating! I grew deathly cold. The door was closing slowly, imperceptibly, silently. Things were whirling around. I shut my eyes. When I opened them again the door was no longer moving; it had closed.

What had Agnes Milton wanted in my room? And the more I asked myself that question the deeper grew the horror.

And then slowly, by degrees, I began to realize there was something wrong within that room, something terribly wrong. But what was it?

I tried to get out of bed; but I seemed unable to move. I strained my eyes, but I could see nothing—only that bright knob, that stream of light, that closed white door.

I listened. It was quiet, very quiet, too quiet. But why too quiet? And then as though there had been a blinding flash of lightning I knew—the breathing wasn't there.

Agnes Milton had taken a pillow off of my bed and smothered her child.

One last word. Jim received word this morning. The door has finished closing for the last time—Agnes Milton is no more. God, I think, may be pitiful, after all.

3 MARY ELIZABETH

Jessie Redmon Fauset

FROM *CRISIS*, DECEMBER 1919

Mary Elizabeth was late that morning. As a direct result, Roger left for work without telling me good-bye, and I spent most of the day fighting the headache which always comes if I cry.

For I cannot get a breakfast. I can manage a dinner,—one just puts the roast in the oven and takes it out again. And I really excel in getting lunch. There is a good delicatessen near us, and with dainty service and flowers, I get along very nicely. But breakfast! In the first place, it's a meal I neither like nor need. And I never, if I live a thousand years, shall learn to like coffee. I suppose that is why I cannot make it.

"Roger," I faltered, when the awful truth burst upon me and I began to realize that Mary Elizabeth wasn't coming, "Roger, couldn't you get breakfast downtown this morning? You know last time you weren't so satisfied with my coffee."

Roger was hostile. I think he had just cut himself, shaving. Anyway, he was horrid.

"No, I can't get my breakfast downtown!" He actually snapped at me. "Really, Sally, I don't believe there's another woman in the world who would send her husband out on a morning like this on an empty stomach. I don't see how you can be so unfeeling."

Well, it wasn't "a morning like this," for it was just the beginning of November. And I had only proposed his doing what I knew he would have to do eventually.

I didn't say anything more, but started on that breakfast. I don't know why I thought I had to have hot cakes! The breakfast really was awful! The cakes were tough and gummy and got cold one second, exactly, after I took them off the stove. And the coffee boiled, or stewed, or scorched, or did whatever the particular thing is that coffee shouldn't do. Roger sawed at one cake, took one mouthful of the dreadful brew, and pushed away his cup.

"It seems to me you might learn to make a decent cup of coffee," he said icily. Then he picked up his hat and flung out of the house.

I think it is stupid of me, too, not to learn how to make coffee. But, really, I'm no worse than Roger is about lots of things. Take "Five Hundred." Roger knows I love cards, and with the Cheltons right around the corner from us and as fond of it as I am, we could spend many a pleasant evening. But Roger will not learn. Only the night before, after I had gone through a whole hand with him, with hearts as trumps, I dealt the cards around again to imaginary opponents and we started playing. Clubs were trumps, and spades led. Roger, having no spades, played triumphantly a Jack of Hearts and proceeded to take the trick.

"But, Roger," I protested, "you threw off."

"Well," he said, deeply injured, "didn't you say hearts were trumps when you were playing before?"

And when I tried to explain, he threw down the cards and wanted to know what difference it made; he'd rather play casino, anyway! I didn't go out and slam the door.

But I couldn't help from crying this particular morning. I not only value Roger's good opinion, but I hate to be considered stupid.

Mary Elizabeth came in about eleven o'clock. She is a small, weazened woman, very dark, somewhat wrinkled, and a model of self-possession. I wish I could make you see her, or that I could reproduce her accent, not that it is especially colored,—Roger's and mine are much more so—but her pronunciation, her way of drawing out her vowels, is so distinctively Mary Elizabethan!

I was ashamed of my red eyes and tried to cover up my embarrassment with sternness.

"Mary Elizabeth," said I, "you are late!" Just as though she didn't know it.

"Yas'm, Mis' Pierson," she said, composedly, taking off her coat. She didn't remove her hat,—she never does until she has been in the house some two or three hours. I can't imagine why. It is a small, black, dusty affair, trimmed with black ribbon, some dingy white roses and a sheaf of wheat. I give Mary Elizabeth a dress and hat now and then, but, although I recognize the dress from time to time, I never see any change in the hat. I don't know what she does with my ex-millinery.

"Yas'm," she said again, and looked comprehensively at the untouched breakfast dishes and the awful viands, which were still where Roger had left them.

"Looks as though you'd had to git breakfast yoreself," she observed brightly. And went out in the kitchen and ate all those cakes and drank that unspeakable coffee! Really she did, and she didn't warm them up either.

I watched her miserably, unable to decide whether Roger was too finicky or Mary Elizabeth a natural-born diplomat.

"Mr. Gales led me an awful chase last night," she explained. "When I got home yestiddy evenin', my cousin whut keeps house fer me (!) tole me Mr. Gales went out in the mornin' en hadn't come back."

"Mr. Gales," let me explain, is Mary Elizabeth's second husband, an octogenarian, and the most original person, I am convinced, in existence.

"Yas'm," she went on, eating a final cold hot-cake, "en I went to look fer 'im, en had the whole perlice station out all night huntin' 'im. Look like they wusn't never goin' to find 'im. But I ses, 'Jes' let me look fer enough en long enough en I'll find 'im,' I ses, en I did. Way out Georgy Avenue, with the hat on ole Mis' give 'im. Sent it to 'im all the way fum Chicaga. He's had it fifteen years,—high silk beaver. I knowed he wusn't goin' too fer with that hat on.

"I went up to 'im, settin' by a fence all muddy, holdin' his hat on with both hands. En I ses, 'Look here, man, you come erlong home with me, en let me put you to bed.' En he come jest as meek! No-o-me, I knowed he wusn't goin' fer with ole Mis' hat on."

"Who was old 'Mis,' Mary Elizabeth?" I asked her.

"Lady I used to work fer in Noo York," she informed me. "Me en Rosy, the cook, lived with her fer years. Ole Mis' was turrible fond of me, though her en Rosy used to querrel all the time. Jes' seemed like they couldn't git erlong. 'Member once Rosy run after her one Sunday with a knife, en I kep 'em apart. Reckon Rosy musta bin right put out with ole Mis' that day. By en by her en Rosy move to Chicaga, en when I married Mr. Gales, she sent 'im that hat. That old white woman shore did like me. It's so late, reckon I'd better put off sweepin' tel termorrer, ma'am."

I acquiesced, following her about from room to room. This was partly to get away from my own doleful thoughts—Roger really had hurt my feelings—but just as much to hear her talk. At first I used not to believe all she said, but after I investigated once and found her truthful in one amazing statement, I capitulated.

She had been telling me some remarkable tale of her first husband and I was listening with the stupefied attention, to which she always reduces me. Remember she was speaking of her first husband.

"En I ses to 'im, I ses, 'Mr. Gale,——'"

"Wait a moment, Mary Elizabeth," I interrupted, meanly delighted to have caught her for once. "You mean your first husband, don't you?

"Yas'm," she replied. "En I ses to 'im, 'Mr. Gale!' I ses——"

"But, Mary Elizabeth," I persisted, "that's your second husband, isn't it,—Mr. Gale?"

She gave me her long-drawn "No-o-me! My first husband was Mr. Gale and my second is Mr. *Gales*. He spells his name with a Z, I reckon. I ain't never see it writ. Ez I wus sayin', I ses to Mr. Gale——"

And it was true! Since then I have never doubted Mary Elizabeth.

She was loquacious that afternoon. She told me about her sister, "where's got a home in the country and where's got eight children." I used to read Lucy Pratt's stories about little Ephraim or Ezekiel, I forget his name, who always said "where's" instead of "who's," but I never believed it really till I heard Mary Elizabeth use it. For some reason or other she never mentions her sister without mentioning the home, too. "My sister where's got a home in the country" is her unvarying phrase.

"Mary Elizabeth," I asked her once, "does your sister live in the country, or does she simply own a house there?"

"Yas'm," she told me.

She is fond of her sister. "If Mr. Gales wus to die," she told me complacently, "I'd go to live with her."

"If he should die," I asked her idly, "would you marry again?"

"Oh, no-o-me!" She was emphatic. "Though I don't know why I shouldn't, I'd come by it hones'. My father wus married four times."

That shocked me out of my headache. "Four times, Mary Elizabeth, and you had all those stepmothers!" My mind refused to take it in.

"Oh, no-o-me! I always lived with mamma. She was his first wife."

I hadn't thought of people in the state in which I had instinctively placed Mary Elizabeth's father and mother as indulging in divorce, but as Roger says slangily, "I wouldn't know."

Mary Elizabeth took off the dingy hat. "You see, papa and mamma—" the ineffable pathos of hearing this woman of sixty-four, with a husband of eighty, use the old childish terms!

"Papa and mamma wus slaves, you know, Mis' Pierson, and so of course they wusn't exackly married. White folks wouldn't let 'em. But they wus awf'ly in love with each other. Heard mamma tell erbout it lots of times, and how papa wus the han'somest man! Reckon she wus long erbout sixteen or seventeen then. So they jumped over a broomstick, en they wus jes as happy! But not long after I come erlong, they sold papa down South, and mamma never see him no mo' fer years and years. Thought he was dead. So she married again."

"And he came back to her, Mary Elizabeth?" I was overwhelmed with the woefulness of it.

"Yas'm. After twenty-six years. Me and my sister where's got a home in the country—she's really my half-sister, see Mis' Pierson,—her en mamma en my step-father en me wus all down in Bumpus, Virginia, workin' fer some white folks, and we used to live in a little cabin, had a front stoop to it. En one day an ole cullud man come by, had a lot o' whiskers. I'd saw him lots of times there in Bumpus, lookin' and peerin' into every cullud woman's face. En jes' then my sister she call out, 'Come here, you Ma'y Elizabeth,' en that old man stopped, en he looked at me en he looked at me, en he ses to me, 'Chile, is yo' name Ma'y Elizabeth?'

"You know, Mis' Pierson, I thought he wus jes' bein' fresh, en I ain't paid no 'tention to 'im. I ain't sed nuthin' ontel he spoke to me three or four times, en then I ses to 'im, 'Go 'way fum here, man, you ain't got no call to be fresh with me. I'm a decent woman. You'd oughta be ashamed of yoreself, an ole man like you.'"

Mary Elizabeth stopped and looked hard at the back of her poor wrinkled hands.

"En he says to me, 'Daughter,' he ses, jes' like that, 'daughter,' he ses, 'hones' I ain't bein' fresh. Is yo' name shore enough Ma'y Elizabeth?'

"En I tole him, 'Yas'r.'

"'Chile,' he ses, 'whar is yo' daddy?'

"'Ain't got no daddy,' I tole him peart-like. 'They done tuk 'im away fum me twenty-six years ago, I wusn't but a mite of a baby. Sol' 'im down the river. My mother often talks about it.' And, oh, Mis' Pierson, you shoulda see the glory come into his face!

"'Yore mother!' he ses, kinda out of breath, 'yore mother! Ma'y Elizabeth, whar is your mother?'

"'Back thar on the stoop,' I tole 'im. 'Why, did you know my daddy?'

"But he didn't pay no 'tention to me, jes' turned and walked up the stoop whar mamma wus settin'! She wus feelin' sorta poorly that day. En you oughta see me steppin' erlong after 'im.

"He walked right up to her and giv' her one look. 'Oh, Maggie,' he shout out, 'oh, Maggie! Ain't you know me? Maggie, ain't you know me?'

"Mamma look at 'im and riz up outa her cheer. 'Who're you?' she ses kinda trimbly, callin' me Maggie thata way? Who're you?'

"He went up real close to her, then, 'Maggie,' he ses, jes' like that, kinda sad 'n tender, 'Maggie!' And hel' out his arms.

"She walked right into them. 'Oh,' she ses, 'it's Cassius! It's Cassius! It's my husban' come back to me! It's Cassius!' They wus like two mad people.

"My sister Minnie and me, we jes' stood and gawped at 'em. There they wus, holding on to each other like two pitiful childrun, en he tuk her hands and kissed 'em.

"'Maggie,' he ses, 'you'll come away with me, won't you? You gona take me back, Maggie? We'll go away, you en Ma'y Elizabeth en me. Won't we, Maggie?'

"Reckon my mother clean fergot my stepfather. 'Yes, Cassius,' she ses, 'we'll go away.' And then she sees Minnie, en it all comes back to her. 'Oh, Cassius,' she ses, 'I cain't go with you, I'm married again, en this time fer real. This here gal's mine and three boys, too, and another chile comin' in November!'"

"But she went with him, Mary Elizabeth," I pleaded. "Surely she went with him after all those years. He really was her husband."

I don't know whether Mary Elizabeth meant to be sarcastic or not. "Oh, no-o-me, mamma couldn't a done that. She wus a good woman. Her ole master, whut done sol' my father down river, brung her up too religious fer that, en anyways, papa was married again, too. Had his fourth wife there in Bumpus with 'im."

The unspeakable tragedy of it!

I left her and went up to my room, and hunted out my dark-blue serge dress which I had meant to wear again that winter. But I had to give Mary Elizabeth something, so I took the dress down to her.

She was delighted with it. I could tell she was, because she used her rare and untranslatable expletive.

"Haytian!" she said. "My sister where's got a home in the country, got a dress looks somethin' like this, but it ain't as good. No-o-me. She got hers to wear at a friend's weddin',—gal she wus riz up with. Thet gal married well, too, lemme tell you; her husband's a Sunday School sup'rintender."

I told her she needn't wait for Mr. Pierson; I would put dinner on the table. So off she went in the gathering dusk, trudging bravely back to her Mr. Gales and his high silk hat.

I watched her from the window till she was out of sight. It had been such a long time since I had thought of slavery. I was born in Pennsylvania, and neither my parents nor grandparents had been slaves; otherwise I might have had the same tale to tell as Mary Elizabeth, or worse yet, Roger and I might have lived in those black days and loved and lost each other and futilely, damnably, met again like Cassius and Maggie.

Whereas it was now, and I had Roger and Roger had me.

How I loved him as I sat there in the hazy dusk. I thought of his dear, bronze perfection, his habit of swearing softly in excitement, his blessed stupidity. Just the same I didn't meet him at the door as usual, but pretended to be busy. He came rushing to me with the *Saturday Evening Post,* which is more to me than rubies. I thanked him warmly, but aloofly, if you can get that combination.

We ate dinner almost in silence for my part. But he praised everything,—the cooking, the table, my appearance.

After dinner we went up to the little sitting-room. He hoped I wasn't tired,—couldn't he fix the pillows for me? So!

I opened the magazine and the first thing I saw was a picture of a woman gazing in stony despair at the figure of a man disappearing around the bend of the road. It was too much. Suppose that were Roger and I! I'm afraid I sniffled. He was at my side in a moment.

"Dear loveliest! Don't cry. It was all my fault. You aren't any worse about coffee than I am about cards! And anyway, I needn't have slammed the door! Forgive me, Sally. I always told you I was hard to get along with. I've had a horrible day,—don't stay cross with me, dearest."

I held him to me and sobbed outright on his shoulder. "It isn't you, Roger," I told him, "I'm crying about Mary Elizabeth."

I regret to say he let me go then, so great was his dismay. Roger will never be half the diplomat that Mary Elizabeth is.

"Holy smokes!" he groaned. "She isn't going to leave us for good, is she?"

So then I told him about Maggie and Cassius. "And oh, Roger," I ended futilely, "to think that they had to separate after all those years, when he had come back, old and with whiskers!" I didn't mean to be so banal, but I was crying too hard to be coherent.

Roger had got up and was walking the floor, but he stopped then aghast.

"Whiskers!" he moaned. "My hat! Isn't that just like a woman?" He had to clear his throat once or twice before he could go on, and I think he wiped his eyes.

"Wasn't it the—" I really can't say what Roger said here,—"wasn't it the darndest hard luck that when he did find her again, she should be married? She might have waited."

I stared at him astounded. "But, Roger," I reminded him, "he had married three other times, he didn't wait."

"Oh—!" said Roger, unquotably, "married three fiddlesticks! He only did that to try to forget her."

Then he came over and knelt beside me again. "Darling, I do think it is a sensible thing for a poor woman to learn how to cook, but I don't care as long as you love me and we are together. Dear loveliest, if I had been Cassius,"—he caught my hands so tight that he hurt them,—"and I had married fifty times and had come back and found you married to someone else, I'd have killed you, killed you."

Well, he wasn't logical, but he was certainly convincing.

So thus, and not otherwise, Mary Elizabeth healed the breach.

1920

- The League of Nations holds its first meeting.
- Mexican president Venustiano Carranza is assassinated.
- The Russian civil war concludes with Communist forces victorious.
- Warren G. Harding elected president.
- Prohibition begins in the United States (Eighteenth Amendment).
- U.S. women granted the right to vote (Nineteenth Amendment).
- Eugene O'Neill's play *The Emperor Jones* premieres with Charles Gilpin in title role.
- James Weldon Johnson becomes the first black executive secretary of the NAACP.
- Marcus Garvey's black nationalist movement reaches its apex.
- The National Negro League is organized for black baseball players.

Black population in United States: 10,463,131 (9.9%)

U.S. unemployment: 5.2%

Lynchings in the United States: 53 blacks, 8 whites

Spingarn Medal:
    W. E. B. Du Bois (author, editor, activist)

Books:
    Raymond Garfield Dandridge, *The Poet and Other Poems* (poetry)
    W. E. B. Du Bois, *Darkwater* (autobiography, poetry, nonfiction, short stories)
    Alice Dunbar-Nelson (ed.), *The Dunbar Speaker and Entertainer* (multigenre anthology)
    Sarah Lee Brown Fleming, *Clouds and Sunshine* (poetry)
    Angelina Weld Grimké, *Rachel* (drama)
    Hubert Harrison, *When Africa Awakes* (nonfiction)

Walter Everette Hawkins, *Chords and Discords* (poetry)
Fenton Johnson, *Tales of Darkest America* (short stories)
Claude McKay, *Spring in New Hampshire and Other Poems* (poetry)
Zara Wright, *Black and White Tangled Threads* (novel)
Zara Wright, *Kenneth* (novel)

Periodicals:
    Brownies' Book (1920–21)
    Competitor (1920–21)

4 THE COMET
W. E. B. Du Bois

From *Darkwater*, 1920

He stood a moment on the steps of the bank, watching the human river that swirled down Broadway. Few noticed him. Few ever noticed him save in a way that stung. He was outside the world—"nothing!" as he said bitterly. Bits of the words of the walkers came to him.

"The comet?"

"The comet——"

Everybody was talking of it. Even the president, as he entered, smiled patronizingly at him, and asked:

"Well, Jim, are you scared?"

"No," said the messenger shortly.

"I thought we'd journeyed through the comet's tail once," broke in the junior clerk affably.

"Oh, that was Halley's," said the president; "this is a new comet, quite a stranger, they say—wonderful, wonderful! I saw it last night. Oh, by the way, Jim," turning again to the messenger, "I want you to go down into the lower vaults today."

The messenger followed the president silently. Of course, they wanted *him* to go down to the lower vaults. It was too dangerous for more valuable men. He smiled grimly and listened.

"Everything of value has been moved out since the water began to seep in," said the president; "but we miss two volumes of old records. Suppose you nose around down there,—it isn't very pleasant, I suppose."

"Not very," said the messenger, as he walked out.

"Well, Jim, the tail of the new comet hits us at noon this time," said the vault clerk, as he passed over the keys; but the messenger passed silently down the stairs. Down he went beneath Broadway, where the dim light filtered through the feet of hurrying men; down to the dark basement beneath; down into the blackness and silence beneath that lowest cavern. Here with his dark lantern he groped in the bowels of the earth, under the world.

He drew a long breath as he threw back the last great iron door and stepped into the fetid slime within. Here at last was peace, and he groped moodily forward. A great rat leaped past him and cobwebs crept across his face. He felt carefully around the room, shelf by shelf, on the muddied floor, and in crevice and corner. Nothing. Then he went back to the far end, where somehow the wall felt different. He sounded and pushed and pried. Nothing. He started away. Then something brought him back. He was sounding and working again when suddenly the whole black wall swung as on mighty hinges, and blackness yawned beyond. He peered in; it was evidently a secret vault—some hiding place of the old bank unknown in newer times. He entered hesitatingly. It was a long, narrow room with shelves, and at the far end, an old iron chest. On a high shelf lay the two missing volumes of records, and others. He put them carefully aside and stepped to the chest. It was old, strong, and rusty. He looked at the vast and old-fashioned lock and flashed his light on the hinges. They were deeply incrusted with rust. Looking about, he found a bit of iron and began to pry. The rust had eaten a hundred years, and it had gone deep. Slowly, wearily, the old lid lifted, and with a last, low groan lay bare its treasure—and he saw the dull sheen of gold!

"Boom!"

A low, grinding, reverberating crash struck upon his ear. He started up and looked about. All was black and still. He groped for his light and swung it about him. Then he knew! The great stone door had swung to. He forgot the gold and looked death squarely in the face. Then with a sigh he went methodically to work. The cold sweat stood on his forehead; but he searched, pounded, pushed, and worked until after what seemed endless hours his hand struck a cold bit of metal and the great door swung again harshly on its hinges, and then, striking against something soft and heavy, stopped. He had just room to squeeze through. There lay the body of the vault clerk, cold and stiff. He stared at it, and then felt sick and nauseated. The air seemed unaccountably foul, with a strong, peculiar odor. He stepped forward, clutched at the air, and fell fainting across the corpse.

He awoke with a sense of horror, leaped from the body, and groped up the stairs, calling to the guard. The watchman sat as if asleep, with the gate swinging free. With one glance at him the messenger hurried up to the sub-vault. In vain he called to the guards. His voice echoed and re-echoed weirdly. Up into the great basement he rushed. Here another guard lay prostrate on his face, cold and still. A fear arose in the messenger's heart. He dashed up to the cellar floor, up into the bank. The stillness of death lay everywhere and everywhere bowed, bent, and stretched the silent forms of men. The messenger paused and glanced about. He was not a man easily moved; but the sight was appalling! "Robbery and murder," he whispered slowly to himself as he saw the twisted, oozing mouth of the president where he lay half-buried on his desk. Then a new thought seized him: If they found him here alone—with all this money and all these dead men—what would his life be worth? He glanced about, tiptoed cautiously to a side door, and again looked behind. Quietly he turned the latch and stepped out into Wall Street.

How silent the street was! Not a soul was stirring, and yet it was high-noon—Wall Street? Broadway? He glanced almost wildly up and down, then across the street, and as he looked, a sickening horror froze in his limbs. With a choking cry of utter fright he lunged, leaned giddily against the cold building, and stared helplessly at the sight.

In the great stone doorway a hundred men and women and children lay crushed and twisted and jammed, forced into that great, gaping doorway like refuse in a can—as if in one wild, frantic rush to safety, they had crushed and ground themselves to death. Slowly the messenger crept along the walls, wetting his parched mouth and trying to comprehend, stilling the tremor in his limbs and the rising terror in his heart. He met a business man, silk-hatted and frock-coated, who had crept, too, along that smooth wall and stood now stone dead with wonder written on his lips. The messenger turned his eyes hastily away and sought the curb. A woman leaned wearily against the signpost, her head bowed motionless on her lace and silken bosom. Before her stood a street car, silent, and within—but the messenger but glanced and hurried on. A grimy newsboy sat in the gutter with the "last edition" in his uplifted hand: "Danger!" screamed its black headlines. "Warnings wired around the world. The Comet's tail sweeps past us at noon. Deadly gases expected. Close doors and windows. Seek the cellar." The messenger read and staggered on. Far out from a window above, a girl lay with gasping face and sleevelets on her arms. On a store step sat a little, sweet-faced girl looking upward toward the skies, and in the carriage by her lay—but the messenger looked no longer. The cords gave way—the terror burst in his veins, and with one great, gasping cry he sprang desperately forward and ran,—ran as only the frightened run, shrieking and fighting the air until with one last wail of pain he sank on the grass of Madison Square and lay prone and still.

When he arose, he gave no glance at the still and silent forms on the benches, but, going to a fountain, bathed his face; then hiding himself in a corner away from the drama of death, he quietly gripped himself and thought the thing through: The comet had swept the earth and this was the end. Was everybody dead? He must search and see.

He knew that he must steady himself and keep calm, or he would go insane. First he must go to a restaurant. He walked up Fifth Avenue to a famous hostelry and entered its gorgeous, ghost-haunted halls. He beat back the nausea, and, seizing a tray from dead hands, hurried into the street and ate ravenously, hiding to keep out the sights.

"Yesterday, they would not have served me," he whispered, as he forced the food down.

Then he started up the street,—looking, peering, telephoning, ringing alarms; silent, silent all. Was nobody—nobody—he dared not think the thought and hurried on.

Suddenly he stopped still. He had forgotten. My God! How could he have forgotten? He must rush to the subway—then he almost laughed. No—a car; if he could find a Ford. He saw one. Gently he lifted off its burden, and took his place on the seat. He tested the throttle. There was gas. He glided off, shivering, and drove up the street. Everywhere stood, leaned, lounged, and lay the dead, in grim and awful silence. On he ran past an automobile, wrecked and overturned; past another, filled with a gay party whose smiles yet lingered on their death-struck lips; on past crowds and groups of cars, pausing by dead policemen; at 42nd Street he had to detour to Park Avenue to avoid the dead congestion. He came back on Fifth Avenue at 57th and flew past the Plaza and by the park with its hushed babies and silent throng, until as he was rushing past 72nd Street he heard a sharp cry, and saw a living form leaning wildly out an upper window. He gasped. The human voice sounded in his ears like the voice of God.

"Hello—hello—help, in God's name!" wailed the woman. "There's a dead girl in here and a man and—and see yonder dead men lying in the street and dead horses—for the love of God go and bring the officers——" And the words trailed off into hysterical tears.

He wheeled the car in a sudden circle, running over the still body of a child and leaping on the curb. Then he rushed up the steps and tried the door and rang violently. There was a long pause, but at last the heavy door swung back. They stared a moment in silence. She had not noticed before that he was a Negro. He had not thought of her as white. She was a woman of perhaps twenty-five—rarely beautiful and richly gowned, with darkly golden hair, and jewels. Yesterday, he thought with bitterness, she would scarcely have looked at him twice. He would have been dirt beneath her silken feet. She stared at him. Of all the sorts of men she had pictured as coming to her rescue she had not dreamed of one like him. Not that he was not human, but he dwelt in a world so far from hers, so infinitely far, that she seldom even entered her thought. Yet as she looked at him curiously he seemed quite commonplace and usual. He was a tall, dark workingman of the better class, with a sensitive face trained to stolidity and a poor man's clothes and hands. His face was soft and slow and his manner at once cold and nervous, like fires long banked, but not out.

So a moment each paused and gauged the other; then the thought of the dead world without rushed in and they started toward each other.

"What has happened?" she cried. "Tell me! Nothing stirs. All is silence! I see the dead strewn before my window as winnowed by the breath of God,—and see——" She dragged him through great, silken hangings to where, beneath the sheen of mahogany and silver, a little French maid lay stretched in quiet, everlasting sleep, and near her a butler lay prone in his livery.

The tears streamed down the woman's cheeks and she clung to his arm until the perfume of her breath swept his face and he felt the tremors racing through her body.

"I had been shut up in my dark room developing pictures of the comet which I took last night; when I came out—I saw the dead!

"What has happened?" she cried again.

He answered slowly:

"Something—comet or devil—swept across the earth this morning and—many are dead!"

"Many? Very many?"

"I have searched and I have seen no other living soul but you."

She gasped and they stared at each other.

"My—father!" she whispered.

"Where is he?"

"He started for the office."

"Where is it?"

"In the Metropolitan Tower."

"Leave a note for him here and come."

Then he stopped.

"No," he said firmly—"first, we must go—to Harlem."

"Harlem!" she cried. Then she understood. She tapped her foot at first impatiently. She looked back and shuddered. Then she came resolutely down the steps.

"There's a swifter car in the garage in the court," she said.

"I don't know how to drive it," he said.

"I do," she answered.

In ten minutes they were flying to Harlem on the wind. The Stutz rose and raced like an airplane. They took the turn at 110th Street on two wheels and slipped with a shriek into 135th.

He was gone but a moment. Then he returned, and his face was gray. She did not look, but said:

"You have lost—somebody?"

"I have lost—everybody," he said, simply— "unless——"

He ran back and was gone several minutes—hours they seemed to her.

"Everybody," he said, and he walked slowly back with something film-like in his hand which he stuffed into his pocket.

"I'm afraid I was selfish," he said. But already the car was moving toward the park among the dark and lined dead of Harlem—the brown, still faces, the knotted hands, the homely garments, and the silence—the wild and haunting silence. Out of the park, and down Fifth Avenue they whirled. In and out among the dead they slipped and quivered, needing no sound of bell or horn, until the great, square Metropolitan Tower hove in sight. Gently he laid the dead elevator boy aside; the car shot upward. The door of the office stood open. On the threshold lay the stenographer, and, staring at her, sat the dead clerk. The inner office was empty, but a note lay on the desk, folded and addressed but unsent:

Dear Daughter:

I've gone for a hundred mile spin in Fred's new Mercedes. Shall not be back before dinner. I'll bring Fred with me.

J. B. H.

"Come," she cried nervously. "We must search the city."

Up and down, over and across, back again—on went that ghostly search. Everywhere was silence and death—death and silence! They hunted from Madison Square to Spuyten Duyvel; they rushed across the Williamsburg Bridge; they swept over Brooklyn; from the Battery and Morningside Heights they scanned the river. Silence, silence everywhere, and no human sign. Haggard and bedraggled they puffed a third time slowly down Broadway, under the broiling sun, and at last stopped. He sniffed the air. An odor—a smell—and with the shifting breeze a sickening stench filled their nostrils and brought its awful warning. The girl settled back helplessly in her seat.

"What can we do?" she cried.

It was his turn now to take the lead, and he did it quickly.

"The long distance telephone—the telegraph and the cable—night rockets and then—flight!"

She looked at him now with strength and confidence. He did not look like men, as she had always pictured men; but he acted like one and she was content. In fifteen minutes they were at the central telephone exchange. As they came to the door he stepped quickly before her and pressed her gently back as he closed it. She heard him moving to and fro, and knew his burdens—the poor, little burdens he bore. When she entered, he was alone in the room. The grim switchboard flashed its metallic face in cryptic, sphinx-like immobility. She seated herself on a stool and donned the bright earpiece. She looked at the mouthpiece. She had never looked at one so closely before. It was wide and black, pimpled with usage; inert; dead; almost sarcastic in its unfeeling curves. It looked—she beat back the thought—but it looked,—it persisted in looking like—she turned her head and found herself alone. One moment she was terrified; then she thanked him silently for his delicacy and turned resolutely, with a quick intaking of breath.

"Hello!" she called in low tones. She was calling to the world. The world *must* answer. Would the world *answer*? Was the world—

Silence!

She had spoken too low.

"Hello!" she cried, full-voiced.

She listened. Silence! Her heart beat quickly. She cried in clear, distinct, loud tones: "Hello—hello—hello!"

What was that whirring? Surely—no—was it the click of a receiver?

She bent close, she moved the pegs in the holes, and called and called, until her voice rose almost to a shriek, and her heart hammered. It was as if she had heard the last flicker of creation, and the evil was silence. Her voice dropped to a sob. She sat stupidly staring into the black and sarcastic mouthpiece, and the thought came again. Hope lay dead within her. Yes, the cable and the rockets remained; but the world—she could not frame the thought or say the word. It was too mighty—too terrible! She turned toward the door with a new fear in her heart. For the first time she seemed to realize that she was alone in the world with a stranger, with something more than a stranger,—with a man alien in blood and culture—unknown, perhaps unknowable. It was awful! She must escape—she must fly; he must not see her again. Who knew what awful thoughts—

She gathered her silken skirts deftly about her young, smooth limbs—listened, and glided into a side-hall. A moment she shrank back: the hall lay filled with dead women; then she leaped to the door and tore at it, with bleeding fingers, until it swung wide. She looked out. He was standing at the top of the alley,—silhouetted, tall and black, motionless. Was he looking at her or away? She did not know—she did not care. She simply leaped and ran—ran until she found herself alone amid the dead and the tall ramparts of towering buildings.

She stopped. She was alone. Alone! Alone on the streets—alone in the city— perhaps alone in the world! There crept in upon her the sense of deception— of creeping hands behind her back—of silent, moving things she could not see,—of voices hushed in fearsome conspiracy. She looked behind and sideways, started at strange sounds and heard still stranger, until every nerve within her stood sharp and quivering, stretched to scream at the barest touch. She whirled and flew back, whimpering like a child, until she found that narrow alley again and the dark, silent figure silhouetted at the top. She stopped and rested; then she walked silently toward him, looked at him timidly; but he said nothing as he handed her into the car. Her voice caught as she whispered:

"Not—that."

And he answered slowly: "No—not that!"

They climbed into the car. She bent forward on the wheel and sobbed, with great, dry, quivering sobs, as they flew toward the cable office on the east side, leaving the world of wealth and prosperity for the world of poverty and work. In the world behind them were death and silence, grave and grim, almost cynical, but always decent; here it was hideous. It clothed itself in every ghastly form of terror, struggle, hate, and suffering. It lay wreathed in crime and squalor, greed and lust. Only in its dread and awful silence was it like to death everywhere.

Yet as the two, flying and alone, looked upon the horror of the world, slowly, gradually, the sense of all-enveloping death deserted them. They seemed to move in a world silent and asleep,—not dead. They moved in quiet reverence, lest somehow they wake these sleeping forms who had, at last, found peace. They moved in some solemn, world-wide *Friedhof,* above which some mighty arm had waved its magic wand. All nature slept until—until, and quick with the same startling thought, they looked into each other's eyes—he, ashen, and she, crimson, with unspoken thought. To both, the vision of a mighty beauty—of vast, unspoken things, swelled in their souls; but they put it away.

Great, dark coils of wire came up from the earth and down from the sun and entered this low lair of witchery. The gathered lightnings of the world centered here, binding with beams of light the ends of the earth. The doors gaped on the gloom within. He paused on the threshold.

"Do you know the code?" she asked.

"I know the call for help—we used it formerly at the bank."

She hardly heard. She heard the lapping of the waters far below,—the dark and restless waters—the cold and luring waters, as they called. He stepped within. Slowly she walked to the wall, where the water called below, and stood and waited. Long she waited, and he did not come. Then with a start she saw him, too, standing beside the black waters. Slowly he removed his coat and stood there silently. She walked quickly to him and laid her hand on his arm. He did not start or look. The waters lapped on in luring, deadly rhythm. He pointed down to the waters, and said quietly:

"The world lies beneath the waters now—may I go?"

She looked into his stricken, tired face, and a great pity surged within her heart. She answered in a voice clear and calm, "No."

Upward they turned toward life again, and he seized the wheel. The world was darkening to twilight, and a great, gray pall was falling mercifully and gently on the sleeping dead. The ghastly glare of reality seemed replaced with the dream of some vast romance. The girl lay silently back, as the motor whizzed along, and looked half-consciously for the elf-queen to wave life into this dead world again. She forgot to wonder at the quickness with which he had learned to drive her car. It seemed natural. And then as they whirled and swung into Madison Square and at the door of the Metropolitan Tower she gave a low cry, and her eyes were great! Perhaps she had seen the elf-queen?

The man led her to the elevator of the tower and deftly they ascended. In her father's office they gathered rugs and chairs, and he wrote a note and laid it on the desk; then they ascended to the roof and he made her comfortable. For a while she rested and sank to dreamy somnolence, watching the worlds above and wondering. Below lay the dark shadows of the city and afar was the shining of the sea. She glanced at him timidly as he set food before her and took a shawl and wound her in it, touching her reverently, yet tenderly. She looked up at him with thankfulness in her eyes, eating what he served. He watched the city. She watched him. He seemed very human,—very near now.

"Have you had to work hard?" she asked softly.

"Always," he said.

"I have always been idle," she said. "I was rich."

"I was poor," he almost echoed.

"The rich and the poor are met together," she began, and he finished:

"The Lord is the Maker of them all."

"Yes," she said slowly; "and how foolish our human distinctions seem—now," looking down to the great dead city stretched below, swimming in unlightened shadows.

"Yes—I was not—human, yesterday," he said.

She looked at him. "And your people were not my people," she said; "but to-day—" She paused. He was a man,—no more; but he was in some larger sense a gentleman,—sensitive, kindly, chivalrous, everything save his hands and—his face. Yet yesterday—

"Death, the leveler!" he muttered.

"And the revealer," she whispered gently, rising to her feet with great eyes. He turned away, and after fumbling a moment sent a rocket into the darkening air. It arose, shrieked, and flew up, a slim path of light, and, scattering its stars abroad, dropped on the city below. She scarcely noticed it. A vision of the world had risen before her. Slowly the mighty prophecy of her destiny overwhelmed her. Above the dead past hovered the Angel of Annunciation. She was no mere woman. She was neither high nor low, white nor black, rich nor poor. She was primal woman; mighty mother of all men to come and Bride of Life. She looked upon the man beside her and forgot all else but his manhood, his strong, vigorous manhood—his sorrow and sacrifice. She saw him glorified. He was no longer a thing apart, a creature below, a strange outcast of another clime and blood, but her Brother Humanity incarnate, Son of God and great All-Father of the race to be.

He did not glimpse the glory in her eyes, but stood looking outward toward the sea and sending rocket after rocket into the unanswering darkness. Dark-purple clouds lay banked and billowed in the west. Behind them and all around, the heavens glowed in dim, weird radiance that suffused the darkening world and made almost a minor music. Suddenly, as though gathered back in some vast hand, the great cloud-curtain fell away. Low on the horizon lay a long, white star—mystic, wonderful! And from it fled upward to the pole, like some wan bridal veil, a pale, wide sheet of flame that lighted all the world and dimmed the stars.

In fascinated silence the man gazed at the heavens and dropped his rockets to the floor. Memories of memories stirred to life in the dead recesses of his mind. The shackles seemed to rattle and fall from his soul. Up from the crass and crushing and cringing of his caste leaped the lone majesty of kings long dead. He arose within the shadows, tall, straight, and stern, with power in his eyes and ghostly scepters hovering to his grasp. It was as though some mighty Pharaoh lived again, or curled Assyrian lord. He turned and looked upon the lady, and found her gazing straight at him.

Silently, immovably, they saw each other face to face—eye to eye. Their souls lay naked to the night. It was not lust; it was not love—it was some vaster, mightier thing that needed neither touch of body nor thrill of soul. It was a thought divine, splendid.

Slowly, noiselessly, they moved toward each other—the heavens above, the seas around, the city grim and dead below. He loomed from out the velvet shadows vast and dark. Pearl-white and slender, she shone beneath the stars. She stretched her jeweled hands abroad. He lifted up his mighty arms, and they cried each to the other, almost with one voice, "The world is dead."

"Long live the——"

"Honk! Honk!" Hoarse and sharp the cry of a motor drifted clearly up from the silence below. They started backward with a cry and gazed upon each other with eyes that faltered and fell, with blood that boiled.

"Honk! Honk! Honk! Honk!" came the mad cry again, and almost from their feet a rocket blazed into the air and scattered its stars upon them. She covered her eyes with her hands, and her shoulders heaved. He dropped and bowed, groped blindly on his knees about the floor. A blue flame spluttered lazily after an age, and she heard the scream of an answering rocket as it flew.

Then they stood still as death, looking to opposite ends of the earth.

"Clang—crash—clang!"

The roar and ring of swift elevators shooting upward from below made the great tower tremble. A murmur and babel of voices swept in upon the night. All over the once dead city the lights blinked, flickered, and flamed; and then with a sudden clanging of doors the entrance to the platform was filled with men, and one with white and flying hair rushed to the girl and lifted her to his breast. "My daughter!" he sobbed.

Behind him hurried a younger, comelier man, carefully clad in motor costume, who bent above the girl with passionate solicitude and gazed into her staring eyes until they narrowed and dropped and her face flushed deeper and deeper crimson.

"Julia," he whispered; "my darling, I thought you were gone forever."

She looked up at him with strange, searching eyes.

"Fred," she murmured, almost vaguely, "is the world—gone?"

"Only New York," he answered; "it is terrible—awful! You know,—but you, how did you escape—how have you endured this horror? Are you well? Unharmed?"

"Unharmed!" she said.

"And this man here?" he asked, encircling her drooping form with one arm and turning toward the Negro. Suddenly he stiffened and his hand flew to his hip. "Why!" he snarled. "It's—a—nigger—Julia! Has he—has he dared——"

She lifted her head and looked at her late companion curiously and then dropped her eyes with a sigh.

"He has dared—all, to rescue me," she said quietly, "and I—thank him—much." But she did not look at him again. As the couple turned away, the father drew a roll of bills from his pockets.

"Here, my good fellow," he said, thrusting the money into the man's hands, "take that,—what's your name?"

"Jim Davis," came the answer, hollow-voiced.

"Well, Jim, I thank you. I've always liked your people. If you ever want a job, call on me." And they were gone.

The crowd poured up and out of the elevators, talking and whispering.

"Who was it?"

"Are they alive?"

"How many?"

"Two!"

"Who was saved?"

"A white girl and a nigger—there she goes."

"A nigger? Where is he? Let's lynch the damned——"

"Shut up—he's all right—he saved her."

"Saved hell! He had no business——"

"Here he comes."

Into the glare of the electric lights the colored man moved slowly, with the eyes of those that walk and sleep.

"Well, what do you think of that?" cried a bystander; "of all New York, just a white girl and a nigger!"

The colored man heard nothing. He stood silently beneath the glare of the light, gazing at the money in his hand and shrinking as he gazed; slowly he put his other hand into his pocket and brought out a baby's filmy cap, and gazed again. A woman mounted to the platform and looked about, shading her eyes. She was brown, small, and toil-worn, and in one arm lay the corpse of a dark baby. The crowd parted and her eyes fell on the colored man; with a cry she tottered toward him.

"Jim!"

He whirled and, with a sob of joy, caught her in his arms.

1921

- The Irish Free State is established.
- Italian-born anarchists Nicola Sacco and Bartolomeo Vanzetti are convicted of murder in the United States amidst ongoing worldwide furor over the case.
- Japanese prime minister Hara Takashi is assassinated.
- Japan, Great Britain, France, and the United States attend the Washington Armaments Conference to come to terms over territorial issues in the Pacific region and naval limitations.
- Swiss psychiatrist Hermann Rorschach introduces the Rorschach ink-blot personality test.
- *Shuffle Along* opens, the first Broadway show authored, produced, and performed by blacks.
- Bessie Coleman becomes the first African American aviatrix to earn a pilot's license.
- The Pace Phonograph Company is established, becoming the first record company owned and operated by blacks.
- A major race riot erupts in Tulsa, Oklahoma.
- Eva B. Dykes (Radcliffe College), Sadi T. Mossell (University of Pennsylvania), and Georgiana R. Simpson (University of Chicago) are the first black women to receive Ph.D. degrees.

U.S. unemployment: 11.7%

Lynchings in the United States: 59 blacks, 5 whites

Spingarn Medal:
    Charles S. Gilpin (actor)

Books:
    Leslie Pinckney Hill, *The Wings of Oppression* (poetry)
    Mary Etta Spencer, *The Resentment* (novel)

5 THE FOOLISH AND THE WISE

Sallie Runner Is Introduced to Socrates

Leila Amos Pendleton

FROM *CRISIS*, MARCH 1921

Mrs. Maxwell Thoro (born Audrey Lemere) tiptoed down the spacious hall toward the kitchen of her dwelling whence issued sounds, not exactly of revelry but—perhaps jubilation would be a better fit. For in a high soprano voice her colored maid-of-all-work, Sallie Runner, for the past half-hour had been informing to the accompaniment of energetic thumps of a flatiron, whomsoever it might concern that she had a robe, a crown, a harp and wings.

Mrs. Thoro moved quietly for, enjoyable as was Sallie's repertoire, one could never tell when she would do some even more enjoyable improvising, and her employer knew from long experience that Sallie's flights were much freer and more artistic when she was unaware of an audience.

Just as Mrs. Thoro reached the kitchen door the soloist started off on the verse, "I gotta shoes," so she stood quietly listening until the verse ended:

"I gotta shoes, yo' gotta shoes,
All a Gawd's chillun gotta shoes;
Wen I getto hebben goin' to put on my shoes
An' skip all ober Gawd's hebben.
Hebben, Hebben! Ever'buddy hollerin' 'bout hebben
Ain't goin' dere.
Hebben, hebben, goin' to skip all ober Gawd's hebben."

As the singer ceased she whirled around upon her employer with a loud laugh. "Ha, ha, Miss Oddry!" cried she. "I knowd yo' was dere. I sho is glad yo' done come, 'cause I'se mighty lonesome an' powerful tired. Jes' was thinkin' to myseff dat I'se goin' to try to swade Brudder Runner to move away fum Starton. Nobuddy don't do nothin' here but git bornd, git married an' git daid, an' wurk, wurk, wurk! Miss Oddry, I'se goin' to tell yo' a secret."

"What is it, Sallie?" inquired Mrs. Thoro.

"I don't lak to wurk. Nuvver did."

"Why, Sallie! That is a surprise," replied her employer. "I should never have guessed it, for there is not a more capable maid in town than you are."

"Yassum, I guess dat's right. I wurks wid my might an' I does whut my hands finds to do, but taint my nature doe. Muss be my Ma's trainin' an' mazin-grace-how-sweet-de-sound mixed togedder, I reckon. Miss Oddry, does yo' know whut I'd ruther do dan anything? I'd ruther know how to read an' write dan anything. I'd ruther know how to read an' write dan anything in de whole, wide world, an' den I'd nuvver do nothin' else but jes' dem two."

"Well, Sallie, I'm sure you would get very tired of reading and writing all the time; but you're not too old to learn."

"Nome, not too ole, mebbe, but too dumb an' too sot in de haid, I reckun. Miss Oddry, couldn't yo' read to me or talk to me on ironin'-days 'bout sumpin' outside uv Starton? Cose I wouldn't want yo' round under my feet on wash-days, but ironin'-days is fine fur lissening."

"Why yes, Sallie, I'd love to do that. Why didn't you ask me before? Mr. Thoro and I are re-reading an old school course, just for the fun of it, and I'll share it with you. I'm sure you would enjoy hearing about some of earth's greatest characters. How would you like to have me tell you about Socrates?"

"Sockertees? Huh! Funny name! Sockertees whut?"

"Well, in his time men seldom had more than one name, Sallie. He was the son of Sophroniscus and Phaenarete. He was a sculptor and a philosopher."

"Gosh!" cried Sallie. "A sculpture an' a lossipede! Wusser an' mo' uv it! But go on, Miss Oddry, tell me mo' 'bout him."

"Socrates was born about 469 years before our Lord, and died at the age of seventy. He is said to have had thick lips, a flat nose, protruding eyes, bald head, a squat figure, and a shambling gait."

"Why!" exclaimed Sallie. "He was a cullud gentmun, warn't he? Musta looked jes' lak Brudder Runner, 'cordin' to dat."

"Oh no, Sallie, he wasn't colored."

"Wal, ef he been daid all dat long time, Miss Oddry, ho kin yo' tell his color?"

"Why he was an Athenian, Sallie. He lived in Greece."

"Dar now! Dat settles it! Ever'buddy knows dat my cullud folks sho do lak grease."

"Oh, Sallie! 'Greece' was the name of his country, just as 'America' is the name of ours." Sallie grunted.

"Socrates," continued Mrs. Thoro, "was a very wise, just, and a good man, and he loved his country and his countrymen very much. He used to delight in wandering through the streets of Athens, conversing with those whom he met, giving them the benefit of the truths he had discovered and seeking to obtain from each more truth or new light. He spent the whole day in public, in the walks, the workshops, the gymnasiums, the porticoes, the schools and the market place at the hour it was most crowded, talking with everyone without distinction of age, sex, rank or condition. It was said that 'as he talked the hearts of all who heard him leaped up and their tears gushed out.'"

"Hole on, Miss Oddry," interrupted Sallie. "Jes' wanta ax yo' one queshun. While ole Sockertees was runnin' round the streets, shootin' off his lip an' makin' peepul cry, who was takin' keer uv his fambly? Sounds mo' an' mo' lak Brudder Runner to me."

"Well, Sallie, he had a very capable wife who bore him three sons and whose name was Xanthippe. No doubt she managed the household. The only fault Socrates found with her was that she had a violent temper."

Sallie slammed the flatiron down and braced herself against the board, arms akimbo, eyes flashing with indignation.

"Vilent temper?" cried she. "Vilent temper? Whut 'oman wouldn't had a vilent temper in a fix lak dat? I sho do symperthize wid Zantipsy an' I doesn't blame her fur gittin' tipsy needer, pore thing. I betcha she was es sweet es a angel befo' she got mahred, 'cause whut it takes to change yo' disposition, a man lak dat sho is got. It's jes' es much es a 'oman kin do to take keer uv her house right an' raise her chillun right wen her husband is doin' all he kin to hepp her, less mo' wen he ain't doin' nothin' but goin' round runnin' he mouf. Dis ain't de fust time I'se met a gentmun whut loves he kentry mo' dan he do he home folks. Go on, Miss Oddry, dear, tell me some mo' 'bout Reveral Eyesire Runner's twin brudder."

"Of course, Sallie," said Mrs. Thoro laughing. "Socrates was human and had his faults, but all in all he was a noble character."

"I hopes so, Miss Oddry, but I'll have to hear mo' fo' I 'cide."

"Socrates," resumed Mrs. Thoro, "believed in signs and omens and in following warnings received in his dreams; he also claimed that there was an inner voice which had guided him from childhood."

"Miss Oddry," expostulated Sallie, "yo' keep on tellin' me Sockertees warn't cullud, but yo' keep on tellin' me cullud things 'bout him. Wen we all b'lieve in signs an' dreams yo'-all allus says, 'It's jes' darky superstishun an' ignunce.' How yo' splain dat?"

"Well, Sallie, in those days the most learned people were very superstitious. Of course we know better now."

"How yo' know yo' knows better, Miss Oddry? How yo' know yo' don't know wusser? Dere's one thing I done found fur sho, an' dat is dat de mo' folks knows de less dey knows. I b'lieves in dreams an' wen I follers dem I goes right. Cose I ain't nuvver heerd no cujjus voice, but ef ole Sockertees say he heard it I b'lieve he heerd it. Nobuddy can't prove he didn't."

"Very true, Sallie, but—"

"Jes' one minute, Miss Oddry, please. Dere's sumpin' I been thinkin' a long time, an' now I knows it. An' dat is dat wen yo' come right down to de fack-trufe uv de inside feelin's, peepul is all alak; black ones is lak white ones an' dem ole ancienty ones lak Sockertees is jes lak dese here ones right now."

"I believe there is some truth in that, Sallie, but shall I go on about Socrates?"

"Oh, yassum, Miss Oddry, I do love to hear 'bout him."

"He tried most earnestly to make people think, to reason out what was right and what wrong in their treatment of each other. He constantly repeated, 'Virtue is knowledge; Vice is ignorance,' while to the young his advice was always, 'Know thyself.'"

"Humph!" interrupted Sallie. "Mighty good advice, Miss Oddry, but it's some job, b'lieve me. I'se es ole es Methusalum's billy goat now an' I ain't nuvver found myseff out yit. Dere's some new kink comin' out ev'ry day. How 'bout you, Miss Oddry?"

"I think you are right, Sallie. But don't you think we are better off if we study ourselves than if we just blunder along blindly?"

"Oh, yassum, I guess so. But how did ole Sockertees come out wid all his runnin' round an' talkin'?"

"Very sadly, I am sorry to say. Very sadly. Most of the Athenians entirely misunderstood him."

"Bound to," said Sallie.

"He made a great many unscrupulous enemies."

"Bound to," said Sallie.

"They accused him of being the very opposite of what he was."

"Bound to," said Sallie.

"And finally they tried him and condemned him to death."

Sallie set down the flatiron and folded her arms, while her eyes flew wide open in astonishment. "What?" she exclaimed. "Jes' fur talkin'? Wal I-will-be-swijjled!"

"Yes," continued Mrs. Thoro. "They imprisoned him and sent him a cup of hemlock, which is a deadly poison, to drink."

"But he had mo' gumption dan to drink it, I hope?"

"It was the law of his country, Sallie, and Socrates was always a law-abiding citizen."

"Wal, fur gosh sake!" cried Sallie. "Whut in de world was de use uv him havin' all dat tongue ef he couldn't use it to show dem peepul wherein? He mouts well been es dumd es a doodlebug!"

"But," explained Mrs. Thoro, "he had spent his whole life in trying to make the Athenians love and honor and obey their laws and he was willing to die for the same cause. He had many friends who loved him truly and they tried to persuade him to escape, but by unanswerable arguments he proved to them how wrong they were."

"Humph!" grunted Sallie. "Tonguey to de last! An' in de wrong way to de wrong ones."

"Plato, who was a friend as well as a pupil," continued Mrs. Thoro, "tells how beautifully Socrates died. He took the cup of hemlock quite calmly and cheerfully and drained it to the dregs. When his friends could not restrain their sorrow for the loss they were about to sustain, he reproved them and urged them to remember that they were about to bury, not Socrates, but the shell which had contained him, for he, himself, was about to enter the joys of the blessed. He tried to the last to make them see that unless they honored and obeyed all laws, their country could not long survive, because lawlessness was the same as suicide."

"Miss Oddry," said Sallie, solemnly, "don't yo' wisht we had one million of dem Sockertees down here in ower sunny Soufland?"

1922

- James Joyce's *Ulysses* and T. S. Eliot's *The Waste Land* are published.
- The International Court of Justice is established at The Hague in the Netherlands.
- Polish president Gabriel Narutowicz is assassinated.
- In India, the British sentence Gandhi to six years in prison.
- Fascist leader Benito Mussolini rises to power in Italy.
- The tomb of Pharaoh Tutankhamen (King Tut) is discovered by archaeologists in Luxor, Egypt.
- Egypt gains independence from Britain.
- René Maran wins France's prestigious Goncourt Prize for *Batouala,* a novel about African tribal life under French colonial rule. Maran is the first black author to receive the award.
- Howard University in Washington, D.C., offers the first course in African history at a U.S. university.
- The Dyer Anti-Lynching Bill dies in the Senate after being passed by the House of Representatives.

U.S. unemployment: 6.7%

Lynchings in the United States: 51 blacks, 6 whites

Deaths: Col. Charles Young (8 Jan.); Bert Williams (4 Mar.)

Spingarn Medal:
>   Mary B. Talbert (activist, stateswoman)

Books:
>   Carrie W. Clifford, *The Widening Light* (poetry)
>   Georgia Douglas Johnson, *Bronze* (poetry)
>   James Weldon Johnson (ed.), *The Book of American Negro Poetry* (anthology)
>   Claude McKay, *Harlem Shadows* (poetry)
>   William Pickens, *The Vengeance of the Gods* (short stories)

6 THE FOOLISH AND THE WISE

Sanctum 777 N. S. D. C. O. U. Meets Cleopatra

Leila Amos Pendleton

From *Crisis*, May 1922

The hour for opening had passed but, strange to say, Sister Sallie Runner, the All Highest Mogul of Sanctum 777, "Notable Sons and Daughters of Come On Up," had not yet arrived. The members stood around in groups and wondered what had happened, for Sis Runner was never late. True the Vice-All Highest, Sister Susan Haslum, was present and technically it was her duty to open the meeting; but the members of the Sanctum had a very poor opinion of her ability. Sallie had once voiced the general feeling when she said to her:

"Sis Haslum, seems lak to me dat yo knowlidge box is allus onjinted an' de mentals of yo mind clean upsot. How yo spect to rule dis Sanctum wen yo time come I cain't tell. Pears lak to me de bes' thing we kin do will be to 'lect yo Grand Past All Highest an' give yo de grand claps now an' be done wid it. Den we won't have to worry wid yo settin' in dis cheer an' tryin to zide."

The suggestion was not acted upon, but as the members waited tonight they wished very earnestly it had been; for then Sister Tulip Bawler would have been in line to preside (as she was Most Mightiest), and no one doubted her ability. When the thoughts of the members had reached this uncertain state, Notable Brother Brown spoke up:

"High Notables, Sons and Daughters, Brothers and Sisters, Officers and Members," he said, "I moves dat we close dis here Sanctum tonight befo' we opens it an' journey 'round to Sis Runner's house to see what all's de matter wid her."

"Sho! Sho! To be certingly," responded the Sanctum unanimously, but just as they were putting on their wraps, in bustled Sallie, breathless but smiling.

"I knowd it," said she, as soon as she could catch her breath. "I jes knowd you all would git tired a waitin'. I tole Reveral Runner so. But dat man is some sick an' whut part ain't sick is scared to death; an' no wonder, as much debilmunt as he's allus up to. Jes as I were puttin' on my hat to come here he dragged in de doe, lookin' lak a ghost. 'Brudder Runner,' says I. 'Is dat yo or yo apparutus?' He diden make no answer but jes pinted to his chist. Wal, yo orter seen me hop 'round. Yo know he already done had newmonny twict. I had some creso an' dats good for de longs; den I chopped up some Turmooda onyuns an' bound him up in dat an' salt. Wen he mence to feel better I turned him over to Obellina. She's jes as gooda nuss as me an' she are wrapped up in her pa 'cause she ain't on to his curbs. Come on, chilluns, less open de lodge. We'll leave off de gowns an' crowns an' mit de regular openin' 'cause it's so late, but I gotta fine ole anncienty story to tel yo an' dis time it's 'bout a cullud lady."

At this the Sanctum was all excitement and officers and members hurriedly took their stations. Sallie gave the altar in front of her five raps, then said she, "High Notibuls, yo kin pass to de secertary's desk one by one an' pay yo dues. Sis Dolum an' Sis Spots tend to passin' de cookies. Does yo all think you kin do all dem things an' lissen to me too?"

"Oh yas, All Highest," came a number of voices. "We's jes crazy to hear yo."

"Wal," proceeded Sallie, in her stateliest manner, "dis here lady I'se goin' to tell 'bout tonight were bornd right spang in Egupt an' dats in Afriky. She were a sho nuff queen too, wid lords an' ladies an' sojers an' servunts. Her name were Clea Patrick."

"All Highest," cautiously inquired Sister Ann Tunkett, Vice-Most Mightiest, "is yo rale sho she were cullud?"

"I is," responded Sallie. "Cose, Mis Oddry beat me down she warnt, but I knows better 'cause I were lookin' right at her. She were one a dese here high browns wid wavy hair an' rosy cheeks, lookin' jes lak dat Donarine Elett whut were runnin' arter Reveral Runner dat time. Least he 'cuse her of runnin' arter him wen dey got cot up wid, but I knows who were doin' de most runnin'."

"Is Mis Oddry got Clea Patrick's picter, All Highest?" inquired Sis Tunkett.

"Yas; an' de nex' time yo come 'round I'll show it to yo. Clea Patrick were one of dese here long-haided, long-nosed, long-eyed, slim gals dat jes nachel come into de world to make trubble. An' she sho made it. Fust off her King pa died wen she were only eighteen years ole an' lef his kentry fur her an' her lil brudder Tallmy to rule over togedder. But whut should Tallmy's gardeens do but grab de whole bisness an' leave Clea wid nuffin."

"Now ain't dat jes lak some men!" exclaimed Sis Bawler. "Seem lak de vurry idear of Wimmin rulin' anything but de cook kitching sets um wild."

"It's de fack—trufe," replied Sallie. "Yo all knows dat as long as I were settin' on dis floor Brudder Runner were a jim-dandy member of de 'Come On Ups.' Soon as I mence to move 'round de cheers, he mence to git restless. Den wen yo all 'lect me All Highest he jes nachel couldn stan' it. So he goes off an' jines dat 'Everlastin' Order of Hezzakites' an' he ain't been back here sence."

"Dats right, All Highest. Dats jes whut he done, but I nuvver seen through it befo'," said Vice-Most Mightiest Tunkett.

"Wal I seen through him. He's jes de same as a winda-pane to me. But ef I'da knowd whut I knows now or ef I'da lissened to my ma he'd nuvver got me in his clinches. Longs as I diden do nuthin but work fur him an' be a skillyun he were as pleased as punch, but jes as soon as peepul act lak dey thot I could do sumpin else sides dat he got sore. An' dat was de vurry way dem men acted wid Clea Patrick. But dey diden know her yit! Ha! Ha! Dey haden foamed her quaintence. She skipped 'round an' got herself a big army an' de way she fout um were sumpin pretty, 'cause evry one of dem sojers was in love wid her. Den right in de middle of all dat here come dat Julyus Siezer."

"Who were he, All Highest?" inquired Sis Haslum.

"Why he were dat great Roaming gineral sumpin lak Elleckzandry, only he were bornd a long time arterward. Wal as soon as he got in gunshot of her, Clea Patrick mence rollin' dem long eyes at him. She done a right cute thing doe— she wind herself all up in a big bufull rug an' make her servunts carry it to Siezer an' say, 'Here's a present Queen Clea Patrick sont you.' Den wen dey onroll it, out she jump an' dat ole jack went crazy over her. Now he were ole nuff to be her grandpa an' he had a wife at home, sides bein' bald-haided, an' dey warnt no scuse fur de way he carried on."

"Wal, All Highest," drawled Most Mightiest Bawler, "yo know whut dey say 'bout a ole fool."

"Yas," returned Sallie, "an' I ain't nuvver seen dat sayin' fail yit. Dis here Siezer were a good zample of it, too. Why he took Clea Patrick back to Roam wid him an' put her in a fine palace an' was gittin' ready to go fum extreemity to extromity. But dem Roamings say, 'Looka here, we's tired a dis foolishness. Nuff's good as a feast. We all cain't die togedder—somebuddy is got to die fust an' it might's well be yo.' So dey jump on Siezer in de State House one day an' fill him fulla daggers."

"Oh! Oh! My! My!" cried the Sanctum.

"Yas indeedy," replied Sallie nonchalantly. "Cose wen I fust got quainted wid dem ole anncienties, dat murdarin' an' momockin' way dey had worried me a lot. But Ise usedta it now. Yo know you kin git usedta anybuddy dyin' but yosef. Wal wen dis here Siezer died, Clea Patrick lit out fur home an' took dey lil son Siezeron wid her. An' it's a good thing dey got away so slick 'cause dem Roamings woulda finished um bofe. But it do seem lak peepul nuvver knows whut dey ralely wants. Wen Siezer were daid evrybuddy got sorry an' wen his will were read an' dey found out dat he had left a whole lotta money to de vurry ones dat had kilt him, why dem Roamings rose up an' made dose killers fly an' burnt up all dey homes an' done um up so bad dey wisht dey nuvver hada seen dat Siezer, less mo' kilt him."

"Wal," Most Mightiest Bawler interposed, "doesn't yo think dat were fair an' square, All Highest?"

"Oh, I guess so," the All Highest replied, "but dem ole anncienties done so many quare things yo nuvver could tell whedder dey was comin' or goin'. Wal, arter Siezer were daid his main frend name Mark an Tony took up de battle. Arter fightin' in evry derection he wint sailin' down to Egupt. Wen Clea Patrick heerd he were comin' she diden git into no carpet dis time. No indeedy! She puts on her gladdes' rags an' jewls an' fumes an' gits in her fines' boat all kivvered wid gold an' silver, an' has her servunts all decked in dey grandes' clothes holdin' parasols over her an' wavin' fans at her an' way she sail to meet Mark an Tony. She already knowd him wen she were in Roam wid dat Siezer an' mebbe dey lak one another den, yo can't tell. Anyhow dey sho lak each udder arter at meetin'. Sho did!"

"Ef she look anything lak Donarina an' was all fixed up lak you says, I knows she were one uvvermo hartbreaker," put in Sis Haslum.

Sallie transfixed her with a look and went on. "Mark an Tony furgot all erbout Roam an' home an' wife an' everything but Clea Patrick. He warnt no ole man lak Siezer so dey was mo' on a quality. Dey played games togedder an' went a huntin' an' a fishin' togedder lak lil boy an' gurl. Sides, Clea would sing to Mark an' play fur him an' talk to him in seben langwitches."

"It's a wunder Mark's wife haden got onto um," commented Sis Tunkett.

"She did. She were one of dem strong-arm wimmin an' she starts up a great war, hopin' dat Mark will come on home an' git into it; but he were too busy. He an' Clea useter dress up in masks an' servunt's clothes at nights an' run up an' down de streets an' play Holler Ween pranks on peepul wen it warnt no Holler Ween. Den agin dey would put on dey grandes' robes an' crowns an' give de bigges' kinda ceptions to dey frends an' eat an' drink tel dey coulden see. An' den in the middle of dem doins Mark's wife upped an' died."

"Ah, de pore soul!" sighed Sis Haslum. "Dat Clea Patrick orta be shamed a hersef."

"Wal," resumed the All Highest, "Mark went on to meet the yuther great Roaming gineral name Tavius an' what should he do but make a match 'tween his sister an' Mark."

"Good gosh!" exclaimed Sis Bawler, "an' Clea Patrick yit livin'? Now don't you know dere's trubble comin' in lobs an' gobs? Diden dat Tavius had gumption nuff to know dat a man whut won't be true to one wife, won't be true to two?"

"Wal," Sallie replied, "pears lak of he uvver knowd it he furgot it or else he were hopin' fur de bes'. Anyhow, fur a while Mark kep' rale straight. But arter while he hadta leave home to go to de wars agin an' wen he got not so fur fum Clea Patrick—uh! uh!—he sont fur her an' give her not rings an' bracelits an' things lak dat, but rivers an' mountings an' cities an' countries."

"Jes whut I knowd!" triumphed Sis Bawler. "Dese here madeup matches allus scares me. Land knows deres times wen it's harda nuff to stand a match yo done made yosef, less mo one dats made fur yo."

"Mark an Tony found dat out aright. He done a lil mo' fightin' 'round erbout den he hikes hissef spang down to Egupt an' dar he stays wid Clea Patrick."

"Ah ha!" Sis Bawler cried. "Tole yo so! Tole yo so!"

"But," Sallie went on, "dem Roamings feel dersef much more degraced by Mark an Tony's doins, an' dey is tired a Clea Patrick hoodoodlin' dey bes' ginerals so dey clar war agin her."

"Serve her jes right!" Sis Tunkett cried indignantly. "Don't care ef she were a cullud queen. I don't hole wid no sich capers. She orta lef dem wimmins' husbunds lone."

"Dats right! Dats right!" chorused the Sanctum.

"Yas," Sallied agreed. "My ole mudder allus said dat 'Right wrongs no one.' Wal, Mark an Tony an' Clea Patrick gethered all dey sojers an' sailurs an' off dey go to fight de Roamings. Wen de battle got hot, Clea got scared an' back home she went ascootin. Stidda Mark an Tony stayin' dere an' fightin' lak a rale sojer, whut muss he do but take a fast boat an' lite out arter Clea Patrick. Cose wen de leaders lef, the sojers stop fightin' an' de inimy captured dem all an' den hiked out arter Clea an' Mark."

"Wal warnt dat sumpin!" exclaimed Sis Haslum.

"Dem two," continued Sallie, "knowd evrything were over den, so dey et an' drunk an' carried on wusser dan uvver, tel dem Roamings come clean into de city. Den Clea Patrick hide hersef wid her maids in a big monimint an' made her servunts tell Mark she were daid. I cain't imagine why she done dat 'cause dat news on top a all de res' of his trubbles jes nachel broke his heart an' he run his own swoad clean fru his body. Den wen dey come back an' say Clea Patrick warnt daid he made dem carry him to her. I reckon dey love one another much as dem kinda peepul kin, 'cause wen she saw him dyin' at her feet, she 'cides she diden wanta live widout him. So she put a pizenous wiper in her breast to sting her an' in a lil while she were dead."

"Poe thing," Sis Haslum sighed. "Poe thing. Mebbe ef her ma hada lived she woulda been a better gurl."

"Mebbe so," answered Sallie, "mebbe so. High Notabuls, de hour is late. We will close by singin' 'Dy soul be on dy guard.'"

7 BECKY

Jean Toomer

FROM *LIBERATOR*, OCTOBER 1922; REPRINTED IN *CANE*, 1923

Becky was the white woman who had two Negro sons. She's dead; they've gone away. The pines whisper to Jesus. The Bible flaps its leaves with an aimless rustle on her mound.

Becky had one Negro son. Who gave it to her? Damn buck nigger, said the white folks' mouths. She wouldnt tell. Common, God-forsaken, insane white shameless wench, said the white folks' mouths. Her eyes were sunken, her neck stringy, her breasts fallen, till then. Taking their words, they filled her, like a bubble rising—then she broke. Mouth setting in a twist that held her eyes, harsh, vacant, staring . . . Who gave it to her? Low-down nigger with no self-respect, said the black folks' mouths. She wouldnt tell. Poor Catholic poor-white crazy woman, said the black folks' mouths. White folks and black folks built her cabin, fed her and her growing baby, prayed secretly to God who'd put His cross upon her and cast her out.

When the first was born, the white folks said they'd have no more to do with her. And black folks, they too joined hands to cast her out . . . The pines whispered to Jesus. The railroad boss said not to say he said it, but she could live, if she wanted to, on the narrow strip of land between the railroad and the road. John Stone, who owned the lumber and the bricks, would have shot the man who told he gave the stuff to Lonnie Deacon, who stole out there at night and built the cabin. A single room held down to earth . . . O fly away to Jesus . . . by a leaning chimney . . .

Six trains each day rumbled past and shook the ground under her cabin. Fords, and horse- and mule-drawn buggies went back and forth along the road. No one ever saw her. Trainmen, and passengers who'd heard about her, threw out papers and food. Threw out little crumpled slips of paper scribbled with prayers, as they passed her eye-shaped piece of sandy ground. Ground islandized between the road and railroad track. Pushed up where a blue-sheen God with listless eyes could look at it. Folks from the town took turns, unknown, of course, to each other, in bringing corn and meat and sweet potatoes. Even sometimes snuff . . . O thank y Jesus . . . Old David Georgia, grinding cane and boiling syrup, never went her way without some sugar sap. No one ever saw her. The boy grew up and ran around. When he was five years old as folks reckoned it, Hugh Jourdon saw him carrying a baby. "Becky has another son," was what the whole town knew. But nothing was said, for the part of man that says things to the likes of that had told itself that if there was a Becky, that Becky now was dead.

The two boys grew. Sullen and cunning . . . O pines, whisper to Jesus; tell Him to come and press sweet Jesus-lips against their lips and eyes . . . It seemed as though with those two big fellows there, there could be no room for Becky. The part that prayed wondered if perhaps she'd really died, and they had buried her. No one dared ask. They'd beat and cut a man who meant nothing at all in mentioning that they lived along the road. White or colored? No one knew, and least of all themselves. They drifted around from job to job. We, who had cast out their mother because of them, could we take them in? They answered black and white folks by shooting up two men and leaving town. "Godam the white folks; godam the niggers," they shouted as they left town. Becky? Smoke curled up from her chimney; she must be there. Trains passing shook the ground. The ground shook the leaning chimney. Nobody noticed it. A creepy feeling came over all who saw that thin wraith of smoke and felt the trembling of the ground. Folks began to take her food again. They quit it soon because they had a fear. Becky if dead might be a hant, and if alive—it took some nerve even to mention it . . . O pines, whisper to Jesus . . .

It was Sunday. Our congregation had been visiting at Pulverton, and were coming home. There was no wind. The autumn sun, the bell from Ebenezer Church, listless and heavy. Even the pines were stale, sticky, like the smell of food that makes you sick. Before we turned the bend of the road that would show us the Becky cabin, the horses stopped stock-still, pushed back their ears, and nervously whinnied. We urged, then whipped them on. Quarter of a mile away thin smoke curled up from the leaning chimney . . . O pines, whisper to Jesus . . . Goose-flesh came on my skin though there still was neither chill nor wind. Eyes left their sockets for the cabin. Ears burned and throbbed. Uncanny eclipse! fear closed my mind. We were just about to pass . . . Pines shout to Jesus! . . . the ground trembled as a ghost train rumbled by. The chimney fell into the cabin. Its thud was like a hollow report, ages having passed since it went off. Barlo and I were pulled out of our seats. Dragged to the door that had swung open. Through the dust we saw the bricks in a mound upon the floor. Becky, if she was there, lay under them. I thought I heard a groan. Barlo, mumbling something, threw his Bible on the pile. (No one has ever touched it.) Somehow we got away. My buggy was still on the road. The last thing that I remember was whipping old Dan like fury; I remember nothing after that—that is, until I reached town and folks crowded round to get the true word of it.

Becky was the white woman who had two Negro sons. She's dead; they've gone away. The pines whisper to Jesus. The Bible flaps its leaves with an aimless rustle on her mound.

1923

- Turkey declares itself a republic, with Mustafa Kemal as president, ending six centuries of Ottoman rule.
- Approximately 140,000 die in a major earthquake in Japan. Tokyo and Yokohama are partially destroyed.
- Bulgarian prime minister Aleksandŭr Stamboliĭski is assassinated.
- In South Africa, Raymond Dart is the first to discover fossil remains of *Australopithecus,* the so-called "missing link" connecting apes and humans.
- Calvin Coolidge assumes presidency following Warren G. Harding's death in office.
- Industry giant U.S. Steel adopts the eight-hour workday, setting a major precedent.
- Robert J. Douglas organizes the New York Rens, the first black professional basketball team.
- Willis Richardson's *The Chip Woman's Fortune* becomes the first serious, nonmusical play by an African American to appear on Broadway.
- Martial law is declared in Oklahoma due to terrorist activities of the Ku Klux Klan.
- Bessie Smith records her first song, "Down Hearted Blues."

U.S. unemployment: 2.4%

Lynchings in the United States: 29 blacks, 4 whites

Spingarn Medal:
    George Washington Carver (scientist)

Books:
> Jean Toomer, *Cane* (short stories, poetry, drama)
> William Pickens, *Bursting Bonds* (autobiography)

Periodical:
> *Opportunity* (1923–49)

8 ESTHER
Jean Toomer

FROM *MODERN REVIEW*, JANUARY 1923;
REPRINTED IN *CANE*, 1923

1

Nine.

Esther's hair falls in soft curls about her high-cheek-boned chalk-white face. Esther's hair would be beautiful if there were more gloss to it. And if her face were not prematurely serious, one would call it pretty. Her cheeks are too flat and dead for a girl of nine. Esther looks like a little white child, starched, frilled, as she walks slowly from her home towards her father's grocery store. She is about to turn in Broad from Maple Street. White and black men loafing on the corner hold no interest for her. Then a strange thing happens. A clean-muscled, magnificent, black-skinned Negro, whom she had heard her father mention as King Barlo, suddenly drops to his knees on a spot called the Spittoon. White men, unaware of him, continue squirting tobacco juice in his direction. The saffron fluid splashes on his face. His smooth black face begins to glisten and to shine. Soon, people notice him, and gather round. His eyes are rapturous upon the heavens. Lips and nostrils quiver. Barlo is in a religious trance. Town folks know it. They are not startled. They are not afraid. They gather round. Some beg boxes from the grocery stores. From old McGregor's notion shop. A coffin-case is pressed into use. Folks line the curb-stones. Business men close shop. And Banker Warply parks his car close by. Silently, all await the prophet's voice. The sheriff, a great florid fellow whose leggings never meet around his bulging calves, swears in three deputies. "Wall, y cant never tell what a nigger like King Barlo might be up t." Soda bottles, five fingers full of shine, are passed to those who want them. A couple of stray dogs start a fight. Old Goodlow's cow comes flopping up the street. Barlo, still as an Indian fakir, has not moved. The town bell strikes six. The sun slips in behind a heavy mass of horizon cloud. The crowd is hushed and expectant. Barlo's under jaw relaxes, and his lips begin to move.

"Jesus has been awhisperin strange words deep down, O way down deep, deep in my ears."

Hums of awe and of excitement.

"He called me to His side an said, 'Git down on your knees beside me, son, Ise gwine t whisper in your ears.'"

An old sister cries, "Ah, Lord."

"'Ise agwine t whisper in your ears,' he said, an I replied, 'Thy will be done on earth as it is in heaven.'"

"Ah, Lord. Amen. Amen."

"An Lord Jesus whispered strange good words deep down, O way down deep, deep in my ears. An He said, 'Tell em till you feel your throat on fire.' I saw a vision. I saw a man arise, an he was big an black an powerful—"

Some one yells, "Preach it, preacher, preach it!"

"—but his head was caught up in th clouds. An while he was agazin at th heavens, heart filled up with th Lord, some little white-ant biddies came an tied his feet to chains. They led him t th coast, they led him t th sea, they led him across th ocean an they didnt set him free. The old coast didnt miss him, an th new coast wasnt free, he left the old-coast brothers, t give birth t you an me. O Lord, great God Almighty, t give birth t you an me."

Barlo pauses. Old gray mothers are in tears. Fragments of melodies are being hummed. White folks are touched and curiously awed. Off to themselves, white and black preachers confer as to how best to rid themselves of the vagrant, usurping fellow. Barlo looks as though he is struggling to continue. People are hushed. One can hear weevils work. Dusk is falling rapidly, and the customary store lights fail to throw their feeble glow across the gray dust and flagging of the Georgia town. Barlo rises to his full height. He is immense. To the people he assumes the outlines of his visioned African. In a mighty voice he bellows:

"Brothers an sisters, turn your faces t th sweet face of the Lord, an fill your hearts with glory. Open your eyes an see th dawnin of th mornin light. Open your ears—"

Years afterwards Esther was told that at that very moment a great, heavy, rumbling voice actually was heard. That hosts of angels and of demons paraded up and down the streets all night. That King Barlo rode out of town astride a pitch-black bull that had a glowing gold ring in its nose. And that old Limp Underwood, who hated niggers, woke up next morning to find that he held a black man in his arms. This much is certain: an inspired Negress, of wide reputation for being sanctified, drew a portrait of a black madonna on the courthouse wall. And King Barlo left town. He left his image indelibly upon the mind of Esther. He became the starting point of the only living patterns that her mind was to know.

2

Sixteen.

Esther begins to dream. The low evening sun sets the windows of McGregor's notion shop aflame. Esther makes believe that they really are aflame. The town fire department rushes madly down the road. It ruthlessly shoves black and white idlers to one side. It whoops. It clangs. It rescues from the second-story window a dimpled infant which she claims for her own. How had she come by it? She thinks of it immaculately. It is a sin to think of it immaculately. She must dream no more. She must repent her sin. Another dream comes. There is no fire department. There are no heroic men. The fire starts. The loafers on the corner form a circle, chew their tobacco faster, and squirt juice just as fast as they can chew. Gallons on top of gallons they squirt upon the flames. The air reeks with the stench of scorched tobacco juice. Women, fat chunky Negro women, lean scrawny white women, pull their skirts up above their heads and display the most ludicrous underclothes. The women scoot in all directions from the danger zone. She alone is left to take the baby in her arms. But what a baby! Black, singed, woolly, tobacco-juice baby—ugly as sin. Once held to her breast, miraculous thing: its breath is sweet and its lips can nibble. She loves it frantically. Her joy in it changes the town folks' jeers to harmless jealousy, and she is left alone.

Twenty-two.

Esther's schooling is over. She works behind the counter of her father's grocery store. "To keep the money in the family," so he said. She is learning to make distinctions between the business and the social worlds. "Good business comes from remembering that the white folks dont divide the niggers, Esther. Be just as black as any man who has a silver dollar." Esther listlessly forgets that she is near white, and that her father is the richest colored man in town. Black folk who drift in to buy lard and snuff and flour of her, call her a sweet-natured, accommodating girl. She learns their names. She forgets them. She thinks about men. "I dont appeal to them. I wonder why." She recalls an affair she had with a little fair boy while still in school. It had ended in her shame when he as much as told her that for sweetness he preferred a lollipop. She remembers the salesman from the North who wanted to take her to the movies that first night he was in town. She refused, of course. And he never came back, having found out who she was. She thinks of Barlo. Barlo's image gives her a slightly stale thrill. She spices it by telling herself his glories. Black. Magnetically so. Best cotton picker in the county, in the state, in the whole world for that matter. Best man with his fists, best man with dice, with a razor. Promoter of church benefits. Of colored fairs. Vagrant preacher. Lover of all the women for miles and miles around. Esther decides that she loves him. And with a vague sense of life slipping by, she resolves that she will tell him so, whatever people say, the next time he comes to town. After the making of this resolution which becomes a sort of wedding cake for her to tuck beneath her pillow and go to sleep upon, she sees nothing of Barlo for five years. Her hair thins. It looks like the dull silk on puny corn ears. Her face pales until it is the color of the gray dust that dances with dead cotton leaves.

3

Esther is twenty-seven.

Esther sells lard and snuff and flour to vague black faces that drift in her store to ask for them. Her eyes hardly see the people to whom she gives change. Her body is lean and beaten. She rests listlessly against the counter, too weary to sit down. From the street some one shouts, "King Barlo has come back to town." He passes her window, driving a large new car. Cut-out open. He veers to the curb, and steps out. Barlo has made money on cotton during the war. He is as rich as anyone. Esther suddenly is animate. She goes to her door. She sees him at a distance, the center of a group of credulous men. She hears the deep-bass rumble of his talk. The sun swings low. McGregor's windows are aflame again. Pale flame. A sharply dressed white girl passes by. For a moment Esther wishes that she might be like her. Not white; she has no need for being that. But sharp, sporty, with get-up about her. Barlo is connected with that wish. She mustnt wish. Wishes only make you restless. Emptiness is a thing that grows by being moved. "I'll not think. Not wish. Just set my mind against it." Then the thought comes to her that those purposeless, easy-going men will possess him, if she doesnt. Purpose is not dead in her, now that she comes to think of it. That loose women will have their arms around him at Nat Bowle's place to-night. As if her veins are full of fired sun-bleached southern shanties, a swift heat sweeps them. Dead dreams, and a forgotten resolution are carried upward by the flames. Pale flames. "They shant have him. Oh, they shall not. Not if it kills me they shant have him." Jerky, aflutter, she closes the store and starts home. Folks lazing on store window-sills wonder what on earth can be the matter with Jim Crane's gal, as she passes them. "Come to remember, she always was a little off, a little crazy, I reckon." Esther seeks her own room, and locks the door. Her mind is a pink mesh-bag filled with baby toes.

Using the noise of the town clock striking twelve to cover the creaks of her departure, Esther slips into the quiet road. The town, her parents, most every-

76   EBONY RISING

one is sound asleep. This fact is a stable thing that comforts her. After sundown a chill wind came up from the west. It is still blowing, but to her it is a steady, settled thing like the cold. She wants her mind to be like that. Solid, contained, and blank as a sheet of darkened ice. She will not permit herself to notice the peculiar phosphorescent glitter of the sweet-gum leaves. Their movement would excite her. Exciting too, the recession of the dull familiar homes she knows so well. She doesnt know them at all. She closes her eyes, and holds them tightly. Wont do. Her being aware that they are closed recalls her purpose. She does not want to think of it. She opens them. She turns now into the deserted business street. The corrugated iron canopies and mule- and horse-gnawed hitching posts bring her a strange composure. Ghosts of the commonplaces of her daily life take stride with her and become her companions. And the echoes of her heels upon the flagging are rhythmically monotonous and soothing. Crossing the street at the corner of McGregor's notion shop, she thinks that the windows are a dull flame. Only a fancy. She walks faster. Then runs. A turn into a side street brings her abruptly to Nat Bowle's place. The house is squat and dark. It is always dark. Barlo is within. Quietly she opens the outside door and steps in. She passes through a small room. Pauses before a flight of stairs down which people's voices, muffled, come. The air is heavy with fresh tobacco smoke. It makes her sick. She wants to turn back. She goes up the steps. As if she were mounting to some great height, her head spins. She is violently dizzy. Blackness rushes to her eyes. And then she finds that she is in a large room. Barlo is before her.

"Well, I'm sholy damned—skuse me, but what, what brought you here, lil milk-white gal?"

"You." Her voice sounds like a frightened child's that calls homeward from some point miles away.

"Me?"

"Yes, you Barlo."

"This aint th place fer y. This aint th place fer y."

"I know. I know. But I've come for you."

"For me for what?"

She manages to look deep and straight into his eyes. He is slow at understanding. Guffaws and giggles break out from all around the room. A coarse woman's voice remarks, "So thats how th dictie niggers does it." Laughs. "Mus give em credit fo their gall."

Esther doesnt hear. Barlo does. His faculties are jogged. She sees a smile, ugly and repulsive to her, working upward through thick licker fumes. Barlo seems hideous. The thought comes suddenly, that conception with a drunken man must be a mighty sin. She draws away, frozen. Like a somnambulist she wheels around and walks stiffly to the stairs. Down them. Jeers and hoots pelter bluntly upon her back. She steps out. There is no air, no street, and the town has completely disappeared.

1924

- Soviet leader Vladimir Ilyich Lenin dies.
- The government of Ethiopia emancipates slaves, although de facto slavery continues in that country for many years to follow.
- The first Winter Olympics opens in Chamonix, France.
- Calvin Coolidge elected president.
- The Indian Citizenship Act declares Native Americans to be U.S. citizens.
- The Immigration Act places severe restrictions on blacks and other ethnic groups entering the United States.
- Singer Roland Hayes is the first African American to give a recital at Carnegie Hall.
- The Civics Club Dinner is held, serving as an unofficial "coming out party" for so-called New Negro writers and inspiring the special Mar. 1925 Harlem issue of *Survey Graphic*.
- Black inventor Garrett A. Morgan receives a patent for his automatic traffic signal.
- First World Series for Negro League baseball teams is held.

U.S. unemployment: 5%

Lynchings in the United States: 16 blacks, 0 whites

Deaths: John Edward Bruce (7 Aug.)

Spingarn Medal: Roland Hayes (singer)

Books:
    W. E. B. Du Bois, *The Gift of Black Folk* (nonfiction)
    Jessie Redmon Fauset, *There Is Confusion* (novel)
    Joshua Henry Jones, *By Sanction of Law* (novel)
    Walter White, *The Fire in the Flint* (novel)

9 VIGNETTES OF THE DUSK
Eric Walrond

FROM *OPPORTUNITY*, JANUARY 1924

It is lunch time. I am in the heart of America's financial seraglio. It is a lovely day. Spring. Oceans of richly clad people sweep by me. In my pockets I jingle coins of gold. Gold! I am tired of eating at Max's Busy Bee. The fellows who dine there are so—so—rough sometimes. Still it is the most democratic eating place I know. There is no class prejudice; no discrimination; newsboys, bootblacks, factory slaves, all eat at Max's.

Today I am "flush" and I think I ought to blow myself to a decent meal. My courage is bolstered up. Rich, I am extravagant today. I rub elbows with bankers and millionaires and comely office girls. Of seraphs and madrigals I dream—nut that I am. I look up at the sparkling gems of architecture and marvel at the beauty that is America. America!

I almost ran past it. There it is, the place with the swinging doors and the chocolate puffs in the show case. Myriads of Babbitts and elfin girls pour into it. Tremblingly I enter. It reminds me of a mediaeval palace. Mirrors, flowers, paintings, candelabra; waiters in gowns as white as alabaster; and at the table a row, two deep, of eager, bright faced youths and maidens.

I stand back in bewilderment. How efficient these waiters are! Don't they ever make mistakes? Don't they ever give wrong change? Don't they ever serve a frappe for a temptation, a soda for a sundae? Don't they ever—

The waiter's inquiring eyes are on mine. He has got round to me. I whisper my order to him.

"Oyster salad—and vanilla temptation."

I put both hands in my coat pockets and think of the beauty and romance to be found in this place. Up my sleeve I laugh at your intellectual immigrants who howl about the barrenness of America. To me it offers exhaustless possibilities. It opens up entirely new and unexpurgated editions to life. Yes, I say to myself,

I must come back again. It is weirdly enchanting. The cuisine is so good. And the people here are such refined eaters! So unlike Max's, where everything is bolted down at a gulp!

Oh, why does he put himself to all that trouble? Couldn't he just hand it to me over there instead of having to come all the way round the counter to make sure that it gets into my hands? Couldn't he have saved himself all that trouble?

He is at my side. Stern and white-lipped he hands me a nice brown paper bag with dusky flowers on it. He holds it off with the tips of his fingers as if its contents were leprous.

"Careful," he warns farsightedly, "else you'll spill the temptation." I do not argue. Sepulchrally I pay the check and waltz out. It is the equivalent of being shoed out. And, listen folks, he was careful *not* to say, "No, we don't serve no colored here."

II.

In 1918 he came to America. That means he is still a foreigner. He is not a citizen—yet! But he is going to be. It is going to be the Big Adventure of his life. But wait—

Sometimes he stops and thinks. He is a Negro. He is a foreign Negro. Every day he reads of lynchings in the South. He is besieged on all sides by vicious soul pricks. No, they'd say to him, you mustn't go South; you won't like it down there. In some places, like Texas, you can't stand up under the same roof with a white man unless you take off your hat. You would rebel against it. You, with your white man's point of view. (Don't you know, the white nurse woman who attends his wife once told him, as she cocked her red head on one side and shut one of her ugly cross eyes, "I think English Negroes are more like white people in their point of view, don't you think so? They're so fine—and not so race conscious.") You, they say to him, you with your white man's ways and outlook will not stand for it. They'd string you up on a tree! They'd. . . .

"But I must go," he screams back at them. "I must! I can't be an American unless I am able to go South! I've got to go."

He thinks of his friend Williams. Williams is a Jamaican. But he is thoroughly, spiritually, euphistically American. Some dusky folks, mistaking him for a native, so perfect is his philological assimilation—I am referring to those Afro-Americans who speak of West Indians as "monkey chasers"—come to him and say, "You know, Bill, dem monkey wimmin is de dummest—"

But Williams, who owns a lovely home in Jersey, and has a pretty wife, a jewel of one of the best colored families of Baltimore, is not a citizen. And he doesn't intend to be one. He has been here twenty years. "America is all right," he'd say, "but I ain't taking no chances!"

III.

I am a listening post. I am anchored in the middle of life's gurgling stream. It is a stream that is anthropologically exotic. Up in the Negro belt.

I am at a chop house on Lenox Avenue. It is a rendezvous for Negro Bohemians. I am amazed at the conglomerateness of it. Quadroons, octoroons, gypsies, yellows, high and low browns, light and dark blacks, of all shades and colors of shades.

"Well, what do you think of this young Negro generation? Think they'll amount to anything?"

"Oh, they'll fizzle out like all the rest. Wind up as porters ... elevator men ... janitors. ..."

Silence.

IV.

I am thinking, thinking, thinking. Of white supremacy; of the Nordic Renaissance. ...

And again I don the armor of the listening post.

Right of me is a Negro, a very black Negro clarionetist, who, as I take my seat, rises to go out. At the table from which he rose two other men sit. One is a mulatto; the other is fair, very fair, almost white. He of the golden hair and thin lips leans back in his chair and looks at the young man about to go out.

"Say," he whispered, "kin—kin ah come along?"

The other played with it. Slowly he took the tooth pick out of his mouth and wagged his head decisively.

"Nope," he said, "I can't take you along, old top. Where I'm going the folks don't like no yalla men."

V.

Out on the street. I whine at the whirl of dust and dirt the wind blasts up on me. I am slowly going down the avenue. In front of me is a jet black trollop. Her hair is bobbed. I snort at the bumps—barber's itch—I am forced to see on the back of her scraped neck. Ugh! Glass bottle!

I stop at Archie's. I always stop at Archie's on the way down. Out on the streaming boulevard he is, as usual. Myriads of men—please don't tell me they all work at night—talk to him about horses, horses, horses. Coming up the avenue is a woman, an anthropological metamorphosis. ...

"May God strike me dead if I ain't telling you the truth," Archie is trying to convince a skeptic of something. "Eight years, I tell you. After me for eight long years. But I didn't bother. And talk about pretty, she was a dream. Her father was one of the richest colored men in Virginia. And she had a lovely bungalow on the South Side. Oberlin graduate too. But I didn't marry her. And I didn't have anything against her. . . . She was so fine and thoughtful. . . . Come any time at the house. I'll show you the little cuff links . . . things like that. . . . I didn't have anything against her. . . . Not a thing. Only thing she was too white. Her hair was a bit too much like old gold. . . . she was too white. . . ."

Coming up the avenue is the anthropological metamorphosis.

"Sure she ain't white, Archie?"

"Ah don't know. . . ."

"Seems lek she. . . ."

Goes the mystery by. Then. . . .

"Naw," Archie spits, "she ain't white. Can't you see her neck?"

10 BLUE ALOES
Ottie B. Graham

FROM *CRISIS*, AUGUST 1924

Who can account for an impulse? Surely not a youth of twenty. Who would account on a day whose skies were blue and whose streams were clearest silver? Oh, not a youth of twenty.

Then Joseph was answering the call that only the young can know when he threw off shoes and top clothes and leaped into the silver of deep, smooth Little River. It flowed in front of Aloe House. Threw off shoes and stockings, and leaping, called to Melrose, living in Aloe House.

"Melrose!" he called, flashing through space and flipping into the water. Across to the opposite bank he swam, speeding like an islander. And climbing up to land by roots and hanging bushes, forth he stepped—youth on a sunny morning! Blessed son of the gods, singing impromptus to a maiden. "Melrose!" And the morning breeze carried the music over the water. Soon the boy followed. He had seen the slender form come out from the little house. But though he swam swiftly and straight, the girl was not there to greet him. He was disappointed but not surprised. Granna had interfered. He knew. Since she could not swim with him, at least they could walk together. So he threw himself flat upon the grass along the bank, stretching out full length to dry.

Little time passed before he heard a dragging footstep. For a moment he thought he was dreaming a dream that was bad. He was supposed to move away upon the approach of the dragging footstep, but he would not move today. He would remain and sing to Melrose if the old woman cursed him doubly. He would—ah, he could not move now if he wanted to. She stood over him.

"Lazy young dog!" she started, and there came such a torrent of maledictions as Joseph had never before heard. At first he had laughed at her. It amused him to hear an old hag going into fury because his young limbs, uncovered, breathed the sun; because he persisted in his love for the girl; because she loved him in return. At first it was funny but soon it ceased to amuse, and he joined in her tirade. Finally Granna dragged away, and she scowled and fussed. Fussed like something from the lower regions. Joseph hurried into his clothes and followed behind her, sullen and determined. Ach! she turned upon him.

"I tell yu, ef I puts a sho nuf curse on yu, yu won't forgit it soon. Runnin' aroun' heah half naked, an' callin' all ovah the place fo that gal, an' she ready an' fixin' to come out in the river with yu lak a young fool. Jus' come on an' take her out ef yu think yu kin. I'll fix yu!"

And the boy put in his part. "Oh, you think I'm afraid of your black magic, you old witch! But I'm not, and I'll teach Melrose not to be. And she'll stop making your aloes cures and the people will stop coming to bring you money for nothing. You old witch, you old wi-hitch! You old witch! Here's what I think of your aloes and your house full of aloes branches. *Now* conjure me!" And his laugh was so wild and shrill with anger it dulled the clanging of the falling tubs he had kicked over in his rage. They held the drippings of aloes.

With the dying away of the furore came a soft crying, then a young, tremulous voice. "Jo!" It wailed softly. "Jo! You don't know what you have done. Jo!" Around the corner of the little house crept the girl, Melrose, frightened and ready to flee. The old woman had disappeared into the house. Soon, however, she returned. Even before the girl could reach her boy.

"Come on, Melrose, come on," called Joseph. The girl had started back. "Come on, she won't hurt you." Granna stopped and glared upon them while the boy talked that she might hear.

"She hates you because you're more beautiful than she would have you; because you are younger than she would have you. She hates you because you love me and her aloes can't stop you!" And he laughed long and lustily. Granna looked on.

Melrose had reached his side. "Hush, Jo, you've done enough. That was the last of the drippings from the blue leaves, and they came from far away. Someone brought them to her on a boat from an island. Listen!"

The woman, already bent from age, was bending farther over, and mumbling, mumbling, mumbling. The violet blue substance, part liquid, part resin, flowed past her in a slow stream. A slow stream from its tumbled tubs. And she, running with it, then running back, mumbled, mumbled, mumbled. The girl and her boy stood looking, the girl, frankly distressed, the boy alarmed in spite of himself.

"It's the curse!" Melrose trembled. Joseph held her hand. They were two children.

"How can it hurt? The stuff is no more than a medicine."

"Oh, but,—"

"It's her foolishness. I'll take you away from the South and its superstitions. Look at her now, the old witch." Granna was on her knees now, splashing handfuls of the substance.

Melrose turned where she stood. "I'll have to go away now, Jo. I can't go back. No! You can't go back either." Joseph had not turned where he stood. Instead, he moved toward the woman. The blue stuff flowed between them.

"Don't cross it, Jo. You can never get rid of the curse if you cross her stream!" And this served only to make him dare. He strode to the stream and jumped across.

"I'm going to take Melrose away!" he yelled. He was quite close upon Granna, but he hollered as though she had been deaf. Perhaps he did not know it. He trembled. "Melrose living under the [same] roof with you. Lord, what a crime! I'll take her from you, old Ashface, out here in the woods. I'll take her from the South and superstition!"

Granna had been kneeling. Now she stood. But she did not measure to the height of the stripling before her. She squinted and blinked up at him, and her wrinkled black face *was* ashen with the heat of temper. She was wont to sing hymns as she brewed aloes, but she seldom talked. This late mad outburst had taken her strength, therefore, and she quivered as she stood. An aloe string hung about her neck. The Negroes of Africa's west coast wore such cords, but that gave no clue to Granna. None knew of her origin. They only knew of the pretty child she had raised. She looked up at Joseph, and he down at her. From a short distance came the soft crying of the young and tremulous voice.

"Takin' my gal, is yu? Well, tell uh don' come back when yu turn to anothuh. Ungrateful yaller devil!" A fresh thunder clap. They gyrated and all but spat in each other's faces. Youth is wild, and sometimes old age too.

"Oh, you say that again, old woman! You judge me by yourself, no doubt. I'll rid you of your hateful self."

"Hi! Yu dar to tuch me." She was witch now, if ever. Her withered old hand touched the cord about her neck, and she snatched it off and dashed it in the face of Joseph. "Yu know what hit yu? Blue aloes!" And she screamed out a grating haw-haw.

Melrose ran to Joseph. For a moment he thought he was blinded. He went, by her hand, to the river, and together they bathed the bruised eyes. Then they started off to the future, empty handed, looking not behind them. Aloe House was still. And the silence deafened, so that neither heard the other catching little breaths at the outset of their journey. Neither heard. The sun now was too hot, the day was now too dry. Melrose coughed. Joseph spoke.

"Her medicines don't cure your cough."

"I got the cough from her."

"Huh!"

"All medicines can't cure a cough." They turned from the road and sat under a tree. Town was still far off.

"What of magic? Can it cure a cough?" They looked at each other.

"There isn't any magic, Jo. I'm not afraid of magic."

"You were afraid back there."

"But I've come away for good. Not afraid now." They resumed their walking—new pilgrims on the search for happiness.

"I'll take you away from the South," said the youth. Brave youth.

"Can't take me from the South, Jo. I have to stay in the South with this cough. It will go, but I'll have to stay here. Jo, where are we going?"

"Up on the hill to my father's house. It is all that I have, my father's house. When I came back last year I closed it. I paddled down Little River and found you. Now I shall open it again. We'll stay there until the cough goes."

"That will be a long time."

They neared the town. Silence had flown, but a town does not exist without its noises. This was called a pretty town, but the girl thought it drab and choky. The country behind was sweet. They entered the town. People stared or nodded, or smiled or shook their heads. In a very short time the whole town knew that Joseph was opening the old home for the girl from Aloe House. One street led up a hill overlooking its section of the town. Up the hill they went, Melrose and Joseph, looking back not once.

The house stood silent like the country along the road; the grounds were silent like the house. The girl felt thankful. They would be away from the town. The afternoon was waning. In its soft, drowsy heat Joseph went down the hill again. Melrose waited under a tree. The trees up here were gracious; their shade was cooling. How could men live in towns—narrow, stuffy places? Where had Jo lived down there? He had lived with the parson. The parson—the parson— oh! There was another thing about towns. They required parsons with love. Well, that would not matter, only it had not occurred to her before this. Love— parsons—what places were towns! Towns—country—country—Granna! But there was no magic. Aloes—just a medicine—no magic. "Till he turned to another—turned to another." But he was coming back already, and someone else was with him. The parson. She knew the parson. He had visited her when she first got the cough. Granna had been very rude. There were others coming too. Was the town moving up to kill the quiet of the hill? She sat still, rising not until Joseph spoke.

"You know who this is, Melrose. We let the others come. They can take back good news now. They'll take back one kind or another, you know." So they were married up on the hill. The crowd, curious, around them. The house, yet unopened. The "guests" carried their news back to the town.

At the parson's house they were feasted, Melrose and Joseph. The parson was kind; so was his wife. The house on the hill was opened and left to the night, that the stale air and the moths might drain out. At the parson's house they were feasted, and taught to look brightly on the future. Youth must never fear the future. These were merely words of advice; there was no fear here. With morning came work for Joseph and gifts from neighbors for the girl. Southerners are good-hearted.

Time brought only happiness. Joseph taught his young wife all he had learned North in schools. He would take her there some day, to the North. Then the girl would cough and he knew she could not go. But it was happiness, this living on the hill where the town was out of sight, and the trees whispered, and the yellow-brown creature moved about singing with the low, tremulous voice. Children from the town came up. He taught her and she taught them. Children from the town—all kinds. Little pale things with scragly locks, little pale things with heavy locks. Brown little things with silken curls, brown little things with kinky curls. They and Melrose. Melrose and they.

Time landed one day a strange cargo. Happiness a bit discolored, came with the bringing of a plant. With a plant. A gardener, an old man working about the town, brought it. A beautiful thing, and rare. Melrose thanked the man with slight strain in her voice. As soon as he had gone she dashed it on the ground, stamping it again and again, until it was bruised and broken. Bruised and broken beyond recovery. She knew most of the species of the aloe. This was akin to the blue. That Joseph might not know of it, she buried the fragments under a great flower jar. But fear and sadness descended upon her. She had brushed aside this silliness long, long ago, and now it had seized her again. Joseph said the mind could be better controlled. This she told herself many times, saying, "It is absurd to fear nothing. It is absurd!" But her cough grew worse and she trembled about her duties. She walked down the hill to meet Joseph.

"Jo, could you ever love anyone else?" They were coming to the house.

"Could anyone else be you, honey?" And he kissed her lightly as they passed the great flower jar. She shook just a little and coughed a lot. That night she sobbed aloud in her sleep.

Melrose grew paler. She felt that the cough was worse. On warm evenings Joseph paddled a canoe. Went drifting down Little River. Joseph was not afraid of things, yet he never took the left branch of the river. The left branch of Little River flowed past Aloe House. It had been several years now since he took Melrose away, and neither of them mentioned it. Whether it still was there he did not know, nor did he go to see. So the right branch of the river was his, and he nosed round the bend automatically. On warm evenings Melrose went with him. Now she stayed home on the hill. She felt that her cough was worse. Now Joseph paddled alone.

On the water he hummed little melodies. He wished Melrose could play the piano better. Then he wished she were here on the water. Here singing with him on the water. No voice sang like hers. In the morning he would send another doctor. She must not be pale. He splashed the water and drifted. The night. Melrose would love the night out here. They had never come this far.

There came on the still air music. When had he heard such music! Music from a piano. He paddled to come nearer to it. Looking around, he saw a huge mansion on a hill. From this mansion came the music. Came the tones of silver.

Light streamed from a topmost window. To a landing he guided the tiny boat and listened. The music stopped and directly the light went out. Surprised, Joseph started back, paddling hard all the way. Melrose stood at the window when he reached the house. He told her of the night. Told her of the music. Told her how he had missed her.

Next night he went again. Went in the little boat down Little River. Down the right branch, drifting and paddling till he heard the silver melody. Music in the night from a mansion on a hill. Melrose would like it so. If she would come but once. Come but once to hear. He listened at the landing. The music ceased and the light went out. Immediately Joseph moved the canoe. At home on his hill Melrose waited. Patiently stood at the window. Again he told her of the night. Of the music.

Melrose next day was weary. She longed for the night to come. She would go this night in the canoe. Please Joseph and go on the river. But the day burned by. It was hot. When evening came she was tired. At the meal she smiled, but the smile was a dismal effort. Joseph set out earlier. Melrose was weary, the air was sultry. He must get out in the boat.

On the river it was cooler. He drifted all the way. And even at the mansion night had not yet come. No music sounded except the whirring of the wind through the trees. At the landing Joseph looked up. At the window, away up high, there stood a woman. The house below her was closed. Joseph started and stared. A paddle slipped from his hand into the river, and he uttered a short cry. "Melrose!" The house was near the river. He could see clearly, but he could not believe.

The woman stepped upon a little balcony outside her window and pitched something to him. It fell by chance into the boat—a beautifully grained paddle, its arm set with a gem of blue. She raised a finger to her lips and motioned him to go. The music came as he paddled away. As he pulled away in a daze. Night had fallen when he reached his hill. Melrose stood by the window. He told her of part of the trip. Of the music and of finding a paddle, but not of a woman who was her second self.

"Let me see the paddle, Jo," she asked. He brought it to her.

"The stone is lapis-lazuli." She was calm like mist on the bog. "The wood is aloe. It is very old; the fragrance is faint." She handed it back to Joseph. He looked at the paddle and then at his wife.

"Shall I throw it away?" She nodded. "I will." Late in the night Joseph awakened talking in his sleep. "I wish I could take her away," he was saying, "take her from the South."

Then he slept again and dreamed of her—of Melrose. But the dream became muddled, and he saw one time his Melrose—saw next time this woman. She came on the balcony and turned to his wife. Melrose came and turned to the woman. Then they came together and submerged into one. He was glad to awake. Glad to find Melrose whom he knew. At sundown he would go once more that he might see this person who was like her.

He went. At sundown he went that he might see. She stood at the window and waved to him. Again she was garbed in blue. Soft, sighing blue. She had worn blue on yesterday. Her window seemed a haze of blue. Joseph seemed rather to sense this than to see it. He gazed only at her face. "Melrose!" It was not her skin alone. There were hundreds in the South like that. Brown-yellow and yellow-brown. Nor was it alone her hair. Black—deep black like crows. Nor yet her gently pushed, red lips. But her sway when she stepped to the balcony. Her eyes like dark, melted pansies. Her waving—her languorous waving. Melrose was in her being.

Joseph returned the next evening, and the next, and the next. Many days he came at dusk, staring and bewildered. He spoke no more of his trips. Melrose asked naught about them. One time a rain came suddenly. All day the heat had stifled, but there had been little sun. Joseph was on the river. He would have turned and hurried back, but the music, more silver than the rain, came through the cooling air. He went to the landing and listened. Soon the woman, beautiful in her blue, appeared at the window. It rained too hard for her to step out, but she beckoned for him to come in. She dropped a big key, an old, rusty thing. A key seldom used, no doubt. Doing her gestured bidding, he opened a large side door. Steps, walled off from the rest of the place, wound straight up from the doorway to the top of the house. The lady, lovely person, met him. From a little anteroom she led him to where she had stood at the window. As he entered this larger room he was struck by the odor of aloes. Pleasant as the perfume was, it sickened him. For a second his head swam and he heard the low crying of Melrose's voice. He wanted to run away. Run like a little boy.

The rain on the roof was cheery but this scented, strange room was sad. It was blue. Blue from floor to ceiling, with rugs and low chairs of velvet and pillows and hangings of silk. A huge, blue opalescent dome hung low from the center ceiling. A piano, a handsome thing, stately in lacquered blue, stood beneath the dome. The walls were like a paneled, morning sky. Joseph gazed at the ceiling— at the floor—all about him. The woman stood at the window. "Like Melrose," Joseph whispered. She had forgotten him, no doubt. She was so still; he continued gazing. Now the dome. The woman turned, and while he gazed at pearl blue opalescence, she rested her eyes on him. He felt her looking and turned. And though he suspected the focusing of her eye, he flinched when their glances met. She came close to him and stood. At this range her face was older than his wife's. Even so, it was rather young, and almost as beautiful.

"The rain will cease," she said. Her voice was that of Melrose grown older. She wore a string of aloes about her throat. Joseph noticed them and gulped.

"I thank you, Madame, for your kind favor. The rain has stopped already. You were good to take me in. Now I must leave." She held his arm lightly to detain him.

"It is almost dark," said she, "and the sky is clearing. The sky from my window is wonderful at night." She returned to her window without asking him to stay. Joseph went with her. Pale stars twinkled through sailing fleece. The sky darkened as it cleared.

"Why have you come in your little boat to watch up at my window every evening?"

"Your playing, Madame, and you." Then she played for him. Played on the blue piano and brought forth silver notes. He listened long to her playing before he arose to go. He thanked her once more and started but she held him again.

"You have not seen my treasures," she said. "I have treasures. Rare things from Sokotra." She turned to a curtained corner and opened a chest of deep drawers. Proudly she drew forth trinkets. Trinkets of many descriptions. Metal necklaces and anklets of aloes. Aloe bracelets and anklets of metal. Rings and head-dresses and luckstones and bangles. Powdered perfumes of aloes and myrrh. Wood of aloes set with jewels. Aloes and cassia for scenting garments. Joseph was in a stupor.

"Rare things from Sokotra—Rare things from Sokotra." The words hummed in his brain. His brain seemed tight and bursting.

"I must go now, Madame. I must go." He heard himself saying this.

"Yes, you must go now, hurry. Hurry or they'll find you here!" The surprise of this statement destroyed the stupor. Joseph fled from the room.

The woman came close behind him. At the top of the stairs they stopped. He would have taken her hand to say goodbye, but she clung to him until he kissed her. Kissed her many times. Half way down the stairs he heard her voice calling—calling to him, "Hurry!"

Outside the night was quiet. The stars, once pale, were glowing. This air was not laden with aloes. He paddled home in a listless fear. A fear that was dull and thumping. Melrose was sleeping—and the room was blue. Oh, this was delusion. He would sleep it away. Sleep it away forever. But the morning came and the room was blue. Melrose dressed in blue. She had draped their room in blue. This was pretty he told her. This change from rose to blue. But he wondered why she made it—why she made it.

Every evening he went on the river. Went before the darkness came. The woman stepped onto the balcony and threw her kisses to him. Each time he looked to see her beckon. But she did not call him, and he wondered who else was there with her. He dared not go unless she beckoned. Beckoned and dropped the key. He listened when she played, and watched her light go out. She made the room dark that the night might come in. The night with its flickering stars. He listened when she played, then paddled home.

At home one night he found aloes. Found his garden set with aloes. Straightway he sought Melrose. She waited at the window.

"Why do you have about you this thing which you fear?" he asked.

"But I do not fear it any longer. You taught me not to fear."

"They are beautiful. You did not find them here?"

"Imported. A species of the Blue from Sokotra."

"Where?"

"Sokotra."

Joseph hushed. Something rang in his mind. "Rare things from Sokotra. Rare things from Sokotra." He looked with unstill eyes at Melrose. She looked quite steadily at him.

"Did you ever have kin in Sokotra?" he queried.

"No one knows but Granna. I know nothing of myself."

"Where is Sokotra, Melrose?"

"Some place on an island." Melrose talked little recently; she moved about more, however. She felt that she was better. That the cough was growing faint.

On the night that Joseph brought the paddle Melrose had felt a quaking. Her heart had sunk within her. Within her something whispered, "When he turns to another. When he turns to another." Why she had felt this she did not know, but the quaking was there in her heart. Somehow she had known that the paddle had not been found. Someone had given it to him. The nights had passed slowly from that time. From that time the day had changed. There was something she must discover. Something was taking Joseph. She had followed him the next night. Down the river he had paddled his tiny craft and she had run behind along the bank. The trees and shrubbery had hidden her. She had followed to the mansion. Had seen the lovely creature; compared her with herself. She had returned the morning after while Joseph was away, but the house had been silent, and the woman's window closed. Again she had gone at evening, after Joseph rode ahead. With him she had seen the greetings and with him heard the music.

Once when rain showered he had entered the house. The woman had tossed him a key. Melrose had come out of hiding and run to go in behind him. The door had locked behind Joseph, and she had dropped to the ground. On her knees she had sobbed aloud. Had called out to her husband. She had not known that her voice reached him, riding on the night like a broken spirit. By the door she had remained until he passed her. Passed her without seeing, and in haste. The odor of aloes had passed with him and she had laughed in pity at herself. At home she had reached the bed just before he came. For some time their room had been blue (she had seen that the woman wore it). But Joseph had first noticed this this night.

Now Melrose felt sorrow in her heart. Sorrow mingled with disdain. Adorned in blue, she had moved about the hill, silent, but stronger and fearless. When the children came up from the town she laughed and told them stories. Stories of Granna, a shrivelled old woman who believed in witchery. Of an island where aloes grow—an island on the way to India. There people dwelt in rubble-built huts, and lived on dates and milk; and aloes kept them well and in health, and scented all their garments. Granna had lived there long ago, chasing goats and wild asses over the hills. Once Joseph listened to the tales, and he searched his wife's face for understanding. He did not know she ever talked of Granna. And Melrose felt sorrow in her heart. Sorrow and disdain. Her husband was bewitched, and she was losing fear. She seldom coughed.

At dusk she ran behind the canoe, trailing him down the river. The woman came on the balcony. She kissed him her hand and he stretched out his arms, pantomiming love. One night she dropped down an aloe leaf. Melrose found it later. At once she filled her home with aloes, rare specimens from the island. Joseph asked about them and found her unperturbed.

Soon one evening, Melrose went ahead of Joseph. Ran swiftly along the river to the mansion on the hill. At the window stood the woman. Waiting already for Joseph. She did not see the figure darting quickly behind trees, stooping under bushes, slipping to her stairway door. But soon she heard a knocking. A knocking, knocking, knocking, and she came very softly down the steps. Without asking from the inside what was wanted, she opened wide the door.

They stood like stone, these women. Stone images reflected in a mirror. Melrose had not seen her close before. She had not seen Melrose ever. But now a look of knowing flitted across her face, then a look of awful fear, and she backed to the steps and turned and ran. Leaped like a frightened deer. Midway she wheeled again. Melrose had not moved. Back down the stairs the woman came, the look of killing in her eyes. She muttered.

"They'll not know," came the words thick and bitten, and away she flew repeating, "They'll not know!"

Melrose started after her, but she knew that Joseph would come. She expected the woman back also, and she must hold her ground. She ascended the stairs trembling. Trembling from what had passed, and what was yet to come. At the top was an antechamber. No one was within. In the large room she had a notion that she had walked into the sky. Into a sky perfumed with aloes. At the window she waited. Looked out on the river. Little River. She listened for the woman, but the woman did not return.

The canoe came gliding. Joseph's brown face was handsome. She would beckon as the woman had once done. Beckon and please him. He would come through the open door and she would kill him. Kill him in this room of blue. Yield to the curse. He looked up smiling and she tried to smile. Joseph frowned and looked harder. He would say goodbye to this woman; she was uncanny. No one should be like Melrose. He did not want this woman's smiles. He would say goodbye. Say goodbye and go. His boat nosed cross-wise. He was turning.

"Jo!" came his name from the window. "Jo!" short and quick. "Jo!" the long wail. Melrose!

She did not call again. She leaned against the window, convulsed with tears and sobbing. Sobbing and shaking. Moaning. Joseph ran to the door and found it open. Found no one upstairs but Melrose. He gathered her up and took her down like a baby in his arms. He could understand nothing, but he did not ask. It was not time to ask. Home he took her in the boat. Through the town they strolled, two lovers. Lovers reconciled.

Little groups of people stood about the streets. At the hill a crowd was jabbering. Eyes centered on Melrose and Joseph. Jabbering started afresh. Faces peered. Faces black and white and yellow, brown and tan and red and black. On the hill policemen guarded. Kept the crowd away. In a porch swing rested the body. The woman was dead. The woman from the mansion. She had tried to kill a white man on the street, and then she had run in the way of a horse. She had been insane. Now she was dead. They were awaiting the ambulance. Awaiting the coming of aid. The woman had been near the hill. People said she belonged there. Joseph chilled through. Melrose burned. They both said it was a mistake. The people had made an error. The ambulance came and took her away.

In the town the people whispered. Some said this woman was the mother of Melrose. Said Granna took Melrose when she was born. Was born of a father not black. Said the woman came from an island. Was brought by a southern family. In the town the secrets spread. "The woman, frightened, had lost her mind. She would not leave the house. The family moved and provided for her there. They left someone to keep her. No one had ever seen the person." Joseph heard the whisperings. "Whoever came, she thought to be her lover. Whoever came, she wooed in careful secrecy. Melrose was her child. Melrose her child." The whispers came to Melrose.

Joseph and Melrose went to find Granna. Back in the country down Little River—down the left branch to Aloe House. After a southern secret. They knocked at the door. Granna was not there. Nothing was there.

11 SLACKENED CAPRICE
Ottie B. Graham

From *Opportunity*, November 1924

Coming home from a long journey, I stopped with Carlotta at a southern city to visit an old friend of her mother's. The trip had been wearisome and we were glad of the few hours to stretch our limbs and rest. The place we wanted was easily reached, and when we arrived there it was so beautiful and still that a feeling of rest came over us in spite of our fatigue.

On the porch was a man standing before a bird cage. He was quiet, with his hands behind him, and he saw only the bird. We walked up the steps and spoke to him before he turned to notice us. He was too old to be young and too young to be even middle-aged. His eyes were soft, very kind and soft, and his smile was slow. He started to speak, but a woman came hurriedly out of the house, interrupting with a laugh and a greeting. She was his mother and the friend Carlotta had come to see. She welcomed us and led us to a sitting-room; then she asked us to excuse her for a few minutes. Her girl was burning something.

As she left the room by one door, her son entered by another. He had us make ourselves comfortable and brought us a cool drink of fruit juice. He sat and talked with us, saying himself very little but making us say much. I believe we were talking about a relative of his or about somebody's new position when he asked very abruptly, "How do you find people as you travel? Are they at all carefree?" His question was directed to Carlotta, but she had chance only for a philosophical, "Well," before he had apparently forgotten that the question was ever in his mind.

"Do you like music?" he asked quite as suddenly as he had made the first query. We said yes, of course.

"Then I shall play for you," he announced very quietly, and without more ado went to the piano. Once seated, he thought no more about us, and his long, bony fingers lifted and sped across the keyboard. For a moment they reminded me of slender, swiftly driven horses. I remember smiling inwardly as I thought that, because the idea seemed far-fetched; but there was something about him that made me draw far-fetched figures. He trilled and lilted through passages as light and airy as flying fairy down. There was something of Grieg wonder in them, but they were not Grieg. Glad, laughing measures repeated themselves, splashing in patches of sharp brilliancy throughout the ascending movement. Then, with what seemed something of reluctance in the long, bony fingers, the allegro stopped its prancing and quieted to a soberer swing. It did not cease descending; it came down, down, losing its gay fire, until only a sweet, crying melody remained. This melody was not at all akin to the start of the composition. Sweet and soft, even yearning, as though it would dance but could not, it merely sang. Here was something of Taylor plaintiveness, but it was not Taylor. And the slender fingers, stopped in their fleet gallop, caressed now tenderly the keys over which they had just sped.

This change of tone and tempo, though beautiful, was to me unusual and I wondered about it as I listened. So engrossed in his rendition was the man, he seemed actually to suffer from his tenseness. His brows raised in despairing frowns which wavered and settled again. He began to sway so that I looked at Carlotta and she at me, both afraid that he would fall from his seat. Just then his mother called to him, cheerily and as though she would check his sad song. Somehow I had imagined he would not leave the instrument even if he stopped playing to answer, but he did. He whirled from the piano, stood a moment, and passed through the door with what seemed a single stride. He said nothing to us—nothing whatever; but before we got over the shock of his leaving he had returned by the other door. He appeared to be annoyed—exceedingly annoyed, and he made a slight glance in our direction as he took his seat again.

The bony, long fingers rested once more upon the keys, impatient to be driven; and the light, dashing measures arose once more—arose and danced away. Then again came the gradual downtoning, and the slackening of pace, down, down, until a mere song remained. A mere song, but a sad one, which sang since it could not dance. The man, as he played on, suffered again, losing himself in the strains that went floating away. This time his mother came into the room, cheerily interrupting him at the place where she had called before. He turned, slowly this time, excusing himself, and quietly left our presence.

The woman made some passing mention of her son's absorbing fondness for the piano, and with an apology for her delay, set upon other conversation. We had well launched upon some interesting thing when the son returned again. He sat close by, listening but saying little, and smiling here and there his slow smile. A woman was mentioned, a master of some instrument, as we turned to talking of music. This made for our hostess' son a livening interest. In a short while he had taken the discussion into details of execution, and arrested the whole with his offer to play again. As though he had not touched the piano for us before, he said very simply, "I will play for you."

His mother seemed a bit nervous as he arose and approached the piano; but he was seated, we were forgotten, and the slender steeds were ready again to obey the will of their master. So splendid a musician was the man, we found ourselves too firmly held by his skill to become amused. A third time he set out upon the same thing—the thing which started in swift beauty and descended, down, down, to a simple, plaintive song.

His mother wanted to stop him again. It was easy to see that she wanted to, but a third time would be too significant of the strange uneasiness which lay behind her son's playing this thing beyond a certain point. Here again I wondered, as I listened, about the gradual, depressing change in the composition, and I wondered whether it pleased me. It was beautiful, to be sure, but I decided that I did not like it. There came then the end of the number. Quite suddenly it ended, and with a crash! A crash in high treble, like a quick, shrill scream. It did something to me that I could never explain; I will never forget that crash.

The son staggered from the piano and out to the porch. He murmured as he went, clutching at his breast and at his head. When his mother reached him, he had stopped at the bird's cage. He was standing still, very still, as though he had never been unsteady. To the bird he talked confidingly, saying low things we could not understand. But when he saw Carlotta and me, he lifted the cage down, quietly excused himself and walked away, down the veranda steps and out to the back of the lawn. All the way he talked to the bird.

"He's been this way now for sometime," his mother said resignedly, looking after him. "He went with the army—volunteered. He came back to me a wreck from gas. His nerves were almost gone, and sometimes his head was wrong; but he began to get back to normal after a while. His music helped a lot—dear boy. He started on his composing again and became wrapped up in a Caprice. That was what he just played. Oh, he was doing so well and I was so proud of him, and one little incident ruined everything. It's strange how it affected him." She stopped a minute as it all came back to her, and when she started again her southern drawl seemed sweeter and sad.

"He went walking one day with me down through the grove. We were just a'laughing and talking, and he kept singing snatches of his Caprice. We stopped to watch a group of children playing in a pretty little park. My boy said that he would work better on his Caprice now that he had seen them. Oh, they were happy little mites. They ran and skipped about, and fell over one another, and laughed and sang as though nothing was anything but their little game. I picked out one who reminded me of the way my boy used to look—brown face and brown curls—brown eyes full of sparkle. Oh, my!" she said, and she sighed.

"Then just as we started to move away, we noticed a sudden hush come over them. There stood a big, burly white man, a watchman or keeper or something, snarling at them and telling them they couldn't stay there. 'No niggers in there.' Well, the poor little things just sauntered away. Nothing else to do. It was mean.

Children are such lovely things—who could hurt them? As they moved away down the grove, one tried to start the others skipping again. They tried it, but it didn't do. They went along their way, several trying to stop the youngest little fellow from crying. He wanted to play in the park.

"Well, my boy didn't talk any more all the way home. He was like something hit in the face. I found him looking at his khaki next day, and later saying something to the bird about his song. He said the cage took something from the bird's song. Then he worked on his Caprice, but it wouldn't go. The first part kept up, but it would just change, it seemed, of itself. My poor boy, he couldn't do a thing with it. It stopped on him every time. Then he got so his head was wrong again. The doctors didn't do much good. They still come, but what's the use? I'm afraid it's all over with him. He can't play anything else. Nothing else but that half Caprice. Funny how one little thing can do so much harm."

Soon we left, as best we could, trying to smile again. Carlotta said later that always within her she could hear that woman saying, "Children are such lovely things—who could hurt them?" And I could hear, and can hear now, the scream in that final crash!

Last year I returned to that city for a longer visit, this time alone. Soon after my arrival there I inquired about the Jaimesons. The mother had died of grief sometime back, upon the son's failure to return home. He had wandered away five years ago without saying anything at all. His mother had stood talking to visitors, bidding them good-bye. The son, bearing a bird in a cage, had gone off through the back garden gate and had not been seen since. This, of course, was like the firing of a cannon to me. I was completely stunned to know that I had figured unknowingly in so grave a tragedy. Had Carlotta and I not been there to take the good woman's time, she might have kept better watch over her demented son.

I asked about their home. It had been sold at auction and torn down, and a theatre now stood in its place. I expressed a desire to see the structure—to attend the theatre, and I was surprised to learn that it was actually possible for me to be admitted. This was the South, and no place in America was any too kind. Always they said the Negro had little or no culture; yet they closed to him, as a rule, all roads to culture. Soon there was to be a concert at this theatre, held through the efforts of a certain music club. Anybody could go. A brown face could not appear on the main floor, to be sure, but a brown face could *appear*. I would go.

I sat, on the night of the concert, awaiting the beginning of the program. To a friend I talked of the Jaimesons. The theatre was pretty—just pretty. It seemed a great shame that so beautiful a home as that of the Jaimesons' should have been destroyed. Oh, well. My friend seemed not to mind. Soon she opened her program and I remembered that I had not looked at mine. The artist of the evening was a well known pianist. He would give a group of his own arrangements of rare and unfinished compositions. In a footnote the name Jaimeson caught my eye. Then I could not believe what I read. An unfinished Caprice by a little known Negro composer had furnished the theme of a number which was very dear to the artist. This thing was next to the last number, and I could scarcely enjoy what went before it. I tried to feel ashamed of not becoming sufficiently absorbed in what at some other time would have taken me from the earth. But I wanted now only to hear this Caprice—to see it executed—and I was not at all ashamed. It was only natural that the rest of the numbers were minor to Jaimeson's.

Finally the Caprice was played and encored. I almost choked to keep from screaming. The old picture came before me, and all that this thing had meant and had failed to mean to its composer whirled round and round in my brain, and I could hear the crash before it came. I waited for the crash. This man did not make it. Then it had not been written in the manuscript. Why should I have thought it had?

The last rendition was a tremendous thing. I tried to concentrate upon it, but instead I sat and wondered about what had gone before it. I supposed that the manuscript of the Caprice had fallen into the hands of the music club during the moving and auctioning of the household goods of the Jaimeson home. Through them it had come into the hands of this artist, no doubt. Thus I pondered and listened at intervals until the music ceased. The artist refused an encore, so the audience started filing out. Now I was wondering why monsieur would not play again. We had reached the lower floor, when there broke upon the air that Caprice.

It was not the artist of the evening. One knew that immediately. I heard three men half whisper, "My God!" I may have said it too. Everyone turned back into the auditorium—also we, even we. Downstairs. Jaimeson sat at the piano. Jaimeson himself. I knew him as soon as I looked. He was like a ghost, long kept from some material thing which he had needed. He was taller, it seemed, and gaunt. His hair had grown long and his profile keener. Like a rail he looked as he leaned forward, driving once more the thin, fiery steeds, his fingers. Nobody stopped him—nobody dared. He played with the frenzy of madness—played as though he were trying to atone for an ill-given rendition of this thing which was his.

The pianist of the concert stood midway the stage, staring and bewildered. Almost the entire audience had returned. They stood staring and astounded. Nobody stopped the player. Midway its dashing course, as five years before it had done, the Caprice checked its wild capering. It changed to something slower, softer, yearning—then came the crash! Like a great mark of exclamation in the midst of the sad, smoothly flowing voice it came. It smote the dazed listeners and I could feel them start—a shortened breath, quickly drawn, *en masse*.

Jaimeson had obeyed his urge; it had taken all his strength; now he collapsed.

No one had noticed the bird cage on the floor beside him until he reached for it at the end of his playing. He must have intended to leave as suddenly as he had come, but he missed the cage (it was empty now), and crumpled to the floor.

There was great and immediate excitement, of course. It was not until special appeals were made to the curious crowd by both the manager and the artist that peace and quiet were secured. Then the curtains were drawn and the onlookers cut off from the little scene. But I held a feeling of intimacy for this poor, crazed soul, hurt forever beyond cure, and I ran, almost unconsciously, to him. Somehow I found my way backstage where they had taken him. The friend who was with me had thought me daring, but I had dismissed her, not caring what she thought. This man was alone and I would help him.

Someone I took to be a doctor asked who I was. "His sister," I answered.

"This fellow was an only child. I knew the family." Here was a tangle. The person speaking was sure of what he said. I knew that certainly.

"Wife, huh?" from someone else, and the words meant more than they asked.

They ignored the glance of defiance I had flashed and accepted my silence for affirmative response. I made no answer, but went to the couch where Jaimeson lay. No one forbade me to touch him, so I sat beside him and rested his head on my breast. He stirred and looked at me, and tears stole down my face. He reached up and fingered a loose ringlet of my hair. I found myself gazing at a man who stood beside me. I was hardly aware of his presence, yet I was speaking to him. "Children are such lovely things—who could hurt them?"

"Was he injured when he was a child?" the man inquired.

"No," I said, "but such a little thing caused it. *Not* a little thing either."

"What was it?" the man asked quickly, and I knew that I had better cease talking while I could.

"Please don't ask me now," I whispered. "It will upset him again." Then, laying Jaimeson's head back upon the couch, I stood up.

"How did he get here tonight? Why wasn't he more closely watched?" the man continued. I had known this question was coming, though I had not prepared an answer.

"I don't know how he came," I said. "I thought he was safe in bed." I felt my face burn, and dropped down upon the couch again beside my strange charge. "I think I can move him now," I ventured, "if you will get me a cab." Heaven knows where I would have taken him. I had not the faintest idea.

"Better wait until the doctor gets here. We've sent for him." Just slightly I trembled.

"Where has he been all these years? In a sanitarium?" the man asked. He seemed wound up to ask questions forever.

"Yes," I whispered again. Anything which sounded plausible would do.

Just then Jaimeson sat up and stared across the room. A piano stood in the corner. Again he was like a ghost. I moved that he might arise. He wanted to.

And I motioned to the others not to interfere. I must show some authority, and it would satisfy him to play, even if the result were adverse. So he moved to the instrument, two of the men and I keeping close behind him. He did not notice us. Once seated, he leaned forward to play. He started the Caprice and stopped. Started again and stopped. Something was wrong. Something wrong. The steeds would not obey their master. First time. First time? I wondered. They started on their dash; then stopped. Started; then stopped. The man looked at me. There was something he knew, yet something he could not understand. He smiled his slow smile and shook his head. Then he played. But it was not the first part he played. That part he could not do. Instead he brought forth the sad, low-singing melody which seemed not at all a part of the Caprice.

Over and over this thing he played, his head sometimes dropped low and forward—sometimes pitched back and high. I stood behind him, and a little to the side. His mouth was partly open. His mouth watered. With a soft, silk kerchief I wiped his watering mouth. Over and over he played the softly wailing measures, his head sometimes dropped low and forward—sometimes pitched back and high.

The others stood watching—simply watching. No one spoke. Finally an arrival was announced.

"Here's the doctor," someone called.

Jaimeson stopped short. I imagined he wanted the bird cage, for he looked around for something. However, he turned and clung to me. He knew that I was someone who cared.

The doctor came toward us. Jaimeson's hold on me relaxed. The doctor spoke lightly. "What seems to be the trouble?"

Jaimeson slipped down and crumpled again to the floor. I answered the doctor. "Nothing now."

I knew without the doctor's word, that the man was dead. I just knew somehow. Just knew. And I was glad for him. It was better that he escape. The others straightaway looked to me. I had seen it this far, I would finish. I sold my rings and paid for the burial.

1925

- U.S. Marines leave Nicaragua (but return the following year).
- Josephine Baker rises to stardom in Paris.
- Approximately 40,000 Ku Klux Klansmen march through Washington, D.C.
- The Scopes "Monkey Trial" concludes, with schoolteacher John T. Scopes convicted and fined for teaching evolution in a public school in Tennessee.
- *Survey Graphic* publishes its special "Harlem number," which will serve as the model for Alain Locke's landmark anthology, *The New Negro*, also published this year.
- Marcus Garvey begins serving time in a federal prison in Atlanta, Georgia.
- NAACP's *Crisis* and the National Urban League's *Opportunity* magazines begin awarding prizes for literature and art.
- Oscar Micheaux's film *Body and Soul* is released with Paul Robeson in his debut screen performance.
- A. Philip Randolph organizes Brotherhood of Sleeping Car Porters labor union.
- Louis Armstrong makes the first of his "Hot Five and Hot Seven" influential jazz recordings.

U.S. unemployment: 3.2%

Lynchings in the United States: 17 blacks, 0 whites

Spingarn Medal:
James Weldon Johnson (author, statesman, activist)

Books:
Countee Cullen, *Color* (poetry)
Harry F. Liscomb, *The Prince of Washington Square* (novel)
Alain Locke (ed.), *The New Negro* (multigenre anthology)

12 THE CITY OF REFUGE

Rudolph Fisher

FROM *ATLANTIC MONTHLY*, FEBRUARY 1925

I

Confronted suddenly by daylight, King Solomon Gillis stood dazed and blinking. The railroad station, the long, white-walled corridor, the impassable slot-machine, the terrifying subway train—he felt as if he had been caught up in the jaws of a steam-shovel, jammed together with other helpless lumps of dirt, swept blindly along for a time, and at last abruptly dumped.

There had been strange and terrible sounds: "New York! Penn Terminal—all change!" "Pohter, hyer, pohter, suh?" Shuffle of a thousand soles, clatter of a thousand heels, innumerable echoes. Cracking rifle-shots—no, snapping turnstiles. "Put a nickel in!" "Harlem? Sure. This side—next train." Distant thunder, nearing. The screeching onslaught of the fiery hosts of hell, headlong, breathtaking. Car doors rattling, sliding, banging open. "Say, wha' d'ye think this is, a baggage car?" Heat, oppression, suffocation—eternity—"Hundred 'n turdy-fif' next!" More turnstiles. Jonah emerging from the whale.

Clean air, blue sky, bright sunlight.

Gillis set down his tan-cardboard extension-case and wiped his black, shining brow. Then slowly, spreadingly, he grinned at what he saw: Negroes at every turn; up and down Lenox Avenue, up and down One Hundred and Thirty-fifth Street; big, lanky Negroes, short, squat Negroes; black ones, brown ones, yellow ones; men standing idle on the curb, women, bundle-laden, trudging reluctantly homeward, children rattle-trapping about the sidewalks; here and there a white face drifting along, but Negroes predominantly, overwhelmingly everywhere. There was assuredly no doubt of his whereabouts. This was Negro Harlem.

Back in North Carolina Gillis had shot a white man and, with the aid of prayer and an automobile, probably escaped a lynching. Carefully avoiding the railroads, he had reached Washington in safety. For his car a Southwest bootlegger had given him a hundred dollars and directions to Harlem; and so he had come to Harlem.

Ever since a traveling preacher had first told him of the place, King Solomon Gillis had longed to come to Harlem. The Uggams were always talking about it; one of their boys had gone to France in the draft and, returning, had never got any nearer home than Harlem. And there were occasional "colored" newspapers from New York: newspapers that mentioned Negroes without comment, but always spoke of a white person as "So-and-so, white." That was the point. In Harlem, black was white. You had rights that could not be denied you; you had privileges, protected by law. And you had money. Everybody in Harlem had money. It was a land of plenty. Why, had not Mouse Uggam sent back as much as fifty dollars at a time to his people in Waxhaw?

The shooting, therefore, simply catalyzed whatever sluggish mental reaction had been already directing King Solomon's fortunes toward Harlem. The land of plenty was more than that now: it was also the city of refuge.

Casting about for direction, the tall newcomer's glance caught inevitably on the most conspicuous thing in sight, a magnificent figure in blue that stood in the middle of the crossing and blew a whistle and waved great white-gloved hands. The Southern Negro's eyes opened wide; his mouth opened wider. If the inside of New York had mystified him, the outside was amazing him. For there stood a handsome, brass-buttoned giant directing the heaviest traffic Gillis had ever seen; halting unnumbered tons of automobiles and trucks and wagons and pushcarts and street-cars; holding then at bay with one hand while he swept similar tons peremptorily on with the other; ruling the wide crossing with supreme self-assurance; and he, too, was a Negro!

Yet most of the vehicles that leaped or crouched at his bidding carried white passengers. One of these overdrove bounds a few feet and Gillis heard the officer's shrill whistle and gruff reproof, saw the driver's face turn red and his car draw back like a threatened pup. It was beyond belief—impossible. Black might be white, but it couldn't be that white!

"Done died an' woke up in Heaven," thought King Solomon, watching, fascinated; and after a while, as if the wonder of it were too great to believe simply by seeing, "Cullud policemans!" he said, half aloud; then repeated over and over, with greater and greater conviction, "Even got cullud policemans—even got cullud—"

"Where y' want to go, big boy?"

Gillis turned. A little, sharp-faced yellow man was addressing him.

"Saw you was a stranger. Thought maybe I could help y' out."

King Solomon located and gratefully extended a slip of paper. "Wha' dis hyeh at, please, suh?"

The other studied it a moment, pushing back his hat and scratching his head. The hat was a tall-crowned, unindented brown felt; the head was brown patent-leather, its glistening brush-back flawless save for a suspicious crimpiness near the clean-grazed edges.

"See that second corner? Turn to the left when you get there. Number forty-five's about halfway [down] the block."

"Thank y', suh."

"You from—Massachusetts?"

"No, suh, Nawth Ca'lina."

"Is 'at so? You look like a Northerner. Be with us long?"

"Till I die," grinned the flattered King Solomon.

"Stoppin' there?"

"Reckon I is. Man in Washin'ton 'lowed I'd find lodgin' at dis ad-dress."

"Good enough. If y' don't, maybe I can fix y' up. Harlem's pretty crowded. This is me." He proffered a card.

"Thank y', suh," said Gillis, and put the card in his pocket.

The little yellow man watched him plod flat-footedly on down the street, long awkward legs never quite straightened, shouldered extension-case bending him sidewise, wonder upon wonder halting or turning him about. Presently, as he proceeded, a pair of bright green stockings caught and held his attention. Tony, the storekeeper, was crossing the sidewalk with a bushel basket of apples. There was a collision; the apples rolled; Tony exploded; King Solomon apologized. The little yellow man laughed shortly, took out a notebook, and put down the address he had seen on King Solomon's slip of paper.

"Guess you're the shine I been waitin' for," he surmised.

As Gillis, approaching his destination, stopped to rest, a haunting notion grew into an insistent idea. "Dat li'l yaller nigger was a sho' 'nuff gen'man to show me de road. Seem lak I knowed him befo'—" He pondered. That receding brow, that sharp-ridged, spreading nose, that tight upper lip over the two big front teeth, that chinless jaw—He fumbled hurriedly for the card he had not looked at and eagerly made out the name.

"Mouse Uggam, sho' 'nuff! Well, dog-gone!"

II

Uggam sought out Tom Edwards, once a Pullman porter, now prosperous proprietor of a cabaret, and told him:—

"Chief, I got him: a baby jess in from the land o' cotton and so dumb he thinks ante bellum's an old woman."

"Where'd you find him?"

"Where you find all the jay birds when they first hit Harlem—at the subway entrance. This one come up the stairs, batted his eyes once or twice, an' froze to the spot—with his mouth wide open. Sure sign he's from 'way down behind the sun an' ripe f' the pluckin'."

Edwards grinned a gold-studded, fat-jowled grin. "Gave him the usual line, I suppose?"

"Didn't miss. An' he fell like a ton o' bricks. 'Course I've got him spotted, but damn 'f I know jess how to switch 'em on to him."

"Get him a job around a store somewhere. Make out you're befriendin' him. Get his confidence."

"Sounds good. Ought to be easy. He's from my state. Maybe I know him or some of his people."

"Make out you do, anyhow. Then tell him some fairy tale that'll switch your trade to him. The cops'll follow the trade. We could even let Froggy flop into some dumb white cop's hands and 'confess' where he got it. See?"

"Chief, you got a head, no lie."

"Don't lose no time. And remember, hereafter, it's better to sacrifice a little than to get squealed on. Never refuse a customer. Give him a little credit. Humor him along till you can get rid of him safe. You don't know what that guy that died may have said; you don't know who's on to you now. And if they get you—I don't know you."

"They won't get *me*," said Uggam.

King Solomon Gillis sat meditating in a room half the size of his hencoop back home, with a single window opening into an airshaft.

An airshaft: cabbage and chitterlings cooking; liver and onions sizzling, sputtering; three player-pianos out-plunking each other; a man and woman calling each other vile things; a sick, neglected baby wailing; a phonograph broadcasting blues; dishes clacking; a girl crying heartbrokenly; waste noises, waste odors of a score of families, seeking issue through a common channel; pollution from bottom to top—a sewer of sounds and smells.

Contemplating this, King Solomon grinned and breathed, "Dog-gone!" A little later, still gazing into the sewer, he grinned again. "Green stockin's," he said; "loud green!" The sewer gradually grew darker. A window lighted up opposite, revealing a woman in camisole and petticoat, arranging her hair. King Solomon, staring vacantly, shook his head and grinned yet again. "Even got cullud policemans!" he mumbled softly.

III

Uggam leaned out of the room's one window and spat maliciously into the dinginess of the airshaft. "Damn glad you got him," he commented, as Gillis finished his story. "They's a thousand shines in Harlem would change places with you in a minute jess f' the honor of killin' a cracker."

"But I didn't go to do it. 'T was a accident."

"That's the only part to keep secret."

"Know whut dey done? Dey killed five o' Mose Joplin's hawses 'fo he lef'. Put groun' glass in de feed-trough. Sam Cheevers come up on three of 'em one night pizenin' his well. Bleesom beat Crinshaw out o' sixty acres o' lan' an' a year's crops. Dass jess how 't is. Soon's a nigger make a li'l sump'n he better git to leavin'. An' 'fo long ev'ybody's goin' be lef'!"

"Hope to hell they don't all come here."

The doorbell of the apartment rang. A crescendo of footfalls in the hallway culminated in a sharp rap on Gillis's door. Gillis jumped. Nobody but a police-man would rap like that. Maybe the landlady had been listening and had called in the law. It came again, loud, quick, angry. King Solomon prayed that the policeman would be a Negro.

Uggam stepped over and opened the door. King Solomon's apprehensive eyes saw framed therein, instead of a gigantic officer, calling for him, a little blot of a creature, quite black against even the darkness of the hallway, except for a dirty, wide-striped silk shirt, collarless, with the sleeves rolled up.

"Ah hahve bill fo' Mr. Gillis." A high, strongly accented Jamaican voice, with its characteristic singsong intonation, interrupted King Solomon's sigh of relief.

"Bill? Bill fo' me? What kin' o' bill?"

"Wan bushel appels. T'ree seventy-fife."

"Apples? I ain' bought no apples." He took the paper and read aloud, labori-ously, "Antonio Gabrielli to K. S. Gillis, Doctor—"

"Mr. Gabrielli say, you not pays him, he send policemon."

"What I had to do wid 'is apples?"

"You bumps into him yesterday, no? Scatter appels everywhere—on de side-walk, in de gutter. Kids pick up an' run away. Others all spoil. So you pays."

Gillis appealed to Uggam. "How 'bout it, Mouse?"

"He's a damn liar. Tony picked up most of 'em; I seen him. Lemme look at that bill—Tony never wrote this thing. This baby's jess playin' you for a sucker."

"Ain' had no apples, ain' payin' fo' none," announced King Solomon, thus prompted. "Didn't have to come to Harlem to git cheated. Plenty o' dat right wha' I come fum."

But the West Indian warmly insisted. "You cahn't do daht, mon. Whaht you t'ink, 'ey? Dis mon loose 'is appels an' 'is money too?"

"What diff'ence it make to you, nigger?"

"Who you call nigger, mon? Ah hahve you understahn'—"

"Oh, well, white folks, den. What all you got t' do wid dis hyeh, anyhow?"

"Mr. Gabrielli send me to collect bill!"

"How I know dat?"

"Do Ah not bring bill? You t'ink Ah steal t'ree dollar, 'ey?"

"Three dollars an' sebenty-fi' cent," corrected Gillis. "'Nuther thing: wha' you ever see me befo'? How you know dis is me?"

"Ah see you, sure. Ah help Mr. Gabrielli in de store. When you knocks down de baskette appels, Ah see. Ah follow you. Ah know you comes in dis house."

"Oh, you does? An' how come you know my name an' flat an' room so good?"

How come dat?"

"Ah fin' out. Sometime Ah brings up here vegetables from de store."

"Humph! Mus' be workin' on shares."

"You pays, 'ey? You pays me or de policemon?"

"Wait a minute," broke in Uggam, who had been thoughtfully contemplating the bill. "Now listen, big shorty. You haul hips on back to Tony. We got your menu all right"—he waved the bill—"but we don't eat your kind o' cookin', see?"

The West Indian flared. "Whaht it is to you, 'ey? You can not mind your own business? Ah hahve not spik to you!"

"No, brother. But this is my friend, an' I'll be john-browned if there's a monkey-chaser in Harlem can gyp him if I know it, see? Bes' thing f' you to do is catch air, toot sweet."

Sensing frustration, the little islander demanded the bill back. Uggam figured he could use the bill himself, maybe. The West Indian hotly persisted; he even menaced. Uggam pocketed the paper and invited him to take it. Wisely enough, the caller preferred to catch air.

When he had gone, King Solomon sought words of thanks.

"Bottle it," said Uggam. "The point is this: I figger you got a job."

"Job? No I ain't! Wha' at?"

"When you show Tony this bill, he'll hit the roof and fire that monk."

"What ef he do?"

"Then you up 'n ask f' the job. He'll be too grateful to refuse. I know Tony some, an' I'll be there to put in a good word. See?"

King Solomon considered this. "Sho' needs a job, but ain' after stealin' none."

"Stealin'? 'T wouldn't be stealin'. Stealin' 's what that damn monkey-chaser tried to do from you. This would be doin' Tony a favor an' gettin' y'self out o' the barrel. What's the hold-back?"

"What make you keep callin' him monkey-chaser?"

"West Indian. That's another thing. Any time y' can knife a monk, do it. They's too damn many of 'em here. They're an achin' pain."

"Jess de way white folks feels 'bout niggers."

"Damn that. How 'bout it? Y' want the job?"

"Hm—well—I'd ruther be a policeman."

"Policeman?" Uggam gasped.

"M-hm. Dass all I wants to be, a policeman, so I kin police all de white folks right plumb in jail!"

Uggam said seriously, "Well, y' might work up to that. But it takes time. An' y've got to eat while y're waitin'." He paused to let this penetrate. "Now, how 'bout this job at Tony's in the meantime? I should think y'd jump at it."

King Solomon was persuaded.

"Hm—well—reckon I does," he said slowly.

"Now y're tootin'!" Uggam's two big front teeth popped out in a grin of genuine pleasure. "Come on. Let's go."

IV

Spitting blood and crying with rage, the West Indian scrambled to his feet. For a moment he stood in front of the store gesticulating furiously and jabbering shrill threats and unintelligible curses. Then abruptly he stopped and took himself off.

King Solomon Gillis, mildly puzzled, watched him from Tony's doorway. "I jess give him a li'l shove," he said to himself, "an' he roll' clean 'cross de sidewalk." And a little later, disgustedly, "Monkey-chaser!" he grunted, and went back to his sweeping.

"Well, big boy, how y' comin' on?"

Gillis dropped his broom. "Hay-o, Mouse. Wha' you been las' two-three days?"

"Oh, around. Gettin' on all right here? Had any trouble?"

"Deed I ain't—'ceptin' jess now I had to throw 'at li'l jigger out."

"Who? The monk?"

"M-hm. He sho' Lawd doan like me in his job. Look like he think I stole it from him, stiddy him tryin' to steal from me. Had to push him down sho' 'nuff 'fo I could git rid of 'im. Den he run off talkin' Wes' Indi'man an' shakin' his fis' at me."

"Ferget it." Uggam glanced about. "Where's Tony?"

"Boss man? He be back direckly."

"Listen—like to make two or three bucks a day extra?"

"Huh?"

"Two or three dollars a day more 'n what you're gettin' already?"

"Ain' I near 'nuff in jail now?"

"Listen." King Solomon listened. Uggam hadn't been in France for nothing. Fact was, in France he'd learned about some valuable French medicine. He'd brought some back with him,—little white pills,—and while in Harlem had found a certain druggist who knew what they were and could supply all he could use. Now there were any number of people who would buy and pay well for as much of this French medicine as Uggam could get. It was good for what ailed them, and they didn't know how to get it except through him. But he had no store in which to set up an agency and hence no single place where his customers could go to get what they wanted. If he had, he could sell three or four times as much as he did.

King Solomon was in a position to help him now, same as he had helped King Solomon. He would leave a dozen packages of the medicine—just small envelopes that could all be carried in a coat pocket—with King Solomon every day. Then he could simply send his customers to King Solomon at Tony's store.

They'd make some trifling purchase, slip him a certain coupon which Uggam had given them, and King Solomon would wrap the little envelope of medicine with their purchase. Mustn't let Tony catch on, because he might object, and then the whole scheme would go gaflooey. Of course it wouldn't really be hurting Tony any. Wouldn't it increase the number of his customers?

Finally, at the end of each day, Uggam would meet King Solomon some place and give him a quarter for each coupon he held. There'd be at least ten or twelve a day—two and a half or three dollars plumb extra! Eighteen or twenty dollars a week!

"Dog-gone!" breathed Gillis.

"Does Tony ever leave you here alone?"

"M-hm. Jess started dis mawnin'. Doan nobody much come 'round 'tween ten an' twelve, so he done took to doin' his buyin' right 'long 'bout dat time. Nobody hyeh but me fo' 'n hour or so."

"Good. I'll try to get my folks to come 'round here mostly while Tony's out, see?"

"I doan miss."

"Sure y' get the idea, now?" Uggam carefully explained it all again. By the time he had finished, King Solomon was wallowing in gratitude.

"Mouse, you sho' is been a friend to me. Why, 'f 't hadn't been fo' you—"

"Bottle it," said Uggam. "I'll be 'round to your room to-night with enough stuff for to-morrer, see? Be sure 'n be there."

"Won't be nowha' else."

"An' remember, this is all jess between you 'n me."

"Nobody else but," vowed King Solomon.

Uggam grinned to himself as he went on his way. "Dumb Oscar! Wonder how much can we make before the cops nab him? French medicine—Hmph!"

V

Tony Gabrielli, an oblate Neapolitan of enormous equator, wabbled heavily out of his store and settled himself over a soap box.

Usually Tony enjoyed sitting out front thus in the evening, when his helper had gone home and his trade was slackest. He liked to watch the little Gabriellis playing over the sidewalk with the little Levys and Johnsons; the trios and quartettes of brightly dressed, dark-skinned girls merrily out for a stroll; the slovenly gaited, darker men, who eyed them up and down and commented to each other with an unsuppressed "Hot damn!" or "Oh no, now!"

But to-night Tony was troubled. Something was wrong in the store; something was different since the arrival of King Solomon Gillis. The new man had seemed to prove himself honest and trustworthy, it was true. Tony had tested him, as he always tested a new man, by apparently leaving him alone in charge for two or three mornings. As a matter of fact, the new man was never under more vigilant observation than during these two or three mornings. Tony's store was a modification of the front rooms of his flat and was in direct communication with it by way of a glass-windowed door in the rear. Tony always managed to get back into his flat via the side-street entrance and watch the new man through this unobtrusive glass-windowed door. If anything excited his suspicion, like unwarranted interest in the cash register, he walked unexpectedly out of this door to surprise the offender in the act. Thereafter he would have no more such trouble. But he had not succeeded in seeing King Solomon steal even an apple.

What he had observed, however, was that the number of customers that came into the store during the morning's slack hour had pronouncedly increased in the last few days. Before, there had been three or four. Now there were twelve or fifteen. The mysterious thing about it was that their purchases totaled little more than those of the original three or four.

Yesterday and to-day Tony had elected to be in the store at the time when, on other days, he had been out. But Gillis had not been overcharging or short-changing; for when Tony waited on the customers himself—strange faces all—he found that they bought something like a yeast cake or a five-cent loaf of bread. It was puzzling. Why should strangers leave their own neighborhoods and repeatedly come to him for a yeast cake or a loaf of bread? They were not new neighbors. New neighbors would have bought more variously and extensively and at different times of day. Living near by, they would have come in, the men often in shirtsleeves and slippers, the women in kimonos, with boudoir caps covering their lumpy heads. They would have sent in strange children for things like yeast cakes and loaves of bread. And why did not some of them come in at night when the new helper was off duty?

As for accosting Gillis on suspicion, Tony was too wise for that. Patronage had a queer way of shifting itself in Harlem. You lost your temper and let slip a single "*nègre.*" A week later you sold your business.

Spread over his soap box, with his pudgy hands clasped on his preposterous paunch, Tony sat and wondered. Two men came up, conspicuous for no other reason than that they were white. They displayed extreme nervousness, looking about as if afraid of being seen; and when one of them spoke to Tony it was in a husky, toneless, blowing voice, like the sound of a dirty phonograph record.

"Are you Antonio Gabrielli?"

"Yes, sure." Strange behavior for such lusty-looking fellows. He who had spoken unsmilingly winked first one eye then the other, and indicated by a gesture of his head that they should enter the store. His companion looked cautiously up and down the Avenue, while Tony, wondering what ailed them, rolled to his feet and puffingly led the way.

Inside, the spokesman snuffled, gave his shoulders a queer little hunch, and asked, "Can you fix us up, buddy?" The other glanced restlessly about the place as if he were constantly hearing unaccountable noises.

Tony thought he understood clearly now. "Booze, 'ey?" he smiled. "Sorry—I no got."

"Booze? Hell, no!" The voice dwindled to a throaty whisper. "Dope. Coke, milk, dice—anything. Name your price. Got to have it."

"Dope?" Tony was entirely at a loss. "What's a dis, dope?"

"Aw, lay off, brother. We're in on this. Here." He handed Tony a piece of paper. "Froggy gave us a coupon. Come on. You can't go wrong."

"I no got," insisted the perplexed Tony; nor could he be budged on that point.

Quite suddenly the manner of both men changed. "All right," said the first angrily, in a voice as robust as his body. "All right, you're clever. You no got. Well, you will get. You'll get twenty years!"

"Twenty year? Whadda you talk?"

"Wait a minute, Mac," said the second caller. "Maybe the wop's on the level. Look here, Tony, we're officers, see? Policemen." He produced a badge. "A couple of weeks ago a guy was brought in dying for the want of a shot, see? Dope—he needed some dope—like this—in his arm. See? Well, we tried to make him tell us where he'd been getting it, but he was too weak. He croaked next day. Evidently he hadn't had money enough to buy any more.

"Well, this morning a little nigger that goes by the name of Froggy was brought into the precinct pretty well doped up. When he finally came to, he swore he got the stuff here at your store. Of course, we've just been trying to trick you into giving yourself away, but you don't bite. Now what's your game? Know anything about this?"

Tony understood. "I dunno," he said slowly; and then his own problem, whose contemplation his callers had interrupted occurred to him. "Sure!" he exclaimed. "Wait. Maybeso I know somet'ing."

"All right. Spill it."

"I got a new man, work-a for me." And he told them what he had noted since King Solomon Gillis came.

"Sounds interesting. Where is this guy?"

"Here in da store—all day."

"Be here to-morrow?"

"Sure. All day."

"All right. We'll drop in to-morrow and give him the eye. Maybe he's our man."

"Sure. Come ten o'clock. I show you," promised Tony.

VI

Even the oldest and rattiest cabarets in Harlem have sense of shame enough to hide themselves under the ground—for instance, Edwards's. To get into Edwards's you casually enter a dimly lighted corner saloon, apparently—only apparently—a subdued memory of brighter days. What was once the family entrance is now a side entrance for ladies. Supporting yourself against close walls, you crouchingly descend a narrow, twisted staircase until, with a final turn, you find yourself in a glaring, long, low basement. In a moment your eyes become accustomed to the haze of tobacco smoke. You see men and women seated at wire-legged, white-topped tables, which are covered with half-empty bottles and glasses; you trace the slow-jazz accompaniment you heard as you came down the stairs to a pianist, a cornetist, and a drummer on a little platform at the far end of the room. There is a cleared space from the foot of the stairs, where you are standing, to the platform where this orchestra is mounted, and in it a tall brown girl is swaying from side to side and rhythmically proclaiming that she has the world in a jug and the stopper in her hand. Behind a counter at your left sits a fat, bald, tea-colored Negro, and you wonder if this is Edwards—Edwards, who stands in with the police, with the political bosses, with the importers of wines and worse. A white-vested waiter hustles you to a seat and takes your order. The song's tempo changes to a quicker [one]; the drum and the cornet rip out a fanfare, almost drowning the piano; the girl catches up her dress and begins to dance. . . .

Gillis's wondering eyes had been roaming about. They stopped.

"Look, Mouse!" he whispered. "Look a-yonder!"

"Look at what?"

"Dog-gone if it ain' de self-same gal!"

"Wha' d' ye mean, self-same girl?"

"Over yonder, wi' de green stockin's. Dass de gal made me knock over dem apples fust day I come to town. 'Member? Been wishin' I could see her ev'y sence."

"What for?" Uggam wondered.

King Solomon grew confidential. "Ain' but two things in dis world, Mouse, I really wants. One is to be a policeman. Been wantin' dat ev'y sence I seen dat cullud traffic-cop dat day. Other is to git myse'f a gal lak dat one over yonder!"

"You'll do it," laughed Uggam, "if you live long enough."

"Who dat wid her?"

"How 'n hell do I know?"

"He cullud?"

"Don't look like it. Why? What of it?"

"Hm—nuthin'—"

"How many coupons y' got to-night?"

"Ten." King Solomon handed them over.

"Y' ought to 've slipt 'em to me under the table, but it's all right now, long as we got this table to ourselves. Here's y' medicine for to-morrer."

"Wha'?"

"Reach under the table."

Gillis secured and pocketed the medicine.

"An' here's two-fifty for a good day's work." Uggam passed the money over. Perhaps he grew careless; certainly the passing this time was above the table, in plain sight.

"Thanks, Mouse."

Two white men had been watching Gillis and Uggam from a table near by. In the tumult of merriment that rewarded the entertainer's most recent and daring effort, one of these men, with a word to the other, came over and took the vacant chair beside Gillis.

"Is your name Gillis?"

"'T ain' nuthin' else."

Uggam's eyes narrowed.

The white man showed King Solomon a police officer's badge.

"You're wanted for dope-peddling. Will you come along without trouble?"

"Fo' what?"

"Violation of the narcotic law—dope-selling."

"Who—me?"

"Come on, now, lay off that stuff. I saw what happened just now myself." He addressed Uggam. "Do you know this fellow?"

"Nope. Never saw him before to-night."

"Didn't I just see him sell you something?"

"Guess you did. We happened to be sittin' here at the same table and got to talkin'. After a while I says I can't seem to sleep nights, so he offers me sump'n he says'll make me sleep, all right. I don't know what it is, but he says he uses it himself an' I offers to pay him what it cost him. That's how I come to take it. Guess he's got more in his pocket there now."

The detective reached deftly into the coat pocket of the dumbfounded King Solomon and withdrew a packet of envelopes. He tore off a corner of one, emptied a half-dozen tiny white tablets into his palm, and sneered triumphantly. "You'll make a good witness," he told Uggam.

The entertainer was issuing an ultimatum to all sweet mammas who dared to monkey 'round her loving man. Her audience was absorbed and delighted, with the exception of one couple—the girl with the green stockings and her escort. They sat directly in the line of vision of King Solomon's wide eyes, which, in the calamity that had descended upon him, for the moment saw nothing.

"Are you coming without trouble?"

Mouse Uggam, his friend. Harlem. Land of plenty. City of refuge—city of refuge. If you live long enough—

Consciousness of what was happening between the pair across the room suddenly broke through Gillis's daze like flame through smoke. The man was trying to kiss the girl and she was resisting. Gillis jumped up. The detective, taking the act for an attempt at escape, jumped with him and was quick enough to intercept him. The second officer came at once to his fellow's aid, blowing his whistle several times as he came.

People overturned chairs getting out of the way, but nobody ran for the door. It was an old crowd. A fight was a treat; and the tall Negro could fight.

"Judas Priest!"

"Did you see that?"

"Damn!"

White—both white. Five of Mose Joplin's horses. Poisoning a well. A year's crops. Green stockings—white—white—

"That's the time, papa!"

"Do it, big boy!"

"Good night!"

Uggam watched tensely, with one eye on the door. The second cop had blown for help—

Downing one of the detectives a third time and turning to grapple again with the other, Gillis found himself face to face with a uniformed black policeman.

He stopped as if stunned. For a moment he simply stared. Into his mind swept his own words like a forgotten song, suddenly recalled: —

"Cullud policemans!"

The officer stood ready, awaiting his rush.

"Even—got—cullud—policemans—"

Very slowly King Solomon's arms relaxed; very slowly he stood erect; and the grin that came over his features had something exultant about it.

13 THE GOLDEN PENKNIFE

S. Miller Johnson

FROM *MESSENGER*, AUGUST 1925

Now Anna was a pretty little devil. Her lips, pursed as if to invite a kiss, were red enough without rouge; and so were her cheeks. Her eyes, clear and light and roaming, fairly beamed with loveliness that clamored for wholesome expression. Anna's life, however, was sadly unguided. She walked spritely as if she were tipping up on something. Sometimes she gasped a little when she talked, but that slight defect added to her attractiveness. This girl was unique in her sphere; she didn't want her golden curls bobbed. Nor did she smoke cigarettes. Nor did she drink—though her dad operated a restaurant and maintained, besides, a flourishing bootlegging business.

At one time Anna had attended church regularly, said her confessions—which were innocent enough when she was a child—observed mass, and Y. W. C. A., and read the *Free Press* and conformed outwardly to its stupid Rotarian philosophy. And yet, she remembered, that ever since the age of puberty, she had suffered as most normal girls suffer during that period; there was the enormous struggle between inward natural desires and conventional morality. Like a father's true daughter, Anna had tried to conform to her father's and her lover's idea of what a good woman should be.

She first told her troubles to the priest, who gave her the conventional advice: "After you are married you'll be all right."

So Anna went home and waited. She wasn't old enough to marry, she thought, and she wouldn't marry if she were old enough. She therefore reacted on the advice of the priest without obtaining any satisfactory results.

And so Anna Paul went again to confer with the good Father Raski. The stupid and pious Father was puzzled to see the shivering figure of the pretty creature standing before him, seeking something spiritual that would calm her raging insides. Only a Freud could have analyzed the thoughts of the good Father that day. Raski prescribed tennis and basket ball and swimming, and wholesome reading and prayer, the Virgin and a lot of other rigamarole. All these Anna tried and found wanting. Why, the idea! Even mother had offered these same remedies once.

The restless girl now started reading in order to find out for herself. After making several excursions into the field of modern literature on sex, freedom of women, ethics, etc., Anna made a final pilgrimage to the venerable Raski.

"You are a fake!" she shouted in the Father's face.

Then she whirled around and rushed from the sanctum sanctorum. This, indeed, ended Anna's relation with Holy Church. * * * From that time on Anna read everything on sex she could get her hands on. Novels, plays, poetry, Freud, Jung, Mencken, Ellis, Nietzsche, et al. She subscribed for the *Smart Set,* ransacked the libraries, haunted bookshops, searched book lists; bought, borrowed and stole books. 'Tis a wonder she didn't develop into a rank sensualist or a Socialist—or even a Bolsheviki, for that matter.

Anna kept her head, however. The more she read, the tamer she became. Even Boccaccio, Balzac, and Casanova didn't upset her. To discover that she had been living a world of lies and lies and lies, sickened and disgusted her. As she saw the clay feet of her idols dissolving, the idols themselves falling and smashing, she grew morose; she wished that she herself could dissolve into nothingness. Unlike many of her more modern sisters under similar conditions, Anna didn't wish to seek solace in mere sensuality; she sought peace of soul and body, she yearned for some one who shared her views, and who would give her sympathy.

Anna was in love with Fred Soskii. Now Fred was of Russian extraction. In him, as in a great many descendants of Russian peasants, East and West had met. And there was a mighty conflict of differing natures—a conflict of the dreamer, the nihilist, and the blood-loving vandal. At present the dreamer was predominating, expressing itself in Babbitism. The other opposing temperaments were not altogether dormant. * * * Anna and Fred were in love.

Their parents had left the land of the Volga and come to live in Detroit, where they hoped to amass a fortune in the grocery business. Fred's folks continued in the food game and achieved considerable financial distinction. They now owned a car and several grocery stores—two in Hamtramck and one in 31st Street in Detroit. The Pauls owned a car too. But they had only one daughter, Anna, once vivacious, pretty and intriguing, now reserved, stern, cynical, truly "anti." * * * The Pauls possessed no grocery stores now. The stimulus given to bootlegging by the passage of the Volstead Act had led the Pauls into a flourishing and respectable liquor business. * * * They went to mass regularly, sold their whiskey and groceries. They were becoming beautifully Americanized.

Fred was the most American of them all, in spite of his Catholicism. He successfully managed his father's grocery stores. In theory he believed he should sacrifice the normal pleasures of youth to business success, and after achieving that success, Fred thought the proper thing to do was to cast aside all liaisons, marry a chaste, pretty woman and settle down, have one or two kids—let the pretty chaste woman nurse his gray hairs—take out insurance, join the Rotarians, denounce law-breakers, boost the Y, be patriotic, etc., etc., etc.

Indeed Fred was a steady lad. He knew the value of putting business before pleasure. His parents liked that in him. Others also liked that in him. But there were other likable qualities and features in and about Fred. His pink cheeks flushed as he smiled good naturedly to the customers who came to his store to purchase a bunch of lettuce, a dozen eggs, or a can or two of pork and beans. With Fred the smile and the ruddy cheeks were natural. But as he dealt with the buyers and sellers about town, he had learned to capitalize his sunny disposition. In other words, this embryo go-getter was developing the traits that distinguishes the self-made American business man in the making.

When he left the market in the morning, smiling inwardly because he had made a good bargain with those elderly fellows there, he could hear at his back muttering appreciations of his ability as a buyer.

"There's Fred Soskii."

"That boy's gonna make something of himself."

"Knows how to buy all right."

"His old man's coining dough too!"

"Bet he is; has a Studebaker for himself and a Buick roadster for his wife."

"Say," drawled one of the salesmen, as he covered the top of a crate of bad tomatoes with some others that were better and redder. "Say, the boy's sweet on Old Paul's daughter, isn't he?"

"What Paul?"

"Aw, you know Paul—Paul's Cafe up on Chene Street?"

"O, yes." Then under his breath, "Sells some mighty fine stuff up there."

"Damn if he didn't. Where's he get it, I wonder?"

"Scotland by way of Canada. He's in the ring. Cars leave Canada destined for Mexico—side tracked here—goods sent to Paul's and to hotels and Grosse Point, Boston Boulevard—same old tale. Fine thing, I calls it."

And he then threw out his well chewed cud of Brown's Mule and spat dignifiedly.

And another spoke: "That's a humdinger, this Paul girl. She *is* a *peach!* She's sometimes at the cafe. You'd think she's a nun. Old man uses her for a drawing card, I suppose."

"Maybe. But she hasn't been 'round there much this winter. I'm in there pretty often. Never seen her yet. About three months ago or something thereabouts, I saw her in there one night. Think she's kinder tamed down now. Soskii, the younger—she's got her eye on the youngster, you see."

"Oh, I see, Ray. I really *do* see. Been seeing her goin' 'round with a stranger lookin' like a wop lately."

———

Fred had had an unusually good day. And to-night as he drove towards Anna Paul's, his heart leapt up in him when he contemplated the joy that would be his when they got together. He visualized Anna. The image of her life-giving personality; her smiling face; her soft, whispering child voice; her warm tender body throbbing against his; her languorous kisses that clung to his lips and flavored deliciously his memories of her! If she'd only lay off reading those silly novels and things! They'd turn her head one of these days.

Soskii could hardly wait until June. He and Anna were to be married then. Six months hence! Damn long time he thought.

A traffic cop blew his whistle. Fred brought his machine to a slow stop.

"Cussed policemen. Holding up time unnecessarily. If I were closer to that guy, I'd bargain with him. Bargain with him by George. That's what I'd do. Hellish cops."

Snow fell fast and thick, frosting his wind shield. Yet Broadway at Gratiot was congested. Cars. Pedestrians. Electric lights glaring out of a gray mist. Newsies running to and fro, yelling, "*Times!* Sunday *Star!*" Autos and pedestrians swarming, police whistles shrilling. What means this hurry? What means this shocking bustle? Nothing—nothing—meaningless—

Again the traffic cop's whistle sounded. Fred stepped on his gas. And off he went spinning towards Anna, his mind completely taken up with his loved one.

What was Anna thinking, he wondered. Her chest was heaving for him, maybe. She was sighing for her Fred perhaps. She wanted to talk to her Freddy. Funny how he kept thinking about Anna in this way. Anna—he hadn't seen her in three weeks. He had called. She had never been there to answer the phone. Anna hadn't *always* been out like those high fliers. Heavens, no! She was the kind of girl he wanted for a wife. He had been busy indeed the last three weeks—saving his father's business— He would tell Anna about that. She would laugh softly and tell him how proud she was of him—Vanity? Well, no—

He swung his car out of Grand Boulevard west into Buchanan.

Anna's!

Fred rang the bell and Anna met him at the door. She held in her hand a translated copy of *Madame Bovary*—unabridged. Anna's pale, uncertain look frightened him. She didn't seem so glad he had come. Why had she called him? Had she called him? Hers was just a momentary coldness, perhaps, that would wear off as soon as he got her in his arms.

"There's my little lady bird!"

Anna looked down at Fred's wet shoes and up again into his capitalized face. A sleeping odor of digested garlic. A vague feeling of disgust mingled with pity flitted through her little body.

Only a little momentary coldness that——

"Hello, Freddy! So glad you came—at last. Mother and father are out. Went to see the Moscow Art Players. The plays are done in Russian, you know. You know our passion for things Russian. Dad and I have had great fun trying to translate Tolstoi's *Anna*. I'm going to make dad teach me more about Russian. Mother's Polish, and dad taught her to speak the Russian."

And somehow Fred sensed that Anna's good humor was feigned. Of course she didn't want him to know she wasn't well.

They sat down together. Fred took the girl's hand.

"Anna, my love, you aren't well. Can't I do something for you?" he said warmly, gazing into her mysterious eyes, that held both a coldness and a warmth—a coldness for something near and a warmth for something far away and unattainable.

"No, there's nothing." Then, as if in after thought, "It's been three weeks since you were here yet."

"Yes, dear, and it seems like a year. I've been very busy. Business at a low ebb those three weeks. It took all my time right on the job, keeping things on the go. Thought about you all the time yet."

She turned slightly away, feeling grossly neglected.

"A strange love that can live on mere thoughts of the loved one."

"A great love, you mean, my dear."

"Yes—I—yes——"

Hesitation.

"Let's just sit here in silence a while," Anna said.

She didn't want to tell him that she wanted time to think. He felt that something was in the air. Why was she so cold toward Fred Soskii to-night? Well, she wasn't feeling well. She hadn't felt well since she accidentally met Alex Tervanovitch a few months ago. * * * Tervanovitch, dark and thoughtful and mystical. Anna had met him in the basement of an old book shop on Grand River Avenue. She didn't think then that the meeting would lead to romance. And the incident hadn't led to romance in the sentimental sense.

Continued silence between Fred and Anna. Anna, kittenlike, rested her head on Fred's shoulder. Anna thought back.

Her meeting with Tervanovitch had happened rather strangely. She had been prowling through the bookshelves in the dimly lighted basement of the bookshop, when suddenly, like a flash, a multitude of expressions, all compressed into one face, stared at her out of the dimness. She was both repelled and attracted by this face which reminded her of the Sphinx, as mysterious as life itself. She wanted to run away, yet she stayed there looking at the man. The owner of the face looked at the same time annoyed, interested and pleased. Anna stammered a meaningless, "Good evening," and then wondered why she had spoken at all. The fellow didn't notice her. He turned expressionlessly and began again peering into a stack of musty, dusty old books that filled the basement with a fog as he moved them about. His back was now turned towards Anna.

She wanted to see that face again. She would move slowly along the shelves until she could get in front of that interesting being. There he sat on a high stool, peering calmly over the books. Occasionally he smiled enigmatically to himself—like an Oriental, somewhat. When he grinned thus, she fidgeted; yet she continued to move toward the figure—like a child who is both frightened and curious in the face of what might be dangerous. Finally she edged around in front of the gentleman, keeping her back to him. She fumbled with books on the shelf and wondered how she could look around without seeming too bold, without embarrassing him or herself. She stood there nervously fumbling the old books, standing there in the dimly lighted basement of [a] downtown bookshop and wondering how she could get a glimpse of a strange face without embarrassing anybody. She grew more and more afraid. Anna moved on, step by step, until she was some distance from the man. Then she ran upstairs and out into the street. Still scared, she jumped into her car and whizzed home, as if she were being pursued by bandits or cannibals——

And then, the very next day——————

"Anna, my love——" Fred's voice awoke her from a sort of lethargy. "Anna, are you better now? Just think! Six months from now we'll be married, and then——"

"Oh, Fred, don't mention it."

Now wasn't that just like Anna? She had such naive ways of expressing her unbounded joy.

"Can't I do something for you, Anna?"

"Yes, Freddy old dear; please leave me alone to-night. I'm not well. My head aches terribly—I'll call you to-morrow and let you know how I'm feeling."

"But Anna——"

"No questions now, Fred——"

"But remember I haven't seen you in three weeks, Anna, and——"

"You love, Freddy?"

"How could you ask that now, Anna?"

"Three weeks," under her breath. Louder, "Well, if you love me, have consideration for my health—Shall I say good night?"

"All right, Anna, my little Anna, I was wrong to insist. Hope you'll feel better to-morrow."

She got his hat and coat and showed him the door. She kissed him rather coldly and turned him out into the cold night.

It all happened so damned quickly. What made Anna act like that? She hadn't done that way before. What could be eating her? As suddenly as a storm comes up over a big lake, something had come between them and sent him out into the night. And it was Anna's— Well, Anna didn't look so well. And yet his experience with women in love had taught him that when a Jane is really sick, she is not so quick to get rid of one who might give her a little sympathy and petting.

But there were exceptions. In this case, perhaps. Anna wouldn't do a thing like that. He knew Anna that well. But something was happening, though. Something had happened. What was it? If she hadn't been so clever—so ill—they would have quarreled to-night, you bet.

Aw, well, women were strange things, anyhow, thought Soskii. He decided to drown his troubles in wine. He'd decided to lay off fast women. Fred would stop at Paul's Cafe and have a drink with the boys before turning in. Must get a long rest to-night. Busy day to-morrow. Carload of oranges from California. Beginning to do things now in a big way. Hooray for the business game!

At the restaurant. Paul's Cafe decorated with red berried holly, palms, ferns, red and green crepe paper. Evergreen. Dancers. Laughter. Jazz. Wine. Laughter, chatter, dancing, wine, song. Women. Sprigs of cedar. Boys. Girls. An added attraction to-night. Dancers whose lithe bodies swayed and bubbled, bubbled and swayed. Snake-like, lithe and rhythmical. Drinks. Laughs. People dancing. Dancing old people. Young people shimmying. Elders outshimmying the wild young generation. Grocer clerks, druggists, restaurant owners, cafe managers, bootleggers. Lively fellows seated at tables and drinking bootleg wine. At other tables—journalists, men high up in the auto and education business, chorus girls, bankers, small store keepers, young dentists, doctors, shop girls, prostitutes, vaudevillians, male and female revellers, etc., etc. Musicians; Jews, Russians, Poles, Italians, Americans—all out for a few hours of innocent gaiety.

Fred Soskii was seated with a gang of lively fellows. Supple bodies swaying—undulating. Fred trying to forget that Anna had stopped loving him. Had she stopped loving him? A woman he knew sat opposite him. He was also trying to forget and ignore her steady dark eyes that were watching him, searching him, questioning him through a cluster of palm leaves. The possessor of those eyes! A sensible looking creature plainly but attractively dressed in a becoming black and gold something consisting of nearly all fringe, ostensibly arranged to show men how far her flesh-colored hose extended above her knees. She wore a black band about her black-haired head and gold bracelets on her wrists. Her black pumps with gold braid carried gilded buckles. Apparently, she was one of the dancers employed at Paul's to-night. Fred sat restless under her gaze. The dancer had been drinking, but now, her sweet legs carelessly and freely crossed, she was smoking a cigarette. She tapped a leg of her table with the tip of her small black satin pump. She eyed Fred constantly.

This woman wore for a locket a tiny gold penknife fastened to an almost invisible golden chain. When she was not smoking her Chesterfield, she kept the gold penknife between her lips—as some women suck the pendants of their lavallieres.

Stanisky—one of Kroger's managers and Fred's buddy—was talking and fumbling in his pocket for smokes. He found none. He beckoned for a waiter. The waiter glided towards him.

"Cigarettes, please," Stanisky demanded.

Then he nodded for one of the dancers. The one eyeing Fred didn't move a peg. But another, more frolicsome and more artificially made up than the one in black fringe, writhed up to him, pitching her hips from side to side, and smiling through her rouge and powder. She danced before the two friends. Fred looked on, his head in a whirl. The liquor and the dancer were responsible for his whirling head. The whiskey, the noise of the orchestra, Anna, the eyes of that woman across the table. God! How could he stand it all?

The frolicsome dancer was a wow! A scarce brassiere she wore. Very scarce, indeed. The nipples of her bubbies were covered with little tips of semi-transparent shiny fabric. Tight tights. A pair of tiny silvery wings, her dark, bewitching eyes, her hair done up in Spanish style with a large fan-like comb, set with sparkling imitation diamonds, her small head thrown back—this gave her the appearance of an artist's interpretation of "The mountain-nymph, sweet Liberty." An almost completely nude dancer dressed scantily in faded pinks and lively lavenders and gliding about under a spot light that gave new and varied colors to everything its beams touched. The effect of rich lavender trimmed with ermine and gold dipped in a mixture of sunset and rainbow lying on white clouds wrapped in azure silken swaddling clothes. A riot of color gyrating about a dancer whose movements bore a close relation to those violent wrigglings made by the earliest dancers, when dancing was intentionally a means of attracting one sex to the other.

The sprite advanced, her body tense, her arms thrust limpidly forward in the manner of the girl in Rodin's *Youth*. She remained thus for a moment, still advancing. Then she stopped suddenly without changing her posture. Rising abruptly on her toes, she leapt wantonly backward, whirled around and then tripped slowly toward Fred Soskii and Stanisky. Standing on the toes of her left foot, she sent the other flying into the air. She looked at the two men out of the corners of her eyes. Around and around! She shimmied violently and ended with a long audible sigh that caused her breasts to rise and fall, her chest to heave turbulently. So much emotional depth, so much powerful expression for such a small slender body! The dancer darted off towards an alcove separated from the revellers by a yellow curtain decorated with black and red cubist-impressionistic figures.

The waiter brought the cigarettes and went back to his stand.

"Know her?" asked Stanisky.

The woman in black fringe was still watching Fred.

"Who?"

"The dancer that just left us."

"No, you?"

"No. Call her."

And so the dancer was called. She curtsied and laughed after the manner of some movie actress she had carefully imitated. She accepted a seat between the two men. She accepted also their wine and their smoke. She laughed and shrugged and shrugged and laughed. And as she did so, her tiny silver wings opened and closed like those of a butterfly. The tips of those silvery wings, still under the changing colors of the spot lights, touched her glittering headdress, as she threw back her head and laughed softly, jocundly.

The dancer in black kept her warm cutting eyes on Fred, luciferous eyes—like those of a woman cheated in love. Once more Fred fidgeted under her gripping stare.

Two policemen sauntered in the cafe, grinning. They touched their caps to the manager. Several Y workers, a couple of ministers, a member of the Board of Recreation and Detective-Lieutenant Daskill—a group detailed by the Department of Uplift to investigate such places as Paul's Cafe—were seated at neighboring tables in a rather dark corner. They were drinking, chattering and flirting with some rather flashy dames whose naked backs fairly glared. When the uplifters saw the cops enter, they hid their whiskey and tried to assume a pious attitude. The policemen looked around casually, smiled, shook their heads helplessly and passed out.

"Say, girl," Fred was saying to the gay dancer at his side. "Think I'll just hire you to dance before me all day long—hic—like to see you trying to kick the moon with your sputtering heels."

The dancer laughed kittenishly.

Stanisky spoke: "What you got in your legs to—hic—to make 'em so kickable—hic—limber?"

They all laughed foolishly. Stanisky ran his hand delicately along the dancer's soft, warm, well-tapered legs, as if he could tell by feeling her flesh wherein lay the flexibility of her members. She continued to laugh and drink the wine offered her. She felt a hand, hidden by the table cover, gently gripping and stroking the tenderness of her sensitive thighs. She leaned towards Stanisky, her quivering lips close to his cheek, her body dilating against his shoulder. Just as he turned, she sprang from the table and glided across the room, whirling and contorting petulantly, like a leaf caught up in a whirlwind. She smiled back at the boys, both of whom wanted to grab the dancer and squeeze from her the delicious essences of love.

The boys drank more wine. They could forget their troubles in this sparkling Canadian wine. The woman in black and gold fringe looked daggers at Fred.

"Well, Fred," said Stanisky, "you'd better make the best of these days; you'll be married soon, won't you? Suppose we take these dames out sometimes. They're easy pickins. Aristocrats of their kind yet. * * * You used to kinder knock around [with] the one in black over there looking at you so hard, didn't you?"

"Pshaw! Lately, every time I see a woman like that, the more I love Anna. I'm not in for this wild life any more, Stan. Going to settle down—hic—yet."

"Hypocrite! Fred, you make me sick with your one-woman mania." (The liquor had broken down barriers of restraint, modesty, et cetera.) "As a friend, Fred, are you blind and crazy? Why do you let a woman put anything over on you? Listen. Hic. You've been engaged to Anna a long time. She's a woman. Hic. You are a man." (He was talking with his hands.) "You have been seeing and enjoying life—its bitterness—its sweetness. You know of the pleasures and honeys a live woman can give. And yet because you think Anna has denied herself much of what you've enjoyed, you call her innocent, pure, virtuous, and what not." (The jazz band shook the structure. Rock, church, rock. Revelers dancing on dimes.) "That's why you take pride in her. I'll bet she hates you for what you expect of her. And in a year or two after you are married—or before you get married, maybe—she'll be a talking about intellectual companionship, soulmates, comraderie. Anna's just that kind. She reads everything. She's ahead of you there—hic—yet."

Silence. * * *

The trombones in the jazz orchestra bellowed softly, the violins whined and moaned, the snare drum crackled convulsively, the cornets and clarinets neighed and neighed, the bodies of the dancers swayed and bubbled and bubbled and swayed. Saxophones tooted madly. Fiddlers on top of the piano. Clarinet player sitting flat on the floor. Snare drummer going through the antics of an African witch doctor. Other performers stamping, kicking, and shouting like Negroes at a camp meeting in Louisiana.

"Stan," Fred replied, "you are crazy. You can't mean that——"

"If you'll hear me out, I'll tell you a few things. I've seen Anna in questionable places with strangers and——"

"Strangers to you, perhaps, but not to Anna. Anna out with strangers. You make me laugh. That girl is pure gold, my friend!"

And yet he couldn't give a satisfactory explanation of Anna's actions lately.

"The case is closed, old boy. She'll be your pure gold whatever I tell you about her. Let's turn in. See the dancers some other time by myself."

"So."

As they arose to go, the dancer in black walked in the direction of their table. They were now at the door. This same dancer accosted Soskii.

"Fred?" she queried.

"Oh. Hello Natalie."

"Going *so* soon?"

"And why not? Hic."

"No reason. Won't you stay a *little* longer?"

"Listen, Nat, I've told you I'm through. Why keep on after me?"

"Because I love. You loved me—you said."

"Aw, forget it. I'm sleepy—hic—old kid. See you some other time."

Fred was in an embarrassing position, with a pretty danseuse, love and madness in her eyes, barring his exit.

"I will dance for you soon. You say you like my dance once."

Stanisky smiled and shook his head. People at other tables became curious. Fred was further embarrassed. He tried to force his way past the woman. He essayed to thrust her aside.

"One question, Fred, please. Just one. Will you, please, my—my—I mean, Fred—just Fred like always? One question?" (She wept bitterly almost choking.)

"Providing you let me by. Damn it!"

"Now. You are not going to—quit your Nat, are you, Fred? You will not marry, no?" as she held the lapels of his coat, her face near his, her eyes searching—searching.

Fred did not know she held open in her hand the gold penknife she once wore as a locket.

Fred was drunk and puzzled. He waited.

"You not marry? No?"

She feared the answer would be "yes."

"Why, yes. I thought you knew it."

The girl grew frightened, mad, wild, ravenous, quiet, beautiful, sour, hurt, pitiable, hateful, satanic all in a moment.

"You joking? No."

"Not joking! Leave me. I'm through, I tell you."

She weakened—then strengthened—turned tigerlike. Amid her tears and grating teeth, she raised her knife.

"You will marry her, hein? Pas du tout!"

Fred caught her arm and twisted the knife out of her hand. It fell to the floor. Tapity-tap. Natalie stood black and blue before him, sobbing, tearing away fitfully at his chest, striking his face with her little fists. Fred pushed her aside and picked up the knife.

"I'll keep this as a souvenir," with a sneer and a shrug.

Stanisky and Soskii were driving leisurely out Chene Street. Fred's mind was a whirl with thoughts of Anna—Anna—Anna—— Was she really sick or did she just want to get rid of him that night? Which? He looked at his watch. Eleven o'clock. Just then a familiar car swept past his. A woman at the wheel. * * * A glimpse of a dark man in the rear seat. * * * Anna Paul's car? Anna—the dark man. Impossible! Did Stanisky tell the truth that night at the cafe?

The next morning Anna left word with her mother that she would be out all day looking for an old book. That was sufficient. Anna went again to the dimly lighted basement of the book shop on Grand River Avenue. Why did she want to go there just to feel the mysterious presence of that stranger with the hard eyes and puzzled face? She would get a good look at his face this time, even if he stabbed her. Pooh. Stab! Who would think of stabbing her?

After that first experience at the old book shop, Anna had returned there almost daily. Most every time she came, she found that same fellow there searching through the old German, French, Greek, Latin and Russian books. Perhaps he had permission of the owner of the store to roam over this pile of apparently useless rubbish. Or he might be hired as janitor. The person, excluding his face, certainly looked like a janitor. Gray unpressed suit, hair unkempt, black and bushy. He needed a shave—a scholar? His heavy eyebrows overhung his slowly blinking eyes. Was he always soused in deep thought? Did he know a lot? His long, thin dark hands cadaverously turned the pages of the books. The man was hardly twenty-five, Anna thought. Was he a sheik? He and Anna were becoming silent friends who met without speaking nearly every day. Later one began to nod as the other entered. Then one day Anna spilled the beans by stammering, "I'd began to think you weren't coming to-day." The stranger acted as if he hadn't heard the remark.

Later. "You are a book lover, I see." He glanced at *Thus Spake Zarathustra* Anna carried under her arm.

She imagined the fellow knew much; she even suspected now that he was a scholar. She found herself, more now than ever, wanting to pour out her heart to this stranger. His face emitted a calm sympathetic glow closely akin to that given out by Murillo's *St. Francis*.

Anna answered with a note of fear in her voice, "No, I can't say I'm such a book lover. I'm just a lost little thing with nothing to hold to."

Silence. Like a child, the fellow sat there gazing at the girl's face. He had met many of her type before, perhaps—"Lost little things holding on to nothing."

"Ah, well, you are not alone; this world is full of lost little things holding on to nothing."

"Not everybody?"

"Almost everybody. The farce of it is that the majority fool themselves by making believe they have found eternal verities; *the* right, *the* wrong, *the* beautiful, *the* truth, and on ad infinitum. There are no such things; 'tis the quality of ignorance that informs thus to their eyes."

The stranger had not raised his head during this recitation.

"You confuse me," Anna said with her head thrown to one side, expressing the profound curiosity of a child.

He went on in a sort of incantation.

"Chastity is right in the sight of God, they tell us; yet it is a matter of common knowledge that this same "God," expressing himself through Nature, plants in every normal human being the arch enemy of chastity. They tell us that God is good, and yet the wicked prosper. They tell us that God is just; while the poor, the weak are so because of what is commonly known as injustice meted out by those whom this same God has permitted to prosper. To me it is a joke, this God-ology. Organized guessing I call it. * * * I should like to live in a world with people who dare to act on convictions and conclusions arrived at through their own individual thinking."

Anna gave him a credulous look.

The stranger continued: "Such people would certainly not gouge out one another's guts with cold steel in the name of democracy, a degenerate theory of government by the weak, for the weak, and of the incompetent."

"What do you mean?" Anna asked.

"I don't know. I'm lost too; I've nothing to cling to."

"Like me."

"And a lot of others."

They looked at each other thoughtfully. Anna looked sad and lost. The stranger was sympathetic.

Anna cried: "I meet so many lies, lies, lies, I don't know what course to take. I don't know what to do or believe. Everybody suffers and suffers, and so unnecessarily, it seems. I'm lost."

"It has always been so. You mustn't cry over the world's suffering. The man who did the most of that died at the age of thirty-three yet—was crucified, you know. You want to live longer than that."

> "'Ah, my beloved, fill the cup that clears
> To-day of past regrets and future fears:
> *To-morrow!*—Why, to-morrow I may be
> Myself with yesterday's sev'n thousand years.'"

"Yes. That's beautiful. But I'm so helpless and unhappy since I started looking through so much dastardly deceitfulness. I've discovered that many of the things I once held most dear and sacred aren't worth talking about yet."

"That's true of most everybody else too. But listen:

> "'Ah Love! Could you and I with Him conspire
> To grasp this sorry Scheme of Things Entire,
> Would not we shatter it to bits—and then
> Remold it nearer to the Heart's desire!'"

There was a peculiar inter-attraction. Anna fell sobbing on the stranger's shoulder. His tears fell hot on her neck and rolled warm down her back and into her bosom. She realized the position she was in, and wanted to move her head. * * * And she didn't want to leave one who she thought felt and thought as she did. They cried there like two old friends meeting after a long separation.

"I'm feeling much better now. I'm going now," Anna whined. * * * "Friday?"

"Any time."

"Friday, then."

Anna reached home and rushed for the telephone.

"Hello * * * Mr. Soskii * * * Yes * * * Mr. Soskii? * * * Fred * * * Feel so much better to-day. Can't you come over to-night. * * * Yes, about eight. * * * News for you. * * * Busy? * * * No. * * * All right at eight. * * * So long."

Eight o'clock. Fred. Faint smell of onions. Anxious. Wondering. Fred Soskii rushing towards his fiancée who he felt had thought her way out of his love. Out of the snow and biting cold Fred Soskii came, shivering, go-gettish. Ready to bargain. Ready to praise purity, Blue Belle canned peaches, Horlick's malted milk, etc., etc. * * * Fresh country eggs. * * *

Fred entered. Some cold-warm-far-off look in Anna's eyes. "Hello, lady bird." * * * "Hello, Fred." Strangeness pervading the room. Fred feeling scared and foolish, as if he had lost a chance to make a good buy. * * * They were seated. Fred took her hands. He tried to kiss her. Anna was neutral, impassive.

"Fred, I can't marry you; I don't love you—any more."

"Anna——"

And yet he had felt this coming all along. He knew she was telling the truth. He knew Anna that well. She meant just what she was saying.

"Anna, you're joking?"

"No."

"But what's the trouble, Anna?"

"You expect what I can't give. I'm not the woman you think you know. I'm wild, ravenous, promiscuous, romantic. Marriage no longer has any fascination for me. I haven't yet had time to express myself. To-day I wept on a stranger's shoulder—a stranger I wanted to rape—though I didn't have the courage. * * * Think I shall rape him one of these days. There are too many lies in the world for you to think of marrying yourself to one of them. I myself am a lie, Fred."

"Anna, you're crazy!"

"I know it. Another reason why you shouldn't marry me."

She baffled him. He wanted to hit her, but dared not.

Anna went on, "I've talked it over with father and mother. They say I am crazy too. That means that none of you understand me. I'm sorry for you—not because of any harm I might be causing, but because you are all so stupid."

"Anna—Anna! You'll ruin me!"

"Quiet, Fred. You'll get over it soon. Just think of all the women you had before you met me."

"Anna, I know I've not been straight as I ought to have been, but I want to be; that's why I want you."

"I've decided not to be straight; in fact, I haven't been at heart. I don't like it. Nor do many others. You especially."

Fred dumbfounded.

"Now run along home and begin learning how to forget about it. Go by dad's and tell Basky to give you that quart of port I left there for you."

And again he was shoved out into the cold, cold snowing snow—flakish, sickly snow that looked like Fred felt. He couldn't believe it. Anna had thrown him over. Anna hadn't thrown him over. Anna *had* thrown him over, *jilted* him. Heavens! Heavens!!

Of late Anna's parents grew inquisitive concerning their daughter's whereabouts. In a way they didn't want to keep her from going out. They were frightened with various reports that came to their ears. Late hours driving alone through the city with a dark man in her car. Some said the man was a Chinaman, some a Jap. Others claimed the stranger was a Philippino, or a Bolsheviki. Or a colored man; a Negro! Great God! Or were these all different men. At the Capitol Theatre, at the New Detroit Opera House. Garrick. Other public places. At the Palms. All this threw the Pauls into a panic. Their daughter was going to elope with a Turk, an Indian. * * * The reports conflicted. Some were stupidly jumbled.

And this was not all. Everybody was trying to find out who Anna's new associate was. Some one had seen them kissing in Palmer Park under the cover of night. Another had seen her driving madly down Brush Street. Still another had seen them enter the Crisis Cafe, a passable eating place frequented by the more decent element among the Detroit Negroes. King Wah Ling's. * * * Statler. * * * The Sindadus Grill Room. * * * Her conduct was pronounced disgraceful. * * * Her father could bear it no longer. His business would certainly be seriously affected by her defiant antics. She must stop.

"Anna, won't you have consideration for your father, yet."

"Father, won't you have more consideration for your Anna yet."

"But, my girlie, Fred's furious, dangerous because you've thrown him over like this, and turned out so——"

"So bad. Exactly. I'm as happy as I have been before—happier. It's none of Fred's business. I don't love him now. I'm not harming anybody."

"Anna—your father——" The old man angered, as his glistening bald spot indicated. "You mind or you get out. There."

"I can certainly go. Thanks for the invitation."

Old Paul's threat didn't work.

They had met again at the book store, Anna and her friend. They embraced calmly, profoundly. She could never remember when he began embracing her. His full lips covered hers. There was a mutual exchange of sweetness, memories of nights and evenings they had spent together in various out-of-the-way rendezvous—all this lingered in their lingering kisses.

"I love you," she was saying. "What is your name? Where do you come from? Why do I love you so? It's going to kill me to love you like this."

"Tervanovitch—Askof Tervanovitch. But what's in a name?" he replied, drawing her close to him. "Your lips are honey dripping from the comb."

A book clerk coughed in a far corner of the basement. * * * This ended their meeting for that day. * * *

———

When Anna first got rid of Fred, he was all shaken up; he groped about trying to forget. He refused to have anything more to do with Natalie. * * * Then one evening he saw Anna and her friend dining at the Sindadus Grill Room on Broadway.

"Look, Stanisky! There's Anna! Well, damn. Is that why she threw me over? For that damn thing. She can't love him. I won't let her!"

He ordered drinks. The dancing began. Tervanovitch was toasting:

"For 'Is' and 'Is-Not' though with rule and line,
And 'Up-and-Down' by logic I define,
Of all that one should care to fathom, I
Was never deep in anything but—*Wine!*"

The orchestra struck up a waltz. Anna and her sheik arose and went gliding over the floor. Fred drank heavily. He'd have a talk with Anna. * * * So it's as he had heard. Anna had thrown him aside for that black dog. (The man was no darker than some Italians.)

Anna's partner wore his evening clothes with a certain Latin dignity. He was helping Anna to her seat. His old world manners attracted the attention of many other women.

"A sheik!"

"Who is he?"

"He doesn't notice anybody else here."

"Why should he?"

Several dissatisfied wives, whose husbands were either elsewhere with their mistresses or attending clubs, tried to catch the stranger's eye by exhibiting vast expanses of their silk-stockinged legs, portions of their bare shoulders, and their girlish smiles. One lady, who had once been Anna's teacher, actually came up and spoke to Anna, with the hope of getting introduced. * * * Nothing doing.

Anna and her partner were now dancing near Fred's table. He could hear the man saying, "This town needs fewer uplifters and more little theatres, my little snow flower." Anna was smiling dreamily under the somnolent influence of the waltz. The orchestra was playing "Moonlight Memories." Her cheek was near her partner's. He could feel her breath against his neck. It is doubtful whether Anna heard what he had said. They graced along as if soaring towards the land of Nirvana on a magic carpet of rose petals.

Stanisky said knowingly, "Fred, that's a colored man yet."

"Impossible. They aren't ever found here."

"Some niggers are mighty light, Fred."

Fred Soskii had become almost Americanized. He bowed his head and sobbed.

"Don't take it so hard, Fred."

"Can't help it, Stan. I love Anna," as he emptied his glass.

Anna saw Fred's face. Nervously to her escort, "Let's go."

Stanisky: "They are leaving. Let's follow."

"I am above that, Stan."

"Fool! Revenge!"

Fred turned blank and white. He unfastened a penknife from his watch charm. He ran his thumb over the keen edge of the blade. They got up and followed.

Outside the snow was falling rapidly. A sharp wind off the lakes swept over lower Detroit and modulated with the voices of yelling newsboys. The Saturday traffic was heavy, in spite of the fast falling flakes. The wind whipped around corners of buildings and lashed—and lashed—and lashed.

"It's no use starting anything, buddy. She don't love me. I tell you."

He stopped his car. "Here's where you live. Jump out and turn in. I'll drive back home. Heavy day to-morrow. Car load of oranges—twenty barrels of sugar—perishables by the car load—a dispatchment of potatoes—market's good now, too."

Stanisky hesitated.

"Come along now," Fred urged. "Snap it up. Can't let one woman break up my business. We'll pick up the dancers later this week."

"Atterboy! You're getting more sense every day. Guess you're right. Good night."

Fred drove slowly towards his home for a block or two. Then he turned suddenly and beat it for Anna's dwelling place. As quietly as possible, he drove his car to the door of Old Paul's garage, stopped the machine and waited. He took out his watch. He looked at it closely. Eleven forty-five. He pretended there was something wrong with his tires. He walked around his machine three times. He counted the number of times. He felt his feet getting cold. The coldness passed. Like the whiskey he had been drinking, the cold helped to numb him. He laughed expressionately, noiselessly. A whispering laugh. He looked at his watch again. He rubbed his hands. He blew his breath on them. Where were his gloves, he wondered? In the car perhaps. He'd get them later. The drink burnt his stomach. He looked at Anna Paul's house. A dim little framed two-story coziness, like Anna used to be. The Pauls were in bed, doubtless. That was funny, the Pauls being in bed. No. It was late enough for that. Surely. Fred looked up at the room Anna told him was hers. How many times she had pointed it out to him! He heard the familiar humming of a motor. Anna's car. He walked around his car twice more. He looked at his watch again. Eleven fifty. What a long five minutes. The car he had heard turned the corner and its lights flashed down upon him. Fred felt in his vest pocket for his penknife. The approaching machine slowed down. Fred was concealed behind his car. * * * He opened his penknife. Again his thumb gently ran over the keen edge of its blade. The whiskey dizzied him. Something else deadened his senses. Anna's Buick rolled up. The car near her father's garage caused her no alarm. It belonged to one of the neighbors, or to one of the neighbors' visitors. She jumped out to open the garage door.

Fred stepped from behind his car. * * * Anna started to scream when she saw him. She didn't know who he was.

"Sh-sh-sh——A friend. Don't scream. Only Fred."

"Fred Soskii! I've a good mind to call father."

"Please don't. Just answer one question and I'll be gone forever. Will you, Anna?"

"Well, what is it?"

He came closer to her meekly. White as the snow under his feet and as cold and as uncontrollable. Anna was steaming and red with anger, which beautified her beaming face, lifted her out of the real and into the ideal.

"Hurry, Mr. Soskii."

"Did you know that fellow's colored you were with to-night?"

"No, I don't know that. Nor do you." She bit her lip. She wanted to hurt. "That's none of your business, anyhow." She wanted to wound him mortally. "What if he is? I *love* him. So there!"

Fred was close to Anna now. She could see his white distorted face. He remembered his golden penknife. He looked straight into Anna's eyes and shook his head slowly. Somehow she couldn't keep her eyes out of his. * * * He raised his hand towards her throat. She thought he was trying to kiss her. Of course she couldn't afford to let him know she was afraid. She threw back her head in scorn.

With a swish and a click, the keen-edged blade lashed her throast. There was a gush of blood, a little hicking, gasping sound. Then faintly from beyond the grave:

"Fred, how could you? My—book—store—man—is——"

Anna staggered and sank.

The snow about her melted, and where her head struck, the snow crimsoned and melted. Fred stood there until the body began to stiffen. He looked at the corpse. He looked at his watch. Twelve o'clock. He looked at his bloody golden penknife. A souvenir. Natalie. He turned Anna's body over with his foot. A milky mist arose from the little pool of steaming blood in which Anna's golden hair lay. Fred Soskii shrugged his shoulders, spat, and turned to go. He felt numb.

The wind off the lakes whipped through the streets, chilling everything it touched. An arc light at the corner sputtered and flared.

Fred Soskii walked calmly towards his machine.

14 MADEMOISELLE 'TASIE
Eloise Bibb Thompson

FROM *OPPORTUNITY*, SEPTEMBER 1925

It was all on account of that last Mardi Gras Ball. Mlle. 'Tasie felt it. Indeed she was absolutely sure of it. The night had been cold and damp and she had not had a wrap suited for such weather. So she had gone in a thin blue organdy dress, the best she owned, with simply a white scarf thrown over her shoulders. A "white" scarf, and a "blue" organdy. It was scandalous! And her "tante" but one year dead. No wonder bad luck in the shape of ill health had followed her ever since—putting off her mourning so soon to go to a Mardi Gras ball. Well, what was the use of thinking of it now? "De milk has been speel, so to speak," she mused, "eet ees a grat wonder, yes, as de doctah say, I deed not go into decline."

But try as she would Mlle. 'Tasie could not stop thinking of it. The heavy cold caught at that Mardi Gras ball was the direct cause of her being about to take the momentous step that she was planning to take to-day. And momentous it was, for a fact; there was not the slightest doubt about that. How it would all end, she was at a loss to comprehend.

Not that it counted so much with her now; for ill health and deprivation had forced her to accept with resignation many things that before had seemed unendurable. But her neighbors, ah! and her relatives who knew how thoroughly she had formerly hated the very thing that she was about to do. Mon Dieu! What were they not saying of her now?

Yes, there was a time in her life when Mlle. 'Tasie would rather have fainted, actually, than to even so much as have been seen on the street with a certain kind of individual, which she and her class designated as a "Negre Americain aux grosses oreilles"—an American Negro with large ears. In a word, with a black American. How many times had she not said of such a contingency, "h-eet h-ees a thing not to be thought h-of h-at h-all." And now—O, now see what she was fixing to do!

For Mlle. 'Tasie was a Creole lady of much less color than a black American.

Be pleased to know first of all, that there are colored Creoles as well as white Creoles, just as there are Creole eggs and Creole cabbages. Any person or article brought up in the French Quarter of old New Orleans, the downtown section across Canal Street, is strictly Creole. And to carry the thought to its final conclusion is, in the highest sense of the word, Superior. Mlle. 'Tasie was what was designated by her lightly colored contemporaries, in a whisper, as "un briquet," that is, she had a reddish yellow complexion, and very crinkled red hair. "In a whisper," because the hair of a "briquet" is usually so short and so crinkled that no one feels flattered at being called one. Yet in spite of all that, Mlle. 'Tasie was a Creole, came of a good family, and spoke "patois French" for the most part, sometimes English, and hence, thinking herself superior, had not mingled with English-speaking Negroes known as Americans. And being yellow, she had never been accustomed, until now, to even be on speaking terms with blacks.

It was a positive fact, Mlle. 'Tasie had come of an exceptional Creole family. Everyone with whom she came in contact knew that well. How could they help knowing it when they had heard it so often? As for the corner grocer from whom Mlle. 'Tasie bought charcoal for her diminutive furnace—she couldn't afford a stove—and various other sundries for her almost empty larder, why, had you awakened him from the soundest sort of sleep, he could have told you about her family, word for word, as she had told it, embellished it with glowing incidents, as she had done. In a word, he could have torn that family tree to pieces for you, from root to apex at the shortest possible notice. That was because, of course, so many circumstances had given rise there in his store, for the frequent telling of her history; having incurred, as she had, the hostility of her English-speaking black neighbors, at whom she rarely ever glanced. By some strange trick of fortune, these black neighbors were much better off than she, and loved to put their little ones up to poking fun at her whenever she came to the store for the small purchases that she made—beans and rice, almost invariably, with a whispered request for meat-scrappings, thrown in by way of courtesy. Poking their heads in roguishly, thru the half-opened door, these taunting, little urchins were wont to scream at her, "Dere she goes, fellahs, look at 'er. A picayune o' red beans, a picayune o' rice, lagricappe salt meat to make it taste nice." Then Mlle. 'Tasie would laugh loudly to hide her embarrassment. Pityingly she would say with up-lifted shoulders and outwardly turned palms, "'Ow you ken h-expec' any bettah fum dem? My own fadda h-own plenty lak dat. —But h-I know, me. H-eet ees dey madda, yes, teach 'em lak dat. She ees mad 'cause h-I doan associate wid 'er. But 'er mahster wheep 'er back plenty, yes. Me—h-I nevva know a mahster, me. H-ask h-any one eef h-eet ees de trufe, and dey will tell you."

None knew better of Mlle. 'Tasie's family than Paul Donseigneur, the clothier of Orleans Street. Paul had been owned by Mlle. 'Tasie's father, Jose Gomez, who belonged to that class of mulattoes known before the Civil War as free men of color. Escaping from the island of Guadaloupe, during a West Indian insurrection, Gomez had settled in New Orleans, purchased a number of slaves and a goodly portion of land, ultimately becoming a "rentier" of some importance. Paul, a tailor by trade, had been assigned to the making of his master's clothes. Because of his efficiency and estimable character, he had rapidly risen in favor. But Paul was aspiring also. He longed for his freedom and begged permission of Gomez to purchase it from him. After much deliberation, the latter surprised him one day with a gift of himself,—that is, with free papers showing a complete bestowal of Paul and all that he possessed, upon himself.

Paul was deeply grateful. It was not in his nature, as it was with so many of his race, to hate the hand that lifted him, when that hand was black. He never forgot the generosity of his master, nor his subsequent assistance in the way of influence, immediately after the Civil War, toward the foundation of the very business into which he was still engaged.

But times had been precarious in New Orleans for any business venture during the early years of reconstruction. Especially so for Paul, efficient and alert though he was, yet an ex-slave, with no capital and no business experience. During the general upheaval, he saw nothing of his master who, like many men of his class, had kept well out of the way of all danger. When the smoke and powder of wrought-up feelings had at last cleared away, Paul again looked about for his old master, with the hope that things had not gone so badly with him. But alas! There was not the slightest trace of him to be found. Had he left the city, or had he only gone uptown? Either step would have been fatal for Paul's finding him. For people in the Faubourg Ste. Marie—the American quarter— were as completely lost at any time, to the people of the French quarter, as if they had gone to New York.

Paul knew that out of that great family of many sons and daughters, only two remained. At least there had been two when last he saw them—his master and Mlle. 'Tasie, the youngest daughter. How had they fared during all those troublous times? Wherever they were, he knew that they were poorer; for the Civil War had stripped them of most of their possessions, and unprepared as they were for service, they would never be able to retrieve them, he was certain. It was all very sad. But there was nothing to be done, since he knew not where to find them.

Chance, however, some ten years later, just before the opening of our story, discovered to him one member of that family at least, Mlle. 'Tasie. He was crossing over to the French Market, one morning, from the old Place D'Armes, en route to his clothing store, when he heard the guttural tones of a Gascon restauranteur raised in heated discussion. Hastening to the spot he saw seated upon one of the high stools, before the oil cloth-covered counter of the "coffee stand," a shabby, little colored woman in a black calico dress, much-worn but speckless gaiters, and a long, cotton crepe veil thrown back from a faded straw hat—a perfect picture of bitter poverty trying to be genteel.

Thru the cracked and much be-scratched mirror that ran around the wall of the "coffee stand" in front of her, he saw reflected her small pinched face, courageously rouged and powdered, and recognized Mlle. 'Tasie.

Wonderingly, Paul took in the situation. The merchant's prices, it seems, were higher than some of the others in the market, or more, anyhow, than Mlle. 'Tasie had been aware of. When the time came to pay for what she had eaten, small tho' it was, she was unprepared to do so completely. Hence the Gasconian war of words.

Mlle. 'Tasie's embarrassment at the turn of affairs was beyond description. With trembling fingers peeping out from cotton lace mittens that time had worn from black to green, she hurriedly lowered her veil, then fumbled about in her lace-covered reticule as if seeking the desired change with absolute fright. Going forward, Paul touched the enraged Gascon on the elbow. The sight of his proffered coin was like oil poured upon troubled waters. Mlle. 'Tasie was saved.

When she lifted her tearful eyes to Paul's pitying face, he saw even through the faded veil what privation had done for her. Gently he took her by the arm and led her to the Place D'Armes thru which he had but just passed. And there upon one of the benches, he coaxed out of her, her whole tragic story. She told him how their poverty becoming greater and greater, she and her father had hidden themselves as he had feared, in the American quarter across Canal Street, away from the people who had known them in brighter days; of her father's subsequent death, and her struggles to support herself with her needle; of her many failures at doing so, because of her complete unpreparedness. To his reproachful query as to why she had not appealed to him, she had answered, shoulders uplifted and mitten-covered palms turned outward, "'Ow h-I could do dat, my deah? Come wid my 'and h-open to you? Me? H-eet was h-impossible."

But he assured her that the success of his tailoring business, slow, to be sure, but very promising always, was such that he might have aided them at the time and was in a still better position of doing so now. She shook her head sadly at the suggestion, and her tears began to flow anew. "Me, h-I would die first!" she exclaimed passionately, "befo' h-I would come to dat."

When she grew calmer, he told her of an innovation that he was planning to bring into his business—the making of blue jeans into trousers for the roustabouts on the Levee, and for other workmen. She mopped her eyes and looked at him with interest. It was jean trousers, she had told him, that she had been attempting to make ever since she had been a breadwinner. But the factories from which she had taken work to be done at home had been so exacting, "docking" her for every mis-stitch, and every mistake in hemming so that there was always very little money coming to her when she finally brought her work back.

Paul surmised as much but had already thought out a plan to meet the situation. He would put her directly under the seamstress in charge, for supervision and instruction. And so, at length, Mlle. 'Tasie was installed into the business of her former slave. Her backwardness in learning to do the work set before her was, at first, disheartening. But for the sake of "Auld Lang Syne," Paul nerved himself into forbearance. When, at last, she gave evidence of beginning to "get the hang" of it, so to speak, she caught a dreadful cold at that Creole Mardi Gras ball.

For Mlle. 'Tasie was still young enough to long for pleasure with something of the ardor of her happier days. She was no "spring chicken," she confessed to herself sadly; she was thirty-seven "come nex' h-All Saints Day," but that did not prevent her from wanting to "h-enjoy herse'f, yes, once een a w'ile h-any 'ow." Since Mardi Gras comes but once a year, she decided to forget everything and go to the ball. Closing her eyes at the horror of the thing—the laying aside of the mourning which she had worn for the past year for an aunt whom she had never seen—she went down into her trunk and pulled out an ancient blue organdy and a thin, white scarf. It had been years since she had seen these things, for some distant relative of Mlle. 'Tasie was always passing away, and custom compelled her to remember them during a long period of mourning.

Perhaps it was her act of rebellion against this custom, she kept telling herself, that had brought such disaster to her health. Oh, if she only had to do it again, how differently would she act. It had meant the almost giving up of her work at Paul Donseigneur's store, for most of her time was now spent at home trying to get well.

Calling one day to ascertain for himself the cause of these frequent absences, Paul became much disturbed at her appearance. She looked more frail than he had ever seen her. Certainly work, he decided, was not what she wanted now, but care and attention. She had already refused from him, in her foolish pride, everything but what she strictly earned by the sweat of her brow. How to help her now in this new extremity was indeed a problem. He must think it out. And Paul left her more perplexed than he had been before.

As he was about to enter his clothing store, he was stopped by a traveling salesman, Titus Johnson, from whom he bought most of the cottonade that he used. Titus was large and black, well-fed and prosperous-looking, with a fat cigar forever in his mouth and a shiny watch-chain forever dangling from his vest. Titus was the idol of his associates, likewise the idol of the "cook-shop" where he ate, for besides ordering the largest and most expensive steaks they carried, together with hot biscuits, rice, French fried potatoes, buck-wheat cakes and coffee, he tipped the waiter lavishly and treated him to a cigar besides. Not only generous, but full of good cheer was Titus, his hearty laugh resounding from one end of the street to the other. Especially so after he had told one of his characteristic jokes, which invariably brought as great a laugh from himself as from his listeners. Simple, whole-hearted and kindly, Titus Johnson met the world with a beaming face and received much of its goodwill in return.

"Hey dere, boss," he shouted to Paul from across the narrow street, as the latter stood upon the sill of his odd-looking suit-store. "I ben waitin' for you. W'at kep' you?" In a stride or two he was at Paul's side. "I hope you ain't gotten so prosperous," he continued, "dat you dodgin' us black folks and fixin' ter pass for white. Hya! Hya! Hya! Hya!" His great voice sounded to the end of the block.

"No danger," smiled back Paul, whose physiognomy forbade any such intention. "I been visitin' de sick. An'—"

"De sick? Who's sick?" Titus' face bespoke concern.

"Mlle. 'Tasie," replied Paul. "De lil' lady who use to sit at dat machine dere by de winda."

"Sho' nuf?" Titus knitted his brow. "I knows her. Leastwise, I mean, I seen her time and time again.—An' you say she's sick?—Very sick? You know, I useter lak ter look at dat lil' body. 'Pere lak dere wuz somepun' so pitiful lak, about her."

"Pitiful," reiterated Paul, his face again wearing its troubled look. "Mais, it is worse yet. It is trageec."

"You doan say!—She ain' goin' die, is she?"

"Ah, I hope not dat, me.—All de same, she need right now plenty of care, yes. An'—you know, some one to see after her—right." He led the way thru a disordered room where women of various shades of color were bending over their work, some at machines, others at long cutting tables. When at length he reached his crowded little office in another wing of the building, he sank heavily into a chair, and motioned Titus to be seated also.

Why talk of business now, he mused, when his mind was so full of Mlle. 'Tasie, and her problems? She was downright troublesome, to say the least, he decided. Why had she let herself get into that weakened condition, just when she was beginning to earn enough to support herself decently? And she was so foolishly proud! It was absurd, it was ridiculous.

Before he knew it, Paul found himself telling the whole story to Titus Johnson—the history of Mlle. 'Tasie and of her remarkable family. Titus was astounded. He had heard that before the Civil War, New Orleans had held a number of men of his race who had not only been free themselves, but had owned a large number of slaves, but he had thought it only a myth. But here, according to Paul, was a representative of that class. He longed to meet her; to really be able, as he expressed it to Paul, to give her "his compliments." Never had he felt so much interest in any one before. When she got better, if Paul would arrange a meeting between them, he would be glad to take her some evening to the Spanish Fort— the great, white way of New Orleans—or to see the Minstrel—some place where she could laugh and forget her troubles.

Titus, like most English-speaking Negroes, felt no inferiority to the better-born of his race, like Mlle. 'Tasie. Had anyone suggested it, he would have scoffed at the possibility of her looking down upon him. For was she not also a Negro? However low his origin, she could never get any higher than he. Her status had been fixed with his by the highest authority.

Paul pondered Titus' proposition. He knew Mlle. 'Tasie's prejudice to color, but he refrained from mentioning it. She was in great extremity and Titus was both prosperous and big-hearted. Suppose a match could be arranged between them in spite of her prejudices. Stranger things than that had happened. Paul was an old man, and had seen women, bigger than Mlle. 'Tasie let go their prejudices under economic stress. When insistently the stomach growls, he mused, and the shoe pinches, women cease to discriminate and take the relief at hand. The thing was worth trying.

Looking up into the eager face of Titus Johnson, Paul promised to arrange a meeting between him and Mlle. 'Tasie at the first possible opportunity. Titus went away highly pleased. Altho he would not have named it so the thing promised an adventure; and, approaching forty tho he was, it was nevertheless very pleasing to contemplate. As for Paul, that man realized with misgiving that there was much preparatory work to be done on Mlle. 'Tasie before the meeting could even be mentioned to her. He, therefore, planned to set about doing so without delay.

But strange to say, when he approached her on the subject, Mlle. 'Tasie was more tractable than he dared hope for. Undoubtedly she had been doing some serious thinking for herself. Here she was, she told herself, rapidly approaching forty, her health broken down, and no help in the way of a husband anywhere in sight. How different it was from what she had dreamed. Long before this, she had thought the "right one" would have turned up—and she would have been settled down for life. But alas! the men she had wanted, had all gone to handsomer and younger women. She had been too discriminating, too exacting. That was her trouble. But all that must stop now. She must feel herself blessed if some well-to-do man, even tho he met but half her requirements, should come along and propose to her.

And so when Paul, after dilating upon the prosperity and big-heartedness of the black "Americain," advised in the most persuasive of language that she permit him to call, instead of flaring up, as he had been sure she would do, she heard him out quietly and consented after a moment or two of sad reflection. Surprised beyond measure at the ready acquiescence, he sat looking at her for a full second in open-mouthed wonderment. Then he congratulated her on her good, common sense; shook hands with her heartily and left, promising to bring Titus as soon as he returned to New Orleans.

But Mlle. 'Tasie's cheerfulness after that seemed to have deserted her. Her health, tho far from being completely restored, enabled her, before long, to resume her duties at the store. And there she sat at her machine, perplexed and miserable, a dumb spectacle of defeat. Since necessity compelled an abandonment of her prejudices, she reflected, if only she could leave the neighborhood before this black man called, so that those who knew her sentiments might not have the pleasure of laughing in her face. But to be compelled to remain right there and receive with a pretense of welcome before a group of peeping, grinning back-biters, the very kind of "Negre aux grosses oreilles" whom she had been known to look down upon—Mon Dieu!—how could one be cheerful after that?

Yet in spite of this dread, the time came at last, when Titus, traveling agent that he was, again arrived in New Orleans. To say that he was eager to meet Mlle. 'Tasie, is far, very far, from the mark, for he fairly lived in the expectation. But Titus was a natural psychologist. On the day of his arrival, contrary to his usual custom, he remained away from Paul's store during the hours that he knew Mlle. 'Tasie was in it, altho he saw to it that Paul got a message that he had not only arrived in town, but would call on Mlle. 'Tasie that evening. For an adventure such as this must not be spoiled thru haste or lack of preparation.

"Ef you wants a lady to 'preciate you," Titus mused, "you must fust have de proper settin'; 'cause settin's everything. You mustn't on'y fix yo'self up for her, but you must git her all worked up fixin' up for you. Den w'en you comes in swaggerin' on yo' cane, a half hour or a hour after she expected you to come, you got her jes' as anxious to meet you, as you is her. All de rest den is clare sailin'."

Arriving in the morning, Titus spent the day shopping. Nothing but the newest apparel must meet her eye when first she beheld him. When Paul, therefore, rather falteringly presented him in the evening after having apprised Mlle. 'Tasie much earlier of his expected visit, Titus was resplendent in brand new "malakoff"-bottom trousers, well creased in the middle, a "coffin-back" shaped coat to match, creaking red brogues, lemon colored tie, and a deep red Camellia in the buttonhole of his coat.

To a man less self-conscious than Titus was at the moment, the meeting would have been a dismal failure. For there was nothing of cordiality in Mlle. 'Tasie's subdued and rather mournful greeting. Paul was so impressed by the chilliness of it, that he beat a hasty retreat, leaving Romeo to the winning of his Juliet unaided. And Titus proved that he was not unequal to the task, for he soon had Mlle. 'Tasie interested in spite of herself. He told her of his travels up and down the State, described the dreary islands of Barataria with their secret passages, where smugglers and robbers nearly a hundred years before had hidden their ill-gotten gains. And had a world of news about the folks of Opoulousas and Point Coupee, places she had not visited since she was a girl. When at length he rose to go, she felt something very much like regret, and before she knew it, entirely forgetful of his color, she had invited him to call again.

Not only was Titus' "gift of gab" an asset to his courting but his frequent absences from town as well. For Mlle. 'Tasie could not help but feel the contrast between the quiet, uneventful evenings without him, and the cheer, the jokes, the kindly gossip that filled the hours when he was there. If only she had not to face the "pryers" with explanations as to why she had become suddenly so "cosmopel" as to bring into her home an American of his complexion. Relatives whom she hadn't seen for months hearing of the strangeness of her conduct, came way from Bayou Rouge and Elysian Fields Street to beg her with tears in their eyes not to disgrace them by allying herself with an American "Negre aux grosses oreilles."

Mlle. 'Tasie became distracted. The opinion of these people meant much to her; but after long thinking she realized that the protection and assistance of a husband would mean vastly more. So she nerved herself to defiance. When at length, Titus proposed marriage to her, she accepted him, not with any feeling stronger than liking, it is true, but with a sense of great satisfaction that now she was for a truth, to have a protector at last.

But now that the marriage day had arrived she felt all the old hesitancy, the repugnance, the sensitiveness because of what the others had been saying, come back upon her, with painful intensity. Yet, nevertheless, she bravely prepared for the event. When, at length, evening came and her shabby, little parlor where the ceremony took place became enlivened by the cheery presence of Titus and the only two invited guests—Paul and the owner of the "cook-shop" where Titus ate—Mlle. 'Tasie felt herself grow calmer.

After partaking lavishly of her "wine sangeree" and her carefully-prepared tea-cakes, the guests finally took their departure, Titus went up to her and putting both his fat hands upon her shoulders, smiled reassuringly into her eyes. "Well, ole 'oman," he said, "you an' me goin' ter make it fine! It's me an' you 'ginst de whole worl', you heah me? You po' lil' critter! You needs somebody ter take care o' you, an' Titus Johnson is de one ter take de job." Then Mlle. 'Tasie felt a sort of peace steal over her, the harbinger, she hoped, of happier days.

1926

- Hirohito succeeds his father as emperor of Japan.
- The first transatlantic telephone call is made.
- Automaker Henry Ford institutes the 40-hour work week.
- Robert Goddard successfully launches the first liquid-fueled rocket.
- White author Carl Van Vechten publishes his controversial best-selling novel, *Nigger Heaven*.
- Negro History Week is established by Carter G. Woodson.
- Jessie Redmon Fauset steps down as literary editor of the NAACP's *Crisis*.
- Violette N. Anderson becomes the first African American woman admitted to practice before the U.S. Supreme Court.
- In response to George S. Schuyler's essay "The Negro-Art Hokum," Langston Hughes publishes his influential essay "The Negro Artist and the Racial Mountain," arguing in favor of artistic independence and race pride.
- Harlem's Savoy Ballroom opens.

U.S. unemployment: 1.8%

Lynchings in the United States: 23 blacks, 7 whites

Deaths:
Bessie Coleman (30 Apr.)

Spingarn Medal:
Carter G. Woodson (historian, educator)

Books:
W. C. Handy (ed.), *The Blues: An Anthology* (music)
Langston Hughes, *The Weary Blues* (poetry)
Eric Walrond, *Tropic Death* (short stories)
Walter White, *Flight* (novel)

Periodical: *Fire!!* (Nov. 1926)

15 GRIST IN THE MILL
Wallace Thurman

FROM *MESSENGER*, JUNE 1926

This is indeed an accidental cosmos, so much so, that even the most divine mechanism takes an occasional opportunity to slip a cog and intensify the reigning chaos. And to make matters more intriguing, more terrifying, there seems to be a universal accompaniment of mocking laughter, coming from the ethereal regions as well as from the more mundane spheres, to each mishap whether that mishap be experienced by a dislodged meteor, a moon-bound planet, a sun-shrunken comet, or a determined man. All of which serves to make this universe of ours a sometimes comic spectacle, serves to push all unexpected cosmic experience just over the deviating border line that divides the comic from the tragic, for there is always something delightfully humorous in an accident even if that accident be as earthly, as insignificant (cosmically speaking) and as fatal as was the accident of Colonel Charles Summers, the second, of Louisiana.

Colonel Charles Summers, the second, was a relic; an anachronistic relic from pre-civil war days, being one of those rare sons of a dyed-in-the-wool southern father who had retained all the traditionary characteristics of his patrician papa. Even his aristocratic blood had escaped being diluted by poor white corpuscles making him indeed a phenomenal person among the decadent first families of the decadent south. Colonel Charles Summers, the second, was your true re-born Confederate, your true transplanted devotee of the doctrines of Jeff Davis, your true contemporary Colonel Charles Summers, the first, even to the petty affectation of an unearned military title, and a chronic case of pernicious anæmia.

It was on one of those placid days when a wary human is always expecting the gods to play a scurvy trick upon him, one of those days when smiling nature might be expected to smirk at any moment, one of those days when all seems to be too well with the world that the first act of Colonel Summers' accident occurred. He should have sensed that all was not to be well with him on that day, for long, lonely, isolated years of living with and nursing a dead ideal, had made him peculiarly attune to the ever variant vibrations of his environment. He had little companionship, for there were few kindred souls in the near vicinity. His wife, to him, was practically non-existent, being considered a once useful commodity now useless. He had no children, had not wanted any, for fear that they would become too seared with the customs and mannerisms of the moment to complacently follow in his footsteps. He could not abide the poor white or mongrel aristocrats who were his neighbors. He shrank from contact with the modern world, and preserved his feudal kingdom religiously, passionately, safeguarding it from the unsympathetic outside. Hence he communed with himself and with nature, and became intensely aware of his own mental and psychical reactions and premonitions, so aware, in fact, that he privately boasted that no accident could befall him without his first receiving a sensory warning, but, of course, he forgot to be aware at the proper time, even tho the day was rampant with danger signals.

Mrs. Summers was an unemotional ninny, being one of those backwoods belles whom the fates failed to attend properly at birth. Her only basis of recognition in this world at all was that she was a direct descendant of an old southern family. She was one of those irritating persons who never think about a thing nor yet feel about it. Rather she met all phenomena dispassionately, practically, and seemed to be more mechanical than most other humans. When an interne from the hospital brought her the news that only a blood transfusion would save her husband's life, she accepted that without the slightest suggestion of having received a shock; and she had accepted the news of his sunstroke, induced by walking beneath a torrid, noonday Louisiana sun, and which had resulted in an acute aggravation of his chronic illness in the same "well, that's no news" manner.

"Blood transfusion," she stated rather than queried, "well, why not?"

"We thought, madame," the interne was polite, "that you might be able to suggest—"

She gave a little shrug, the nearest approach to the expression of an emotion that she ever allowed herself. "I am no physician," and the door was closed deliberately, yet normally.

The hospital staff was thus placed in an embarrassing dilemma, for there was no professional blood donor available, and no volunteers forthcoming either from the village center or the outlying plantations. One must suffer from not having friends as well as suffer from having them—so the Colonel's life line continued to fray, his wife made perfunctory visits, and continued to appear disinterested, while the hospital staff pondered and felt criminal, not too criminal, you know, for they remembered that the Colonel had most insultingly refrained from ever donating to their building or upkeep fund, yet they could not let him die while there was a possible chance of saving him, so being both human and humanitarian they played a joke on the doughty old Colonel and at the same time saved his life.

Zacharia Davis had a suppressed desire, and the suppression of that desire was necessarily more potent than the desire itself, for Zacharia wished to make a happy hegira to the northland, and being in the south decided that it was best to keep this desire under cover until such time came that he would have what he called the "necessary mazuma."

Zacharia had been born and schooled in Illinois, and had been perfectly willing to remain there until a certain war-time conscription measure had made Mexico seem more desirable. Once in Mexico he had remained until the ink of the Armistice signatures had been dry five years, and then he had recrossed the border into the cattle lands of western Texas. There he had parked, and attempted to amass sufficient coin to enable him to return to and dazzle Chicago's south side black belt, but an untimely discovery of a pair of loaded dice on his person during an exciting crap game had made it necessary for him to journey by night, and by freight to the cane-brake country of Southern Louisiana.

Here he had occupied himself by doing odd jobs about the various plantations and village shops, and by gambling down by the river bottom at night with the rice field and cane-brake laborers. He avoided trouble either with his fellow black men who were somewhat suspicious of this smooth talking "furriner," and with that white portion of his environment that demanded his quiescent respect. Consciously he adopted a protective cloak of meekness, and at first glance could not be distinguished from the native southern blacks; in fact, only a keen analyst could have discerned that Zacharia was continually laughing at all those about him, both white and black, and that he, unlike the southern native Negro suffered little, even unconsciously, and laughed much. Then, too, Zacharia washed the hospital windows every Saturday morning, and was thus drawn into the little comedy in which Colonel Summers was to play the star role.

Meanwhile there were other factors working to deter Zacharia from ever realizing the fruition of his desire. The sheriff of the parish had finally decided to clamp down on the river bottom gambling activities where there had lately been a siege of serious cuttings and fatal shootings. Of course, normally it did not matter if all the "coons" insisted upon killing one another, but it did matter when northern migration was at its highest peak, and labor was both scarce and valuable to the plantation owners and it was at the instigation of these persons that the sheriff was moved to act. He planned his raid secretly and carefully, seeking the aid of the local K. K. K. and the more adventurous villagers. They had no intention of using firearms or of jailing any of the game participants.

Neither did they have any intention of stopping the games completely. They merely hoped to lessen the attendance, and to inspire caution in those who would attend about the advisability of carrying firearms and knives.

Of course, it was in line with Zacharia's general luck that he should be in the midst of a winning streak on the night when the eager vigilantes swooped down upon the river bottom rendezvous like revengeful phantoms in the moonlight, and proceeded to do their chosen duty. And, of course, it was in line with Zacharia's general procedure to forego immediate flight in order to gather up forsaken cash piles.

There was much confusion there in the damp darkness. The fiery, white demons reveled in the raucous riot they had created, while the scuttling blacks cursed and cried out against the lash sting and the club beat. The rendezvous was surrounded, there was only one means of escape, the river, and the cornered ones shrank back from its cold, slimy, swift currents. Hysteria descended upon the more terrified. Knives were drawn, and temporarily reflected the gleaming moonlight as they were hurled recklessly into the mad white-black crowd. Periodic pistol shots punctuated the hoarse shouts of the conquerors and the pained moans of the vanquished. Torchlight flares carried by the invaders gave the scene the color and passion of a Walpurgis night. Marsh grass was trampled, its dew turned red by dripping blood. And the river—the muddy river—became riotous with struggling men, and chuckled to itself as an occasional body was unable to withstand the current, or unable to reach the other shore.

There was much more confusion there in the damp darkness. Bleeding heads emitted mournful groans, emitted fresh blood streams, more groans, more blood, and then grew still, grew horribly inanimate. Wounded bodies squirmed and moaned. The flares were all extinguished. The river was once more quietly rippling undisturbed by super-imposed freight. The round-up had commenced, the injured whites were being carefully carried into the village hospital, while the wounded blacks were being dragged to jail. Thus the night wore on, and seemed a little weary of having witnessed such a carnal spectacle, such elemental chaos.

Among those hapless blacks who regained consciousness in the crowded jail was Zacharia, who was nonchalantly nursing a cracked head, and a sock full of coin. Being in jail was no novelty, nor was having a cracked head an entirely new experience, but the sock of money, the sock that contained his pecuniary emancipation, the sock that contained the "necessary mazuma," ah, that was new, saliently new, and comforting.

The town was in an uproar. A deputy sheriff had died from a knife wound inflicted by some infuriated black during the conflict. No one had expected any of the invaders to come back wounded. No one had considered that the cornered colored man might stand at bay like a wild, jungle animal, and fight back. Everyone had considered the whole episode as an unusual chance to sock a few niggers upon the head, and to flay a few black hides with a long unused lash, but instead most of the blacks had fought their way to freedom, only a mere handful of the more seriously wounded were in custody, and they were being claimed by their plantation employers. Moreover, the hospital was overcrowded with wounded whites, and now, this death, this death of a white man at the hands of a nigger. Of course, some one had to pay. The plantation owners were not willing to part with any of their hired help, considering the cultivation of the rice and sugar cane crop of more importance now than the punishment of some unknown assailant. Oh, yes, catch some one and punish him, but don't take this nigger of mine, who is one of my best workmen, seemed to be the general attitude.

No one came to claim Zacharia, and he remained in his cell, awaiting to be released, and amusing himself meanwhile by trying to compute in his mind just how much money his beloved sock, so carefully hidden away, contained. No one came to claim him and finally he was accused of having murdered the deputy sheriff.

The trial was conducted rather leisurely. There was no hurry to cash in on the mob's vengeance. Their call for blood had been satiated by that river bottom battle. It was enough that they had a victim in custody whom they could torture at will, and whom they could put to death legally. Thus Zacharia found himself a participant in a mock trial, found himself being legally railroaded to the gallows, found himself being kept away from freedom—from Chicago—when he had the cash, the long desired cash. He was too amazed at first to realize just how completely he had been enveloped by a decidedly hostile environment. Realization came slowly, and noticeably. His bronze colored face grew wan and sickly. His beady eyes became more and more screwed up until it seemed as if they would completely retreat into the protective folds of their wrinkled sockets. Even the firm lower lip, his one sign of forceful character, drooped, and mutely asked for pity.

He was found guilty, and made ready to take his journey to the state penitentiary where he would be held until the date set for his hanging. The date of his departure drew near, and Zacharia became pitifully panic stricken. The four walls of his lousy cell seemed to be gyrating mirrors sordidly reflecting his certain doom. The bars running diagonally across the cell door and standing upright in the cell window all seemed to assume the personality of ballet dancers attired in hemp, and forming twirling circular figures, lunging at him with menacing loops. Everything choked him, his food—the air—even thought. Incipient nausea tortured him. And then one thought flashed across his mind, lingered there, shimmering with the glorified heat of potential hope. A spasm of grotesque smiles distorted the uneven, thick features, and the quivering lips called to the guards, and begged them to send for Colonel Summers.

Had Zacharia asked for anyone else besides Colonel Summers his request would have been either roughly refused, or rudely ignored, but to have a con-demned "nigger" ask for old stuck up Colonel Summers, well, well, well, what a chance for some fun at the Colonel's expense. The question was would the Colonel come. In all probability he wouldn't. Since he had recovered from that last illness of his he had drawn more and more into himself. His wife had im-ported a sister for company, but the Colonel continued to tramp about his plan-tation, continued to commune with himself.

It was sheer accident that Colonel Summers happened to be in town on the same day that Zacharia had asked to see him. His wife's sister had had an attack of indigestion. In fact it seemed to Colonel Summers that she was always hav-ing an attack of something. And she was always having prescriptions filled, al-ways dispatching a servant to the drug store. Damned frump, the Colonel called her. Worrisum bitch, was what the black servants called her. However, on this day she had sent for medicine twice, and each time the little black boys had come back with the wrong brand, so impatient at both his sister-in-law, the stu-pid black boys, and the crafty druggist, the Colonel went into town himself.

Of course, once there the Colonel did the usual thing, id est, wandered aim-lessly about the streets and enjoyed himself by cursing the activities of these ambitious, pettily so, of course, poor trash. And in his wanderings he walked past the jail, was hailed, stopped to see what the insolent fellow wanted, gaped slightly when he heard, and without a word, or without an idea why he did so except that his pride would not let him appear to be placed at a disadvantage, strode into the jail, and asked to see Zacharia.

Fifteen minutes later the amused eavesdropping guards and jail loiterers rushed into the cell passageway to see the Colonel striking through the bars with his cane, perspiring dreadfully, his face inordinately infused with blood, and to find Zacharia cowed against the further wall, his face a study in perplexity and pleading, his lips whimpering, "I didn't lie, I didn't lie, it was me, it was me," on and on in ceaseless reiteration.

The surprised and amused men plied the old Colonel with questions in a vain effort to find out what was wrong, but the old southern gentleman was incoher-ent with rage, and sick, both in body and in mind. He seemed on the verge of collapse and the more solicitous men in the group attempted to lead him into the warden's quarters where he could lie down. Someone even suggested a doc-tor, but all were overruled by Colonel Summers, who had meanwhile regained some of his strength and cried out, "The hospital, the hospital," and to the hos-pital the men carried him, not knowing that he did not wish to go there for treatment, or that he was seeking for verification—verification of what the doomed Zacharia had told him.

Twenty-four hours later he was taken home, babbling, unconscious, and piti-ful. The hospital authorities had verified Zacharia's statement, and Colonel Summers now knew that it was the black man's blood that had saved his life.

———

It commenced to rain about twilight time. Colonel Summers suddenly sat up in his bed, the most ambitious move that he had made in a week. He was alone in the room, alone with himself, and his fear, alone in the defeated twilight.

The rain drops increased in volume and velocity. Colonel Summers threw the covers back, struggled out of the bed, and staggered laboriously to the panel mirror set in his clothes closet door. Eagerly, insanely he peered into it, and what he saw there evidently pleased him, for the drawn features relaxed a trifle, and only the eyes, the weak, pitiful eyes, remained intensely animate as they peered and peered into the mirror. Then his strength gave out, and he sank with a groan to the floor.

The rain drops began to come down in torrents, urged on by a rising wind. Colonel Summers once more drew himself up with the aid of the door knob, and once more peered and peered into the mirror. By this time he had ripped his night shirt from him, and stood there naked, his wasted body perspiring from the effort. Soon his strength gave out again, and as he sank to the floor there was a peaceful half smile striving for expression on his pained and fear-racked face.

"Still white, still white," he muttered, and then more loudly, "still white, still white, still white," the voice became hoarse again, "still white, thank God, A'hm still white."

Night came, greeted by the whistle of the frolicsome wind and the ceaseless chorus of the scampering rain drops. The bedroom became dark, and once more gaining consciousness the naked Colonel crawled across the carpeted floor to the nearest window. The darkness frightened him, he was seeking for light, and since the interior offered none, he sought for it or a reflection of it through the window panes. But on the outside was also the black night plus the cachinnating rain drops, and the playful wind. He shrank back in abject terror only to be confronted with the same terrifying darkness behind him.

He looked out of the window once more. A flash of lightning provided the wanted light, but it brought no release, brought only additional terror, for the tree tops, glistening wet and swaying with the wind, assumed the shapes of savage men, rhythmically moving to the tune of a tom-tom, rhythmically tossing to the intermittent thud of the reverberating thunder.

"Darkies," he murmured, and tried to draw away from the window, "My God—darkies." Then the scene changed. His insane eyes set in a bearded skull conjured up strange figures when the lightning flashed. Each tree assumed a definite personality. That broken limb dangling from the tree just beyond the fence was Zacharia, and as it gyrated wildly in the mad night, it seemed to whisper to the wind, "He is my brother, my brother, my brother," while the wind broadcasted the whisper through the night. And then that tallest tree so close to the house was himself, a black reproduction of himself with savage sap surging through its veins. It too reveled in the wildness of the night; it too exulted in being pelted by the wind-driven rain drops and in responding to the rough rhythm of the thunder-gods tom-tom.

Someone lit a light in the hall, and laid their hand on the door knob preparatory to opening the door to the Colonel's room. Then someone else across the hall called, and the first person released their grip on the knob and treaded softly away.

The Colonel fell prostrate to the floor, and attempted to burrow his head deep into the thick protective nap of the carpet. He felt an inky blackness enveloping him, his whole form seemed to be seared with some indigo stain that burned and burned like an avid acid. Then his body began to revolt against this dusky intruder, began to writhe and wriggle upon the floor, began to twitch and turn, trying to rub itself clean, trying to shed this super-imposed cloak, but the blackness could not be shed—it was sprouting from the inside, and being fertilized by the night.

Time passed. Voices were heard whispering in the hall. A door closed. More whispering. Outdoors all was jubilantly mad. In the bedroom the Colonel still lay upon the floor, panting, perspiring, exhausted from his insane efforts. His reason was now completely gone. His last ounce of life was being slowly nibbled away. The blackness became more intense, and then a black crow, stranded, befuddled by the storm, sought refuge upon the window ledge, and finding none there cawed out in distress, and to the dying maniac on the floor, it seemed to caw, "nigaw, nigaw, nigaw"——

Someone opened the door, turned on the light, and screamed.

16 HANNAH BYDE
Dorothy West

FROM *MESSENGER*, JULY 1926

One comes upon Hannah in her usual attitude of bitter resignation, gazing listlessly out of the window of her small, conventionally, cheaply furnished parlor. Hannah, a gentle woman crushed by environment, looking dully down the stretch of drab tomorrows littered with the ruins of shattered dreams.

She had got to the point, in these last few weeks, when the touch of her husband's hand on hers, the inevitable proximity in a four-room flat, the very sound of his breathing swept a sudden wave of nausea through her body, sickened her, soul and body and mind.

There were moments—frightful even to her—when she pictured her husband's dead body, and herself, in hypocritical black, weeping by his bier; or she saw her own repellent corpse swirling in a turgid pool and laughed a little madly at the image.

But there were times, too—when she took up her unfinished sack for the Joneses' new baby—when a fierce, strange pain would rack her, and she, breath coming in little gasps, would sink to the floor, clutching at the tiny garment, and, somehow, soothed, would be a little girl again with plaited hair, a little eager, visioning girl—"Mama, don't cry! Some day I'll be rich an' ev'rything. You'll see, mama!"—instead of a spiritless woman of thirty who, having neither the courage nor strength to struggle out of the mire of mediocrity, had married, at twenty, George Byde, simply because the enticing honeymoon to Niagara would mark the first break in the uneventful circle of her life.

Holiday crowds hurrying in the street.... bits of gay banter floating up to her. ... George noisily rustling his paper.... Wreaths in the shop window across the street.... a proud black family in a new red car.... George uttering intermittent, expressive little grunts.... A blind beggar finding a lost dollar bill.... a bullying policeman running in a drunk.... George, in reflective mood, beating a pencil against his teeth—

With a sharp intake of breath she turned on him fiercely, her voice trembling with stifled rage, angry tears filming her eyes.

"For God's sake, stop! You'll drive me mad!"

He dropped his paper. His mouth fell open. He got to his feet, a great, coarse, not unkindly, startled giant. "Hannah, I ain't—What under the sun's the matter with you?"

She struggled for composure. "It's nothing. I'm sorry. Sorry, George." But her eyes filled with pain.

He started toward her and stopped as he saw her stiffen. He said quietly, "Hannah, you ain't well. You ain't never bin like this."

She was suddenly forced into the open. "No," she said clearly, "I'm not well. I'm sick—sick to death of you, and your flat, and your cheap little friends. Oh," she said, her voice choked with passion, "I'd like to throw myself out of this window. Anything—anything to get away! I hate you!"

She swayed like some yellow flower in the wind, and for a moment there was the dreadful silence of partial revelation.

He fumbled, "No, no, hon. You're jes' nervous. I know you women. Jes' you set down. I'll go see if Doc's home."

She gave a deep sigh. Habitual apathy dulled her tone. "Please don't bother. I'm all right. It's nerves, I guess. Sometimes the emptiness of my life frightens me."

A slow anger crept over him. His lips seemed to thicken. "Look here, Hannah. I'm tiahed of your foolishness. There's limits to what a man will stand. Guess I give you ev'rything anybody else's got. You never have nothing much to do here. Y' got a phonygraph—and all them new records. Y' got a piano. I give you money las' week to buy a new dress. And yesterday y' got new shoes. I ain't no millionaire, Hannah. Ain't no man livin' c'n do better'n his best."

She made a restless, weary little gesture. She began to loathe him. She felt an almost insane desire to hurt him deeply, cruelly. She was like a taunting mother goading her child to tears.

"Of course I appreciate your sacrifice." Her voice shook a little with rising hysteria. "You're being perfectly splendid. You feed me. You clothe me. You've bought me a player piano which I loathe—flaunting emblem of middle-class existence—Oh, don't go to the trouble of trying to understand that—And a stupid victrola stocked with the dreadful noises of your incomparable Mamie Waters. Oh, I'm a happy, contented woman! 'There never is anything to do here.'" She mocked in a shrill, choked voice. "Why, what in God's name is there to do in a dark, badly furnished, four-room flat? Oh, if I weren't such a cowardly fool, I'd find a way out of all this!"

The look of a dangerous, savage beast dominated his face. He stood, in this moment, revealed. Every vestige of civilization had fled. One saw then the flatness of his close-cropped head, the thick, bull-like shortness of his neck, the heavy nose spreading now in a fierce gust of uncontrollable anger, the beads of perspiration that had sprung out on his upper lip, one wondered then how the gentlewoman Hannah could have married him. Shut her eyes against his brutal coarseness, his unredeemed ignorance—here no occasional, illiterate appreciation of the beautiful—his lack of spiritual needs, his bodily wants.

And yet one sees them daily, these sensitive, spiritless Negro women caught fast in the tentacles of awful despair. Almost, it seems, they shut their eyes and make a blind plunge, inevitably to be sucked down, down into the depths of dreadful existence.

He started toward her, and she watched his approach with contemptuous interest. She had long ago ceased to fear him. She had learned to whip him out of a mood with the lash of her scathing tongue. And now she waited, almost hoping for the miracle of his heavy hand blotting out her weary life.

He was trembling. His eyes were black with rage. His speech was thick. "By God, you drive me mad! If I was any kind of man I'd beat you till you ran blood. I must have been crazy to marry you. You—you—!"

There was a sharp rapping at the door, drowning his crazy words. Hannah smiled faintly, almost compassionately.

"The psychological moment. What a pity, George."

She crossed the floor, staggering for an instant with a sudden, sharp pain. She opened the door and unconsciously caught her lip in vexation as she admitted her visitor.

"Do come in," she said, almost dryly.

Tillie entered. Tillie, the very recent, very pretty, very silly wife of Doctor Hill: a newly wed popular girl finding matrimony just a big cramping.

She entered boldly, anticipating and ignoring the palpable annoyance in the stern set of Hannah's face. She even shrugged a little, a kind of wriggling that her friends undoubtedly called "cute." She spoke in the unmistakable tone of the middle-class Negro.

"Hello, you! And big boy George! I heard you all walking about downstairs, so I came on up. I bin sittin' by myself all evenin'. Even the gas went out. Here it's New Year's eve, I'm all dolled up, got an invite to a swell shebang sittin' pretty on my dresser—and my sweet daddy walks out on a case! Say, wouldn't that make you leave your happy home?"

George enjoyed it. He grinned sympathetically. Here was a congenial, jazz-loving soul, and, child-like, he promptly shelved his present grievance. He wanted to show off. He wanted, a little pathetically, to blot out the hovering bitterness of Hannah in the gay camaraderie of Tillie.

He said eagerly, "Got some new records, Tillie."

She was instantly delighted. "Yeh? Run 'em round the green."

She settled herself in a comfortable chair and crossed her slim legs. Hannah went to the window in customary isolation.

George made a vain search of the cabinet. "Where're them records, Hannah?" he asked.

"On the table ledge," she murmured fretfully.

He struggled to his feet and shuffled over to the table. "Lord," he grumbled, "you ain't undone 'em yet?"

"I've been too tired," she answered wearily.

He and Tillie exchanged mocking glances. He sighed expressively, and Tillie snickered audibly. But their malicious little shafts fell short of the unheeding woman who was beating a sharp, impatient tattoo on the window pane.

George swore softly.

"Whassa matter?" asked Tillie. "Knot?"

He jerked at it furiously. "This devilish string."

"Will do," she asserted companionably. "Got a knife?"

"Yep." He fished in his pocket, produced it. "Here we go." The razor-sharp knife split the twine. "All set." He flung the knife, still open, on the table.

The raucous notes of a jazz singer filled the room. The awful blare of a frenzied colored orchestra, the woman's strident voice swelling, a great deal of "high brown baby" and "low down papa" to offend sensitive ears, and Tillie saying admiringly, "Ain't that the monkey's itch?"

From below came the faint sound of someone clumping, a heavy man stamping snow from his boots. Tillie sprang up, fluttered toward George.

"Jim, I'll bet. Back. You come down with me, G. B., and maybe you c'n coax him to come on up. I got a bottle of somethin' good. We'll watch the new year in and drink its health."

George obediently followed after. "Not so worse. And there oughta be plenty o' stuff in our ice-box. Scare up a little somethin', Hannah. We'll be right back."

As the door banged noisily, Hannah, with a dreadful rush of suppressed sobs, swiftly crossed the carpeted floor, cut short the fearful din of the record, and stood, for a trembling moment, with her hands pressed against her eyes.

Presently her sobs quieted, and she moaned a little, whimpering, too, like a fretful child. She began to walk restlessly up and down, whispering crazily to herself. Sometimes she beat her doubled fists against her head, and ugly words befouled her twisted lips. Sometimes she fell upon her knees, face buried in her outflung arms, and cried aloud to God.

Once, in her mad, sick circle of the room, she staggered against the table, and the hand that went out to steady her closed on a bit of sharp steel. For a moment she stood quite still. Then she opened her eyes, blinking them free of tears. She stared fixedly at the knife in her hand. She noted it for the first time: initialed, heavy, black, four blades, the open one broken off at the point. She ran her fingers along its edge. A drop of blood spurted and dripped from the tip of her finger. It fascinated her. She began to think: this is the tide of my life ebbing out. And suddenly she wanted to see it run swiftly. She wanted terribly to be drained dry of life. She wanted to feel the outgoing tide of existence.

She flung back her head. Her voice rang out in a strange, wild cry of freedom.

But in the instant when she would have freed her soul, darkness swirled down upon her. Wave upon wave of impenetrable blackness in a mad surge. The knife fell away. Her groping hands were like bits of aimless driftwood. She could not fight her way through to consciousness. She plunged deeply into the terrible vastness that roared about her ears.

And almost in awful mockery the bells burst into sound, ushering out the old, heralding the new: for Hannah, only a long, grey twelve month of pain-filled, soul-starved days.

As the last, loud note died away, Tillie burst into the room, followed by George and her husband, voluble in noisy badinage. Instantly she saw the prostrate figure of Hannah and uttered a piercing shriek of terror.

"Oh, my God! Jim!" she cried, and cowered fearfully against the wall, peering through the lattice of her fingers.

George, too, stood quite still, an half empty bottle clutched in his hand, his eyes bulging grotesquely, his mouth falling open, his lips ashen. Instinctively although the knife lay hidden in the folds of her dress, he felt that she was dead. Her every prophetic, fevered word leaped to his suddenly sharpened brain. He wanted to run away and hide. It wasn't fair of Hannah to be lying there mockingly dead. His mind raced ahead to the dreadful details of inquest and burial, and a great resentment welled in his heart. He began to hate the woman he thought lay dead.

Doctor Hill, puffing a little, bent expertly over Hannah. His eye caught the gleam of steel. Surreptitiously he pocketed the knife and sighed. He was a kindly, fat, little bald man with an exhaustless fund of sympathy. Immediately he had understood. That was the way with morbid, self-centered women like Hannah.

He raised himself. "Poor girl, she's fainted. Help me with her, you all."

When they had laid her on the couch, the gay, frayed, red couch with the ugly rent in the centre Hannah's nerve-tipped fingers had torn, Jim sent them into the kitchen.

"I want to talk to her alone. She'll come around in a minute."

He stood above her, looking down at her with incurious pity. The great black circles under her eyes enhanced the sad dark beauty of her face. He knew suddenly, with a tinge of pain, how different would have been her life, how wide the avenues of achievement, how eager the acclaiming crowd, how soft her bed of ease, had this gloriously golden woman been born white. But there was little bitterness in his thoughts. He did not resignedly accept the black man's unequal struggle, but he philosophically foresaw the eventual crashing down of all unjust barriers.

Hannah stirred, moaned a little, opened her eyes, in a quick flash of realization stifled a cry with her hand fiercely pressed to her lips. Doctor Hill bent over her, and suddenly she began to laugh, ending it dreadfully in a sob.

"Hello, Jim," she said. "I'm not dead, am I? I wanted so badly to die."

Weakly she tried to rise, but he forced her down with a gentle hand. "Lie quiet, Hannah," he said.

Obediently she lay back on the cushion, and he sat beside her, letting her hot hand grip his own. She smiled, a wistful, tragic, little smile.

"I had planned it all so nicely, Jim. George was to stumble upon my dead body—his own knife buried in my throat—and grovel beside me in fear and self-reproach. And Tillie, of course, would begin extolling my virtues, while you—Now it's all spoilt!"

He released her hand and patted it gently. He got to his feet. "You must never do this again, Hannah."

She shook her head like a wilful child. "I shan't promise."

His near-sighted, kindly eyes bored into hers. "There is a reason why you must, my dear."

For a long moment she stared questioningly at him, and the words of refutation that leaped to her lips died of despairing certainty at the answer in his eyes.

She rose, swaying, and steadied herself by her feverish grip on his arms. "No," she wailed, "no! no! no!!"

He put an arm about her. "Steady, dear."

She jerked herself free, and flung herself on the couch, burying her stricken face in her hands.

"Jim, I can't! I can't! Don't you see how it is with me?"

He told her seriously, "You must be very careful, Hannah."

Her eyes were tearless, wild. "But, Jim, you know—You've watched me. Jim! I hate my husband. I can't breathe when he's near. He—stifles me. I can't go through with it. I can't! Oh, why couldn't I have died?"

He took both her hands in his and sat beside her, waiting until his quiet presence should soothe her. Finally she gave a great, quivering sigh and was still.

"Listen, Hannah," he began, "you are nervous and distraught. After all, a natural state for a woman of your temperament. But you do not want to die. You want to live. Because you must, my dear. There is a life within you demanding birth. If you seek your life again, your child dies, too. I am quite sure you could not be a murderer.

"You must listen very closely and remember all I say. For with this new year—a new beginning, Hannah—you must see things clearly and rationally, and build your strength against your hour of delivery."

Slowly she raised her eyes to his. She shook her head dumbly. "There's no way out. My hands are tied. Life itself has beaten me."

"Hannah?"

"No. I understand, Jim. I see."

"Right," he said, rising cheerfully. "Just you think it all over." He crossed to the door and called, "George! Tillie! You all can come in now."

They entered timorously, and Doctor Hill smiled reassuringly at them. He took his wife's hand and led her to the outer door.

"Out with you and me, my dear. We'll drink the health of the new year downstairs. Mrs. Byde has something very important to say to Mr. Byde. Night, G. B. Be very gentle with Hannah."

George shut the door behind them and went to Hannah. He stood before her, embarrassed, mumbling inaudibly.

"There's going to be a child," she said dully.

She paled before the instant gleam in his eyes.

"You're—glad?"

There was a swell of passion in his voice. "Hannah!" He caught her up in his arms.

"Don't," she cried, her hands a shield against him, "you're—stifling me."

He pressed his mouth to hers and awkwardly released her.

She brushed her hands across her lips. "You've been drinking. I can't bear it."

He was humble. "Just to steady myself. In the kitchen. Me and Tillie."

She was suddenly almost sorry for him. "It's all right, George. It doesn't matter. It's—nothing."

Timidly he put his hand on her shoulder. "You're shivering. Lemme get you a shawl."

"No." She fought against hysteria. "I'm all right, George. It's only that I'm tired . . . tired." She went unsteadily to her bedroom door, and her groping hand closed on the knob. "You—you'll sleep on the couch tonight? I—I just want to be alone. Good night, George. I shall be all right. Good night."

He stood alone, at a loss, his hands going out to the closed door in clumsy sympathy. He thought: I'll play a piece while she's gettin' undressed. A little jazz'll do her good.

He crossed to the phonograph, his shoes squeaking fearfully. There was something pathetic in his awkward attempt to walk lightly. He started the record where Hannah had cut it short, grinning delightedly as it began to whir.

The jazz notes burst on the air, filled the narrow room, crowded out.

And the woman behind the closed door flung herself across the bed and laughed and laughed and laughed.

17 MUTTSY

Zora Neale Hurston

From *Opportunity*, August 1926

The piano in Ma Turner's back parlor stuttered and wailed. The pianist kept time with his heel and informed an imaginary deserter that "she might leave and go to Halimufack, but his slow-drag would bring her back," mournfully with a memory of tom-toms running rhythm through the plaint.

Fewclothes burst through the portieres, a brown chrysalis from a dingy red cocoon, and touched the player on the shoulder.

"Say, Muttsy," he stage whispered, "Ma's got a new lil' biddy in there—just come. And say—her foot would make all of dese Harlem babies a Sunday face."

"Whut she look like?" Muttsy drawled, trying to maintain his characteristic pose of indifference to the female.

"Brown skin, patent leather grass on her knob, kinder tallish. She's a lil' skinny," he added apologetically, "but ah'm willing to buy corn for that lil' chicken."

Muttsy lifted his six feet from the piano bench as slowly as his curiosity would let him and sauntered to the portieres for a peep.

The sight was as pleasing as Fewclothes had stated—only more so. He went on in the room which Ma always kept empty. It was her receiving room—her "front."

From Ma's manner it was evident that she was very glad to see the girl. She could see that the girl was not overjoyed in her presence, but attributed that to southern greenness.

"Who you say sentcher heah, dearie?" Ma asked, her face trying to beam, but looking harder and more forbidding.

"Uh-a-a man down at the boat landing where I got off—North River. I jus' come in on the boat."

Ma's husband from his corner spoke up.

"Musta been Bluefront."

"Yeah, musta been him," Muttsy agreed.

"Oh, it's all right, honey, we New Yorkers likes to know who we'se takin' in, dearie. We has to be keerful. Whut did you say yo' name was?"

"Pinkie, yes, mam, Pinkie Jones."

Ma stared hard at the little old battered reticule that the girl carried for luggage—not many clothes if that was all—she reflected. But Pinkie had everything she needed in her face—many, many trunks full. Several of them for Ma. She noticed the cold-reddened knuckles of her bare hands too.

"Come on upstairs to yo' room—thass all right 'bout the price—we'll come to some 'greement tomorrow. Jes' go up and take off yo' things."

Pinkie put back the little rusty leather purse of another generation and followed Ma. She didn't like Ma—her smile resembled the smile of the Wolf in Red Riding Hood. Anyway back in Eatonville, Florida, "ladies," especially old ones, didn't put powder and paint on the face.

"Forty-dollars-Kate sure landed a pippin' dis time," said Muttsy, sotto voce, to Fewclothes back at the piano. "If she ain't, then there ain't a hound dawk in Georgy. Ah'm goin' home an' dress."

No one else in the crowded back parlor let alone the house knew of Pinkie's coming. They danced on, played on, sang their "blues" and lived on hotly their intense lives. The two men who had seen her—no one counted ole man Turner—went on playing too, but kept an ear cocked for her coming.

She followed Ma downstairs and seated herself in the parlor with the old man. He sat in a big rocker before a copper-lined gas stove, indolence in every gesture.

"Ah'm Ma's husband," he announced by way of making conversation.

"Now you jus' shut up!" Ma commanded severely. "You gointer git yo' teeth knocked down yo' throat yit for runnin' yo' tongue. Lemme talk to dis gal—dis is *mah* house. You sets on the stool un do nothin' too much tuh have anything tuh talk over!"

"Oh, Lawd," groaned the old man feeling a knee that always pained him at the mention of work. "Oh, Lawd, will you sen' yo' fiery chariot an' take me 'way from heah?"

"Aw shet up!" the woman spit out. "Lawd don't wantcher—devil wouldn't have yuh." She peered into the girl's face and leaned back satisfied.

"Well, girlie, you kin be a lotta help tuh me 'round dis house if you takes un intrus' in things—oh Lawd!" She leaped up from her seat. "That's mah bread ah smell burnin! . . ."

No sooner had Ma's feet cleared the room than the old man came to life again. He peered furtively after the broad back of his wife.

"Know who she is," he asked Pinkie in an awed whisper. She shook her head. "You don't? Dat's Forty-dollars-Kate!"

"Forty-dollars-Kate?" Pinkie repeated open eyed. "Naw, I don't know nothin' 'bout her."

"Sh-h," cautioned the old man. "Course you don't. I fuhgits you ain't nothin' tall but a young 'un. Twenty-five years ago they all called her dat 'cause she *wuz* 'Forty-dollars-Kate.' She sho' wuz some p'utty 'oman—great big robus' lookin' gal. Men wuz glad 'nough to spend forty dollars on her if dey had it. She didn't lose no time wid dem dat didn't have it."

He grinned ingratiatingly at Pinkie and leaned nearer.

"But you'se better lookin' than she ever wuz, you might—taint no tellin' whut you might do ef you git some sense. I'm a gointer teach you, hear?"

"Yessuh," the girl managed to answer with an almost paralyzed tongue.

"Thass a good girl. You jus' lissen to me an' you'll pull thew alright."

He glanced at the girl sitting timidly upon the edge of the chair and scolded.

"Don't set dataway," he ejaculated. "Yo' back bone ain't no ram rod. Kinda scooch down on the for'ard edge uh de chear lak dis." (He demonstrated by "scooching" forward so far that he was almost sitting on his shoulder-blades.) The girl slumped a trifle.

"Is you got a job yit?"

"Nawsuh," she answered slowly, "but I reckon I'll have one soon. Ain't been in town a day yet."

"You looks kinda young—kinda little biddy. Is you been to school much?"

"Yessuh, went thew eight reader. I'm goin' again when I get a chance."

"Dat so? Well ah reckon ah kin talk some Latin tuh yuh den." He cleared his throat loudly. "Whut's you entitlum?"

"I don't know," said the girl in confusion.

"Well, den, whut's you entrimmins," he queried with a bit of braggadocio in his voice.

"I don't know," from the girl, after a long awkward pause.

"You chillun don't learn nothin' in school dese days. Is you got to 'goes into' yit?"

"You mean long division?"

"Ain't askin' 'bout de longness of it, dat don't make no difference," he retorted. "Sence you goin' stay heah ah'll edgecate yuh—do yuh know how to eat a fish— uh nice brown fried fish?"

"Yessuh," she answered quickly, looking about for the fish.

"How?"

"Why, you jus' eat it with corn bread," she said, a bit disappointed at the non-appearance of the fish.

"Well, ah'll tell yuh," he patronized. "You starts at de tail and liffs de meat off de bones sorter gentle and eats him clear tuh de head on dat side; den you turn 'im ovah an' commence at de tail agin and eat right up tuh de head; den you push *dem* bones way tuh one side an' takes another fish an' so on 'till de end— well, 'till der ain't no mo'!"

He mentally digested the fish and went on. "See," he pointed accusingly at her feet, "you don't even know how tuh warm yoself! You settin' dere wid yo' feet ev'y which a way. Dat ain't de way tuh git wahm. Now look at *mah* feet. Dass right put bofe big toes right togethah—now shove 'em close up tuh de fiah; now lean back so! Dass de way. Ah knows uh heap uh things tuh teach yuh sense you gointer live heah—ah learns all of 'em while de ole lady is paddlin' roun' out dere in de yard."

Ma appeared at the door and the old man withdrew so far into his rags that he all but disappeared. They went to supper where there was fried fish but forgot all rules for eating it and just ate heartily. She helped with the dishes and returned to the parlor. A little later some more men and women knocked and were admitted after the same furtive peering out through the nearest crack of the door. Ma carried them all back to the kitchen and Pinkie heard the clink of glasses and much loud laughter.

Women came in by ones and twos, some in shabby coats turned up about the ears, and with various cheap but showy hats crushed down over unkempt hair. More men, more women, more trips to the kitchen with loud laughter.

Pinkie grew uneasy. Both men and women stared at her. She kept strictly to her place. Ma came in and tried to make her join the others.

"Come on in, honey, a lil' toddy ain't gointer hurt nobody. Evebody knows *me*, ah wouldn't touch a hair on yo' head. Come on in, dearie, all th' men wants tuh meetcher."

Pinkie smelt the liquor on Ma's breath and felt contaminated at her touch. She wished herself back home again even with the ill treatment and squalor. She thought of the three dollars she had secreted in her shoe—she had been warned against pickpockets—and flight but where? Nowhere. For there was no home to which *she* could return, nor any place else she knew of. But when she got a job, she'd scrape herself clear of people who took toddies.

A very black man sat on the piano stool playing as only a Negro can with hands, stamping with his feet and the rest of his body keeping time.

> "Ahm gointer make me a graveyard of mah own
> Ahm gointer make me a graveyard of mah own
> Carried me down on de Smoky Road"—

Pinkie, weary of Ma's maudlin coaxing, caught these lines as she was being pulled and coaxed into the kitchen. Everyone in there was shaking shimmies to music, rolling eyes heavenward as they picked imaginary grapes out of the air, or drinking. "Folkes," shouted Ma. "Look a heah! Shut up dis racket! Ah wantcher tuh meet Pinkie Jones. She's de bes' frien' ah got." Ma flopped into a chair and began to cry into her whiskey glass.

"Mah comperments!" The men almost shouted. The women were less, much less enthusiastic.

"Dass de las' run uh shad," laughed a woman called Ada, pointing to Pinkie's slenderness.

"Jes' lak a bar uh soap aftah uh hard week's wash," Bertha chimed in and laughed uproariously. The men didn't help.

"Oh, Miss Pinkie," said Bluefront, removing his Stetson for the first time. "Ma'am, also Ma'am, ef you wuz tuh see me settin' straddle of uh Mud-cat leadin' a minner whut ud you think?"

"I-er, oh, I don't know, suh. I didn't know you-er anybody could ride uh fish."

"Stick uh roun' me, baby, an' you'll wear diamon's." Bluefront swaggered. "Look heah, lil' Pigmeat, youse *some* sharp! If you didn't had but one eye ah'd think you wuz a needle—thass how sharp you looks to me. Say, mah right foot is itchin'. Do dat mean ah'm gointer walk on some strange ground wid you?"

"Naw, indeedy," cut in Fewclothes. "It jes' means you feet needs to walk in some strange water—wid a lil' red seal lye thowed in."

But he was not to have a monopoly. Fewclothes and Shorty joined the chase and poor Pinkie found it impossible to retreat to her place beside the old man. She hung her head, embarrassed that she did not understand their mode of speech; she felt the unfriendly eyes of the women, and she loathed the smell of liquor that filled the house now. The piano still rumbled and wailed that same song—

> "Carried me down on de Smoky Road
> Brought me back on de coolin' board
> Ahm gointer make me a graveyard of mah own."

A surge of cold, fresh air from the outside stirred the smoke and liquor fumes and Pinkie knew that the front door was open. She turned her eyes that way and thought of flight to the clean outside. The door stood wide open and a tall figure in an overcoat with a fur collar stood there.

"Good Gawd, Muttsy! Shet 'at do," cried Shorty. "Dass a pure razor blowing out dere tonight. Ah didn't know you wuz outa here nohow."

> "Carried me down on de Smoky Road
> Brought me back on de coolin' board
> Ahm gointer make me a graveyard of mah own,"

sang Muttsy, looking as if he sought someone and banged the door shut on the last words. He strode on in without removing hat or coat.

Pinkie saw in this short space that all the men deferred to him, that all the women sought his notice. She tried timidly to squeeze between two of the men and return to the quiet place beside old man Turner, thinking that Muttsy would hold the attention of her captors until she had escaped. But Muttsy spied her through the men about her and joined them. By this time her exasperation and embarrassment had her on the point of tears.

"Well, whadda yuh know about dis!" he exclaimed, "A real lil' pullet."

"Look out dere, Muttsy," drawled Dramsleg with objection, catching Pinkie by the arm and trying to draw her toward him. "Lemme tell dis lil' Pink Mama how crazy ah is 'bout her mahself. Ah ain't got no lady atall an'—"

"Aw, shut up, Drams," Muttsy said sternly, "put yo' pocketbook where yo' mouf is, an' somebody will lissen. Ah'm a heavy-sugar papa. Ah eats fried chicken when the rest of you niggers is drinking rain water."

He thrust some of the others aside and stood squarely before her. With her downcast eyes, she saw his well polished shoes, creased trousers, gloved hands and at last timidly raised her eyes to his face.

"Look a heah!" he frowned, "you roughnecks done got dis baby ready tuh cry."

He put his forefinger under her chin and made her look at him. And for some reason he removed his hat.

"Come on in the sittin' room an' le's talk. Come on befo' some uh dese niggers sprinkle some salt on yuh and eat yuh clean up lak uh radish." Dramsleg looked after Muttsy and the girl as they swam through the smoke into the front room. He beckoned to Bluefront.

"Hey, Bluefront! Ain't you mah fren'?"

"Yep," answered Bluefront.

"Well, then why caint you help me? Muttsy done done me dirt wid the lil' pig-meat—throw a louse on 'im."

Pinkie's hair was slipping down. She felt it, but her selfconsciousness prevented her catching it and down it fell in a heavy roll that spread out and covered her nearly to the waist. She followed Muttsy into the front room and again sat shrinking in the corner. She did not wish to talk to Muttsy nor anyone else in that house, but there were fewer people in this room.

"Phew!" cried Bluefront, "dat baby sho got some righteous moss on her keg—dass reg'lar 'nearrow mah Gawd tuh thee' stuff." He made a lengthy gesture with his arms as if combing out long, silky hair.

"Shux," sneered Ada in a moist, alcoholic voice. "Dat ain't nothin' mah haih useter be so's ah could set on it."

There was general laughter from the men.

"Yas, ah know it's de truth!" shouted Shorty. "It's jes' ez close tuh yo' head *now* ez ninety-nine is tuh uh hund'ed."

"Ah'll call Muttsy tuh you," Ada threatened.

"Oh, 'oman, Muttsy ain't got you tuh study 'bout no mo' cause he's parkin' his heart wid dat lil' chicken wid white-folks' haih. Why, dat lil' chicken's foot would make you a Sunday face."

General laughter again. Ada dashed the whiskey glass upon the floor with the determined stalk of an angry tiger and arose and started forward.

"Muttsy Owens, uh nobody else ain't to gointer make no fool outer *me*. Dat lil' kack girl ain't gointer put *me* on de bricks—not much."

Perhaps Muttsy heard her, perhaps he saw her out of the corner of his eye and read her mood. But knowing the woman as he did he might have known what she would do under such circumstances. At any rate he got to his feet as she entered the room where he sat with Pinkie.

"Ah know you ain't lost yo' head sho' 'nuff, 'oman. 'Deed, Gawd knows you bettah go 'way f'um me." He said this in a low, steady voice. The music stopped, the talking stopped and even the drinkers paused. Nothing happened, for Ada looked straight into Muttsy's eyes and went on outside.

"Miss Pinkie, Ah votes you g'wan tuh bed," Muttsy said suddenly to the girl.

"Yes-suh."

"An' don't you worry 'bout no job. Ah knows where you kin git a good one. Ah'll go see 'em first an' tell yuh tomorrow night."

She went off to bed upstairs. The rich baritone of the pianoplayer came up to her as did laughter and shouting. But she was tired and slept soundly.

Ma shuffled in after eight the next morning. "Darlin', ain't you got 'nuff sleep yit?"

Pinkie opened her eyes a trifle. "Ain't you the puttiest lil' trick! An' Muttsy done gone crazy 'bout yuh! Chile, he's lousy wid money an' diamon's an' every-thing— Yuh better grab him quick. Some folks has all de luck. Heah ah is—got uh man dat hates work lak de devil hates holy water. Ah gotta make dis house pay!"

Pinkie's eyes opened wide. "What does Mr. Muttsy do?"

"Mah Gawd, chile! He's de bes' gambler in three states, cards, craps un hawses. He could be a boss stevedore if he so wanted. The big boss down on de dock would give him a fat job—just begs him to take it cause he can manage the men. He's the biggest hero they got since Harry Wills left the waterfront. But he won't take it cause he makes so much wid the games."

"He's awful good-lookin," Pinkie agreed, "an' he been mighty nice tuh me— but I like men to work. I wish he would. Gamblin' ain't nice."

"Yeah, 'tis, ef you makes money lak Muttsy. Maybe yo' ain't noticed dat diamon' set in his tooth. He picks women up when he wants tuh an' puts 'em down when he choose."

Pinkie turned her face to the wall and shuddered. Ma paid no attention.

"You doan hafta git up till you git good an' ready, Muttsy says. Ah mean you kin stay roun' the house 'till you come to, sorter."

Another day passed. Its darkness woke up the land east of Lenox—all that land between the railroad tracks and the river. It was very ugly by day, and night kindly hid some of its sordid homeliness. Yes, nighttime gave it life.

The same women, or others just like them, came to Ma Turner's. The same men, or men just like them, came also and treated them to liquor or mistreated them with fists or cruel jibes. Ma got half drunk as usual and cried over every-one who would let her.

Muttsy came alone and went straight to Pinkie where she sat trying to shrink into the wall. She had feared that he would not come.

"Howdy do, Miss Pinkie."

"How'do do, Mistah Owens," she actually achieved a smile. "Did you see bout m'job?"

"Well, yeah—but the lady says she won't needya fuh uh week yet. Doan' worry, Ma ain't gointer push yuh foh room rent. Mah wrist ain't got no cramps."

Pinkie half sobbed: "Ah wantsa job now!"

"Didn't ah say dass alright? Well, Muttsy doan lie. Shux! Ah might jes' es well tell yuh—ahm crazy 'bout yuh—money no objeck."

It was the girl herself who first mentioned "bed" this night. He suffered her to go without protest.

The next night she did not come into the sitting room. She went to bed as soon as the dinner things had been cleared. Ma begged and cried, but Pinkie pretended illness and kept to her bed. This she repeated the next night and the next. Every night Muttsy came and every night he added to his sartorial splendor; but each night he went away, disappointed, more evidently crestfallen than before.

But the insistence for escape from her strange surroundings grew on the girl. When Ma was busy elsewhere, she would take out the three one dollar bills from her shoe and reconsider her limitations. If that job would only come on! She felt shut in, imprisoned, walled in with these women who talked of nothing but men and the numbers and drink, and men who talked of nothing but the numbers and drink and women. And desperation took her.

One night she was still waiting for the job—Ma's alcoholic tears prevailed. Pinkie took a drink. She drank the stuff mixed with sugar and water and crept to bed even as the dizziness came on. She would not wake tonight. Tomorrow, maybe, the job would come and freedom.

The piano thumped but Pinkie did not hear; the shouts, laughter and cries did not reach her that night. Downstairs Muttsy pushed Ma into a corner.

"Looky heah, Ma. Dat girl done played me long enough. Ah pays her room rent, ah pays her boahd an' all ah gets is uh hunk of ice. Now you said you wuz gointer fix things—you tole me so las' night an' heah she done gone tuh bed on me agin."

"Deed, ah caint do nothin' wid huh. She's thinkin' sho' nuff you goin' git her uh job and she fret so cause tain't come, dat she drunk uh toddy un hits knocked her down jes lak uh log."

"Ada an' all uh them laffin—they say ah done crapped." He felt injured. "Caint ah go talk to her?"

"Lawdy, Muttsy, dat gal dead drunk an' sleepin' lak she's buried."

"Well, caint ah go up an'—an' speak tuh her jus' the same." A yellow backed bill from Muttsy's roll found itself in Ma's hand and put her in such good humor that she let old man Turner talk all he wanted for the rest of the night.

"Yas, Muttsy, gwan in. Youse *mah* frien'."

Muttsy hurried up to the room indicated. He felt shaky inside there with Pinkie, somehow, but he approached the bed and stood for a while looking down upon her. Her hair in confusion about her face and swinging off the bedside; the brown arms revealed and the soft lips. He blew out the match he had struck and kissed her full in the mouth, kissed her several times and passed his hand over her neck and throat and then hungrily down upon her breast. But here he drew back.

"Naw," he said sternly to himself, "ah ain't goin' ter play her wid no loaded dice." Then quickly he covered her with the blanket to her chin, kissed her again upon the lips and tipped down into the darkness of the vestibule.

"Ah reckon ah bettah git married." He soliloquized. "B'lieve me, ah will, an' go uptown wid dicties."

He lit a cigar and stood there on the steps puffing and thinking for some time. His name was called inside the sitting room several times but he pretended not to hear. At last he stole back into the room where slept the girl who unwittingly and unwillingly was making him do queer things. He tipped up to the bed again and knelt there holding her hands so fiercely that she groaned without waking. He watched her and he wanted her so that he wished to crush her in his love; crush and crush and hurt her against himself, but somehow he resisted the impulse and merely kissed her lips again, kissed her hands back and front, removed the largest diamond ring from his hand and slipped it on her engagement finger. It was much too large so he closed her hand and tucked it securely beneath the covers.

"She's *mine!*" he said triumphantly. "All mine!"

He switched off the light and softly closed the door as he went out again to the steps. He had gone up to the bed room from the sitting room boldly, caring not who knew that Muttsy Owens took what he wanted. He was stealing forth afraid that someone might *suspect* that he had been there. There is no secret love in those barrens; it is a thing to be approached boisterously and without delay or dalliance. One loves when one wills, and ceases when it palls. There is nothing sacred or hidden—all subject to coarse jokes. So Muttsy re-entered the sitting room from the steps as if he had been into the street.

"Where you been, Muttsy?" whined Ada with an awkward attempt at coyness.

"What *you* wanta know for?" he asked roughly.

"Now, Muttsy, you know you ain't treatin' me right, honey. How come you runnin' de hawg ovah me lak you do?"

"Git outa mah face, 'oman. Keep yo' han's offa me." He clapped on his hat and strode from the house.

Pinkie awoke with a gripping stomach and thumping head.

Ma bustled in. "How yuh feelin', darlin'? Youse jes lak a lil' doll baby."

"I got a headache, terrible from that ole whiskey. Thass mah first und las' drink long as I live." She felt the ring.

"Whut's this?" she asked and drew her hand out to the light.

"Dat's Muttsy' ring. Ah seen him wid it fuh two years. How'd y'all make out? He sho is one thur'bred."

"Muttsy? When? I didn't see no Muttsy."

"Dearie, you doan' hafta tell yo' bizniss ef you doan wanta. Ahm a hush-mouf. Thass all right, keep yo' bizniss to yo' self." Ma bleared her eyes wisely. "But ah know Muttsy wuz up heah tuh see yuh las' night. Doan' mine *me*, honey, gwan wid 'im. He'll treat yuh right. Ah *knows* he's crazy 'bout yuh. An' all de women is crazy 'bout *him*. Lawd! lookit dat ring!" Ma regarded it greedily for a long time, but she turned and walked toward the door at last. "Git up darlin'. Ah got fried chicking fuh breckfus' un mush melon."

She went on to the kitchen. Ma's revelation sunk deeper, then there was the ring. Pinkie hurled the ring across the room and leaped out of bed.

"He ain't goin' to make *me* none of his women—I'll die first! I'm goin' outa this house if I starve, lemme starve!"

She got up and plunged her face into the cold water on the washstand in the corner and hurled herself into the shabby clothes, thrust the three dollars which she had never had occasion to spend, under the pillow where Ma would be sure to find them and slipped noiselessly out of the house and fled down Fifth Avenue toward the Park that marked the beginning of the Barrens. She did not know where she was going, and cared little so long as she removed herself as far as possible from the house where the great evil threatened her.

At ten o'clock that same morning, Muttsy Owens, dressed his flashiest best, drove up to Ma's door in a cab, the most luxurious that could be hired. He had gone so far as to stick two one hundred dollar notes to the inside of the windshield. Ma was overcome.

"Muttsy, dearie, what you doin' heah so soon? Pinkie sho has got you goin'. Un in a swell cab too—gee!"

"Ahm gointer git mah'ried tuh de doll baby, thass how come. An' ahm gointer treat her white too."

"Umhumh! Thass how come de ring! You oughtn't never fuhgit me, Muttsy, fuh puttin' y'all together. But ah never thought you'd mah'ry *nobody*—you allus said you wouldn't."

"An' ah wouldn't neither ef ah hadn't of seen *her*. Where she is?"

"In de room dressin'. She never tole me nothin' 'bout dis."

"She doan' know. She wuz sleep when ah made up mah mind an' slipped on de ring. But ah never miss no girl ah wants, you knows me."

"Everybody in this man's town knows you gets whut you wants."

"Naw, ah come tuh take her to brek'fus 'fo we goes tuh de cote-house."

"An' y'all stay heah and eat wid me. You go call her whilst ah set de grub on table."

Muttsy, with a lordly stride, went up to Pinkie's door and rapped and waited and rapped and waited three times. Growing impatient or thinking her still asleep, he flung open the door and entered.

The first thing that struck him was the empty bed; the next was the glitter of his diamond ring upon the floor. He stumbled out to Ma. She was gone, no doubt of that.

"She looked awful funny when ah tole her you wuz in heah, but ah thought she wuz puttin' on airs," Ma declared finally.

"She thinks ah played her wid a marked deck, but ah didn't. Ef ah could see her she'd love me. Ah know she would. 'Cause ah'd make her," Muttsy lamented.

"I don't know, Muttsy. She ain't no New Yorker, and she thinks gamblin' is awful."

"Zat all she got against me? Ah'll fix that up in a minute. You help me find her and ah'll do anything she says jus' so she marries me." He laughed ruefully. "Looks like ah crapped this time, don't it, Ma?"

The next day Muttsy was foreman of two hundred stevedores. How he did make them work. But oh how cheerfully they did their best for him. The company begrudged not one cent of his pay. He searched diligently, paid money to other searchers, went every night to Ma's to see if by chance the girl had returned or if any clues had turned up.

Two weeks passed this way. Black empty days for Muttsy.

Then he found her. He was coming home from work. When crossing Seventh Avenue at 135th Street they almost collided. He seized her and began pleading before she even had time to recognize him.

He turned and followed her; took the employment office slip from her hand and destroyed it, took her arm and held it. He must have been very convincing for at 125th Street they entered a taxi that headed uptown again. Muttsy was smiling amiably upon the whole round world.

A month later, as Muttsy stood on the dock hustling his men to greater endeavor, Bluefront flashed past with his truck. "Say, Muttsy, you don't know what you missin' since you quit de game. Ah cleaned out de whole bunch las' night." He flashed a roll and laughed. "It don't seem like a month ago you wuz king uh de bones in Harlem." He vanished down the gangplank into the ship's hold.

As he raced back up the gangplank with his loaded truck Muttsy answered him. "And now, I'm King of the Boneheads—which being interpreted means stevedores. Come on over behind dis crate wid yo' roll. Mah wrist ain't got no cramp 'cause ah'm married. You'se gettin' too sassy."

"Thought you wuzn't gointer shoot no mo'!" Bluefront temporized.

"Aw Hell! Come on back heah," he said impatiently. "Ah'll shoot you any way you wants to—hard or soft roll—you'se trying to stall. You know ah don't crap neither. Come on, mah Pinkie needs a fur coat and you stevedores is got to buy it."

He was on his knees with Bluefront. There was a quick movement of Muttsy's wrist, and the cubes flew out on a piece of burlap spread for the purpose—a perfect seven.

"Hot dog!" he exulted. "Look at dem babies gallop!" His wrist quivered again. "Nine for point!" he gloated. "Hah!" There was another quick shake and nine turned up again. "Shove in, Bluefront, shove in dat roll, dese babies is crying fuh it."

Bluefront laid down two dollars grudgingly. "You said you wuzn't gointer roll no mo' dice after you got married," he grumbled.

But Muttsy had tasted blood. His flexible wrist was already in the midst of the next play.

"Come on, Bluefront, stop bellyachin'. Ah shoots huy for de roll!" He reached for his own pocket and laid down a roll of yellow bills beside Bluefront's. His hand quivered and the cubes skipped out again. "Nine!" He snapped his fingers like a trap-drum and gathered in the money.

"Doxology, Bluefront. Git back in de line wid yo' truck an' send de others roun' heah one by one. What man can't keep one lil' wife an' two lil' bones? Hurry 'em up, Blue!"

18 THE EATONVILLE ANTHOLOGY

Zora Neale Hurston

From *Messenger*, September–November 1926

I
THE PLEADING WOMAN

Mrs. Tony Roberts is the pleading woman. She just loves to ask for things. Her husband gives her all he can rake and scrape, which is considerably more than most wives get for their housekeeping, but she goes from door to door begging for things.

She starts at the store. "Mist' Clarke," she sing-songs in a high keening voice, "gimme lil' piece uh meat tuh boil a pot uh greens wid. Lawd knows me an' mah chillen is SO hongry! Hits uh SHAME! Tony don't fee-ee-eee-ed me!"

Mr. Clarke knows that she has money and that her larder is well stocked, for Tony Roberts is the best provider on his list. But her keening annoys him and he arises heavily. The pleader at this shows all the joy of a starving man being seated at a feast.

"Thass right Mist' Clarke. De Lawd loveth de cheerful giver. Gimme jes' a lil' piece 'bout dis big (indicating the width of her hand) an' de Lawd'll bless yuh."

She follows this angel-on-earth to his meat tub and superintends the cutting, crying out in pain when he refuses to move the knife over just a teeny bit mo'.

Finally, meat in hand, she departs, remarking on the meanness of some people who give a piece of salt meat only two-fingers wide when they were plainly asked for a hand-wide piece. Clarke puts it down to Tony's account and resumes his reading.

With the slab of salt pork as a foundation, she visits various homes until she has collected all she wants for the day. At the Piersons, for instance: "Sister Pierson, plee-ee-ease gimme uh han'ful uh collard greens fuh me an' mah po' chillen! 'Deed, me an' mah chillen is SO hongry. Tony doan' fee-ee-eed me!"

Mrs. Pierson picks a bunch of greens for her, but she springs away from them as if they were poison. "Lawd a mussy, Mis' Pierson, you ain't gonna gimme dat lil' eye-full uh greens fuh me an' mah chillen, is you? Don't be so graspin'; Gawd won't bless yuh. Gimme uh han'full mo'. Lawd, some folks is got everything, an' theys jes' as gripin' an stingy!"

Mrs. Pierson raises the ante, and the pleading woman moves on to the next place, and on and on. The next day, it commences all over.

II
TURPENTINE LOVE

Jim Merchant is always in good humor—even with his wife. He says he fell in love with her at first sight. That was some years ago. She has had all her teeth pulled out, but they still get along splendidly.

He says the first time he called on her he found out that she was subject to fits. This didn't cool his love, however. She had several in his presence.

One Sunday, while he was there, she had one, and her mother tried to give her a dose of turpentine to stop it. Accidentally, she spilled it in her eye and it cured her. She never had another fit, so they got married and have kept each other in good humor ever since.

III

Becky Moore has eleven children of assorted colors and sizes. She has never been married, but that is not her fault. She has never stopped any of the fathers of her children from proposing, so if she has no father for her children it's not her fault. The men round about are entirely to blame.

The other mothers of the town are afraid that it is catching. They won't let their children play with hers.

IV
TIPPY

Sykes Jones' family all shoot craps. The most interesting member of the family—also fond of bones, but of another kind—is Tippy, the Jones' dog.

He is so thin, that it amazes one that he lives at all. He sneaks into village kitchens if the housewives are careless about the doors and steals meats, even off the stoves. He also sucks eggs.

For these offenses he has been sentenced to death dozens of times, and the sentences executed upon him, only they didn't work. He has been fed bluestone, strychnine, nux vomica, even an entire Peruna bottle beaten up. It didn't fatten him, but it didn't kill him. So Eatonville has resigned itself to the plague of Tippy, reflecting that it has erred in certain matters and is being chastened.

In spite of all the attempts upon his life, Tippy is still willing to be friendly with anyone who will let him.

V

THE WAY OF A MAN WITH A TRAIN

Old Man Anderson lived seven or eight miles out in the country from Eatonville. Over by Lake Apopka. He raised feed-corn and cassava and went to market with it two or three times a year. He bought all of his victuals wholesale so he wouldn't have to come to town for several months more.

He was different from us citybred folks. He had never seen a train. Everybody laughed at him, for even the smallest child in Eatonville had either been to Maitland or Orlando and watched a train go by. On Sunday afternoons all of the young people of the village would go over to Maitland, a mile away, to see Number 35 whizz southward on its way to Tampa and wave at the passengers. So we looked down on him a little. Even we children felt superior in the presence of a person so lacking in worldly knowledge.

The grown-ups kept telling him he ought to go see a train. He always said he didn't have time to wait so long. Only two trains a day passed through Maitland. But patronage and ridicule finally had its effect and Old Man Anderson drove in one morning early. Number 78 went north to Jacksonville at 10:20. He drove his light wagon over in the woods beside the railroad below Maitland, and sat down to wait. He began to fear that his horse would get frightened and run away with the wagon. So he took him out and led him deeper into the grove and tied him securely. Then he returned to his wagon and waited some more. Then he remembered that some of the train-wise villagers had said the engine belched fire and smoke. He had better move his wagon out of danger. It might catch afire. He climbed down from the seat and placed himself between the shafts to draw it away. Just then 78 came thundering over the trestle spouting smoke, and suddenly began blowing for Maitland. Old Man Anderson became so frightened he ran away with the wagon through the woods and tore it up worse than the horse ever could have done. He doesn't know yet what a train looks like, and says he doesn't care.

VI
COON TAYLOR

Coon Taylor never did any real stealing. Of course, if he saw a chicken or a watermelon or muskmelon or anything like that that he wanted he'd take it. The people used to get mad but they never could catch him. He took so many melons from Joe Clarke that he set up in the melon patch one night with his shotgun loaded with rock salt. He was going to fix Coon. But he was tired. It is hard work being a mayor, postmaster, storekeeper and everything. He dropped asleep sitting on a stump in the middle of the patch. So he didn't see Coon when he came. Coon didn't see him either, that is, not at first. He knew the stump was there, however. He had opened many of Clarke's juicy Florida Favorite on it. He selected his fruit, walked over to the stump and burst the melon on it. That is, he thought it was the stump until it fell over with a yell. Then he knew it was no stump and departed hastily from those parts. He had cleared the fence when Clarke came to, as it were. So the charge of rock-salt was wasted on the desert air.

During the sugar-cane season, he found he couldn't resist Clarke's soft green cane, but Clarke did not go to sleep this time. So after he had cut six or eight stalks by the moonlight, Clarke rose up out of the cane strippings with his shot-gun and made Coon sit right down and chew up the last one of them on the spot. And the next day he made Coon leave his town for three months.

VII
VILLAGE FICTION

Joe Lindsay is said by Lum Boger to be the largest manufacturer of prevarications in Eatonville; Brazzle (late owner of the world's leanest and meanest mule) contends that his business is the largest in the state and his wife holds that he is the biggest liar in the world.

Exhibit A—He claims that while he was in Orlando one day he saw a doctor cut open a woman, remove everything—liver, lights and heart included—clean each of them separately; the doctor then washed out the empty woman, dried her out neatly with a towel and replaced the organs so expertly that she was up and about her work in a couple of weeks.

VIII

Sewell is a man who lives all to himself. He moves a great deal. So often, that 'Lige Moseley says his chickens are so used to moving that every time he comes out into his backyard the chickens lie down and cross their legs, ready to be tied up again.

He is baldheaded; but he says he doesn't mind that, because he wants as little as possible between him and God.

IX

Mrs. Clarke is Joe Clarke's wife. She is a soft-looking, middle-aged woman, whose bust and stomach are always holding a get-together.

She waits on the store sometimes and cries every time he yells at her, which he does every time she makes a mistake, which is quite often. She calls her husband "Jody." They say he used to beat her in the store when he was a young man, but he is not so impatient now. He can wait until he goes home.

She shouts in Church every Sunday and shakes the hand of fellowship with everybody in the Church with her eyes closed, but somehow always misses her husband.

X

Mrs. McDuffy goes to Church every Sunday and always shouts and tells her "determination." Her husband always sits in the back row and beats her as soon as they get home. He says there's no sense in her shouting, as big a devil as she is. She just does it to slur him. Elijah Moseley asked her why she didn't stop shouting, seeing she always got a beating about it. She says she can't "squinch the sperrit." Then Elijah asked Mr. McDuffy to stop beating her, seeing that she was going to shout anyway. He answered that she just did it for spite and that his fist was just as hard as her head. He could last just as long as she. So the village let the matter rest.

XI
DOUBLE-SHUFFLE

Back in the good old days before the World War, things were very simple in Eatonville. People didn't fox-trot. When the town wanted to put on its Sunday clothes and wash behind the ears, it put on a "breakdown." The daring younger set would two-step and waltz, but the good church members and the elders stuck to the grand march. By rural canons dancing is wicked, but one is not held to have danced until the feet have been crossed. Feet don't get crossed when one grand marches.

At elaborate affairs the organ from the Methodist church was moved up to the hall and Lizzimore, the blind man, presided. When informal gatherings were held, he merely played his guitar assisted by any volunteer with mouth organs or accordions.

Among white people the march is as mild as if it had been passed on by Volstead. But it still has a kick in Eatonville. Everybody happy, shining eyes, gleaming teeth. Feet dragged 'shhlap, shhlap! to beat out the time. No orchestra needed. Round and round! Back again, parse-me-la! shlap! shlap! Strut! Strut! Seaboard! Shlap! Shlap! Tiddy bumm! Mr. Clarke in the lead with Mrs. Mosely.

It's too much for some of the young folks. Double shuffling commences. Buck and wing. Lizzimore about to break his guitar. Accordion doing contortions. People fall back against the walls, and let the soloist have it, shouting as they clap the old, old double shuffle songs.

> "Me an' mah honey got two mo' days
> Two mo' days tuh do de buck"

Sweating bodies, laughing mouths, grotesque faces, feet drumming fiercely. Deacons clapping as hard as the rest.

> "Great big nigger, black as tar
> Trying tuh git tuh hebben on uh 'lectric car."

> "Some love cabbage, some love kale
> But I love a gal wid a short skirt tail."

> Long tall angel—steppin' down,
> Long white robe an' starry crown.

'Ah would not marry uh black gal (bumm bumm!)
Tell yuh de reason why
Every time she comb her hair
She make de goo-goo eye.

Would not marry a yaller gal (bumm bumm!)
Tell yuh de reason why
Her neck so long an' stringy
Ahm 'fraid she'd never die.

Would not marry uh preacher
Tell yuh de reason why
Every time he comes tuh town
He makes de chicken fly.

When the buck dance was over, the boys would give the floor to the girls and they would parse-me-la with a slye eye out of the corner to see if anybody was looking who might "have them up in church" on conference night. Then there would be more dancing. Then Mr. Clarke would call for everybody's best attention and announce that *'freshments was served! Every gent'man would please take his lady by the arm and scorch her right up to de table fur a treat!*

Then the men would stick their arms out with a flourish and ask their ladies: "You lak chicken? Well, then, take a wing." And the ladies would take the proffered "wings" and parade up to the long table and be served. Of course most of them had brought baskets in which were heaps of jointed and fried chicken, two or three kinds of pies, cakes, potato pone and chicken purlo. The hall would separate into happy groups about the baskets until time for more dancing.

But the boys and girls got scattered about during the war, and now they dance the fox-trot by a brand new piano. They do waltz and two-step still, but no one now considers it good form to lock his chin over his partner's shoulder and stick out behind. One night just for fun and to humor the old folks, they danced, that is, they grand marched, but everyone picked up their feet. *Bah!!*

XII
THE HEAD OF THE NAIL

Daisy Taylor was the town vamp. Not that she was pretty. But sirens were all but non-existent in the town. Perhaps she was forced to it by circumstances. She was quite dark, with little brushy patches of hair squatting over her head. These were held down by shingle-nails often. No one knows whether she did this for artistic effect or for lack of hair-pins, but there they were shining in the little patches of hair when she got all dressed for the afternoon and came up to Clarke's store to see if there was any mail for her.

It was seldom that anyone wrote to Daisy, but she knew that the men of the town would be assembled there by five o'clock, and some one could usually be induced to buy her some soda water or peanuts.

Daisy flirted with married men. There were only two single men in town. Lum Boger, who was engaged to the assistant school-teacher, and Hiram Lester, who had been off to school at Tuskegee and wouldn't look at a person like Daisy. In addition to other drawbacks, she was pigeon-toed and her petticoat was always showing so perhaps he was justified. There was nothing else to do except flirt with married men.

This went on for a long time. First one wife then another complained of her, or drove her from the preserves by threat.

But the affair with Crooms was the most prolonged and serious. He was even known to have bought her a pair of shoes.

Mrs. Laura Crooms was a meek little woman who took all of her troubles crying, and talked a great deal of leaving things in the hands of God.

The affair came to a head one night in orange picking time. Crooms was over at Oneido picking oranges. Many fruit pickers move from one town to the other during the season.

The *town* was collected at the store-postoffice as is customary on Saturday nights. The *town* has had its bath and with its week's pay in pocket fares forth to be merry. The men tell stories and treat the ladies to soda water, peanuts and peppermint candy.

Daisy was trying to get treats, but the porch was cold to her that night.

"Ah don't keer if you don't treat me. What's a dirty lil' nickel?" She flung this at Walter Thomas. "The ever-loving Mister Crooms will gimme anything atall Ah wants."

"You better shet up yo' mouf talking 'bout Albert Crooms. Heah his wife comes right now."

Daisy went akimbo. "Who? Me! Ah don't keer whut Laura Crooms think. If she ain't a heavy hip-ted Mama enough to keep him, she don't need to come crying to me."

She stood making goo-goo eyes as Mrs. Crooms walked upon the porch. Daisy laughed loud, made several references to Albert Crooms, and when she saw the mail-bag come in from Maitland she said, "Ah better go in an' see if Ah ain't got a letter from Oneido."

The more Daisy played the game of getting Mrs. Crooms' goat, the better she liked it. She ran in and out of the store laughing until she could scarcely stand. Some of the people present began to talk to Mrs. Crooms—to egg her on to halt Daisy's boasting, but she was for leaving it all in the hands of God. Walter Thomas kept on after Mrs. Crooms until she stiffened and resolved to fight. Daisy was inside when she came to this resolve and never dreamed anything of the kind could happen. She had gotten hold of an envelope and came laughing and shouting, "Oh, Ah can't stand to see Oneido lose!"

There was a box of ax-handles on display on the porch, propped up against the door jamb. As Daisy stepped upon the porch, Mrs. Crooms leaned the heavy end of one of those handles heavily upon her head. She staggered from the porch to the ground and the timid Laura, fearful of a counter-attack, struck again and Daisy toppled into the town ditch. There was not enough water in there to do more than muss her up. Every time she tried to rise, down would come that ax-handle again. Laura was fighting a scared fight. With Daisy thoroughly licked, she retired to the store porch and left her fallen enemy in the ditch. None of the men helped Daisy—even to get out of the ditch. But Elijah Moseley, who was some distance down the street when the trouble began, arrived as the victor was withdrawing. He rushed up and picked Daisy out of the mud and began feeling her head.

"Is she hurt much?" Joe Clarke asked from the doorway.

"I don't know," Elijah answered. "I was just looking to see if Laura had been lucky enough to hit one of those nails on the head and drive it in."

Before a week was up, Daisy moved to Orlando. There in a wider sphere, perhaps, her talents as a vamp were appreciated.

XIII
PANTS AND CAL'LINE

Sister Cal'line Potts was a silent woman. Did all of her laughing down inside, but did the thing that kept the town in an uproar of laughter. It was the general opinion of the village that Cal'line would do anything she had a mind to. And she had a mind to do several things.

Mitchell Potts, her husband, had a weakness for women. No one ever believed that she was jealous. She did things to the women, surely. But most any townsman would have said that she did them because she liked the novel situation and the queer things she could bring out of it.

Once he took up with Delphine—called Mis' Pheeny by the town. She lived on the outskirts on the edge of the piney woods. The town winked and talked. People don't make secrets of such things in villages. Cal'line went about her business with her thin black lips pursed tight as ever, and her shiny black eyes unchanged.

"Dat devil of a Cal'line's got somethin' up her sleeve!" The town smiled in anticipation.

"Delphine is too big a cigar for her to smoke. She ain't crazy," said some as the weeks went on and nothing happened. Even Pheeny herself would give an extra flirt to her over-starched petticoats as she rustled into church past her of Sundays.

Mitch Potts said furthermore, that he was tired of Cal'line's foolishness. She had to stay where he put her. His African soup-bone (arm) was too strong to let a woman run over him. 'Nough was 'nough. And he did some fancy cussing, and he was the fanciest cusser in the county.

So the town waited and the longer it waited, the odds changed slowly from the wife to the husband.

One Saturday, Mitch knocked off work at two o'clock and went over to Maitland. He came back with a rectangular box under his arm and kept straight on out to the barn and put it away. He ducked around the corner of the house quickly, but even so, his wife glimpsed the package. Very much like a shoe-box. So!

He put on the kettle and took a bath. She stood in her bare feet at the ironing board and kept on ironing. He dressed. It was about five o'clock but still very light. He fiddled around outside. She kept on with her ironing. As soon as the sun got red, he sauntered out to the barn, got the parcel and walked away down the road, past the store and out into the piney woods. As soon as he left the house, Cal'line slipped on her shoes without taking time to don stockings, put on one of her husband's old Stetsons, worn and floppy, slung the axe over her shoulder and followed in his wake. He was hailed cheerily as he passed the sitters on the store porch and answered smiling sheepishly and passed on. Two minutes later passed his wife, silently, unsmilingly, and set the porch to giggling and betting.

An hour passed perhaps. It was dark. Clarke had long ago lighted the swinging kerosene lamp inside.

Once 'way back yonder before the stars fell all the animals used to talk just like people. In them days dogs and rabbits was the best of friends—even tho both of them was stuck on the same gal—which was Miss Nancy Coon. She had the sweetest smile and the prettiest striped and bushy tail to be found anywhere.

They both run their legs nigh off trying to win her for themselves—fetching nice ripe persimmons and such. But she never give one or the other no satisfaction.

Finally one night Mr. Dog popped the question right out. "Miss Coon," he says, "Ma'am, also Ma'am which would you ruther be—a lark flyin' or a dove a settin'?"

Course Miss Nancy she blushed and laughed a little and hid her face behind her bushy tail for a spell. Then she said sorter shy like, "I does love yo' sweet voice, brother dawg—but—but I ain't jes' exactly set in my mind yit."

Her and Mr. Dog set on a spell, when up comes hopping Mr. Rabbit wid his tail fresh washed and his whiskers shining. He got right down to business and asked Miss Coon to marry him, too.

"Oh, Miss Nancy," he says, "Ma'am, also Ma'am, if you'd see me settin' straddle of a mud-cat leadin' a minnow, what would you think? Ma'am also Ma'am?" Which is a out and out proposal as everybody knows.

"Youse awful nice, Brother Rabbit, and a beautiful dancer, but you cannot sing like Brother Dog. Both you uns come back next week to gimme time for to decide."

They both left arm-in-arm. Finally Mr. Rabbit says to Mr. Dog, "Taint no use in me going back—she ain't gwinter have me. So I mought as well give up. She loves singing, and I ain't got nothing but a squeak."

"Oh, don't talk that a' way," says Mr. Dog, tho' he is glad that Mr. Rabbit can't sing none.

"Thass all right, Brer Dog. But if I had a sweet voice like you got, I'd have it worked on and make it sweeter."

"How! How! How!" Mr. Dog cried, jumping up and down.

"Lemme fix it for you, like I do for Sister Lark and Sister Mocking-bird."

"When? Where?" asked Mr. Dog, all excited. He was figuring that if he could sing just a little better Miss Coon would be bound to have him.

"Just you meet me t'morrer in de huckleberry patch," says the rabbit and off they both goes to bed.

The dog is there on time next day and after a while the rabbit comes loping up.

"Mawnin', Brer Dawg," he says kinder chippy like. "Ready to git yo' voice sweetened?"

"Sholy, sholy, Brer Rabbit. Let's we all hurry about it. I wants tuh serenade Miss Nancy from de piney woods tuh night."

"Well, den, open yo' mouf and poke out yo' tongue," says the rabbit.

No sooner did Mr. Dog poke out his tongue than Mr. Rabbit split it with a knife and ran for all he was worth to a hollow stump and hid hisself.

The dog has been mad at the rabbit ever since.

Anybody who don't believe it happened, just look at the dog's tongue and he can see for himself where the rabbit slit it right up the middle.

Stepped on a tin, mah story ends.

19 CORDELIA THE CRUDE

Wallace Thurman

FROM *FIRE!!*, NOVEMBER 1926

Physically, if not mentally, Cordelia was a potential prostitute, meaning that although she had not yet realized the moral import of her wanton promiscuity nor become mercenary, she had, nevertheless, become quite blasé and bountiful in the matter of bestowing sexual favors upon persuasive and likely young men. Yet, despite her seeming lack of discrimination, Cordelia was quite particular about the type of male to whom she submitted, for numbers do not necessarily denote a lack of taste, and Cordelia had discovered after several months of active observation that one could find the qualities one admires or reacts positively to in a varied hodge-podge of outwardly different individuals.

The scene of Cordelia's activities was The Roosevelt Motion Picture Theatre on Seventh Avenue near 145th Street. Thrice weekly the program changed, and thrice weekly Cordelia would plunk down the necessary twenty-five cents evening admission fee, and saunter gaily into the foul-smelling depths of her favorite cinema shrine. The Roosevelt Theatre presented all of the latest pictures, also, twice weekly, treated its audiences to a vaudeville bill, then too, one could always have the most delightful physical contacts . . . hmm. . . .

Cordelia had not consciously chosen this locale nor had there been any conscious effort upon her part to take advantage of the extra opportunities afforded for physical pleasure. It had just happened that The Roosevelt Theatre was more close to her home than any other neighborhood picture palace, and it had also just happened that Cordelia had become almost immediately initiated into the ways of a Harlem theatre chippie soon after her discovery of the theatre itself.

It is the custom of certain men and boys who frequent these places to idle up and down the aisle until some female is seen sitting alone, to slouch down into a seat beside her, to touch her foot or else press her leg in such a way that it can be construed as accidental if necessary, and then, if the female is wise or else shows signs of willingness to become wise, to make more obvious approaches until, if successful, the approached female will soon be chatting with her baiter about the picture being shown, lolling in his arms, and helping to formulate plans for an after-theatre rendezvous. Cordelia had, you see, shown a willingness to become wise upon her second visit to The Roosevelt. In a short while she had even learned how to squelch the bloated, lewd faced Jews and eager middle aged Negroes who might approach as well as how to inveigle the likeable little yellow or brown half men, embryo avenue sweetbacks, with their well modeled heads, stickily plastered hair, flaming cravats, silken or broadcloth shirts, dirty underwear, low cut vests, form fitting coats, bell-bottom trousers and shiny shoes with metal cornered heels clicking with a brave, brazen rhythm upon the bare concrete floor as their owners angled and searched for prey.

Cordelia, sixteen years old, matronly mature, was an undisciplined, half literate product of rustic South Carolina, and had come to Harlem very much against her will with her parents and her six brothers and sisters. Against her will because she had not been at all anxious to leave the lackadaisical life of the little corn pone settlement where she had been born, to go trooping into the unknown vastness of New York, for she had been in love, passionately in love with one John Stokes who raised pigs, and who, like his father before him, found the raising of pigs so profitable that he could not even consider leaving Lintonville. Cordelia had blankly informed her parents that she would not go with them when they decided to be lured to New York by an older son who had remained there after the demobilization of the war time troops. She had even threatened to run away with John until they should be gone, but of course John could not leave his pigs, and John's mother was not very keen on having Cordelia for a daughter-in-law—those Joneses have bad mixed blood in 'em—so Cordelia had had to join the Gotham bound caravan and leave her lover to his succulent porkers.

However, the mere moving to Harlem had not doused the rebellious flame. Upon arriving Cordelia had not only refused to go to school and refused to hold even the most easily held job, but had also victoriously defied her harassed parents so frequently when it came to matters of discipline that she soon found herself with a mesmerizing lack of home restraint, for the stress of trying to maintain themselves and their family in the new environment was far too much of a task for Mr. and Mrs. Jones to attend to facilely and at the same time try to control a recalcitrant child. So, when Cordelia had refused either to work or to attend school, Mrs. Jones herself had gone out for day's work, leaving Cordelia at home to take care of their five room railroad flat, the front room of which was rented out to a couple "living together," and to see that the younger children, all of whom were school age, made their four trips daily between home and the nearby public school—as well as see that they had their greasy, if slim, food rations and an occasional change of clothing. Thus Cordelia's days were full— and so were her nights. The only difference being that the days belonged to the folks at home while the nights (since the folks were too tired or too sleepy to know or care when she came in or went out) belonged to her and to—well—whosoever will, let them come.

Cordelia had been playing this hectic, entrancing game for six months and was widely known among a certain group of young men and girls on the avenue as a fus' class chippie when she and I happened to enter the theatre simultaneously. She had clumped down the aisle before me, her open galoshes swishing noisily, her two arms busy wriggling themselves free from the torn sleeve lining of a shoddy imitation fur coat that one of her mother's wash clients had sent to her. She was of medium height and build, with overly developed legs and bust, and had a clear, keen light brown complexion. Her too slick, too naturally bobbed hair, mussed by the removing of a tight, black turban was of an undecided nature, i.e., it was undecided whether to be kinky or to be kind, and her body, as she sauntered along in the partial light, had such a conscious sway of invitation that unthinkingly I followed, slid into the same row of seats and sat down beside her.

Naturally she had noticed my pursuit, and thinking that I was eager to play the game, let me know immediately that she was wise, and not the least bit averse to spooning with me during the evening's performance. Interested, and, I might as well confess, intrigued physically, I too became wise, and played up to her with all the fervor, or so I thought, of an old timer, but Cordelia soon remarked that I was different from mos' of des' sheiks, and when pressed for an explanation brazenly told me in a slightly scandalized and patronizing tone that I had not even felt her legs . . . !

At one o'clock in the morning we strolled through the snowy bleakness of one hundred and forty-fourth street between Lenox and Fifth Avenues to the walk-up tenement flat in which she lived, and after stamping the snow from our feet, pushed through the double outside doors, and followed the dismal hallway to the rear of the building where we began the tedious climbing of the crooked, creaking, inconveniently narrow stairway. Cordelia had informed me earlier in the evening that she lived on the top floor—four flights up east side rear—and on our way we rested at each floor and at each half way landing, rested long enough to mingle the snowy dampness of our respective coats, and to hug clumsily while our lips met in an animal kiss.

Finally only another half flight remained, and instead of proceeding as was usual after our amorous demonstration I abruptly drew away from her, opened my overcoat, plunged my hand into my pants pocket, and drew out two crumpled one dollar bills which I handed to her, and then, while she stared at me foolishly, I muttered good-night, confusedly pecked her on her cold brown cheek, and darted down into the creaking darkness.

Six months later I was taking two friends of mine, lately from the provinces, to a Saturday night house-rent party in a well known whore house on one hundred and thirty-fourth street near Lenox Avenue. The place as we entered seemed to be a chaotic riot of raucous noise and clashing color all rhythmically merging in the red, smoke filled room. And there I saw Cordelia savagely careening in a drunken abortion of the Charleston and surrounded by a perspiring circle of handclapping enthusiasts. Finally fatigued, she whirled into an abrupt finish, and stopped so that she stared directly into my face, but being dizzy from the calisthenic turns and the cauterizing liquor she doubted that her eyes recognized someone out of the past, and, visibly trying to sober herself, languidly began to dance a slow drag with a lean hipped pimply faced yellow man who had walked between her and me. At last he released her, and seeing that she was about to leave the room I rushed forward calling Cordelia?—as if I was not yet sure who it was. Stopping in the doorway, she turned to see who had called, and finally recognizing me said simply, without the least trace of emotion,—'Lo kid. . . .

And without another word turned her back and walked into the hall to where she joined four girls standing there. Still eager to speak, I followed and heard one of the girls ask: Who's the dicty kid? . . .

And Cordelia answered: The guy who gimme ma' firs' two bucks. . . .

20 SMOKE, LILIES AND JADE

Richard Bruce Nugent

FROM *FIRE!!*, NOVEMBER 1926

He wanted to do something . . . to write or draw . . . or something . . . but it was so comfortable just to lie there on the bed . . . his shoes off . . . and think . . . think of everything . . . short disconnected thoughts . . . to wonder . . . to remember . . . to think and smoke . . . why wasn't he worried that he had no money . . . he *had* had five cents . . . but he had been hungry . . . he *was* hungry and still . . . all he wanted to do was . . . lie there comfortably smoking . . . think . . . wishing he were writing . . . or drawing . . . or something . . . something about the things he felt and thought . . . but what did he think . . . he remembered how his mother had awakened him one night . . . ages ago . . . six years ago . . . Alex . . . he had always wondered at the strangeness of it . . . she had seemed so . . . so . . . so just the same . . . Alex . . . I think your father is dead . . . and it hadn't seemed so strange . . . yet . . . one's mother didn't say that . . . didn't wake one at midnight every night to say . . . feel him . . . put your hand on his head . . . then whisper with a catch in her voice . . . I'm afraid . . . ssh don't wake Lam . . . yet it hadn't seemed as it should have seemed . . . even when he had felt his father's cool wet forehead . . . it hadn't been tragic . . . the light had been turned very low . . . and flickered . . . yet it hadn't been tragic . . . or weird . . . not at all as one should feel when one's father died . . . even his reply of . . . yes he is dead . . . had been commonplace . . . hadn't been dramatic . . . there had been no tears . . . no sobs . . . not even a sorrow . . . and yet he must have realized that one's father couldn't smile . . . or sing anymore . . . after he had died . . . everyone remembered his father's voice . . . it had been a lush voice . . . a promise . . . then that dressing together . . . his mother and himself . . . in the bathroom . . . why was the bathroom always the warmest room in the winter . . . as they had put on their clothes . . . his mother had been telling him what he must do . . . and cried softly . . . and that had made him cry too but you mustn't cry Alex . . . remember you have to be a little man now . . . and that was all . . . didn't other wives and sons cry more for their dead than that . . . anyway people never cried for beautiful sunsets . . . or music . . . and those were the things that hurt . . . the things to sympathize with . . . then out into the snow and dark of the morning . . . first to the undertaker's . . . no first to Uncle Frank's . . . why did Aunt Lula have to act like that . . . to ask again and again . . . but when did he die . . . when did he die . . . I just can't believe it . . . poor Minerva . . . then out into the snow and dark again . . . how had his mother expected him to know where to find the night bell at the undertaker's . . . he was the most sensible of them all though . . . all he had said was . . . what . . . Harry Francis . . . too bad . . . tell mamma I'll be there first thing in the morning . . . then down the deserted streets again . . . to grandmother's . . . it was growing light now . . . it must be terrible to die in daylight . . . grandpa had been sweeping the snow off the yard . . . he had been glad of that because . . . well he could tell him better than grandma . . . grandpa . . . father's dead . . . and he hadn't acted strange either . . . books lied . . . he had just looked at Alex a moment then continued sweeping . . . all he said was . . . what time did he die . . . she'll want to know . . . then passing through the lonesome street toward home . . . Mrs. Mamie Grant was closing a window and spied him . . . hallow Alex . . . an' how's your father this mornin' . . . dead . . . get out . . . tch tch tch an' I was just around there with a cup a' custard yesterday . . . Alex puffed contentedly on his cigarette . . . he was hungry and comfortable . . . and he had an ivory holder inlaid with red jade and green . . . funny how the smoke seemed to climb up that ray of sunlight . . . went up the slant just like imagination . . . was imagination blue . . . or was it because he had spent his last five cents and couldn't worry . . . anyway it was nice to lie there and wonder . . . and remember . . . why was he so different from other people . . . the only things he remembered of his father's funeral were the crowded church and the ride in the hack . . . so many people there in the church . . . and ladies with tears in their eyes . . . and on their cheeks . . . and some men too . . . why did people cry . . . vanity that was all . . . yet they weren't exactly hypocrites . . . but why . . . it had made him furious . . . all these people crying . . . it wasn't *their* father . . . and he wasn't crying . . . couldn't cry for sorrow although he had loved his father more than . . . than . . . it had made him so angry that tears had come to his eyes . . . and he had been ashamed of his mother . . . crying into a hand-kerchief . . . so ashamed that tears had run down his cheeks and he had frowned . . . and someone . . . a woman . . . had said . . . look at that poor little dear . . . Alex is just like his father . . . and the tears had run fast . . . because he *wasn't* like his father . . . he couldn't sing . . . he didn't want to sing . . . he didn't want to sing . . . Alex blew a cloud of smoke . . . blue smoke . . . when they had taken his father from the vault three weeks later . . . he had grown beautiful . . . his nose had become perfect and clear . . . his hair had turned jet black and glossy and silky . . . and his skin was a transparent green . . . like the sea only not so deep . . . and where it was drawn over the cheek bones a pale beautiful red appeared . . . like a blush . . . why hadn't his father looked like that always . . . but no . . . to have sung would have broken the wondrous repose of his lips and maybe that was his beauty . . . maybe it was wrong to think thoughts like these . . . but they were nice and pleasant and comfortable . . . when one was smoking a cigarette through an ivory holder . . . inlaid with red jade and green . . . .

he wondered why he couldn't find work . . . a job . . . when he had first come to New York he had . . . and he had only been fourteen then . . . was it because he was nineteen now that he felt so idle . . . and contented . . . or because he was an artist . . . but was he an artist . . . was one an artist until one became known . . . of course he was an artist . . . and strangely enough so were all his friends . . . he should be ashamed that he didn't work . . . but . . . was it five years in New York . . . or the fact that he was an artist . . . when his mother said she couldn't understand him . . . why did he vaguely pity her instead of being ashamed . . . he should be . . . his mother and all his relatives said so . . . his brother was three years younger than he and yet he had already been away from home a year . . . on the stage . . . making thirty-five dollars a week . . . had three suits and many clothes and was going to help mother . . . while he . . . Alex . . . was content to lay and smoke and meet friends at night . . . to argue and read Wilde . . . Freud . . . Boccaccio and Schnitzler . . . to attend Gurdjieff meetings and know things . . . Why did they scoff at him for knowing such people as Carl . . . Mencken . . . Toomer . . . Hughes . . . Cullen . . . Wood . . . Cabell . . . oh the whole lot of them . . . was it because it seemed incongruous that he . . . who was so little known . . . should call by first names people they would like to know . . . were they jealous . . . no mothers aren't jealous of their sons . . . they are proud of them . . . why then . . . when these friends accepted and liked him . . . no matter how he dressed . . . why did mother ask . . . and you went looking like that . . . Langston was a fine fellow . . . he knew there was something in Alex . . . and so did Rene and Borgia . . . and Zora and Clement and Miguel . . . and . . . and . . . and all of them . . . if he went to see mother she would ask . . . how do you feel Alex with nothing in your pockets . . . I don't see how you can be satisfied . . . Really you're a mystery to me . . . and who you take after . . . I'm sure I don't know . . . none of my brothers were lazy and shiftless . . . I can never remember the time when they weren't sending money home and when your father was your age he was supporting a family . . . where you get your nerve I don't know . . . just because you've tried to write one or two little poems and stories that no one understands . . . you seem to think the world owes you a living . . . you should see by now how much is thought of them . . . you can't sell anything . . . and you won't do anything to make money . . . wake up Alex . . . I don't know what will become of you . . . .

it was hard to believe in one's self after that . . . did Wilde's parents or Shelley's or Goya's talk to them like that . . . but it was depressing to think in that vein . . . Alex stretched and yawned . . . Max had died . . . Margaret had died . . . so had Sonia . . . Cynthia . . . Juan-Jose and Harry . . . all people he had loved . . . loved one by one and together . . . and all had died . . . he never loved a person long before they died . . . in truth he was tragic . . . that was a lovely appellation . . . The Tragic Genius . . . think . . . to go through life known as The Tragic Genius . . . romantic . . . but it was more or less true . . . Alex turned over and blew another cloud of smoke . . . was all life like that . . . smoke . . . blue smoke from an ivory holder . . . he wished he were in New Bedford . . . New Bedford was a nice place . . . snug little houses set complacently behind protecting lawns . . . half-open windows showing prim interiors from behind waving cool curtains . . . inviting . . . like precise courtesans winking from behind lace fans . . . and trees . . . many trees . . . casting lacy patterns of shade on the sun-dipped sidewalks . . . small stores . . . naively proud of their pseudo grandeur . . . banks . . . called institutions for saving . . . all naive . . . that was it . . . New Bedford was naive . . . after the sophistication of New York it would fan one like a refreshing breeze . . . and yet he had returned to New York . . . and sophistication . . . was he sophisticated . . . no because he was seldom bored . . . seldom bored by anything . . . and weren't the sophisticated continually suffering from ennui . . . on the contrary . . . he was amused . . . amused by the artificiality of naiveté and sophistication alike . . . but maybe that in itself was the essence of sophistication or . . . was it cynicism . . . or were the two identical . . . he blew a cloud of smoke . . . it was growing dark now . . . and the smoke no longer had a ladder to climb . . . but soon the moon would rise and then he would clothe the silver moon in blue smoke garments . . . truly smoke was like imagination . . . .

Alex sat up . . . pulled on his shoes and went out . . . it was a beautiful night . . . and so large . . . the dusky blue hung like a curtain in an immense arched doorway . . . fastened with silver tacks . . . to wander in the night was wonderful . . . myriads of inquisitive lights . . . curiously prying into the dark . . . and fading unsatisfied . . . he passed a woman . . . she was not beautiful . . . and he was sad because she did not weep that she would never be beautiful . . . was it Wilde who had said . . . a cigarette is the most perfect pleasure because it leaves one unsatisfied . . . the breeze gave to him a perfume stolen from some wandering lady of the evening . . . it pleased him . . . why was it that men wouldn't use perfumes . . . they should . . . each and every one of them liked perfumes . . . the man who denied that was a liar . . . or a coward . . . but if ever he were to voice that thought . . . express it . . . he would be misunderstood . . . a fine feeling that . . . to be misunderstood . . . it made him feel tragic and great . . . but maybe it would be nicer to be understood . . . but no . . . no great artist is . . . then again neither were fools . . . they were strangely akin these two . . . Alex thought of a sketch he would make . . . a personality sketch of Fania . . . straight classic features tinted proud purple . . . sensuous fine lips . . . gilded for truth . . . eyes . . . half opened and lids colored mysterious green . . . hair black and straight . . . drawn sternly mocking back from the false puritanical forehead . . . maybe he would make Edith too . . . skin a blue . . . infinite like night . . . and eyes . . . slant and gray . . .

very complacent like a cat's . . . Mona Lisa lips . . . red and seductive as . . . as pomegranate juice . . . in truth it was fine to be young and hungry and an artist . . . to blow blue smoke from an ivory holder . . . .

here was the cafeteria . . . it was almost as though it had journeyed to meet him . . . the night was so blue . . . how does blue feel . . . or red or gold or any other color . . . if colors could be heard he could paint most wondrous tunes . . . symphonious . . . think . . . the dulcet clear tone of a blue like night . . . of a red like pomegranate juice . . . like Edith's lips . . . of the fairy tones to be heard in a sunset . . . like rubies shaken in a crystal cup . . . of the symphony of Fania . . . and silver . . . and gold . . . he had heard the sound of gold . . . but they weren't the sounds he wanted to catch . . . no . . . they must be liquid . . . not so staccato but flowing variations of the same caliber . . . there was no one in the cafe as yet . . . he sat and waited . . . that was a clever idea he had had about color music . . . but after all he was a monstrous clever fellow . . . Jurgen had said that . . . funny how characters in books said the things one wanted to say . . . he would like to know Jurgen . . . how does one go about getting an introduction to a fiction character . . . go up to the brown cover of the book and knock gently . . . and say hello . . . then timidly . . . is Duke Jurgen there . . . or . . . no because if one entered the book in the beginning Jurgen would only be a pawnbroker . . . and one didn't enter a book in the center . . . but what foolishness . . . Alex lit a cigarette . . . but Cabell was a master to have written Jurgen . . . and an artist . . . and a poet . . . Alex blew a cloud of smoke . . . a few lines of one of Langston's poems came to describe Jurgen . . . . .

> Somewhat like Ariel
> Somewhat like Puck
> Somewhat like a gutter boy
> Who loves to play in muck.
> Somewhat like Bacchus
> Somewhat like Pan
> And a way with women
> Like a sailor man . . . .

Langston must have known Jurgen . . . suppose Jurgen had met Tonio Kroeger . . . what a vagrant thought . . . Kroeger . . . Kroeger . . . Kroeger . . . why here was Rene . . . Alex had almost gone to sleep . . . Alex blew a cone of smoke as he took Rene's hand . . . it was nice to have friends like Rene . . . so comfortable . . . Rene was speaking . . . Borgia joined them . . . and de Diego Padro . . . their talk veered to . . . James Branch Cabell . . . beautiful . . . marvelous . . . Rene had an enchanting accent . . . said sank for thank and souse for south . . . but they couldn't know Cabell's greatness . . . Alex searched the smoke for expression . . . he . . . he . . . well he has created a fantasy mire . . . that's it . . . from clear rich imagery . . . life and silver sands . . . that's nice . . . and silver sands . . . imagine lilies growing in such a mire . . . when they close at night their gilded underside would protect . . . but that's not it at all . . . his thoughts just carried and mingled like . . . like odors . . . suggested but never definite . . . Rene was leaving . . . they all were leaving . . . Alex sauntered slowly back . . . the houses all looked sleepy . . . funny . . . made him feel like writing poetry . . . and about death too . . . an elevated crashed by overhead scattering all his thoughts with its noise . . . making them spread . . . in circles . . . then larger circles . . . just like a splash in a calm pool . . . what had he been thinking . . . of . . . a poem about death . . . but he no longer felt that urge . . . just walk and think and wonder . . . think and remember and smoke . . . blow smoke that mixed with his thoughts and the night . . . he would like to live in a large white palace . . . to wear a long black cape . . . very full and lined with vermilion . . . to have many cushions and to lie there among them . . . talking to his friends . . . lie there in a yellow silk shirt and black velvet trousers . . . like music-review artists talking and pouring strange liquors from curiously beautiful bottles . . . bottles with long slender necks . . . he climbed the noisy stair of the odorous tenement . . . smelled of fish . . . of stale fried fish and dirty milk bottles . . . he rather liked it . . . he liked the acrid smell of horse manure too . . . strong . . . thoughts . . . yes to lie back among strangely fashioned cushions and sip eastern wines and talk . . . Alex threw himself on the bed . . . removed his shoes . . . stretched and relaxed . . . yes and have music waft softly into the darkened and incensed room . . . he blew a cloud of smoke . . . oh the joy of being an artist and of blowing blue smoke through an ivory holder inlaid with red jade and green . . .

the street was so long and narrow . . . so long and narrow . . . and blue . . . in the distance it reached the stars . . . and if he walked long enough . . . far enough . . . he could reach the stars too . . . the narrow blue was so empty . . . quiet . . . Alex walked music . . . it was nice to walk in the blue after a party . . . Zora had shone again . . . her stories . . . she always shone . . . and Monty was glad . . . everyone was glad when Zora shone . . . he was glad he had gone to Monty's party . . . Monty had a nice place in the village . . . nice lights . . . and friends and wine . . . mother would be scandalized that he could think of going to a party . . . without a copper to his name . . . but then mother had never been to Monty's . . . and mother had never seen the street seem long and narrow and blue . . . Alex walked music . . . the click of his heels kept time with a tune in his mind . . . he glanced into a lighted cafe window . . . inside were people sipping coffee . . . men . . . why did they sit there in the loud light . . . didn't they know that outside the street . . . the narrow blue street met the stars . . . that if they walked long enough . . . far enough . . . Alex walked and the click of his heels sounded . . . and had an echo . . . sound being tossed back and forth . . . back and forth . . . someone was approaching . . . and their echoes mingled . . . and gave the sound of castanets . . . Alex liked the sound of the approaching man's footsteps . . . he walked music also . . . he knew the beauty of the narrow blue . . . Alex knew that by the way their echoes mingled . . . he wished he would speak . . . but strangers don't speak at four o'clock in the morning . . . at least if they did he couldn't imagine what would be said . . . maybe pardon me but are you walking toward the stars . . . yes, sir, and if you walk long enough . . . then may I walk with you . . . I want to reach the stars too . . . perdone me señor tiene usted fósforo . . . Alex was glad he had been addressed in Spanish . . . to have been asked for a match in English . . . or to have been addressed in English at all . . . would have been blasphemy just then . . . Alex handed him a match . . . he glanced at his companion apprehensively in the match glow . . . he was afraid that his appearance would shatter the blue thoughts . . . and stars . . . ah . . . his face was a perfect compliment to his voice . . . and the echo of their steps mingled . . . they walked in silence . . . the casta-nets of their heels clicking accompaniment . . . the stranger inhaled deeply and with a nod of content and a smile . . . blew a cloud of smoke . . . Alex felt like singing . . . the stranger knew the magic of blue smoke also . . . they continued in silence . . . the castanets of their heels clicking rhythmically . . . Alex turned in his doorway . . . up the stairs and the stranger waited for him to light the room . . . no need for words . . . they had always known each other . . . .

as they undressed by the blue dawn . . . Alex knew he had never seen a more perfect being . . . his body was all symmetry and music . . . and Alex called him Beauty . . . long they lay . . . blowing smoke and exchanging thoughts . . . and Alex swallowed with difficulty . . . he felt a glow of tremor . . . and they talked and . . . slept . . .

Alex wondered more and more why he liked Adrian so . . . he liked many people . . . Wallie . . . Zora . . . Clement . . . Gloria . . . Langston . . . John . . . Gwenny . . . oh many people . . . and they were friends . . . but Beauty . . . it was different . . . once Alex had admired Beauty's strength . . . and Beauty's eyes had grown soft and he had said . . . I like you more than anyone Dulce . . . Adrian always called him Dulce . . . and Alex had become confused . . . was it that he was so susceptible to beauty that Alex liked Adrian so much . . . but no . . . he knew other people who were beautiful . . . Fania and Gloria . . . Monty and Bunny . . . but he was never confused before them . . . while Beauty . . . Beauty could make him believe in Buddha . . . or imps . . . and no one else could do that . . . that is no one but Melva . . . but then he was in love with Melva . . . and that explained that . . . he would like Beauty to know Melva . . . they were both so perfect . . . such compliments . . . yes he would like Beauty to know Melva because he loved them both . . . there . . . he had thought it . . . actually dared to think it . . . but Beauty must never know . . . Beauty couldn't understand . . . indeed Alex couldn't understand . . . and it pained him . . . almost physically . . . and tired his mind . . . Beauty . . . Beauty was in the air . . . the smoke . . . Beauty . . . Melva . . . Beauty . . . Melva . . . Alex slept . . . and dreamed . . . . .

he was in a field . . . a field of blue smoke and black poppies and red calla lilies . . . he was searching . . . on his hands and knees . . . searching . . . among black poppies and red calla lilies . . . he was searching and pushed aside poppy stems . . . and saw two strong white legs . . . dancer's legs . . . the contours pleased him . . . his eyes wandered . . . on past the muscular hocks to the firm white thighs . . . the rounded buttocks . . . then the lithe narrow waist . . . strong torso and broad deep chest . . . the heavy shoulders . . . the graceful muscled neck . . . squared chin and quizzical lips . . . Grecian nose with its temperamental nostrils . . . the brown eyes looking at him . . . like . . . Monty looked at Zora . . . his hair curly and black and all tousled . . . and it was Beauty . . . and Beauty smiled and looked at him and smiled . . . said . . . I'll wait Alex . . . and Alex became confused and continued his search . . . on his hands and knees . . . pushing aside poppy stems and lily stems . . . a poppy . . . a black poppy . . . a lily . . . a red lily . . . and when he looked back he could no longer see Beauty . . . Alex continued his search . . . through poppies . . . lilies . . . poppies and red calla lilies . . . and suddenly he saw . . . two small feet olive-ivory . . . two well-turned legs curving gracefully from slender ankles . . . and the contours soothed him . . . he followed them . . . past the narrow rounded hips to the tiny waist . . . the fragile firm breasts . . . the graceful slender throat . . . the soft rounded chin . . . slightly parting lips and straight little nose with its slightly flaring nostrils . . . the black eyes with lights in them . . . looking at him . . . the forehead and straight cut black hair . . . and it was Melva . . . and she looked at him and smiled and said . . . I'll wait Alex . . . and Alex became confused and kissed her . . . became confused and continued his search . . . on his hands and knees . . . pushed aside a poppy stem . . . a black-poppy stem . . . pushed aside a lily stem . . . a red-lily stem . . . a poppy . . . a poppy . . . a lily . . . and suddenly he stood erect . . . exultant . . . and in his hand he held . . . an ivory holder . . . inlaid with red jade . . . and green . . . .

and Alex awoke . . . Beauty's hair tickled his nose . . . Beauty was smiling in his sleep . . . half his face stained flush color by the sun . . . the other half in shadow . . . blue shadow . . . his eyelashes casting cobwebby blue shadows on his cheek . . . his lips were so beautiful . . . quizzical . . . Alex wondered why he always thought of that passage from Wilde's Salome . . . when he looked at Beauty's lips . . . I would kiss your lips . . . he *would* like to kiss Beauty's lips . . . Alex flushed warm . . . with shame . . . or was it shame . . . he reached across Beauty for a cigarette . . . Beauty's cheek felt cool to his arm . . . his hair felt soft . . . Alex lay smoking . . . such a dream . . . red calla lilies . . . red calla lilies . . . and . . . what could it all mean . . . did dreams have meanings . . . Fania said . . . and black poppies . . . thousands . . . millions . . . Beauty stirred . . . Alex put out his cigarette . . . closed his eyes . . . he mustn't see Beauty yet . . . speak to him . . . his lips were too hot . . . dry . . . the palms of his hands too cool and moist . . . through his half-closed eyes he could see Beauty . . . propped . . . cheek in hand . . . on one elbow . . . looking at him . . . lips smiling quizzically . . . he wished Beauty wouldn't look so hard . . . Alex was finding it difficult to breathe . . . breathe normally . . . why *must* Beauty look so long . . . and smile *that* way . . . his face seemed nearer . . . it was . . . Alex could feel Beauty's hair on his forehead . . . breathe normally . . . breathe normally . . . could feel Beauty's breath on his nostrils and lips . . . and it was clean and faintly colored with tobacco . . . breathe normally Alex . . . Beauty's lips were nearer . . . Alex closed his eyes . . . how did one act . . . his pulse was hammering . . . from wrist to finger tip . . . wrist to finger tip . . . Beauty's lips touched his . . . his temples throbbed . . . throbbed . . . his pulse hammered from wrist to finger tip . . . Beauty's breath came short now . . . softly staccato . . . breathe normally Alex . . . you are asleep . . . Beauty's lips touched his . . . breathe normally . . . and pressed . . . pressed hard . . . cool . . . his body trembled . . . breathe normally Alex . . . Beauty's lips pressed cool . . . cool and hard . . . how much pressure does it take to waken one . . . Alex sighed . . . moved softly . . . how does one act . . . Beauty's hair barely touched him now . . . his breath was faint on . . . Alex's nostrils and lips . . . Alex stretched and opened his eyes . . . Beauty was looking at him . . . propped on one elbow . . . cheek in his palm . . . Beauty spoke . . . scratch my head please Dulce . . . Alex was breathing normally now . . . propped against the bed head . . . Beauty's head in his lap . . . Beauty spoke . . . I wonder why I like to look at some things Dulce . . . things like smoke and cats . . . and you . . . Alex's pulse no longer hammered from . . . wrist to finger tip . . . wrist to finger tip . . . the rose dusk had become blue night . . . and soon . . . soon they would go out into the blue. . . . . . .

the little church was crowded . . . warm . . . the rows of benches were brown and sticky . . . Harold was there . . . and Constance and Langston and Bruce and John . . . there was Mr. Robeson . . . how are you Paul . . . a young man was singing . . . Caver . . . Caver was a very self-assured young man . . . such a dream . . . poppies . . . black poppies . . . they were applauding . . . Constance and John were exchanging notes . . . the benches were sticky . . . a young lady was playing the piano . . . fair . . . and red calla lilies . . . who had ever heard of red calla lilies . . . they were applauding . . . a young man was playing the viola . . . what could it all mean . . . so many poppies . . . and Beauty looking at him like . . . like Monty looked at Zora . . . another young man was playing a violin . . . he was the first real artist to perform . . . he had a touch of soul . . . or was it only feeling . . . they were hard to differentiate on the violin . . . and Melva standing in the poppies and lilies . . . Mr. Phillips was singing . . . Mr. Phillips was billed as a basso . . . and he had kissed her . . . they were applauding . . . the first young man was singing again . . . Langston's spiritual . . . Fy-ah-fy-ah-Lawd . . . fy-ah's gonna burn ma soul . . . Beauty's hair was so black and curly . . . they were applauding . . . encore . . . Fy-ah Lawd had been a success . . . Langston bowed . . . Langston had written the words . . . Hall bowed . . . Hall had written the music . . . the young man was singing it again . . . Beauty's lips had pressed hard . . . cool . . . cool . . . fy-ah Lawd . . . his breath had trembled . . . fy-ah's gonna burn ma soul . . . they were

all leaving . . . first to the roof dance . . . fy-ah Lawd . . . there was Catherine . . .
she was beautiful tonight . . . she always was at night . . . Beauty's lips . . . fy-ah
Lawd . . . hello Dot . . . why don't you take a boat that sails . . . when are you leaving again . . . and there's Estelle . . . everyone was there . . . fy-ah Lawd . . . Beauty's
body had pressed close . . . close . . . fy-ah's gonna burn my soul . . . let's leave . . .
have to meet some people at the New World . . . then to Augusta's party . . .
Harold . . . John . . . Bruce . . . Connie . . . Langston . . . ready . . . down one hundred thirty-fifth street . . . fy-ah . . . meet these people and leave . . . fy-ah Lawd
. . . now to Augusta's party . . . fy-ah's gonna burn ma soul . . . they were at
Augusta's . . . Alex half lay . . . half sat on the floor . . . sipping a cocktail . . . such
a dream . . . red calla lilies . . . Alex left . . . down the narrow streets . . . fy-ah . . .
up the long noisy stairs . . . fy-ahs gonna bu'n ma soul . . . his head felt swollen
. . . expanding . . . contracting . . . expanding . . . contracting . . . he had never
been like this before . . . expanding . . . contracting . . . it was that . . . fy-ah . . . fy-
ah Lawd . . . and the cocktails . . . and Beauty . . . he felt two cool strong hands
on his shoulders . . . it was Beauty . . . lie down Dulce . . . Alex lay down . . .
Beauty . . . Alex stopped . . . no no . . . don't say it . . . Beauty mustn't know . . .
Beauty couldn't understand . . . are you going to lie down too Beauty . . . the light
went out expanding . . . contracting . . . he felt the bed sink as Beauty lay beside
him . . . his lips were dry . . . hot . . . the palms of his hands so moist and cool . . .
Alex partly closed his eyes . . . from beneath his lashes he could see Beauty's face
over his . . . nearer . . . nearer . . . Beauty's hair touched his forehead now . . . he
could feel his breath on his nostrils and lips . . . Beauty's breath came short . . .
breathe normally Beauty . . . breathe normally . . . Beauty's lips touched his . . .
pressed hard . . . cool . . . opened slightly . . . Alex opened his eyes . . . into
Beauty's . . . parted his lips . . . Dulce . . . Beauty's breath was hot and short . . .
Alex ran his hand through Beauty's hair . . . Beauty's lips pressed hard against
his teeth . . . Alex trembled . . . could feel Beauty's body . . . close against his . . .
hot . . . tense . . . white . . . and soft . . . soft . . . soft . . . .

they were at Forno's . . . everyone came to Forno's once . . . maybe only once . . . but
they came . . . see that big fat woman Beauty . . . Alex pointed to an overly stout
and bejeweled lady making her way through the maze of chairs . . . that's Maria
Guerrero . . . Beauty looked to see a lady guiding almost the whole opera company to an immense table . . . really Dulce . . . for one who appreciates beauty
you do use the most abominable English . . . Alex lit a cigarette . . . and that florid
man with white hair . . . that's Carl . . . Beauty smiled . . . The Blind Bow-Boy . . .
he asked . . . Alex wondered . . . everything seemed so . . . so just the same . . . here
they were laughing and joking about people . . . there's Rene . . . Rene this is my
friend Adrian . . . after that night . . . and he felt so unembarrassed . . . Rene and
Adrian were talking . . . there was Lucrecia Bori . . . she was bowing at their table
. . . oh her cousin was with them . . . and Peggy Joyce . . . everyone came to

Forno's . . . Alex looked toward the door . . . there was Melva . . . Alex beckoned . . . Melva this is Adrian . . . Beauty held her hand . . . they talked . . . smoked . . . Alex loved Melva . . . in Forno's . . . everyone came there sooner or later . . . maybe only once . . . but . . . .

up . . . up . . . slow . . . jerk up . . . up . . . not fast . . . not glorious . . . but slow . . . up . . . up into the sun . . . slow . . . sure like fate . . . poised on the brim . . . the brim of life . . . two shining rails straight down . . . Melva's head was on his shoulder . . . his arm was around her . . . poised . . . down . . . gasping . . . straight down . . . straight like sin . . . down . . . the curving shiny rail rushed up to meet them . . . hit the bottom then . . . shoot up . . . fast . . . glorious . . . up into the sun . . . Melva gasped . . . Alex's arm tightened . . . all goes up . . . then down . . . straight like hell . . . all breath squeezed out of them . . . Melva's head on his shoulder . . . up . . . up . . . Alex kissed her . . . down . . . they stepped out of the car . . . walking music . . . now over to the Ferris Wheel . . . out and up . . . Melva's hand was soft in his . . . out and up . . . over mortals . . . mortals drinking nectar . . . five cents a glass . . . her cheek was soft on his . . . up . . . up . . . till the world seemed small . . . tiny . . . the ocean seemed tiny and blue . . . up . . . up and out . . . over the sun . . . the tiny red sun . . . Alex kissed her . . . up . . . up . . . their tongues touched . . . up . . . seventh heaven . . . the sea had swallowed the sun . . . up and out . . . her breath was perfumed . . . Alex kissed her . . . drift down . . . soft . . . soft . . . the sun had left the sky flushed . . . drift down . . . soft down . . . back to earth . . . visit the mortals sipping nectar at five cents a glass . . . Melva's lips brushed his . . . then out among the mortals . . . and the sun had left a flush on Melva's cheeks . . . they walked hand in hand . . . and the moon came out . . . they walked in silence on the silver strip . . . and the sea sang for them . . . they walked toward the moon . . . we'll hang our hats on the crook of the moon Melva . . . softly on the silver strip . . . his hands molded her features and her cheeks were soft and warm to his touch . . . where is Adrian . . . Alex . . . Melva trod silver . . . Alex trod sand . . . Alex trod sand . . . the sea *sang* for her . . . Beauty . . . her hand felt cold in his . . . Beauty . . . the sea *dinned* . . . Beauty . . . he led the way to the train . . . and the train dinned. . . Beauty . . . dinned . . . dinned . . . her cheek *had* been soft . . . Beauty . . . Beauty . . . her breath *had* been perfumed . . . Beauty . . . Beauty . . . the sands *had* been silver . . . Beauty . . . Beauty . . . they left the train . . . Melva walked music . . . Melva said . . . don't make me blush again . . . and kissed him . . . Alex stood on the steps after she left him . . . and the night was black . . . down long streets to . . . Alex lit a cigarette . . . and his heels clicked . . . Beauty . . . Melva . . . Beauty . . . Melva . . . and the smoke made the night blue . . .

Melva had said . . . don't make me blush again . . . and kissed him . . . and the street had been blue . . . one *can* love two at the same time . . . Melva had kissed him . . . one *can* . . . and the street had been blue . . . one *can* . . . and the room was clouded with blue smoke . . . drifting vapors of smoke and thoughts . . . Beauty's hair was so black . . . and soft . . . blue smoke from an ivory holder . . . was that why he loved Beauty . . . one *can* . . . or because his body was beautiful . . . and white and warm . . . or because his eyes . . . one *can* love . . . .

. . . To Be Continued . . .

21 WEDDING DAY
Gwendolyn B. Bennett

FROM *FIRE!!*, NOVEMBER 1926

His name was Paul Watson and as he shambled down rue Pigalle he might have been any other Negro of enormous height and size. But as I have said, his name was Paul Watson. Passing him on the street, you might not have known or cared who he was, but any one of the residents about the great Montmartre district of Paris could have told you who he was as well as many interesting bits of his personal history.

He had come to Paris in the days before colored jazz bands were the style. Back home he had been a prize fighter. In the days when Joe Gans was in his glory Paul was following the ring, too. He didn't have that fine way about him that Gans had and for that reason luck seemed to go against him. When he was in the ring he was like a mad bull, especially if his opponent was a white man. In those days there wasn't any sympathy or nicety about the ring and so pretty soon all the ringmasters got down on Paul and he found it pretty hard to get a bout with anyone. Then it was that he worked his way across the Atlantic Ocean on a big liner—in the days before colored jazz bands were the style in Paris.

Things flowed along smoothly for the first few years with Paul's working here and there in the unfrequented places of Paris. On the side he used to give boxing lessons to aspiring youths or gymnastic young women. At that time he was working so steadily that he had little chance to find out what was going on around Paris. Pretty soon, however, he grew to be known among the trainers and managers began to fix up bouts for him. After one or two successful bouts a little fame began to come into being for him. So it was that after one of the prize-fights, a colored fellow came to his dressing room to congratulate him on his success as well as invite him to go to Montmartre to meet "the boys."

Paul had a way about him and seemed to get on with the colored fellows who lived in Montmartre and when the first Negro jazz band played in a tiny Parisian cafe Paul was among them playing the banjo. Those first years were without event so far as Paul was concerned. The members of that first band often say now that they wonder how it was that nothing happened during those first seven years, for it was generally known how great was Paul's hatred for American white people. I suppose the tranquility in the light of what happened afterwards was due to the fact that the cafe in which they worked was one in which mostly French people drank and danced and then too, that was before there were so many Americans visiting Paris. However, everyone had heard Paul speak of his intense hatred of American white folks. It only took two Benedictines to make him start talking about what he would do to the first "Yank" that called him "nigger." But the seven years came to an end and Paul Watson went to work in a larger cafe with a larger band, patronized almost solely by Americans.

I've heard almost every Negro in Montmartre tell about the night that a drunken Kentuckian came into the cafe where Paul was playing and said:

"Look heah, Bruther, what you all doin' ovah heah?"

"None ya bizness. And looka here, I ain't your brother, see?"

"Jack, do you heah that nigger talkin' lak that tah me?"

As he said this, he turned to speak to his companion. I have often wished that I had been there to have seen the thing happen myself. Every tale I have heard about it was different and yet there was something of truth in each of them. Perhaps the nearest one can come to the truth is by saying that Paul beat up about four full-sized white men that night besides doing a great deal of damage to the furniture about the cafe. I couldn't tell you just what did happen. Some of the fellows say that Paul seized the nearest table and mowed down men right and left, others say he took a bottle, then again the story runs that a chair was the instrument of his fury. At any rate, that started Paul Watson on his siege against the American white person who brings his native prejudices into the life of Paris.

It is a verity that Paul was the "black terror." The last syllable of the word, nigger, never passed the lips of a white man without the quick reflex action of Paul's arm and fist to the speaker's jaw. He paid for more glassware and cafe furnishings in the course of the next few years than is easily imaginable. And yet, there was something likable about Paul. Perhaps that's the reason that he stood in so well with the policemen of the neighborhood. Always some divine power seemed to intervene in his behalf and he was excused after the payment of a small fine with advice about his future conduct. Finally, there came the night when in a frenzy he shot the two American sailors.

They had not died from the wounds he had given them hence his sentence had not been one of death but rather a long term of imprisonment. It was a pitiable sight to see Paul sitting in the corner of his cell with his great body hunched almost double. He seldom talked and when he did his words were interspersed with oaths about the lowness of "crackers." Then the World War came.

It seems strange that anything so horrible as that wholesale slaughter could bring about any good and yet there was something of a smoothing quality about even its baseness. There has never been such equality before or since such as that which the World War brought. Rich men fought by the side of paupers; poets swapped yarns with dry-goods salesmen, while Jews and Christians ate corned beef out of the same tin. Along with the general leveling influence came France's pardon of her prisoners in order that they might enter the army. Paul Watson became free and a French soldier. Because he was strong and had innate daring in his heart he was placed in the aerial squad and cited many times for bravery. The close of the war gave him his place in French society as a hero. With only a memory of the war and an ugly scar on his left cheek he took up his old life.

His firm resolutions about American white people still remained intact and many chance encounters that followed the war are told from lip to lip proving that the war and his previous imprisonment had changed him little. He was the same Paul Watson to Montmartre as he shambled up rue Pigalle.

Rue Pigalle in the early evening has a somber beauty—gray as are most Paris streets and other-worldish. To those who know the district it is the Harlem of Paris and rue Pigalle is its dusky Seventh Avenue. Most of the colored musicians that furnish Parisians and their visitors with entertainment live somewhere in the neighborhood of rue Pigalle. Some time during every day each of these musicians makes a point of passing through rue Pigalle. Little wonder that almost any day will find Paul Watson going his shuffling way up the same street.

He reached the corner of rue de la Bruyere and with sure instinct his feet stopped. Without half thinking he turned into "the Pit." Its full name is The Flea Pit. If you should ask one of the musicians why it was so called, he would answer you to the effect that it was called "the pit" because all the "fleas" hang out there. If you did not get the full import of this explanation, he would go further and say that there were always "spades" in the pit and they were as thick as fleas. Unless you could understand this latter attempt at clarity you could not fully grasp what the Flea-Pit means to the Negro musicians in Montmartre. It is a tiny cafe of the genus that is called *bistro* in France. Here the fiddle players, saxophone blowers, drumbeaters and ivory ticklers gather at four in the afternoon for a porto or a game of billiards. Here the cabaret entertainers and supper musicians meet at one o'clock at night or thereafter for a whiskey and soda, or more billiards. Occasional sandwiches and a "quiet game" also play their parts in the popularity of the place. After a season or two it becomes a settled fact just what time you may catch so-and-so at the famous "Pit."

The musicians were very fond of Paul and took particular delight in teasing him. He was one of the chosen few that all of the musicians conceded as being "regular." It was the pet joke of the habitues of the cafe that Paul never bothered with girls. They always said that he could beat up ten men but was scared to death of one woman.

"Say fellow, when ya goin' a get hooked up?"

"Can't say, Bo. Ain't so much on skirts."

"Man alive, ya don't know what you're missin'—somebody little and cute telling ya sweet things in your ear. Paris is full of women folks."

"I ain't much on 'em all the same. Then too, they're all white."

"What's it to ya? This ain't America."

"Can't help that. Get this—I'm collud, see? I ain't got nothing for no white meat to do. If a woman eva called me nigger I'd have to kill her, that's all!"

"You for it, son. I can't give you a thing on this Mr. Jefferson Lawd way of lookin' at women."

"Oh, tain't that. I guess they're all right for those that wants 'em. Not me!"

"Oh you ain't so forty. You'll fall like all the other spades I've ever seen. Your kind falls hardest."

And so Paul went his way—alone. He smoked and drank with the fellows and sat for hours in the Montmartre cafes and never knew the companionship of a woman. Then one night after his work he was walking along the street in his queer shuffling way when a woman stepped up to his side.

"Voulez vous."

"Naw, gowan away from here."

"Oh, you speak English, don't you?"

"You an 'merican woman?"

"Used to be 'fore I went on the stage and got stranded over here."

"Well, get away from here. I don't like your kind!"

"Aw, Buddy, don't say that. I ain't prejudiced like some fool women."

"You don't know who I am, do you? I'm Paul Watson and I hate American white folks, see?"

He pushed her aside and went on walking alone. He hadn't gone far when she caught up to him and said with sobs in her voice:—

"Oh, Lordy, please don't hate me cause I was born white and an American. I ain't got a sou to my name and all the men pass me by cause I ain't spruced up. Now you come along and won't look at me cause I'm white."

Paul strode along with her clinging to his arm. He tried to shake her off several times but there was no use. She clung all the more desperately to him. He looked down at her frail body shaken with sobs, and something caught at his heart. Before he knew what he was doing he had said:—

"Naw, I ain't that mean. I'll get you some grub. Quit your cryin'. Don't like seein' women folks cry."

It was the talk of Montmartre. Paul Watson takes a woman to Gavarnni's every night for dinner. He comes to the Flea Pit less frequently, thus giving the other musicians plenty of opportunity to discuss him.

"How times do change. Paul, the woman-hater, has a Jane now."

"You ain't said nothing, fella. That ain't all. She's white and an 'merican, too."

"That's the way with these spades. They beat up all the white men they can lay their hands on but as soon as a gang of golden hair with blue eyes rubs up close to them they forget all they ever said about hatin' white folks."

"Guess he thinks that skirt's gone on him. Dumb fool!"

"Don' be no chineeman. That old gag don' fit for Paul. He cain't understand it no more'n we can. Says he jess can't help himself, every time she looks up into his eyes and asks him does he love her. They sure are happy together. Paul's goin' to marry her, too. At first she kept saying that she didn't want to get married cause she wasn't the marrying kind and all that talk. Paul jus' laid down the law to her and told her he never would live with no woman without being married to her. Then she began to tell him all about her past life. He told her he didn't care nothing about what she used to be jus' so long as they loved each other now. Guess they'll make it."

"Yeah, Paul told me the same tale last night. He's sure gone on her all right."

"They're gettin' tied up next Sunday. So glad it's not me. Don't trust these American dames. Me for the Frenchies."

"She ain't so worse for looks, Bud. Now that he's been furnishing the green for the rags."

"Yeah, but I don't see no reason for the wedding bells. She was right—she ain't the marrying kind."

... and so Montmartre talked. In every cafe where the Negro musicians congregated Paul Watson was the topic for conversation. He had suddenly fallen from his place as bronze God to almost less than the dust.

The morning sun made queer patterns on Paul's sleeping face. He grimaced several times in his slumber, then finally half-opened his eyes. After a succession of dream-laden blinks he gave a great yawn, and rubbing his eyes, looked at the open window through which the sun shone brightly. His first conscious thought was that this was the bride's day and that bright sunshine prophesied happiness for the bride throughout her married life. His first impulse was to settle back into the covers and think drowsily about Mary and the queer twists life brings about, as is the wont of most bridegrooms on their last morning of bachelorhood. He put this impulse aside in favor of dressing quickly and rushing downstairs to telephone to Mary to say "happy wedding day" to her.

One huge foot slipped into a worn bedroom slipper and then the other dragged painfully out of the warm bed were the courageous beginnings of his bridal toilette. With a look of triumph he put on his new grey suit that he had ordered from an English tailor. He carefully pulled a taffeta tie into place beneath his chin, noting as he looked at his face in the mirror that the scar he had received in the army was very ugly—funny, marrying an ugly man like him.

French telephones are such human faults. After trying for about fifteen minutes to get Central 32.01 he decided that he might as well walk around to Mary's hotel to give his greeting as to stand there in the lobby of his own, wasting his time. He debated this in his mind a great deal. They were to be married at four o'clock. It was eleven now and it did seem a shame not to let her have a minute or two by herself. As he went walking down the street towards her hotel he laughed to think of how one always cogitates over doing something and finally does the thing he wanted to in the beginning anyway.

Mud on his nice gray suit that the English tailor had made for him. Damn—gray suit—what did he have a gray suit on for, anyway. Folks with black faces shouldn't wear gray suits. Gawd, but it was funny that time when he beat up that cracker at the Periquet. Fool couldn't shut his mouth he was so surprised. Crackers—damn 'em—he was one nigger that wasn't 'fraid of 'em. Wouldn't he have a hell of a time if he went back to America where black was black. Wasn't white nowhere, black wasn't. What was that thought he was trying to get ahold of—bumping around in his head—something he started to think about but couldn't remember it somehow.

The shrill whistle that is typical of the French subway pierced its way into his thoughts. Subway—why was he in the subway—he didn't want to go any place. He heard doors slamming and saw the blue uniforms of the conductors swinging on to the cars as the trains began to pull out of the station. With one or two strides he reached the last coach as it began to move up the platform. A bit out of breath he stood inside the train and looking down at what he had in his hand he saw that it was a tiny pink ticket. A first class ticket in a second class coach. The idea set him to laughing. Everyone in the car turned and eyed him, but that did not bother him. Wonder what stop he'd get off—funny how these French said descend when they meant get off—funny he couldn't pick up French—been here so long. First class ticket in a second class coach!—that was one on him. Wedding day today, and that damn letter from Mary. How'd she say it now, "just couldn't go through with it," white women just don't marry colored men, and she was a street woman, too. Why couldn't she have told him flat that she was just getting back on her feet at his expense. Funny that first class ticket he bought, wish he could see Mary—him a-going there to wish her "happy wedding day," too. Wonder what that French woman was looking at him so hard for? Guess it was the mud.

1927

- Belgian astronomer Georges Lemaître proposes a theory for the creation of the universe, serving as the foundation for what will come to be known as the Big Bang theory.
- The first successful demonstration of television takes place.
- Regular transatlantic telephone service begins.
- Charles Lindbergh successfully completes the first nonstop solo transatlantic flight.
- *The Jazz Singer,* with Al Jolson, is the first full-length feature film with sound. Its release marks the beginning of the end of the silent film era.
- White playwright Paul Green wins a Pulitzer Prize for his drama *In Abraham's Bosom,* which portrays three decades in the life of a black family.
- The Harlem Globetrotters professional basketball team is organized.
- Duke Ellington and his band open at the Cotton Club in Harlem.
- U.S. Supreme Court rules against white-only primary elections in *Nixon v. Herndon.*
- Marcus Garvey has his prison sentence commuted and is deported to Jamaica.

U.S. unemployment: 3.3%

Lynchings in the United States: 16 blacks, 0 whites

Deaths:
    Florence Mills (1 Nov.)
    Hubert Harrison (17 Dec.)

Spingarn Medal:
    Anthony Overton (businessman)

Books:

    Countee Cullen, *The Ballad of the Brown Girl* (poetry)

    Countee Cullen (ed.), *Caroling Dusk* (poetry anthology)

    Countee Cullen, *Copper Sun* (poetry)

    Langston Hughes, *Fine Clothes to the Jew* (poetry)

    Charles S. Johnson (ed.), *Ebony and Topaz* (multigenre anthology)

    Georgia Douglas Johnson, *Plumes* (drama)

    James Weldon Johnson, *The Autobiography of an Ex-Colored Man* (novel)

    James Weldon Johnson, *God's Trombones* (poetry)

    Alain Locke and Montgomery Gregory (eds.), *Plays of Negro Life* (anthology)

Periodical:

    Black Opals (1927–28)

22 CITY LOVE
Eric Walrond

FROM *THE AMERICAN CARAVAN*, 1927

From a gulf in the dark low sea of rooftops there came mounting skyward the fiery reflexes of some gaudy Convention Night on Lenox Avenue. With the fate of a sinning angel the eye went *carombolling* 'cross the fizzing of a street lamp, caught the rickety vision of a bus, topheavy with a lot of fat, fanning Jews, tottering by on the cloudy August asphalt; flitted from the moon-shingled edges of elm and oak, onward, finally settling on the dark murmuring folk enlivening the park's green dusk rim.

"Quit that, honey!" warned the girl, softly. "I's skeert o' dirt, baby, don't you do that." She steered the lad's menacing hand out the way.

"No tellin' wheh some o' dat grabble might go," continued Nicey, making a pirate's cross bones of her legs.

A silence, dramatic to St. Louis, ensued. He was hurt, put out, ashamed of himself at Nicey's gently unanswerable rebuke.

He risked a pair of greedy, sun-red eyes round at her, and his courage took fresh impetus. "I know a place," he bristled suddenly with conviction, and Nicey's head turned involuntarily. "An' here Ah wuz——," he chuckled self-condemningly. "Come on, le's chance it."

"A nice place?" Nicey asked, quietly, not wishing to seem eager.

"Ah mean!" breathed Primus with deep-felt ardor.

"Yo' talk like yo' know it, like yo' done bin they orreadly," was what she was on the verge of saying, but large immediate interests possessed her, and she said instead, half-coyly, "No kiddin' now!"

"Honest," he said, getting up, "I ain't foolin'. I ain't green as I look. I bin there——"

"Oh yeah?" risked Nicey with surgical placidity.

"I mean," he stammered, admitting the error, but she checked the ripening flow of advances, and stood up. "That'll do," she said sagely, and walked, hips swinging, on down the hill in front of him.

He kept a little ways behind, feeling insecure and moody at his silly measure of self-puffing.

A flower coursed by, and she caught it, pressing the white dewy petals to her mouth. Dissatisfied, she flung it in a curdle of nettles. "Ah likes flowers dat got pa'fune," she said, "dis one ain't got a bit o' smell."

As they sped out on the flaky stone flight of steps leading toward St. Nicholas, clots of lovers, in twos and more than twos, leaned against the bowing foliage, forcing the dicks, bronze and pale-faced ones, to take refuge upon their fobs and palms behind the dark viny hedge.

A big muddy touring car filled with a lot of drinking Bolita Negroes skidded recklessly by into the gulch to One Hundred Thirty-Fifth Street. Pebbly dust bombarded the lids of Nicey's and Primus' eyes.

". . . fur to go, baby?"

"Thutty fo'th . . . not fur . . . come . . . look out . . . you'll get run ovah, too."

A shanty, lodged beside an aerial railway track, with switches and cross ties, hovered dark and low above the street. A mob of Negroes passing underneath it hurried on as the trains rushed by, the lusty pressure chipping dust and rust off the girders.

Cars lurched in and out of side streets, assuming and unloading cargoes of vari-hued browns and blacks of conflicting shades of ebony splendor.

"How much furrer we got to go, honey?" cried Nicey, dusty, eager, ill-at-ease.

"Not fur, honey, here we's at——"

They stopt before a brown stone dwelling. In the thickening night-light they glimpsed a fat butter-yellow Negress lolling in a rocker on the stoop and fanning herself with the long end of her apron.

There they stood, naked of pleats and tucks, frills and laces . . . orphans.

"Go on down t' the basement," the woman directed, with a wave of her heavy hand.

"You'd better wait here, Nicey," Primus said, with a show of manly vigor. Skipping to the basement the smells of a Negro cook shop came somersaulting at him. His senses were placid beside the sickening essences of corn and pork and candied yams.

The man who shared in this riotous obscenity was spotted by a kerosene torch swaying from a hook nailed in the wall. He was bald and tall and huge and spade black. He wore a shirt and flabby blue jeans and braces. Under such a low ceiling his fading oak skull threatened to violate the plumbing. In such a tiny passageway he seemed with his thick rotund figure to be as squat as an inflated bull frog.

He turned, at the shadow absorbing a length of the trembling light, and there was hair on both sides of his broad black face. He looked into Primus' eyes and a mist of mutuality sprang between them.

"Wha' yo' wife at?" he muttered in a whining Southern voice.

"I'll call 'er——"

"No, yo' don't hav' to call her," he assured him. "She outside?"

"Yeah."

"That's orright."

"Any bags?" he plied further, eyeing St. Louis closely. "Wha' yo' bags at? Outside, too? Don't le' 'em stay dere. Bring 'em on down in yah."

"Bags?" cried Primus, quickly. "I ain't got no bags. Wha' kind o' bags?" He hung on eagerly for the rest.

"Ain't yo' know," the man said, with that faculty for understatement which seems to be the pride of Negroes of the late plantation class, "that yo can't register at no hotel without bags? Go git yo'self a armful o' bags!"

He fled, breathless, to the girl on the pavement.

"Well!" Nicey said, both hands on her spreading hips.

He was excited and hurt, and he stuttered. "They—he—won't take us like this. I mean—we got to git weself some bags—bags—bags—"

Nicey sighed, a plaintive sigh of relief—a sigh that was a monumental perplexity to him. "Don't look at me like that!" he swore, angry at his ineffectuality. "I did my darndest to git 'im to take us, but he won't do it. Says it's 'gainst the law."

"What yo' gwine do now?" she cut in, distrustful of self-defenses.

"Git me a bag, that's all! Ain't nothin' else to do. C'm awn!"

2.

In the resistless languor of the summer evening the Negroes wandered restively over the tar-daubed roofs, squatted negligeed on shelterless window sills, carried on connubial pantomimic chatter across the circumscribed courts, swarmed, six to a square inch, upon curb and step, blasphemously jesting.

"I'll run up," he said, pausing before the portals of a greasy tower of flats. "You wait here, baby, I ain' gwine b' long."

And he cut a slanting passage through the mob, leaped up half a dozen crumbling steps, through a long narrow corridor, ending, blowing, before a knob on the sixth floor.

He rattled a key in the lock, and entered. A strip of oilcloth, dimly silvery in the shadowy interior, flashed at him. He put the strip behind him, flicked on the lights, and stared in Son Son's big starry eyes. The child was the browning purple of star apple and was gorgeously animated. He was strapped in a ram-upholstered chair cocked against the window opening out upon a canyon of street. He jiggled at Primus a plumed African Knight of a doll.

The doll, profuse with bells and spangled half-discs, tinkled annoyingly. "Less noise, sah!" shouted Primus, descending on all fours and industriously examining the debris piled under the davenport which separated the cluttered room in two. Dimples of satanic delight brightened the child's face. He jiggled his toy, wagged his legs, carolling. He puffed his cheeks and booed, scattering mouth-mist about.

"Ain't I tell you to less noise, yo' lil' water mout' imp yo'," cried St. Louis, flying up, seizing and confiscating the tasseled ebony knight and slapping the kid's dusk-down wrists. "Ain't I tell yo' not to botha' yo' pappy when 'e come 'ome, to less yo' noise?" The youngster's sudden recourse to imperturbability annoyed him. "Yo' ain't gwine cry no? Well, tek dat, an' dat, an' dat! Cry, Uh say, Cry! Yo' won't open yo' mout', no, yo' won't buss loose, yo'——"

A pair of claws fell viciously on Primus' back, and, combined with the soaring quality of Tiny's voice, served to wheel him aboutface with a swift downing jolt.

He had forgotten, alas! to push the bath room door when he came in.

"Look yah, man, wha' de hell yo' tink yo' his, hennyhow? Yo' tink yo' dey down in de Back Swamp whey yo' come from, wha' dem don' know nutton but fi' beat up people? Hey, dis yah sinting yo' Ah see 'tan' up yah, 'im tink 'im his back in Lucy a prog bout fi' yampies an' hunions in de picknee head. Come tumpin' de po' picknee roun' like him hone him!"

A fit of conquering rage narrowed and hardened and glistened Tiny's small, tight, mole-flecked face.

From the piano she flew to Son Son's side. The child was bashful, and in a dazed, defensive mood. "Hit dis yah picknee a next time 'n see if me don' cahl a policeman fi' yo' hay. Hey, yo' na'h ashame' o' yo'self, no, fi' come down pon' a puny liggle picknee like dis 'n a show arf yo' strengt'? Why yo' didn't knock de man de oddah day when 'im bruk 'im wheel barrow 'cross yo' neck back 'pon de wharf? Why yo' didn't ram yo' hook in 'im gizzard, yo' dutty old cowrd yo', yo' can't fight yo' match, but yo' must wait till yo' get 'ome an' tek it out pon' me po' boy picknee."

He was on his knees, ransacking the amassing litter.

"Yo' a prowl 'bout now," Tiny went on, hugging Son Son to her bosom, "like a cock sparrow, but go 'long. Me na'h say nutton to yo', me jes' ah wait till de cole weddah come roun' again. An', boy, me will see yo' faht blue hice fuss befor' yo' get anyt'ing from me to shub in yo' stinkin' guts! The day yo' say yo' got de back ache, an de foot ache, an' de turrah ache, don't le' me hear yo' wit' me name 'pon yo' mout', yo' hear? Fo' if yo' tink yo' gwine get me fo' go out fi' scrub me finger nail dem white fi' cram bittle down a neygah man troat like yo', yo' is lie! Yo' bes' mek up yo' mine now it warm 'n get yo'self a helevator job fo' when de winter come. Fo' so 'elp me Gawd me will see yo' in holy hell fuss befo' yo' a see me trudge hup an' down dem yah stair' like I is any whore fi' do as yo' dam well please."

"Oh, woman," he chuckled, unconcernedly, "tun yo'self out o' me way, yo' smell bad." He banged the door after him, a frayed straw valise under his arm.

3.

He espied her, not leaning toward the frog-ringed moon rising out the river, against the red-spotted rods barricading the way to the cellar, where he had left her; but standing facing him, a speck in the dusk, on the opposing piazza, in an arrow of shadow in the court. He crossed the street, and was inside the marbled sink.

Nicey detached herself from the wall and waved a red, exacting mouth before his tense, sweating face. "Got any idea o' de time," she asked, impatiently.

He had taken a virgin pride in the valise, and was wrestling with it. "Le' me see——" He yanked out the coruscant disc, and Nicey's calm was star-cut. "Ten nine," he said, looking full and composed at her. It broke him up to be there facing her with the lamplight, stealing past her clouded face, giving an added lustre to the curves and brackets of her body.

"Well," she cried, aroused, "I'll be jail housed! You mean to tell me you had me waitin' down here fo' you fo' nearly a hour, yo' lanky suck egg son of a bitch!" She swung herself free of his grovelling embraces.

"Oh, Nicey," he begged, running after her, "don't go, sweet, I got de bag—"

"An' now yo' got it," she turned, interrogatively, "wha' yo' expect to do with it?"

"Tek it on back there!" he avowed in one of his recurrent moments of self-assertiveness.

"Like hell we do!" she swore. "I'm gwine home."

"Oh, don't go, Nicey," he cried, swinishly. "I know a place. Don't let's go home after all the trouble we bin to."

"Aw, hell, boy, yo' give me a pain in the hip. Yo' know a place me eye! Where is this place at?"

"Come awn, I'll show yah! Don't be skeert, I know what I'm talkin' 'bout—"

"Like hell you do."

". . . it ain't the same one we bin to orready."

"Fur?" she perked up, with returning curiosity.

"Oh, no, jes' roun' de corner, I'll show yo'. Yo' tink it's fur? It ain't fur." His lurid efforts at self-assertion were taking a strange weight with her.

And so they peddled on. The dust, the city's dissoluteness, the sensory pursuits, gave a rigorous continuity to themselves, and to their needs, sent them burning against the sinister sovereignty of Upper Fifth Avenue.

Here there was a cluster of figures aloft. "Come on up," cried the man, "look out, lady, fo' dat ole runnin' hoss. Little Bits, ain't I tell you not to leave yo' things knockin' 'bout like dat? Come 'n tek 'em in miss . . . look out, mistah, get up there, Mignon, an' let the gemman pass."

As a sort of imposed ritual the woman remarked, with a friendly frown suggestive of a discovery of startling import, "Ain't it hot tonight?"

"Ain't it though?" returned Nicey, flopping grandly by.

"This way, folks," cried the man, showing them to the parlor.

Passing the opulent hangings, sinking ankle deep in the rugs, Nicey was moved to observe, "Gee, I'd like to sleep in a swell place like this." As the female of the occasion she was led to the reddest plush couch in the room. Outside by the coat rack the two men stopt.

Primus' head bared, he was dabbing for the sweat sizzling in the rim of his hat. He put the valise down and went through his pockets for the money.

A princely urbanity governed the man. He edged the light behind him and scanned the most vagrant impulses lurking in Primus' eyes.

"Why don't you people come right?" he scolded in fatherly fashion. "Yo' don't come right," he insisted, trusting to the fleetness of the young man's mind.

Of the two listening there was no doubt that Nicey's ears were cocked nearer the big man's voice.

"Now take the lady," he went on, with disarming felicity. "Why—why don't she wear a hat?"

With the feet of a deer, the girl shot out the parlor, sped past St. Louis, through the vestibule and out into the Harlem night.

"I keep on tellin' 'em they won't come right," he said, as Primus trotted, valise in hand, down the stairs. "Don't they know that folks don't travel that-a-way?"

As she was about to merge in with the dusk saturating Lenox Avenue, he caught up with her.

"Jee, you're an unlucky bastard!"

"I'm sorry, Nicey."

"I never heard o' anybody with your kind o' luck. Yo' must o' spit on a hot brick or somethin'."

"I'd give anything to prove to you, Nicey, that I ain't nobody's simp."

"You're a long time provin' it, big boy."

"Oh, honey, giv' me time!"

"Say, big fellah, go to the judge, don't come to me. I can't giv' yo' any mo' time."

"I'd do anything—"

"Go stick yo' head in a sewer then."

"Let's go back, sweet, come, let's."

"Go back where?"

"I mean—with a hat. I'll go git yo' a hat."

"Christ, what next, buyin' me a hat. All I got to do is stick roun' you long enough an' you'll be buyin' me a teddy aftah awhile."

At a Hebrew hat shop on the Avenue they stopt and when they came out again Nicey was none the worse for a prim little bonnet with bluebells galloping wildly over it.

———

Crowds of high-hitting Negroes, stevedores from the North River docks—Cubans prattling in sugar lofts on the Brooklyn water front—discarding overalls and gas masks and cargo hooks—revelling in canes and stickpins and cravats—strutting light browns and high blacks—overswept the Avenue. And the emotion of being part of one vast questing whole quickened the hunger in Nicey's and Primus' breasts.

Waddling down the long moldy corridor, he let the girl go on ahead of him. The man was behind him, carrying the candle and jingling keys, ready to exact the casuallest ounce of tribute. "Don't forget," he said, "that if you want hot water in the morning, it'll be fifty cents extra."

23 LYNCHING FOR PROFIT
George S. Schuyler

FROM *MESSENGER*, MARCH 1927

(Address of Hon. I. M. A. Sapp, prominent advertising man of Moronville, Georgia, delivered to a group of up-and-coming men of vision assembled in the metropolis of that great state.)

Gentlemen: The great money-making possibilities of lynching have been overlooked. All of you will agree that these outbreaks of righteous indignation are necessary to protect our women (our *white* women, if you please) and maintain forever inviolate the supremacy of the white race. Even among the black leaders of a certain type there is a tendency to condone what others call a "crime" because a cessation of lynching would mean monetary loss to them. Since lynching will probably exist for some time to come, why not control and direct it into profitable channels? It is about the only activity in the United States that is not carefully organized and planned with an eye to financial return, yet we have neglected to organize it all these years.

And how can we do this? Well, you all know that the news of a lynching to be held always draws a large audience of white people. They will come from miles around to see that justice is done, and perhaps to carry a souvenir back home. I have known hangings and burnings in this state that have drawn spontaneous gatherings of as high as 2,000 people.

Now if it is possible to bring together that many people to witness lynching with only by-word-of-mouth advertising, why isn't it possible to bring 50,000 people from all parts of the state by inaugurating the same advertising methods we have found so potent in the sale of soap, underwear, cigarettes, and overalls? Why can't we do it? Why can't we make this practice more profitable? Why can't we inject the spirit of Service into it? That's the word, gentlemen—Service!

Just think of it, friends! Fifty thousand visitors! What does this mean to the

railroads, the hotels, the garages, the restaurants, the street cars, the storekeep-
ers, the merchants? Think it over! Fifty thousand people with good money in
their pockets! Fifty thousand people imbued with the holiday spirit! Fifty thousand people unmindful of the morrow! Here is a golden opportunity. We have
lynched 500 blacks in Georgia since 1882 in defense of our ideals, and while it
is a record of which we are very proud, I think we should deplore the fact that
we have not made it yield us direct returns.

I am not theorizing, gentlemen. We did this very thing in Moronville a few
weeks ago and the results were exceedingly gratifying. At a meeting of the solid
and substantial business men of the city, I brought up this matter and it was
enthusiastically endorsed by all. Everybody promised to cooperate and a fund
of $1,000 was raised to finance the advertising. Then we went to work.

The editor of the Moronville Gazette printed a news article about a white
woman being insulted by a big, burly, black brute. He worked that assiduously
every day for a week in his news and editorial columns. The local Klavern of the
K. K. K. bought thousands of copies and distributed them throughout our section. On Sunday the preachers delivered strong sermons against the menace of
lecherous brutes. Then the Sheriff announced that he had not yet been able to
locate the culprits but promised an arrest soon. Several white women wrote
letters to the editor claiming to have been insulted. The white people began to
clamor for action. Finally the Sheriff arrested a troublesome darkey on suspicion and put him in the county jail. Everything was all set then, so we ran a half
page advertisement in the Moronville Gazette and the Klan distributed copies
free for fifty miles around.

Let me pause here to read a copy of the advertisement:

NEGRO TO BE BURNED AT STAKE

In Moronville, Ga.
At the Cretin County Fairgrounds
Come One!   Come All!

Bring the Family and Spend a Pleasant Day.
Plenty of Refreshments Served.

———

Excursions from All Neighboring Towns at Half Price.
Street Cars Will Take You Directly to the Fairgrounds.

———

COME AND SEE THE GHASTLY SIGHT!

HEAR THE BLACK VILLAIN SCREAM!

SMELL THE ROASTING FLESH!

TAKE HOME A KNUCKLE OR RIB!

The Biggest Lynching Ever Staged!

———

ADMISSION ONE DOLLAR

Including War Tax.

A Seat for Every Man, Woman and Child.
Come and Be Comfortable—No Rowdyism.

Perfect Order Will Be Maintained by
THE MORONVILLE POLICE DEPARTMENT.

The results, gentlemen, far exceeded our expectations. We made more money in one day than we had made in the previous week. During the excitement we easily persuaded a wealthy old darkey to sell out a valuable piece of ground we had been trying to get for many years. The cotton mill owners were able to reduce wages 5 cents an hour without a clamor by subscribing $1,000 to the local K. K. K. The Negro ministers reported increased collections, the darkies became much more polite than formerly, and their leaders drew up a resolution expressing confidence in the *good* white people of the town and condemning the Negro criminal element. Insurance collections leaped from 60 per cent to 99 per cent in the next two weeks. Our white churches reported that contributions for foreign missionary work broke all previous records. The number of Negro migrants was small and were mostly from the more assertive element that seems to have difficulty in knowing its place, especially since the late War for Democracy. Even the better type of Negroes were glad to see them go because it was felt that they disturbed the cordial relations existing between the races. In the North, we learned the Negro agitational organizations increased revenues by 25 per cent and the principal Negro newspapers all reported leaps in circulation.

You can see, therefore, with what great possibilities this project is pregnant. We have in our favor the easily stirred indignation of our white people (b) an almost inexhaustible supply of Negroes, (c) the support of all business interests, the K. K. K., and the white and black clergy. There is no danger that the Negro leaders will attempt to stir up their people except to religious ecstasy, and experience has shown that we need not fear the interference of the Federal Government. Moreover, even if some politician in Washington should protest, we can easily show our increase in income tax payments and that will quell the outburst of any politician.

It is unnecessary and unsound to lynch many Negroes—one a month will be sufficient to bring the desired results, and at the same time will keep our lynching record low enough to appease the tender-hearted. All the police chiefs have privately promised to cooperate, the Klan will furnish ushers at $5 a head, the sawmills will supply fuel, and the railroads will give 5 per cent of their excursion revenue for the erection of health clinics and schools for Negroes. Thus the success of this project is assured in every way.

With the enthusiasm of our hard-headed business men and the support of almost all elements of the population, this new venture can be made a marvelous success and a credit to our business acumen. (Prolonged and deafening applause.)

24 HIGHBALL
Claude McKay

FROM *OPPORTUNITY*, MAY–JUNE 1927;

REPRINTED IN *GINGERTOWN*, 1932

I

In the early afternoon Nation Roe was seated at the piano, practicing his latest blues. He was a stout man, thirty-seven, clean-shaven, with large hands, thick fingers, and a brown lap of fat bulging over his collar.

He was singing a blues song.

His curious alto voice, emphasizing the sudden quavering variations and subtle semitones that delighted New York's lovers of syncopation, now filled every corner of his flat, escaping through window and door to tickle the happy ears of his humble Harlem neighbors.

He paused, and a voice called from the next room, "Nation, I am thirsty."

"What do you want?"

"You know what I want without asking—a ginger ale highball."

He opened a cabinet and, taking out a decanter of whisky, went into the adjoining room.

"No ginger ale, Myra dear," he said. "I drank the last bottle when I came in this morning."

The woman sat up in bed and with an irritated smack of her lips said: "Send Esther for some. I forgot to put in an order yesterday. But why did you drink the last bottle when you know I can't do without it?"

He mumbled some excuse and went to call the colored maid. And as he left the room she said between her teeth, "That black fool!"

"I think I'll take a straight, anyhow," she said to herself. And she reached for the decanter and poured out a big drink. She was rather a coarse-fleshed woman, with freckled hands, beet-colored elbows, dull-blue eyes, and lumpy hair of the color of varnish.

Her husband returned and sat on the edge of a chair.

"Where did you go last night?" she asked him.

"I was out with Lieberman and some more of the fellows."

"Was it a stag?"

"No, there was a few gals there from the *Argus*; it was pretty good. You should have been there, but I didn't know about it till I was finished at the theater. And when I tried to phone you, you wasn't here."

"If your gang wanted me, Nation, they'd let me know, all right. . . ."

"But they just thought it up all of a sudden, Myra."

"They can fool you, but they can't fool me. I am one of them. They all treat me mean because I'm married to a black man, but I don't give that much for them."

She snapped her fingers.

"Don't talk like that none at all, Myra. Want me to think my white friends could really feel that way? If that was so, they'd take it out on me. Now, what d'you say about that? You think Lieberman he's got any feeling against us, honest now?"

"Oh, I don't mean him," cried Myra. "He and Judith are nice enough. But they pity us, that's what. Can't you see?"

"I kain see many things, but I kaint see any pity for us in George and Judith, nor kain I see, anyhow, that my friends resent your being my wife, Myra. I know there's lots of prejudice about that, you know—but not among mah friends."

"You're just a big boob. That's why you can't see," she said, angrily. "Don't they send you invitations without mentioning me? And when I just made bold and went along with you to that party for Mae Farine, didn't they all treat me as if I was nothing?"

"I didn't notice no such thing. They were polite . . ."

"Yes, like a roomful of pokers."

The maid knocked at the door and brought in the ginger ale. She was young, soft-skinned, and chestnut-complexioned. Myra poured herself a highball.

"Come, dress and let's go to the 'Skipper' for eats, Myra. You drink too much."

"Leave me alone," she cried. "I'm sick of that old 'Skipper.' They don't like me there, either. Guess because I'm your wife."

"For Christ's sake, Myra. What's the matter with you? You say my white friends are against you and you imagine the colored ones are, too."

"I'm right about it, too," she insisted. "I think I'll eat at home."

Nation knew, of course, that the respectable Negroes, especially the women of his race, resented intermarriage as much as the whites. That did not worry him. What did worry him was Myra's constant hints that his white friends slighted her because she was his wife. He did not want to believe that.

From a colored cabaret in Baltimore to the glory of Broadway. That was Nation's achievement.

A freak of chance brought the thing about. An actor-manager had an evening in Baltimore. He had no means of amusing himself in that town and took a curious walk down Druid Hill Avenue, the street of Aframerican respectability.

He had asked for the Belt and was directed there. Druid Hill Avenue disappointed him. The atmosphere was as austere as that of Park Avenue. The man turned off into a side street and saw a pink flare of light which advertised a Negro cabaret. It was a cheap singing-and-drinking joint.

Nation was singing when the curious visitor entered. The regular customers eyed him furtively. For it was unusual to have a well-dressed white man dropping in at their joint. Nation sang with all his heart, as he always did when a personage came to the cabaret. He sang his own songs, blues that he made up himself in bad grammar and false rhymes. Shrewd comments and sidelights on American life from a Negro's point-of-view. And that very night the actor-manager made a contract with him.

During his first year on Broadway, Nation's manager had enough trouble with him, the sort of trouble that his manager had never expected when he contracted with Nation.

The Metropolitan writers had praised his technique extravagantly. But Nation had become one of the big men of the Belt, having the right of entry to the best homes. The Negro journals said that Nation was among the few living men of the race who served as an example and incentive to all Aframericans, but they also said that Nation's bad grammar and false rhymes were old coon stuff and not in keeping with the modern Negro spirit. Little by little Nation was persuaded to put rhyme and grammar in his songs, but they failed to get across to his audiences as his earlier things did, and so at last Nation's manager put a firm foot down on all academic improvements.

II

Nation had a friend in George Lieberman, the successful black-face actor. George (one day when he was half blacked up) said that he wished he had been born colored. To which Nation answered: "You wouldn't never ha' said that so easy at all ef you'd known what it was to live colored."

George retorted that he knew what it was to live as a Jew.

"It ain't the same thing, though," said Nation, smiling broadly and good-naturedly shaking his great kinky head. "It ain't the same I tell you, brother; you kain be one of the crowd when I kaint never."

George introduced Nation to a group of his colleagues and in that group Nation found and gained needed confidence in himself. Among them Nation came to some understanding of the subtleties critics call artistry. He became certain of the finest accents of his voice, qualities that he always possessed but of which he was never surely aware.

Nation's artistic contacts helped to give his voice a wider range and greater power. His audiences grew bigger. His pay also. And his manager smiled.

Nation's new friends invited him to parties in the downtown district. In the earlier days of his career his walnut-brown wife from Baltimore often went with him to those parties. The first Mrs. Roe was a little home woman. She had drum-stick legs, but the lines of her shoulders were perfect, and white women liked her way of plaiting her fuzzy hair and making it look like a turban.

Mrs. Roe always said very little at those parties. She really had very little to say at any time—even to Nation at home. But she enjoyed the parties, and Nation's white colleagues were nice to her. They liked her because she possessed the quality of simple charm. But Nation on his side acquired a critical attitude toward his wife. All the girls at the downtown parties were gossipy and brightly entertaining, and Nation began wishing that he had a brilliant-talking wife like one of the white actresses. . . .

It was at a Negro cabaret in the Belt that Nation met Myra Peck. Myra did not belong to the circle in which Nation's white friends moved. Her set was made up of jockeys, bookmakers, successful salesmen, and cabaret actors—people who read the *Morning Telegraph* when it is hawked around in the first hours of a new day. It was a set that patronized certain cabarets in the Belt, cabarets where the proprietor, the musicians, the singers and waiters were colored, and the patrons almost all white. The common cabaret-going Negroes were not catered to at these cabarets. The few who were welcomed were known in the Belt as "Big Money" Negroes. At those cabarets white and colored people drank, chatted, and danced together in a happy atmosphere.

When Myra heard who Nation was, she was extremely charming to him. Perhaps he might have been flattered and over-softened by any other white girl who was as nice to him as Myra. For, until his success on the stage, he had never moved freely and naturally among white people. He had grown up in the atmosphere and knowledge of hostility between white and colored and therefore had regulated his public life to avoid as much as possible unpleasant contacts.

Even when success brought him white applause and new associates, he was never quite sure of his ground among his white friends. Often in their company he felt instinctively that there were some things left unsaid, some things left undone, that would have been said and done if a Negro had not been among them.

But Myra showed herself to him wide open in every way. She brought the alien white world close to him. The commonplace in her turned his head, because to him the commonplace had always been strange. He felt a mysterious charm in her sallow complexion; he saw a golden foam in her lumpy corn-colored hair. He divorced his wife and married Myra.

Nation himself had noticed no change in the attitude of his white associates since his second marriage. But when Myra began worrying him with her bitter resentments, he reluctantly began to take notice. At the café where they usually met downtown, his friends were very cordial, and at any special affairs he stood out as Nation Roe, the singer. He was always called upon to make a speech, often the principal speech.

He was forced to admit, however, that his white friends did not visit him very often in Harlem now. They used to, before his second marriage. And they used to ask his little brown wife to visit them. But now it seemed that they managed to ask him without including Myra. He was so wrapped up in Myra, so much in love with her, that he had been blind to the slights of his friends. . . .

A little hatred began stirring in him now for all of them. What business was it of theirs if he chose to marry a white girl? And if they resented that, why should they make his wife suffer for it?

They are nice to me only because I am successful. White folks care for fame and fortune only. I won't let them start any trouble between me and Myra.

III

Myra sat with her fat arms laid carelessly upon the table, a green scarf thrown over her shoulders. She always began eating with a ginger ale highball and finished with it. She couldn't help drinking to excess and was often ill. Some days she could not get up for luncheon, and had to put ice on her forehead and temples. And the more she drank the more irritable and unreasonable she became about Nation's friends.

"When I see George today, Myra, I'm going to look him square in his eyes and ask him if they've got anything against we two."

"What's the good of saying anything to that old dumb-bell?"

"He's true blue, Myra. Would never go back on me. George and Judith are A-number-1 spohts. They don't mind coming up here to see us."

"It's good business for him to keep in right with you."

"I'm sure they like us, Myra. Don't be sore on George and Judith because the others p'raps . . ."

"I'm not sore on anybody. . . . I don't care if none of those downtown snobs ever come here."

Myra hated George Lieberman and his wife. Myra said that George liked Nation because he could learn useful things from him to further his career as a black-face comedian. Nation defended George and Judith. His simple mind made him see simple things clearly despite his blind infatuation for Myra. He could not understand, of course, that Myra was afraid of George and Judith, that she was afraid of their obvious superiority to her, afraid that Nation would see that superiority. George and Judith paired nicely together and Myra couldn't stand that. She hated to sit down with them at table and see them so chummy together. And she felt almost hysterical when Nation said tender things to her before them.

"But, Myra, if you're nice to George he could fix things up. I was going to tell him everything about this affair and ask his advice."

"I don't care about them . . . but I would like to go to some of those downtown parties."

"They're mostly stags, though. . . ."

"Stags," she sneered, "*you* men! Don't mind about me, Nation. In fact, I really don't want to go to those affairs. Honest, I don't. It's just some sort of jealousy. I don't care about anybody, as long as Dinah sticks to me."

"And me?" asked Nation. "What about me?" he laughed.

"Oh, you know! I don't mean you. I mean Dinah compared to those downtown snobs."

"You're a strange mixture, Myra. I kaint tell just what you want. I wish I could, for I want to please you always."

She drank another highball.

"Don't mind me, Nation. It's nothing, really. I think I want things that I really don't want, but I have to want them because my friends think I should have them. I don't want anything and I want everything."

"That's beyond me, Myra, like something outa big books." He went to his room to dress.

He returned tall, big, in a heavy brown overcoat. The bell rang and Dinah D'Aguilar came in. She kissed Myra affectionately with a great deal of fuss, and cried, "Hello, Nation," at him in a very offhand manner.

Nation hated Dinah. She was the only white person that stirred up an instinctive feeling of aversion in him. That night when he first met Myra at the cabaret Dinah was with her. And when he married Myra, Dinah became a permanent visitor to their flat. Dinah and Myra were everlastingly embracing and kissing each other and swilling highballs. And Nation sometimes felt that Myra was more affectionate towards Dinah than she was towards him.

Moreover, he had a suspicion that Dinah was laughing at him always. In her eyes, in her voice, in her attitude, he saw mockery. When he went alone to parties, Dinah and Myra went together to cabarets, where they caroused with their old friends. Myra was forever talking about her dear Dinah. Whatever could she do without dear Dinah? Dinah went with her shopping. Dinah went with her to the cabarets of the Belt. Dinah accompanied her to downtown places of amusement where Nation was not admitted. Myra was always giving presents to Dinah. And they were costly enough presents.

Dinah was tall and black-haired, sharp-featured and snub-nosed. Her arms were uncommonly long. Her nails were manicured to sharp and exceedingly long points. Her lips were carmine—excessively rouged. And she affected black dresses with a touch of red, black velvet slippers and purple stockings. She used to act in burlesque shows, but that was long ago. She managed to marry well, divorced her husband, got some money, and now she lived without working.

Nation's dislike of her was increased by one incident which filled him with burning hate whenever he remembered it. And he remembered it very often; indeed, every time he saw her.

The incident occurred when they were all three of them dining at Skipper's

Restaurant on Seventh Avenue. They had been drinking and joking, and Myra said they ought to find another person and go and dance. Nation said to Dinah, "Why don't you get you'self a permanent partner?"

Dinah answered, "I didn't get rid of a dumb-bell to pick up a millstone."

"All of us ain't dumb-bells and millstones," retorted Nation.

"Well, you're a good old skate, all right," said Dinah. "But there aren't many like you."

"I'll look out for a good chappie for you," laughed Nation.

"Thanks," answered Dinah, "but I don't like prunes." She clapped her hand on her mouth almost before the word was off her tongue. And she added, red and embarrassed: "I don't mean you, Nation. Hope you don't mind it."

But he was terribly offended. He explained that he had really meant that he would find Dinah a friend among his white associates. And the thing was only a joke, after all. Dinah agreed that the whole incident was a joke, and therefore Nation shouldn't try to explain anything. If she didn't like prunes, she didn't like onions, either, she said, making an awkward effort to set things right.

But Nation was raging inside of him. He kept thinking and wondering if Dinah always referred to Negroes as prunes and what else among white people. Perhaps she had even said it to Myra, his own dear wife. And perhaps they had laughed together over "prunes." And he was a "prune." . . . He laughed and told Dinah it was all right. But he could never forget.

Buttoning up his overcoat and readjusting his brown Derby on his head, he kissed Myra good-by. His hand was on the door knob when Dinah said:

"Say, what about the Stunts Annual, Nation? I heard some girls talking about it last night at Fearon's Cabaret. Of course you and Myra are going. Can't you try and wheedle a ticket out of somebody for me? I'd love to go."

"I don't know that I kain. I'll try, though, and I . . ."

"It would be awful nice of you, Nation. I've never been to one of their affairs."

"Nor I," said Myra. "I hear they're awful swell and funny and awfully free."

The Stunts Annual was the great yearly event of a group of actors to which George Lieberman belonged. Nation had attended the last celebration with his first wife. They had both had a very happy night of it. Walking towards the Subway station Nation recalled how specially nice the guests had been to his wife. Somebody had called upon her for a speech, and when she wouldn't budge, everybody cried: "Speech! Speech! Speech! Mrs. Roe," amid waving of glasses and clapping of hands. And Ethel had stood up, timid, smiling, and said, "It's a great pleasure to be here among Nation's friends, but I must leave the stage entirely to him."

That made a great hit with the revelers and Nation was happy that Ethel did her simple part so well.

The feeling of his white friends for Ethel had been genuine. But Myra. . . . It hurt him to think that they should be concerned about his marrying a woman of their race. He did not want to believe that that was true. Why should they mind about his private life? If Myra pleased him . . .

IV

George Lieberman was seated in a large, comfortable leather chair, indolently looking at the photographs in the *Theater News,* when Nation greeted him. George's club was perhaps the only one frequented by white people in New York where a man of Nation's complexion could be received. George was delighted to see Nation. His delight shone frankly in his brown eyes and roundish face. He was a compact, jolly type. Nation sat down on the other side of the newspaper-strewn table. Two other actors came in. One leaned against Nation, putting his elbow on his shoulder.

"Let's go round to Cruse's for a drink, fellows," he suggested.

"Excuse me, brother," said Nation. "I have a personal message for George."

George got up, and he and Nation went out together. They knew a quiet café a few blocks away. The roar of the Sixth Avenue Elevated train drove them towards Broadway. The crowd of the great thoroughfare drove them into a taxi-cab. . . .

"George," said Nation, "I am worried a tall lot about some'n'. And you sure kain tell me what I want to know about this business. Don't imagine that I minds hearing the truth, even if it's a hard dose to swallow. I'd like to know just how things stand."

"Well," asked George, "what is it?"

"It's about Myra, my wife . . ."

He hesitated, took a sip of his fizz and twirled his gold chain.

"A fight?" asked George, expectantly and in a joyful tone.

"O Lord, no!" exclaimed Nation. "It's . . . Have you fellows anything against me 'cause I'm married to a white girl?"

He said it hastily, as if he were spitting a nasty fly out of his mouth.

"Gracious! No, Nation. Aren't we all just the same to you?"

"To me, sure you're all right, you all are. But youse different with Myra. The fellows don't come up to Harlem any more. And I don't seem to get any invites out with her. Mind you, I didn't notice the change mahself. But Myra did. And when she spoke I saw it sure enough."

"I don't think it's anybody's business who your wife is," said George, dryly. "And if we—if any of us fellows resented your marriage to a white woman—don't you think you would feel it, old man?"

"I think that, too," Nation said in a low, half-ashamed voice. "But Myra says I'm blind. She sees everything clear as daylight."

"Perhaps she does see something. . . ."

Nation finished his fizz and asked for another. He had been hoping that there was nothing in Myra's allegations, after all, and that he could go home and tell her so. In his big body there was the sensitiveness of a child. He wanted to live in simple peace, to sing his songs perfectly at each performance, chum with his white friends, and go home to the exotic bosom of his Myra, reeking of Luckystrike and ginger ale highballs. But George's "Perhaps she does see something" made Nation ask, pointedly:

"Well, is there anything against Myra herself?"

George hesitated to answer.

"Tell me. You kain tell me the truth," urged Nation, "and I won't mind. Honest to God, George, I won't mind. It'll make me feel better."

"It's nothing, really," said George, guardedly, "except that your wife doesn't belong with our crowd. Doesn't fit in at our affairs. But nobody holds anything against you for that. How could we?"

"I see," said Nation. "Leastways I'm trying to see. But why kaint she come in with the bunch same as me?"

"Well, I'll tell you what one of the chaps thinks about it and that was exactly how the crowd felt . . . if you won't be offended. . . ."

"No, I tell you again. It's better I hear. Let's hear it."

"It was put like this," said George. "If we were talking about a fish, Myra would want to gut it right on the table; if it was about pigs, she'd want to bring in the slops from the pen. . . . That's awful strong talk, Nation, but you said you wanted to hear. It isn't anything, really. But Myra couldn't fit in like you. Lots of the fellows don't bring their women around, and the women have sense enough not to want it, either."

Nation winced.

"Who was it said that about Myra, George?" he asked.

"Gracious, Nation! Don't ask me that. You've just said you wanted to know the truth, but only in a general way. Myra is your wife, after all, and I hate the idea of me sitting here discussing her with you."

"All right, Georgie. Don't mind me, thanks," Nation said, putting his hand on his friend's shoulder. "It was a bonehead question. Honest, I really don't want to know who said it!"

George asked Nation to have dinner with him at home. . . .

The table was laid for five persons. Judith Lieberman's cousin, Joseph Hyman, with his wife, was dining with them.

When they were seated around the table Nation thought to himself that it would be a nice even party if Myra were there.

Judith was a pleasant hostess. She was pretty, with her shiny, short, black hair and plump peach-colored cheeks. Nation liked Judith for her simple, free manners.

Judith asked about Myra.

"I left Dinah with her. They have a date for this evening, I guess. Some cabaret or other. Dinah is crazy about cabarets."

"I don't care much for cabarets since I got married," commented Judith.

"I like them sometimes," said Nation.

"Me, too," agreed George. "Remember, Judith, I met you in a cabaret."

"And after that I had no reason to go any more," laughed Judith.

"I should like to go to a cabaret sometimes," said the sweet and soft Mrs. Dr. Hyman. "But Joe won't go further than the theater. He's so busy with his practice, he can't stay up late."

"You could go with my brother," said her husband. "He goes to all the dens and dives."

Mrs. Hyman pretended not to hear.

"I should think actors have a swell time of it spending all their life in theaters and cabarets," she said.

The others laughed, even her husband.

"We spend a little time at home, too," said George. "But you should see some real cabaret life, Mabel. Sometimes it's just a little more tiresome than a church. What about getting up a party one of these nights?"

"I'm game if Doctor ——"

"Sure, Doc, you've got to run away from your patients one night. . . . Let them live, Doc."

"Why not come to Harlem?" suggested Nation. "And I'll show you all of the news that the jazz-hounds up there are putting on."

"A good idea," agreed Judith. "Last time I was up your way, Dinah told me she didn't have any more time for downtown cabarets. Only the colored ones have the real spirit, she says."

"I think she's right," agreed George. "Harlem has the real hot stuff."

Nation was feeling glad that he had turned the cabaret talk Harlemwards when Judith said:

"Why not let's go to one of these downtown places tonight after the theater? Joe can't excuse himself out of it now. We'll just keep him here. I love to go off on a party like that without planning beforehand. It's such fun."

"All right," agreed George, "and some night we'll make up a big party for Harlem."

"That's fine!" Mrs. Hyman clapped her hands and nodded and smiled like a nice bird at her husband.

"Nation," said Judith, "you'd better telephone Myra now and tell her to meet us after the theater with Dinah."

Nation looked embarrassed and did not answer. George, remembering their talk in the café, said:

"Come on, Nation, phone Myra, and we'll have a real night of it among ourselves."

"But I couldn't go," said Nation, helplessly.

"Why not?" asked Mrs. Hyman.

"Oh, come on, Nation," insisted George. "It will be good fun."

"But you know I can't go," said Nation in a vexed and hurt tone, "because I'm Negro." He blurted that out almost angrily.

The others grew red and confused. Nation excused himself to get his cigarette-case from his overcoat. "It's a shocking shame!" he heard Mrs. Hyman say as he went along the hall.

It was, indeed. He shrugged his heavy shoulders. He had been placed in similar embarrassing situations and had heard those identical words so often, that the phrase had grown trite and meaningless for him. He knew that George and Judith were the most considerate persons in the world, yet they had unwittingly got him in such an equivocal position.

Nation knew that his friends resented the petty limitations to which he was subjected. Yet sometimes in a burning wave of resentment he felt that his white friends made blunders like that because their humanity was not all-human enough.

Their way of ordering their life of work and love and play was based upon hundreds of years of tradition among themselves. It had become a commonplace routine to them, and it seemed it was just impossible for them to imagine themselves in the place of a colored man within that pattern.

They all went into the sitting-room for coffee and smoking. And a little later George and Nation left for the theater. They strode along in silence. George desired to say something soothing to Nation, knowing that he was hurt, but he could not find a precisely appropriate phrase. Nation apprehended George's mood. He preferred that nothing further should be said about the incident, so he talked a great deal about nothing.

At Times Square they parted a little awkwardly, each one going to his own theater.

V

Ten o'clock in the evening. Myra, stumpy and panting, wearing a maroon hat and overcoat to match, waddled lazily up the stairs. Dinah, slim, lizard-like, crept after her. Reaching the third floor, Myra looked in her red leather handbag for her key, inserted it in the lock, and opened the door. Nation was sprawling half-dressed against the piano.

"Aren't you gone yet?" asked Myra in a loud raw voice.

"No. I don't know that I should. . . ."

"Why not? What's the good lying around the house like this? It's so trying."

"I don't care about going without you, Myra," said Nation, despondently.

"Oh, nonsense! What's the good in talking like that? I should have liked to go, and Dinah, too, if you'd gotten the invites for us. But it's not any fault of yourn that we didn't. And why shouldn't you go and enjoy yourself? I'm not selfish."

"I won't enjoy the damned ole show at all without you . . . of course most of the fellows ain't taking their women. . . ."

Dinah had seated herself and listened to the dialogue with a contemptuous and bored expression.

"You'd better finish dressing and skate along, Nation," said Myra. "I couldn't grudge you a little fun like that. Look at all the places *I* can go to when you can't."

"I don't want to hear about that, Myra. I don't like it. It woulda been better we two went everywhere together, or stays home together. That would make me feel a whole lot happier."

"We can't have everything just as we want," she said. "You go on along to the Stunts. You can't afford to miss such things if you want to hold your place on the stage. Don't mind me at all. I can look after myself."

Two hours before, they had quarreled and Myra had flung herself out of the flat, raging. She had thought Nation would be gone by the time she returned, and she was intensely annoyed to find him still at home. She thought that, sitting there so dejected, he looked ever so much like a stupid black stump of a tree, spoiling the landscape of life.

Nation went out, closing the door. Dinah, standing behind Myra's chair, put her long slim arms, enveloped in tight black-satin sleeves, around her friend's fat, freckled neck. Myra put her hands up to her breast and squeezed Dinah's pretty hands.

"Darling," murmured Dinah, "sometimes I get a feeling that you really like that great big plug-ugly."

"O Lord, Dinah: What makes you think that way? I've got to nag at him, and be discontented, you know, acting superior-like. For he must never get it into his head that I'm like any of the cheap nigger women he's been used to."

"You clever dear," Dinah kissed Myra.

"He's a good-natured old thing, though, Dinah. Better than any hard-fisted brute of a white male."

"I should say he is," agreed Dinah.

"He pays the bills without asking any questions. And I do use up gallons of highball. He's all right as a reliable stand-by, even if I've got to imagine sometimes he's somebody else."

Nation had been very upset when George gave him the invitation and Myra was not included in it. He almost felt that it was an insult.

"And Myra!" he protested. "Myra . . ."

"I know," said George. "I understand. Judith isn't going, either, nor Bert Roach's wife. It's nothing personal why Myra isn't invited."

George explained to Nation that they had taken in many new members in the course of the year, and that it had been a problem to hold the party down to the usual size so that it should keep its old intimate and friendly atmosphere. For that reason the committee had decided to have as guests only a few people actively connected with the stage, and many friends and relations had been left out.

George was angry with himself for having lied. Yet he could not tell Nation that the committee had barred Myra because she was undesirable. Now he would have to ask Anna Roach and Judith to stay away from the party. George wondered if he could persuade Anna! The Roaches did not understand and feel about Nation as George and Judith did.

As George walked away he thought how dreadful it was that Nation should be burdened with Myra. Good God! How could a man with such a beautiful voice put up with such a coarse cow? I wonder if something is always lacking in Negroes the way they say? Was Nation blind? Had he no discriminating faculties? He had sung his way into the heart of the great white public. How could he forget about his race? Forget that he was a living life-long problem, and pick up the burden of a Myra on top of that?

Nation received a rare ovation when he walked into the reception-room of the Stunts Annual. The hall was decorated with ferns and palms. The platform was banked with a profusion of large white chrysanthemums, pink carnations, and red geraniums. Half-hidden behind the palms were the Negro musicians from the Harmony Club. The banqueting-table was crowned with three green baskets filled with American Beauties. A Stars and Stripes was suspended like a vast bowl over the platform. Buntings of blue, white, and red zig-zagged around the ceiling, and paper streamers, hung low, ran diagonally across. The evening's surprise, planned by the recreation committee, was the tiny pennant bearing the name of his theater that each actor found beside his plate. The pennants were in various colors and very pretty.

The actors had dressed as they pleased, some in Tuxedo coats and soft white shirts, and some in dark sports suits. There were many Pierrots and some Harlequins. And the women were radiant in warm tropical colors.

Nation was seated between George and the petite, sunny-haired Mae Farine, the clever actress of sentimental comedies, whose skin was white and sweet like the petal of an apple blossom. Opposite were the Roaches. Anna smiled intimately at Nation, and he wondered that she was there, and remarked it to George.

"She came in just a little before you with a message for Bert," George explained, "and the fellows wouldn't let her go. You know how it is when they are stewed a little."

Nation also noticed a sprinkling of gay girls that he knew were not connected with the stage. But Judith, at any rate, was conspicuously absent. Nation felt confident that George had not hoaxed him.

The cocktails were very dry and worked rapidly. And before the plum cake and the ice-cream were served, the champagne had already reduced everyone present to a happy, playful state of relaxation. The green-uniformed servitors were having their own high time downstairs. You could tell that by the way they lifted up their feet and by the hot color of their ears. Those black boys behind the white chrysanthemums were having their share, too. You knew that they were by the gleam of their teeth.

A playful boy tossed a tangerine at Mae Farine's golden head, and immediately a little war was on. Fruits, candies, American Beauties, and light bits of things were commandeered and sent flying at ducking heads amid cascades of laughter. Seats were exchanged, seats left vacant, windowsills invaded.

And Nation forgot everything and entered wholeheartedly into the fun. Down in one corner of the room, Anna Roach and a group of girls had tied a red-silk handkerchief over his eyes and were playing Blind Man's Bluff with him. And while they were laughing at his heavy antics he was yelled at to do something, sing a little song or make a little speech before the dancing began.

And in the midst of the whistling and hand-clapping for Nation, Judith walked in, wrapped up in a little fortune of furs. She said her taxicab was waiting outside. She was passing and dropped in to say a word to George. Some one cried, "You should have been here long ago!" Mae Farine shrilled, "Send the taxi away!" Judith was surrounded and divested of her furs. She was beautiful in a fine-fitting pink party dress.

Nation's thoughts immediately darkened. Surely he had been fooled. Judith's coming at that hour could not be accidental. George had planned it. Nation's head was heavy from champagne, but his faculties were working all right enough. The party became a rotten and cheap affair for him. I won't stand this cussed crowd any longer, he thought. Trying to make a fool baby of me. Myra is as good as any of them here. Why should they object to her? It's a slap at me. If there's any difference between her and these here women I kaint see it. Myra was right. They despise me because I'm married to a white woman. . . .

"Speech, speech, Nation!" . . . "Ho, Nation! sing us the Brownboy Blues." . . . "No, let's have the Harlem Blues!" . . . "No! No! Not Harlem. . . . The Baltimore Blues! Sing the Baltimore Blues!" cried a chorus of voices.

Nation's head reeled. He gripped the table. . . . "Leave me be. . . . Youse all a gang of damned hypocrites! Just Crackers!"

The revelers were struck dumb with amazement; shocked into soberness.

Horrified, George rushed up to Nation and took hold of his arms. But Nation shook him off with an angry gesture. He felt like a wild bull. He dashed from the room. The green-uniformed Greek in the cloakroom helped him into his overcoat. He took the first taxicab for Harlem.

"I don't care . . . I don't care . . . I don't care," he kept on repeating to himself. "I don't care for stupid gaiety and a cheap bunch of hypocritical friends. All I want is Myra, nothing more than Myra. . . ."

When Nation let himself into the apartment house he heard an unusual noise. And as he mounted to the third floor sounds of laughter and intermittent chords from the piano came from his flat.

Myra must have gotten lonely and asked a few friends up to amuse herself. Poor Myra! I'll enjoy this better than the Stunts.

His hand was on the door knob when he heard Dinah say: "Here's your high-ball, Myra. Let's all drink to the success of the good old prune."

There was a general clinking of glasses and a tipsy young male voice cried: "Here's to prune, prune, prune, our nation . . . al prune."

Nation recognized the voice as that of a pretty young *habitué* of Fearon's cabaret who often went dancing with Dinah. He was nicknamed Lord Percy.

Nation stood stone still, dropping his hand. He heard Myra call imperiously, precisely as she used to call to him: "Hand me another drink. . . . God damn you, Percy, I don't want a straight. I want a . . ."

Perhaps Nation's spirit blazed so fiercely that the flames reached through to Myra inside. For without visible reason she staggered over to the door and opened it and saw Nation standing there. She backed and fluttered heavily away into the center of the room like a frightened duck.

Nation walked into the midst of them. Myra's guests glanced at his dark face and sneaked away as quickly as they could.

But Dinah remained.

"Get out!" cried Nation.

Dinah fled.

"And you, too!" he exclaimed, jerking his thumb at Myra.

"Me! I can't leave here like this. . . . My things . . ."

"You'll find them on the sidewalk tomorrow."

"But what have I done? Where can I go? I am—am I not—ain't I married to you . . . your wife?"

"Looka here, white woman. . . . Go on away from me *right now.* Leave me alone with God!"

She had never before heard his voice like that. She looked into his eyes and cleared out.

Nation looked round the room at the glasses half-filled with red and yellow liquor. It seemed as though a crowd of white insects were still sitting there and screaming: "Prune! Prune!! Prune!!!"

He had a sharp thought of George Lieberman and the friends he had so grossly insulted. He remembered his first wife, Ethel Roe. She could never have said "prune" and made it hurt him.

He quivered. His heavy frame shook. He knelt down against the liquor-stained piano and bellowed like a wounded bull.

25 GAME
Eugene Gordon

From *Opportunity*, September 1927

As Sam Desmond, porter of the Greater Boston Meat Market, entered that concern's front door, he noticed the deliveryman Roberts returning the telephone to its accustomed place. He noticed also that a mirthful grin was playing havoc with the deliveryman's countenance, breaking its black surface into numberless shining facets. He knew that a message had come for him, and, in the light of many experiences, suspected that it was not a pleasant one. Roberts grinned like that only when there was a possibility of making his colleague uncomfortable.

Sam shuffled the length of the sawdusty aisle of chop-blocks and display cases of a variety of meats to a rear room of the store, where, removing his overcoat and hat, he put on a soiled white jacket, and a skull cap made from the upper portion of a woman's stocking. He knew that Roberts' unconscious love for the dramatic would never permit him to deliver the message before it was asked for, and as he returned to the shop he was resolved to have it out.

"Well, Black Boy," he began, "what's nibblin' at *your* funnybone?"

Roberts carried a basket of meats to the delivery truck at the curb and returned before he had decided to satisfy Sam's curiosity.

"Matter with me, little Snow White? Why, th' aint nothin' the matter with *me*. Is it, Mr. Bamberger?" Mr. Bamberger was president of the Greater Boston Meat Market, and occasionally revealed his democratic nature by joking and laughing with his colored employees. Now he merely smiled discreetly and continued taking turns about the floor.

"That telephone call," Roberts announced, "came from your better three-quarters, Sam. She want you should tell her how long it take you to eat your lunch. Say ever time she call you up you jus' gone to lunch or jus' gettin' back. Say don't she feed you 'nough? She say—"

Sam held up his hand. "Never mind no more Miller and Lyles, Black Boy. What she wants? That's what I want you to tell me."

Roberts was moving from one clerk to another picking up parcels, and, reading the addresses scribbled on them, arranging them in a basket he carried. He stopped in the midst of this occupation and said impressively:

"What she say, Snow White? She say you better bring her home some game, that's what she say. She say she want a rabbit or a squirrel or a ven'son steak, or somp'n like that: she don't care what, jus' so long's it's game. He delivered his parcels to the truck and, returning, "She say and don't forget somp'n nice for Mussolini," he called, his voice shattering into loud laughter.

The six clerks, Miss Schulte (the cashier), and Mr. Bamberger all laughed at this.

"Damn Mussolini!" Sam was busy now at the big refrigerator, attending to the long-deferred task of top-to-bottom cleansing. "I wish that lousy yaller devil 'ud die or something," he muttered.

"Yeah, damn the cat!" Roberts retorted with gleeful scorn. "Damn Mussolini all you want to, but be mighty particler you don't do it to home. Ef Marguerita ever hear you talk like that 'bout her cat you be lookin' for another place to hang out at."

"Is that so!" Sam threw the scrub brush down, the better to use his hands for gesticulating. "Is *that* so!" He approached the deliveryman, who lolled against a showcase watching a clerk quarter a small pig. "Well, let me tell *you* something, Black Boy. You say she better not catch me cussin' round the house. All right! You watch what I say. She's gonna catch me doin' more than that yet. I'm gettin' sicken tired of bein' bossed round by a woman and a dirty yaller cat. And when I get sicken tired anything I put my foot down and stop it. That aint no hot air; I mean it. You jus' watch, Black Boy; I'm tellin' you."

For a moment he glowered, his runted gnarled little black figure tense and purposeful under the heat of his synthetic anger. Roberts alone laughed, a jeering guffaw that was weighted with scorn and scepticism. "What you think, Mr. Bamberger?" he called, pausing on his way to the truck. "When Sam's better three-quarters start naggin' at him old Mussolini join in and spit on Sam. Gee, but that make little Snow White mad." Mr. Bamberger and the clerks immediately donned sober faces. Probably the memory of a tale Roberts occasionally repeated of Sam's running wild with a cleaver at the Roxbury Market, from which place he had come to Bamberger's, sobered them. They probably thought it wiser—and perhaps safer—to enjoy Sam's discomfiture with straight faces. They had never seen Sam's wife, about whom Roberts had built for their amusement a tradition of pugnacious determination. Roberts admitted that Marguerita had been engaged to him before Sam came along, but insisted that he passed her up because he thought it foolish in a man so black marrying a yaller woman like Rita. They would attract embarrassing attention on the street. Sam said Roberts was a wall-eyed liar.

When he finally heard the spasmodic back-spitting of the delivery truck and saw Roberts scoot with it across the soiled front of the plate glass window, Sam sidled up to Mr. Bamberger, who was talking to Miss Schulte at the cashier's cage. The porter's tone was deeply confidential.

"Mr. Bamberger, I want to get a rabbit or a squ'rrel or a ven'son steak, or some sort of game, to take home to my wife. She's jus' crazy about game, you know, an' she called up an' said—"

"Yes, I know, Sam," interrupted the rotund head of the Greater Boston Meat Market. "I heard Roberts telling you about it. And I said then to myself, I said, 'It's too bad we didn't know sooner,' I said to myself, 'because,' I said, 'I'd like to accommodate Sam.' But there aint any more in the shop, Sam." The small gray eyes were sympathetic. "If you'd just been about a half hour earlier," he appended in a regretful voice. "As it is, Sam, Roberts got the last order of game now delivering it in Brookline. Sorry, Sam. Save you a rabbit tomorrow, if you want me to."

Sam declared that this would be satisfactory, and requested that Mr. Bamberger charge it. "But, Mr. Bamberger, you can give me something for that lousy yaller cat, though, can't you?"

"Sure thing, Sam! Just tell Mike over there . . . O Mike! Fix up some liver or something for Mussolini, will you? . . . Charge that to Sam, Miss Schulte. And tomorrow, Sam, you'll have the game for your wife. We're getting in a fresh supply in the morning, see? . . . Got the refrigerator all cleaned out, eh? Well, finish that up before you go tonight, Sam." He turned and resumed his tete-a-tete with the cashier.

II

Through six years of diligent service to the Greater Boston Meat Market Sam had attained the full confidence of the management and certain prized prerogatives. One of these was the privilege of remaining until every one had gone every night and closing the store. It had been a long time since Mr. Bamberger or Miss Schulte or Mike had locked up. Even when he had an engagement to go out with Marguerite, Sam preferred to exercise his prerogative. Being black offered few enough prerogatives, God knew, and he would be a fool not to grab those proffered him. At home a mere cipher, he felt like a man of some consequence when he was allowed the staggering responsibility of putting out the lights (all except the one over the cash register) and closing and locking the front door. It must have impressed people who passed along Tremont street and saw him. They must have thought him a partner in the concern.

As usual Sam put out the lights, except the one over the cash register, looked about proprietarily to see that everything was all right, and then went out into the cold January night and locked the door. The liver for Mussolini was concealed in an outer wrapper made of a sheet of the Boston *Transcript,* left in the store by a Back Bay customer, and Sam carried it pressed under his arm. Turning north on Tremont street, he boarded at Northampton a car for Cambridge.

As always when going home he was painfully aware of every step he took from the door of the shop to the car stop, and of each revolution of the wheels of the car from Tremont and Northampton streets to his stop in Cambridge. He was going home after a hard day's work; taking fresh meat to a lousy yaller cat that spit at him to show its contempt; thinking up a presentable lie for a lazy yaller woman. What had he married her for, anyway? Because she was pretty? Well, she was pretty, all right, and no getting away from that. She was a little broad acrosswise and rather heavy on her slippered, slip-slap feet about the small apartment; but pretty, just the same. An ugly little runt like him was lucky to have a woman like Marguerita. . . . Lucky? Well, he didn't know so much about that. After all, why was *he* lucky? Why wasn't *she* the lucky one? Of course he had a good looking high yaller woman for a wife, but what didn't *she* have? She had a little runt of a black man who would slave for her; somebody who would show up her handsomeness by contrast; somebody who was just crazy about her, and she knew it; somebody she could boss around; somebody who'd continue to slave like a fool the rest of his life for her. That's what she had. And in spite of all this she seemed to love that lousy yaller cat better than she loved him. "What you call him Mussolini for?" he had once asked her. "Because," she had responded, so promptly she must have been thinking about it, "I want to kid myself there's a real man round the house." Of course she loved the cat better than she loved him.

Straight down the middle of his meandering thoughts the car rumbled across the Harvard Bridge, then rattled down Massachusetts Avenue past Technology, and, at Sam's signal, came to a hissing, wheezing, grumbling stop at Lafayette Square. Sam observed the window display of ornate furniture in the store before him as a crazy fantasy. He could feel the complete petering out of his earlier incipient spirit of rebellion. Oh, what was the use, anyway? Straight down Massachusetts Avenue, about two blocks away, lay Central Square. If he had any money . . . He shrugged, then cut across Lafayette Square into Columbia street.

The second-floor-rear window was alight, an indication that Marguerita was in the kitchen. Now what would he say? The truth? Yes, but suppose she wanted to know why he had not gone elsewhere? Bamberger's wasn't the only market on earth, he very well knew. What was the matter with the Manhattan right there in Cambridge? But she knew that he had no penny above his scant allowance.

He removed his hat and overcoat at the top of the stairs. From the kitchen a triangle of yellowish gaslight cut into the darkness of the hallway. There came also the sound of frying meat hissing above that of Marguerita's padded footfalls, and an odor of hot pork-chops floating on a haze of gray smoke. He wondered whether she had heard him enter; was certain that she had not, since she had not called for the game. He stood still, trying to decide what to do. Mussolini came out the kitchen door, resembling in his sleek-sided massive bulk a lion cub, and stopped to look Sam over. Then the cat advanced down the hallway toward his mistress' lesser portion, his yellow back arched, his stiff tail standing up like a malignant finger, accusingly. Mussolini rubbed against Sam's legs, almost unbalancing him; sniffed curiously at the parcel of liver, uttering deep throaty supplications.

Sam's reason warned him to observe restraint, yet he disobeyed, and shoved the cat with his foot. It was not a kick, but merely a vigorous push, that made Mussolini sprawl on his side. Immediately the hallway was filled with a yowl of angry protest. Marguerita came hastening from the kitchen, wiping her hands on her soiled apron, slip-slapping glidingly, and peering into the twilight haziness of the hallway. Mussolini ran to meet her, casting backward at his mistress' husband baleful and reproachful glances.

"Wassa matter, Mussolini, darlin'? What's happened to Mother's 'ittle darlin'? What—"

Sam stepped briskly forward, as though he had but that moment entered the hallway. His wife was glaring.

"Sam Desmond, what you—"

"Dark out here," he said, rather hurriedly. "Stumbled over him. Guess he smelt his meat. I—"

"I thought 'twas you. Slinkin' round here worse'n Mussolini. What you up to now? I know it's something you ashamed of. I bet you didn't get my game." She waited for him either to confirm or abrogate her suspicion. He was silent, which indicated confirmation. She went on: "That's it, now, aint it? You didn't get my game. You didn't get my game. I knew it. Give me that meat. I knew you wouldn't."

She left him standing miserable in the semi-dark hallway. Mussolini stalked ahead of her into the kitchen. For a moment Sam listened. . . .

"I knew you wouldn't. You never do. . . . Come on, Mussolini, and get your dinner, pet. You're the only real male around here . . ." Sam could easily distinguish the part of her address meant for him: "Some day you're going to find yourself looking for another woman . . ." Yes, that was his. He had memorized it years since. He stood motionless, waiting for the rest of it. There it was: "I'm sicken tired of your carelessness. You don't think about doin' nothin' to please me once in a while . . ." Every time he heard this accusation he resented it anew. He felt that it was maliciously untrue. He renounced it with a surging burning resentment. She interrupted his smoldering meditation: "I ask you to bring me—"

"But they didn't *have* any, Rita! You might know they must not've had any if—"

"Oh, that's no excuse! Suppose they *didn't* have any. Is old Bamberger's the only meat market in town? What's the matter with the Manhattan right here at Central Square? No, that aint the reason. You just didn't—"

"But you know I haven't got no account at the Manhattan, Rita. An' I didn't have a pen—"

"Account! Account! Don't make me choke myself laughin'. You haven't got any charge account anywhere, if that's what you mean. Old Bamberger only takes pity on you and lets you have things because he knows you're too dumb to walk out on him and look for a decent job . . . " He could hear the loud frying of something freshly laid in the skillet. The hissing momentarily blanketed her voice. Presently, however, it broke through: "Account! Account! No, you aint got any account. And *you* aint any account, either."

Making a gesture of resignation to the smoke-filled odor-laden dusk of the hallway, Sam shuffled toward the bathroom. His narrow shoulders drooped lower than usual, and he was angry with himself because he could think of none of the fine set-speeches he often rehearsed on the car going home. He closed the bathroom door and lighted the gas. Above the sound of running water he could hear Marguerita's baby talk addressed to Mussolini: "Come on, oo po' 'ittle hung'y kittsy cat, an' get its supper. Come on, dear!"

Mussolini! The lousy yaller beast! Oh, if he could only do something with that cat! Perhaps then his wife would transfer some of these generous affections to her husband. But he did not pursue the notion. It was a will-o'-the-wisp, and not worth pursuit. Mussolini was already twelve years old; he was wiser than most cats of greater age, and as truly an institution of the Desmond household as Marguerita herself. There existed about as much likelihood of his getting rid of that husky feline as there was of his making up to resemble Valentino. Mussolini! The lousy yaller . . . Sam buried his face in the cold water, holding his breath; removed his face and rubbed it with a towel until it glistened in the mirror above the wash basin like polished patent leather. He preferred cold water for his face even in winter, he said, for it soothed his nerves. He studied himself for a moment in the glass, then grimaced.

"So she wishes I wasn't so black, does she?" he muttered, recalling the oft-told tale. "Oh, well, I should worry! I sure don't look like nobody's little Snow-White, 'spite what Roberts calls me."

"Sam, come out that bathroom and get your dinner—if you want any. You must think I'm gonna stay in the kitchen all night."

Sam chuckled grimly as he shambled toward the kitchen. "What a difference when she speaks to me'n when she speaks to that lousy yaller beast."

There being no dining room, they ate in the kitchen, utilizing a folding camp-table which was kept in the kitchen closet between meals. As Sam took his place he watched his wife's face covertly, hoping to determine the extent of her displeasure. She slip-slapped about, jolting the table when her soft ample person made contact with it; filled his plate with bony fried fish, his cup with inky black coffee, and his soul with leaping, shrieking passion for revenge on Mussolini. Why should *he* have to eat fish? He hated it, and Marguerita knew he hated it.

He noticed that *her* plate held two browned pork-chops, and suspected that punishment was being visited upon his appetite and stomach for his failure to bring her game. And this angered him, for he had bought those chops with the natural and logical intention of eating one of them himself. He felt resentment swelling, bubbling, in his breast; rising to his throat, and clogging it; to his eyes, making the tears burn beneath his lids; making him blink his eyes rapidly and lower his head as if looking for something under the table.

Marguerita took her place opposite him, scanning him from squinting eyes. Her full fleshy jaw was set, and as she struck back from her moist cheek the vagrant lock of black straight hair, Sam knew that she not only was prepared for a quarrel but would welcome one. He was still reluctant to give her cause, provided she did not think she had cause enough already. There was so far no sound reason for *his* exploding. If he did, of course, it would be just *too bad*. Yes, he would hold his temper inside. She merely sought an excuse to jump on him; he knew that, and swore that he would give her nothing that even resembled a cue. So he began slowly to thread the fish, picking out with his fingers the innumerable needle-like bones.

The cat sat to one side, regarding them from slitted yellow eyes. Glimpsing what he considered Mussolini's contemptuous regard of the master of the house, Sam sensed a sudden desire to injure it. There Mussolini sat, its great sleek yellow back hunched, its massive head, like a wise old man's, tilted to one side, and a diabolical smirk on its too human features. He wanted to see it squirm in pain, to hear it yowl and spit defiance to no avail. He did not doubt that but for the lousy yaller beast Marguerita would be a better wife.

"You make me sick, Sam Desmond! Here I am all day workin' my head off to make a home for you, an' you can't even do me a little favor."

Sam munched distastefully his fried fish and boiled potato, dropping his eyes from the angry gaze of his wife's; then he looked across at the kingly usurper on the floor. Mussolini, with long, slithering strides, came forward as if once more to demonstrate his priority rights. Crouching slightly, he sprang upon his mistress' lap and thrust his yellow head into her plate. He sniffed about for a moment but, presumably finding nothing to his taste, he sat back with lazy and smug complaisance, almond eyes indifferently fixed on the man opposite.

Then, as if to show further the extent of *his* prerogatives, he lifted a soiled white paw and did what Sam in delirious lapses dreamed of doing but which in sane moments haunted him only sub-consciously: Mussolini slapped Marguerita's face. With a petulant shove she sent him to the floor. "Get down, Mussolini. I don't feel like playing tonight. I'm mad."

The cat stretched, curled over on the crescent of his back to wash himself, then stalked around the table and sprang upon Sam's lap. For an instant the man shrank in confounded amazement. Why, the damn, lousy, yaller! . . . Why, he'd never dared to do that before! It was downright defiance, that was it;

defiance in the presence of his—of *their*—mistress. With a quick, vicious gesture he hurled the cat to the floor. Mussolini made no sound, but stood lashing his tail and looking from the man to the woman; seeming in his attitude to demand the woman's intervention.

The next moment Marguerita had bounded from her seat, nearly upsetting the light table, and had planked Mussolini in Sam's plate. "There, Mussolini," she cried. "And you," she snarled, "Mr. Nice-Nasty, you just touch that cat again if you dare! Just lay your black hands on him again—just go ahead and do it. . . . I'm sicken tired of you goin' round here actin' like you was just too disgusted to live under the same roof with me and my cat. . . . That's right Mussolini, eat! . . . If you're so disgusted why don't you find somewhere else to stay? You make me . . ." She resumed her seat and glared at him.

With an impatient quirk of the body Sam sent the table skidding against the set tubs. There was a clatter of broken crockery on the floor, the scurrying of heavy footfalls of a frenzied yellow cat, the wide-eyed incredulity of an over-sized yellow woman.

Sam left the scene in silent triumph. It had occurred so suddenly, so instantaneously, that he was confused as to how it had happened. Certainly he had done nothing so radical before in all his married life. Marguerite said nothing. In silence too she took down the folding table and put it into the closet. Then she began to wash the dishes. . . . Sam did not often exhibit such temper.

Sam was now in the front room with the radio. He had the earphones on and did not hear his wife's calling until she screeched near his head. He felt that the first round of this fight was his; every detail of her present demeanor seemed to proclaim it. Clearly she was upset. He removed the earphones with methodical slowness and frowned at her, thrilling at the experience.

He heard her say: "Well, why don't you *do* something? Didn't you hear me? He's chokin'!"

She had already turned and slip-slapped quickly back to the kitchen. Muttering, Sam followed. "*He's* chokin'? *Who's* chokin'? What you talkin' 'bout?" He disliked having to admit that her seeming discomfiture at his sudden exhibition of temper was due to something else.

In the kitchen Sam saw Marguerita on her knees with the coughing Mussolini squeezed to her pillowy breast. Tears were on Marguerita's cheek, and she was rocking from side to side as though trying to soothe a fretful child.

"O Sam, Mussolini's got a fish bone in his throat! See if you can get it out. I've tried everything I know," she whined, "an' nothin' don't seem to work. Oh, he's chokin' to death! Oh! Oh!"

Sam straightened his frail shoulders. "Then let the yaller lousy beast choke to death! He can die and go to heaven for all I care." Sam returned to the radio.

For a while he stood holding the earphones in his hands, listening to Mussolini's coughing and Marguerita's baby talk. Then there was silence. Presently he heard his wife coming back, and he hastened to put the phones over his ears and sink into the cushioned armchair. One glimpse of her face told him that she was contrite. He did not like to see her angry or upset. She sat beside him, on the arm of his chair, and pulled his head down against her breast.

He tried to think of Mussolini's recently lying there, but her caresses dulled his senses and exhilarated him. "Naughty boy," she scolded playfully. "Naughty boy, not to bring mama what she wanted. And mama was mad, too; yes, she was. Mama just as mad as she could be." She fondled his head, running her soft fingers through his tight hair. In spite of himself his soothing rebellion cooled under her ministrations. It always did. "Naughty boy! If you had brought mama's rabbit Mussolini wouldn't 've got a bone in his little pink throat, 'cause you've had the chops then, an' . . ."

Sam shook himself free.

"Oh, you still angry with mama, is you, naughty boy? Why you still angry with your mama?"

"You like that lousy yaller cat better than you do me! I'm gettin' sicken—"

"Oh, that's it, is it! Naughty boy jealous of Mussolini!" Her soft deft fingers stroked his cheeks, his throat, his eyelids. He lay back, half listening to the dance music from the Copley Plaza, half hypnotized by the woman's caresses. Resentment was all burned out. He lay back, feeling the throb of her heart beneath the warm soft breast.

"You won't forget tomorrow, will you, Sammy Boy? And you won't be nasty to Mussolini any more, will you?"

His senses were dissolved and merged. "No, never. . . . You got the bone out all right? Thas good. . . . Tomorrow I'm gonna bring you the nicest, biggest, fattest . . . Les go to bed. I'm all in."

III

The ever-recurrent flare of resentment at Mussolini's presence in the bed flickered for an instant, then glowed angrily thru the rest of Sam's waking hours. The beast lay between him and Marguerita, its warm furry body wedged close. Sam could hear its throaty purr at intervals, like the distant whirr of an aeroplane. Thus was husband separated from wife. He knew that if he moved nearer her Mussolini would challenge him with spitting and scratches; yet, if he lifted the lousy yaller beast by the scruff of the neck and dropped it to the floor, he would suffer verbal attack from Marguerita. His thoughts became an irrational patchwork; he wondered whether she permitted the cat to sleep between them solely to keep him away; speculated dully on ways and means of banishing it forever; listened to his wife's deep regular breathing . . .

Rabbits, squ'rrels, ven'son steak—game; a big yaller cat caressed by a big yaller woman. . . . He slept . . .

His wife, sitting up in bed, was shaking him and calling his name loudly.

Through the murk of drowsiness he heard her saying: "That fish bone's still in his throat, Sam! *Please* see if you can't get it out. If we don't do something he'll die! Don't you guess you could call up some doctor now? Mr. Williams downstairs would let you use his telephone. Oh, listen to the poor little darlin'! He's just gaspin' for breath. . . . Sam Desmond, would you lay up there an' let a poor innocent dumb animal suffer? . . . Well, you're even worsen I thought you was. Don't you ever speak to me again, so there!"

She was out of the bed, the cat pressed to her bosom, pulling down the shades, lowering the window, fumbling for matches and the gas jet. There was in her actions all the intense, compact suffering of the mother whose babe lies dangerously ill. Finding it impossible to sleep longer Sam sat up, scratching and rubbing his eyes. The cat was coughing and clawing at its throat. Sam felt suddenly an overwhelming sense of compunction, but before it could move him to action Marguerita had dragged him, cover and all, to the floor.

"What's the matter with you, Sam Desmond? You crazy? I told you to call up a doctor! D'you want Mussolini to die?" She tossed her husband his old bathrobe from the foot of the bed. "Put that on and go downstairs and call up a doctor."

But Sam caught up the old garment and hurled it at the choking feline, who, momentarily terrified, wriggled from Marguerita's arms and scampered under the bed. Its coughing had ceased. Sam stood glaring down at it for a moment, then turned to his wife.

"Damn that cat! I'm gettin' awfully tired of so much foolishness, d'you understand? I mean it, Marguerita! I'm sicken tired of playin' butler and chambermaid to that lousy yaller cat. First thing you know you'll wake up some mornin' an' find you aint got no cat nor husband neither. An' another thing," he cut in, raising his hand to check Marguerita's impending retort. "I'm sick of sleepin' in bed with a cat. I'm tired of that nasty beast layin' up there between us. I didn't marry no cat, an' I aint going to sleep with none no more. I mean that, believe me! I think it's about time I put my foot down roun' here."

He scowled at her for a moment, but she stood in stupefied silence, her eyes fixed on his. Then he crawled into bed, dragging the covers with him, and turned his back to her. After a little while he sensed that she had turned out the light. He heard her push up the window and run up the window shade, then get heavily into bed. A flood of exultation overswept him as he realized more fully the prodigious extent of his victory—a victory without bowls. For a long while both lay silent. Presently he heard Mussolini's pat-pat-pat, noted the abrupt cessation of the footfalls, then, before he could speculate on the cat's intention, Mussolini was walking across Sam's head seeking its place between the man and his wife.

With a muttered "damn!" the man sprang up, dragging the covers with him and, seizing the animal, tossed it across the room. It uttered a howling wail of protest, an imprecation, Sam thought, and spit at him. Sam wondered whether in its defiance it would spring at him in the dark. But Marguerita was out of the bed again; pulling down the window and the shade; making a light. Sam hastened to return to the covers. He lay silent and disturbed, his face to the wall. Without a word to her husband Marguerita picked up the cat, crooning brokenly over it; then kissing it noisily, she placed it again in the bed. Sam wondered how much resentment a man's breast would hold before it exploded like an overfilled gas bag. . . .

IV

In the morning Sam heard his wife slip-slapping, slipper-shod as usual, in the kitchen. He rose and went into the bathroom. Above the noise of running water he heard her calling to him: "The cat's still got that fish bone in his throat. I want you to take him to the animal hospital in the Fenway on your way to work. You won't have time to eat no breakfast, but I got you a cup of coffee ready."

Sam found Mussolini caged in an old basket. Marguerita had padded it with clean cloths and covered it with old window screening. Grumbling, his shoulders hopelessly drooped, Sam gulped his coffee, then picked up the basket and left the house. At the hospital examination disclosed nothing more than an inflamed throat. There probably *had* been a bone, it was explained, but certainly there was none now. Sam proceeded to his work, arriving half an hour late.

Roberts observed to the clerical force sometime during the afternoon that "maybe you folks don't know Sam here's Mussolini's nurse maid." "Yeah," he called loudly, from the rear of the store, "Sam nursin' Mussolini now. 'S'wife make him take the cat out to walk when he come to work in the mornin', then walk home with it at night. See that basket Sam bring in here this mornin'? Well, Mussolini's in that. Jus' as nice an' comfy. Aint he, Sam?"

The porter listened in pretended good humor.

The telephone rang, Mr. Bamberger answering it. "Why, yes, Mrs. Desmond, your husband's right here. No, no trouble at all. Just a minute."

Sam was laconic to the point of gruffness. "What's that? Yup! . . . Oh, the cat? Well, it's . . . dead. I said he's dead! Yup, dead. D-E-A-D, dead! Finee! Compree? Expired. Passed out. . . . Yup, at the hospital . . ." He hung up the receiver and turned to the questioning stares of the house. To the proprietor he said: "Never mind the rabbit, Mr. Bamberger. She don't want it now. Lost her appetite, I guess."

Sam swept the floor. He sprinkled fresh sawdust all round, cleaned out the back room, and washed the rear and front windows, inside and out, despite the biting cold! Coincidentally, it was a busy afternoon for the others, too, being Saturday; for which Sam was thankful. He didn't feel like a lot of cheap talk. . . .

It was nearly closing time. Roberts came in from the rear, calling loudly and somewhat excitedly: "Say, Snow White, what's the big idea? Mussolini aint no more dead'n I is. Why—"

"If he aint no more dead'n you, then he's all ready for the embalmin' fluid—an' don't know it. That cat's dead, I'm tellin' you . . ."

Sam closed the shop as usual that night, leaving fully an hour later than the others. He carried no basket, but, instead, a parcel in butcher's wrapping paper, which, in turn, was wrapped within a newspaper; a parcel which may have contained a dressed rabbit or a squirrel or a venison steak. As he waited for a car at Tremont and Northampton streets he grinned into the frigid semi-darkness; then, holding the parcel aloft before his face:

"Why don't you yowl for your mama, you lousy yaller rascal?" he apostrophized, in a low tense voice. "Why don't you spit on me? . . . So she wants game, does she? Well, she'll *get* game!"

26 MASKS
Eloise Bibb Thompson

From *Opportunity*, October 1927

Paupet, an octoroon and born free, was a man of considerable insight. That was because, having brains, he used them. The cause of Julie's, his wife's, trouble was no secret to him. Although it never dawned upon him fully until after she died. Then he dictated the words to be placed upon her tombstone. The inscription proved to be unique, but not more than the cemeteries themselves of old New Orleans. The motto written in 1832 read as follows: "Because she saw with the eyes of her grandfather, she died at the sight of her babe's face."

This grandfather, Aristile Blanchard, had been an enigma to the whole Quadroon Quarter of New Orleans. But he was no enigma to Paupet although he had never lain eyes upon him. Seeing him had not been necessary, for Paupet had heard his whole life's history from Paul, Julie's brother, whom he met in Mobile before he had known Julie. Paul, although a ne'er do well who had left the home-fires early, admired his grandfather immensely. Hence he had found delight even as a youth in securing from the old man those facts of his life which had proved so interesting to Paupet.

Now Paupet, among other things, was a natural psychologist albeit an unconscious one. He was accustomed to ponder the motives of men, their peculiar mental traits and their similarity to those of their parents whom he happened to know. No one was more interesting to Paupet than Julie, his wife. So of course he gave much thought to her. But the occasion is always necessary for the knowledge of a soul, and the opportunity for really knowing Julie came only when she was expecting her offspring. But even then Paupet would not have known where to place the blame for her peculiarity had he not known, as we have said, all there was to know about old Aristile Blanchard.

That Aristile was a man to be pitied Paupet felt there was no question. For what man does not deserve pity who sees his fondest dream fall with the swiftness of a rocket from a starlit sky to the darkness of midnight? No wonder that hallucination then seized him. With such a nature as his that was to be expected. But that the influence of such a delusion should have blighted Julie's young life was the thing of which Paupet most bitterly complained.

Aristile, Paul told Paupet, had been a native of Hayti. Coming to New Orleans in 1795 when the slave insurrection was hottest, he had set up an atmosphere of revolt as forceful as the one he had left behind him. Of course when Julie entered the world, the revolution had long been over; Toussaint L'Ouverture had demonstrated his fitness to rule, had eventually been thrown in an ignominious dungeon and been mouldering in the grave some five years or more. But the fact that distressed Paupet was that Aristile lived on to throw his baneful influence over the granddaughter entrusted by a dying mother to his care.

Of all the free men of color in Hayti at the time none were more favored than Aristile. A quadroon of prepossessing appearance with some capital at hand, he had been sent to Bordeaux, France, by a doting mother to study the arts for which he was thought to show marked predilection. In reality he was but a dabbler in the arts, returning at length to his native land with some acquaintance with most of them, as for instance sculpture, painting, woodcarving and the like but with no very comprehensive knowledge of any one of them. There was one thing, however, that did not escape him—being there at the time when France was a hotbed of that revolt which finally stormed the Bastile—and that was the spirit of liberty. "Liberty, Fraternity, Equality" was in the very air he breathed. He returned from France with revolutionary tendencies far in advance of any free man in the island, tendencies that awaited but the opportunity to blossom into the strongest sort of heroism.

Although he burned to be of service to his race on returning to his native land he forced himself to resume his usual tenor of life. He sought apprenticeship to an Oriental mask-maker, a rare genius in his line where the rich French planters were wont to go in preparation for their masquerades and feast-day festivities. Masks had always had a strange fascination for Aristile. He would often sit lost in thought beside their maker, his mind full of conflicting emotions. But when the French slave-owners assembled at Cape Haitien to formulate measures against the free men of color to whom the National Assemble in France had decreed full citizenship, he forgot everything and throwing down his tools immediately headed the revolt that followed.

With Rigaud, the mulatto captain of the slaves, he gave himself to the cause of France, offering at the risk of his life to spy upon the English when they came to the support of the native French planters bent upon re-establishing slavery upon the island.

Making up as a white man as best he could, he boldly entered the port of Jeremie where the English had but recently landed. His ruse would have succeeded had it not been for a native white planter all too familiar with his African earmarks, who standing by at the time readily spotted him out. Without warning, Aristile was seized, flogged unmercifully and thrown into a dungeon to die. But he was rescued after a time by a good angel in the form of an octoroon planter identified with whites all his life because of a face that defied detection; not only rescued but shipped with his daughter in safety to New Orleans. Then the octoroon rescuer took up the work of spy upon the English which Aristile had been forced to relinquish. That he was successful is manifested in the subsequent work of Toussaint L'Ouverture who because of him was able before very long to drive in all the troops of the English, to invest their strongholds, to assault their forts, and ultimately to destroy them totally.

This incident had a lifelong effect upon Aristile. Full of despondency, disappointment over his failure in the work he had set himself to do with the enthusiasm and glow of a martyr, his mind dwelt wholly upon the facial lineaments that had brought about his defeat. "Cheated!" he would exclaim bitterly. "Cheated out of the opportunity of doing the highest service because of a face four degrees from the pattern prescribed for success. Fate has been against me.—Nature has been against me. It was never meant that I should do the thing I burned to do.—O, why did not Nature give me the face of my father?—Then all things would have been possible to me. Other quadroons have been so blessed. Hundreds of them—thousands of them! Save for a slight sallowness of the skin there was absolutely nothing to show their African lineage. But Nature in projecting my lips and expanding my nose has set me apart for the contumely of the world.—The ancients lied when they said the gods made man's face from the nose upwards, leaving their lower portion for him to make himself. Try as I may I will never be able to change the mask that Nature has imposed upon me."

Day and night these thoughts were with him. Paul described this state to Paupet declaring that his mother had feared for Aristile's mind. At length this mood suddenly changed to one of exultation and he rose from his bed a new man.

"I have found the formula for greatness!" he told those about him. "It reads, Thou shalt be seen wearing a white man's face.—But only a fraction being able to carry out this prescription it is left for me to create a symbol so perfect in its imitation of Nature that the remainder of mankind may likewise receive a place in the sun. My brothers and I shall no longer be marked for defeat. I shall make a mask that will defy Nature herself. There shall be no more distinct and unmistakable signs that will determine whether a man shall be master or slave. All men in future shall have the privilege of being what they will."

With this end in view he repaired to the Quadroon Quarter of New Orleans and set up a workshop that soon became the talk of the district because of the strange-looking objects it contained. Paupet could vouch for their strangeness for they were still in existence when he came to the place. Upon the walls of this room hung many attempts of the thing Aristile had set himself to do. There were masks of paper patiently glued in small bits together in a brave effort to imitate Nature in the making of a white man's face. Likewise masks of wood, of papier mache and of some soft, clinging, leaf-like material which it is very likely he discovered in Louisiana's wondrous woods. Interesting-looking objects they were, every one of them; most of them, however, were far from the goal; but a few in their skin-like possibility of stretching over a man's face might have been made perfect—who knows—greater marvels have been seen—had their completion not been suddenly broken off. There was about the whole of this room an unmistakable depression, an atmosphere of shattered hope as if the maker of these objects had set out with high purpose toward their completion then suddenly been chilled by some unforeseen happening that filled him with despair. And so it really had been. While Negro supremacy existed in his beloved country Aristile worked with ever-increasing enthusiasm toward his cherished dream. He had been unable, he told himself, to assist his brothers as a soldier because of the lineaments that Nature had imposed. But he would present them with a talisman like unto Aladdin's lamp that would work wonders for them in a world where to be blessed was to be white. But when the news reached him that Toussaint, the savior of his race, had been tricked and thrown into a French prison to die, he was plunged into the deepest sorrow and turned from his purpose in despair. Laying aside his implements, for a long time he could not be induced to take interest in anything. At length when his funds began to dwindle, it was borne in upon him that men must work if they would live. Then he turned to the making of those limp figures in sweeping gowns that when Paupet saw them were no doubt of his own distorted mind, designed for standing in the farthest corner of the room—grotesque figures wearing hideous masks, the reflection, clowns and actors of the comic stage.

It was not very long before the place began to be frequented by patrons of the Quadroon Masques and of those open-air African dances and debaucheries known as "Voodoo Carousals" held in the Congo Square. Later actors from the French Opera looked in upon him. Then he conceived the idea of having Clotile, his daughter, already an expert with the needle, prepare for his patrons of the masque and stage to be rented at a nominal fee, those gowns and wraps that were now fading behind the glass doors of yonder cabinets. But though he worked continuously it had no power, apparently, to change his usual course of thought. His mind ever dwelt upon the disaster that had blighted his life.

And then came Julie in this atmosphere of depression to take up in time the work which fate decreed Clotile should lay down. As apt with the needle as her dead mother had been she was able, when her grandfather through age and ill-health became enfeebled, to maintain them both. And those were formative years for the young Julie, obliged to listen to her grandfather's half-crazed tirade against Nature's way of fixing a man to his clan through the color of his skin. Unaccustomed to thinking independently she, however, could see something of the disastrousness of it all because of the stringent laws confronting her in New Orleans. As much as she longed to do so, for instance, she dared not wear any of the head-gear of the times, although much of it was made by her own fingers, because of the law forbidding it; a bandana handkerchief being decreed to all free women of color so that they might easily be distinguished from white ladies. And that was only one of the minor laws. There were others graver and more disastrous by far. So these conditions forced her to realize early that her grandfather had good reason for his lament. She too deplored the failure of his design—the making of a mask that would open the barred and bolted doors of privilege for those who knocked thereon. Without anything like bitterness for these conditions, she began to reason that color and not mental endowment or loftiness of character determined the caliber of a man. For did not color determine his destiny? He was rich or poor, happy or unhappy according to his complexion and not according to his efforts at all. And so the words superior and inferior were invariably dependent upon the color of his skin. She, a brunette-like quadroon, the counterpart of her grandfather, was far superior to the black slave-peddlers who sometimes came into the Quadroon Quarter begging a place to rest. And that was why the Quarter guarded the section so jealously from all black dwellers, however free they might be, because they wanted only superior people in their midst.

One morning some months after her grandfather's death she awoke trembling with a great discovery. For years she reflected in wonderment her revered relative had tried to make a mask that when fitted to a man's face would change his entire future and had failed. And lo! the secret had just been whispered to her. "To me," she whispered to herself ecstatically, "to po' lil' me. An' I know it ees tr-rue, yes. It got to be tr-rue. 'Cause madda Nature, she will help in de work, an' w'at else you want?" For the life-mate she would choose for herself would be an octoroon, as fair as a lily. With her complexion and his she knew that she would be able to give to her children the mask which her grandfather had yearned. She saw now why he had failed. No doubt it was never meant for men to know anything about it at all. It must be in the keepings of mothers alone. "Now we will see," she told herself exultantly. "Ef my daughter got to wear a head handgcher lak me. Fo' me it ees notting. I cannot help. But jes' de same a son of mine goin' be king of some Carnival yet. You watch out fo' me."

And so when Paupet, the whitest octoroon that she had ever seen, came to the Quarter, she showed her preference for him at once. When, after their marriage, in the course of time their first born was expected she was like an experimentalist in the mating of cross-breeds, painfully nervous and full of the greatest anxiety over the outcome of a situation that she had been planning so long. What preparations she made! She fitted up a room especially for the event. She was extravagance itself in the selection of the garments, buying enough material to clothe half a dozen infants. She literally covered the fly leaves of the Bible with male and female names in preparation for the Christening; and made so many trips to town for all sorts of purchases that Paupet became full of anxiety for the outcome of it all.

To him she talked very freely now of her readiness in marrying him—it was really for the good of the child that was about to come to them. Her trials would not be her infant's. She had seen to that. He would look like Paupet, and could therefore choose his own way in life unhampered by custom or law.

To the midwife too she communicated her hopes and expectations, dwelling at great length upon the future of the child the whiteness of whose face would be a charm against every prevailing ill. Such optimism augured ill to the midwife who rarely vouchsafed her a word. When at length the child was born, the midwife tarried a long time before placing it into Julie's arms. It was sympathy upon her part that caused the delay. But Julie could not understand it. In the midst of her great sufferings she marvelled at it, until at length she caught a glimpse of her child's face. Then she screamed. With horror she saw that it was identical with the one in the locket about her neck. It was the image of her chocolate-colored mother.

1928

- The Kellogg-Briand Pact, a multilateral agreement renouncing war, is first signed. Eventually over 60 nations will sign; however, the lack of provision for enforcement renders the pact all but useless.
- Chiang Kai-shek and the Chinese Nationalists take control of China.
- The Soviet Union announces its first Five-Year Plan to collectivize agriculture.
- Ras Tafari becomes king of Ethiopia.
- Mexican president Alvaro Obregón is assassinated.
- British bacteriologist Alexander Fleming discovers penicillin.
- Mickey Mouse makes his film debut.
- Herbert Hoover elected president.
- Oscar DePriest becomes the first African American from a nonsouthern state to be elected to Congress.
- An experimental cooperative housing project, the Dunbar Apartments, opens in Harlem.

U.S. unemployment: 4.2%

Lynchings in the United States: 10 blacks, 1 white

Deaths:
> Eloise Bibb Thompson (8 Jan.)
> Lewis H. Latimer (11 Dec.)

Spingarn Medal:
> Charles W. Chesnutt (author)

Books:
> Raymond Garfield Dandridge, *Zalka Peetruza and Other Poems* (poetry)
> W. E. B. Du Bois, *Dark Princess* (novel)

Rudolph Fisher, *The Walls of Jericho* (novel)
Leslie Pinckney Hill, *Toussaint L'Ouverture: A Dramatic History*
    (drama)
Georgia Douglas Johnson, *An Autumn Love Cycle* (poetry)
Nella Larsen, *Quicksand* (novel)
Claude McKay, *Home to Harlem* (novel)

Periodicals:
    Harlem (Nov. 1928)
    Saturday Evening Quill (1928–30)

27 BATHESDA OF SINNERS RUN

Maude Irwin Owens

FROM *CRISIS*, MARCH–APRIL 1928

It was like reading the Books of Chronicles, to read in the Thornton family history of the attending succession of slave women that formed the single line of Bathesda's ancestry. The Thorntons had always boasted of their seven generations of slave housekeepers who had directly descended from the housekeeper of the first American Thornton. They would proudly point out the precious, faded entries, so faithfully recorded in the old genealogy. The paternal side of the issue was always politely ignored in strict accordance with the manners and customs of the South.

The scapegrace of the younger son of an English baron, Richard Thornton, was founder of the family. When gambling debts and foul dueling forced him to flee his native land, he decided upon the colony of George II under Governor Oglethorpe. His first slave purchase was written in two sentences, which seemed to wink and laugh up at the reader with its tan ink and old fashioned lettering. It read:

"On this day did I barter my gold hilted sword, some lace and several shillings to that villain from the Virginia colony whom I do sorely despise—for a black wench to cook my porridge, brew my tea and wash my linen. She is comely withal and methinks, the temper of a noble blooded colt; so I have named the vixen, Jezebel."

From this Jezebel on the issue became mulatto and less mulatto: for it was written that Jezebel foaled a likely mustard-colored filly whose father and master, with malicious humor, named for his King and the colony.

So Jezebel became the mother of Georgie; who begat Abigail; whose brat was Callie; whose offspring was Ruth; whose child was Viney; whose daughter was Anne; and twenty years after slavery, came Bathesda.

To the utter amazement and chagrin of her erstwhile master and mistress, when the bell of freedom tolled for those in bondage, Anne betook herself from under the Thornton roof, in spite of all the inducements and cajoleries the Thorntons offered.

She married Enoch Creek, a fusion of Creek Indian, Negro and white and who chose to select his surname from the Indian blood which dominated his being. He was a bitter man, having no faith or belief in mankind or the institutions and principles of mankind; a religion of hatred that banned all but Anne and, much later, little Bathesda.

They founded a tiny home at Sinners Run, the Negro suburb of Thorntonville, Georgia, that had been called after a famous camp-meeting revival sermon preached there, years back. Their cabin was a little apart and elevated from the other huts and shacks of the Sinners Run people, so that they could look down upon the road which was alternatingly red clay or yellow mud and note the comings and goings of those who lived upon it.

Anne attended the Sinners Run Baptist Church regularly and prayed that her husband find salvation. Enoch traded at the store because it was necessary—but after that, all socializing with their neighbors ceased; unless in the case of illness, when Anne was administering angel and healer of the small community. Within her lean yellow hands was the strange, soothing power to allay pain, and from her husband, she learned much of the Indian mysteries of roots and herbs for medicinal use.

They were thrifty and got along. For twenty years they worked, saved, improved their little two room home, and the acre upon which it stood. Anne was an expert needle-woman as Viney, Ruth and Callie had been before her; and she was in great demand in all the big houses down in Thorntonville. Enoch hired himself out as a plantation farmer, and in spite of his scowling silence, was known as a good hand.

Then, at the age of forty—when all hope of bearing the traditional one girl-child had flown from the heart of Anne, it happened; and Bathesda made her advent into the life of Sinners Run.

Enoch smiled for the first time—his squinting Indian eyes snapping with delight at the yellow gypsy-like Anne in the role of Madonna, with the robust little papoose that was his. Of course the Thorntons got wind of it, investigated and greedily annexed one more generation to old Jezebel's descendants, although the essence of reflected glory had lost its flavor since the inconvenient Emancipation. The distinction of being the first of her line born out of slavery was the most disgraceful thing that could have been written about Bathesda into the sacred Annals, according to Thornton opinion.

Two weeks later, Enoch stepped on a rusty spike. Blood-poisoning set in and, in spite of their combined knowledge of medicine and healing—his time had come to leave Anne and Bathesda, before Anne had convinced him there was a God.

Anne turned from the unmarked grave, and faced the world alone with her baby, unflinchingly—with that calm independence that asked no pity. She went about her sewing at the houses of her patrons, for a while, carrying her infant with her.

But as Bathesda began to toddle about, Anne realized her child should have home life, and be allowed to play in the vegetable patch and flower garden which Enoch had so painstakingly planted. So Anne took only work such as she could do at home, and her little daughter grew to be the marvel of the countryside—a healthy, lovely child.

She attended the broken down school-house to be taught by a wizened old maid from Connecticut a few months a year, and she sat at her mother's knee, during the school period . . . both struggling eagerly to master a clear fluent English. Anne, being ardently religious, insisted that the little girl read her Bible and attend church regularly, in which she was reluctantly obeyed.

Thus Bathesda grew up to womanhood. Beautiful—of deep-rooted intelligence handicapped by inadequate schooling, a pagan love for the gorgeous wonders of Nature and a passion for all things artistic. She became adept at the fine French seams and hemming; learned to feather-stitch the picturesque quilts on the huge frame, to weave highly imaginative Indian designs out of the bright silken rags into rugs and mats, to make the difficult Yankee hook rug, the knowledge of which had been introduced South by a Yankee Thornton bride; and best of all, she became an expert copier of the old ante-bellum samplers. Anne's sampler embroidering frame looked worm-eaten—it was so old; and Bathesda considered it with great reverence.

They made a picture to be remembered, sitting together at their artistic labors—the older woman and her daughter. Anne invariably talked religion to Bathesda having sensed a silent indifference which bespoke much of Enoch's atheism. When at the stuffy little church, the sermon had become highly exhortive, and the worshipers' down-trodden souls burst forth in howling primitive devotion to a God they desperately believed in—even when great tears spilled down her quiet mother's cheeks, Bathesda's sole reaction was a disdainfully cold squinting of her pretty black eyes.

"It's Enoch! It's Enoch!" mourned old Anne, as she watched the child of her old age flower into radiant womanhood with no change of heart.

"But Mother," Bathesda would say, "you take on so 'bout nothin'. Ain't we happy? We have always been different from them in our way of livin' and doin' things and so how can you expect me to be like them in their church doin's? You are not like them when you feel the spirit, Mother. You cry a little bit, but I have never seen you rear and tear and stomp and scream 'halleluliah' like someone crazy. . . . I hate it! My church is the purple mist stealin' ahead of the red dawn—the chirpin' wood-chucks; wild wood blossoms! If I ever 'get religion' Mother 'twill be in that kind of church, and not among the sweaty, hysterical hypocrites of your church. Why! I believe to my soul, Mother, you are the only real Christian among them, and do the least testifyin'!"

"Child—you don't understand. It is as real with them as life itself! It is given to each to work out his own destiny in the Lord, in his own way. It is the feelin' that they are weak and sinful that overpowers them so—in their strivin' to follow the Good Book."

"I don't care 'bout them anyways, Mother. We are better colored folks . . . that's all. It just ain't in them to be better. Look at their homes! Bare plank floors that all their scrubbin' and scourin' don't improve; walls plastered with newspapers full of pictures that they think are pretty; gunny-sacks tacked up to the windows . . . ugh! Give them their winter supply of potatoes, rice and hog meat . . . let them go to church and give chitterlin' suppers . . . plenty of shoutin' and back-bitin' and they are happy all winter long, Mother. But—look at our home!"

She waved her pale brown hand proudly around the room in which they sat. The walls were whitewashed. The floor was covered with a huge rag rug rich with colorful stripes and the single square window was draped with deep rose curtains that fluttered happily in the breeze. They had been made from flour bags soaked in kerosene to remove the printing, and dyed with berry juice. There were two fine old pieces of colonial mahogany in this outer room—a gigantic highboy and a marble-topped medicine chest. The other articles of furniture were three rush-bottomed chairs and a table that Enoch had made, and carved all over with the weirdly grotesque totem-pole gargoyles. Upon the mantel over the fireplace were a brilliant basket and two odd potteries also relics of the Creek strain in the father of Bathesda. Small painted tubs and cans were in interesting groups about the room, filled with plants of various sorts.

"I don't suppose I should say I hate them, Mother dear," Bathesda continued, "but I can get along without them. I shall do as you have always done . . . when they're sick, I'll make them well if they call upon me—but I don't . . . I can't be one of them in religion or otherwise."

"Ah, my child," sadly smiled Anne, "you may have inherited the sense of medicine from Enoch, your father, but the Divine gift of healing can never descend upon a disbeliever . . . and you are the first of us women who has not been born with the gift since Mother Jezebel. She, even in her early day, was a Christian convert."

At this, Bathesda would shake her head impatiently as if flinging aside the admonitions of her mother, and the two long black braids would flare about her arms and shoulders. Then, bowing earnestly over her work, she would concentrate upon the exact copying of probably old Viney's intricately designed sampler with the words—"Little flakes make the biggest snow," ordered by an antique dealer from Savannah.

Bathesda's mother died in her sixtieth year, and never had there been such a funeral in the history of Sinners Run. Unlike her husband who had only a faithful wife and new born babe to follow him to his grave—the entire countryside turned out to do honor to Anne Creek. All of the present generation of Thorntons came from their town house in Savannah, in full force, much to the awe of the Sinners Run folk. They even hinted about how appropriate and fitting it would be if Anne were buried beside Viney, in Thorntonville; but Bathesda was obdurate.

"Thank you, Mr. and Mrs. Thornton, but my mother's place is beside her husband. My father has been alone out there, long enough."

So the Thorntons had a second lesson in Negro independence.

"Promise me, my daughter, that you will seek Jesus!" gasped Anne in her last consciousness. "Go to the church—seek Him until you find Him . . . and He will give you your birthright like he has given it to all the rest of us. Promise your poor old Mammy, Bathesda . . . baby!"

And so she had promised to seek religion and the power to heal the sick.

Bathesda lived on, as the years rolled by, much as when Anne lived. She made beautiful things with her graceful slender hands, and more money than she needed in her simple mode of living. She lived alone with the spirit presences of her parents, except for the loyal protection of a watch dog. She cared for the gay little flower garden tenderly and kept her graves freshly decorated in flower season. She grew her vegetables, also the roots and herbs with which she concocted her famous medicinal recipes. She attended the Sinners Run Baptist Church and contributed to its support; but the Indian in her worshipped only the wonders of Nature and she put no other gods before the beauty of the earth.

The colored people of Sinners Run envied and hated her, yet maintained a deceitful courtesy that permitted them to call upon her when in need of intervention with white people, money or in sickness. Her ability to always smooth the way for them, in any form of distress, was known with a certainty that was uncanny to their superstitious minds. She could do all except smooth out actual pain like her mother had done. However, she did her all, in the name of Anne . . . she herself caring little for these crude mean-hearted and petty people, who grinned in her face for favors, and hissed "half white bastard" behind her back. This last amused her, however, since her intelligence allowed her to see no difference between the black and yellow progeny of the illicit unions of slavery.

"What queer religion these folks have," laughed the woman, "it breaks forth in a certain place, and at a certain fixed time, then they lose it 'til the next time."

The women were especially incensed against her, because—if they married at all, they invariably married men who Bathesda had rejected. She allowed each suitor in his time to visit her, sit as long as he pleased admiring her at the embroidering rack, while she, with serene indifference, hoped he would make his departure in time for her to take her dog and go to the crest for the sunset, or some such solitary jaunt. She could say "no" with a cool pleasantness that retained their goodwill; but the wives to whom she gave the men up hated her venomously for so doing. Hated her for wrapping her long glossy braids around and around her head in a coronet which made her a queen among them. Hated her for appearing so youthful despite her forty-seven years. Hated her for not shouting at church, and for failing to testify or profess. Hated her for having the prettiest house and garden in the community—for making the medicine that cured them. Hated her for weaving and embroidering while they took in washing, or labored beside their men in the cotton and corn fields. Hated her for her chaste aloofness of man, while they bore large families in the morass of poverty and misery. Hated her for showing contempt for the edicts of fashions and mail order houses up North or the cheap stores in Thorntonville and Savannah and for wearing the simply made, richly embroidered garments which none could duplicate. For all these reasons, the women of Sinners Run despised Bathesda.

Among them, she had one sincere friend in the person of young Becky Johnson. The dark-skinned girl had sought Bathesda in a frenzy one stormy midnight. Bathesda had donned her cape and accompanied the wild young mother to the bedside of her baby who was strangling with diphtheria. It was a simple deed; the swabbing of the little throat with boiled vinegar and salt, with a few directions, but the brown girl had hugged Bathesda's knees and kissed her comfortably shod feet in feverish adoration. The father, too, had looked dumb gratitude with brimming eyes. After this incident, Becky took Li'l Jim up to see Bathesda regularly, and Bathesda became greatly attached to the small family, such devotion from Becky having awakened within her cold nature, something akin to affection.

Becky's sister, mother and grandmother, strongly disapproved of this friendship. The sister, whose name was Cisseretta, was somewhat of a belle, and when rigged up in the cast-off clothes of the white people for whom she worked, was, for Sinners Run, quite elegant. She was light brown, with hazel eyes that were sly and coquettish. Her hair was of that yellowish cotton-batten sort, known as riney. She meant to marry better than had her older sister, and scorned the field hands as prospective husbands, although she was not averse to keeping them from dancing attendance on the less discriminating girls of her set.

The mother, Eliza Lambert, was about Bathesda's age and a malicious "yes" woman to gossip and trouble making, although too stupid herself to even instigate a healthy lie.

The grandmother, Granny Lou, was an ancient crone, black as pitch, who had lost trace of her age, but knew everything pertaining to a scandalous nature concerning the families of both races for miles around. She sat in one corner year in and year out, wrapped in filthy shawls and hoods summer and winter, smoking her foul clay pipe, and spitting snuff into the maw of the tumble-down stove, or gumming her vicious old tales. She was reputed to be the oldest woman in that section of Georgia, and to have borne more children than she herself knew; Eliza, being her youngest, to whom she had hitched herself. Just as most of the trouble making and under-current of evilness in the neighborhood could usually be traced to the chair of Granny Lou and Lambert household, so was she guilty of inciting most of the fierce antipathy among the women, against Bathesda.

One particular early autumn morning, she pursed and screwed her shrunken lips around to settle the snuff and saliva making a "Mpwhumn-mpwhumn" noise, and began lisping to Eliza who was washing:

"Heh, heh! Ah sees whar dat-ar new ministah done gine sottin' up to Thesdy's already—heh, heh! 'Pears lak to me dat you 'omans ain't slaves no moah an' oughten't go fer to put up wid sich cayin' on. Lize . . . Yo' Cissy tryin' to sot huh cap foah him, but 'pears lak to me, effen she gits him, won't be twell dat Thesdy's chawed 'im up an' spat him back at huh! Heh, heh!" and as if to suit the word with the action, she spat into the pink wood ashes which were falling out of the stove pit.

"'Tain't nothin' to them Jezebel 'omans, noways. De white folks make me sick cayin' on so high 'bout dem. Day all sold dere souls to de debbil. Don't dey fool 'round wid roots 'n things? . . . mind how dey nebber show dere natchul age lak we'uns does?"

The silence that followed was broken by the sudsy slapping of wet clothes with home made lye soap. Eliza was too busy to bother about her old mother's chatter this morning, but Granny Lou was nothing loath to amusing herself.

"Becky, lak a li'l fool . . . she run up dere case day yaller 'oman do foah dat brat ahern, jis what any of ussen coulda did. Ah knows, chal! Yo' Granny Lou knowed dem f'om way back to Callie!"

"Kyah, kyah, kyah! Granny Lou—hush yo' mouf," laughingly yelled Eliza above the suds, steam and slop, with perspiration dripping from her corn-rowed head into the tub.

Cisseretta, who had entered the room unnoticed, flared up angrily at the old hag's challenge—

"I wants Brother Parson Brown, and I's shore goin' to git him. 'Tain't goin' to be after Thesdy done chawed him, either, Granny!" So saying, she jammed her hands down upon her hips with her legs astride and frowned belligerently from her mother to her grinning grandmother.

The pine door swung open admitting Becky, resplendent in a soft white dress carrying Li'l Jim who was sportive in a blue smock and cap. The three women were aghast at the sudden picture. Poor Becky who was content to drudge in a one room cabin with her baby, for a husband who scarcely could pay for his fat back and meal down at the store,—what right had she to look nicer than Cisseretta, the acknowledged social leader of Sinners Run!

"Whar'd je git dem cloes?" darkly inquired Eliza of her daughter.

"Oh Mammy! Ain't dey jist swell? Miss Thesdy done made dis up special foh me out o' brand new goods case Ah told huh 'twas my second year married, today! See Li'l Jim? Ain't he grand? I has a big suppah foh Big Jim when he gits home and thought I would run in an' let you folks see us."

"Humph! 'Miss' Thesdy! Since whin did we start 'Missin'' yaller niggers? Was Parson Brown anywhere bouts up there?" this from Cisseretta.

"Seems to me dat dose cloes would scorch yo' skin, chal. Dat Thesdy is a woman wid no religion whatsomever," exasperatingly sighed Eliza.

"Jes' gib yo' all dose cloes fuh to git yo' wrapped up in huh, fudder—dan she gine conjuh yo' . . . heah me, now, heah me!" snapped old Granny Lou with a portentious shaking of her beshawled head.

Poor Becky! All her joyous happiness so quickly transformed to bitter antagonism.

"How come yo'all hates that pore woman so? What she done done aginst you? All I seed she done was good! She's up dere in huh own pretty li'l house, amindin' huh business, and you folks down heah hatin' huh! Cisseretta? You won't make no hit wid Parson Brown . . . hatin' Miss Thesdy, 'case he thinks she is jest grand! As for me and Big Jim, she saved our boy's life which is moah dan you what's his own kin-folks done, and we loves huh, even ef she ain't done professed 'ligion. From what I seed of huh and knowed of younes, she's a heap sight nigh to God dan you folks who eat out yo' hearts wid hatin' huh!"

She gathered the bewildered Li'l Jim up and left the scene of unsympathetic relatives, muttering to herself— "Gawd! Effen I stayed widdem any longer I would lose my own 'ligion. They's my own folks, but dey simply breed evilness, and I doesn't blame sweet Miss Thesdy from not minglin' wid 'em 'ceptin' when she has to."

In the Lambert cabin, Granny Lou was grunting— "See dat? She done got dat chal tu'ned agin huh own folks already . . . an' de preachuh eatin' out ob huh hand,"—with a cunning glance at Cisseretta.

"For two cents, Granny—" whined Cisseretta, petulantly, "I'd git the women together and go up to her ol' house and beat her up!"

"Kyah kyah! Lawsy me! Hush yo' mouf, chal!" elaborately guffawed her mother.

"Go hade, den . . . go hade! Do moah—an' talk less, honey!" huskily whimpered the old woman to her infuriated grandchild.

The day had been a busy one for Bathesda. She had contracted to make reproductions of the old samplers for an important Jewish antique dealer of Atlanta. Little Alice Thornton, quite grown up, and home from college, had motored out to see her, bringing with her her fiancé from Boston, an artist. He had begged for the privilege of painting Bathesda in all the glory of her little cottage and embroidering frames. To please Alice, she consented, on condition that it wouldn't interfere with her work.

"Like one of Millet's peasant women," he had said—"and that interior! Worthy of the old Dutch masters."

The young minister had sat awhile, explaining his well meant plan of progress for his congregation, which she knew would never be accepted by the deluded Sinners Run folks, the present pastor being their first seminary man. They understood only the old fashioned untrained "called-but-not-sent" type of ministering.

Becky and Li'l Jim dropped in with the new things she had made for them, and the sight of the mother and child transformed by her handiwork, thrilled her deeply.

She bent her queenly head over the crimson, green and purple threads she was interweaving so intricately into the words—"Heart within, God without" on the square of yellow, and smiled the smile of the middle-aged who had all they wanted in life—peace, pleasant labor, and contentment. Why should she be sad because of a God who withheld Himself, or the doubtful power of healing a people who despised her?

She decided to pick a fresh cabbage for her supper, and going to the door, was surprised to see Cisseretta Lambert approaching. With shifting eyes, and lowered brow, she informed Bathesda they had come to fetch her for a friend. At the little picket gate stood an old rickety home-made cart with ill matched wheels, drawn by a sorry nag whose hips punctured his skin in miss-meal significance. Eliza was driving and perched beside her for all the world like a bundled up mummy, sat Granny Lou.

"We kin fotch you there and back in no time, Thesdy. New folks jest come to Sinners Run, and powerful sick."

Bathesda hurriedly threw a light shawl around her shoulders with a strong sense of foreboding which she forcibly thrust out of her mind, and joined the trio at the cart.

She and Cisseretta rode backwards with their feet swinging, and nothing was said by the four women as the half dead animal faltered along the lonely road pulling the unbalanced, lurching, wabbling vehicle behind them.

Then Eliza . . .

"Kyah kyah! Heah we all is, folksies! Kyah kyah! Lawdy, Lawdy, Lawd!"

Bathesda turned from the back end of the wagon and saw glaring malevolently at her, the dark faces of ten or twelve women. They were as a pack of hungry hounds eager to be off on the chase. Cisseretta leaped from her seat on the wagon and rudely grabbed Bathesda, causing her to stumble to the ground on her knees. As if waiting for the initiative action from their leader, they pounced upon her, dragging her by the arms up the sloping hillside. The decrepit conveyance with the beswaddled old woman, was left standing on the road.

The maddened women yelled violent invectives—brandished whips, twigs and sticks aloft, dragging her roughly uphill, not allowing her to regain her foothold or the freedom of her arms.

"Thought you'd git yo' claws on Revern Bro Brown, didn't you? We see 'bout dat, won't we? Cain't feed him none o' yo' hoodoo vittles . . . nuh-uh!"

"Yes indeedy. We is gwine to see 'bout all dis heah monkey business yo' been cayin' on all dese yeahs wid de men folks. . . ."

"Think you better dan ussens, doesn't you? Humph! Old half white niggers make me sick . . . cain't be white an' cain't be black!"

"Naw! We niggers don't want you and de white folks won't hab you!"

"Lawdy, Lawdy, Lawd today! Yeowh!"

"Pull huh ol' plaits down! Make me tiahd wid huh ol' dawg har! Wouldn't have straight har, mahself—Revelations say as plain as day—'har lak lambs wool' like ussen got. . . ."

"Sis Grenn? Dis is shoah a holy deed Cisseretta done called on us to do . . . to protect ouah poah pastor from de wiles ob dis sinner woman. . . ."

"Kyah kyah! Lawd today!"

They reached the summit of the hill which was capped with a small patch of woods. A few of the trees had recently been chopped down, judging by the fresh stumps. The several women in whose clutches Bathesda had fallen, suddenly released their hold on her and jumped back out of her reach. But Bathesda merely stomped the caked dirt from her shoes and torn skirt, threw a quiet searching glance around the semicircle of women, and made to swing her loosened braids around her head.

This action galled Cisseretta, who saw in it a self assurance, a composure that was shaking the courage of her vigilance committee. She sprang at Bathesda heavily with an angry snarl, pushing her back into a tree which instantaneously crashed to the earth, sideways, sending Cisseretta and all the women scrambling and yelping down the hill.

"Conjuh woman! conjuh . . . Lawd Ah's feared!"

"Hoodoo stuff! Told yo'all we oughten to bother wid huh!"

"Lawd! Jist 'low me to git home once moah . . . please!"

"Cisseretta done got ussen into dis mess . . . !"

From the opposite direction came two white men, hurrying toward Bathesda who stood arranging her hair beside the fallen tree.

"Anybody hurt, Auntie? We are clearing these here woods for Ben Lovett who has bought the strip, and my buddy here—he sprained his joint while chopping down that 'un a few minutes ago. We went up to my shack after some liniment and we didn't 'reckon anyone would come along before we got back. The tree was nearly cut thru and I 'spec a slight jostle knocked her over."

"No one was hurt. It fell to the side," murmured the yellow woman absently—eyes searching into the distance.

A delicate tenderness played over her face, and kindly wrinkles appeared about her mouth and forehead. Like Haggard's "She," Bathesda unexpectedly looked her age, all at once. She had dropped the cloak of a hardened, held-over youth, and taken on the ethereal robe of an inner beauty—a soul transformation had taken place.

She, for the first time, turned directly to the lumberjacks, and asked of the one with the bandaged arm—

"Is it bad?"

"Hurts mightily and swellin' every second."

She unwrapped the crude bandage, wiped away the stench of liniment, cupped her two hands about the swollen arm and gazed upward—her thin lips moving almost imperceptibly while the men stood transfixed.

She finally withdrew her hands, clenched them into tight fists and then shook them open and away from her, as if throwing off the contamination of alien flesh.

"Now . . . it is well!"

"Bill! Honest to John! She's right! The dadburned misery has gone completely, and look! The swellin' is goin' down right before my very eyes!"

"Good God! 'tis a miracle we've just witnessed! The woman's a saint." And he hastily crossed himself, while the other man tested his healed arm by swinging an ax.

Bathesda went down the hill with wide masculine strides—the light winds causing her snagged skirt and white apron to billow and flurry. Her eyes were two muddy pools of tears. She was testifying.

"Up Calvary's rugged brow did I go, this day with Thee, dear Lord . . . To the very foot of the Cross . . . and I saw the bloody nails in Thy precious feet . . . the cruel thorns . . . and the bitter cup was spared me . . . me, a worthless worm . . . but Thou didst drink it to the dregs!"

And she went home with a new power—with understanding, tolerance and forgiveness; to be one of her people; to take care of Becky with her Li'l Jim and Big Jim; and the fragrant drops of rain pelted her in gentle benediction.

28 HE MUST THINK IT OUT
Florida Ruffin Ridley

FROM *SATURDAY EVENING QUILL*, JUNE 1928

Henry Fitts took up Gray's letter. It was the last in his mail to be reached and he had avoided the big document largely because of its bulkiness. With pressing financial adjustments to make, Fitts was in no mood for discursiveness in any form.

While he was frowningly considering his mail, Henry's daughter Irene had interrupted. Fitts had resignedly pushed aside the disturbing literature to look upon his daughter, equally disturbing in her way, and now bound upon an expedition of "week-ending."

Irene had found her father in a familiar attitude, and had rallied him, as was her habit.

"Cheer up, darling!" she had said, as with calm assurance she had swept the sheets from before him and established herself upon his desk. "This outfit is not entirely to the bad. I expect it to land me on Hazard's staff. I have a hunch it made a big impression on Minnie Hazard at the class luncheon today. I'd like to embrace you, but haven't time to trifle with my make-up. Now, brace up, dearest. You were nice to marry early so as to have many years to enjoy the prosperity to be achieved by your wonder child!"

Although Irene had drawn the usual caressing smile, her banter had slipped off the edge of her father's mood. There was quiet, approving fondness in his eyes, as he watched the youthful figure whose vitality and poise were so clearly revealed in its costuming.

Irene was talking now seriously but practically and vividly, talking of her plans, but Fitts was not following her, although his mind and heart were absorbed in her.

What had it meant to produce this clear-cut, adorable young thing, this vigorous, healthy body in its absurd yet fascinating clothes, the clear, responsive mind, the cultivated taste? It had cost more than money, and money had never come easily to him. It had cost frayed nerves and anxious days. But her ambition was no greater than his. He was proud of his children—how proud!—how fondly proud! Irene, the eldest, the best beloved, she was his gift to posterity.

It had been nearly closing time when Irene had taken her affectionate and lively departure from his office. Fitts took up the letter and saw with surprise that it was from Gray, Ephraim Gray. Why should Gray, whose office was in the same building, whom he ran across in or out of court, almost any day—why should he send a letter, a long letter in long hand, and in his own hand, at that?

In the growing quiet he began to read. The outer office was by now deserted. His own stenographer had long since clicked daintily down the corridor. The doors of the elevators had given their last clank, and a few belated passengers were running down the stairs.

Fitts glanced at his watch as he picked up Gray's letter. It was time to go home, and he would take the letter with him; and yet, somehow, he would rather read it here. Besides, it would take only a few minutes to run it over.

What the deuce, anyway, had Gray to say on paper? True, they had been thrown together, in a way, on government cases, but Gray was counted in another race; was, in fact, a Negro, and except in the courts, very seldom seen.

In a way, Fitts had been an admirer of Gray. He had admired the strong personality of the big man whose deep, arresting voice carried an irresistible human, as well as logical, appeal. He had wondered at the poise which held through circumstances of so persistently tragic a flavor. They had been drawn together in a certain kind of restricted companionship, and Fitts had enjoyed the dry and genial humor of the man. It had been only a few days ago that they had laughed together over an old photograph, which Fitts produced, of one of his forebears wearing the strained expression and painful best clothes called for in photographs of the "sixties."

"If they could only have caught him unawares, Gray. By George, he has the same lion head as yourself!"

He had lingered as Gray had told some incidents of his own life and experiences, a field which the man had seemed loth to enter, but from which, under the spell of Fitts' sympathy, he drew tales of tragic interest. They had sat late that day, so late that Fitts had a passing regret, more or less poignant, that it was not possible to take the man home with him, to eat dinner with them, to charm Bella and Irene. But of course that was unthinkable; the idea had been hurriedly, almost frantically, dismissed!

Harassed as Fitts had been, and was, by the many demands of a growing family, he naturally had his ears open for any current tale of opportunities for big money; although it had never happened, he was always hoping for some ideas, some suggestions that might be grasped for his own benefit; so when Gray had approached him a short time before with a tale of possible wealth for a client of his, Fitts had been an interested listener.

Gray's story had been about a recently built highway leading to a newly developed manufacturing center which had brought some old forgotten woodlots and their to-be-found owners into prominence and prosperity. During the telling it had been impossible for Fitts to suppress a twinge of envy and a surge of bitterness. Of course Gray's clients must be Negroes—Negroes inheriting American land! while he, Fitts . . . It was a damned shame that he had had no help. With the hope of getting, without reading the letter, an idea of what it was all about, Fitts began to glance hastily through the many sheets he had taken from the envelope. There were enclosures. There were arresting phrases. He snapped on his desk light and sat down to read:

My Dear Fitts:

The information which I am passing on to you, in this statement, I have withheld until I was absolutely sure of its validity; more than this, I have not brought myself to give you these facts until I had become convinced myself that it was the right and proper step for me to take.

I have been weeks in coming to this conclusion, and now that the decision that you should have the facts has been reached, I shall not weary or annoy you by beating around the bush.

In investigating my client's claim to the tract of woodland whose ownership has recently come into dispute and of which we have so often talked, I found that there was an adjacent lot in demand and waiting the appearance of a legal owner. Naturally I interested myself in an endeavor to trace the ownership of this property. So successfully have I done this that I tracked the original owner to Texas, and then identified him as the original owner of a tract of land there on which oil wells were afterwards discovered, and which lately has gained much notoriety as the "Garden Oil Fields."

Stephen Griggs, in whose name the title of the Ardley Woodlots (those of which we have talked) rests, was the brother of Eben Griggs, who owned adjoining lots, those claimed by my client as a descendant of Eben Griggs. Stephen Griggs disappeared while a young man,—in fact, while a boy,—and was entirely lost sight of by relatives and friends. Eben Griggs had two daughters, both of whom left the lonely homestead. One appears to have dropped out of sight, after taking service in a distant city; the other moved away upon her marriage, but her descendants never lost sight of their claim to Eben Griggs' property, for the title was redeemed by his grandson in recent years. This grandson, in the absence of other known heirs, had also claimed title to the lots left by his great-uncle Stephen.

In settling this claim for my client, who is the great-grandson of Eben Griggs, I have given much time to an effort to track and locate the descendants of Stephen Griggs, should he have any. It has been a long and tiring process, the details of which I will submit to you at another time. Here and now I will briefly outline the results.

I have found that Stephen Griggs never married, and that he wandered by degrees into the far southwest. Then he evidently took up a small tract of land of little apparent value, but which probably kept him alive. At his death he left his little property to be held by the courts until a legal claimant should appear.

For many years those sixty lonely acres of Stephen Griggs went almost unnoticed. At one time they were rented in order to obtain land fees, but in the main they were overlooked. Recently a tenant discovered oil upon this land and made a frenzied attempt to purchase and obtain a clear title. It was through the broadcasting of this sensational news that my attention was attracted, and that, after a long investigation, I connected the owner of the land upon which these oil wells were located with the original unknown owner of the Ardley woodlots, whose sale I was negotiating. I am now convinced that Stephen Griggs was the owner of both and that the collateral descendants of Stephen Griggs can claim title not only to his share in the Ardley woods, but also to one of the best yielding oil fields now operating. You may be asking of what interest this can be to you?

Simply this, I have found through my investigations that you are indisputably a lineal descendant of the brother, and, with one other, the only legal heir, of Stephen Griggs!

You will recall my interest in an old portrait of your great-grandfather's which you showed me, your sole heirloom, you said. My client has its duplicate. It is his great-grandfather, also, which would make him (my client) your cousin one degree removed. Further proof will be found in enclosed papers and in those which I am forwarding, which are copies of birth and death and marriage certificates that have been secured to prove your claim.

If there should seem to be impropriety in my using our acquaintance to help obtain this knowledge, you must lay it to a lawyer's propensity to investigate, and my natural desire to push my client's interest.

At this, Fitts threw down the sheets and leaped excitedly to his feet.

"My God, man, make no excuses! You've saved my life!" He spoke aloud, the words tumbling from his lips.

With hands trembling and blood pounding in his temples, he went back to his reading.

Among the papers I am sending you, you will find description of both properties and of the great potential wealth within your grasp.

Before allowing you to publicly investigate and corroborate this claim, there is one other piece of information which I must pass on to you. I do it reluctantly, for although it is so, yet it is dastardly that these facts should be a matter of such vital import. However, there is no course open to me but to tell you that my client, co-heir with you, the great-grandson of your great-grandfather, the son of your mother's cousin and the great-nephew of Stephen Griggs is, myself, Ephraim Gray!

With bulging eyes Fitts read again and yet again. "The son of your mother's cousin"—what did the man mean? What was he driving at? How could Gray, who was almost black in color, be the son of *his* mother's cousin? Was this a fool joke? Was it possible that Gray was trying to blackmail him?

"The black rascal! How dare he?" He almost shouted the words.

Then he stopped short, stabbed with a remembrance of Gray's impressive sincerity. Suppose it were true—impossible of course, but just suppose . . . Tied up with a black family!

"No, no!" he almost shrieked, as he threw down the papers and rushed to open the window. "Damn him, no, no!"

So violent was his instinctive protest that a feeling of nausea overcame him as he leaned against the open window seeking air. For some minutes he stood there, fighting down the mental and physical surge which was becoming chaos within him.

Regaining, after a while, a measure of composure, he stumbled back to his desk and attempted to take up the disordered sheets of Gray's letter, but the full sense of the hideous implications again overwhelmed him. He— "a nigger" and Irene, his Irene, his gay, lovely daughter . . . It was a lie! a *lie!*

He flung his arms over his desk, and in doing so uncovered a snapshot of Gray,—one taken in the corridor by an amateur photographer in the building. Glancing at it with eyes dulled by pain and anguish, his slow gaze was caught by something familiar in the picture: the outline, the poise of the body, the set of the head suggested some one—he hadn't noticed it before, but there it was. Yes, the resemblance was there—no need to bring out the portrait of old Eben.

Fitts tore the card in two and sank his head into his hands. Well, it might be true. No, not *really* true, never, *never,* but how to keep down any suspicion that any one had thought it to be true. It was Gray that must be handled. He must be made to swallow his words; they must be forced down his throat.

He fumbled for Gray's letter and steeled himself to go on.

I will not, for obvious reasons, make extended comment upon the situation; the papers accompanying will make clear many things which may seem inexplicable. At any rate, it may not be out of place to emphasize the fact that there were many unions in the backwoods of our state, and that these mingled the blood of Indians, Negroes and whites, and many cases are on record where traces of Negro blood have grown faint with subsequent white infusions. Lois Griggs, your grandmother and sister to Nancy Griggs, my grandmother, seems, as I said, to have left home early in life to take service with a family in a distant city. Her movements were never checked by her family, but you will find among the papers a true record which leads straight to your birth, the son of a white mother and a supposedly white man; but, really, the grandson of old Eben Griggs, Negro and Indian.

After the signature came a postscript:

It is no reflection upon my regard for you or on the sincerity of our intercourse that from the first I have had an idea of our relationship. In fact, from letters which were left by my father and which you will be allowed to examine, I judged that just such a situation would develop. I confess I have been on the outlook, ready to follow any and every clue. America's attitude in such relationships made it impossible for me to be more open with you. Even now, whatever may be your future plans, they may be made without reference to me.

Fitts straightened himself stiffly. The impressiveness of Gray's personality was too strong upon him to allow a complete rejection of the whole matter. He arose from his chair and dragged himself to the door of his coat closet, stumbling over a chair in his way. He turned on the light and consulted the mirror sunk in the door.

Yes, he had the same face, a face which was even a little whiter than it was before he had received the staggering news that he was no longer a white man. If this thing proved to be true, what was he, and where did he belong? Where would he look for friends? He gave himself a prolonged stare. He was the same man identically, the same man that he was at this time yesterday, and yet he must be damned by what—for what . . .

And what about his family? Fitts' eyes grew wild as the thought of Bella, of Irene, came into his mind, and then he laughed at his reflection in the glass. Was it not ridiculous for him to be afraid to face facts? But his laugh cracked. He *was* afraid, miserably afraid! He shivered as his imagination leaped forward and tortured him with the pictures it drew. Doors closed on Irene, his loved and lovely Irene, so adequately prepared and so gallantly facing a friendly world— doors closed everywhere and on every side—in schools and stores and churches and homes!

And then, that Jim Crow business, with sheriffs waiting for objectors! He would shoot, kill! Let any one dare insult his daughter! Yes, he would show how this thing should be met! But how absurd to imagine that Irene would be treated like a common black girl! And he laughed again, and again the laugh broke.

There was that incident of last winter. He had seen the girl in Gray's office—a girl as fair as his Irene. It was a judgment against him that he hadn't been more outspoken. But now—he would cry their crimes from the house tops.

Of all persons why should this curse come upon *him*, upon him who had always been tolerant and sympathetic? Why hadn't some of those ugly fanatics, Negro-haters,—why hadn't they been the ones to suffer?

It wasn't fair—it was unjust that a good man, that a sweet girl, should be so punished. Punished? *Cursed!* Talk about a merciful God! Hadn't he been a Christian—hadn't he been upright? And God had let this come upon him. He would not submit—he would maim, he would murder! He would rather see Irene dead!

"Better dead!" he whispered as, spent with emotion, he slumped into a nearby chair. His overwrought feelings gave way, and for a while he sprawled motionless and blessedly thoughtless. Into this lethargy other thoughts began to creep. Why need the truth be divulged? Why couldn't that be managed? It shouldn't be hard!

Fitts jerked up straight, his head lifted, the light returned to his eyes. He was foolish to despair. There was always a way.

Gray was leaving America. He would get Gray's promise of secrecy. He would not appear as a claimant of the fortune. He would pay *that* price for secrecy. Gray could be trusted! And Fitts laughed again. He threw up the window and drew deep breaths of the cool night air. The world was all right again—everything was all right—all right! What a fool he had been to give way! To let himself get worked up to such a frenzy! It was a good thing no one had seen or heard him.

The thing to do was to swear Gray to secrecy and to avoid all contact with him or people of his kind.

And now for home and his delayed dinner. Get away, get away—The phrase persisted in his mind! But if he was to get away, why not take the money? Think what it would do! If he didn't take the money, Gray would know the secret just the same. Would there be any advantage not to take the money? In either case, he would be at the mercy of Gray. *Could* Gray be trusted? And if he could, why couldn't they manage together that the world shouldn't know the truth?

What would happen should Gray die? That would have to be arranged; could it be arranged?

Would it be better to refuse the money, after all? What difference would it make, except that he would be poor instead of rich? He was getting confused again; but another gleam shot through his confusion.

"Bella!" he almost shouted in his relief. "I'll talk with Bella! She'll know what is best. She always does." Why hadn't he thought of her before? She always saw light in the darkest problems. Why, of course.

But he stopped short again. Tell Bella what?—that in marrying him she had been deceived, betrayed, condemned? No, he could not tell Bella. Even that comfort was denied him. Fate was giving the last twist to the implements of torture!

Well, what was it he was trying to decide?

He must concentrate!

He must think it out before he saw Bella.

He must think it out.

He must think it out alone.

The bell of the telephone shrilled again and again, unheard in the darkened room.

Henry Fitts was thinking it out—and alone!

29 ANTHROPOI
John F. Matheus

FROM *OPPORTUNITY*, AUGUST 1928

There were visible several shades of green—the deep verdure of the trees on the West Virginia hill-sides, the bright green of the trees, lighted by the noon sun on the Ohio shore, then the dull, oily green of the river and the green, differing from all, that shone in the grey eyes of Bushrod Winter—the green of envy and exasperation.

Bush Winter had long held bitter feelings against Demetrius Pappaniasus. The latter had come from Greece by way of the Latin Quarter of Paris, where he had drudged for months in a tailor shop on the Boulevard Raspail until he had garnered enough francs to pay for steerage passage to New York. Wandering about like his famous countryman of classical times he drifted West and finally settled down in the Tri-State Valley, where the Ohio river touches Pennsylvania, West Virginia, and the commonwealth which is that river's namesake.

Bush Winter was an American of African descent. Born in Ohio in the last year of the Civil War he had grown up in a free and friendly atmosphere, a tradition handed down from the establishment of the Northwest Territory. He had gone through the grammar school and had acquired quite early an argumentative interest in public activities which developed into petty leadership among his group in local politics.

Demetrius Pappaniasus was an undersized, swarthy, black haired Greek.

Bush Winter was an oversized, swarthy, black haired mulatto.

When Bush Winter first knew the Greek the men and boys around town called him John, a general appellation then coming into vogue among native Americans of the eighteen-nineties to designate the foreigner. Bush was driving a dray for a living. It was a big dray pulled by powerful Percheron horses. He was an expert in moving heavy objects, iron safes and pianos. Daily he drove up Market street to meet the Panhandle trains and daily he was greeted from all sides in hale small town intimacy, "Hello, Bush. How goes 'er?"

In those days Bush had not been long married and he found much joy in coming back to town on Saturday nights to buy groceries and gossip in the "Equal Rights Barber Shop" where black and white could have their tonsorial needs attended to. Sometimes he would drop in Pappaniasus's bootblack stand on the corner of Market and Westmoreland Avenue and pay him a nickel to shine his broad shoes. And the little man shined them well, bending over his task with the finesse of an artist, rubbing the paste in with his fingers, gnarled and dirty with blacking under the nails.

Pappaniasus lived then on Water street with his brown-skin Syrian wife. All the newly arrived wops and hunkies lived on Water street: Croatians, Poles, Bohemians, Italians, Greeks, Syrians. They were piled up in little racial clumps and then lumped together by the town's old residents without the least regard for age old feuds and demarcations.

Their children had already begun to multiply, whereat his wife was glad, since these swarthy babies were coming in free America, where people did not live in hovels and had hydrant water right in the yard.

When Pappaniasus took out his first naturalization papers he shortened his name to Pappan. It was better so for business, because the Americans always protested against dago names that were more than two syllables long.

By the time Pappaniasus had reduced his name to Pappan he had saved enough nickels to open a little restaurant on Market street. There anybody who would come could buy cheap, filling food; beans, baked and boiled, buttermilk, ham sandwiches, hot coffee, hot soup and so the rounds of cheap and wholesome menus. And Pappan continued to save money, learning the English language and absorbing American customs.

When he was able to add a candy kitchen and a soda water counter he had become naturalized and adept in imitating the slangy banter he heard in his restaurant. He moved his family from Water street into a house on Eighth street, a neighborhood being invaded by the more prosperous of the Greek colony. He had the house all alone for his family save for two boys who flunkied for him in the restaurant. But it still smelled of garlic.

It so happened that Bush Winter lived on Eighth street too, on the higher, hillier section of that street. From his upstairs window could be seen the Ohio river meandering through the hazy valley in lazy curves, the trains, puffing across the Panhandle bridge, the boats, with hoarse, raucous steam whistles, slipping down stream to Cincinnati and Louisville.

On Sundays he enjoyed watching this placid scenery and sometimes in the afternoon he would go down town and hire a buggy for two dollars and hitch up one of his draught horses and give his wife and boy and girl the treat of a drive along the river bank. The Greeks never did this, not a bit more than they would buy chicken for dinner or spend their money for fine clothes.

Bush believed in good clothes for the adornment of the body. He always had an account at Bergstein's Emporium or at some of the gentile establishments. On the other hand styles meant nothing to the Pappans. Clothes had but one function for their point of view—the prime function of covering the body.

These were the little details which led Bush Winter to think of Pappan with the patronizing air of the rest of the native born members of the community. It never occurred to him to ponder upon what was Pappan's attitude toward him, not even when they were exchanging crude, bluff jokes. But he found out unexpectedly.

On a certain sultry August Sunday in the midst of the heat of dog days Bush brought his family into the inviting coolness of the Pappan Ice Cream Parlor for the refreshing pleasure of some cold carbonated drink.

"Hello, John," shouted Bush with brisk joviality, "give us something cold to drink."

One of the boy flunkies darted forward obligingly. He was gathering up the red bottles, sweating cold drops of condensed vapor as the hot air struck the frigid glass.

Pappan was standing near, stretching his face in a forced smile and rubbing his hands together nervously, as though he were washing them in the humid air. He said something in the Greek language to his clerk, rapid, guttural words.

"No can drink him here," said the boy.

Pappan bowed politely.

Bush did not grasp what it was all about, but his quicker witted wife sensed the meaning immediately.

"He doesn't want us to drink his pop in here, Bush."

"What—what do you mean?" roared Bush.

"Me no can help. My beezness—these 'leukoi'—these I mean other Americans, they no like black. You all right, Bush, but eet is beezness."

He continued rubbing his hands, a mimicry of helpless Pilate.

"Why you dirty—," began Bush, reaching for one of the bottles, the cold drops dripping down his coat sleeve; but his sensible wife grabbed his uplifted arm and the glass smashed on the tile floor.

So began their feud. And Bush stood green with impotent rage and exasperation. He had lived to see the day when an Esau had stolen his birthright. He would seek redress in the courts. He could do that. Thinking such thoughts, he turned on his heel and stalked out, his family behind him.

He consulted a lawyer on Monday morning. After hearing the facts, the attorney doubted the wisdom of his bringing suit, since there had been no refusal to sell or denial of service, save the request to drink outside of his parlor.

"There is a technicality that may beat you," observed the lawyer.

The weeks slipped by. Bush worked hard, rising early and turning in late, endeavoring to offset the competition of a rival who had bought a truck. His wife had urged him to sell his horses and purchase a truck too, but he was hard to convince because the initial investment was high and their home had not been completely paid for.

Demetrius Pappan in the meantime flourished like the green bay tree. His trade grew. He had to enlarge his quarters. In the front of his restaurant now appeared the sign—WHITE.

Bush winced when he saw it, as he jostled down Market street, perched on the lofty front seat of the heavy dray.

Worry over the effrontery of Pappan, fuming and fretting about the unfairness of it all, was becoming an obsession with Bush. His children took it up. They had heard their father berate the "dirty dagoes" so much, and their mother's indignant agreement had penetrated so deeply in their consciousness, that they involuntarily began to vie with Pappan's son and daughter in the local High School.

Mary Pappan was quite as dark as Edith Winter and there was a shade of color in favor of Bush's son, Bush Winter, Jr., when the critical High School students compared him with young Demetrius Pappan.

"Mary Pappan is as black as a nigger!" whispered some of the girls behind her back, and when some tattler told Mary, the girl was beside herself with rage.

But anyway the native born Americans began to concede a grudging respect for the thrifty Greek. He was a good business investment. That was why the Savings Trust Company had loaned money to Pappan for his project to open a moving picture theatre that would monopolize the amusement business in the little valley town. So much was it worth to have inherited acumen, handed down from the sharp practices of ancestors who matched wits with the Turk, the Armenian, and the Jew of the Levant.

The opening of Pappan's Palace Theatre was widely advertised, especially in the local Republican and Democratic papers. They agreed that the theatre would eclipse all others in the valley, become the center of the community's entertainment.

Pappan knew how to spend his money.

The opening was quite an event. Bush had made reluctant promise to his children to allow them to go, after admitting that he did not believe in cutting off the nose to spite the face. So on inauguration night they were in the crowd. Bush hurried to buy a ticket.

Mary Pappan was the ticket seller. Bush waited. She did not notice him. He knocked impatiently with his hard silver money on the smooth glass counter.

"Ticket, please."

She pointed to a sign. He had not noticed it. He read, "We do not cater to the Ethiopian race."

The Ethiopian race? What had he to do with the Ethiopian race? Her renegade father was as black as he was, and wasn't Mary Pappan the color of his quadroon wife and daughter?

But she held out and would not sell him a ticket.

He had a clear case against him now, and he lost no time in bringing suit for damages. He hired a lawyer, one Solomon Lavinsky, who in turn subpoenaed the needed witnesses.

The case came to trial in the Mayor's Court. Lawyer Lavinsky reviewed the history of the case, stressing the violation of the Civil Rights Law of the State of Ohio that was involved, and its infringement of democratic principles in general.

The attorney for the defendant argued that his client had been within his legal rights, that he was in no way responsible for the state of public opinion and should be protected in making such rules as would defend his business from unwarranted losses.

Of course the race issue was drawn in with all of its nasty complications. But there could be no denial of the clear violation of the Civil Rights Law.

Bush Winter was given one dollar damages and Pappan was ordered to remove the offending sign.

A lot of publicity was given the decision. Bush considered the award a victory, for he was contending for the principle involved and not for pecuniary damages. His sense of triumph was further exhilarated by the news that was brought home from High School, that his son had won highest honors in scholarship.

But this triumph was shortlived. Adroit lawyers have so many clever suggestions to foil the laws. News came that the Pappan Palace Theatre was drawing a line in seating. He hoped somebody would test the ugly discrimination. But nobody did.

"I will test it," he said.

He went alone this time, seeking to save his family humiliation. He was not refused a ticket, but there they were all huddled together in the most undesirable section of the balcony. He called the usher.

"Get me another seat."

He went away and came back shortly.

"All sold out, mister," he said bumptiously.

Then he went himself. The ticket seller made the same excuse and then sold a man a ticket in the section he had asked for.

Now he was to learn the intimate secrets of the court, the law's delay, and the wearing sacrifice of the fight. His suit was lost this time.

The old obsession was growing. He was outraged. He took the matter to his lodge and then to his church. He preached boycott. But no money came, for some of the dark skinned folk said, "Humph! Serves him right. Tryin' to be white."

Others were interested and willing to help but their fate was hard enough already. They were poor and exhausted with their daily struggle for sustenance.

So Bush Winter became a bitter man, complaining against his lot and communicating his disgust to his children.

Then came the great Alembic of the War, into which the sons of the families of the Nation were fed. Bush Winter and Demetrius Pappan both gave theirs. But Fate was merciful to them both, for the sons were returned unharmed and the fathers were glad to tears to behold them once again.

"Now," said Pappan, "I can do what I have planned. Turn my business over to him while I go back to my native heaths once more before I die and enjoy with my wife a bit [of] the fruit of long years of toil."

"If I could only give my boy a college education," grieved Bush Winter, but how could he? Bad luck had overtaken him.

While moving a safe he had strained himself severely. The rope had slipped and he had to bear the load for a while or be crushed. The doctor told him to stop all work if he wanted to live.

And so he had been compelled to rent out his dray and depend upon haphazard and untrustworthy hirelings to bring in what they chose.

Edith Winter had inherited her father's pessimistic discouragement. She had finished High School, but never had been able to adjust herself to the blow her pride had received when Mary Pappan had been able to secure at once a position as stenographer in the Savings Trust Company's offices, while she, who had made better marks, had been offered nothing but a kitchen job.

But young Bush Winter had opened his eyes in the army and taught himself to think. Away from the smug ways of his valley home he began to study things as they were. He saw clearly the futile strivings of his father, seeking redress in the courts from a usurper of what was there for him to get. He pictured old man Pappan forsaking his native ties and emigrating to America with the flaming spirit of the pioneer. He saw it all clearly and determined that he would study this secret mastery of the purse strings. If only he had capital he would build up his father's business. He would get power and erect his own theatre and then he could determine where people should sit.

He broached the difficult subject to his father but could find no solution, for the broken man had to confess his poverty.

"All that you say is mighty fine, son, but they are a young fellow's dream. It takes money to buy trucks and do all you want, and—and—the house is already mortgaged."

Those were trying days after the War. Foolish laborers who never looked beyond their noses were not prepared for the sudden slump in wages and for the unemployment which followed the closing of the munition factories. Yet prices soared, while statesmen wrangled and passed the dastard word, "profiteering," in councils of state and nation. And there were charges and counter charges.

People of the age of Bush Winter and his wife and the Pappans wondered if the younger generation were going to the dogs. The safe old moorings had all been swept away and there seemed to be no stakes to which the drifters could be anchored.

Edith Winter and her set were caught in the vortex of this moral maelstrom. Mary Pappan and her younger sister lost their heads. The fathers and mothers worried and begged, cajoled and threatened without avail. Bobbed hair, short skirts, loose language, suggestive dances—and behold, the flapper appeared.

Young Bush Winter and young Demetrius Pappan, returned home, leaving that long isolation from currents of home thought, found themselves entangled in the meshes of a baffling reaction.

So it happened one autumn night after a day of fruitless worry, feeling that the bottom had fallen out of things, young Bush Winter followed his sister to the Idle Dream Hall where the boys and girls of their group toddled to the strains of jazz. Across the street one square below in the Knights of Columbus Hall, white youth were swaying in the same unbridled revelry, body to body beneath the reddish glare of low burning lights.

Resentment at first welled up in the harassed spirits of the young ex-soldiers and each in his set upbraided his sister in the stinging chastisement of a protecting brother who is worldly wise. But what the use? The blandishments of passionate music bring surcease of trouble. They had paid and paid, they had suffered, and why refuse this little fling? Let us all throw the barriers down and drink life, feel life, for yesterday was hell, and to-morrow. . . .

Sudden sound of shooting, muffled detonations, and dancers stopped and music ceased. Eager, curious faces pressed against window panes, jumping for some new excitement. The Ku-Kluxers were burning a cross on the hill above the town, the fiery cross, casting sinister shadows against the sky, and many remembered veiled, unfounded rumors. Aftermath of War!

That lowing, composite roar of crowds gushed down the street, now mounting loudly, now fading to a whisper. A great throng was in procession, automobiles with flying flags, men in long white robes and cone-shaped hoods.

Young Demetrius Pappan led the gang that rushed from Knights of Columbus Hall, hatless, breathless, in the mood for anything. In one piercing glance he sensed it all, the automobile leading the way, fluttering flag of his country on the hood. A white wave of anger swept over him and young Demetrius Pappan stepped boldly before the honking machine, arms upraised, a dramatic figure in the blinding glare of the headlights.

"Stop," he cried. "Take down that flag. I didn't fight in France to see it desecrated by cowards who hide behind a mask. Why don't you take off your masks, I say?"

He grabbed the flag and broke the fragile stick that fitted into the ornament on top of the hood.

"A riot! A riot!" echoed in the hall where Edith Winter danced. Young Bush Winter tried to find his sister in the stampede for the door.

Hats were thrown away; overcoats forgotten.

"Git off o' my arm, girl," somebody yelled. "This ain't no time to faint."

Clatter down the stairs. Confusion in the streets. Shots are fired. The police are coming—the Fire Department clangs out, throwing water on the squirming mass.

After the fight a wreck of automobiles, punctured tires, broken glass, wasted gasoline, and Demetrius Pappan's son, beaten half to death, unconscious on the ground.

He lay many days in the Valley Hospital, hovering between life and death. During those trying days old man Pappan's form grew bent and deep wrinkles seared his brow. He thought as he never thought before, walking silently through the streets.

Bush Winter saw him one evening, pottering before his house—his enemy, his grudge of years in person, the obsession of agonizing meditations.

"How-do, Bush," greeted Pappan.

"How-do, John," grunted Bush.

"Ah, I have much troubles."

"How is your boy, Pappan? I was sorry to hear of his being hurt."

"Ah—what can I say? The doctors, they don't say. And your boy—he's fine feller, too. You can be proud of heem."

And in the talk that flowed a rapprochement grew.

"Tell your girl it ees a good beesness head on her shoulders. My Mary will help her get trade. Shurr—there ees no Beauty Parlor een thees town," he confided as he sauntered slowly on.

They understood each other, these old, worn fathers, after all.

And many an evening they talked, and Bush was glad to review his hopes and Pappan listened, comprehending.

"Such a life," commented Pappan. "You because you not white must suffer and I because I be born in Greece. Your son he can fight, but mine, maybe he die."

But he did not die. His strong young vitality would pull him through and the next day after the doctors had pronounced their verdict, Demetrius Pappan came pottering to Bush's house.

"I want see you," he said.

Bush took him upstairs to his room where they could see the river's yellow stream in the fading light. Pappan pulled out his check book, coughing uneasily and speaking brusquely.

"How much money your boy want to buy them truck and open garage. 'Tis good beesness head he hev. Fine feller that boy."

"No, no!" he waved to Bush's wild-eyed protest. "I like mek invest. Take it from me, Bush, when I see beesness, I know beesness."

"That's what my wife always said," assented Bush.

"An' my old woman, too," laughed Pappan.

Old Bush Winter out of his window saw the deep verdure of the trees on the distant West Virginia hillsides, the brighter green of trees on the Ohio shore, lighted by the last rays of the evening sun, and the shimmering, oily green of the river, but the reflected emerald in his eyes gleamed with tears.

1929

- The Vatican City becomes an independent state.
- Political rivals Leon Trotsky and Nikolai Bukharin are expelled from the Soviet Union, leaving Josef Stalin as the sole controlling Communist leader.
- Growing anti-American sentiment in Haiti results in protests that are quickly quashed by U.S. Marines.
- The term *apartheid* ("separateness") is used for the first time.
- The U.S. stock market crash signals the onset of the Great Depression.
- The Museum of Modern Art opens in New York City.
- In Chicago, Al Capone's mob executes seven members of a rival gang in what will become known as the St. Valentine's Day Massacre.
- White author Julia Peterkin wins a Pulitzer Prize for her novel *Scarlet Sister Mary*, a folk tragedy depicting South Carolina's Gullah culture.
- King Vidor's *Hallelujah* and *Hearts in Dixie* are released, marking the first full-length films to feature all-black casts.
- The Harlem Broadcasting Corporation begins airing radio programs.

U.S. unemployment: 3.2%

Lynchings in the United States: 7 blacks, 3 whites

Spingarn Medal: Mordecai Wyatt Johnson (educator)

Books:
> Countee Cullen, *The Black Christ and Other Poems* (poetry)
> Jessie Redmon Fauset, *Plum Bun* (novel)
> Taylor Gordon, *Born to Be* (autobiography)
> Nella Larsen, *Passing* (novel)
> Claude McKay, *Banjo* (novel)
> Wallace Thurman, *The Blacker the Berry* (novel)
> Walter White, *Rope and Faggot* (nonfiction)

Periodical: *Bronzeman* (1929–33)

30 PROLOGUE TO A LIFE
Dorothy West

From *Saturday Evening Quill*, April 1929

In 1896 Luke Kane had met and married Lily Bemis. He had been very much in love with her. And she had literally fallen at his feet, stumbling over his bicycle, lying flat before the back door, and sprawling before him, her full skirts billowing about her, and quite all of the calves of her legs showing.

Luke, in an instant, was out of the kitchen, and had gathered the hired girl in his arms, and was cursing his bicycle and soothing her in the same breath.

She was small and soft. Though her face was hidden against his breast, he saw that her arms were golden and her dark hair wavy and long.

"Is that your old bicycle?" Lily asked tearfully. "You're fixin' to kill somebody."

"Ain't I the biggest fool!" he agreed.

She got herself out of his arms and, sitting down on the steps, she tried to do things with her clothes and hair.

"What anybody'd put an old bicycle right in the doorway for—"

But he was staring into her eyes.

"How long you been working for Miz Trainor?"

"I've seen you before," she told him. "Lots."

"Yeh? Don't you speak to nobody?"

"Gentlemen to whom I been introduced. Oh, yes."

"I'm somebody round these parts," he boasted. "Ever heard of Manda Kane?"

"Sure. We get our fancy cakes from her when we're having parties and things."

"I'm her son," he informed her, proudly. "I been up here delivering. My name's Luke."

"Yeh?" Her eyes were bright with interest. "Mine's Lily Bemis."

"Come from the South?"

"Born there. Yes. But I came up with the Mitchells when they came. That's been five years. But then old Miz Mitchell died, and the two girls got married. I never cared much for old Mister Mitchell, so I came on to Springfield. 'Cause

Mamie Cole went on to Boston and said I could take her place here. I knew Miz Trainor was good and all, and didn't have no small children. So I sorta thought I'd try it. Gee, I'm young and everything. If I don't like it here, I can travel on."

He plumped down beside her.

"Listen," he said softly, "I hope you'll like it here."

Her eyes were two slits and dangerous.

"Why—Luke?"

"'Cause, then," he said huskily, "you'll stay. And I can be likin' you."

She bent to him suddenly. "You're the funniest coon. Your eyes are blue as blue."

"Yeh. It's funny, black as I am," he said modestly.

She put two slim yellow fingers against his cheek. "You're not black at all. You're just dark brown. I think you're a beautiful color."

His eyes that were like a deep sea glowed with gratitude. "I sorta like yours the best."

"Oh, me, I'm not much!" she said carelessly. "What makes you think I'm pretty?"

"I dunno. You're so little and soft and sweet. And you ain't so shy."

She was instantly on her feet. "If you think I'm bold, sitting out here with you, when we never been introduced—"

"Looka here!" He was on his feet, too. "Women's the funniest things. I'm liking you 'cause you're not like everyone else, and you're bristling! I can have any girl in this little old town of Springfield I want. But I'm not making up to any 'cause I ain't found none that suited me. My mother's orful particular. We got a name in this town. You're the first girl I'm liking, and you're cutting up!"

But she was inside of the screen door now, and he saw her hook it. She came very close to it, but she was careful not to press her nose against it.

"Listen, Mr. Kane, I like you, too. I want to meet you proper. What would folks say if they knew we met like this? Me with two buttons off my shirtwaist and my hair net torn? But tomorrow's prayer meeting night, and I'm going. I'm an A. M. E. If that's your church, too, you come on over. I'll get Miz Hill to get Reverend Hill to introduce us proper."

He gulped. "Can I bring you home after?"

She considered it. "Maybe I'll let you be keeping my company," she promised.

There followed a whirlwind month of courtship. Lily had a hundred moods. They were a hundred magnets drawing Luke. She did not love him. Deep within her was an abiding ambition to see her race perpetuated. Though she felt that her talents were of a high order, she knew she would escape greatness through her lack of early training. And she had the mother instinct. Thus she would rather bear a clever child. In her supreme egoism she believed the male seed would only generate it. She would not conceive of its becoming blood of her child's blood and flesh of her child's flesh. Men were chiefly important as providers. She would have married any healthy man with prospects. . . .

Late in the summer Lily and Luke were married. Lily didn't want a church wedding. They were married in Reverend Hill's front parlor. Miz Hill and Manda Kane stood up with them. Ma Manda was tearful. She was losing her only son to a low-voiced yellow woman. She knew the inescapable bond of soft skin and hair.

Lily, standing quietly by Luke's side, felt a vast contentment. She respected the man she was marrying. She faced the future calmly. She only wanted their passion to be strong enough to yield a smart and sturdy son.

Later that day they were on a train that was bound, by the back door route, for Boston. They sat in the coach with their little belongings piled all about them. Luke made sheep's eyes at Lily and felt very proud. He was wondering whether it was obvious that they had just been married. He rather wanted the phlegmatic passengers to admire his golden bride.

He drew her round dark head on to his shoulder, and caught his hand in the tendrils of her hair.

"Guess I'm the happiest man in the world, and the proudest."

"Ho, you're not proud of me!"

"You are the moon and the stars, Lily, and the bright sun."

She twisted her head and looked deep into his kind eyes.

"Luke, do you love me as much as that?"

"You watch me," he told her. "I'll bring you the world on a silver platter. Lily, I'll make you a queen."

She rubbed her little hand up and down his arm.

"How much money we got now, Luke?"

"Enough," he boasted, "to live like millionaires for maybe a week in Boston."

"Luke," she said earnestly, "we're not going back. Ever."

He was pleased. "Our honeymoon will last wherever we are."

She was almost impatient. "It ain't that!"

He drew away from her and stared down at her hard.

"What in the name of God—"

"Let's eat," she said, and dug about for Ma Manda's hamper.

She put the linen napkin on her lap and laid out the sandwiches, licking her fingers when the mayonnaise or jam or butter had oozed through.

"Chicken," she announced, "and ham, and I reckon this is po'k, Luke!"

He balanced the coffee on his knee. "There's cups somewheres, Lily."

Presently they were hungrily eating, Luke almost wolfishly.

"We've caught our train," said Lily, with a little nervous laugh. He was making her rather ill.

He took a great gulp of coffee.

"Always was a fast eater. Father before me was."

Her hand tightened over his. "You could die," she said with real concern, "of indigestion."

He ducked his head suddenly and kissed her wrist.

"But I'll make you your million before I do."

Thus she let him go back to his eating, and she gave him an almost indulgent smile.

Once in the vast South Station they stood for a moment, bewildered. They both felt newly married and foolishly young. Lily had a sudden sense of panic. Suppose Ma Manda never forgave them. Suppose Luke died or deserted her. Suppose she was never able to bear a child.

And then she saw Mamie Cole coming toward them. She flew into her arms.

"The blushing bride and groom!" cried Mamie, and offered her cheek to Luke.

"Well, it's nice to see you," said Luke, rather shyly kissing her.

"I'm only off for an hour," she explained, "so we better get up to the flat. I got you three real nice rooms, Lily, in front."

"Three—?" echoed Luke. His voice fell in disappointment. "I kinda thought—a hotel—"

"Luke!" Lily caught his arm fast. Her brown eyes were dark with pleading. "Luke, it's not a hotel room I want. It's a home."

He asked in bewilderment: "Here—in Boston?"

"Listen, we're not going back. We're laying our corner-stone here. There's far and away more business in Boston than in Springfield. Just you see. I want my husband. Luke, I want my home. I want my—son. Back home we'd have to live with your mother. She's got that big house. And, Luke, I can't get along with no women. I almost hate women. They're not honest. They're weaklings. They care about cheap things. God knows you're going to find it hard to live with me—and *you* love me. I don't want nothing but my man and my son. That's me, Luke."

He had the most terrible longing to take her in his arms.

"Your man and your son? Lily, my girl, you've got your man. By God, you'll have your son. . . ."

In 1898 Lily gave birth to twins.

They were boys, with Lily's soft yellow skin and fine brown eyes, and all about them the look of her, somehow. Jamie and John. They were completely sons of Lily. To her they were gods.

Luke had been getting on in a fair sort of way before the twins were born. He had opened a tiny lunch stand in the South End. Lily had been helping with the cooking. After a barely perceptible start, business had picked up nicely. Luke could cook almost as well as his mother. And Lily, growing prettier and plumper every day, and rapidly learning badinage, was an obvious attraction.

She worked until the week before the twins were born. Then Ma Manda, in panicky self-reproach, hurried on to Boston, saw to it that a proper girl was hired, packed Lily off to the New England Hospital, and looked about at houses. She decided on a red-brick one on a quiet street in Brookline, and bought it through a profiteering agent. She ordered atrocious furniture on the credit plan (Lily returned it piece by piece later), and awaited the birth of her grandchild in grim satisfaction.

To the triumphant Lily the world existed for two golden babies. These were her lives to shape and guide. These were her souls to expand. She, with her constant faith, must quicken their geniuses.

So the years passed. Jamie and John were three and able to read. Then John at four could bang out a harmony on the new upright piano. Jamie at six was doing third grade lessons. . . .

They were nine. And Lily's pride, and joy, and love, and life. They had not cried in their cradle. They had never been jealous of each other. They had given her and Luke wholeheartedly their love. They wrote regularly and beautifully to their grandmother. Their teachers adored them. Despite their talents, they were manly and popular with children. They had never been ill. They were growing like weeds. John, at the Boston Conservatory, had been singled out as an extraordinary pupil. His little sensitive face had stared out of many daily papers. Jamie, in the seventh grade, leading his class, was the marvel of his school. He could solve the mathematical problems of high school students. He could also discuss his future with calm assurance. . . .

Lily was thirty-two now. And a housewife. Occasionally she swept into the shop which had been yearly enlarged until it comprised three wide windows and twenty-two tables. The doctors and lawyers who frequented the place would rise and eagerly greet her. She was completely complacent. She was fat, but her skin was firm and soft to Luke's touch. Her eyes were clear and content. There were always tender anecdotes about her boys. Jamie and John. The realization of her dreams, the growing fulfillment of her hopes, the latent genius quickening.

She walked in peace. She knew ten years of utter harmony. She was therefore totally unprepared for any swift disruption.

In 1908 the twins were ten. Though they were young men now with certain futures, they were still very charming, and went swimming or skating with the boys on their block whenever they were called for. . . .

It was on the last day of March, going all too meekly like a lamb, that Lily, in her kitchen, making the raisin-stuffed bread pudding the twins adored, sat down suddenly with her hand to her throat, and her heart in a lump against it. She was alone, but she knew she was not ill. She made no attempt to cry out to a neighbor. She could see, as clearly as though she stood at the pond's edge, the twins, their arms tight about each other, crashing through the treacherous ice, making no outcry, their eyes wide with despair, dragged swiftly down, brought up again to break her heart forever, and Jamie's red scarf, that Ma Manda had knitted for him, floating. . . .

Within twenty minutes three frightened children brought her the news. Two days later their bodies were found. Lily identified them in a dim dank morgue.

The twins lay together in a satin-lined casket in the flower-filled parlor. They were very lovely in their last sleep. The undertaker's art had restored them and enhanced them. There was about their mouths that too exquisite beauty that death brings to the mouths of children who die in pain. Dead, they were more similar than living. And it was James who looked like John. . . .

James and John were Lily. James and John were dead. Only the fact that she had watched her heart and soul flung into the earth with her sons kept Lily's body alive. She was spiritually a dead woman walking in the patient hope of physical release. There was no youth in her any more. Her body was no longer firm, but flabby. Her eyes were lustreless. Her lips that had always been a little too thin were a line now that went sharply down at each corner. And the voice that had bantered richly with her boys, that had thrilled like a girl's at the intimate bass of a man, was quavering, and querulous, and, all too often, still. . . .

Ma Manda stayed on. Lily wanted it. They were held by their mutual bereavement. The twins, dead, were more potent than ever they could have been, living. Now Lily and Ma Manda knew there was nothing these boys could not have done, no world they would not have conquered, had they lived.

Ma Manda one week-end returned to Springfield, sold her house and the two fine mares, and her business and her lease to a prosperous German. Her only sentimentalities were two ribboned packets of letters.

Luke was sorry that the twins were dead, but his heart was not broken. Lily was his world. While she lived there was hope, and love, and life. He had no real conception of the genius of the twins. He had always thought of them as smart little boys. Now death had shattered their spell for him. He even wondered vaguely why it did not occur to Lily she might have another child.

One night, after a silent meal that Luke had cooked himself to tempt the too light appetite of his women, Lily rose abruptly from the supper table, and with the knuckles of her clenched fists showing white, said in a voice that she tried to keep steady: "Luke, I'm sleeping in the twins' room tonight. I—I guess I'll go on up now. G'night, Ma Manda. 'Night, Luke."

An hour later, when he softly tried the door, it was locked.

———

A year passed. Lily, a little mad in her constant communion with her dead, had grown somehow hauntingly lovely, with her loosened hair always tangled, her face thin and pale and exquisite, and her eyes large and brightly knowing. Now she was voluble with Ma Manda, though there were no notes in her voice. She kept up a continual stream of pathetic reminiscences. And she went about her house with her hands outstretched briefly to caress some memorial to her boys.

Ma Manda indulged her. To her there was only beauty in Lily's crazy devotion. She had loved Luke's golden sons more than she had ever loved Luke. As with Lily, throughout their growing, they had become her sole reality. With the ancient's idea of duty, she kept their memory fresh, her sorrow keen. She went regularly to a Baptist church and wailed when the preacher harangued the dead.

And always for Luke, in his starved normal passion, surprisingly not the brute, Lily's light body was a golden mesh.

Lily had sat by an open window, staring up at the stars, her bare feet on a chilled floor, her nightgown fluting in the wind. Presently she had begun to sneeze. Soon her eyes and her nose were running. When she got into Jamie's white bed, she felt a great wave engulf her. In the morning she was very ill.

Lily felt that she was dying. And she was afraid to die. She hated pain. She had given no thought to death before the death of her twins. After that she had thought of her going as only a dreamless sleeping and a waking with her sons. Now there was something in her chest that was making her last hours torture. And a cough that tore her from the hot pillows and started that jerk and pull in her heart. Sometimes her breath was a shudder that shook her body.

In the first hours of the third night, she clutched at Ma Manda and stared up at her with eyes so full of piteous appeal that Ma Manda said sharply and involuntarily: "Lily, my child, you best let Luke in. He's a great one for healing. There's the power of the Almighty in his hands."

Lily made a little gesture of acquiescence. Ma Manda went softly, fumbling in her tears.

Luke bent over Lily. His blue eyes burned. They were dark and deep and glowing. She felt her own eyes caught in them. Felt her senses drowning. He flung one hand up to the sky, the fingers apart and unbending. The other he pressed against her chest till his flesh and her flesh were one.

He was exalted and inspired. The muscles leaped in his arm. He was trembling and black and mysterious.

"Lily, my girl, God's going to help you. God in His heaven's got to hear my prayer! Just put your faith in me, my darling. I got my faith in Him. I got a gift from the heavenly Father. Praise His name! Lily, my Lily, I got the power to heal!"

Strength surged out of him—went swinging down through the arm upraised, flashed through his straining body, then shot down and tingled in his fingers which had melted into her breast. They were like rays, destroying. Five streams of life, pouring into her sick veins, fierce, tumultuous, until the poison and the pain burst into rivulets of sweat that ran swift and long down her quivering body, and presently left her washed clean and quiet and very, very tired.

Then Luke's words came in a rush, in the voice of one who had fought a hard fight, or run a long race, yet deep and tremblingly beautiful.

"God, be praised! God, the Maker, we humbly thank Thee! Thou heard! Thou heard!! Thou gave me strength to heal! O God, this poor child—my Lily—she's well! She can rise and take up her bed and walk! O God, Thou art the Father of all living! Thou art life! Thou art love! Thou art love!! Thou art love!!!"

He slumped down on his knees and burst into wild tears. His head went bumping against Lily's breast.

In her relief and gratitude and wonderment, she felt her first compassion for her husband. In his weakness she was strong. She was a mother.

He clung to her. He was a man sick with passion.

Presently she said: "Lie with me, Luke," and drew him up into her arms.

For Lily, and for Luke, and for Ma Manda, after a week or two, that night, crowded out of their consciousness, might have never been. Lily went back to her inner life; Ma Manda to the spiritual needs of her daughter-in-law and the physical needs of her son; Luke to the old apathetic content in Lily's apparent contentment.

But one Sunday morning as he lay staring at a bright patch of sunlight on the wall and hearing faintly the bells of the Mission Church without emotion, the door creaked sharply.

Lily came in and stood at the foot of his bed.

He sat up in real surprise and made a vague gesture toward his bathrobe.

Her eyes were level into his and full of scorn. Her face was pale and proud. Her lips were a thin twist of contempt.

She was so lovely and so terrible in her fury that he caught his breath.

He scuttled down to the foot of the bed and gripped her wrist tight.

"Lily, you sick? For God's sake, what ails you?"

She flung her arm free. "I'm going to have a child. Another child! Well, it's yours. I've borne my babies. And I've buried them. This is your little black brat, d'you hear? You can keep it or kill it. If it wasn't for my babies in heaven, I'd get rid of it with the deadliest poison. But I can't damn my soul to hell for a wretched child that may be born dead. And if it lives"—her voice was a wail—"I curse it to my despair!"

For the first time since his childhood, Luke flung himself down full length on the bed and cried. . . .

In the months that followed, Ma Manda and Luke, in their terrific watchfulness, had a nine months' travail, too.

Lily's child was born on a spring morning in a labor so fierce that both of them, after hours of struggle, lay utterly spent; the child in the big white crib that had been the twins', the mother, for the last time, on her own great mahogany bed.

Lily was conscious and calm. She was dying as she had wanted to die, painlessly. She felt no curiosity about her baby. She had heard a sharp whisper, "It's a girl," which she had half expected, and had turned her face from the sound of it to summon all of her strength for a bitter chuckle.

Presently Luke came to stare down at her. His eyes were filled with great desperation. He, too, had forgotten the new baby. Lily was dying.

"Lily"—his voice was deep and tender—"just put your faith in God. My Father has never failed me. He'll pull you through."

She was quietly exalted. "I have come through."

"Lily, I love you. Don't act that way. Put your hand in mine. Let me help you, my darling."

His hand went out to her. She saw the fingers stiffen, straighten, and the muscles pulling in his arm.

But she made no move.

"Are you too weak? Let me raise your hand. The power of God is in me. It leaps like a young ram. Only touch me, Lily!"

Ma Manda, kneeling at the foot of the bed, wrung her hands and wailed, "Only touch him, Lily!"

Her eyes were wide and seeking. Her mouth was tremulous and beautiful. With a tremendous effort she raised herself up from her pillow. Her braids went lopping over her breasts.

Her hands went out, slowly, gropingly. Luke waited, quivering, his heart in his mouth.

But then she sighed sharply. Her hands clasped tightly. Her eyes were passionate. Her face was glorious.

It was Ma Manda who scrambled to her feet and laid her back on the pillow, and knew that she was dead, and gently brushed the lids over her eyes.

In the instant when her soul leaped to the sun, the new baby whimpered, once, then again, and was still. Luke turned toward it with a furious oath. He bent over the crib and looked down at the tiny dark bundle that was scarcely anything at all, with its quiet hands and shut eyes.

In the sudden hope that it had died, he put his hand over its heart.

The baby opened its eyes. They were blue—as deeply blue as his own, but enormous and infinitely sad. It was their utter despairing that moved him. He felt for this child a possessive tenderness such as the twins had never inspired. It was a woman-child. He understood her frailty.

So he knelt and slapped her face hard, and breathed into her mouth, and cried out *Lily! Lily!* naming her. He urged the strength in his spatulate fingers to quicken the beat of her heart. He prayed, "God, be merciful!" again and again.

She broke into a lusty wail and fell into a normal sleep, with the tears still wet on her cheeks.

Lily was dead, and Lily was not dead. A mother is the creator of life. And God cannot die.

1930

- Pluto is discovered by astronomers.
- Haile Selassie is crowned emperor of Ethiopia.
- Japanese prime minister Hamaguchi Osachi is shot during an assassination attempt (dies the following year).
- A joint U.S.–League of Nations commission reports that slavery is still practiced in Liberia.
- White women in South Africa gain the right to vote, but blacks remain disenfranchised.
- *The New York Times* formally announces it will begin capitalizing the word *Negro,* the first major U.S. newspaper to do so.
- The NAACP is victorious in its campaign to block confirmation of U.S. Supreme Court nominee John H. Parker, an alleged racist.
- White playwright Marc Connelly wins a Pulitzer Prize for his drama *The Green Pastures*, an African American folklife adaptation of Bible stories.
- Wallace D. Fard founds the Nation of Islam.
- Josh Gibson joins the Pittsburgh Homestead Grays, beginning a 15-year professional career as one of the greatest American baseball players.

Black population in the United States: 11,891,143 (9.69%)

U.S. unemployment: 8.7%

Lynchings in the United States: 20 blacks, 1 white

Deaths:
> Raymond Garfield Dandridge (24 Feb.)
> Charles S. Gilpin (6 May)
> Pauline Elizabeth Hopkins (13 Aug.)

Spingarn Medal:
    Henry A. Hunt (educator)

Books:
    Randolph Edmonds, *Shades and Shadows* (drama)
    Langston Hughes, *Not without Laughter* (novel)
    James Weldon Johnson, *Black Manhattan* (nonfiction)
    Willis Richardson (ed.), *Plays and Pageants from the Life of the Negro*
        (anthology)

Periodical:
    Abbott's Monthly (1930–33)

31 SANCTUARY
Nella Larsen

FROM *FORUM*, JANUARY 1930

I

On the Southern coast, between Merton and Shawboro, there is a strip of desolation some half a mile wide and nearly ten miles long between the sea and old fields of ruined plantations. Skirting the edge of this narrow jungle is a partly grown-over road which still shows traces of furrows made by the wheels of wagons that have long since rotted away or been cut into firewood. This road is little used, now that the state has built its new highway a bit to the west and wagons are less numerous than automobiles.

In the forsaken road a man was walking swiftly. But in spite of his hurry, at every step he set down his feet with infinite care, for the night was windless and the heavy silence intensified each sound; even the breaking of a twig could be plainly heard. And the man had need of caution as well as haste.

Before a lonely cottage that shrank timidly back from the road the man hesitated a moment, then struck out across the patch of green in front of it. Stepping behind a clump of bushes close to the house, he looked in through the lighted window at Annie Poole, standing at her kitchen table mixing the supper biscuits.

He was a big, black man with pale brown eyes in which there was an odd mixture of fear and amazement. The light showed streaks of gray soil on his heavy, sweating face and great hands, and on his torn clothes. In his wooly hair clung bits of dried leaves and dead grass.

He made a gesture as if to tap on the window, but turned away to the door instead. Without knocking he opened it and went in.

II

The woman's brown gaze was immediately on him, though she did not move. She said, "You ain't in no hurry, is you, Jim Hammer?" It wasn't, however, entirely a question.

"Ah's in trubble, Mis' Poole," the man explained, his voice shaking, his fingers twitching.

"W'at you done done now?"

"Shot a man, Mis' Poole."

"Trufe?" The woman seemed calm. But the word was spat out.

"Yas'm. Shot 'im." In the man's tone was something of wonder, as if he himself could not quite believe that he had really done this thing which he affirmed.

"Daid?"

"Dunno, Mis' Poole. Dunno."

"White man o' niggah?"

"Cain't say, Mis' Poole. White man, Ah reckons."

Annie Poole looked at him with cold contempt. She was a tiny, withered woman—fifty perhaps—with a wrinkled face the color of old copper, framed by a crinkly mass of white hair. But about her small figure was some quality of hardness that belied her appearance of frailty. At last she spoke, boring her sharp little eyes into those of the anxious creature before her.

"An' w'at am you lookin' foh me to do 'bout et?"

"Jes' lemme stop till dey's gone by. Hide me till dey passes. Reckon dey ain't fur off now." His begging voice changed to a frightened whimper. "Foh de Lawd's sake, Mis' Poole, lemme stop."

And why, the woman inquired caustically, should she run the dangerous risk of hiding him?

"Obadiah, he'd lemme stop ef he was to home," the man whined.

Annie Poole sighed. "Yas," she admitted, slowly, reluctantly, "Ah spec' he would. Obadiah, he's too good to youall no 'count trash." Her slight shoulders lifted in a hopeless shrug. "Yas, Ah reckon he'd do et. Emspecial' seein how he allus set such a heap o' store by you. Cain't see w'at foh, mahse'f. Ah shuah don' see nuffin' in you but a heap o' dirt."

But a look of irony, of cunning, of complicity passed over her face. She went on, "Still, 'siderin' all an' all, how Obadiah's right fon' o' you, an' how white folks is white folks, Ah'm a-gwine hide you dis one time."

Crossing the kitchen, she opened a door leading into a small bedroom, saying, "Git yo'se'f in dat dere feather baid an' Ah'm a-gwine put de clo's on de top. Don' reckon dey'll fin' you ef dey does look foh you in mah house. An Ah don' spec' dey'll go foh to do dat. Not lessen you been keerless an' let 'em smell you out gittin' hyah." She turned on him a withering look. "But you allus been triflin'. Cain't do nuffin' propah. An' Ah'm a-tellin' you ef dey warn't white folks an' you a po' niggah, Ah shuah wouldn't be lettin' you mess up mah feather baid dis ebenin', 'cose Ah jes' plain don' want you hyah. Ah done kep' mahse'f outen trubble all mah life. So's Obadiah."

"Ah's powahful 'bliged to you, Mis' Poole. You shuah am one good 'oman. De Lawd'll mos' suttinly—"

Annie Poole cut him off. "Dis ain't no time foh all dat kin' o' fiddle-de-roll. Ah does mah duty as Ah sees et 'thout no thanks from you. Ef de Lawd had gib you a white face 'stead o' dat dere black one, Ah shuah would turn you out. Now hush yo' mouf an' git yo'se'f in. An' don' git movin' and scrunchin' undah dose covahs and git yo'se'f kotched in mah house."

Without further comment the man did as he was told. After he had laid his soiled body and grimy garments between her snowy sheets, Annie Poole carefully rearranged the covering and placed piles of freshly laundered linen on top. Then she gave a pat here and there, eyed the result, and finding it satisfactory, went back to her cooking.

III

Jim Hammer settled down to the racking business of waiting until the approaching danger should have passed him by. Soon savory odors seeped in to him and he realized that he was hungry. He wished that Annie Poole would bring him something to eat. Just one biscuit. But she wouldn't, he knew. Not she. She was a hard one, Obadiah's mother.

By and by he fell into a sleep from which he was dragged back by the rumbling sound of wheels in the road outside. For a second fear clutched so tightly at him that he almost leaped from the suffocating shelter of the bed in order to make some active attempt to escape the horror that his capture meant. There was a spasm at his heart, a pain so sharp, so slashing that he had to suppress an impulse to cry out. He felt himself falling. Down, down, down. . . . Everything grew dim and very distant in his memory. . . . Vanished. . . . Came rushing back.

Outside there was silence. He strained his ears. Nothing. No footsteps. No voices. They had gone on then. Gone without even stopping to ask Annie Poole if she had seen him pass that way. A sigh of relief slipped from him. His thick lips curled in an ugly, cunning smile. It had been smart of him to think of coming to Obadiah's mother's to hide. She was an old demon, but he was safe in her house.

He lay a short while longer listening intently, and, hearing nothing, started to get up. But immediately he stopped, his yellow eyes glowing like pale flames. He had heard the unmistakable sound of men coming toward the house. Swiftly he slid back into the heavy, hot stuffiness of the bed and lay listening fearfully.

The terrifying sounds drew nearer. Slowly. Heavily. Just for a moment he thought they were not coming in—they took so long. But there was a light knock and the noise of a door being opened. His whole body went taut. His feet felt frozen, his hands clammy, his tongue like a weighted, dying thing. His pounding heart made it hard for his straining ears to hear what they were saying out there.

"Ebenin', Mistah Lowndes." Annie Poole's voice sounded as it always did, sharp and dry.

There was no answer. Or had he missed it? With slow care he shifted his position, bringing his head nearer the edge of the bed. Still he heard nothing. What were they waiting for? Why didn't they ask about him?

Annie Poole, it seemed, was of the same mind. "Ah don' reckon youall done traipsed 'way out hyah jes' foh yo' healf," she hinted.

"There's bad news for you, Annie, I'm 'fraid." The sheriff's voice was low and queer.

Jim Hammer visualized him standing out there—a tall, stooped man, his white tobacco-stained mustache drooping limply at the ends, his nose hooked and sharp, his eyes blue and cold. Bill Lowndes was a hard one too. And white.

"W'atall bad news, Mistah Lowndes?" The woman put the question quietly, directly.

"Obadiah—," the sheriff began—hesitated—began again. "Obadiah—ah—er—he's outside, Annie. I'm 'fraid—"

"Shucks! You done missed. Obadiah, he ain't done nuffin', Mistah Lowndes. Obadiah!" she called stridently. "Obadiah! git hyah an' splain yo'se'f."

But Obadiah didn't answer, didn't come in. Other men came in. Came in with steps that dragged and halted. No one spoke. Not even Annie Poole. Something was laid carefully upon the floor.

"Obadiah, chile," his mother said softly, "Obadiah, chile." Then, with sudden alarm, "He ain't daid, is he? Mistah Lowndes! Obadiah, he ain't daid?"

Jim Hammer didn't catch the answer to that pleading question. A new fear was stealing over him.

"There was a to-do, Annie," Bill Lowndes explained gently, "at the garage back o' the factory. Fellow tryin' to steal tires. Obadiah heerd a noise an' run out with two or three others. Scared the rascal all right. Fired off his gun an' run. We allow et to be Jim Hammer. Picked up his cap back there. Never was no 'count. Thievin' an' sly. But we'll git 'im, Annie. We'll git 'im."

The man huddled in the feather bed prayed silently. "Oh, Lawd! Ah didn't go to do et. Not Obadiah, Lawd. You knows dat. You knows et." And into his frenzied brain came the thought that it would be better for him to get up and go out to them before Annie Poole gave him away. For he was lost now. With all his great strength he tried to get himself out of the bed. But he couldn't.

"Oh Lawd!" he moaned. "Oh Lawd!" His thoughts were bitter and they ran through his mind like panic. He knew that it had come to pass as it said somewhere in the Bible about the wicked. The Lord had stretched out his hand and smitten him. He was paralyzed. He couldn't move hand or foot. He moaned again. It was all there was left for him to do. For in the terror of this new calamity that had come upon him he had forgotten the waiting danger which was so near out there in the kitchen.

His hunters, however, didn't hear him. Bill Lowndes was saying, "We been a-lookin' for Jim out along the old road. Figured he'd make tracks for Shawboro. You ain't noticed anybody pass this evenin', Annie?"

The reply came promptly, unwaveringly. "No, Ah ain't sees nobody pass. Not yet."

IV

Jim Hammer caught his breath.

"Well," the sheriff concluded, "we'll be gittin' along. Obadiah was a mighty fine boy. Ef they was all like him——. I'm sorry, Annie. Anything I c'n do let me know."

"Thank you, Mistah Lowndes."

With the sound of the door closing on the departing men, power to move came back to the man in the bedroom. He pushed his dirt-caked feet out from the covers and rose up, but crouched down again. He wasn't cold now, but hot all over and burning. Almost he wished that Bill Lowndes and his men had taken him with them.

Annie Poole had come into the room.

It seemed a long time before Obadiah's mother spoke. When she did there were no tears, no reproaches; but there was a raging fury in her voice as she lashed out, "Git outen mah feather baid, Jim Hammer, an' outen mah house, an' don' nevah stop thankin' yo' Jesus he done gib you dat black face."

32 DOOR-STOPS
May Miller

From *Carolina Magazine*, May 1930

Green Willow Street never boasted of virgins; not, of course, that one could be certain that such did not exist within its narrow confines but rather that one would never have associated such an anomaly with such a street. Indeed, the reputation of this little section was due entirely to ladies who plied a most distinctive trade, nor would the casual passerby have hesitated to add to the long list of artful traffickers the plump brown girl who sprawled indolently over the stoop at number ———. She herself did not expect anyone to believe the truth; moreover did not want anyone to. With unnatural horror she dreaded the disclosure of the fact—so much did she desire to be like all the others.

Spring had stolen up the street so insidiously that few recognized it. There were no trees to herald its coming, and the closely laid bricks of the pavements and cobblestones of the street brooked no intruding grass. Tonight, however, one knew of the season's arrival. The stoops were cluttered with lounging figures—thermometers were not needed in Green Willow Street so well did the appearance of the stoops register changes in weather. At number ——— the feeble cries of Nannie Bowen's new baby (it was her fourth fatherless brat) could be heard through the open window. Next door Easy Jones began to pump the pedals of his new pianola, and in the streets the children were mimicking life—choosing and losing lovers to rhythmic clapping and tuneful repetition of the barely intelligible words,

> "That ol' man ain't got no wife, Mis Liza Jane,
> Shouldn't have mine to save his life, Mis Liza Jane.
> Oh, Mis Liza, Mis Liza Jane."

A slender, dark form towering for an instant above the enthusiastic singers, a gruff exchange of greetings with the half-dozing stoop-loungers, an unusual alertness on the part of the plump brown girl—Joe had arrived.

"Hey, Irma, you ready? We ain't got much time; it's after ten now," was the youth's abrupt greeting.

"Uh huh, what's yo' hurry?" the girl rejoined.

"We want seats, don't we? The place was crowded when I come past."

"Be wid you in a minute." Irma rose and went into the house.

It was a gala night at the Bucket of Blood. Count and his far famed troubadours from Atlantic City were the visiting artists and the cabaret was delightfully crowded. Smoke ascended to the low ceiling and returned to sting the eyes and mingle with the products of fresh cigarets. Gracefully draped half-pint, pint, and quart bottles were furtively produced from the most unexpected places. A stout, dark diva was crooning in a deep contralto voice, "I can't give you anything but love, baby."

Irma, a tingling warmth stealing over her, surveyed the sea of black, brown, and yellow faces. They harmoniously blended into one effective background from which the only real visage that emerged was the one that stood out in bold relief, face to face with hers. The smoke from Joe's cigaret circled their heads and inclosed them in a little paradise of their own. She leaned dizzily over the rickety table.

"Love me, Joe?" she asked thickly.

"How do I know?" the youth grumbled.

"You don' know? How come you don' know? I knows I loves you."

"I ain't sayin' nothin' 'bout you; Ise talkin' 'bout mahself an' I ain't got no ways of tellin' yit."

The youth reached down beside the table leg, brought up a bottle and filled the two glasses with a clear liquid which the proprietors called gin and sold at sixty-five cents a half-pint. Irma drained her glass and persisted.

"Whatcha mean, Joe?"

"You know damned well what I mean, but this ain't no time to talk 'bout that. Let's dance."

Joe gulped down the liquor, pushed his chair back violently and lurched toward Irma. She rose unsteadily. Joe's arms encircled her and they swayed to the saxophone's wail. After five minutes of movement in which they had progressed merely five feet from their table, they realized that the selection had ended and stumbled back to their places. Joe filled the glasses again. Irma drank and questioned anew.

"Joe, you ain't meaning you ain't lovin' me an' count of that?"

"I ain't said that yit, but I been goin' wid yuh foh two weeks now an' I guess we'd better be gittin' somewheres."

"Somewheres!" Irma opened her heavy eyes in alarm.

Joe sensed another explanation. "Forgit it, kid," he retorted harshly and emptied his glass.

And so a new day was born and grew older with the same round repeated—a drink, a question, a dance—a question, a dance, a drink. At two Joe muttered something about that ride to Sparrow's Point in the morning, kicked the empty bottle, grabbed his hat from the table and started toward the door. Irma snatched her threadbare black coat from the back of the chair and staggered after him.

The fresh air cleared her eyes and cooled her brow, but she clutched desperately at Joe's arm as he strode rapidly toward her home. Why couldn't they go on like this—just Joe and her—her and Joe—liquor warming her body and April's breeze in her face? But he was waiting—just waiting—and when the time came, she had nothing to say. She could not talk of that; it had been so long ago she had forgotten—forgotten—there was no forgetting that. She shuddered and tightened her grasp on Joe's arm.

They had reached her stoop and Joe's voice cut in on her reverie.

"Listen, Irma," he was murmuring, "am I goin' in wid you tonight or not?"

"Joe, tonight?" she floundered helplessly.

"Yes, tonight. Ise tired of this tomorrow—tomorrow. I ain't takin' no mo' chances."

"But ————"

"There ain't no but. We lef' yo' ant down at The Bucket an' there ain't no one else to kick. Aw, come on, kid."

Joe reached out and with hands as gentle as a mother's drew Irma into his arms. She went willingly and nestled close. He covered her forehead, face, and neck with hot, hurried kisses. Irma was limp in his arms. She closed her eyes in a dizzy whirl.

"Come on, let's go in." Joe had turned the knob and kicked the door open. They were half way over the sill.

Irma was sober in a minute. She jerked herself away stammering, "Joe, you know—you know—"

"Sure, I knows," he interrupted harshly. "You don' like me an' you don' like mah kisses. Gawd, Irma, what does you 'spect of a feller?"

"I don' know, Joe. Hones' to Gawd, I loves you—I loves you better'n anythin' else, but I jus' can't now."

"Now! It's been two weeks."

"Yes, I knows, but somethin'—somethin' happened once an' ——"

"Somethin' happened! What happened?" Joe was frankly puzzled.

"Somethin'—somethin'————Oh, I can't talk 'bout it, but I ain't never been like all the others since."

"Ain't like all the others! What you mean?" The boy eyed the girl with open suspicion.

Irma drew back as if to hide herself from her sweetheart's scrutiny. "No, not that but—but—" She stopped, attempted once more to explain, then ended in a burst of tears.

"Tears ain't helpin' none," Joe cried exasperated. "Ise been 'bout as decent as any feller could be an' this is what I gets foh it. You'se jus' the queerest gal I ever met. You makes believe you loves me an' then you acts like this. 'Course you'se been good company, I don' know a better sport; but there's a time when a feller wants a girl, an' you don' know how to be a girl. Ise quittin'. Understan' I likes you awright but you gotta learn." He concluded his statement with [an] air of finality and turned sullenly away from Irma.

"Joe! Joe!" the girl cried brokenly and clutched at his arm, but he swung himself violently away, walked down the steps and up the street without a backward glance. Regretfully she followed his retreating form until the shadows swallowed it, then bewildered passed through the open door.

She made no light but groped her way to the staircase and mounted wearily. Behind the dowdy cretonne curtain that divided her own sleeping quarters from those of her aunt and her mate, Irma jerked her red dress over her head and flung it carelessly over the back of a chair.

She dropped to her knees beside the sagging bed and muttered half audibly the Lord's Prayer. Her lips moved as she repeated the words, but her mind was sauntering down Green Willow Street with the departing Joe. The prayer was ended; Irma, however, unconscious that her lips had made the "Amen," remained crouched there with her head buried in her arms. Finally she realized that her duty to God had been executed and started to rise, then sank back again. A new thought had come. She did as much for God every night; maybe God could help her. No longer were lips alone moving to the words of memory; a teeming brain was driving them to some greater being who could chain wayward men and convert virgins to adultery. If God would only answer this plea, she'd go to church every Sunday—every Sunday, honest to God—and she'd sing and shout louder than all the rest, if God would only bring Joe back.

A load lifted. Irma climbed contentedly into the bed, confident of Joe's hasty return, for hadn't she promised God what she would do? Now a new dress to charm him when he sulked shamefacedly back. She thought with satisfaction of the three dollars she had been hoarding for a butterfly skirt that she had seen in the window at the corner of Biddle and the Avenue for two ninety-eight. She'd hang on Joe's arm as she went down the street, both alike rejoicing in the sneering glances of its envious residents. Irma smiled drowsily, nestling contentedly under the disarranged cover. Then with a start and a dull emptiness that was almost physical pain, she returned to consciousness.

The glorious creature in a red checkered butterfly skirt had vanished. In her place stood a cringing ten-year-old girl trying hard to remember everything that the big white man with the thundering voice commanded. Oh, if only God would help her forget the little of it she did remember!

It had been a morning seven years ago that her mother had started to work. Irma had always wanted to cry when her mother left for work, partially because she, Irma, hated to be left alone but more because her frail mother had never seemed strong enough to work. Irma had felt particularly sorry for her that hot summer morning because she was sick. Her face was black and swollen where Steve had hit her and she walked with a limp. Steve always quarreled and beat her when he had been drinking; but that last night the quarrel had seemed more violent and lengthy and the beating, more severe. Then, too, it was strange that her mother, who usually left at six, had waited until Steve had departed at seven before going to work. Irma and she had stood in the doorway together and watched him scuffle down the street.

"An' foh Gawd's sake, Steve, don' git no mo' of that kind of licker," her mother hollered after him.

"Shut yo' damned mouth an' git yo' lazy self tuh work," he retorted thickly.

"Yes," her mother half muttered as she drew Irma gently over the threshold, "I wasn't fixin' tuh leab this chile in no house alone wid you, wid all that licker in you an' another pint on yo' hip. She ain't the worse lookin' creature an' you ain't got no sense. I been watchin'."

"Watchin' what?" the child in curiosity questioned and forgot to wait for an answer. It came shortly after noon. (It wasn't hard for Irma to remember that, for the whistles of all the factories had announced in chorus the hour.)

The answer was Steve. About twelve-thirty he thrust his head warily in the door and asked gruffly, "Yo' mother gone?"

"Uh huh," the child replied noticing that Steve was uglier than usual. He shut the door as cautiously as any sober man could have but reeled as he caught at the edge of the table and sank in a chair.

"Come here," he mumbled.

"Whatcha want?" she asked.

"Damn you, don' cha hear me say come?" Irma was silent in her confusion. "Don' make me come fah you," Steve added harshly and glowered at her threateningly.

Irma now thoroughly frightened retreated toward the back door. Steve rose with an oath and flung himself between her and the door. She sought the corner. He followed. She didn't know this Steve. His eyes were red and bulging; his mouth was open and his nostrils moved with labored breathing. Heavy hands moved over her body and she felt smothered in her corner. The hands moved swiftly; she must evade them. She sank to the floor as the outer door flung open. Her mother stood there—a woman she did not know.

After that, things happened quickly—things that the man of the booming voice and the large, hushed court room waited to hear. That heavy iron lion that had held the front door back—they had thrust it in front of her face—and asked if she had ever seen it before. How had her mother grasped it when she hit Steve?

Why did they think she knew? She had thrown her arm before her face and not until a heavy thud, her mother's shriek and an awful silence had alarmed her, had she uncovered her eyes. She opened them then to a picture she had never forgotten—a frail, little woman bending over a huge form stretched still on the floor—a bloody Steve who could not answer a pleading voice that wailed, "I ain't never meant to, Steve, but you ought n' had of touched her. Steve! Steve——"

Irma did not remember much, but others did. The whole street seemed to know that her mother and Steve had quarreled the night before, and a number of quiet men listened as they told what they knew. Especially did Martha Lewis remember and once she shook her finger in Irma's mother's face to help her remember.

The men went out. There were twelve of them, for Irma, proud of her number work and anxious to do something, counted them as they filed past. Evidently everyone had forgotten a child of ten who sat cramped between two towering men. An age passed—an age filled with the restless walking back and forth of men, the hushed whispers of women, and the periodic sobs of her mother.

"Come on, kid. They're waitin' fer you." An officer stood over her and spoke in a gruff, not unkindly voice. She must have been sleeping, for she opened her eyes on a room that was practically deserted.

Martha Lewis, state's witness, rushed up to her and encircling her with fat, motherly arms, sobbed, "How'd I know they'd send her up? Gee, honey, I'm sorry."

Irma looked at her in bewilderment. "Where's Ma?" she asked.

"That's what I jus' said. She's goin' away an' might not never come back no mo'. I'm goin' be yo' ant from now on an' take care of you."

"Yes," Irma persisted, "but where's Ma?"

"She's gone," Martha sobbed audibly.

Irma had never seen her mother again. Years later Martha told her how her mother had fainted on hearing the sentence and had been carried unconscious from the room. Prison routine had soon put an end to a frail, unhappy life.

Irma had grown up much as all of Green Willow Street's illegitimates, living under the protection of first one and then another of Martha's lovers whom the street called husbands. She was one of the group of ragged children who barefoot raced madly up and down the cobblestones. In "Mis Liza" she sang louder and swayed more energetically to the rhythm than all the other participants. On the cluttered stoops at night it was Irma who told the most frightful ghost story or out-argued the wisest boy. The only sport from which she apologetically, almost shamefacedly, excused herself was the secret ceremony which was conducted under the door-steps and in the narrow passage-ways between the houses. From these mystic rites she fled precipitantly driven by a very vivid memory.

The same vivid memory that haunted her now as she pulled the ragged sheet almost over her head to shut out the picture of a ten-year-old girl cringing in a corner, a twelve-year-old barred from the holy councils, and a maid in her teens losing sweethearts to less attractive but more fortunate rivals.

The cover over her head, however, did not smother her thoughts and the endless torture continued. Suppose Joe did return, it would only mean that he would leave again unless———. There her imagination failed her as she realized the hopelessness of the situation. It was like getting out of bed in the morning. No matter how long you delayed, you still had to get up. The thing just waited. Once up, however, it was over. One might as well arise at once then and have it over, since delay brought only dreaded anticipation and no less effort in the end. If Joe left her now, at least it would be ended; but if he returned———. Thus she thought and having resigned herself to a Joe-less tomorrow fell into a heavy slumber.

The morrow held no such resignation. She woke conscious of a lack and with a heaviness which at first puzzled her; then with an indefinable ache she realized anew that Joe had left her. The day brought its usual routine but no forgetfulness for Irma. She worked swiftly and efficiently at her tasks for Mrs. Davis on Madison Avenue trying to hide from her own thoughts. She scrubbed the marble steps with vengeance as his features outlined themselves there. She rubbed vigorously on the silver service to blot out a familiar visage that shone from its lustrous surface. Joe was everywhere.

Evening again—childhood at its sportive pranks—youth at nature's eternal game of love-making—and sleep coming to tired old age. Alone on her stoop Irma slouched defiantly. Nobody had to know. She'd just lounge rather indifferently like all the others waiting for their fellows. Of course, she knew Joe was not coming, but the others need not know. She slouched more carelessly on the steps.

In the medley of street sounds she heard a strumming. Her body quivered in response as if those practiced fingers were playing on its nerves. Irma jerked herself to an upright position and listened tensely. She did not need the feeble rays of the street lamp to distinguish his figure on Bessie Briggs' stoop. No one could miss Joe's uke—certainly not Irma. Even Easy's heartiest rendition could not drown altogether the strain. Throbbing and passionate it ran, a seductive undercurrent. God! why didn't Easy stop just a minute? She might hear what Joe was playing. At last a break! Easy was changing the roll. Now she could hear plainly. The clear, unmistakable tenor of Green Willow Street's bard unashamed cried its love message to the street,

> "Say gal, say gal,
> Ain't you mine—
> Ain't you mine?"

Why had she listened? Joe and Bessie—Bessie and her Joe! It wasn't fair. Bessie with all her knowledge of hospital clinics—Bessie who had all the street's fellows—and now her Joe. God! how she hated her. No, that wasn't hatred; it was just envy. Wouldn't she change places with Bessie tomorrow—didn't she wish that she could die and be born again, a Bessie? She crouched lower on the step, her ear alert to every sound and her body unrelaxed.

No, she couldn't blame Joe either. He played the game as he saw it. He was only seeking the kind of love he understood. No use talking to Joe; he couldn't see—others had not understood. Sometimes Irma wondered if she herself understood. Even in her confusion, however, there was one fact that she did understand with unusual perception—she must have Joe back.

He had said she had to learn to be a girl. Very well, she would learn. Slumped there on the stoop with his song ringing in her ears she made the resolution. Almost triumphantly she raised her head and watched them. The song was ended. Bessie rose and took Joe's uke. She went into the house and returned almost immediately. Together they went down the street arm in arm. Irma smiled at their retreating backs. They were going to the Bucket. Let Bessie make good of this night; it would be her last. Tomorrow belonged to her, Irma.

Irma outlined her plan of attack carefully as she lay in bed. The next day she executed it without faltering. She worked until six as usual. By six-thirty she had visited the department store and had procured the much desired butterfly skirt. She added to her list, moreover, a new item—a black and red slip-on sweater. At home she brushed vigorously on a rebellious bob and heightened her rich brown complexion with dabs of rouge. At last she donned the butterfly skirt and slip-on sweater and mumbling something about a movie date fared forth on her adventure.

Seven o'clock found her walking rather aimlessly back and forth on the Avenue between McMechen and Wilson Streets, avidly eyeing every prospect. An early show was ended and the crowd issued from the theatre joyous, nonchalant. Delayed dinners and more pressing engagements called a limited number who rudely zig-zagged through the crowd; but the majority leisurely wended their way letting the spell of April and the shrieking melodrama, which they had just seen, take effect. They passed one apparently nervous girl whose eyes eagerly sought theirs without recognition or surprise.

Substituting disgust for misgiving she abruptly decided that a Green Willow Street virgin seeking prey would work more successfully below Dolphin Street. These hinkty folks uptown didn't even pause for a swell outfit like hers. She didn't want to go down among Joe's crowd; but then she had to learn. A little discouraged but none the less determined, she mingled with the south bound line of pedestrians. So intent was she on her newly decided territory and its prospects that she hardly felt a body that brushed hers so gently that she should have doubted the accident of the contact. A husky, pleasant voice burst so suddenly on her consciousness that she wheeled abruptly to look into the smiling face of a stout brown man.

"'Scuse me please, Miss, but ain't you—" He had caught her steps and was walking close by her side.

"You know damned well I ain't," Irma responded in a not unfriendly voice giving the stranger a sly side glance.

"Sho, I knew you wasn't no Miss ah ——but how's a feller goin' to meet a good lookin' girl if he don' asx is you Miss——." He looked Irma frankly in the face now and grinned an infectious grin. Irma found it easy to respond.

"Can't be that you ain't got nothin' to do a nice evenin' like this?"

"Nothin' particular," Irma answered thoroughly at ease.

"I don' see why we can't git together." He grinned again in his good natured ease.

"I don' neither."

"Oh, I almost forgot to asx you yo' name."

"Irma," she replied simply.

He was satisfied. In this world where lives touch and pass Christian or nick-names alone are required. It never occurred to him to question further and in turn he answered without cunning. "An' they calls me Chubby."

The rest was managed swiftly and efficiently—pint and a two dollar room in a nearby hotel. Irma thought learning might be easier than she had anticipated, but she drank little of the liquor. Liquor did something to you that got your mind turned upside down and she needed more sense than she usually had without the liquor. She encouraged her companion to drink freely, however, gaily joking as he drank. Once she even essayed a song. There was little time for selection and Irma shocked even herself when she heard herself singing,

> "Say gal, ain't you mine,
> Ain't you mine?"

That was Joe's song and she must not think of him until this other was over. Joe had said "Until you learn." The song was ended. Irma, still a little uneasy that her thoughts would not be controlled, sauntered to the open window. April's breeze in her face; liquor warming her body and——. She looked toward the bed. Chubby, half stupefied from the bad liquor, had kicked off his shoes and stretched himself at full length.

"Come on, girl." The inevitable grin mocked the haste of the man's words.

"Awright, Chubby," Irma answered calmly. Chubby was good-natured. Maybe after all it was not going to be as horrible as she had anticipated. If all men were only like Chubby——. Bessie needn't any longer feel superior and Joe needn't stop there because Bessie understood. She, Irma, would understand hereafter.

How would she tell Joe? Maybe she could get Chubby to take her to the Bucket. In this new outfit and with a strange fellow, she would most certainly attract Joe to her table. Again, it might be better just to sit on the stoop tomorrow night and when Joe started past on his way to Bessie's, to call him rather half-heartedly. She could hear him even now asking in surprise, "Yeah, kid, what cha want?"

Then she would answer, "Nothin' only you."

"Oh no, you ain't wantin' me 'cause I wants a girl."

"Well, can't I be yo' girl?"

"You don' know how."

"Oh, don't I?" An almost beatific expression illumined Irma's features for a minute as she reviewed the reconciliation that would follow.

"Oh, come on," Chubby called again bringing Irma back to the realization of the present.

"Uh huh," she grunted distractedly and turned away from the window. She stumbled and cursing her own awkwardness looked down. Only a heavy iron lion that held a door (hundreds had once been cast in the same pattern), but Irma stopped as still as the figure over which she had tripped.

33 CROSS CROSSINGS CAUTIOUSLY

Anita Scott Coleman

FROM *OPPORTUNITY,* JUNE 1930

Sam Timons rarely thought in the abstract. His thoughts as were his affections were marshalled concretely. His affections were rolled into a compact and unbreakable ball which encircled his wife Lettie and his young son Sammy. His thoughts—he did not think much—but such as his thoughts were, they involved this, if he did a good turn for somebody, somebody else would quite naturally do him or his a good turn also.

Usually Sam was a cheerful creature. Work and love; love and work, that, boiled down to brass tacks is the gist of all life, and Sam possessed both. Even though, at present, he was out of a job.

He walked along the sandy road stirring up miniature dust clouds with every step for his heavy feet shuffled wearily with the burden of his dejected body.

He felt down and out. He was at the end of his rope. One dollar in his pocket. He gripped it in his fingers. All he had. But he could not give up. The ball of his affection, as it were, trundled along before him luring him on. He was "hoofing it" to another town to try again.

"Saw wood . . . clean house, paint barns, chop weeds . . . plow, anything, suh. . . . Just so it's work so's I can earn somethin'. I'm a welder by trade, but they don't hire cullud."

Behind him stretched the long, dusty way he had come. Before him a railroad zigzagged his path. As his feet lifted to the incline, he raised his eyes, and met advice from a railroad crossing sign:

CROSS CROSSINGS CAUTIOUSLY

He paused to spell out the words, repeating them painstakingly. Then he went on. A little beyond and across the tracks another huge sign caught his attention.

Soon, he had halted beside this one, letting his eyes sidle up and down and over the gaily painted board. Now he was staring open-mouthed at the glaring yellow lion who crouched to spring, now, at the flashy blond lady pirouetting on a snow white mount. He stood quite still thinking. Wouldn't Lettie and little Sam be wild to see such a show.

"'Lo Mister."
Sam swung around like a heavy plummet loosed from its mooring.
"Gee . . . Mister, you 'fraid of me?"
A little girl hardly more than a baby addressed him. She was regarding him with the straight unabashed gaze of the very innocent and of the very wise.
"I want you to carry me to the circus," she announced, when their mutual survey of one another seemed to her enough.
Sam's eyes were fixed on the web-fine, golden hair escaping from two torn places in the child's hat. Already he had seen that the eyes searching his were blue. . . . He fidgeted. He made a move to go.
"Oh, don't, don't go," beseeched the child. "Mother has to 'tend a meeting, and father is always busy. There is no one else. Mother said I might if only somebody'd take me. See." She thrust out a little smudgy fist—and opening it, revealed a shiny new fifty-cent piece. "This is mine," she said plaintively. "Can't we go?"

Mrs. Maximus McMarr was a busy woman. She managed to attend fourteen clubs each week, but that excluded any time to manage Claudia, her five-year-old daughter. Claudia's father considered children woman's responsibility. One advantage or disadvantage this sort of bringing up gave Claudia, she always got what she wanted.
Something about her made Sam do her bidding now.
They were half way between the McMarr place and the circus grounds before he thought about what he was doing. He clutched at the dollar in his pocket. He wanted to laugh, guessed he was nervous. Suddenly, he stopped abruptly—there was another of those signs where the train's right-of-way intersected another dusty country road.

CROSS CROSSINGS CAUTIOUSLY

"Oh do come on," urged the child jerking his hand in an ecstasy of delight and impatience.
Further on a half-grown lad passed them, but stopped and turned to watch them down the road. As the man and the little girl drew out of sight, he faced about and pelted up the road.
The noise of the circus leapt up to meet and welcome Sam and Claudia. The music of the band was sweet to their ears. Sam reveled in it and Claudia's little feet danced over the road. Even the bellowing and roars of the wild animals left them undismayed. It was circus day.

Mrs. McMarr had alighted from a friend's car and remained standing beside it, to talk. Both women observed the runner at the same time. Mrs. McMarr felt her heart skid upward into her throat. Claudia had not appeared. She divined that the messenger tended evil for no other than her precious baby. She made up her mind to swoon even before she received the tidings.

The friend went in search of McMarr who for once allowed himself an interruption. Close-lipped, he tumbled off his harvester and rushed pell-mell across his field.

All afternoon, Claudia had been surfeited with care. One after another had tendered and petted and caressed her. Even her father had been solicitous. She curled up, drowsy and very tired, in the big arm chair.

The rain that had threatened to fall all day suddenly commenced like the tat-a-rat-tat of far-off drums. Claudia was wide awake. She sat up. Remembering. The circus band! The monkeys in their little red coats! Her circus man! Something had happened. What?

The impulse to know surmounted the fear she harbored of her father. She slipped over to his chair. He had been very kind today. Perhaps . . . he wouldn't mind telling her . . . Where her circus man was?

1931

- The Benguela-Katanga railroad is completed, the first trans-African railway.
- Flooding in China results in the deaths of 3.7 million people.
- Japan invades Manchuria.
- The British Commonwealth of Nations is founded, establishing the autonomy and equality of status of Britain and her Dominions (Australia, New Zealand, South Africa, and Canada).
- The first long-playing record (33⅓) is released.
- Francis Scott Key's "Star-Spangled Banner" is made the official national anthem.
- The Empire State Building in New York City is completed, becoming the world's tallest building.
- U.S. gangster boss Al Capone is sentenced to prison after being found guilty of income tax evasion.
- Walter White succeeds James Weldon Johnson as executive secretary of the NAACP.
- Nine African Americans, the so-called Scottsboro Boys, are arrested and tried in Scottsboro, Alabama, for allegedly raping two white women, resulting in a national and international outcry.

U.S. unemployment: 15.9%

Lynchings in the United States: 12 blacks, 1 white

Deaths:
    Ida B. Wells-Barnett (25 Mar.)
    A'Lelia Walker (17 Aug.)

Spingarn Medal:
    Richard B. Harrison (actor)

Books:

Arna Bontemps, *God Sends Sunday* (novel)

Jessie Redmon Fauset, *The Chinaberry Tree* (novel)

Mercedes Gilbert, *Selected Gems of Poetry, Comedy and Drama* (poetry, fiction, drama)

Langston Hughes, *The Negro Mother and Other Dramatic Recitations* (poetry)

James Weldon Johnson (ed.), *The Book of American Negro Poetry* (anthology, rev. ed.)

George S. Schuyler, *Black No More* (novel)

George S. Schuyler, *Slaves Today* (novel)

34 WHY ADAM ATE THE APPLE

Mercedes Gilbert

FROM *SELECTED GEMS OF POETRY,*
COMEDY AND DRAMA, 1931

Fust I'm gonna tell you how come Adam to take up wid dat gal Eve.

Well, you see to start wid, little Eve was a chorus gal, and Adam saw her one night when he was sittin' in the front row. He fell for her, and fell hard. So he ups and writes her a note, askin' to take her out to Coney Island, after the show. She agreed, and dey started out to make whoopee. Well, Adam drank so much near beer, dat he got drunk, dat's dey last he remembered, 'til Eve woke him up in de subway station, by pokin' him in de ribs, with a marriage certificate. From den on de trouble started.

Adam got a job out in Long Island, keepin' a garden, and dey had a bungalow, to live in, right on de place. Adam was some lazy, he wouldn't do a thing, but, lay 'round under de apple trees.

As for Eve, she spent all of her time, in de movies, listenin' to de talkies, and she and Adam use to have some fights, when she come home.

Well, dar was a lot of apple trees in dat garden, but Adam didn't lak' but one. Dat was a tree dat had great big red apples on it, and every one of dem apples had a worm in it, and dey was all female worms. So dat made Eve mad.

Eve told Adam if he dared to eat one of dem apples, she'd sue him for divorce and alimony.

One day Eve stayed in town longer den usual, the reason for dat was, she was at a bargain sale down at Gimbles. Dey had a sale on pajamas.

When she got home dar was no supper done, and Adam was some mad. Eve tried to git him to eat some apple sauce, but nothin' doin'. He started to rave, and jes' raised Cain. Eve stood it as long as she was able, den she got tired of hearin' him carry on, so she jes' grab'd de rollin' pin, and said to poor Adam, in a terrible voice, "Aw', go eat an apple."

Adam was so excited he runned right out and grab'd one, an' started eatin' it, right off dat tree, dat he had been told to lay off. But what else was the poor fellow to do?

35 THE NEEDLE'S POINT

J. Saunders Redding

FROM *ABBOTT'S MONTHLY*, JANUARY 1931

All day a slow, hot wind had been seeping up from the river, filling the air with the heavy odor of ripe tomatoes, peaches, melons, loaded on the sagging barges floating up the river to Chester. But now the wind had stopped, the air was breathless, thick with the flat smell of mud and dead fish, and as evening came on the clouds that all day had given promise of rain receded and left the sky a deep flame-blue. In front of the gray shacks along the river the mud of the road was baked and serrated: in the ruts there were dust-heaps ankle-deep. Three children, black, brown, yellow, played in the tall reed grass along the shore, unmindful of the mosquitoes that, even before the sunset, were beginning to buzz and sing. The road, ending abruptly in a dismantled warehouse, was patched with ashes and cracked oyster shells.

"Hey'o, Miss Vigil," one of the children screamed.

In the door of the last shack Vigil Clark stood watching the houses up the road. Her bulk filled the doorway. Her huge black arms were crossed over her breast, meat-heavy.

"Hey'o," she answered, and went on watching the houses up the road. When all the children screamed at her and ducked in the grass, Vigil did not look at them.

Three doors up Clissy Segars came out. She was a little pinched-face yellow woman with bleary eyes set in red rims of skin. She balanced herself precariously on the edge of her worn sill and gazed across the river. In her own good time she said to Vigil, by way of greeting:

"Has she come yit?"

Vigil pretended ignorance. She hated Clissy for being yellow and for some other unknown reason. She shifted her great weight from one foot to the other and eyed Clissy angrily.

"Whocomeyit?"

"Peacie," Clissy answered in a sibilant half-whisper. She leaned far out, lost her footing, laughed nervously, and started toward Vigil.

"Walks like a bantam hen," Vigil thought. Aloud she said: "Ain't see'd her."

Clissy smiled archly, roguishly, catering to Vigil's hatred of Peacie, as she catered to everyone's whims.

"Ain't it time she was come?"

Vigil looked at her and their eyes met. Then she turned her head the other way, only to turn it back again.

"Her time's up today," she said, smiling a thick smile of hate. "An' they let 'em out jest after lunch."

Clissy wagged her little head and started back toward her door. "I wouldn't trust no dopey," she said over her shoulder. "Oscie's a fool."

Vigil grunted.

The five o'clock whistle blew and, observing some rite, more women crowded into their doorways. The children came up from the shore fighting mosquitoes. The women passed talk between themselves. Soon afterward little groups of men came into the road from across the field that stretched behind the houses up into the city. For the most part they were dressed in thin jersey jackets with khaki breeches stuffed into the tops of yellow-stained rubber boots—the garb of the leather worker. They greeted the women casually.

In front of the last house Osceola John stopped with two or three others. His room was at the top of the stairs that ran up the outside of Vigil's house.

"What you goin'a do tonight, Oscie?"

"Nothin'. Too hot." He tilted back his oily cap and scratched the front of his head. His nostrils dilated, spreading above his heavy lips like liquid flesh. "Wish it'd rain." His crossed eyes, set in the shining smoothness of his black face like mismated beads on a cushion, swept the river melting away into gray up by The Point.

"Cronin bites goin'a ape tonight," someone said.

"Yeh," Oscie said. He saw Vigil out of the corner of his eye. His face hardened.

"Yeh! Vigil, where's Shef?" someone asked her. "Don't see him much no more since he got took off'n the day shif'."

"Sleep."

The men moved off up the road and Osceola, avoiding looking at Vigil, climbed the stairs.

His room was hot under the low ceiling. The pine board floor, warped from the heat, cracked under his heavy tread. Comic sheets nailed to the walls relieved the white tedium [of] kalsomine, iron bed and coverlet. A cook-stove and a table crowded one side of the room. Hanging on the closet door, its arms and bodice stuffed with paper, was a woman's faded purple dress.

"Wonder what time she'll git here?" Oscie said to himself. Sinking into a chair by the window, he pulled off his stained shirt and boots.

"Wish it'd rain," he mumbled.

Stripped to the waist and barefooted, he got a three gallon can from the closet and went down the steps to the river. Mosquitoes swarmed about his head and he fanned at them with one hand while he managed the can with the other. He waded out to his knees and dropped the can on the bottom, keeping it submerged with his foot.

Vigil, watching from her doorway, grunted, admiring John's broad, heavy shoulders. She scanned the now empty road, then, raising her voice, called maliciously:

"Ain't Peace come yit?"

John looked up frowning. He lifted the can from the bottom and poured the muddy water out. Then he lowered the can again. "Not yit."

"Ain't she s'pose to come today?" Jealously, and with it hot desire, welled up in her. She came out of the door and sat on the step, resting her fat arms on her knees.

"Yeh. But she ain't come. I ain't 'spectin' her none 'fore night," John said.

"They mos' and gen'ally let 'em out 'bout one o'clock."

John made his way through the mud and stood by the step, holding the full can easily. They looked at each other. The threads of their understanding touched, broke.

"Tend your damn business!" John said.

Vigil grunted.

When he had started a fire in the stove, he put on two small buckets of water, and taking from the closet a large tin tub put it in the middle of the floor. Then he sat out on his landing waiting for the water to heat.

Night had already settled over the river. Here and there red and green lights twinkled and the soft chug-chug of a small boat came up to him. That would be old Nutsy Segars going up to The Point for whisky. The first star shone just in front of him and low down in the sky. "It ain't goin'a rain none," he thought. Around the high chimney of the warehouse a bat circled and John could hear the blubber-like beat of its wings as it flapped clumsily by. "Star, star," he said, vaguely remembering. Then he got up abruptly, put more wood on the fire, and fetched his mandolin. Something queer and heavy was going on inside him when he sat down again. The first note he struck trembled through the hot dark night. After a desultory chord or two he began to sing softly.

> *"Flame an' fiah done burnt my soul*
> *An' I'm goin'a Jesis to be made whole.*
> *Ride on, my Gawd, ride on."*

———

His voice was rich as a tropical sunset.

Vigil came out and sat at the bottom of the stairs, leaning against the rail. Osceola knew it was Vigil. He sang another verse and stopped. Still plucking the strings, he looked down at her uncertainly, caught in a spell of his own making.

"Don't you'all feel kinda blue-like?" he said queerly.

"For what? Ma belly's full."

Her laugh stung him like a curse. He felt ashamed. He got up mumbling and went into his room. In the hot darkness he stripped himself and bathed. The hot water against his hot flesh was soothing. The odor of his wet body filled the room, strong, earth-like, penetrating to his brain like the sight of a naked woman. Again and again he lathered himself for the pleasure of feeling his hands run over his smooth body. In place of the melancholy heaviness came a drunken tingling feeling. Bending perilously over the edge of the tub, he lifted the other bucket of steaming water from the stove and doused himself with it.

While he was drying, Vigil came up and peered in at the door. In a moment he had stepped into his trousers and stood towering above her, black, immense. She slumped down on the step of the landing and he laughed softly, patting his bare stomach with the palm of his hand.

"S'pose Peace don't come," she said after a while.

He looked at her quickly. "Jes' s'pose," he said.

They fell silent, a full silence, like the pause between two cries of pain. John leaned his elbows over the rail and stared out into the night. Her shoulders were hunched as if to ward off a blow. John braced himself with his elbows against the rail, his nostrils spread, his trembling leg shook the little balcony.

"Shef works tonight," Vigil said without turning.

"I knowed it."

They both relaxed after that. Vigil's shoulders drooped and she bent lower over her knees. Osceola sat on the sill and tried to define the outlines of the warehouse, thinking queer things. When the tense air had fully cleared he reached inside the door for his mandolin.

That is how they were when Peacie came. She stopped uncertainly at the bottom of the stairs, then, with a bold laugh, mounted swiftly. Vigil's back stiffened, but she did not move to let her by. Peacie looked over Vigil toward John and he could see her eyes shining in the darkness like twin lights. It seemed a long while before she spoke.

"Hello, Oscie. Hello, Vigil," she said in her strident voice. She leaned against the step rail catching her breath. She drew her tall slender body between Vigil and the side of the house, came up to John and stood vibrant from head to foot looking down at him with restless eyes.

"Hello, Peacie," he said.

Vigil got up slowly, like some giant animal after a long nap. Oscie held his breath. She turned around on the narrow step and faced them.

"I see you got your ear-rings of'en the shelf," Vigil said.

"Them's my heart." Peacie laughed. The glass balls, pendant from a thin chain attached to her ears, made a tinkling music.

Vigil started down the steps. Half way down she called back: "Glad you didn't buy no snow." And there was scorn, knife-edged, in her voice.

"Go to hell," Peacie said. Then she brushed by John into the room.

The hardest part, the meeting, was over. For ten minutes John sat on the sill, looking over the dark river. He pulled the flat air into his lungs in great nosefuls and let it out slowly, bit by bit, until his heart pounded. Under his resting arms his knees trembled. He could feel the sweat drop from the pits of his arms to his ribs. When he went in he found her lying supine on the bed. Her eyes were on him as soon as his shadow crossed the sill. Pretending to himself that she was asleep, he moved cautiously between the stove and the closet putting away the cans and the tub. When he had finished a feeling of exhaustion came on him.

Out of the darkness Peacie asked: "What you been doing all this time since I been gone?"

He stopped in the middle of the floor, the weight of his averted head stooping his shoulders.

"You ain't been gone so long," he protested mildly.

Peacie laughed shortly. "I ain't talkin' 'bout that," she said. She closed her eyes. He could see the light of them go out. Now her body was a blub of shadow on the bed.

"Six months ain't long," she said derisively. "Oh, no, six months ain't long." Suddenly her voice became higher, more strident. "Six months is too damn long for a woman like me."

He had nothing to say to that. He could only look at her hopelessly. He stood perfectly still and a silent misery pressed down on him, smothering, like a wet blanket. When he moved he realized that all his muscles were tight, aching.

"You all right now, ain't you, Peacie?"

"All right!" She laughed. Then as if she were suddenly tired, she said: "Oh, yeh. I'm all right. Six months would make anybody all right."

She swung her legs over the side of the bed and began unlacing her shoes. She looked up at him. "All right," she said again.

He grabbed at her words for assurance. With a mad feverishness he slipped on his shirt and shoes, going over in his mind what to get for her to eat. The heat, forgotten for a time, renewed life in him. He remembered that he had not eaten.

"I'm goin'a git sum'en t' eat," he said.

"Oscie."

He stopped at the door and turned toward her. Her voice was subdued, intense, like the voice of one in great joy, or sorrow. John moved closer to her, drawn by the spell of her eyes.

"I'm cured this time, sure." She got up and went to him, her stockinged feet making soft sounds on the bare floor. "I ain't never goin' back there no more." She raised her head slowly and her lean face seemed all alight. "Never!" Then, loving, pitying, she drew his face down to hers and for an instant there was nothing, nothing.

"I'm goin'a git sum'en t' eat." He was gone, laughing happily, stumbling down the steps in mad haste.

Peacie threw herself back on the bed, feeling that kiss burn in her blood like a live thing. She laughed and it broke on a high note, falling like rain in the hot bare room. "I ain't never goin' back there no more," she thought. No more. No more. The kiss was burning out in her blood. She sighed: . . . Women in gray in a long bare room, bent over buzzing machines . . . glad you didn't buy no snow . . . nothing but the buzz of the machines, like a million steel-voiced bees . . . and a craving, such a craving! . . . work hard as hell and time'll go quicker . . . sewing straps on overalls . . . a million straps, a million women, a million machines, and endless time . . . didn't buy no snow . . . work, woman, work . . . no snow. . . .

Now she was in a hurry. It seemed if she did not move, every muscle, every nerve of her would snap and jangle. In a pain of stillness, her muscles aching, she controlled herself, breathing like a blown dog. It was somehow good to exercise this control, a sort of paying up. Fighting haste, she lifted her skirt and took a hypodermic from under her garter. She peeled the thin sleeve of her dress back to her elbow and rubbed the little puckers, forcing herself to wait. Finally, slowly she plunged the needle deep into her arm and prolonged the pain of the wound. In an ecstasy of pain she pressed the pump. With elaborate care she replaced the needle under her garter, smoothed out her skirts and, feeling a heavy surge of slumber, settled her head in the crumpled pillow.

John found her there when he came back. As he crossed the sill he called to her: "Peacie," but there was no answer. For a moment he stood uncertainly, merging with the night. Then he heard her slow, quiet breathing and thought he would not wake her. When he had put the food on the cold stove, he got down his mandolin and sat bent over it by the window, like some overgrown hobgoblin, quietly picking note after note and humming through his thick nose:

"Rivah's wide, rivah's deep: It's Jordan."

Then smiling and patting his foot,

"Jordan, Jordan . . ."

———

Suddenly something that had been making a great noise stopped. He didn't know what it was. He got up, tense. With bulging eyes he tried to make out Peacie's form on the bed, and he saw, or thought he saw, a slow tremor shake her body. Fascinated by the fear in his mind, he made his way to the table and lighted the lamp. The washed-out yellow light threw his contorted shadow on the wall. He kept his eyes on it, fearing to turn around, for he knew now what noise had stopped.

With eyes on the shadow and still clutching the mandolin, he backed toward the bed and stood like a dumb beast awaiting the snap of a whip. Life seemed to stand still. With all his effort he turned his head slowly around and down, until his eyes, red with fear, fell on her puckered forehead. Between her lips one small froth bubble burst and her open mouth made a small black hole in the empty tenseness of her face. Her long fingers, flexed and brittle looking, were spread palm downwards on the bed. Already she smelt cold and sickly sweet. Involuntarily his thumb and forefinger swept the protesting strings and he dropped heavily to his knees, his mandolin on the bed, his head on the instrument.

"Peac-ie," he cried.

1932

- French president Paul Doumer and Japanese prime minister Inukai Tsuyoshi are assassinated.
- The Indian National Congress is outlawed and Gandhi is arrested.
- War breaks out between Bolivia and Paraguay.
- Franklin D. Roosevelt elected president.
- Amelia Earhart becomes the first woman to make a solo transatlantic flight.
- Charles Lindbergh's infant son is kidnapped; later found murdered.
- *Atlanta Daily World* becomes the first black U.S. daily newspaper since Reconstruction.
- The New York Rens, a black professional basketball team, defeat the Boston Celtics, marking the first world championship by blacks in any sport.
- African American James W. Ford is nominated as the Communist Party's vice presidential candidate.
- Langston Hughes, Dorothy West, Ted Poston, and nineteen other African Americans embark for the Soviet Union to make *Black and White,* a never completed Soviet film about the history of blacks in the United States.

U.S. unemployment: 23.6%

Lynchings in United States: 6 blacks, 2 whites

Deaths:
    Bill Pickett (2 Apr.)
    Charles W. Chesnutt (15 Nov.)

Spingarn Medal:
    Robert Russa Moton (educator)

Books:

Arna Bontemps and Langston Hughes, *Popo and Fifina* (juvenile fiction)

Sterling A. Brown, *Southern Road* (poetry)

Countee Cullen, *One Way to Heaven* (novel)

Victor Daly, *Not Only War* (novel)

Rudolph Fisher, *The Conjure-Man Dies* (novel)

Langston Hughes, *The Dream Keeper and Other Poems* (poetry)

Langston Hughes, *Scottsboro Limited* (poetry, drama)

Claude McKay, *Gingertown* (short stories)

Wallace Thurman, *Infants of the Spring* (novel)

Wallace Thurman and A. L. Furman, *The Interne* (novel)

Periodical:

Journal of Negro Education (1932–current)

36 CRAZY MARY
Claude McKay

FROM *GINGERTOWN*, 1932

Miss Mary startled the village for the first time in her strange life that day when she turned herself up and showed her naked self to them. Suddenly the villagers realized that after many years of harmless craziness something was perhaps dangerously wrong with Mary, but before they could do anything about it she settled the matter herself.

For a long time she had been accepted as an eccentric village character. Ever since she had recovered from her long sad illness and started going round the village with a bunch of roses in her arms.

Before that she had been the sewing-mistress of the village school. She was a pretty young yellow woman then. Her parents, following the custom of those peasants with a little means, had sent her to a sewing-school in Gingertown. She had gone away in short frocks, with her hair down and a bright bow pinned to it.

When she returned for good after three years she was in long skirts, with her hair up in what the villagers called a "Chinese bump."

Her father bought her a Singer finer than those of the other peasant women, a foot-working one similar to that owned by the village tailor. She subscribed to *Weldon's Ladies' Journal* and the *Home Magazine,* and opened a little school in her home for girls to learn to sew and design and cut. Her girls called her Miss Mary, and a few superior folk, such as the parson and family, the schoolmaster, and the postmistress, called her Miss Dean.

The schoolmaster's wife was the sewing-mistress then. But two years later the schoolmaster left for a better-paying school. He was succeeded by a bachelor, and Miss Mary applied for and got the sewing-mistress's job. The sewing-mistress went to the school twice a week for two hours during the afternoon session.

Miss Mary sometimes took two or three of her bigger girls along to help teach the tots to sew.

Girls came from other villages to learn Miss Mary's art. She was much admired, for she was charming. She was nice-shaped, something like a ripened wild cane, and could look a perfect piece of elegance in a princess gown.

Naturally much of Miss Mary's spare time was spent with the schoolmaster. Often they went out walking together in the afternoon after school until twilight. And sometimes they rode horseback to Gingertown together. The villagers got to liking to see them together. The parson approved of it. So did Miss Mary's parents. And everybody thought the two would certainly get married. . . .

The schoolmaster was a pure ebony, shining and popular. He played cricket with the young men. He was of middle size, stocky, and an excellent underhand bowler. He organized a cricket club, and during the short days let school out earlier than usual to go to field practice.

Sometimes the schoolmaster and Miss Mary took tea together at the parsonage. And the schoolmaster would talk about the choir and new anthems with the minister's wife, who was the organist. Miss Mary was not in the choir, for she hadn't a singing voice nor any knowledge of music.

As a constant visitor to the Dean home the schoolmaster became almost like one of the family. The villagers indulged in friendly gossip about the couple, anticipating a happy termination of the idyll. Nothing could enrapture the people more than a big village wedding with bells and saddle horses and carriages.

But bang came the scandal one day.

The girls who attended Miss Mary's sewing-classes at home were nearly all girls just out of elementary school, between fourteen and fifteen years. There were a few younger who for some reason had not finished school, and also a few older who were considered and treated as young ladies.

Among those who accompanied Miss Mary to the school was a little bird-brown one plump as a squab, just turned thirteen, curiously cat-faced and forever smiling. They called her Freshy because she was precocious in her manners.

Sometimes the schoolmaster would tell one of the girls to do something in the teacher's cottage. To do a little cleaning up or prepare a beverage of bitter oranges or pineapple or a soursop-cup during the recreation hours. And it seems that Freshy, always forward, had got herself asked to do things many times.

And one morning while the classes were humming with work, the schoolmaster at his desk, the mother of Freshy, with her bluejean skirt tucked high up and bandanna flying as if for war, rushed into the school and slapped the schoolmaster's face and collared and shook him, bellowing that he had ruined her little daughter.

The schoolmaster was in a pitiful state, trying to hold his dignity and the woman off, until the monitors interfered and the woman was at last mastered and put out.

The village was shaken as if by an earthquake. Of course, the schoolmaster denied that he had ruined Freshy, but the girl maintained by the mouth of her mother that he had.

The village midwife, after seeing Freshy, insisted that she had not been ruined. But the midwife was the sister of Miss Mary's father, who was a leader in the church.

The parson was constrained to relieve the schoolmaster of his duties and put his wife in temporary charge of the school. For the protection of his pastorate, he said. Then there was the religious side. The schoolmaster being a member of the church and lay preacher, a church meeting was called to air the affair.

The village was divided for and against the schoolmaster. Curiously, it was the older heads who were more favorable to him. The young folk and chiefly the bucks were already calling the man a rogue and turning the whole thing into a salacious song. It began to be bruited that the schoolmaster was secretly a wild one who abused the innocence of schoolgirls. But there were some who maintained that even at her age Freshy had already passed the age of innocence with the apples of her bosom so prettily tempting.

Freshy was very conscious of the notoriety she had attained, and, fortified by the aggressiveness of her mother, when she went about the village she tossed her head and turned her lips in scorn like a petulant little actress at those who whispered and stared at her.

The first church meeting, with the parson presiding, broke up in a babel of recriminations, when Freshy's mother became bellicose and abusive to those who had dared to insinuate that her daughter was not a mere child.

It was then that Miss Mary acted. Freshy had not returned to the sewing-school since the day the trouble began. Meeting her in the lane one afternoon, Miss Mary took her home. And alone with Freshy in a room she third-degreed her until the girl cried out that the schoolmaster had not touched her.

At the next church meeting Miss Mary gave an account of Freshy's confession. Speaking quietly in her refined way and holding all attention with her pretty personality, she was almost convincing the whole meeting. But Freshy's mother jumped up, interrupting her, and related how Miss Mary had prevailed upon her child to confess, accusing her of being a little woman and having been with the boys. In her turn Freshy's mother charged Miss Mary with being the schoolmaster's mistress, and in a rage she threatened to box her ears and made a rush for her. Women shrieked as if filled with the spirit for a public fight, but some men held back Freshy's mother and she was put out.

Again the church meeting broke up. The young men especially did not want to believe that a person so nice as Miss Mary could say dirty things to Freshy. But the women shook their heads dubiously and repeated the saying, "Still river run deep." The declaration of Freshy's mother started a big gossip, for it was locally conceded that Miss Mary was a virgin. There was nothing dishonorable in the fact that girls were deflowered at a tender age and young virgins were few in the country; nevertheless, the village folk took a pride-like interest in any young woman of whom it could be said she was a virgin up until the time of her marriage.

It seemed as if the church and the village were going to rags over the affair, until a member named Jabez Fearon suggested taking the case to the law courts and having Freshy examined by a doctor from Gingertown. Jabez Fearon was the local tax-collector, commonly called the bailiff. His outstretched hand carried much weight among the peasants, but they had never considered his mind of any weight at all.

Now, however, his opinion appeared intelligent and worth acting upon. How strange that nobody had thought of the legal course before! After all the church-meeting bickering and disagreement! The younger church members thought that that was the most excellent way of settling the trouble. A doctor's examination and the decision of a judge.

But before any step was taken and another church meeting called, the school-master quietly disappeared.

And a few weeks after his disappearance Miss Mary went to the city and stayed there a long time. Her people said that she had had a breakdown from nervous trouble and they had had to take her to a doctor in the city.

But the weeks became months before she returned. And then she was confined to the house for as many months more. The village thought she was surely consumptive. Especially when they glimpsed her so tiny and strange in the portico of the house or on the barbecue.

Then at long last, when she could not be detained at home and away from people any longer, she came out, and the village became aware that she was not consumptive, but a little crazy. Her parents stayed away from the church and were never the same charming folk again. Their village respectability became a sour thing.

Miss Mary went about with her hair down like a girl. And it was lovely hair, thick, black and frizzly. The first day she went out she gathered a bunch of flowers and took it to the schoolhouse and placed it on the teacher's desk without a word, and walked out. The new schoolmaster was a married man. The parson said that he would never engage an unmarried man again.

Miss Mary got rid of her shoes, too, and went about barefooted like a common peasant girl. Every day she gathered her flowers, and there was always plenty of red—hibiscus, poinsettias, dragon's-blood. And she had a strange way of holding the bouquet in her arm as if she were nursing it. Sometime she talked to herself, but never to anybody, and when anyone tried to talk to her she answered with a cracked little laugh.

Her people kept her clean. And the village folk settled down into familiarity with her as a strange character. Nobody thought that she should be sent to the madhouse, for she was harmless.

And the months turned into years, the village changed schoolmasters again, and even the parson was called to a church in a little town where he earned more money. The village had long ceased from wondering about the disappearance of the schoolmaster, and Freshy had had three children for three different black bucks before she was nineteen.

Then one day the schoolmaster returned. He had been away in Panama. He was a changed man after being so long free from semi-religious duties, a little dapper with a gait the islanders called "the Yankee strut." He was married to a girl he met over there, a saucy brown dressed in an extreme mode of the Boston dip of the day.

It was on a Sunday and they went to church. And after the service the schoolmaster and his wife stood in the yard, surrounded by an admiring group of old friends and young admirers who wanted to hear all about the life and prospects in Colon and Panama.

Nobody had thought of Miss Mary, poor crazy thing in that social center of the village, where new acquaintances were introduced and sweethearts met and children skipped about.

But she must have heard of his arrival somehow, for suddenly she appeared in the churchyard and, pushing through the folk around the schoolmaster, she threw the bouquet of flowers at him and, turning, she ran up the broad church steps and turned herself up at everybody, looking at them from under with a lecherous laugh.

There was a sudden bewildered pause. And then a young church member dashed up the steps after Mary and the church crowd recovered from the shock, remembering that she was crazy. But before he could reach and seize her she had jumped down the steps, shrieking strange laughter, and started running towards the graveyard.

Just outside the gate she turned again, repeated her act, and laughed. The young villager gave chase after her, followed by others. Mary ran like a rabbit in a mad zigzag. And whenever she saw herself at a safe distance from her pursuers she performed her act with laughter.

She ran past the graveyard and, striking the main road, she headed straight for the river. A little below where the river crossed the road there was a high narrow waterfall that from the churchyard looked like a gorgeous flowing of gold.

Mary ran down a little track leading to the waterfall. Her pursuers stopped in the road, paralysed by her evident intention, and began shouting to her to stop. And watching from the churchyard, the folk began to bawl and howl.

But Mary kept straight on. On the perilous edge of the waterfall she halted and did her stuff again, then with a high laugh she went sheer over.

37 HIS LAST DAY
Chester Himes

FROM *ABBOTT'S MONTHLY*, NOVEMBER 1932

The small, bright lights screwed to the sockets in the ceiling of the corridor, one in front of each cell, illumined the narrow passage-way, the dead-white walls and ceiling, the grayish concrete floor with a brilliant, eye-stabbing glare. The first five cells were bare and empty. On one of the horizontal bars of the sixth hung a white wooden label with the name Wilson painted in a black arc across the top, and underneath it the number 13289 connected the edges of the arc.

Immediately outside the cell, across the four-foot corridor, a uniformed guard sat tilted back against the wall in an unsympathetic straight-back chair. His cap visor was pulled low over his forehead to shade his eyes from the over-head glare, and his head nodded slowly up and down as he dozed fitfully. When his chin sagged below a subconscious danger point he would awake with a jerk and glance sharply about him as if to recall where he was and what it was that he was supposed to be doing. The dull black stock of a pistol appeared projecting from a holster at his side.

The corridor light shone obliquely within the cell forming a checker-board pattern by the shadow of the bars halfway across the smooth concrete floor and illumined the entire cell with a sharp twilight. A chair stood beside the bunk partly within the light, laden with clothes strung over its back in careless disorder. The bunk abutted the right wall, extending from within two feet of the rear wall to within two feet of the bars which comprised the front of the cell. A wash basin and a sanitary commode were built out from the rear wall opposite the bunk and immediately above them was a small, narrow tin-shelf. The cell was devoid of any other furnishings.

A man lay stretched out on the grayish-white sheet of the narrow bunk snoring slightly. His full-length, dingy-white underwear were twisted about his body as if he had been turning over in his sleep. But now he lay on his back, perfectly still except for the rhythmic rising and falling of his chest as he breathed. His left arm was flung across his chest, the hand clenched in a tight fist. The other arm rested at his side, the fingers curled loosely inward. His left leg was twisted under his right.

The sheet was creased in a hundred places and the drab gray blanket lay in a heap on the floor at the foot of the bunk.

An oblique shaft of light struck across the man's face, throwing his features into relief. Tiny beads of perspiration glistened on his forehead, and his dark brown skin shone with a film of perspiration and oil that had seeped through its pores.

His short, black hair curled over his head in disorder. Tiny lines had begun to form in crow's feet at the corners of his eyes, otherwise his face was smooth as a baby's, giving to him a youthful appearance that he did not merit. His forehead was high and intelligent, his nose was large and prominent with wide, flaring nostrils, and his mouth was thick-lipped and sensuous. There was an indefinable sense of weakness about his mouth. One felt it rather than saw it. A stubble of thick, blue beard decorated his square, bulldog chin.

His large, powerful body reached the full length of the bunk and his head rested on the very edge of a lumpy pillow. One would have received the impression of jungle strength and animal cunning by careful observation.

The man moved his hand across his face as if some imaginary object was bothering him. Suddenly his eyes opened wide. He lay without moving for a moment, staring about the cell with his muddy, sleep-heavy eyes. After a while he turned over on his side and pushed the chair away from the bed. He reached his hand underneath the bed, took out a red coffee can and rolled a cigaret from the tobacco flakes and rice papers within it.

He sprawled back obliquely across the bed with his heels resting on the wall at his side and his torso lying flat and stuck the cigaret in his mouth. He struck a match from a safety box and applied it to his cigaret. The flame painted the white walls a flickering crimson and outlined grotesque shadows of his cupped hands on the rear wall. He blew the match out, inhaled deeply on the cigaret, and thumbed the match in the direction of the guard.

The guard was sitting straight in his chair now, and peering intently into the cell.

"Taking a drag, eh, Spats?" he asked, trying to keep his voice from betraying the uneasiness he was feeling.

The warden had instructed him to keep a sharp eye on the condemned men to prevent them from committing suicide. Burning was effective even if it was rather gruesome and some guys would try anything to beat the chair, the guard reasoned. Jobs were scarce and he didn't want to have to look for another one.

Spats took another deep inhalation and let smoke dribble through his nostrils.

"Just taking my mawnin's mawnin', Bill," he replied. His voice was as harsh as the fog-horn on a Duluth bound ore-ship.

Things were different now, he thought idly. When he was in before on that robbery rap over in the regular cells a guard would have marched him across the yard to the "hole" and probably have stood him up for four or five hours had he seen him smoking in bed at any time while the cell lights were off. Now he could smoke in bed all he wanted to and they didn't make a peep. Well, that's progress, he mused and gave a harsh snort of laughter at the thought.

The guard jumped at the unmirthful sound. He stared at the side of Spats' face as if to read his mind, but he could only see the red glow of the cigaret as Spats puffed intermittently.

"Well, today's the day, eh, Spats," he remarked.

Spats' thoughts swerved sharply back again to the immediate present.

"Yep, if the governor don't change his mind and give me a last minute reprieve, which ain't likely. He ain't got any reason to do it, anyway."

"Wel-l-l?" the guard questioned. He was curious to know how Spats was taking it.

"Oh, I'm ready," Spats explained. "I don't give a damn now that all chance is gone. I just made the fight for a new trial because I didn't want to overlook any bets. I'm too good a gambler for that. I never would feel just right taking the lightning ride if I thought that I'd had a chance to beat it and then overlooked it."

The guard nodded understandingly.

Spats relapsed again into silence. He reviewed the chain of circumstances that led up to his present confinement in the death row at Big Meadows where he had spent ten years on a robbery charge, and had returned in less than a year after his release to ride the lightning in the hot-squat.

His mind turned back to that Sunday morning out in the Texas Club in Center City. He hadn't intended to pull off that bit of shooting, but he had been wary and sort of prison scared too. Ten years in the big house had taught him not to take any chances, to shoot when the occasion called for shooting, and shoot straight, and pay for his blanks with his freedom.

He'd been heisting the manager of the Club in the ground floor foyer as he came down from the Club above with the Saturday night's receipts.

His mouth crooked in a mocking grin as he thought of the wide, frightened eyes of the little Jew when he commanded him to get 'em up. Why, the little sucker trembled so that he could hardly hold his arms above his shoulders, and just because a guy had a heat in his face.

Then the dicks busted in like rosy-cheeked heroes in an 1890 melodrama. He didn't even have time to clip the little tyke for his layers. One dick stepped in from the street and the other came thumping down the stairs. And he, Spats, standing in the floor with his heat in his hand. It was a tight squeeze and he had to smoke his way out. But of all the tough breaks that he ever had had, the one who lived was the one who saw his fawn colored spats and remembered them. He'd been a fool for wearing spats on the job but then he thought it safe as a drink of water.

He always would believe that the tip-off came from a frail, one whom he had gone nuts over the night before and spilled his plans about the job trying to impress her.

He frowned and flipped the cigaret against the wall at the back of the cell. He was conscious of a dull burning pain somewhere about his heart. Tricked to the chair by a lousy frail. He didn't claim to be smart but he didn't usually act that dumb. Well, a jane had been many a con's Waterloo, but that didn't ease the choking, self-contemptuous intensity of his chagrin.

Suddenly the small round globe in the exact center of the ceiling flashed on, flooding the cell with brilliant, yellow light.

Spats stretched and yawned loudly and tested the cold concrete floor with his bare feet. He pulled the chair containing his clothes over to the bunk and began to dress. Heavy cotton socks, dark blue trousers wrinkled and bagged, blue cotton shirt freshly laundered and given to him the night before to wear to the chair—to the chair.

And he wouldn't be doing this tomorrow. He would be dead—burnt to death in the chair—and crammed into one of those small wooden coffins that fundless executed men were buried in. A stifling sensation came in his chest and his breath whistled through his mouth. His fingers turned to thumbs and he found it impossible to button his shirt.

Then the disturbing thought left as suddenly as it had come. Jeeze, he would be glad to get it over with, he thought. This suspense was giving him the jitters. He had lived long enough, anyway.

When he finished dressing he washed his face and hands in the bowl and dried himself with the towel that had been given to him at his bath a few days before. He took his toothbrush from his vest pocket and lathered some soap on it. Then a little voice whispered in his ear, mocking him. "What are you cleaning up so much for?" it asked. "You're not going anywhere but to hell, and it don't make any difference how you look going there."

He broke the handle of the brush with a savage snap and hurled the pieces through the bars, cursing horribly under his breath.

The guard got up from his chair and kicked the pieces to one side of the corridor.

"Take it e-e-easy, take it e-easy, Spats," he cautioned. "You'll just make a fool out of yourself and have the papers poking fun at you in the late editions."

Spats quickly got himself under control and managed a smile. "Just got a tooth-ache," he defended.

The guard's words made him conscious of his most fervid desire other than that of beating the rap altogether—which was very improbable—and that was for the papers to say that he had gone to the chair with a smile. He wanted to take the last stroll down the stone-flagged corridor with a sneer on his lips and a mocking, devil-may-care spirit in his stride, and the other inmates seeing him pass, would say:

"Jeeze, there goes Spats as cool as if he was taking an afternoon stroll—and damned if he ain't grinning. Jeeze, what-a-nerve, what-a-man."

He understood the convicts' intense curiosity concerning the condemned men and knew that their topic of conversation for days after an electrocution would be how the condemned man acted when he walked across the yard.

He turned back to his bed, carefully folding and spreading the blanket over the sheet, then drew the chair to the center of the floor and slumped down into it, cocking his feet on the bars at the front of the cell.

"I hope it don't rain today, Bill. I'd hate to get wet when we crossed the yard on the way to the chair," he joked.

"Aw, a little water won't hurt you. Just make the juice shoot through you that much quicker," Bill informed him with the self-satisfied assurance born of complete ignorance.

"Well, if that's the case I guess I'll wet my head before I go out. They tell me that a man lives two or three seconds after they turn the juice on him," Spats said. He shuddered involuntarily at the thought.

"Well," opined the guard, "they'll leave your head kinda damp when they shave it. But you'll have first hand information concerning how long a man lives after they turn the juice on you." He chuckled at his grim humor.

Spats jumped to his feet. Beads of perspiration formed on his forehead and his face turned three shades paler. "What the hell are you trying to do, get my goat?" he snarled hoarsely.

The guard eyed him indifferently. "Well, here comes your breakfast. After you get a belly-full you might feel better," he remarked as a blue clad convict approached, carrying a heavy aluminum plate and a small aluminum bucket of coffee.

The attendant slid the plate and bucket through a cut-out in the bars at the base of the door.

"What do you want for dinner, old kid?" he asked Spats.

Spats remembered that the condemned men were given whatever they desired for their last meal and he didn't want to think about last meals.

"Just bring the regular dinner," he replied.

The attendant stuck a spoon through the bars. "O.K. That'll be chicken. That's the regular last meal."

Last meal. The phrase kept popping up. It had a disturbing effect upon Spats' appetite. "Beat it, rat," he snarled at the attendant.

The man hastened away.

Spats eyed his breakfast with a complete absence of enthusiasm. There were two doughnuts, some fried potatoes and gravy, two thick slices of bread and a chip of butter. The coffee was sugarless and slightly muddied with milk.

He wolfed the food, not tasting it, kicked the tins through the door, tossed the spoon out on the corridor floor and rolled and lighted a cigaret. He took several deep inhalations before taking the cigaret from his lips and explained to the guard:

"I guess I must to've been hungry, Bill. That slop sure tasted good this morning."

The guard looked up and nodded.

And then the thought suddenly assailed Spats that this was the last breakfast he would eat, ever. His hands began trembling. He quickly stuck the cigaret back into his mouth and jammed them into his pockets. He glanced sharply toward the guard to see if he had noticed the action.

But the guard was preparing to leave. His hours were over. Another guard took his place in the chair and nodded a good morning to Spats.

"The time nears, young man," he observed.

"Sure be glad when it's over with," Spats rejoined.

"Young man," the guard asked in a soft, sympathetic voice, "have you got right with God?"

Spats' lips curled in a sneer. "Has God got right with me?" he argued. "I didn't ask to come here into this world. He brought me here. He didn't make any provision for me to eat or to get the things I needed to live, so I got them the best way I could." His voice relieved the congestion that was forming in his lungs, the tautness that was pulling at his muscles. He continued, speaking faster: "That way was robbery. A sucker got in my way and I bumped him, maybe. I didn't ask that dick to come after me that Sunday morning. Perhaps God sent him there. If he did he sure as hell got him killed. I ain't a damn bit sorry to see a meddling dick get croaked. It was him or me or whoever the guy was who bumped him. You kept me here ten years and then turned me out into the world where I was ten years late to make a living and because I get accused of bumping a dick making that living you say: 'Young man, have you got right with God?' To hell . . ."

"Young man, young man, I wouldn't say that if I were you," the guard remonstrated gently. "You are on the brink of eternity and you have done enough already without adding to your other sins that of unforgivable profanity."

"All right, all right, deacon, if you're scared to listen to facts," Spats sneered. "But I want you to know that I ain't a damn bit worried, anyway," he added and lapsed into silence.

He took his hands from his pockets and struck a match to relight the dead butt in his lips. He noticed that his hands were still trembling so he held them in his lap and forced the muscles to steadiness through an exertion of his will.

Trembling like a panicky rat, he upbraided himself. Just like that tyke he had lined that Sunday morning in the Texas Club.

His mind spanned the months and returned to that Sunday morning. He remembered how he had made a panicky retreat from the scene of the shooting and beat it to Pony Boy's flat on Thackery Avenue.

The same Pony Boy who had given him that moniker, Spats, years ago when he was a kid in his teens and used to gamble in Pony Boy's drive. That had been long before he had taken his first tumble and got the saw-buck in the big house. The name stuck through the years just as had his exaggerated fondness for fawn colored spats.

He and Pony Boy had been the best of friends then. He brought plenty layers to fatten the games in Pony Boy's joint.

Later, when he saw Pony Boy kill an unwilling dame one night in a rented room by striking her on the temple with his fist, they became better friends. He had dangled the sharp edge of a prison sentence over Pony Boy's head and made him dance to his tunes.

That had been the only place in the entire city where he felt safe to go that morning. He got there hungry and broke just as the sun began to turn red in the eastern sky. His luck had served him well for he had found Pony Boy alone in the flat. His wife was away on a visit at the time.

He had been safe enough there but he got to thinking of five grands he had left with his pal, the manager of a nearby cabaret. A couple of nights later, when he thought the hunt had dimmed a little, he slipped down to the cabaret. He told himself that he needed the dough in case he should get a chance to clear the city.

"Someone to see you," the guard called, interrupting his chain of reminiscences.

Spats lifted his gaze and scowled at the bars. Two neatly dressed men came up and nodded to him.

The guard moved his chair in closer so that he could keep a sharper watch.

"We're from the Graphic," one of the men explained. "Want to interview you."

Spats forced a smile to his face. "How do you do, gentlemen," he greeted.

"Fine day for an electrocution," the reporter remarked, testing Spats' nerve.

Spats paled slightly, but his smile remained, frozen.

"Do you want a picture of him, Dan?" the other reporter asked. He took a small camera from his pocket and began to adjust it.

"No, don't bother. He isn't that important," Dan replied.

"Do you still maintain your innocence?" he questioned Spats.

"Sure do," Spats contended. "I was home and in bed when that killing jumped off."

"That's what I told this kid here," Dan smiled, nodding toward his companion. "They haven't electrocuted a guilty man during the twenty-two years I've been on the sheet. Do you hold any ill feelings toward the people who sent you here? The judge, the prosecutor, the cop who testified against you?"

"No, I don't. I know that the judge and the prosecutor were just doing their duty. And that dumb copper was just mistaken. I believe that he was sincere in thinking that the party he saw was me," Spats conceded. "You know my record influenced the jury. Just a chain of circumstances that an excon hadn't a chance to beat."

"Yeah, that's copy. Smiling Joe Collotti said the same thing seventeen years ago. Well, I see that you're not afraid of the chair, anyway," Dan noted.

"Afraid of what? Why, I'm laughing," Spats assured them, and let out a snort of unclassifiable noise to prove it.

"Well, I'll give you a line about going to the hot-seat with a smile on your lips. How'll that suit you?"

"Fine, Dan."

"Now don't break down and make me out a liar," Dan cautioned, as he closed his notebook and turned to go.

"I'll be smiling when the juice is turned on," Spats called after him. "I'm a man."

No sooner had the reporters left than a little, sallow faced man with nose glasses attached to a ribbon around his neck appeared before the bars, as if he had been waiting his turn.

"This must be your busy day, Spats," he greeted, wearing a mechanical smile.

"Hello, Zanny. Any news?" Spats asked. He couldn't quite keep the note of desperate hope from his voice.

"Nope. I just came over to tell you goodbye. I did everything that I could for you. The appellate court was almost compelled to uphold the verdict. You're so conspicuously guilty. And then there wasn't a flaw in the prosecution to get a grip on. You didn't expect any aid from the governor, anyway."

The hope died in Spats' eyes. "Nope, I didn't expect to beat it but I was just playing my hand to the end." His voice was resigned. "Well, so long, Zanny. I'll pick you up later in hell." He tried to smile. He failed.

"By the way, Spats," Zanny spoke as if a sudden thought had flashed to his mind, "where is that jewelry that you promised to turn over to me for fighting your case? You said it was in a safety box in the Guardian Trust Company. I have a statement for you to sign so that I can get it. Then you can tell me the number of the box. The guard here will witness the transaction, won't you, sir?" he turned to the guard.

The guard nodded.

Spats gave a snort of mirthless laughter. "There ain't any jewelry, Zanny. You got beat that time. You'll remember me when everybody else has forgotten me, because I stung you."

Blood surged to the attorney's face, mottling it with a dirty red. "Well, you'll get burnt yourself, Spats," he sneered.

Spats jumped toward the bars, a savage snarl issuing from his lips. The attorney retreated hastily as if he thought that Spats might get through the bars. He kept on down the corridor and didn't slacken his pace until he was out of sight.

Spats indulged in a fit of blood-curdling, insane laughter. "That's one lousy tyke fixer who gave his services for nothing," he muttered.

A few minutes later the same attendant who had brought him his breakfast appeared with a large tray covered with a white linen napkin. Spats wondered what it was that they were feeding him today.

And then he remembered that this was his last meal. Last meal. The words stuck in his mind, leech-like, and a hollow feeling came to his stomach. His appetite was suddenly dissipated. He felt that the least tiny crumb would stick in his throat and choke him.

But when the attendant stuck the food through the door and the savory odors wafted across his nostrils his appetite returned. He examined the dinner, picked up the different plates and laid them on his bunk. There was chicken, dressing, candied sweet potatoes, salad, celery, ice cream and cake—and a spoon to eat it with. Spats ate as much as he could hold and shoved the dishes back through the door.

A feeling of well-being pervaded him. He lit a cigaret and found to his surprise that it really tasted good. That was all he had needed, he told himself, just something good to eat. He had been hungry and had thought he was turning yellow.

Sure, he was going tonight. What the hell did he care? He wouldn't let a little thing like that faze him. He exploded with a snort of mirthless laughter and the guard looked up to see what the trouble was.

"I guess you think that because a man is going to die he should be crying and praying, eh, brother," Spats sneered, noting the guard's quick interest. "Well, I'm not like those sniveling rats. I'm a man."

He stretched out on his bunk, feeling drowsy, and slowly puffed on his cigaret.

A whiskey glass and a woman, he mused. Well, he had steered pretty clear of whiskey, but he hadn't always been able to keep clear of the women.

Like that night when he went to the cabaret to get the five grands from his pal. He had gone in and seen his pal and got by the two dicks that were there on the look-out for him, trying to corral that five grands reward the citizens had put out for him, dead or alive.

He could remember it as plain as if it had just happened.

He had bumped into Eloise coming out of the cabaret and she had recognized him. But he had her number. She liked money well enough to sell him to the first policeman who hove into view, but she was yellow. However, he had chilled her monetary ambitions with a few sharp threats and she had beat it down the street one way while he beat it another.

But it was when he had returned to Pony Boy's that the bottom dropped out of his world.

Pony Boy was dead, shot by a woman named Margaret, whom he had been keeping. Margaret said that Pony Boy had been jealous of the attention she gave her twelve-year-old boy and had taken him away from her. And she had come down and demanded him to tell her where the boy was. One word led to another, and that led to the shot that killed Pony Boy.

Spats had recognized Margaret. He knew her well. They had been childhood sweethearts wrapped up in each other, once. But he had left her flat—with the callous indifference of youth—when she told him that she was going to have a baby. Remorse from that action, burning in his soul like an eternal fuse down through the years, goading him to deeds of extreme recklessness and cruelty, had made his name a byword in police headquarters for crimes of unusual viciousness.

It was this baby, now a twelve-year-old boy, whom Margaret called Little Spats, that Pony Boy had taken away from her.

It was funny, Spats thought, how he had always been a sucker for a good sob story.

If at that moment, Margaret had said: "Let's go unicorn hunting," he would have put on his unicorn clothes.

But she just stood and looked at him through her large, dumb-animal eyes so he had given her the five grands that he had got from his pal and sent her out to look for the kid. Then he cleaned all traces that she might have left in the flat and left a trade-mark of his own—finger prints and a fawn-colored spat.

And a few minutes later he had taken hot lead in the guts from a Tommy gun wielded by a squad of coppers.

His trial, four months later, when he had recovered from his wounds, was merely a formality of justice. The jury had convicted him long before.

He lit another cigaret and turned over on his side, puffing leisurely. Well, he thought, he had had his day, anyway. He was living on someone else's time now. He'd hoisted many a guy and had beat some tough raps. He had even put a few guys to sleep with a spade in their face, too. But he had known that he wouldn't beat that last rap, cop-killing. He had known it ever since that Sunday morning when he made that panicky get-away from the Texas Club. He had known he would burn—if he lived. It might have been within the week, it might have been within the month, or the year; but he had known that he would burn—if he lived.

He'd been a lone wolf: no friends, one woman, and he never would be quite sure that she didn't turn him up for that other five grands. Not even a mother to grieve for him when he was gone. Well, he was glad for that.

He'd just been a good spender, a fast liver, a hard guy.

And now he was in the condemned men's row in the state prison. And today was his last day.

His throat felt suddenly dry. He jumped from the bed and gulped great swallows of water, spilling some of it down his shirt front.

The guard eyed him speculatively.

Spats noticed the guard's gaze. "Just had a nice nap," he lied, trying vainly to keep his voice casual.

"You'll have a long nap directly," the guard reminded him.

Blind panic boiled up within him at the words. His last day. In just a few more hours he would be dead. Fear increased within him in cold stifling waves. A definite sensation of ice chilled him. He began to tremble all over as if he had the ague. His thoughts became vague beyond endurance and his craven fear intensified to the point where it would break beyond all control.

He tried to steady himself. If this kept up he would go to the chair like a blubbering, sniveling rat. He might even have to be carried, for now his legs were so weak that he could hardly stand.

The thought brought some semblance of control back to his distraught senses. He thought of the article they would have about him in the papers—"He went to the chair with a smile on his lips." He became more calm and even experimented with a smile. Why, what the hell was the matter with him? He was a man, he wasn't scared.

A shadow appeared in front of him. He looked up and noticed a tall, gray-headed man with the garb of the clergy standing by his door. Deep brown eyes which gleamed with infinite pity shone from the minister's seamed, tan face. The prison chaplain stood at his side.

The prison chaplain said: "I've brought Reverend Brown from one of the city churches to give you a few words of consolation. I thought that perhaps you would like to have one of your own race to spend the last few hours with you."

"Last few hours!" The words seared Spats' mind like tongues of flame. He tried to rise from the chair but his knees buckled together and collapsed under him. His teeth began to chatter and the words, "last few hours," raced through his mind like white fire, expelling all other thought. He tried to speak but his tongue stuck to the roof of his mouth.

The guard pushed his chair forward to the minister. Reverend Brown seated himself and moved nearer the bars so that he could be heard without having to raise his voice.

"Mr. Wilson," he began, addressing Spats. "Have you got a mother, sir?" Spats trembled visibly.

"If you have," Reverend Brown continued, "she would want you to get right with God this day."

"Stop! Stop!" Spats cried, his voice rising to a shrill yell. "Get away! Get away! I don't want to hear it."

"I'm not trying to make you feel bad, Mr. Wilson," Reverend Brown explained in sterling sincerity. "My heart goes out to you. You're a young man. Perhaps society hasn't given you the breaks that you have deserved. I can't remedy that, I have no control over the machinery of society. Perhaps at times you have wanted to go straight and live according to the word of God, and the callous and ungodly peoples of your environment would not let you.

"But the glory of it all is that there is a forgiving God. He will give you a chance to do better in the next world, a chance to atone for the mistakes you have made in this one—if you only confess Him, my son, if you only confess Him, and have faith in Him. Get on your knees, humble your spirit and ask His forgiveness. I'm sure he won't deny it."

"Get away, get away, I say," Spats yelled, springing to his feet and raising his clenched hand as if he would smash the bars and tear the good minister limb from limb. "Take him away, take him away," he commanded the chaplain standing nearby. "I don't want to hear his sniveling prattle about God."

The chaplain shook his head.

The minister slowly arose from his seat. He placed one hand on the bars and leaned forward trying to look Spats in the eyes. "My son," he said, "I would gladly take your place, your mother, if she is living, would gladly take your place in that chair of death, if this day you would confess God and ask His forgiveness." There was the ring of unalloyed truth in the minister's voice.

Spats flung himself on his bunk and turned his face toward the wall. "I'm a man," he muttered. "I don't need God to go to the chair with me. I didn't have Him when I croaked that lousy meddling dick and I don't need Him now."

A look of infinite sadness spread over the old minister's face. "Son, isn't there anything I can say that may give you comfort in your last few minutes of life? Isn't there anything that will influence you to see the light, and show you that you are taking the wrong attitude? Isn't there any way or anything that I can do that will persuade you to take God into your heart before it is too late?" he pleaded.

Spats maintained a sullen silence. The old minister turned away with drooping shoulders and departed. "This is the saddest day of my life. I have failed," he confessed to the chaplain.

The guard resumed his seat eyeing Spats with unveiled contempt. "I'd like to tell you what I think of you," he said.

But Spats didn't hear him. The words, "LAST FEW MINUTES OF LIFE," were disseminating through his blood like tiny crystals of ice. He felt numb, drenched with a sense of unspeakable shame. He shouldn't have treated the old minister like he had, he regretted. He should have listened to him politely and after his sermon he should have told him that he confessed God. It wouldn't have hurt him and it would have made the old minister so happy.

But then people reading that he had got religion on his last day would have thought him yellow, and said that he had had to go to God to get the nerve to go to the chair. Nope, he would take his medicine just as it came.

But the words, "LAST FEW MINUTES OF LIFE," drew his mind back, like great fingers, to the horrible death that awaited him. He could visualize himself sitting in the chair with his head shaved. He could feel the officers strapping his arms down to the metal arms of the chair. He could feel the black cap slipping down over his head, over his eyes.

He sprang from his bunk with a muttered curse on his lips and a driving, haunting fear in his eyes.

Maybe there was some truth in this hereafter stuff, after all. Most of the people of the civilized world believed in some kind of hereafter. And he had scorned the idea, turned down a chance to get in line for a ticket to this everlasting paradise. Now, perhaps he would have to burn through eternity in hell. But then the fact that everybody believed in it didn't prove it to be so. How the hell did they know, anyway?

He began to fight for control as the fear increased within him. He forced all thoughts from his mind by a strenuous exertion of his will. He then rolled a cigaret, his hands moving in short, jerky movements as he exerted great control to keep them from trembling.

He took a dozen deep inhalations before he removed the cigaret from his lips. The smoke tasted like burning straw in his mouth but after a while it created a sort of dullness in his mind. He threw the cigaret from him and rolled and lit another one.

"What time is it, captain?" he questioned the guard.

The guard took his watch out of his pocket, glanced at it, and said: "A quarter to two." He put his watch back in his pocket, folded his arms and maintained a distinct attitude of silence toward Spats.

"I guess they'll be around directly to take me out," Spats remarked. His voice relieved that freezing, gnawing fear that was creeping through his heart and slowly deadening his muscles.

The guard didn't show any inclination to talk.

"You don't have to talk to me, brother," Spats sneered, noticing his attitude.

He rolled and lit another cigaret and slumped down into his chair eyeing the guard through hate-laden eyes.

In a few minutes the officials came and took him out of the cell and marched him across the yard to the little brick house at the end of the road.

Spats walked rigidly erect, like a drunken man trying to keep from staggering. He said a few words to the deputy warden in a snarling whisper through the corner of his mouth. He gave a snort of harsh, mirthless laughter once. And on his lips he wore a frozen, sneering, mocking smile. But in his eyes there was the subtle hint of utter fear.

1933

- Japan and Germany both announce their intention to leave the League of Nations.
- Romanian prime minister Ion Duca, Peruvian president Luis M. Sánchez Cerro, and Afghan king Muhammad Nadir Shah are assassinated.
- The National Socialists (Nazis), with Adolf Hitler as chancellor, gain dictatorial powers in Germany.
- The first concentration camp in Germany is established at Dachau.
- Congress approves a measure granting independence to the Philippines, but the measure is later rejected by the Philippine legislature.
- Prohibition is repealed in the United States (Twenty-First Amendment).
- The United States officially recognizes the Soviet Union.
- President Roosevelt creates what comes to be known as his "Black Cabinet," an advisory panel composed of prominent African Americans.
- United Artists film *Emperor Jones,* starring Paul Robeson, is first major movie release to star an African American and have whites in supporting roles.
- Katherine Dunham debuts in her first lead dance role in the ballet *La Guiablesse.*

U.S. unemployment: 24.9%

Lynchings in the United States: 24 blacks, 4 whites

Deaths:
Sissieretta Jones (24 June)

Spingarn Medal:
Max Yergan (missionary, activist)

Books:

    Jessie Redmon Fauset, *Comedy: American Style* (novel)
    John H. Hill, *Princess Malah* (novel)
    James Weldon Johnson, *Along This Way* (autobiography)
    Claude McKay, *Banana Bottom* (novel)

38 A SUMMER TRAGEDY
Arna Bontemps

From *Opportunity*, June 1933

Old Jeff Patton, the black share farmer, fumbled with his bow tie. His fingers trembled and the high, stiff collar pinched his throat. A fellow loses his hand for such vanities after thirty or forty years of simple life. Once a year, or maybe twice if there's a wedding among his kinfolks, he may spruce up; but generally fancy clothes do nothing but adorn the wall of the big room and feed the moths. That had been Jeff Patton's experience. He had not worn his stiff-bosomed shirt more than a dozen times in all his married life. His swallowtailed coat lay on the bed beside him, freshly brushed and pressed, but it was as full of holes as the overalls in which he worked on week days. The moths had used it badly. Jeff twisted his mouth into a hideous toothless grimace as he contended with the obstinate bow. He stamped his good foot and decided to give up the struggle.

"Jennie," he called.

"What's that, Jeff?" His wife's shrunken voice came out of the adjoining room like an echo. It was hardly bigger than a whisper.

"I reckon you'll have to he'p me wid this heah bow tie, baby," he said meekly. "Dog if I can hitch it up."

Her answer was not strong enough to reach him, but presently the old woman came to the door, feeling her way with a stick. She had a wasted, dead-leaf appearance. Her body, as scrawny and gnarled as a string bean, seemed less than nothing in the ocean of frayed and faded petticoats that surrounded her. These hung an inch or two above the tops of her heavy unlaced shoes and showed little grotesque piles where the stockings had fallen down from her negligible legs.

"You oughta could do a heap mo' wid a thing like that 'n me—beingst as you got yo' good sight."

"Looks like I *oughta* could," he admitted. "But ma fingers is gone democrat on me. I get all mixed up in the looking glass an' can't tell whicha way to twist the devilish thing."

Jennie sat on the side of the bed and old Jeff Patton got down on one knee while she tied the bow knot. It was a slow and painful ordeal for each of them in this position. Jeff's bones cracked, his knee ached, and it was only after a half dozen attempts that Jennie worked a semblance of a bow into the tie.

"I got to dress maself now," the old woman whispered. "These is ma old shoes an' stockings, and I ain't so much as unwrapped ma dress."

"Well, don't worry 'bout me no mo', baby," Jeff said. "That 'bout finishes me. All I gotta do now is slip on that old coat 'n ves' an' I'll be fixed to leave."

Jennie disappeared again through the dim passage into the shed room. Being blind was no handicap to her in that black hole. Jeff heard the cane placed against the wall beside the door and knew that his wife was on easy ground. He put on his coat, took a battered top hat from the bed post and hobbled to the front door. He was ready to travel. As soon as Jennie could get on her Sunday shoes and her old black silk dress, they would start.

Outside the tiny log house, the day was warm and mellow with sunshine. A host of wasps was humming with busy excitement in the trunk of a dead sycamore. Grey squirrels were searching through the grass for hickory nuts and blue jays were in the trees, hopping from branch to branch. Pine woods stretched away to the left like a black sea. Among them were scattered scores of log houses like Jeff's, houses of black share farmers. Cows and pigs wandered freely among the trees. There was no danger of loss. Each farmer knew his own stock and knew his neighbor's as well as he knew his neighbor's children.

Down the slope to the right were the cultivated acres on which the colored folks worked. They extended to the river, more than two miles away, and they were today green with the unmade cotton crop. A tiny thread of a road, which passed directly in front of Jeff's place, ran through these green fields like a pencil mark.

Jeff, standing outside the door, with his absurd hat in his left hand, surveyed the wide scene tenderly. He had been forty-five years on these acres. He loved them with the unexplained affection that others have for the countries to which they belong.

The sun was hot on his head, his collar still pinched his throat, and the Sunday clothes were intolerably hot. Jeff transferred the hat to his right hand and began fanning with it. Suddenly the whisper that was Jennie's voice came out of the shed room.

"You can bring the car round front whilst you's waitin'," it said feebly. There was a tired pause; then it added, "I'll soon be fixed to go."

"A'right, baby," Jeff answered. "I'll get it in a minute."

But he didn't move. A thought struck him that made his mouth fall open. The mention of the car brought to his mind, with new intensity, the trip he and Jennie were about to take. Fear came into his eyes; excitement took his breath. Lord, Jesus!

"Jeff. . . . O Jeff," the old woman's whisper called.

He awakened with a jolt. "Hunh, baby?"

"What you doin'?"

"Nuthin. Jes studyin'. I jes been turnin' things round 'n round in ma mind."

"You could be gettin' the car," she said.

"Oh yes, right away, baby."

He started round to the shed, limping heavily on his bad leg. There were three frizzly chickens in the yard. All his other chickens had been killed or stolen recently. But the frizzly chickens had been saved somehow. That was fortunate indeed, for these curious creatures had a way of devouring "poison" from the yard and in that way protecting against conjure and bad luck and spells. But even the frizzly chickens seemed now to be in a stupor. Jeff thought they had some ailment; he expected all three of them to die shortly.

The shed in which the old T-model Ford stood was only a grass roof held up by four corner poles. It had been built by tremulous hands at a time when the little rattle trap car had been regarded as a peculiar treasure. And, miraculously, despite wind and downpour, it still stood.

Jeff adjusted the crank and put his weight upon it. The engine came to life with a sputter and bang that rattled the old car from radiator to tail light. Jeff hopped into the seat and put his foot on the accelerator. The sputtering and banging increased. The rattling became more violent. That was good. It was good banging, good sputtering and rattling, and it meant that the aged car was still in running condition. She could be depended on for this trip.

Again Jeff's thought halted as if paralyzed. The suggestion of the trip fell into the machinery of his mind like a wrench. He felt dazed and weak. He swung the car out into the yard, made a half turn and drove around to the front door. When he took his hands off the wheel, he noticed that he was trembling violently. He cut off the motor and climbed to the ground to wait for Jennie.

A few moments later she was at the window, her voice rattling against the pane like a broken shutter.

"I'm ready, Jeff."

He did not answer, but limped into the house and took her by the arm. He led her slowly through the big room, down the step and across the yard.

"You reckon I'd oughta lock the do'?" he asked softly.

They stopped and Jennie weighed the question. Finally she shook her head. "Ne' mind the do'," she said. "I don't see no cause to lock up things."

"You right," Jeff agreed. "No cause to lock up."

Jeff opened the door and helped his wife into the car. A quick shudder passed over him. Jesus! Again he trembled.

"How come you shaking so?" Jennie whispered.

"I don't know," he said.

"You mus' be scairt, Jeff."

"No, baby, I ain't scairt."

He slammed the door after her and went around to crank up again. The motor started easily. Jeff wished that it had not been so responsive. He would have liked a few more minutes in which to turn things around in his head. As it was, with Jennie chiding him about being afraid, he had to keep going. He swung the car into the little pencil-mark road and started off toward the river, driving very slowly, very cautiously.

Chugging across the green countryside, the small battered Ford seemed tiny indeed. Jeff felt a familiar excitement, a thrill, as they came down the first slope to the immense levels on which the cotton was growing. He could not help reflecting that the crops were good. He knew what that meant, too; he had made forty-five of them with his own hands. It was true that he had worn out nearly a dozen mules, but that was the fault of old man Stevenson, the owner of the land. Major Stevenson had the odd notion that one mule was all a share farmer needed to work a thirty-acre plot. It was an expensive notion, the way it killed mules from overwork, but the old man held to it. Jeff thought it killed a good many share farmers as well as mules, but he had no sympathy for them. He had always been strong, and he had been taught to have no patience with weakness in men. Women or children might be tolerated if they were puny, but a weak man was a curse. Of course, his own children—

Jeff's thought halted there. He and Jennie never mentioned their dead children anymore. And naturally, he did not wish to dwell upon them in his mind. Before he knew it, some remark would slip out of his mouth and that would make Jennie feel blue. Perhaps she would cry. A woman like Jennie could not easily throw off the grief that comes from losing five grown children within two years. Even Jeff was still staggered by the blow. His memory had not been much good recently. He frequently talked to himself. And, although he had kept it a secret, he knew that his courage had left him. He was terrified by the least unfamiliar sound at night. He was reluctant to venture far from home in the daytime. And that habit of trembling when he felt fearful was now far beyond his control. Sometimes he became afraid and trembled without knowing what had frightened him. The feeling would just come over him like a chill.

The car rattled slowly over the dusty road. Jennie sat erect and silent with a little absurd hat pinned to her hair. Her useless eyes seemed very large, very white in their deep sockets. Suddenly Jeff heard her voice, and he inclined his head to catch the words.

"Is we passed Delia Moore's house yet?" she asked.

"Not yet," he said.

"You must be drivin' mighty slow, Jeff."

"We jes as well take our time, baby."

There was a pause. A little puff of steam was coming out of the radiator of the car. Heat wavered above the hood. Delia Moore's house was nearly half a mile away. After a moment Jennie spoke again.

"You ain't really scairt, is you, Jeff?"

"Nah, baby, I ain't scairt."

"You know how we agreed—we gotta keep on goin'."

Jewels of perspiration appeared on Jeff's forehead. His eyes rounded, blinked, became fixed on the road.

"I don't know," he said with a shiver, "I reckon it's the only thing to do."

"Hm."

A flock of guinea fowls, pecking in the road, were scattered by the passing car. Some of them took to their wings; others hid under bushes. A blue jay, swaying on a leafy twig, was annoying a roadside squirrel. Jeff held an even speed till he came near Delia's place. Then he slowed down noticeably.

Delia's house was really no house at all, but an abandoned store building converted into a dwelling. It sat near a crossroads, beneath a single black cedar tree. There Delia, a catish old creature of Jennie's age, lived alone. She had been there more years than anybody could remember, and long ago had won the disfavor of such women as Jennie. For in her young days Delia had been gayer, yellower and saucier than seemed proper in those parts. Her ways with menfolks had been dark and suspicious. And the fact that she had had as many husbands as children did not help her reputation.

"Yonder's old Delia," Jeff said as they passed.

"What she doin'?"

"Jes sittin' in the do'," he said.

"She see us?"

"Hm," Jeff said. "Musta did."

That relieved Jennie. It strengthened her to know that her old enemy had seen her pass in her best clothes. That would give the old she-devil something to chew her gums and fret about, Jennie thought. Wouldn't she have a fit if she didn't find out? Old evil Delia! This would be just the thing for her. It would pay her back for being so evil. It would also pay her, Jennie thought, for the way she used to grin at Jeff—long ago when her teeth were good.

The road became smooth and red, and Jeff could tell by the smell of the air that they were nearing the river. He could see the rise where the road turned and ran along parallel to the stream. The car chugged on monotonously. After a long silent spell, Jennie leaned against Jeff and spoke.

"How many bale o' cotton you think we got standin'?" she said.

Jeff wrinkled his forehead as he calculated.

"'Bout twenty-five, I reckon."

"How many you make las' year?"

"Twenty-eight," he said. "How come you ask that?"

"I's jes thinkin'," Jennie said quietly.

"It don't make a speck o' diff'ence though," Jeff reflected. "If we get much or if we get little, we still gonna be in debt to old man Stevenson when he gets through counting up agin us. It's took us a long time to learn that."

Jennie was not listening to these words. She had fallen into a trance-like meditation. Her lips twitched. She chewed her gums and rubbed her old gnarled hands nervously. Suddenly, she leaned forward, buried her face in the nervous hands and burst into tears. She cried aloud in a dry cracked voice that suggested the rattle of fodder on dead stalks. She cried aloud like a child, for she had never learned to suppress a genuine sob. Her slight old frame shook heavily and seemed hardly able to sustain such violent grief.

"What's the matter, baby?" Jeff asked awkwardly. "Why you cryin' like all that?"

"I's jes thinkin'," she said.

"So you the one what's scairt now, hunh?"

"I ain't scairt, Jeff. I's jes thinkin' 'bout leavin' eve'thing like this—eve'thing we been used to. It's right sad-like."

Jeff did not answer, and presently Jennie buried her face again and cried.

The sun was almost overhead. It beat down furiously on the dusty wagon path road, on the parched roadside grass and the tiny battered car. Jeff's hands, gripping the wheel, became wet with perspiration; his forehead sparkled. Jeff's lips parted. His mouth shaped a hideous grimace. His face suggested the face of a man being burned. But the torture passed and his expression softened again.

"You mustn't cry, baby," he said to his wife. "We gotta be strong. We can't break down."

Jennie waited a few seconds, then said, "You reckon we oughta do it, Jeff? You reckon we oughta go 'head an' do it, really?"

Jeff's voice choked; his eyes blurred. He was terrified to hear Jennie say the thing that had been in his mind all morning. She had egged him on when he had wanted more than anything in the world to wait, to reconsider, to think things over a little longer. Now *she* was getting cold feet. Actually, there was no need of thinking the question through again. It would only end in making the same painful decision once more. Jeff knew that. There was no need of fooling around longer.

"We jes as well to do like we planned," he said. "They ain't nothin' else for us now—it's the bes' thing."

Jeff thought of the handicaps, the near impossibility, of making another crop with his leg bothering him more and more each week. Then there was always the chance that he would have another stroke, like the one that had made him lame. Another one might kill him. The least it could do would be to leave him helpless. Jeff gasped. . . . Lord, Jesus! He could not bear to think of being help-less, like a baby, on Jennie's hands. Frail, blind Jennie.

The little pounding motor of the car worked harder and harder. The puff of steam from the cracked radiator became larger. Jeff realized that they were climbing a little rise. A moment later the road turned abruptly and he looked down upon the face of the river.

"Jeff."

"Hunh?"

"Is that the water I hear?"

"Hm. Tha's it."

"Well, which way you goin' now?"

"Down this-a way," he said. "The road runs 'long 'side o' the water a lil piece."

She waited a while calmly. Then she said, "Drive faster."

"A'right, baby," Jeff said.

The water roared in the bed of the river. It was fifty or sixty feet below the level of the road. Between the road and the water there was a long smooth slope, sharply inclined. The slope was dry, the clay hardened by prolonged summer heat. The water below, roaring in a narrow channel, was noisy and wild.

"Jeff."

"Hunh?"

"How far you goin'?"

"Jes a lil piece down the road."

"You ain't scairt is you, Jeff?"

"Nah, baby," he said trembling. "I ain't scairt."

"Remember how we planned it, Jeff. We gotta do it like we said. Brave-like."

"Hm."

Jeff's brain darkened. Things suddenly seemed unreal, like figures in a dream. Thoughts swam in his mind foolishly, hysterically, like little blind fish in a pool within a dense cave. They rushed, crossed one another, jostled, collided, retreated and rushed again. Jeff soon became dizzy. He shuddered violently and turned to his wife.

"Jennie, I can't do it. I can't." His voice broke pitifully.

She did not appear to be listening. All the grief had gone from her face. She sat erect, her unseeing eyes wide open, strained and frightful. Her glossy black skin had become dull. She seemed as thin, as sharp and bony, as a starved bird. Now, having suffered and endured the sadness of tearing herself away from beloved things, she showed no anguish. She was absorbed with her own thoughts, and she didn't even hear Jeff's voice shouting in her ear.

Jeff said nothing more. For an instant there was light in his cavernous brain. The great chamber was, for less than a second, peopled by characters he knew and loved. They were simple, healthy creatures, and they behaved in a manner that he could understand. They had quality. But since he had already taken leave of them long ago, the remembrance did not break his heart again. Young Jeff Patton was among them, the Jeff Patton of fifty years ago who went down to New Orleans with a crowd of country boys to the *Mardi Gras* doings. The gay young crowd, boys with candy-striped shirts and rouged-brown girls in noisy silks, was like a picture in his head. Yet it did not make him sad. On that very trip Slim Burns had killed Joe Beasley—the crowd had been broken up. Since then

Jeff Patton's world had been the Greenbrier Plantation. If there had been other *Mardi Gras* carnivals, he had not heard of them. Since then there had been no time; the years had fallen on him like waves. Now he was old, worn out. Another paralytic stroke (like the one he had already suffered) would put him on his back for keeps. In that condition, with a frail blind woman to look after him, he would be worse off than if he were dead.

Suddenly Jeff's hands became steady. He actually felt brave. He slowed down the motor of the car and carefully pulled off the road. Below, the water of the stream boomed, a soft thunder in the deep channel. Jeff ran the car onto the clay slope, pointed it directly toward the stream and put his foot heavily on the accelerator. The little car leaped furiously down the steep incline toward the water. The movement was nearly as swift and direct as a fall. The two old black folks, sitting quietly side by side, showed no excitement. In another instant the car hit the water and dropped immediately out of sight.

A little later it lodged in the mud of a shallow place. One wheel of the crushed and upturned little Ford became visible above the rushing water.

1934

- Chinese Communists, led by Mao Tse-tung, begin their Long March, relocating 6,000 miles to the north in China.
- In India, Gandhi suspends the civil disobedience campaign.
- Yugoslavian king Alexander I, French foreign minister Jean Louis Barthou, and Australian chancellor Engelbert Dollfuss are assassinated.
- British heiress Nancy Cunard publishes her extensive anthology, *Negro*.
- U.S. military occupation of Haiti ends.
- Elijah Muhammad becomes head of the Nation of Islam.
- W. E. B. Du Bois resigns as editor of NAACP's *Crisis*.
- Arthur W. Mitchell of Chicago becomes the first African American Democrat elected to the U.S. House of Representatives.
- Harlem's Apollo Theater opens.
- Aaron Douglas completes work on his *Aspects of Negro Life* murals for the 135th Street branch of the New York Public Library.

U.S. unemployment: 21.7%

Lynchings in the United States: 15 blacks, 0 whites

Deaths:
> Wallace Thurman (Dec. 22)
> Rudolph Fisher (Dec. 26)

Spingarn Medal: William T. B. Williams (educator)

Books:
> Arna Bontemps, *You Can't Pet a Possum* (juvenile fiction)
> Randolph Edmonds, *Six Plays for a Negro Theatre* (drama)
> Langston Hughes, *The Ways of White Folks* (short stories)
> Zora Neale Hurston, *Jonah's Gourd Vine* (novel)
> George W. Lee, *Beale Street: Where the Blues Began* (nonfiction)

Periodical: *Challenge* (1934–37)

39 BARREL STAVES
Arna Bontemps

FROM *CHALLENGE*, MARCH 1934

Skeeter Gordon was an exile. His friends in Harlem had turned on him. His young chocolate-colored wife had bristled like a porcupine and evicted him with sudden dispatch and finality. When the door banged behind him, Skeeter was sprawled face downward on a small landing a dozen steps below. He was convinced that Harlem was no longer safe for him. He had been cast from his last stronghold.

The explanation is simple: Skeeter was dishonest. He had double-crossed his young friends, the black boys who had stood by him; and he had deceived the girl who had taken up with him when he was ragged as a picked sparrow. He was a no-'count, ungrateful nigger, and he deserved the worst thing that could happen to him.

During his exile the lean spidery black boy took refuge in the upper Bronx. There, in the vicinity of East 225th Street, he found many other black faces sprinkled like pepper over the Jewish and Italian neighborhood. Here in this far end of the Bronx, however, he was a total stranger; and if he had no friends, neither had he enemies. Life, miserably tangled in Harlem, seemed to him very simple here; and best of all, it was safe.

He shuffled serenely down White Plains Avenue, his hands in his hip pockets, a tune on his lips.

> Walked de streets from sun to sun,
> > Lawd, Lawd!
> Walked de streets from sun to sun—
> Ain't got no money an' don't want none.

He was coatless, with a frayed shirt and a pair of purplish blue pants that hit him six inches above the ankles; but as he walked he flapped his long comical feet proudly, swaying from one side of the pavement to the other, as if he owned the street.

"Heah's where I gits a fresh start," he told himself. "I gonna 'gin all over 'gin. I gonna git me a lil odd job an' a steady hard-workin' gal whut ain't so hot-haided an' settle down. Tha's whut I gonna do. I ain't gonna be no mo' devilish tramp. Hm!"

He turned into 223rd Street and lazied eastward in the bright afternoon sunlight. His slick round head glistened like ebony. After a month of stuffy Harlem pigeon-holes, this fresh air was a blessing. The Skeeter was feeling good and he didn't care who knew it. He was as happy as a colt in a new pasture.

"If it wa'n't so hot, I'd jus break and run," he said. "I feels lak another nigger. I done almost forgit ma name's bad-luck Skeeter."

There were two or three small apartment houses at long intervals in the block between the rows of private dwellings. On the sidewalk, in front of one of the smallest of these tenements, Skeeter saw black youngsters playing. That indicated the sort of place he had been seeking. He flopped on the step, scratched his incredible legs, produced from his pockets a mashed-up palm-leaf fan and leaned back to refresh himself.

"Ah!" he grunted. "Hm!"

The children frisked wildly about his feet. Since he had decided to remain in this part of the city, his interest kept running out to those features of the neighborhood that might affect his living. He wondered about the sources of food, about a place to sleep. Given a chance, he could at that very moment have punished a stiff bait of victuals. And as for sleeping, that was never out of the question. He could always sleep. He could sleep standing up. The fact that he felt drowsy there in the sunshine, on the warm concrete steps, was neither odd or significant.

Presently an old rheumatic Negro came up from the basement and eyed Skeeter pleasantly. The old fellow wore a pair of striped overalls and a battered cap that had once, perhaps, belonged to some steamboat man. His face was matted with frizzly whiskers, and Skeeter noticed that he was not more than five feet tall.

"He-o, Cap'n," Skeeter grinned.

"Is you a Harlem boy?"

"Hm. I was, [but] I ain't no mo'. I done leave town."

"Dis heah is a slow-time place for city niggers."

"You reckon I can find me a lil odd job an' a place to sleep round heah, Cap'n?"

The old sawed-off black looked the long indolent boy up and down.

"Is you any 'count?"

"Me? I's one mo' hard workin' nigger, Cap'n. I's de workingest nigger you mos' ever set eyes on."

"Yo' look is kind o' deceivin'. Reckon you could tote a ash can up these heah steps by yo'self?"

Skeeter tried to show scorn. "Shucks! I could come up them there steps wid a ash can under both arms an' one on ma back."

"Lemme study a minute. If you's worth a dime, you might could stay heah an' sleep in de boiler room an' help me wid de garbage an' wid de ash cans."

They descended the steps to the basement and Skeeter followed the Cap'n down a dark hallway. The old fellow pointed out the boiler room, the little hot-water furnace, the coal bins, and the dumb waiter shafts. Half a dozen large cans were arranged against the wall.

"Heah they is," the Cap'n said.

But Skeeter was no longer interested. His head was raised; his eyes were turned skyward; he had caught a glimpse of something two floors above that deflected his attention. A glossy velvet-skinned young woman was standing at the window, her face split with a huge smile.

The black girl was evidently in the midst of her cooking. In one hand she held a dish rag, in the other a long-handled spoon. And there was an odor of food pouring from her window, an odor so strong and compelling it made Skeeter's jaws hang apart like a pair of tongs.

Suddenly the young woman turned away from the window and burst into song:

"Ma daddy is a business man, a business man,
Keys in his pocket an' a diamond on his han."

"I done decide, Cap'n," Skeeter said.

"It's yourn if it suits you."

"It suits me good, Cap'n. Look out o' ma way now whilst I shows you how to tote three ash cans at a time."

Skeeter's little gesture in the areaway did not go unnoticed. Adina, the velvety gal at the kitchen window, saw him juggling the heavy cans and she was deeply impressed.

"Hush ma mouth wide open," she exclaimed. "Wonder where de Super' found dat ole good-lookin' devil."

She forgot her pots. Resting her elbows on the window sill, leaning as far out as she dared, she became engrossed in the performance below. Suddenly she shouted:

"Hey Super! Look lak you gonna have some help?"

"Yeah, Miss Dina, I done got me a 'sistant."

"Reckon he any 'count?"

"Don't know yet, but I gonna put him through de mill directly."

"Whyn't you send him up heah an' start him on dis sink o' mine, whut I been tryin' to git you fix ever since las' month?"

"Das a notion, Miss Dina." The Cap'n dropped his eyes. Skeeter was returning empty-handed. The old fellow pointed to the gal in the window. "Dat lady yonder is havin' trouble wid her sink. You mind lookin' at it for me?"

Skeeter threw another glance upwards.

"Open de door, Miss Sheba, I's comin' up fas' an' I is apt to bus' it down."

He made a break for the tools. When Adina reached the door he was already there. He arched his neck and entered the little kitchen. The room was bursting with the odors of frying meat and onions, boiling vegetables and ham hocks. Skeeter stood in the center of the floor, dazed by his surroundings.

"M-m-m!" He shook his head expressively. "I ain't been this close to a bait o' good ole home cookin' in mo' days'n I can count."

"You's right pitiful."

"Sho is. De womens in Harlem was fixin' to let me die. Tha's how come me out heah."

"Dis heah is a mo' betta place to die," she said compassionately. "Was you to pass out in one o' dem cellars in Harlem, de rats'd eat you."

He shuddered. "Dat dey would. But I gonna die out heah on y'all's hands."

"Whyn't you try me on a lil smell o' dem victuals you's cookin'? You'll see what a big diff'ence it'll make in papa Skeeter."

Adina was a short, big-hipped girl. She wore a checkered house dress without sleeves, and as she carried on with Skeeter she leaned against the ice box with obvious coquetry.

"Maby I will an' maby I won't," she said. "I gonna wait an' see how good you fixes ma sink."

Skeeter banged the tool box on the floor.

"You ole big eyed sumpin' o' nuther."

He quickly disconnected the drain, fitted a new washer, then reattached the pipe. It was like sleight-of-hand. Skeeter was a case. He was one of the most handiest boys Adina had ever set eyes on.

"How dat suit you, Miss?"

"Ah, so-so," she said. "I 'spect you'll do."

Adina took a large plate from the shelf, heaped it to capacity and placed it at a tiny rickety table. Skeeter adjusted a chair, stretched his legs and went to work.

That one mighty meal did not satisfy Skeeter for long, however, and the next day he was out job-hunting. The sun had come up strong and the streets were dry and dusty. Dust had settled on the leaves of the trees like powder. A string of empty milk wagons lined the curb near 219th Street. The proprietors of countless fruit stands were busy arranging their displays. These impressed Skeeter. He planted himself in front of one, drew his fan and stood calmly inspecting the pyramids of red apples, ripe oranges and yellow pears.

"Dog if dat ain't a sight," he mused. "Tha's jest nachal-born putty."

Around the heaps of bright fruit were designs of fresh mustard greens, lettuce, spinach, cabbages and collards, green onions, carrots, beets, asparagus—all looking fresh and moist as if they had never been harvested, as if the natural dew was still on them. From the ceiling suspended great bunches of bananas, ripe and yellow and fine. And elsewhere strings of crimson peppers hung against the walls, strings of dried figs and mushrooms. Mountains of earth-colored potatoes rose in the background, and cocoanuts were scattered among the green things as if literally dropped there from the trees. Watermelons lay about the floor, between the sacks and baskets.

Skeeter was too absorbed to move. He stood in the middle of the sidewalk, the palm leaf fan in his hand, mouth open. His little glossy head suggested a billiard ball.

The fruit man's small motor truck, parked at the curb, was still partly loaded with crates and boxes of vegetables from the wholesale market. Angelo had neglected it for the moment and was passing over his display with a water sprinkler to protect the greens from the wilting heat of the sun. A few morning customers, too, had begun to require his attention. He was a short, thickly built Italian with loose curly hair, a white apron, and a tiny cap on the back of his head. At the moment his face was red with the hurry and excitement of setting his stand in order.

"M-m!" Skeeter ejaculated. "Dat gits it. Tha's a purty howdy-do, I thank you."

"Yeah? You like um?"

"I'm tellin' you."

"You wanna buy some nice sweet oranges? bananas? apples?"

"You done mistook me, Mistah. I couldn't buy a pair o' slippers for a musketeer. Money an' me ain't speakin'. I's jes studyin' 'bout you in dis great big fruit sto' by yo'self. You oughta have a black boy to keep it all sweep up nice an' clean an' unload de truck an' one thing an' another."

Angelo inspected the long boy carefully. Then he looked at his floor and his half-loaded truck. That was an idea, especially since Skeeter appeared to be such inexpensive help. A boy as ragged as this bare-headed stranger surely wouldn't have a large salary in mind.

"You t'ink so, hunh? You like-a job?"

"Yes suh, me 'like-a,'" Skeeter grinned. "Me 'like-a' plenty."

"Al'ight. Sweep um up." He thrust a broom into Skeeter's hands. "You good boy, maybe I keep you."

"Yes suh!"

Skeeter commenced working with a flourish that won the Italian's eye immediately. His broom danced over the floor with a grace and skill like magic. Not a straw or leaf was missed. That finished he turned to the truck, unloaded the remainder of the vegetables, quickly transported them through the store out into the shady back yard, and covered them with wet sacks.

Angelo sat on a box watching the performance. He became limber with amusement and good humor. When Skeeter finished, the fruit man gave him a handful of over-ripe bananas and sent him into the back yard to eat. Skeeter grinned as he disappeared. He felt sure that he had at last landed on his feet.

"I knows when I's well off," he told himself. "I done got lucky again. I done got dat fresh start, an' I ain't fixin' to muff it neither. No suh."

He sat down beneath the horse-chestnut tree that leaned across the fence and began skinning and devouring the ripe fruit.

Later in the afternoon Skeeter discovered a little two-wheeled delivery cart upturned behind a stack of old boxes, out of use. That gave him another thought. He could now become delivery man for Angelo. And that would give him an opportunity to go about the neighborhood and seek amusement during the midday lull. He visualized himself majestically piloting the empty cart over the rugged side streets, bumping and rattling it with an air of great importance. He could imagine the womenfolks of the neighborhood high-balling him from the kitchen windows, beseeching him to hurry back with a soup bunch or a mess of new potatoes.

"Heah where I puts some git-up in these lil ole sleepy streets," he thought. "When papa Skeeter gits on de road, folks gonna sit up an' take notice. To heah me comin', they gonna think I's drivin' de fire wagon, cause I aims to travel wid horns and drums."

He adjusted a small flat strip of wood on the body of the cart in such a manner as to clap against each spoke when the wheel turned. He hung a tin can to the axle by a string just long enough to let the bottom of the can reach the ground. In the can he put nails and bits of iron, such things as he thought would make a first rate noise to help remind folks that papa Skeeter was on the road.

Angelo was satisfied. If this overgrown black idiot wanted to rattle around the neighborhood with that old discarded cart, he was welcome to do so. Angelo frequently had need of a delivery boy; had in fact on several occasions hired school boys for this purpose, but he saw no reason why the cart would be needed. In that, however, he let Skeeter have his wish.

Angelo was so well pleased with the comical boy he had hired that on the third day he made the mistake of leaving Skeeter alone in the fruit store. Skeeter began immediately to explore the spaces beneath the counter, the backs of the shelves, and the dark corners of the back room. Within a few moments he had found and substantially damaged a jug of Angelo's private wine.

Meanwhile Skeeter's interest in Adina had stood still. Once or twice since his meal in her kitchen, she had yelled at him pleasantly in the areaway. But he was no better acquainted than he had been the first day he saw her. He wasn't even sure that she would be eligible for his attentions; not knowing her well, he couldn't guess what she would require of a gentleman who came to court her regularly. Now that he was settled, with a job in the fruit store and a cot in the furnace room, she got on his mind again.

"Wonder whut ole good-lookin' 'Dina's doin'," he worried. "Guess she think I done plum forget her. She right, too; I been had me mind on work, an' I been eatin' and drinkin' so much on de side I wa'nt fittin' for nuthin' but sleep when I knocked off in de evenin'."

Skeeter was returning to the fruit store with his empty cart, down a quiet tree-shaded street. The sun was low, the yellow light flashing directly in the black boy's eyes. He had walked rapidly and was dripping with sweat, but he felt good. He felt like chewing the rag with some such big-eyed gal as Adina.

He brought his cart booming into the back alley and wheeled it into the yard behind the fruit store. Then he went inside to tell Angelo he was ready to go home. The fat Italian was nodding on his box. He grunted when Skeeter spoke but paid him no attention. Skeeter's eyes rolled in their deep sockets. As Angelo sank back into slumber the boy quickly grabbed up a small bunch of bananas, perhaps a dozen, and three large cocoanuts. With these under his arms he flashed through the back door.

Skeeter went directly to Adina's apartment and rang the bell. She came to the door, mopping the perspiration from her face with the corner of her apron.

"Look lak I's too late," Skeeter said.

"Too late for what?"

"For supper. Ain't you done boarded?"

"Is you hungry?" Adina settled back on her heels and seemed exasperated.

"I ain't huntin' grub, sweetness," Skeeter smiled. "I's bringin' you sumpin'. Reckon you could make 'way wid these?"

"Could I! I done et a lil bit," she admitted, "but I ain't half full."

"Well, pitch in, baby. Gimme sumpin' to crack these heah cocoanuts wid."

Skeeter went to work on the hard shells with the aid of a flat iron.

Adina was a matter-of-fact young woman, and one who was not ashamed to eat in the presence of masculine company. Neither was she embarrassed by her weight and the surplus flesh under her chin. She smacked her lips with pleasure as she masticated the cocoanut meat.

Skeeter enjoyed watching her. Tilted backwards and rocking on two legs of his chair, it occurred to him that he and Adina had a great deal in common. Each of them had ravenous appetites and they seemed to like the same foods. That had not been true of the thin hot-tempered girl in Harlem with whom he had failed to live in harmony and from whom he had fled. She liked cold meats, pickles, delicatessen foods; and that sort of thing had irked the Skeeter. Adina was more like his kind, a gal with a taste for tropical fruits, green vegetables, and pork meat. It was time, he figured, they become better acquainted.

"Is you a single gal, 'Dina?"

"Well yes 'n no. I's a widder woman."

"Oh."

"Ma ole man got hisself a job on de railroad an' I ain't seen head or tail o' him since."

"He done disert you?"

"Um hunh! Tha's it."

"Devilish scoundrel! A nigger lak dat ain't fit to have a good steady woman."

"Sho ain't. But y'all menfolks is putty much all de same."

"Don't say dat, sweetness." Skeeter was deeply serious. "I ain't one o' dem jack rabbit mens. I's a true-love boy."

"Yo' looks is kinda deceivin', papa Skeeter."

"Eve'ybody tell me dat," he said. "That de firs' thing de Cap'n met me wid. I don't know whut cause it neither."

"Maybe it's a birthmark."

"Mus' be is."

"You ain't never run off an' lef' a lovin' woman whut was good to you?"

"Not lessen she sent me 'way," he vowed. "I been married wid a ole hot-haided gal once—signed up at de cou't house an' got a receipt an' ev'ything—but it ain't 'mounted to a hill o' beans. Dat gal kicked me out head foremost an' tore up the permit an' th'owed it at me."

"So you's a widder, too?"

"I mean."

"An' you ain't goin' back?"

"How can I go back when she done tore up de permit. I's free as a jay bird."

"Tha's a notion," she said. "I b'lieve I'll tear up mine, too."

Skeeter rolled his eyes at Adina. "Hmp! Tha's whut you gonna have to do," he said. "I gonna see to dat."

"Why you so worried up?"

"I feels ma love comin' down. Tha's how come I's worried. You an' me's gonna be sweet if I's got anything to say 'bout it."

"Hm. You ain't got nuthin' to say 'bout it though, long boy. I'm gonna wait an' make up ma own mind 'bout dat."

"You betta make it up in a hurry," he commanded, "'cause if yo' don't I'm apt to make it up for you."

They understood each other. Skeeter reared back, opened his mouth wide enough to swallow a cocoanut and emitted a gale of laughter that could be heard half a mile. Adina chirped and giggled so hard tears came to her eyes, and the fat on her shoulders shook like jelly.

The next day Skeeter brought Adina a half dozen of Angelo's biggest and finest yams. He hid them in his shirt and slipped away with them while the Italian fruit store man nodded in the entrance of his shop. Adina was delighted and, in return, invited the long boy to stay for dinner. While the two were bending over the steaming plates, she mentioned something to him that was on her mind.

"Is you goin' to de New Covenant bus ride?"

"Whut ole New Covenant bus ride?" Skeeter corrugated his brow. "I ain't heared 'bout no sich come-off."

"No? It's gonna be next week. It's sumpin'."

"Good time, hunh?"

"I mean. Righteous."

"How come you ain't invited me to come an' be yo' company?"

"Cause you ain't give me time. I's jes fixin' to say would you like to 'tend?"

"I like to go anywheres you gonna be, honey. All I wants to do is to be wid you. Tha's all I studies 'bout now."

"Well now, 'bout goin' wid me, I er. . . . . . . I gotta 'splain dat. Brother Sam Chalmers, de 'sistant shepherd at New Covenant, got his head set on bein' ma company, too."

Skeeter's mouth fell open. It closed and opened again, but no words came. His eyes blinked. He swallowed a lump in his throat. Still he was unable to talk. Adina, seeing that he was paralyzed, hurried to his rescue.

"Course I ain't give him ma word yet," she said. "I jes waitin' to see how you'd take it."

Skeeter regained his strength with a long sigh.

"Honey," he said, "I gonna be so close to you dat day de Brother Sam Chalmers ain't gonna be able to see you for me. An' dat ain't all. I'm gonna bring you an' me mo' good stuff from de fruit sto' 'n you can shake a stick at."

"Dat suits me, son. I'll jest mix up some fried chicken an' sandwiches an' things like that. An' if you makes a good showin' wid de fruits we'll be set for de day."

"'Pend on me, baby."

"You'll have to be on de spot early, too. De bus gonna pull out at eight o'clock sharp."

Skeeter smiled broadly. "I'm gonna be sittin' on de church house steps at ha'-past seben."

During the days that intervened, Skeeter walked on air. Time after time he unfolded the prospects of that bus ride and picnic in his mind as he expected them to materialize. He would work late the preceding night, however, and while the boss was busy with the last of the customers he would sneak the fruit he wanted into the back room, put it in a basket and cover it. Then he would be careful to unlock the back window. This would enable him to come in by way of the alley, get the fruit and carry it away while Angelo was off with the truck doing the regular wholesale marketing. On the bus and at the picnic, there would be nothing but bliss. Skeeter could see himself lolling on a green spot, legs crossed, a chicken bone in his hand and Adina smiling affectionately at his side, while Brother Sam Chalmers shot malicious glances at them and wrung his hands.

He planned and selected the basket of fruit with an eye toward impressing Adina. The gift should be the last necessary ounce. He had started well, he would be sure to finish strong. To be Adina's company on that bus ride, in the presence of all the church folks, would be like a banner in his hand. That was what he wanted. He wanted the world to know he was papa Skeeter from Harlem, the shiniest black boy in that end of town and a devil with the gals.

With these notions stirring in his head, he began the pleasant chore of selecting the fruit. He hid a basket under a pile of sacks in the back room. Then, throughout the day, at such times as he found Angelo's back turned, he slipped oranges, apples, pears, bananas, cocoanuts and cantaloupes into it. Skeeter was deft on this business. It was not new to him. And when the day preceding the bus ride came, he had a lunch basket assortment worthy of any picnic. It was so "worthy," in fact, Skeeter wondered how he could get the thing away. He lifted it at a time to make sure he could handle it conveniently. Yes, he could manage. The Skeeter put his shoulders back, smiled from ear to ear, and poked out his chest.

The next morning he was out at the crack of day. And when the time came for Angelo to be away with the truck, Skeeter slipped quietly into the yard behind the fruit store.

The window, through which it was necessary to get the basket, had no weight or pulleys. It was a heavy window, and Skeeter could not hold it up while lifting the fruit. So he found a stick of suitable length and with it propped the pane. He then put his head and shoulders through the waist-high window and reached for his treasure.

But as he leaned forward in this position a surprising thing happened. The window came down suddenly with a bang that left Skeeter pinned as tightly as a mouse in a trap, his head and shoulders inside, his body and legs outside.

Angelo, suspecting his store-boy's dishonesty for some days, had discerned Skeeter's plans and set himself accordingly. When Skeeter got his head well through the window, the Italian had quickly slipped from behind the boxes where he was crouched and withdrawn the stick supporting the heavy pane.

So the Skeeter was helpless. Inside, his little head was all mouth and eyes, bellowing like forty bulls and blazing fire. Outside, his lean frog-like hind-parts wriggled and twisted and beat the air. Angelo went calmly to the corner of the yard, selected a barrel, crushed it, returned with an arm full of staves, took a firm position with his heels braced, and began studiously breaking the staves one at a time across the protruding legs and body.

In the meantime a crowd gathered in front of the New Covenant Church. The bus was filled. The driver insisted on getting away on schedule. The motor rumbled and the heavy vehicle pulled out.

Skeeter came around the corner limping like a man with rheumatism, bruised, crestfallen, and empty-handed. He stood with stooped shoulders, nursing his bruises and watching the diminishing picture of his own dreams plowing down the yellow road, obscured by a cloud of dust.

One thing was very distinct. In the back seat was old big-eyed Adina, and beside her the Brother Sam Chalmers. The glossy black deacon was wearing a new milk-white straw hat. His face was split by a smile that rippled like an ocean wave. He was swollen worse than a pouter pigeon, and as he leaned back caressing Adina's broad shoulders with affection and triumph, he shot mean and spiteful glances over his shoulder.

Skeeter blinked, rubbed his tiny slick head and turned his face in the opposite direction. He drew the palm-leaf fan from his pocket, refreshed himself and started walking.

"I'm going back to Harlem," he decided. "This heah place is bad luck."

40 WHY, YOU RECKON
Langston Hughes

FROM *New Yorker*, MARCH 1934

Well, sir, I ain't never been mixed up in nothin' like that before nor since, and don't intend to be agin, but I was hongry as hell that night, indeed, I was! You-all standin' here with me now in this here beggin' grub line knows how hongry a man can get. So I was goin' down a Hundred Thirty-third Street when another colored fellow what looks hongry sidetracks me and says, "Say, buddy, you wanta make a little jack?"

"Sure," I says. "How?"

"Stickin' up a guy," he says. "The first white guy what comes out o' one o' these speaks and looks like bucks, we gonna grab him!"

"Oh, no," says I.

"Oh, yes, we will," says this other guy. "Man, ain't you hongry? Didn't I see you down there at the charities today, not gettin' nothin'—like me, neither? You didn't get it, did you? Hell, no! Well, you gotta *take* it, that's all, reach out and *take* it," he says. "Even if you are starvin', don't be no fool. You must be in love with white folks, or something. Do you think they care anything about you?"

"No," I says.

"They sure don't," he says. "These here rich white folks come up to Harlem spendin' forty or fifty dollars down in these night clubs and speakeasies, and don't care nothin' 'bout you and me out here in the street, do they? Well, they gonna give me some o' their money tonight before one of 'em gets back home"

"What about the cops?"

"To hell with the cops! Now listen, now. I live right here, sleep on the ash pile back o' the furnace down in this here basement. Don't nobody never come down there after dark. They let me stay here for keepin' the furnace goin' at night. It's kind of a fast house upstairs, you understand. Now, you grab this here guy we pick out, push him down to the basement door, right here, I'll pull him in, and we'll drag him on back yonder to the furnace-room and rob him, money, watch, clothes, and all. Then push him out in the rear court. If he hollers, and he sure will holler when that cold air hits him, folks'll just think he's some drunken white man what's fell out with a chocolate baby upstairs, and has had to run and leave his clothes behind him, 'cause some o' these fast-house mad-ams don't take no foolishness. And by that time we'll be long gone. What you say, boy?"

Well, sir, I'm tellin' you, I was so tired and hongry I didn't hardly know what to say, so I said all right, and we decided to do it. Looked like to me 'bout that time a Hundred Thirty-third Street was just workin' with people, taxis cruisin', women hustlin', white folks from downtown lookin' for hot spots. It were just about midnight.

This guy's front basement door was right near the floor o' the Rufus Bar, where that yellow woman sings them blues what all the o'fays is crazy about. And well, sir! Just what we wanted to happen happened right off.

A big party o' young white folks in furs and things came down the street. They musta parked their car on Lenox, 'cause they wasn't in no taxi. They was walkin' in the snow. And just when they got right by us, one of them white women says to a young man with her, she says, "Ed-ward," but she didn't say it like we say Edward. She said, "Ed-*ward*," she said, "Oh, darlin', don't you know I left my purse and cigarettes and compact in the car. Please go and ask the chauffeur to give 'em to you." And they went on in the Rufus. The boy started toward Lenox agin.

Well, sir, Edward never did get back no more that evenin' to the Rufus Bar. No, sir, 'cause we nabbed him. When he came back down the street in his evenin' clothes and all, with a swell black overcoat on that I wished I had, just a-tippin' so as not to slip up and fall on the hard snow, we grabbed him. Before he could say Jack Robinson, I pulled him down the steps to the basement door, the other fellow jerked him in, and by the time he knew where he was, we had that white boy back yonder behind the furnace in the coal bin.

"Don't you holler," I said.

There wasn't much light back there, just the raw gas comin' out of a jet, kinder blue-like, blinkin' in the coal dust. Took a few minutes before we could see what he looked like.

"Ed-*ward*," the other fellow said, "don't you holler."

But Edward didn't holler. He just sat right down on the coal. I reckon he was sorta scared weak-like.

"Don't you throw no coal neither," the other fellow said. But Edward didn't look like he was gonna throw coal.

"What do you want?" he said by and by in a nice white-folks kind o' voice. "Am I kidnapped?"

Well, sir, we never thought o' that, kidnappin'. I reckon we both looked puzzled. I could see the other guy thinkin' maybe we *ought* to hold him for ransom. Then the other fellow musta decided that that weren't wise, 'cause he says to this white boy, "No, you ain't kidnapped," he says. "We ain't got time for that. We's hongry *now*, so, buddy, gimme your money."

The white boy handed out o' his coat pocket amongst other things the lady's pretty white beaded bag that he'd been sent after. The other fellow held it up. "Doggone!" he said. "My gal could go for this. She likes purty things. Stand up and lemme see what else you got."

The white guy got up and the other fellow went through his pockets. He took out a wallet and a gold watch and a cigarette-lighter and he got a swell key ring and some other little things that colored never use.

"Thank you," said the other guy, when he got through friskin' the white boy, "I guess I'll eat tomorrow! And smoke right now," he said, openin' up the white boy's cigarette case. "Have one," and he passed them swell fags around to me and the white boy, too. "What kind is these?" he wanted to know.

"Benson's Hedges," said the white boy, kinder scared-like, 'cause the other fellow was making an awful face over the cigarette.

"Well, I don't like 'em," the other fellow said, frownin' up. "Why don't you smoke decent cigarettes? Where do you get off, anyhow?" he said to this white boy standin' there in the coal bin. "Where do you get off comin' up here to Harlem with these kind o' cigarettes? Don't you know don't no colored folks smoke these kind o' cigarettes? And what're you doin' bringin' a lot o' purty rich women up here wearin' white fur coats? Don't you know it's more'n we colored folks can do to get a black fur coat, let alone a white one? I'm askin' you a question," the other fellow said. The poor little white fellow looked like he was gonna cry. "Don't you know," the colored fellow went on, "that I been walkin' up and down Lenox Avenue for three or four months tryin' to find some way to earn money to get my shoes half-soled? Here, look at 'em." He held up the palms o' his feet for the white boy to see. There were sure big holes in his shoes. "Looka here!" he said to that white boy. "And still you got the nerve to come up here to Harlem all dressed up in a tuxedo suit with a stiff shirt on and diamonds shinin' out o' the front o' it, and a silk muffler on and a big heavy overcoat! Gimme that overcoat," the other fellow said.

He grabbed the little white guy and took off his overcoat.

"We can't use that John Barrymore outfit you got on," he said, talking about the tux. "But we might be able to make earrings for our janes out o' them studs. Take 'em off," he said to the white kid.

All this time, I was just standin' there, wasn't doin' nothin'. The other fellow had taken all the stuff, so far, and had his arms full.

"Wearin' diamonds up here to Harlem, and me starvin'!" the other fellow said. "Goddamn! You wearin' diamonds and Harlem starvin'."

"I'm sorry," said the white fellow.

"Sorry?" said the other guy. "What's your name?"

"Edward Peedee McGill, III," said the white fellow.

"What third?" said the colored fellow. "Where's the other two?"

"My father and grandfather," said the white boy. "I'm the third."

"I had a father and grandfather, too," said the other fellow, "but I ain't no third. I'm the first. Ain't never been another black bastard like me. I'm a new model." And he laughed out loud.

When he laughed, the white boy looked real scared. He looked like he wanted to holler. He sat down in the coal again. The front of his shirt was all black where he'd took the diamonds out. The wind came in through a broken pane above the coal bin and the white fellow sat there shiverin'. He was just a kid—eighteen or twenty maybe—runnin' around to night clubs.

"We ain't gonna kill you," the other fellow kept laughin'. "We ain't got time. But if you sit in that coal long enough, white boy, you'll be black as me. Gimme your shoes. I might maybe can sell 'em."

The white fellow took off his shoes. As he handed them to the colored fellow, he had to laugh, hisself. It looked so crazy handin' somebody else your shoes. We all laughed.

"But I'm laughin' last," said the other fellow. "You two can stay here and laugh if you want to, but I'm gone. So long!"

And man, don't you know he went on out from that basement and took all that stuff! Left me standin' just as empty-handed as when I come in there. Yes, sir! He left me with that white boy standin' in the coal. He'd done took the money, the diamonds, and everythin', even the shoes! And me with nothin'! Was I stung? I'm askin' you!

"Ain't you gonna gimme none?" I hollered, runnin' after him down the dark hall. "Where's my part?" I couldn't even see him in the dark—but I *heard* him.

"Get back there," he yelled at me, "and watch that white boy till I get out o' here. Get back there," he hollered, "or I'll knock your livin' gizzard out! I don't know you."

I got back. And there me and that white boy was standin' in a strange coal bin, him lookin' like a picked chicken—and me *feelin'* like a fool. Well, sir, we both had to laugh agin.

"Say," said the white boy, "is he gone?"

"He ain't here," I said.

"Gee, this was exciting," said the white fellow, turning up his tux collar. "This was thrilling!"

"What?" I says.

"This is the first exciting thing that's ever happened to me," said the white guy. "The first time in my life I had a good time in Harlem. Everything else's been fake. You know, something you pay for. This was real."

"Say, buddy," I says, "if I had your money, I'd be always having a good time."

Then I went out and looked, and there wasn't no cops or nobody much in the streets, so I said "So long" to that white boy and left him standin' in the door there in his stocking feet. Say, what do you suppose is the matter with rich folks. Why, you reckon, they ain't happy?

41 SPANISH BLOOD
Langston Hughes

From *Metropolis*, December 1934; reprinted in *Stag*, August 1937

In that amazing city of Manhattan where people are forever building things anew, during prohibition times there lived a young Negro called Valerio Gutierrez whose mother was a Harlem laundress, but whose father was a Puerto Rican sailor. Valerio grew up in the streets. He was never much good at school, but he was swell at selling papers, pitching pennies, or shooting pool. In his teens he became one of the smoothest dancers in the Latin-American quarter north of Central Park. Long before the rhumba became popular, he knew how to do it in the real Cuban way that made all the girls afraid to dance with him. Besides, he was very good looking.

At seventeen, an elderly Chilean lady who owned a beauty parlor called La Flor began to buy his neckties. At eighteen, she kept him in pocket money and let him drive her car. At nineteen, younger and prettier women—a certain comely Spanish widow, also one Dr. Barrios' pale wife—began to see that he kept well dressed.

"You'll never amount to nothin'," Hattie, his brown-skinned mother, said. "Why don't you get a job and work? It's that foreign blood in you, that's what it is. Just like your father."

"*Que va?*" Valerio replied, grinning.

"Don't you speak Spanish to me," his mama said. "You know I don't under-stand it."

"O.K., mama," Valerio said. "*Yo voy a trabajar.*"

"You better *trabajar*," his mama answered. "And I mean work, too! I'm tired o' comin' home every night from that Chinee laundry and findin' you gone to the dogs. I'm gonna move out o' this here Spanish neighborhood anyhow, way up into Harlem where some real *colored* people is, I mean American Negroes. There ain't nobody settin' a decent example for you down here 'mongst all these

Cubans and Puerto Ricans and things. I don't care if your father was one of 'em, I never did like 'em real well."

"Aw, ma, why didn't you ever learn Spanish and stop talking like a spook?"

"Don't you spook me, you young hound, you! I won't stand it. Just because you're straight-haired and yellow and got that foreign blood in you, don't you spook me. I'm your mother and I won't stand for it. You hear me?"

"Yes, m'am. But you know what I mean. I mean stop talking like most colored folks—just because you're not white you don't have to get back in a corner and stay there. Can't we live nowhere else but way up in Harlem, for instance? Down here in 106th Street, white and colored families live in the same house—Spanish-speaking families, some white and some black. What do you want to move further up in Harlem for, where everybody's all black? Lots of my friends down here are Spanish and Italian, and we get along swell."

"That's just what I'm talkin' about," said his mother. "That's just why I'm gonna move. I can't keep track of you, runnin' around with a fast foreign crowd, all mixed up with every what-cha-ma-call-it, lettin' all shades o' women give you money. Besides, no matter where you move, or what language you speak, you're still colored less'n your skin is white."

"Well, I won't be," said Valerio. "I'm American, Latin-American."

"Huh!" said his mama. "It's just by luck that you even got good hair."

"What's that got to do with being American?"

"A mighty lot," said his mama, "in America."

They moved. They moved up to 143rd Street, in the very middle of "American" Harlem. There Hattie Gutierrez was happier—for in her youth her name had been Jones, not Gutierrez, just plain colored Jones. She had come from Virginia, not Latin America. She had met the Puerto Rican seaman in Norfolk, had lived with him there and in New York for some ten or twelve years and borne him a son, meanwhile working hard to keep him and their house in style. Then one winter he just disappeared, probably missed his boat in some far-off port town, settled down with another woman, and went on dancing rhumbas and drinking rum without worry.

Valerio, whom Gutierrez left behind, was a handsome child, not quite as light as his father, but with olive-yellow skin and Spanish-black hair, more foreign than Negro. As he grew up, he became steadily taller and better looking. Most of his friends were Spanish-speaking, so he possessed their language as well as English. He was smart and amusing out of school. But he wouldn't work. That was what worried his mother; he just wouldn't work. The long hours and low wages most colored fellows received during depression times never appealed to him. He could live without struggling, so he did.

He liked to dance and play billiards. He hung out near the Cuban theater at

110th Street, around the pool halls and gambling places, in the taxi dance emporiums. He was all for getting the good things out of life. His mother's moving up to black 143rd Street didn't improve conditions any. Indeed, it just started the ball rolling faster, for here Valerio became what is known in Harlem as a big-timer, a young sport, a hep cat. In other words, a man-about-town.

His sleek-haired yellow star rose in a chocolate sky. He was seen at all the formal invitational affairs given by the exclusive clubs of Harlem's younger set, although he belonged to no clubs. He was seen at midnight shows stretching into the dawn. He was even asked to Florita Sutton's famous Thursday midnight-at-homes where visiting dukes, English authors, colored tap dancers, and dinner-coated downtowners vied for elbow room in her small Sugar Hill apartment. Hattie, Valerio's mama, still kept her job ironing in the Chinese laundry—but nobody bothered about his mama.

Valerio was a nice enough boy, though, about sharing his income with her, about pawning a ring or something someone would give him to help her out on the rent or the insurance policies. And maybe, once or twice a week, mama might see her son coming in as she went out in the morning or leaving as she came in at night, for Valerio often slept all day. And she would mutter, "The Lord knows, cause I don't, what will become of you, boy! You're just like your father!"

Then, strangely enough, one day Valerio got a job. A good job, too—at least, it paid him well. A friend of his ran an after-hours night club on upper St. Nicholas Avenue. Gangsters owned the place, but they let a Negro run it. They had a red-hot jazz band, a high-yellow revue, and bootleg liquor. When the Cuban music began to hit Harlem, they hired Valerio to introduce the rhumba. That was something he was really cut out to do, the rhumba. That wasn't work. Not at all, *hombre*! But it was a job, and his mama was glad.

Attired in a yellow silk shirt, white satin trousers, and a bright red sash, Valerio danced nightly to the throbbing drums and seed-filled rattles of the tropics—accompanied by the orchestra's usual instruments of joy. Valerio danced with a little brown Cuban girl in a red dress, Concha, whose hair was a mat of darkness and whose hips were nobody's business.

Their dance became the talk of the town—at least, of that part of the town composed of night-lifers—for Valerio danced the rhumba as his father had taught him to dance it in Norfolk when he was ten years old, innocently—unexpurgated, happy, funny, but beautiful, too—like a gay, sweet longing for something that might be had, some time, maybe, some place or other.

Anyhow, business boomed. Ringside tables filled with people who came expressly to see Valerio dance.

"He's marvelous," gasped ladies who ate at the Ritz any time they wanted to.

"That boy can dance," said portly gentlemen with offices full of lawyers to keep track of their income tax. "He can dance!" And they wished they could, too.

"Hot stuff," said young rum-runners, smoking reefers and drinking gin—for these were prohibition days.

"A natural-born eastman," cried a tan-skin lady with a diamond wrist-watch. "He can have anything I got."

That was the trouble! Too many people felt that Valerio could have anything they had, so he lived on the fat of the land without making half an effort. He began to be invited to fashionable cocktail parties downtown. He often went out to dinner in the East 50's with white folks. But his mama still kept her job in the Chinese laundry.

Perhaps it was a good thing she did in view of what finally happened, for to Valerio the world was nothing but a swagger world tingling with lights, music, drinks, money, and people who had everything—or thought they had. Each night, at the club, the orchestra beat out its astounding songs, shook its rattles, fingered its drums. Valerio put on his satin trousers with the fiery red sash to dance with the little Cuban girl who always had a look of pleased surprise on her face, as though amazed to find dancing so good. Somehow she and Valerio made their rhumba, for all their hip-shaking, clean as a summer sun.

Offers began to come in from other night clubs and from small producers as well. "Wait for something big, kid," said the man who ran the cabaret. "Wait till the Winter Garden calls you."

Valerio waited. Meanwhile, a dark young rounder named Sonny, who wrote number bets for a living, had an idea for making money off of Valerio. They would open an apartment together where people could come after the night clubs closed—come and drink and dance—and love a little if they wanted to. The money would be made from the sale of drinks—charging very high prices to keep the riffraff out. With Valerio as host, a lot of good spenders would surely call. They could get rich.

"O.K. by me," said Valerio.

"I'll run the place," said Sonny, "and all you gotta do is just be there and dance a little, maybe—you know—and make people feel at home."

"O.K.," said Valerio.

"And we'll split the profit two ways—me and you."

"O.K."

So they got a big Seventh Avenue apartment, furnished it with deep, soft sofas and lots of little tables and a huge icebox and opened up. They paid off the police every week. They had good whisky. They sent out cards to a hundred downtown people who didn't care about money. They informed the best patrons of the cabaret where Valerio danced—the white folks who thrilled at becoming real Harlem initiates going home with Valerio.

From the opening night on, Valerio's flat filled with white people from midnight till the sun came up. Mostly a sporty crowd, young blades accompanied by ladies of the chorus, race-track gentlemen, white cabaret entertainers out for amusement after their own places closed, musical-comedy stars in search of new dance steps—and perhaps three or four brown-skin ladies-of-the-evening and a couple of chocolate gigolos, to add color.

There was a piano player. Valerio danced. There was impromptu entertaining by the guests. Often famous radio stars would get up and croon. Expensive night-club names might rise to do a number—or several numbers if they were tight enough. And sometimes it would be hard to stop them when they really got going.

Occasionally guests would get very drunk and stay all night, sleeping well into the day. Sometimes one might sleep with Valerio.

Shortly all Harlem began to talk about the big red roadster Valerio drove up and down Seventh Avenue. It was all nickel-plated—and a little blonde revue star known on two continents had given it to him, so folks said. Valerio was on his way to becoming a gigolo de luxe.

"That boy sure don't draw no color lines," Harlem commented. "No, sir!

"And why should he?" Harlem then asked itself rhetorically. "Colored folks ain't got no money—and money's what he's after, ain't it?"

But Harlem was wrong. Valerio seldom gave a thought to money—he was having too good a time. That's why it was well his mama kept her job in the Chinese laundry, for one day Sonny received a warning, "Close up that flat of yours, and close it damn quick!"

Gangsters!

"What the hell?" Sonny answered the racketeers. "We're payin' off, ain't we—you and the police, both? So what's wrong?"

"Close up, or we'll break you up," the warning came back. "We don't like the way you're running things, black boy. And tell Valerio to send that white chick's car back to her—and quick!"

"Aw, nuts!" said Sonny. "We're paying the police! You guys lay off."

But Sonny wasn't wise. He knew very well how little the police count when gangsters give orders, yet he kept right on. The profits had gone to his head. He didn't even tell Valerio they had been warned, for Sonny, who was trying to make enough money to start a number bank of his own, was afraid the boy might quit. Sonny should have known better.

One Sunday night about 3:30 A.M., the piano was going like mad. Fourteen couples packed the front room, dancing close and warm. There were at least a dozen folks whose names you'd know if you saw them in any paper, famous from Hollywood to Westport.

They were feeling good.

Sonny was busy at the door, and a brown bar-boy was collecting highball glasses, as Valerio came in from the club where he still worked. He went in the bedroom to change his dancing shoes, for it was snowing and his feet were cold.

> *O, rock me, pretty mama, till the cows come home . . .*

sang a sleek-haired Harlemite at the piano.

> *Rock me, rock me, baby, from night to morn . . .*

when, just then, a crash like the wreck of the Hesperus resounded through the hall and shook the whole house as five Italian gentlemen in evening clothes who looked exactly like gangsters walked in. They had broken down the door.

Without a word they began to smash up the place with long axes each of them carried. Women began to scream, men to shout, and the piano vibrated, not from jazz-playing fingers, but from axes breaking its hidden heart.

"Lemme out," the piano player yelled. "Lemme out!" But there was panic at the door.

"I can't leave without my wrap," a woman cried. "Where is my wrap? Sonny, my ermine coat!"

"Don't move," one of the gangsters said to Sonny.

A big white fist flattened his brown nose.

"I ought to kill you," said a second gangster. "You was warned. Take this!"

Sonny spit out two teeth.

Crash went the axes on furniture and bar. Splintered glass flew, wood cracked. Guests fled, hatless and coatless. About that time the police arrived.

Strangely enough, the police, instead of helping protect the place from the gangsters, began themselves to break, not only the furniture, but also the *heads* of every Negro in sight. They started with Sonny. They laid the barman and the waiter low. They grabbed Valerio as he emerged from the bedroom. They beat his face to a pulp. They whacked the piano player twice across the buttocks. They had a grand time with their night sticks. Then they arrested all the colored fellows (and no whites) as the gangsters took their axes and left. That was the end of Valerio's apartment.

In jail Valerio learned that the woman who gave him the red roadster was being kept by a gangster who controlled prohibition's whole champagne racket and owned dozens of rum-running boats.

"No wonder!" said Sonny, through his bandages. "He got them guys to break up our place! He probably told the police to beat hell out of us, too!"

"Wonder how he knew she gave me that car?" asked Valerio innocently.

"White folks know everything," said Sonny

"Aw, stop talking like a spook," said Valerio.

When he got out of jail, Valerio's face had a long night-stick scar across it that would never disappear. He still felt weak and sick and hungry. The gangsters had forbidden any of the night clubs to employ him again, so he went back home to mama.

"Umm-huh!" she told him. "Good thing I kept my job in that Chinee laundry. It's a good thing. . . . Sit down and eat, son. . . . What you gonna do now?"

"Start practicing dancing again. I got an offer to go to Brazil—a big club in Rio."

"Who's gonna pay your fare way down yonder to Brazil?"

"Concha," Valerio answered—the name of his Cuban rhumba partner whose hair was a mat of darkness. "Concha."

"A woman!" cried his mother. "I might a-knowed it! We're weak that way. My God, I don't know, boy! I don't know!"

"You don't know what?" asked Valerio, grinning.

"How women can help it," said his mama. "The Lord knows you're *just* like your father—and I took care o' him for ten years. I reckon it's that Spanish blood."

"*Que va!*" said Valerio.

1935

- Italy invades Ethiopia.
- An estimated 50,000 people die in an earthquake in Quetta, India.
- Persia is officially renamed Iran.
- Nuremburg Laws deprive Jews of their rights of citizenship in Germany.
- Senator Huey P. Long of Louisiana is assassinated.
- The Social Security Act is passed.
- The National Council of Negro Women is founded by Mary McLeod Bethune, who serves as its president.
- A race riot in Harlem results in over $2 million in property damage.
- The WPA's Federal Theater Project (FTP) and Federal Writers' Project (FWP) are both launched, programs designed in part to promote African American arts. Several FTP productions will be staged in Harlem's Lafayette Theatre while African American authors—Arna Bontemps, Chester Himes, Zora Neale Hurston, and Richard Wright, for example—will write under the FWP's auspices.
- *Porgy and Bess* opens on Broadway.

U.S. unemployment: 20.7%

Lynchings in the United States: 18 blacks, 2 whites

Deaths:
> Richard B. Harrison (14 Mar.)
> Alice Dunbar-Nelson (18 Sept.)

Spingarn Medal:
> Mary McLeod Bethune (educator, activist)

Books:
> Countee Cullen, *The Medea and Some Poems* (drama, poetry)
> Frank Marshall Davis, *Black Man's Verse* (poetry)

George Wylie Henderson, *Ollie Miss* (novel)
Zora Neale Hurston, *Mules and Men* (nonfiction)
James Weldon Johnson, *Saint Peter Relates an Incident: Selected Poems* (poetry)
Willis Richardson and May Miller (eds.), *Negro History in Thirteen Plays* (anthology)

Periodicals:
Negro Needs Education (1935–36)
Metropolitan (Jan. 1935)

42 JOHN ARCHER'S NOSE
Rudolph Fisher

FROM *METROPOLITAN*, JANUARY 1935

Whenever Detective Sergeant Perry Dart felt especially weary of the foibles and follies of his Harlem, he knew where to find stimulation: he could always count on his friend, Dr. John Archer. Spiritually the two bachelors were as opposite as the two halves of a circle—and as complementary. The detective had only to seek out the physician at the latter's office-apartment, flop into a chair, and make an observation. His tall, lean comrade in crime, sober of face but twinkling of eye, would produce a bottle, fill glasses, hold a match first to Dart's cigar then to his own, and murmur a word of disagreement. Promptly an argument would be on.

Tonight however the formula had failed to work. It was shortly after midnight, an excellent hour for profound argumentation, and the sounds from the avenue outside, still alive with the gay crowds that a warm spring night invariably calls forth, hardly penetrated into the consulting-room where they sat. But Dart's provocative remark had evoked no disagreement.

"Your folks," Dart had said, "are the most superstitious idiots on the face of the earth."

The characteristic response would have been:

"Perry, you'll have to cut out drinking. It's curdling your milk of human kindness." Or, "*My* folks?—Really!" Or, "Avoid unscientific generalizations, my dear Sherlock. They are ninety-one and six-thirteenths percent wrong by actual measurement."

But tonight the physician simply looked at him and said nothing. Dart prodded further:

"They can be as dark as me or as light as you, but their ignorance is the same damned color wherever you find it—black."

That should have brought some demurring comment on the leprechauns of the Irish, the totems of the Indians, or the prayer-wheels of the Tibetans. Still the doctor said nothing.

"So you won't talk, hey?"

Whereupon John Archer said quietly:

"I believe you're right."

Dart's leg came off its perch across his chair-arm. He set down his glass untasted on the doctor's desk, leaned forward, staring.

"Heresy!" he cried, incredulous. "Heresy, b'gosh!—I'll have you read out of church. What the hell? Don't you know you aren't supposed to agree with me?"

"Spare me, your grace." The twinkle which kindled for an instant in Dr. Archer's eyes flickered quickly out. "I've had a cogent example today of what you complain of."

"Superstition?"

"Of a very dark hue."

"State the case. Let's see if you can exonerate yourself."

"I lost a kid."

Dart reached for his glass. "Didn't know you had one."

"A patient, you jackass."

Dart grinned. "Didn't know you had a patient, either."

"That's not funny. Neither was this. Beautiful, plump little brown rascal— eighteen months old—perfectly developed, bright-eyed, alert—and it passes out in a convulsion, and I was standing there looking on—helpless."

"If it was so perfect, what killed it?"

"Superstition."

"Humph. Anything for an alibi, hey?"

"Superstition," repeated Archer in a tone which stilled his friend's banter. "That baby ought to be alive and well, now."

"What's the gag line?"

"Status lymphaticus."

"Hell. And I was just getting serious."

"That's as serious as anything could be. The kid had a retained thymus."

"I'll bite. What's a retained thymus?"

"A big gland here in the chest. Usually disappears after birth. Sometimes doesn't. Untreated, it produces this status lymphaticus—convulsions—death."

"Why didn't you treat it?"

"I did what I could. Been seeing it for some time. Could have cleared it up over night. What I couldn't treat was the superstition of the parents."

"Oh."

"Specially the father. The kid should have had X-ray treatments. Melt the thing away. These kids, literally choking to death in a fit, clear up and recover— zip—like that. Most spectacular thing in medicine. But the old man wouldn't hear of it. None of this new-fangled stuff for *his* only child."

"I see."

"You can't see. I haven't told you yet. I noticed today, for the first time, a small, evil-smelling packet on a string around the baby's neck. In spite of the shock immediately following death, my curiosity got the better of me. I suppose there was also a natural impulse to—well—change the subject, sort of. I asked what it was."

"You would."

"The father didn't answer. He'd gone cataleptic. He simply stood there, looking. It seemed to me he was looking rather at the packet than at the child, and if ever there was the light of madness in a man's eyes, it was in his. The mother, grief-stricken though she was, managed to pull herself together long enough to answer."

"What was it?"

"Fried hair."

"What?"

"Fried hair.—No—not just kinky hair, straightened with hot irons and grease, as the term usually implies. That packet—I examined it—contained a wad of human hair, fried, if you please, in snake oil."

Dart expelled a large volume of disgusted smoke. "The fools."

"A charm. The father had got it that morning from some conjure-woman. Guaranteed to cure the baby's fits."

"He'd try that in preference to X-rays."

"And his name," the doctor concluded with a reflective smile, "was Bright—Solomon Bright."

After a moment of silence, Dart said:

"Well—your sins are forgiven. No wonder you agreed with me."

"Did I?" Having unburdened his story, John Archer's habit of heckling, aided by a normal desire to dismiss an unpleasant memory, began now to assert itself. The twinkle returned to his eyes. "I am of course in error. A single graphic example, while impressive, does not warrant a general conclusion. Such reasoning, as pointed out by no less an authority than the great Bacon—"

"I prefer ham," cut in Dart as the phone rang. His friend, murmuring something to the effect that "like begets like," reached for the instrument.

"Hello . . . Yes . . . Yes. I can come at once. Where? 15 West 134th Street, Apartment 51 . . . Yes—right away."

Deliberately he replaced the receiver. "I'm going to post a reward," he said wearily, "for the first person who calls a doctor and says, 'Doctor, take your time.' Right away—right away—"

He rose, put away the bottle, reached for hat and bag.

"Want to come along?"

"You're not really going right away?"

"In spite of my better judgement. That girl was scared."

"O.K. All I've got to do before morning is sleep."

"Don't count on it. Got your gun?"

"Gun? Of course. But what for?"

"Just a hunch. Come on."

"Hunch?" Dart jumped up to follow. "Say—what is this? A shooting?"

"Not yet." They reached the street.

"So what?"

"Girl said her brother's been stabbed."

"Yea?—here—let's use my car!"

"Righto. But lay off that siren. It gives me the itch."

"Well, scratch," Dart said as his phaeton leaped forward. "You've got finger-nails, haven't you?" And with deliberate perversity he made the siren howl.

In three minutes they reached their destination and were panting up endless stairs.

"It's a cowardly trick, that siren," breathed the doctor.

"Why?"

"Just a stunt to scare all the bad men away from the scene of the crime."

"Well, it wouldn't work up here. This high up, they couldn't hear a thing in the street."

"You're getting old. It's only five flights."

Dart's retort was cut off by the appearance of a girl's form at the head of the stairway.

"Dr. Archer?" Her voice was trembling. "This way.—Please—hurry—"

They followed her into the hallway of an apartment. They caught a glimpse of a man and woman as they passed the front living-room. The girl stopped and directed them with wide, frightened eyes into a bed-chamber off the hall. They stepped past her into the chamber, Dart pausing automatically to look about before following the physician in.

An old lady sat motionless beside the bed, her distorted face a spasm of grief. She looked up at the doctor, a pitifully frantic appeal in her eyes, then looked back toward the bed without speaking.

Dr. Archer dropped his bag and bent over the patient, a lean-faced boy of perhaps twenty. He lay on his left side facing the wall, his knees slightly drawn up in a sleeping posture. But his eyes were open and fixed. The doctor grasped his thin shoulders and pulled him gently a little way, to reveal a wide stain of blood on the bedclothing below; pulled him a little farther over, bent in a moment's inspection, then summoned Dart with a movement of his head. To-gether they observed the black-pearl handle of a knife, protruding from the chest. The boy had been stabbed through his pajama coat, and the blade was unquestionably in his heart.

Dr. Archer released the shoulder. The body rolled softly back to its original posture. The physician stood erect.

"Are you his mother?" he asked the old lady.

Dumbly, she nodded.

"You saw the knife, of course?"

"I seen it," she said in almost a whisper, and with an effort added, "I—I didn't pull it out for fear of startin' him bleedin' ag'in."

"He won't bleed any more," Dr. Archer said gently. "He hasn't bled for an hour—maybe two."

The girl behind them gasped sharply. "You mean he's been—dead—that long?"

"At least. The blood stain beneath him is dry."

A sob escaped the old lady. "Sonny—"

"Oh Ma—!" The girl moved to the old lady's side, encircled her with compassionate arms.

"I knowed it," the old lady whispered. "I knowed it—the minute I seen him, I knowed—"

Dr. Archer terminated a long silence by addressing the girl. "It was you who called me?"

She nodded.

"When you said your brother had been stabbed, I knew the case would have to be reported to the police. Detective Sergeant Dart was with me at the time. I thought it might save embarrassment if he came along."

The girl looked at Dart and after a moment nodded again.

"I understand.—But we—we don't know who did it."

A quick glance passed between the two men.

"Then it's lucky I came," Dart said. "Perhaps I can help you."

"Yes.—Yes, perhaps you can."

"Whose knife is that?"

"His own."

"His own?—Where did you last see it?"

"On the bureau by the head of the bed."

"When?"

"This afternoon, when I was cleaning up."

"Tell me how you found him."

"Just like that. I'd been out. I came in and along the hall on the way to my room, I noticed his door was closed. He hasn't been coming in till much later recently. I stopped to speak to him—he hadn't been well.—I opened the door and spoke. He didn't answer. I pushed on the light. He looked funny. I went over to him and saw the blood—"

"Shall we go into another room?"

"Yes, please.—Come, Ma—"

Stiffly, with the girl's assistance, the mother got to her feet and permitted herself to be guided toward the door. There she paused, turned, and looked back at the still figure lying on the bed. Her eyes were dry, but the depth of her shocked grief was unmistakable. Then, almost inaudibly, she said a curious thing:

"God forgive me."

And slowly she turned again and stumbled forward.

Again Dart and Archer exchanged glances. The former's brows lifted. The latter shook his head thoughtfully as he picked up his bag. As the girl and her mother went out, he stood erect and sniffed. He went over to the room's one window, which was open, near the foot of the bed. Dart followed. Together they looked out into the darkness of an airshaft. Above, one more story and the edge of the roof. Below, an occasional lighted window and a blend of diverse sounds welling up: a baby wailing, someone coughing spasmodically, a radio rasping labored jazz, a woman's laugh, quickly stifled.

"God forgive her what?" said Dart.

The doctor sniffed again. "It didn't come from out there."

"What didn't?"

"What I smelt."

"All I smell is a rat."

"This is far more subtle."

"Smell up the answer to my question."

The physician sniffed again, said nothing, turned and started out. He and Dart overtook the others in the hallway. A moment later, they were all in the living-room.

The man and woman, whom they had seen in passing, waited there, looking toward them expectantly. The woman, clad in gold-figured black silk Chinese pajamas, was well under thirty, slender, with yellow skin which retained a decided make-up even at this hour. Her boyish bob was reddish with frequent "frying," and her eyes were cold and hard. The man, in shirt-sleeves and slippers, was approximately the same age, of medium build and that complexion known as "riny"—light, sallow skin and sand-colored kinky hair. His eyes were green.

The girl got the old lady into a chair before speaking. Then, in a dull, absent sort of way, she said:

"This is the doctor. He's already turned the case over to this gentleman that came with him."

"And who," the woman inquired, "is the gentleman that came with him?"

"A policeman—a detective."

"Hmph!" commented the woman.

"Fast work," added the man unpleasantly.

"Thank you," returned Dart, eyeing him coolly. "May I know to whom I owe the compliment?"

The man matched his stare before answering.

"I am Ben Dewey. This is my wife. Petal there is my sister. Sonny was my brother." There was unnecessary insolence in the enumeration.

"'Was' your brother?"

"Yes, was." Mr. Dewey was evidently not hard to incense. He bristled.

"Then you are already aware of his—misfortune?"

"Of course."

"In fact, you were aware of it before Dr. Archer arrived."

"What do you mean?"

"I mean that no one has stated your brother's condition since we came into this room. You were not in the bedroom when Dr. Archer did state it. Yet you know it."

Ben Dewey glared. "Certainly I know it."

"How?"

The elder brother's wife interrupted. "This is hardly the time, Mr. Detective, for a lot of questions."

Dart looked at her. "I see," he said quietly. "I have been in error. Miss Petal said, in the other room just now, 'We don't know who did it.' Naturally I assumed that her 'we' included all the members of the family. I see now that she meant only herself and her mother. So, Mrs. Dewey, if you or your husband will be kind enough to name the guilty party, we can easily avoid a 'lot of questions.'"

"That ain't what I meant!" flared the wife. "We don't know who did it either."

"Oh. And you are not anxious to find out—as quickly as possible?"

Dr. Archer mediated. "Sergeant Dart naturally felt that in performing his duty he would also be serving you all. He regrets, of course, the intrusion upon your—er—moment of sorrow."

"A sorrow which all of you do not seem to share alike," appended Dart, who believed in making people so angry that they would blurt out the truth. "May I use your phone?"

He went to the instrument, resting on a table near the hall door, called the precinct station, reported the case, asked for a medical examiner, and declined assistants.

"I'm sure the family would prefer to have me act alone for the time being."

Only Dr. Archer realized what these words meant: that within five minutes half a dozen men would be just outside the door of the apartment, ready to break in at the sergeant's first signal.

But Dart turned and smiled at the brother and his wife. "Am I right in assuming that?" he asked courteously.

"Yes—of course," Ben said, somewhat subdued.

Swiftly the courteous smile vanished. The detective's voice was incisive and hard. "Then perhaps you will tell me how you knew so well that your brother was dead."

"Why—I saw him. I saw the knife in—"

"When?"

"When Petal screamed. Letty and I had gone to bed. And when Petal screamed, naturally we jumped up and rushed into Sonny's room, where she was. She was standing there looking at him. I went over to him and looked. I guess I shook him. Anybody could see—"

"What time was that?"

"Just a few minutes ago. Just before the doctor was called. I told her to call him."

"About ten minutes ago, then?"

"Yes."

"How many times did your sister scream?"

"Only once."

"You're sure?"

"Yes."

"You had retired. You heard one scream. You jumped up and went straight to it."

"Why not?"

"Extraordinary sense of direction, that's all.—Whose knife is that?"

"Sonny's."

"How do you know?"

"I've seen him with it. Couldn't miss that black pearl handle."

"Who else was in the house at the time?"

"No one but Ma. She was already in the room when we got there. She's got an extraordinary sense of direction, too."

"Any one else here during the evening?"

"No—not that I know of. My wife and I have been in practically all evening."

"Practically?"

"I mean she was in all evening. I went out for a few minutes—down to the corner for a pack of cigarettes."

"What time?"

"About ten o'clock."

"And you've heard nothing—no suspicious sounds of any kind?"

"No. At least *I* didn't. Did you, Letty?"

"All I heard was Sonny himself coming in."

"What time was that?"

"'Bout nine o'clock. He went in his room and stayed there."

"Just what was everyone doing at that time?"

"The rest of us were in the back of the flat—except Petal. She'd gone out. Ben and I were in the kitchen. I was washing the dishes, he was sitting at the table, smoking. We'd just finished eating supper."

"Your usual supper hour?"

"Ben doesn't get home from the Post Office till late."

"Where was Mother Dewey?"

"In the dining-room, reading the paper."

"Anyone else here now?"

"Not that I know of."

"Do you mind if we look?"

"If I minded, would that stop you?"

Dart indulged in an appraising pause, then said:

"It might. I should hate to embarrass you."

"Embarrass me!—Go ahead—I've nothing to hide."

"That's good. Doc, if you can spare the time, will you take a look around with me?"

Dr. Archer nodded with his tongue in his cheek. Dart knew very well that a cash-in-advance major operation could not have dragged the physician away.

"Before we do, though," the detective said, "let me say this: Here are four of you, all closely related to the victim, all surely more or less familiar with his habits and associates. Yet not one of you offers so much as a suggestion as to who might have done this."

"You haven't given us time," remarked Letty Dewey.

Dart looked at his watch. "I've given you five minutes."

"Who's been doing all the talking?"

"All right. Take your turn now. Who do *you* think did it?"

"I haven't the remotest idea."

"M-m—so you said before—while I was doing all the talking." He smiled. "Strange that none of you should have the remotest idea. The shock, no doubt. I should rather expect a flood of accusations. Unless, of course, there is some very good reason to the contrary."

"What do you mean?"

"I mean"—the detective was pleasantly casual—"unless you are protecting each other. In which case, if I may remind you, you become accessory.—Come on, Doc. No doubt the family would like a little private conference."

During the next few minutes the two went through the apartment. Alert against surprise, they missed no potential hiding-place, satisfying themselves that nobody had modestly secreted himself in some out-of-the-way corner. The place possessed no apparent entrance or exit other than its one outside door, and there was nothing unusual about its arrangement of rooms—several bedchambers off a central hallway, with the living-room at the front end and a kitchen and dining-room at the back.

Characteristically, the doctor indulged in wordy and somewhat irrelevant reflection during the tour of inspection. Exchanges of comment punctuated their progress.

"Back here," Dr. Archer said, "I don't get it. But up there where they are, I do. And in the boy's room, *I* did.

"Get what—that smell?"

"M-m. Peculiar—very. Curious thing, odors. Discernible in higher dilution than any other material stimulus. Ridiculous that we don't make greater use of them."

"I never noticed any particular restriction of 'em in Harlem."

On the dining-room table a Harlem newspaper was spread out. Dart glanced at the page, which was bordered with advertisements.

"Here it is again," he said, pointing. "'Do you want success in love, business, a profession?' These 'ads' are all that keep this sheet going. Your folks' superstition—"

Dr. Archer's eyes traveled down the column but he seemed to ignore the interruption.

"Odors *should* be restricted," he pursued. "They should be captured, classified, and numbered like the lines of the spectrum. We let them run wild—"

"Check."

"And sacrifice a wealth of information. In a language of a quarter of a million words, we haven't a single specific direct denotation of a smell."

"Oh, no?"

"No. Whatever you're thinking of, it is an indirect and non-specific denotation, liking the odor in mind to something else. We are content with 'fragrant' and 'foul' or general terms of that character, or at best 'alcoholic' or 'moldy,' which are obviously indirect. We haven't even such general direct terms as apply to colors—red, green, and blue. We name what we see but don't name what we smell."

"Which is just as well."

"On the contrary. If we could designate each smell by number—"

"We'd know right off who killed Sonny."

"Perhaps. I daresay every crime has its peculiar odor."

"Old stuff. They used bloodhounds in *Uncle Tom's Cabin*."

"We could use one here."

"Do tell?"

"This crime has a specific smell—"

"It stinks all right."

"—which I think we should find significant if we could place it."

"Rave on, Aristotle."

"Two smells, in fact. First, alcohol."

"We brought that with us."

"No. Another vintage I'm sure. Didn't you get it in the boy's bedroom?"

"Not especially."

"It's meaning was clear enough. The boy was stabbed while sleeping under the effect of alcohol."

"How'd you sneak up on that answer?"

"There was no sign of struggle. He'd simply drawn up his knees a little and died."

"Don't tell me you smelt alcohol on a dead man's breath."

"No. What I smelt was the alcoholic breath he'd expelled into that room before he died. Enough to leave a discernible—er—fragrance for over an hour afterward."

"Hm—Stabbed in his sleep."

"But that simply accounts for the lack of struggle and the tranquil posture of the corpse. It does indicate, of course, that for a boy of twenty Sonny was developing bad habits—a fact corroborated by his sister's remark about late hours. But that's all. This other odor which I get from time to time I consider far more important. It might even lead to the identity of the killer—if we could trace it."

"Then keep sniffing, Fido. Y' know, I had a dog like you once. Only he didn't do a lot of talking about what he smelt."

"Too bad he couldn't talk, Sergeant. *You* could have learned a great deal from him."

As they approached the front door the bell rang. Dart stepped to the door and opened it. A large pink-faced man carrying a doctor's bag stood puffing on the threshold. He blinked through his glasses and grinned.

"Dr. Finkelbaum!" exclaimed the detective. "Some service! Come in. You know Dr. Archer." He looked quickly out into the corridor, noted his men, grinned, signaled silence, stepped back.

"Sure. Hello, doctor," greeted the newcomer. "Whew! Thank your stars you're not a medical examiner."

"You must have been uptown already," said Dr. Archer.

"Yea. Little love affair over on Lenox Avenue. I always phone in before leaving the neighborhood—they don't do things by halves up here. Where's the stiff?"

"In the second room," said Dart. "Come on, I'll show you."

"At least," murmured Dr. Archer, "it was in there a moment ago."

Despite his skepticism, which derived from sudden mysterious disappearances of corpses on two previous occasions in his experience, they found the contents of Sonny's bedchamber unchanged.

"Who did this?" inquired the medical examiner.

"At present," Dart said, "there are four denials—his mother, his sister, his brother, and his brother's wife."

"All in the family, eh?"

"I haven't finished talking to them yet. You and Dr. Archer carry on here. I'll go back and try some more browbeating."

"Righto."

Now Dart returned to the living-room. The four people seemed not to have moved. The brother stood in the middle of the floor, meditating. The wife sat in a chair, bristling. The girl was on the arm of another chair in which her eld-erly mother still slumped, staring forward with eyes that saw nothing—or per-haps everything.

The detective looked about. "Finished your conference?"

"Conference about what?" said Ben.

"The national debt. What's happened since I left here?"

"Nothing."

"No conversation at all?"

"No."

"Then who used this telephone?"

"Why—nobody."

"No? I suppose it moved itself? I left it like this, with the mouthpiece facing the door. Now the mouthpiece faces the center of the room. One of the miracles of modern science or what?"

Nobody spoke.

"Now listen." There was a menacing placidity in the detective's voice. "This conspiracy of silence stuff may make it hard for me, but it's going to make it a lot harder for you. You people are going to talk. Personally, I don't care whether you talk here or around at the precinct. But whatever you're holding out for, it's no use. The circumstances warrant arresting all of you, right now."

"We've answered your questions," said Letty angrily. "Do you want us to lie and say one of *us* did it—just to make your job easier?"

"Lawd—Lawd!" whispered the old lady and Petal's arm went about her again, vainly comforting.

"Who else lives here?" Dart asked suddenly.

As if sparing them the necessity of answering, the outside door clicked and opened. Dart turned to see a young man enter the hallway. The young man looked toward them, his pale face a picture of bewilderment, closed the door behind him, mechanically put his key back into his pocket, and came into the living-room.

"What's up," he asked. "What do those guys want outside?"

"Guys outside?" Ben looked at Dart. "So the joint's pinched?"

"Not yet," returned Dart. "It's up to you people." He addressed the newcomer. "Who are you?"

"Me? I'm Red Brown. I live here."

"Really? Odd nobody's mentioned you."

"He hasn't been here all day," said Letty.

"What's happened?" insisted Red Brown. "Who is this guy?"

"He's a policeman," Petal answered. "Somebody stabbed—Sonny."

"Stabbed Sonny—!" Dart saw the boy's wide eyes turn swiftly from Petal and fix themselves on Ben.

"A flesh wound," the detective said quickly.

"Oh," said Red, still staring with a touch of horror at Ben. His look could not have been clearer had he accused the elder brother in words.

"You and Sonny are good friends?" pursued Dart.

"Yea—buddies. We room together."

"It might make it easier for Ben if you told me why he stabbed his brother."

Red's look, still fixed, darkened.

"Why should I make it easier for him?"

There was silence, sudden and tense. Ben drew a deep, sharp breath, amazement changing to rage.

"Why—you stinking little pup!"

He charged forward. Letty yelled, "Ben!" Red, obvious child of the city, ducked low and sidewise, thrusting out one leg, over which his assailant tripped and crashed to the floor. Dart stepped forward and grabbed Ben as he struggled up. There was no breaking the detective's hold.

"Easy. What do you want to do—prove he's right?"

"Let me go and I'll prove plenty! I'll make him—"

"It's a lie!" breathed Letty. "Ben didn't kill him."

Unexpectedly Dart released Ben.

"All right," said he. "Get to proving. But don't let me have to bean you."

The impulse to assault was spent. Ben pulled himself together.

"What's the idea?" he glowered at Red. "I even call up the poolroom where you work, trying to keep you out of this. And you walk in and try to make me out a murderer."

"Murderer?" Red looked about, engaged Dart. "You—you said—flesh wound."

"Yes," the detective returned drily. "The flesh of his heart."

"Gee! Gee, Ben. I didn't know you'd killed him."

"I didn't kill him! Why do you keep saying so?"

Red looked from Ben to Letty, encountering a glare of the most intense hatred Dart had ever seen. The woman would obviously have tried to claw his eyes out had not circumstance restrained her.

"Go on," she said through her teeth. "Tell your tale."

Her menace held the boy silent for an uncertain moment. It was outweighed by the cooler threat of Dart's next words:

"Not scared to talk, are you, Red?"

"Scared? No, I ain't scared. But murder—gee!"

"You and Sonny were buddies, weren't you?"

"Yea—that's right."

"Slept in the same bed."

"Yea."

"Supposing it had been you in that bed instead of Sonny?"

"Yea—it might 'a been."

"Sonny wouldn't have let you down, would he?"

"He never did."

"All right. Speak up. What do you know?"

"I know—I mean—maybe—maybe Ben figured there was somethin' goin' on between Sonny and—." He did not look at Letty now.

"Was there?"

"Wouldn't matter whether there was or not—if Ben thought so."

"True enough. Well, Mr. Dewey, what about that?"

Ben Dewey did not answer—seemed not to have heard the detective's last word. His mouth hung open as he stared dumbfounded at his wife.

His wife, however, still transfixed Red with gleaming eyes.

"It should have been you instead of Sonny," she said evenly. "You rat."

Abruptly Dart remembered the presence of the old lady and the girl. He turned toward them, somewhat contrite for not having spared them the shock of this last disclosure, but got a shock of his own which silenced his intended apology: The girl's face held precisely the expression of stunned unbelief that he had expected to find. But the old lady sat huddled in the same posture that she had held throughout the questioning. Her steadfast gaze was still far away, and apparently she had not heard or seen a single item of what had just transpired in the room.

Dart stepped into the hall to meet Dr. Archer and the medical examiner as they returned from the death room.

"I'm through," said Dr. Finkelbaum. "Immediate autopsy on this. Here's the knife. He handed Dart the instrument, wrapped in a dressing. "I don't believe—"

Dart interrupted him with a quick gesture, then said loudly enough to be heard by those in the living-room:

"You don't believe it could have been suicide, do you, doctor?"

"Suicide? I should say not." The medical examiner caught Dart's cue and matched his tone. "He wasn't left-handed, was he?"

Dart turned back, asking through the living-room doorway, "Was your brother left-handed, Mr. Dewey?"

Ben had not taken his eyes off Letty.

"Seems like he was," he said in a low voice, which included his wife in his indictment.

"Is that true, Miss Petal?"

"No, sir. He was right-handed."

"Then it wasn't suicide," said the medical examiner. "The site of the wound and the angle of the thrust rule out a right hand. The depth of it makes even a left hand unlikely."

"Thanks, doctor. We can forget the fact that it was his own knife."

"Absolutely."

"And," Dart winked as he added, "we can expect to find the killer's fingerprints on this black pearl handle, don't you think?"

"Oh, unquestionably," replied Dr. Finkelbaum. "That handle will name the guilty party even if he wore a glove. The new method, you know."

"So I thought," said Dart. "Well, on your way?"

"Yep. I'll get him downtown and let you have a report first thing in the morning. See you later, gentlemen."

"I'm afraid you will," murmured Dr. Archer.

Dr. Finkelbaum departed. Dr. Archer and the detective conferred a brief moment in inaudible tones, then entered the living-room.

"Mr. Dewey," said Dart, "do you deny having committed this crime in the face of the circumstances?"

"What circumstances?"

"The existence of ample motive, as testified by Red Brown, here, and of ample opportunity, as testified by your wife."

"What do you mean, opportunity?"

"She corroborated your statement that at about ten o'clock you went out for a few minutes on the pretext of getting a pack of cigarettes."

"I did go out and I got the cigarettes."

"The time when you say you went out happens to correspond with the time when the doctors say the crime was committed."

"And if I was out, how could I have done it?"

"You couldn't. But suppose you weren't out? Suppose you went down the hall, opened and shut the front door, crept back silently into Sonny's room—only a few steps—did what you had to do, and, after the proper lapse of time, crept back to the front door, opened and shut it again, and walked back up the hall as if you had been out the whole time? Your wife says that you went out. But she can not swear that you actually left the apartment."

"Of course I can!" said Letty sharply.

"Yes? Then, Mrs. Dewey, you must have been in the hallway the whole time Mr. Dewey was out. You can not see the length of that hallway from any room in this house. The only way you can swear there was nobody in it throughout that time is to swear that you were in it throughout that time. Could you swear that?"

Letty hesitated only a moment before answering hotly, "Yes!"

"Careful, Mrs. Dewey. Why should you stand idle for ten minutes alone in an empty hallway?"

"I—I was measuring it for wallpaper."

"Strange. I noted that it had recently been re-papered."

"I didn't like the new paper. I was planning to have it changed."

"I see. Then you insist that you were in that hallway all that time?"

"Yes."

"And that Mr. Dewey was not?"

"Yes."

"And that no one else was?"

"No one."

"Madam, you have accused yourself."

"Wh—what?"

"You have just accused yourself of killing your brother-in-law."

"What are you talking about?"

"I'll make it plainer. The only doorway to Sonny's room is on the hall. Assuming that the doctors are right about the time of death, and assuming that the killer used the only door, which is on the hallway you so carefully kept under observation, no one but yourself was within striking distance at the time Sonny was stabbed. You follow my reasoning?"

"Why—"

"Therefore by your own statement—which you are willing to swear to—you must have killed him yourself."

"I never said any such thing!"

"You wish to retract your statement?"

"I—I—"

"And admit that your husband may have been in the hallway?"

Completely confused and dismayed, the woman burst into tears.

But disloyal or not, this was Ben Dewey's wife; he came to her rescue:

"Wait a minute, officer. At least you had a reason for accusing me. What would she want to do that for?"

"I'd rather not guess, Mr. Dewey. But it shouldn't be hard."

Only Letty's sobs broke the next moment's silence. Finally Ben said in a dull, low voice:

"She didn't do it."

"Did you?" asked Dart quickly.

"No. I didn't either. It's—it's all cockeyed."

The man's change of attitude from arrogance to humility was more touching than the woman's tears.

"Are we under arrest?"

Dart's answer was surprising. "No."

"No?"

"No. You are free to go about as usual. You will all hold yourselves ready for questioning at any time, of course. But I shall not make an arrest until this knife is examined."

Letty stopped sobbing to follow the general trend of eyes toward the gauze-wrapped knife in Dart's hand.

"Here is the answer," said the detective, looking about and raising the object. "Of course—a confession would save us a bit of time and trouble."

Nobody uttered a word.

"Well—in the morning we'll know. Dr. Archer, put this in your bag, please. And do you mind keeping it for me until morning? I've got a bit of checking up to do meanwhile."

"Not at all." The doctor took the knife, placed it carefully in a side pocket of his bag. "It'll be safe there till you come for it."

"Of course. Thanks a lot. We'll be going now."

The two started out. Dart halted as his companion went on toward the outside door.

"I might say before going, Mr. Dewey," he remarked, "that anything that happens to Red Brown here will make things look even worse for you and your wife. Both of you threatened him, if I remember."

"I can take care of myself," said Red Brown coolly.

"I'm glad to know that," returned Dart. "And—oh yes. I'd like to see you all here in the morning at nine. That's all. Good night."

"From your instructions to your men," observed Dr. Archer, as he and the detective rode back toward his office, "I gather the purpose of not making an arrest."

"It's the only way," Dart said. "Let 'em go and keep an eye on 'em. Their actions will always tell more than their words. I hadn't got anywhere until Red Brown looked at brother Ben. Yet he didn't say a word."

"And," Dr. Archer continued, "I gather also that Exhibit A, which rests enshrouded in my bag, is to be a decoy."

"Sure. That was all stuff—about prints and the new method. Probably not a thing on that knife but they don't know that. Somebody's going to try and get that lethal weapon back."

"But"—the doctor's words disregarded the detective's interruptions—"what I fail to gather is the reason for dragging in me and my bag."

"You dragged me in, didn't you?"

"I see. One good murder deserves another."

"No. Look. The thing had to be planted where the guilty person figured it could be recovered. They wouldn't attempt to get it away from me. But you're different."

"Different from you?"

"Exactly."

"It's a relief to know that."

"You're no happier over it than I am."

"You'll be nearby, I trust?"

"Under your bed, if you like."

"No. The girl might come for it."

"That's just why I'll be nearby. Leave you alone and she'll get it."

"Shouldn't be at all surprised. Lovely little thing."

"But not too little."

"Nor too lovely."

"Aren't you ashamed of yourself?"

"Not at all. You see—"

"Yea, I see. Never mind the long explanation. Adam saw, too."

"Ah, but what did Adam see? An apple. Only an apple."

"Well, if it's the girl—which it won't be—she'd better bring an apple along—to keep the doctor away."

"Sergeant, how you admire me. What makes you think it won't be the girl?"

"You don't think she killed her brother, do you?"

"I hope not. But I wouldn't—er—express an opinion in cash."

"Couldn't you just say you wouldn't bet on it?"

"Never use a word of one syllable, sergeant, when you can find one of six."

"Why wouldn't you bet on it? She's just a kid. A rather nice kid."

"How did you find out?"

Dart ignored him. "She screamed. She telephoned for you."

"Nice girls of nineteen have been known to do such things."

"Kill their sweethearts, maybe—their ex-sweethearts. Not their brothers."

"True. Usually it is the brother who kills his sister's sweetheart, isn't it? Whereupon the sweetheart is known as a betrayer."

"Yea. Family honor. Course I've never seen it, but—"

"Cynic. Here we are."

But Dart drove on past the doctor's apartment.

"Whither, pray?"

"Get smart. They may recognize the detective's license-plates. Around the corner'll be better."

"And me with no roller-skates."

Shortly they returned to the apartment on foot, and soon were engaged in smooth hypotheses, well oiled.

"One of these things is going to fool us yet," meditated the physician between sips.

"They all fool us."

"Modesty ill becomes you, Perry. I mean the party who obviously did the thing from the outset sometimes does it."

"That party is always obvious from the outset—when it's all over. What I'd like to see is a case in which the party who is obvious from the outset is obvious *at* the outset."

"The trouble is with the obviousness—the kind of obviousness. One person is obviously guilty because everything points to him. Another is obviously guilty because nothing points to him. In the present case, Ben is the one example, Red the other."

"You're drinking. How can a man be guilty because nothing points to him?"

"Because, of course, too perfect an alibi is no alibi, just as too perfect a case is no case. Perfection doesn't exist. Hence the perfect thing is false."

"This is false whiskey."

"May it continue to deceive us. Consider this: Can you imagine a lad like Red Brown living in a house with a girl like Petal not being—er—affected?"

"I was thinking of the brother-sweetheart complex you suggested."

"With the brother getting the worst of it? But Letty said Red had been out all day. How could Red—?"

"Just as you said Ben could. Only he didn't slam the front door."

"Of course Letty was lying about being in the hall all that time. Maybe Red could have sneaked in and out, at that. But that's taking it pretty far. Nothing that we know indicates Red."

"Nothing except that he's altogether too un-indicated."

"Well, if you really want to get fancy, listen to this."

"Go ahead."

"Red knows that Letty is two-timing."

"Yes."

"Ben doesn't."

"No."

"If Ben finds it out, it's her hips."

"Yes."

"She's rather partial to her hips."

"Naturally."

"A blab from either Sonny or Red—and bye-bye."

"Hips."

"So, tired of Sonny and afraid of Red, she decides on what is known as murder for elimination."

"Murder of Sonny?"

"No. Of Red. With Sonny implicated by his knife."

"Go on. How'd she get Sonny and Red mixed?"

"She heard Sonny come in—'way down the hall where she couldn't see. But Sonny, having developed bad habits, never comes in so early. She believes this is Red. When Ben steps out, she slips into the dark room and hurriedly acts in self-defense."

"Hip-defense."

"M-m. Only it happens to be Sonny.

"Well, what about it?"

"Utterly fantastic. Yet not utterly impossible."

"O.K. Your turn."

"You leave me the most fantastic possibility of all."

"The old lady?"

"No. The mother." The doctor paused a moment, then said, "There's quite a difference. Can you imagine anything that would make a mother kill her son?"

"That smell you mentioned, maybe."

"No. Seriously."

"I don't know. It's pretty hard to believe. But it could happen, I suppose. By mistake, for instance. Suppose the old lady thought it was Red—just as Letty might have. Red—leading her child down the road to hell. . . . That would explain why she said, 'God forgive me!'"

"Let's forget your 'mistake' for a while."

"Well then, look. When I was walking a beat, a woman came to me once and begged me to put her son in jail. He was a dope. She said when she saw him like that, she wanted to kill him."

"But did she?"

"No. But why can't mother-love turn to hate like any other love?"

"I guess the fact that it doesn't is what makes it mother-love."

"What about those hospital cases where unmarried girls try to smother their kids—and sometimes succeed?"

"Quite different, I should say. Those girls aren't yet mothers, emotionally. They're just parents, biologically. With a wholly unwanted and recently very painful obstruction between themselves and happiness. Mother-love must develop, like anything else. It grows as the child grows, becomes a personal bond only as the child becomes a person."

"All right. But mothers can go crazy."

"Yes. There are cases of that kind."

"That old lady acted kind o' crazy, I thought."

"Probably just grief. Or concern over the whereabouts of Sonny's soul."

"Maybe. I wouldn't press the point. But as long as we're guessing, I don't want to slight anybody."

"I did have a case once where, I believe, a fairly sane mother would have killed her son if she'd been able. He was a lad about Sonny's age, with a sarcoma of the jaw. It involved half his head—he suffered terrifically. Death was just a matter of time. She repeatedly begged me to give him an overdose of morphine."

"What prevented her from killing him?"

"I sent him to a hospital."

"Well—"

"Yes, I know. Sonny could have had a sort of moral sarcoma—eating up his soul, if you like. The sight of him going down and down might have been more than his mother could bear. But unless she was actually insane at the moment, she'd keep hoping and praying for a change—a turn for the better. That hope would prevent any drastic action. After all, sarcoma of the soul is not incurable."

"The only way it could be his mother, then, is if she went temporarily off her nut?"

"Exquisitely phrased, my friend. Have another drink."

Dr. Archer's apartment, which combined office and residence, was on the ground floor of a five-story house. Its front door was immediately within and to one side of the house entrance, off a large rectangular foyer at the rear of which a marble staircase wound upward and around an elevator-shaft. At this hour the elevator was not running.

Inside, the front rooms of the apartment constituted the physician's office—waiting-room, consultation-room, laboratory. Beyond these were a living-room, bedroom and kitchen.

It was agreed that Dart should occupy the bedroom for the rest of the night, while Dr. Archer made the best of the living-room couch. Dart could thus remain behind the scene of any forthcoming action, observe unseen, and step forward when occasion demanded.

Neither undressed, each lying down in shirt-sleeves and trousers. In the event of a caller, Dart agreed that, barring physical danger, he would not interfere unless the doctor summoned him.

"Still hoping it'll be the girl, hey?" grinned the detective.

"Nothing would amaze me more," returned Archer. "Go on—lie down. This is my party." He stretched his considerable length on the couch. Dart went into the adjacent bedroom, leaving the intervening door ajar.

As if some unseen director had awaited this moment, the apartment bell promptly rang, first briefly, timidly, then longer, with resolute determination. "I didn't want to sleep anyway," murmured the doctor. "Keep your ears open. Here goes."

He went through the office rooms to the front door, cracked the little trap-window designed against rent-collectors and other robbers, snapped it to with a gasp of astonishment, unlocked and opened the door.

His preliminary glance was corroborated. Before him stood Petal, bare-headed, with a handbag under her arm.

"I know it's late," she was saying, a little breathlessly, "but—"

"Not at all. Come in."

"Thank you." She looked behind her.

He closed the door quickly. "Someone following you?"

"I—I thought so. Just—nervousness I hope."

"Come back this way."

She followed him through the waiting-room into the consulting office. He slipped on an office coat from a rack.

"Who would be following you at this hour?" he asked, giving her a chair and seating himself at his desk.

"Detectives, maybe."

"Hardly. You're the last person to be suspected in this affair."

She was silent a moment. Her eyes rested on the doctor's bag, which sat conspicuously on top of his desk. Then she began still breathlessly to talk. She leaned forward in her chair, dark eyes wide and bright, gentle breasts rising and falling, small fingers moving restlessly over the flat handbag on her lap.

"Are—are we alone?"

He smiled. "Would you care to look about?"

She accepted this with a feeble reflection of his smile.

"I came here to—to warn you. About Ben."

"Ben?"

"He's—wild. He blames you. He says if you hadn't brought in that detective, he wouldn't be in a jam."

"But that's ridiculous. The thing couldn't have been covered up. The same facts would have been brought out sooner or later."

"I know. But he—he's a little crazy, I guess. Finding out about Letty and everything. He thinks he could have managed."

"Managed—what?"

"Keeping the thing quiet."

"Why should he want to keep it quiet?"

"I don't know. His job—his wife—it's all such a mess. I guess he wants to take it out on somebody and he can't—on Sonny."

"I see. What does he intend to do?"

"He's coming here and hold you up for that knife. If you refuse to give it to him—he'll take it."

"How?"

"He has a pistol. He has to have it when he's loading mail, you know. The way he is now, he'd use it."

"In which case he might be actually guilty of a crime of which he is now only suspected."

"Yes. He might kill you."

"And naturally you want to save him from that."

"Him—and you."

"Hm. . . . What do you suggest?"

"Give me the knife."

He smiled. "But I've promised Sergeant Dart to turn it over to him in the morning."

"I know. But I'll give it back to you, I swear I will."

"My dear child, I couldn't do that. Don't you see—it would make my position very awkward? Obstructing the due course of justice and all that?"

"Oh—I was afraid you wouldn't.—Please! Don't you see? It may mean your life—and Ben's. I tell you he's crazy."

"How is it that he didn't get here first?"

"He had to stay with Ma. She passed out. I'm supposed to be out looking for medicine. As soon as I get back, he's coming."

"As soon as you get back. Well, that makes it simple."

"What do you mean?"

"Don't go back. Stay here. Sergeant Dart will come for the knife at eight o'clock in the morning. It's three now. When it has been examined, he will come back for us. It will be too late for Ben to do anything to me then."

"Stay here the rest of the night?"

"You'll be quite safe. I should hardly be—ungrateful for your effort to protect me."

"But—but—what about Ma's medicine?"

"If she simply fainted, she's in no danger."

"I couldn't stay away. If anything happened to Ma—"

The physician meditated.

"Well," he said after a moment, "strange how the simplest solution is often the last to occur to one. I can easily take care of both the danger to myself and the further implication of your brother."

"How?" Petal asked eagerly.

"By just spending the rest of the night elsewhere. Parts unknown."

"Oh."

"Come. That will settle everything. You run along now. Get your mother's medicine. When brother Ben arrives I'll be far, far away."

Reluctantly the girl arose. Suddenly she swayed, threw a hand up to her face, and slumped back down into the chair. Dr. Archer sprang forward. She was quite limp. He felt her pulse and grinned. She stirred, opened her eyes, smiled wanly.

"A little water—?" she murmured.

He filled a paper cup from a washstand faucet in the corner and brought it to her.

"It's so warm," she protested.

"I'll get a bit of ice."

He went through the next room into the kitchen, put ice in a glass, filled it and returned. She had not apparently moved, but the flap of his bag on the desk was unsecured at one end. She drank the water.

"Thank you. That's so much better. I'm sorry. I feel all right now."

Again she arose and now preceded him through the waiting-room. At the front door she turned and smiled. She was really very pretty.

"You've been swell," she said. "I guess everything will turn out all right now."

"I hope so. You've done bravely."

She looked at him, turned quickly away as if eluding some hidden meaning in his words, and stepped across the threshold. As she did so, the bang of a pistol shot shook the foyer. Archer reached out, seized the girl's arm, yanked her back, slammed the door. He secured its lock, then hustled her back into the consulting-room.

There, both drew breath.

"Somebody means business. Sit down."

She obeyed, wordless, while he went back to reassure Dart. When he returned a moment later, he found a thoroughly frightened girl.

"I—I heard it hit the side of the doorway," she breathed. "Who—who'd shoot at me?"

"I can't imagine who'd shoot at either of us. Even your brother would try to get what he came for before shooting."

"It was at me," she insisted. "You were still inside the room. It was from the stairs at the back."

"Well. Looks as if we both have to stay here a while now."

"There's no other way out?"

"Yes. The kitchen. But that door opens on the same foyer."

She gave a sigh of despair. Slowly her eyes filled.

"Spoils your whole scheme, doesn't it?"

She said nothing.

"Don't feel too bad about it. It was spoiled already."

Her wet eyes lifted, questioning.

"Look in your bag," he said.

She opened the handbag, took out a gauze-wrapped object.

"Unwrap it."

She obeyed. The knife was not Sonny's pearl-handled weapon, but a shining surgeon's scalpel.

"I anticipated some such attempt as you made, of course. The real thing is already under inspection."

He felt almost ashamed at her look.

After a brief silence, she shrugged hopelessly. "Well—I tried."

He stood before her. "I wish you'd tell me the whole story."

"I can't. It's too awful."

"I'd really like to help you if I could."

"You could give me the knife."

"What could you do with it now? You don't dare leave, with somebody shooting at you."

"If Ben comes—"

"Ben has surely had time to come—come to his senses, anyway. Don't you see what it would mean? If Ben would go so far as to kill—as you claim—to get that knife, it can only mean one thing: He knows whom it would implicate." He paused, continued: "That might be himself."

Inspiration kindled her eyes for a brief instant. Before he was sure he saw it, the lids drooped.

"Or," he leaned a little closer, "would it be Letty? Letty, who killed Sonny for betraying her, then begged her husband to forgive her and recover the one thing that would identify her?"

She looked up at him, dropped her eyes again, and said:

"Neither."

"Who then?"

"Me."

"You!"

"Me." She drew deep breath. "Don't you think I know what it means for me to come here and try to get that thing? Why make it hard? It means I killed Sonny, that's all. It means I told them tonight after you left. Ben would have come here and done anything to get the knife, to save me. But Ma passed out when I told. And I ran out while Ben was holding her, saying I'd get something for her. And then I came here. . . . Why would I let Ben risk his neck for something I did?"

Dr. Archer sat down. "Petal, you're lying."

"No. It's true. I did it. I didn't know it was Sonny. I didn't go out as Letty said. I hid in the room closet. I thought it was Red that came in. When he went to sleep I came out of the closet. It was dark. . . . I meant to—to hang on to the knife, but I couldn't pull it out." She halted, went on: "Then I went out, quietly. It was Ma who really discovered him as I came back in, later. That's why I screamed so when—" She halted again.

"But Petal—why?"

"Can't you guess?" she said, low.

"Good Lord!" He sat back in his chair. "If that's a lie, it's a good one."

"It's not a lie. You said you'd help me if you could. Will you give me the knife now? Just long enough to let me clean the handle?"

He was silent.

"It's my life I'm asking for."

"No, Petal," he said gently. "The beauty of your story is that if it stands up you might get off very lightly. Juries are funny about a woman's honor. It's certainly not a question of your life."

"Lightly! What good is a jailbird's life?"

"I can't believe this."

She stood up, her bag dropping to the floor.

"Look at me," she said. He looked. "I'll do anything you want me to, any time, from now till I die, if you'll give me the knife for five minutes. Anything on earth."

And, whatever her falsehood up to that moment, he had no doubt of her sincerity now.

"Sit down, Petal."

She sat down and began to cry softly.

"It's a lie. But it's a grand lie."

"Why do you keep saying that?"

"Because it's so. Don't you see how inconsistent you are?"

She stopped crying.

"Look," he went on. "You come to me, whom you know nothing about except that I'm a doctor. Nothing personal at all. You say you've killed for the sake of your—let us say—honor. Yet the same honor, which you prize highly enough to commit murder for, you offer to sacrifice to me if I will save you from the consequences of what you've done for it. Does that make sense?"

She did not answer.

"How can you hold so cheap now a thing which you held so dear a few hours ago?"

"I'm not. It's worth all it ever was. Something else is worth more, that's all."

"How you must love your brother."

"Myself."

"No. You wouldn't do this for yourself. If you were the only one involved, you'd still be defending your honor—not trading it in."

"Please—you said you'd help me."

"I'm going to help you—though not in the way you suggest—nor at the price."

"Then—how?"

"You'll have to leave that to me, Petal."

There was complete defeat in her voice. "It certainly looks that way."

"Now call your home and say that you've been detained by the police, but will be there in the morning. Tell Ben you were detained for trying to see me. That will keep him safe at home."

She obeyed, replaced the receiver, turned to him. "Now what?"

"Now lie down on that sofa and rest till morning. I'll be in the next room, there."

With utmost dejection in every movement, she went toward the sofa. John Archer turned and went out, back through the living-room into the bedroom where Dart waited, and went into whispered close communion with the detective.

An hour later he came softly back to the consulting-room, cracked the door, looked through. Petal lay face-down on the sofa, her shoulders shaking with silent sobs.

During that hour of whispered conference, the physician and the detective had engaged in one of their characteristic disagreements.

"You yourself said," Dart reminded the doctor, "that the party who is obviously guilty *is* guilty. That party is Ben. He is the only one with sufficient motive. This Letty and Petal stuff is hooey. Women don't kill guys that trick 'em any more. They sue 'em. But men still kill guys that trick their wives."

"You're barking up the wrong sycamore, Perry. Ben didn't know anything about Letty's two-timing—delightful phrase, 'two-timing'—till Red spilt it over two hours *after* the stabbing. The way you say he acted proves that. Why, he was still staring dumbfounded at Letty when the medical examiner and I came back on the scene. Men may kill guys that trick their wives—if I may borrow your elegant diction—but surely not till after they know the worst. It is still customary, is it not, for a cause to precede its effect?"

"You needn't get nasty. Maybe there was some other motive."

"You wouldn't abandon your motive, would you, Sergeant? 'Love is all,' 'Seek the woman' and all that?"

"It's been known to play a part," said the other drily.

"I wish I could place that smell."

"I wish you could place it, too—as far away as possible."

"Let's see now. I got it in the dead boy's room when we first went in. But I didn't get it when the medical examiner and I went in."

"So?"

"So it must have been upon someone who was present the first time and absent the second."

"Yea."

"Don't growl—you're not the hound you think you are. That would mean it was one of four people—Sonny, Petal, Ma, or you."

"Wake me up when this is over."

"Then I got it in the front of the flat during the first period of questioning. So it couldn't have been Sonny. And I did not get it anywhere else in the flat when you and I were looking around. Hence it couldn't have been you."

"Nope. I use Life-Buoy."

"That leaves Petal and Ma. But I didn't get it when Petal greeted us at the head of the stairs, nor while I was talking to her just now. I actually leaned close to her to be sure."

"You leaned close to her—why?"

"To be sure."

"Oh. To be sure."

"That leaves Ma."

"Hmph. So Ma killed Sonny. I begin to smell something myself."

"I didn't say the bearer of the odor killed Sonny."

"No. You only said the odor would lead to the killer. You had a hunch."

"I've still got it—bigger than ever. Ma may not have killed Sonny, but I'll bet you champagne to Rochelle salts that if it hadn't been for Ma, Sonny wouldn't have been killed."

"It's a bet. And the one that wins has to drink his winnings on the spot."

"In other words, Ma is inextricably bound up in the answer to this little riddle."

"Anything besides an odor leading you on?"

"Yes. There are two things I can believe out of Petal's story: first, Petal is awfully anxious to protect somebody. Second, Ben—who was coming here also if Petal had returned home—is also very anxious to protect somebody. There was time for plenty of talk after we left, so it's unlikely that Ben and Petal are concerned over two different people. Ben and Petal, brother and sister, are trying to protect the *same* person. It wouldn't be Red, whom Ben tried to beat. It wouldn't be Letty, whom Petal has shown no special affection for. But it would be Ma, their mother, the one person in the picture whom both love."

"Are you trying to say that Ma killed her own son, and that Ben and Petal know she did?"

"Not exactly. I'm saying that Ben and Petal believe that that knife will incriminate Ma."

Dart became serious for a moment. "I get it. Ben's ignorance of Letty's two-timing eliminates him. Petal's inconsistency eliminates her. Yet each of them wants the knife, because it may incriminate Ma."

"Beautifully summarized, professor. With the aid of a smell."

"Where do you want to smell next?"

"At their apartment in the morning. Have everybody there—and a few trusty fallen arches. I'm going to locate that odor if it asphyxiates me."

"Y' know, maybe I ought to put you on a leash."

"Have the leash ready. I'll get you somebody to put on it."

In the morning about eight-thirty the two men and the girl had coffee together, Dart pretending to have just arrived. Petal exhibited a forced cheerfulness that in no wise concealed the despair in her eyes.

Even the hard habits of long police experience had not wholly stifled the detective's chivalry, and in an effort to match the girl's courageous masquerade, he said lightly:

"You know, this case is no cinch. I'm beginning to believe some of your folks must walk in their sleep."

As if struck, the girl jumped up. It was as if the tide of her terror, which had receded during the early morning hours, suddenly swung back with his remark, lifting her against her will to her feet. Controlling herself with the greatest effort, she turned from the table and disappeared into the next room.

"Gee!" said Dart. "Bull's eye—in the dark."

"M-m," murmured Archer. "Ma. But I hope I'm wrong."

"I hope so, too."

Petal reappeared.

"I'm sorry. I'm so upset."

"Better finish your coffee," said the doctor.

"My fault," Dart apologized. "I might have let you out a few more minutes."

"It's all right—about me. But there's someone I wish you would let out—as far as you can."

"Who?"

"Ma."

"I don't understand. Surely you don't mean that your mother—"

"No. Of course not. But—perhaps I should have mentioned it sooner—but it's not something we talk much about. You ought to know it though."

"I'll certainly try to protect your confidence."

"My mother is—well—not entirely—right."

"You mean she's—insane?"

"She goes off—has spells in which she doesn't know what she's saying. You saw how she was last night—she just sat there."

"But," the physician put in, "anybody—any mother, certainly—might act that way under the circumstances. The shock must have been terrific."

"Yes, but it is more than that. Ma has—I don't know—she sees things. As long as she's quiet it doesn't matter. But when she starts talking, she says the most impossible things. When you see her again, she's likely to have a complete story of all this. She's likely to say anybody did it—anybody." Her voice dropped. "Even herself."

The two men looked at her, Dart quizzically, Archer gravely.

"That's why I'm asking you to—let her out. If ever she had reason to be unresponsible for what she says, it's now."

"Quite so," the doctor said. "I'm sure Sergeant Dart will give your mother every consideration."

Dart nodded. "Don't worry, young lady. Policemen are people, too, you know."

"I just thought I'd better tell you beforehand."

"Glad you did. Now let's get around to your place and see if we can't clear up the whole thing. Some of the boys are to meet me there at nine. Perhaps something has developed that will put your mind at rest."

"Perhaps," said the girl with no trace of conviction or hope.

When, a few minutes later, they reached the Dewey apartment, they found a bluecoat in the corridor outside the door and two of Dart's subordinates already awaiting him, with the other members of the family, in the living-room.

"Isn't Red Brown here?" was the detective's first question.

"No," Ben told him. "He left right after you did last night and hasn't come back."

"The first law of nature," murmured Dr. Archer.

"Yea," Dart agreed, "but who is he protecting himself from—Mr. and Mrs. Dewey here or the law?"

"It could be both," remarked the tight-lipped Letty.

"Or neither," the doctor added. "He's probably stayed out all night before. And I doubt that I should care to occupy Sonny's bed under the circumstances."

"I told him to be here," Dart said. "This doesn't look too good for him."

One of the headquarters men called Dart aside.

"Autopsy report," he said, low. "Tuberculosis both lungs. Due to go anyway, sooner or later."

"M-m."

"Here's the knife."

"Anything on it?"

"Nothing."

And the detective, knowing that every Dewey's eyes had followed where their ears could not reach, pretended a satisfaction which only valuable information could have given.

"Thanks," said he aloud. "This is all I've been waiting for."

He surveyed the four members of the household—Ma, seated in the same chair she had occupied last night, much as if she had not left it since; Petal, again protectively by her side; Letty, still disagreeably defiant, standing beside Ben, her scowling husband. But the far-away expression was no longer in Ma's eyes; she was staring now at the detective with the same fearful expectancy as the others.

After a moment of complete silence, Dart, looking meditatively at the knife which he balanced in his hand, said almost casually:

"If I were the guilty party, I think I'd speak now."

Ma Dewey drew a quick breath so sharply that all eyes turned upon her.

"Yes," she said in a dull but resolute voice. "Yes. That's right. It's time to speak."

"Ma!" cried Petal and Ben together.

"Hush, chillun. You all don' know. I got to tell it. It's got to come out."

"Yes, Mrs. Dewey?"

"Oh Ma!" the girl sobbed, while Ben's shoulders dropped suddenly and Letty gave a sardonic shrug.

"I don't know," Ma said, "what you all's found on that knife. It don't matter. One thing I do know—my hand—this hand"—she extended a clenched, withered fist—"had hold o' that knife when it went into Sonny's heart."

Petal turned desperate, appealing eyes to Dart. No one else moved or spoke.

"I told the chillun las' night after you all had lef'."

Dr. Archer gave Petal a glance that at last comprehended all she had tried to accomplish in his office last night.

"You all don' know," the old lady resumed with a deliberate calmness of voice that held no hint of insanity. "You don' know what it means to a mother to see a child goin' down and down. Sonny was my youngest child, my baby. He was sick, body and soul."

She stopped a moment, went doggedly on.

"He got to runnin' around with the wrong crowd here in Harlem. Took to drinkin' and comin' in all hours o' the night—or not at all. Nothin' I say or do seem to have no effect on him. Then I see he's beginnin' to fall off—gettin' thinner by the minute. Well, I made him go 'round to the hospital and let them doctors examine him. They say he got the T.B. in his lungs and if he don' go 'way to a cemetarium he'll die in a year. And I knowed it was so, 'cause his father died o' the same thing."

She was looking back over the years now, and into her eyes came last night's distant stare.

"But he wouldn' go. Jes' like his father. Say if he go'n' die he go'n' die at home and have a good time befo' he go. I tried ev'ything—prayer, charms—God and the devil. But I'd done seen his father go and I reckon I didn' have no faith in neither one. And I begun to think how his father suffered befo' he went, and look like when I thought 'bout Sonny goin' through the same thing I couldn' stand it. Seem like sump'm kep' tellin' me, 'Don' let him suffer like that—Don' let him suffer like that.'

"It weighed on my mind. When I went to sleep nights I kep' dreamin' 'bout it. 'Bout how I could save him from goin' through all that sufferin' befo' he actually come down to it. And las' night I had sech a dream. I seen myself kneelin' by my bed, prayin' for strength to save him from what was in store for him—strength to make his death quick and easy, 'stead o' slow and mis'able. Then I seen myself get up and slip into the hall and make into Sonny's room like sump'm was leadin' me. Same sump'm say, 'If he die in his sleep he won' feel it.' Same sump'm took my hand and moved it 'long the bureau-top till it hit Sonny's knife. I felt myself pick it up and move over to the bed . . . and strike. . . ."

Her voice dwindled to a strained whisper.

"That's all. When I opened my eyes, I was in my own bed. I thought it was jes' another dream. . . . Now I know better. It happened. I killed him."

She had straightened up in her chair as she spoke. Now she slumped back as if her strength was spent.

Dr. Archer went quickly to her. Dart saw him lean over her, grow abruptly rigid, then fumble at the bosom of her dress, loosening her clothing. After a moment, the doctor stood erect and turned around, and upon his face was the light of discovery.

"She's all right," he said. "Wait a minute. Don't do anything till I get back."

He went into the hallway, calling back, "Petal, just fan your mother a bit. She'll be all right"—and disappeared toward the dining-room at the rear of the apartment.

In a few moments, during which attention centered on reviving Ma Dewey, he returned with a newspaper in his hand.

"This was on the dining-room table, open at this page, last night," he said proffering the paper to Dart. "Read it. I'll be right back."

He turned and went out again, this time leaving the apartment altogether, by way of its front door.

Dart looked after his vanished figure a moment, wondering perhaps if his friend might not also be acting in a trance. Then his eyes fell on the page which advertised columns of guaranteed charms.

Before he could find just what it was Dr. Archer had wanted him to read, a curious sound made him look up. From the hallway, in the direction of the rear, came a succession of sharp raps.

"What's that?" whispered Letty, awe-struck.

Dart stepped into the hallway, Ben, Letty, and the two officers crowding into the living-room doorway behind him. Again came the sharp succession of taps, and this time there was no mistaking their source. They came from within the closed door of Sonny's room.

Letty stifled a cry as Dart turned and asked:

"Who's in that room?"

"Nobody," Ben answered, bewildered. "They took Sonny away last night—the door's locked."

Again came the taps.

"Where's the key?"

Ben produced a key, Dart seized it, quickly unlocked the door and flung it wide.

Dr. Archer stood smiling in the doorway.

"What the hell?" said Dart.

"Unquestionably," returned his friend. "May I give an order to your two men?"

He wrote something on his prescription pad and handed it to one of the two men behind Dart. The latter read it.

"O.K., Doc. Come on, Bud."

They departed.

"As I remarked before," Dart growled, "what the hell?"

The physician backed into the room. "The missing link," he said blandly.

"Red Brown?"

"You heard Ma Dewey's story?"

"Of course I heard it."

"She was quite right. She did kill Sonny. But not in the way she believes. I'm just working out the details. See you in the living-room. Lock this door again, will you?" And he shut the door between himself and the detective.

With consummate self-control Dart suppressed comment and question and obeyed.

Then he went back into the living-room with the others. The local newspaper was still in his hand, somewhat crumpled. He smoothed the pages.

"Take it easy, everybody," he advised the members of the family, with whom he was now alone. "We'll wait for Dr. Archer and Red Brown." And he began to peruse in earnest the columns of ads:

BLACK CAT LODESTONE.

Draw anything you want to you.
Free—Hot foot and attracting powders
with your order.

Pay the postman only $1.95 on delivery and
it is all yours to keep and enjoy forever.

Burn Lucky Stars and surround yourself
with good fortune.

Win Your Loved One

Let us send you our Sacred Controlling
Love Powder.

Do you suffer from lack of Friends, Money, Health?

Oriental Wishing Ring

He had read to the bottom of the right-hand column before something caught his eye, an address which seemed somehow familiar.

"15 West 134th Street, Apt. 51—Why, that's here!"

He re-read the advertisement:

Faith Charm

Faith can move mountains.

Develop your faith by using our special charm.

Secret formula. Bound to bring health and
happiness to the wearer.

"Say!"

The front door rattled. Dart stepped out and admitted Dr. Archer. "What kind of hide-and-seek is this?"

"It isn't," smiled the physician. "It's a practical demonstration in entrances and exits. It shows that even if Sonny's door had been locked, his assailant could have entered and left his room, undetected."

"How?"

"The next apartment is empty. Its entrance is not locked—you know how vacant apartments are hereabouts: the tenants bring their own locks and take them when they move. One room has a window on the same airshaft with

Sonny's, at right angles to it, close enough to step across—if you don't look down."

"You jackass! You'd risk your hindquarters like that?"

"Sergeant—please."

"But what's the use? We've got the old lady's confession, haven't we?"

"Yes."

"And you admitted she did it—you were working out details. Good grief— would she go around to the next apartment and climb across an airshaft—at her age? What do you want me to believe?"

"Believe in the value of an odor, old snoop. Come on."

They re-entered the living-room. Dr. Archer went to Ma Dewey.

"Tell me, Mother Dewey, where do you keep the oil?"

She looked up at him. "I don't keep it. I gets it jes' as I needs it."

"When did you last need it?"

"Yestiddy mornin'."

"After it had failed so long to help Sonny?"

"I didn' have faith. I'd done seen his father die. But somebody else might 'a' had faith."

"Curious," reflected the doctor, "but common."

Dart's patience gave out.

"Would you cut out the clowning and state in plain English what this is all about?"

"I mean the mixture of Christian faith and primitive mysticism. But I suppose every religion is a confusion of superstitions."

The doorbell saved Dart from exploding. He went to the door and flung it open with unnecessary violence.

His two subordinates stood before him, holding between them a stranger— a sullen little black man whose eyes smoldered malevolence.

As they brought him into the living-room, those eyes first encountered Ben. Their malevolence kindled to a blaze. The captive writhed from the hands that held him and leaped upon the brother, and there was no mistaking his intention.

His captors got hold of him again almost before Ben realized what had happened.

"Who the devil's this?" Dart asked the physician.

"Someone for your leash. The man that killed Sonny."

"Yea—," panted the captive. "I got him. And"—indicating Petal— "I come near gettin' her las' night. And if you turn me loose, I'll get *him*." Vainly he struggled toward Ben.

"Three for one," said the doctor. "Rather unfair, isn't it, Mr. Bright?"

"She took all *we* had, didn' she? Give my wife that thing what killed *our* kid. We got to pay her back—all for all."

"Solomon Bright," breathed Dart. "The guy that lost his kid yesterday."

Dr. Archer said to the man, "What good will it do to pay Mother Dewey back?"

The little man turned red eyes on the quiet-voiced physician. "They ain' no other way to get our chile back, is they?"

Dr. Archer gave a gesture of despair, then said to Dart:

"Mother Dewey made the charm yesterday."

"'Twasn' no charm," Solomon Bright glowered. "'Twas a curse. Cast a spell on our chile, tha's what it done."

"Its odor," John Archer went on, "was characteristic. But I couldn't place it till Mother Dewey fainted just now and I saw the cord around her neck. On the end of it hangs the same sort of packet that I saw on Mr. Bright's baby."

Dart nodded. "I get it. . . . When she made that charm, she was unwittingly killing her own son. This bird's poison."

"Grief-crazed—doesn't realize what he's doing. Look at him."

"Realize or no realize, he killed Sonny."

"No," said the doctor. "Superstition killed Sonny." He sighed. "But I doubt that we'll ever capture that."

1936

- Spanish Civil War begins.
- France institutes the 40-hour work week.
- The British Broadcasting Corporation (BBC) initiates regular television broadcasts.
- In violation of the Treaty of Versailles, Germany reoccupies the demilitarized zone of the Rhineland.
- King Edward VIII of Great Britain voluntarily abdicates in order to marry American-born divorcée Wallis Warfield Simpson. He is succeeded by George VI.
- Italy annexes Ethiopia.
- Franklin D. Roosevelt reelected.
- Composer William Grant Still, serving as guest conductor of the Los Angeles Symphony Orchestra, becomes the first African American to lead a major symphony orchestra.
- Mary McLeod Bethune becomes the first black woman to receive an important federal appointment as the National Youth Administration's director of Negro affairs.
- Jesse Owens earns 4 gold medals in Berlin Olympics; black athletes win 13 Olympic medals altogether.

U.S. unemployment: 16.9%

Lynchings in the United States: 8 blacks, 0 whites

Deaths:
	Rose McClendon (12 July)

Spingarn Medal:
	John Hope (educator)

Books:

Arna Bontemps, *Black Thunder* (novel)
Mae V. Cowdery, *We Lift Our Voices* (poetry)
Marion Vera Cuthbert, *April Grasses* (poetry)
Juanita Harrison, *My Great, Wide, Beautiful World* (autobiography)
Arthur Joseph [pseud. John Arthur], *Dark Metropolis* (novel)
O'Wendell Shaw, *Greater Need Below* (novel)

Periodical:

Brown American (1936–45)

43 MOB MADNESS
Marion Vera Cuthbert

FROM *CRISIS*, APRIL 1936

Lizzie watched Jim stir his coffee. Her eyes were wide with fever and horror. Around and around he stirred, and the thin stuff slopped over and filled the saucer. But he did not notice because he was talking to their son.

"Shore, we got 'im at the very spot I showed you and Jeff. Lem would o' slit his throat right then, but the fellers back on the pike was waitin' an' wanted to be in on it, too, so we drug 'im out o' the brush. The boys wanted ter git at 'im to once, but some o' the more experienced of 'em cooled us down. You was there last night, so you know as much o' that end o' it as anybody."

He turned to the neglected coffee now and downed it in great gulps. The thirteen-year-old boy watched, his face set in a foolish grin of admiration and wonder.

"Jeff said he heard a man down to the square say you all got the wrong nigger. Said this one didn't do it."

"Guess he did it all right. An' if he didn't, one of the black ——— stretched out Ole Man Dan'l, an' the smell o' this one roastin' will teach the rest o' 'em they can't lay hands on a white man, b'Gawd!"

"Les see the toe again."

The man took a filthy handkerchief out of his overalls pocket, and unwrapped carefully a black object.

Lizzie swayed, and fearing to fall against the hot woodstove, sank into a chair.

Then Jim and the boy finished breakfast and went out.

For a long time Lizzie sat in the chair. After a while she got up shakily and went in the other room. Little Bessie was still sleeping heavily. She was ailing and her mother had been up with her most of the night.

But she would have been up all of that night, that terrible night, anyway. Neighbors had run in on their way to the square to ask her if she was not going, too.

She was not going.

Jim had come in long past midnight, little Jim with him. His eyes were blood-shot. She would have believed him drunk, but there was no smell of liquor on him. The boy was babbling incoherently.

"Maw, you should a seed it!"

Big Jim shut him up. The two fell into bed and slept at once.

After a time it was day, and Lizzie moved like a sick woman to get breakfast.

She stood looking down now on little Bessie. The child's yellow hair had fallen across her face. This she brushed back and looked for a long time on the thin little oval of a face. The purple veined eyelids were closed upon deep blue-gray eyes. Lizzie's own mother had said she was the living image of little Bessie when she was a child. Delicate and finicky. But when she was sixteen she had married six-foot, red-faced Jim. He was always rough, but men seemed all like that. She did not know then that he would . . .

After a little the child awoke. She gave her some breakfast, but would not let her get up. Allie Sneed from next door ran in.

"Everything's as quiet as kin be this mornin'. Not a nigger on the street. Lizzie, you missed it last night!"

Jim drove the truck for the store. He had gone to Terryville and did not come for lunch. Little Jim came in, swallowed his food and was off. It was cold, so Lizzie kept the woodstove going smartly. She held little Bessie in her arms and rocked back and forth. All day she had not eaten, but she was not hungry. She rocked back and forth . . .

. . . they got It down in the brush on the other side of the branch . . . they took It into the woods . . . at dark they tied It to a car and dragged It back to the town . . . at the square they piled up a huge bonfire . . .

. . . Jim had helped by bringing crates from the store . . .

. . . they had cut parts of It away . . .

. . . Jim had something black in a handkerchief . . .

. . . then they put what was left of It on the fire . . . their house was quite a way from the square, but she had heard the shouting. Every house around was emp-tied . . .

. . . once her brother had had an argument with another man. They fought, and pulled knives on each other. Both were cut pretty badly and they feared the other man would die. But she never shrank from her brother after that. All hot words and anger. He did not shout, crazy. Afterwards he did not brag . . .

. . . they did not fight It . . . they caught It like an animal in the brush . . . if It had been an animal they would have killed It at once . . . but This they took in the woods . . . before they killed It outright they cut off Its fingers and toes . . .

. . . Jim had something black in a handkerchief . . .

———

She put the child back in bed and went out in the yard to pump some water. She leaned her hot face against the porch post. In the dark by the fence something moved. It came nearer.

"Mis' Lizzie? O my Gawd, Mis' Lizzie! Dey burned me out las' night. Ah bin hidin' in de shacks by de railroad. Waitin' fo' de dahk. You allays good to us po' cullud people. Hope yo' Jim put me in de truck an' take me to Terryville tonight. Tell 'im he'p me, Mis' Lizzie, tell 'im he'p me!"

She could only stare at her. The voice of the black woman seemed far away, lost in the shouting in her head.

Their home was quite a way from the square, but she had heard the shouting.

The voice of the black woman seemed to go away altogether. So Lizzie went inside and began supper.

Soon after Jim came home and ate his supper. He was weary and dour. As soon as he was through he went to bed, and the boy, too.

Lizzie sat by the fire. Little Bessie was better and sleeping soundly.

. . . if Jim had not been so tired he would have come to her . . .

. . . he did not yet know she was going to have another child. This child, and little Bessie, and little Jim, had a father who helped catch a Thing in the brush . . . and cut off the quivering flesh. It seemed that all the men in the town had thought this a good thing to do. The women, too. They had all gone down to the square . . .

. . . little Jim was like his father. The other day he had spoken sharp to her. As big Jim so often did. He said she was too soft and finicky for her own good. Most boys were like Jim. When little Bessie grew up she would marry a boy like this . . .

. . . when little Bessie grew up . . .

. . . some boy who could touch her soft, fair flesh at night, and go forth into the day to hunt a thing in the brush, and hack at its flesh alive . . .

Lizzie looked and looked at the child. She remembered things which she had thought were true when she was a child. She was a woman now, and she knew that these things were not true. But she had thought they were true when she was a child.

The fire in the stove went down, then out. She made no effort to replenish it. Toward morning she went to the table drawer and took something out. She went in the other room and looked down on the uncouth figures of the sprawling man and boy. It was over the boy that she finally bent, but she straightened at once, remembering that the man and the boy were one. So she turned to the little girl, and the lifted blade of steel did not gleam any more.

Jim had had a good rest and awakened early. He found the bodies, already cold.

When the shock of the first terror let him find his voice he declared he would kill with his own hands every black man, woman and child within a hundred miles of the town. But the sheriff made him see that it was not murder. All this she had done with her own hand.

"She didn't touch me, ner the boy. When they go mad like this, sometimes they wipes out all."

Out in the yard Allie Sneed said to an awestruck group, "I know it was somethin' wrong with her when she held back from seein' the burnin'. A rare, uncommon sight, that, and she hid in her house missin' it!"

44 GESTURE

Georgia Douglas Johnson

From *Challenge*, June 1936

(under pseudonym Paul Tremaine)

Clouds of dust spun skyward in swirls of fury, behind the speeding automobile, going north on the desert highway. It hovered an instant and then settled slowly over the terrain as it had been doing for countless ages. The highway wound in and out among the rocky bluffs and deep gullies, to end somewhere out of sight in the distant mountains. The auto soon disappeared beyond that last tiny line that marked the end of the road, to the seeing eye. Once more it was quiet and still along the Hassayampa river road in the Arizona desert.

A hundred feet or so from the highway, in a clump of bushes, that afforded shade from the hot sun, a young man lay flat on his back gazing up into the dusty skies. The noise of the roaring motor had wakened him. He listened intently for a moment to determine the direction taken by the automobile, then yawning and stretching luxuriously, sat up grinning, and said aloud, "Well old man, better be getting out on that highway and thumbing yourself a ride or else . . . ?" He studied the sun and the skies a little while and decided it must be about four o'clock.

Searching thru his pockets for a cigarette, he found the butt of one he had smoked the night before. Carefully he smoothed it out with his fingers, put it between his lips and searched again for a match. At last he had a light. There were not more than two or three drags left in the short butt, but he inhaled deeply and let the smoke out thru his nostrils slowly with a sigh of deep satisfaction. His eyes roved slowly around his immediate tiny horizon, and a grin of appreciation stole slowly over his boyish countenance as he drank in the strange beauty of the desert.

A bee droned noisily above him. A grey bit of bird chirped tonelessly somewhere in a mosquito clump. A tiny lizard crawled out on a small dead limb and blinked at him in unwavering study. The cigarette burned his fingers and he quickly flipped it away. The suddenness of his movement frightened the lizard and it scuttled away with a great noise for so small an animal. The man threw back his head and laughed loud and heartily. He was amused.

Suddenly he stopped laughing. He spied an old desert cow and calf standing near in some bushes eyeing him curiously. Soberly the old cow's jaw moved in continuous chewing on her cud, her eyes unblinking as she stared at the man. The calf stood close to its mother with lifted head, as if trying to satisfy its own small-brained curiosity. The man studied them in silent amusement, then laughed loudly, frightening the cow, who suddenly broke into a fast lope, with the calf running close beside her. She looked back once or twice, but the sound of the man's continued laughter seemed to make her run faster. They disappeared beyond a fringe of bushes and desert growth along the river. Once more the man was alone, and now even the tiny noises were stilled.

His face sobered. Anxiously he listened again with his ears to the earth, then quickly got to his feet, looked down at his dusty blue serge, and flicked the dust carelessly with his hands before stepping out to the highway to hail the car he had heard. Desert dust brushes off easily. He did not look like a fellow who had been out in the desert most all night nor like one who had slept on the ground most of the hot hours of the day. His shoulders squared as he walked.

The night before he had ridden out from Phoenix with a fellow who had turned off somewhere back down the road. So he had walked on, stopping now and then to sit on a rock and smoke. Daylight had come and with it no rides with friendly motorists. When it had become too hot he had found the shade of the bushes and slept as comfortably as if he had been in a hotel.

The motor he had heard coming turned out to be a stage. It bore down upon him rapidly. He stepped out of the road to watch it go past. Passengers turned to stare at the lonely fellow in the middle of the desert. Some of them waved and he waved back, muttering, "Why in the world do people always wave and grin at a fellow walking when they are riding." He laughed deep in his throat as he watched the stage move out of sight on the winding road. Then he turned and looked back south a long time. No other car was coming. He faced north and began walking. His steps were slow and careless. He might have been any man strolling in a city park.

As he walked he began to recite a few lines to himself and to the silence of the desert at large.

> "Strange about thuh desert—how it sorta gits a man
> Thuh rusty, dusty desert wheh no rivahs eveh ran
> Thuh eart' so hot below yuh, thuh hot blue skies above,
> A funny sort of country for a man to learn to love."

He didn't know about those lines; whether he had read them somewhere long before, or whether he had made them up in his own mind as he thought and walked. A roaring motor coming from behind him stopped his reciting. He looked back. A large shiny car was coming, and a horse looked at him from a trailer hauled behind. He stood one side, ready to hail the car for a ride. It neared, and he waved his hand politely. The car didn't slow down. The cowboy driver looked a bit guilty as he passed by but the lone woman passenger in the rear seat ignored the man in the road. Only the horse looked over his shoulder curiously as they passed. In a cloud of dust, they were gone. The man in the road cursed as they disappeared. "Goddam such lowdown stingy scared to death people. Great, big empty car and wouldn't give me a ride."

His anger passed and he grinned. "What to hell," he chided himself. "It is their car, ain't it? They don't have to give a bum a ride if they don't want to. A good hombre will come along any time anyway!"

Far ahead up the road he saw the car top a rise, the trailer with the horse bobbing after them. Then they passed out of sight. He shrugged his shoulders carelessly and dismissed them from his mind. Once again his thoughts returned to the poem he had been reciting.

> "Yuh have t' learn t' love thuh desert for at first yuh hate it
> all—
> Thuh cactus and the sage brush and the sands where
> lizards crawl—"

He stopped reciting, searched for a smoke again, and not finding one, walked on, up one rise and down thru a gully, and then up another long rise, climbing easily and unhurriedly. He halted and stared as he topped the rise. A little way below him the shiny car with the trailer had stopped. The cowboy driver was out and kneeling beside a rear wheel. The man grinned and walked carelessly toward the car, stopping first at the horse and looking him over admiringly. The two people were unaware that he had neared them, and not until he had spoken did either of them look up.

"Cowboy," he said, "I reckon you could shoe a hoss much handier than you can fix that tire."

The cowboy looked up at him, grinning. "Sure could, stranger. Never did fix one of these nohow. I gotta fix one tho this time. We ain't got no more spares. Been having lots of tire trouble."

The woman stared coldly at the newcomer, her eyes pale and unfriendly. For a second the man looked into her eyes just as coldly. Then he said to the cowboy, "All right, Buddy, you sit on that rock, and I'll fix it for you."

He took his coat off and flung it over the side of the car, then knelt and expertly removed the tire from the rim. He yanked the tube out, and walking over to a rock, began to patch the hole with the repair kit he had picked up from the running board.

The cowboy rolled a cigarette and smoked, eyeing the stranger with a knowing expression in his eyes. The woman smoked and watched also. In a very few minutes the man had the tire back on the rim. "There yuh are, cowboy, pump it up. I'll take the makin's while you're doing it. I'm plumb out of smokes."

The cowboy handed the sack of tobacco and papers over to him and went to work on the pumping business. Soon the tools were in the car, and they were ready to travel once more.

The tramp took his coat from the car door, saying, "That sure is a fine looking hoss to be bringing out in this country. Bet my shoes he's a long way from where he was born." He turned to the horse and said, "Old fellow, you sure are going to miss that bluegrass out here."

The woman was studying him closely. Now she asked, "What are you doing way out here alone in the middle of the desert?"

The fellow grinned. The cowboy turned and looked soberly. "I was walking, mam. Slept out here most all day." He looked toward dark mountains. "Walking to Prescott."

The woman asked, "Don't you want to ride with us? We are going to Prescott."

The fellow smiled oddly, and shook his head, "No mam, I don't want to ride. I'll walk."

Her voice was tense with surprise. "It's getting dark already. The sun is going down. You'll be out here all night!"

"I know it, mam. I like it in the desert at night."

"Why don't you want a ride now?" she demanded. "You hailed us for one back there."

"Oh did I? Well, I must have changed my mind."

He looked into her eyes with a cold smile.

"Can I pay you for fixing my tire for me?" she asked indifferently as she picked up her purse.

He shook his head. "You don't owe me nothing, mam. You understand, courtesy of the road. We're in the west now."

Curtly she ordered the grinning cowboy to drive on. Her face settled into haughty indifference as she stared straight ahead toward the distant mountains. The cowboy started the motor and shifted slowly, looking around and winking slyly at the vagabond as the car moved away. His left hand dropped over the side of the car and a sack of tobacco and papers slipped through his fingers to the road.

Like a graven image the man stood and watched the car and horse pass out of sight again. Then once more he began to walk and recite,

> "Yuh come t' find it beautiful 'n' glorious and grand
> With its colors splashed regardless by some giant's careless
>   hand."

He shivered and walked faster, drawing his coat closer around him. The sun had gone down behind the western hills. The coolness of the desert night was rolling down from the darkening hills. He walked faster as he recited,

> "Yuh come to love thuh desert where the air is crystal like
>   and clear
> Where the stars come down at night time sorta friendly like
>   and near."

He shivered again and pulled his collar higher, shoving his hands deeper into his pockets and walking faster.

Far ahead in the mountains he could hear the echoing of a roaring motor as it labored up some steep grade. He stared at the darkness approaching from the mountain side, then swore an oath and raised a heel of his shoe hard into the seat of his trousers.

"Damn, damn fool," he muttered.

1937

- Japan initiates a full-scale military conflict with China. Resulting from this is the Rape of Nanjing, in which a reported 20,000 rapes occur at the hands of the invading Japanese. As many as 300,000 Chinese are killed at Nanjing, including 42,000 civilians (mostly women and children).
- The first jet engine is developed independently in England and Germany.
- Iraqi military dictator Bakr Sidqi is assassinated.
- The dirigible *Hindenburg* explodes at Lakehurst, New Jersey.
- American aviatrix Amelia Earhart is lost at sea.
- In the United States, the Marijuana Tax Act outlaws the nonmedical untaxed possession or sale of the drug.
- William H. Hastie becomes the first black to serve as U.S. federal judge (Virgin Islands).
- Hugo L. Black is appointed to the Supreme Court. His appointment is followed soon thereafter by controversy once the public learns that Black was a member of the Ku Klux Klan for two years during the 1920s.
- Joe Louis wins the heavyweight boxing championship of the world.
- William Edmondson becomes the first African American to have a solo exhibition at New York City's Museum of Modern Art.

U.S. unemployment: 14.3%

Lynchings in the United States: 8 blacks, 0 whites

Deaths:
    Henry Ossawa Tanner (25 May)
    Bessie Smith (26 Sept.)

Spingarn Medal:
    Walter White (author, activist)

Books:
> Arna Bontemps, *Sad-Faced Boy* (juvenile fiction)
> Anita Scott Coleman [pseud. Elizabeth Stapleton Stokes], *Small Wisdom* (poetry)
> Frank Marshall Davis, *I Am the American Negro* (poetry)
> Zora Neale Hurston, *Their Eyes Were Watching God* (novel)
> George W. Lee, *River George* (novel)
> Claude McKay, *A Long Way from Home* (autobiography)
> Waters E. Turpin, *These Low Grounds* (novel)

Periodicals:
> *New Challenge* (Fall 1937)
> *Negro History Bulletin* (1937–current)

45 POPE PIUS THE ONLY
Richard Bruce Nugent

FROM *CHALLENGE*, APRIL 1937

It was decidedly uncomfortable. But then Rome had burned, so who was he? Algy sniffed his smoke and burned. The fire around his feet was beginning. Slowly and hotly they burned and then—poof—the acrid trail singed clean his legs, and—poof—his crotch—poof-poof—his eyebrows. So Algy just stood and burned, and the heat on his feet was so great as to seem cold, and he remembered how hot a tub of water could be before adequate testing. Like dry ice. He had seen dry ice smoke under water once. Algy floated along and turned over on his back, his little gills fanning. And knew he was no longer a cinder with black face and hands, because the noise of the waters had washed him clean, washed him in the blood of the lamb. So he'd have lamb with mint sauce for the asking. As long as he lived and burned like hell. Algy turned over and swam with flaccid strokes, for his gills were very, very weary.

It was then that he met the merman, a truly remarkable creature with his legs each going off into a tail. And Algy remembered mermaids and thought, "how comfortable, how cozy" and burrowed deep into the bowels of the earth. He had been smoking "reefers," known in better circles as marijuana. In yet other and different circles as weed, or griefer. But Algy had been smoking "reefers"—and he let his head drop forward, where it hung heavy and pleasant on his chest while he thought for hours about tossing it back to wobble pleasingly unstable atop his spine. For hours he thought, forcing his will to lift his head from his chest and juggle it precariously above his shoulders. And it was a full minute before he did. He knew that it was only a minute, that the hours of time had somehow been cramped into that one minute, only he knew that it was hours too. Time was very unimportant, or maybe he meant elastic. But it had been of greatest importance that he drop his head, first forward, then back, and let it loll. The simple combined movement would "set his gauge." Then space would converge, and thoughts and time; dimensions would become distorted and correct; he would become aware and super aware and aware of awareness and on and on in a chain of dovetailings and separate importances. Everything would have its correct perspectives—time, thought, deed and the physical surrounding him and surrounding that and—first first dimension, second dimension, third, fourth and fifth dimension—no need to stop there—the incredible dimension of the pin point, the worm, the man—at one and the same time blending yet separate. Not only did he have to imagine the fourth side of things now, he could see it. See all sides—top, bottom, four sides, outside *and* inside.

And when he arose his slow maneuverings would be swift as an arrow, while all the while they would be as slow as death and normal. Above all, normal, despite conflicting sensations which did not conflict. So he swiftly at a snail-like pace rose from his seat. And his eyes dilated contractedly and his vision was photographic, stereoscopic and omnipotent.

He went on down Seventh Avenue. Nineteen thirty-five, summer and fall. E.R.A., N.R.A., P.W.A., W.P.A. Almost like Russia for initials. Huey P. Long and General Hugh Johnson, only Long was dead and so was Pushkin. Long live Pushkin.

Algy stepped through an idea, and the glamour of a Russian court warmed him after the icy blasts outside. On all sides of him, and inside too, the white faces surrounding him were red or pink or other than white. They were the white man. White Russia, coursing about him and through him. His insides must be quite white by now because he was Pushkin, and somehow, somewhere there was a blending which made his yellow skin black. White Russia with red faces, or at least so he felt as he reached for a sable with which to soothe his hurt and waxed prophetic. Hannibal had crossed the Alps with elephants, so Pushkin smiled a grin across Mongolia and thought of Catherine the Great as an army whispered by. And he withdrew into his red boots lined with black and white and wrote a poem.

His elephant slipped and an avalanche cascaded down the Roman side. He only smiled and wept when his army thought, "Hannibal, be careful." Formerly he thought Rome warm, but that was near the sea, and it is cold on the heights. Oh, he was great with future, but he thought, "Oh, Hannibal, I weep for an olive," and sighed as he bit into a Turkish delight. Alexander the Beautiful, the youthful soldier with Greek behavior.

The taste of Turkish delight was strange to Crispus Attucks. It filled his mouth with strangeness. Boston was a wheel within a wheel high up in the middle of the air. He bowed pleasantly to Phillis Wheatley as he passed, for she had passed on. And thought, "What a thing indeed is Sunday school, springing as it did with biblical flourish through Africa." And his black hands did not tremble as he laughed to see the dish run away with the spoon. But he stumbled and fell, his head was so high, his palms so pink. And as his blood foamed on his lips, he only wished he were in other circles, breathing in to dry his throat. "Reefers." He most decidedly wanted to be in the vernacular.

But he lit instead a star. There was a rite connected with this. He loosened first the end of Capricorn with his thumb and forefinger, caressing it gently into useful shape; then, stars converging, stars diminishing, he struck a match to his reefer. So he strolled on down Seventh Avenue, "trucked on down the midway," alive and atingle the whole dead length of him, aware and dreaming from his "stomps" to his "conk," and thought I could have meant "kicks" or even feet— and skull or even head—but only in circles where words were English instead of "jive"—

> stomps—feet
> sky-piece—hat
> skull—head—

atingle and dead from toe to head. He must not make a poem on Seventh Avenue. Or be Ira Aldridge or Dumas *père.* Instead—instead—from toe to head—glide—slide—ride the crest—breast—best of Seventh Avenue. So he walked on down Seventh Avenue and then crossed One Hundred and Twenty-Fifth Street. And he stood in the crowd and was Georgia and Mississippi, a sort of walking delegate, and when they hanged John Brown he was a shadow, the sun full upon him. He sorrowed as he laughed and took off his head with a courtly bow and said, "Good evening white folks." Then he ran like hell. He had forgotten to say Mister White Folks. He giggled. It sounded so funny. "Mr. White Folks. Mr. White—*Monsieur Blanc.*" He tittered as he ran and led an army to revolt in French. It was fine. A fine language being Toussaint or Christophe or Dessalines. It was too fine—with scarlet breeches, mulatto bitches, and high black places for whites to stumble from. And the fires of the burning sugar fields made a nice light to see him by and a pungent acrid caramel smell to carve words in the dark of a French dungeon. But they cut him to pieces, and that was confusing—cut him into one Herndon and nine Scottsboro pieces of eight. So he walked in glory and was Emperor Jones and sang whenever he was hailed the title the people called him.

Shim-sham-shimmy, and Charleston. He danced the gri-gri down Seventh Avenue and stopped for another gri-gri-griefer. Algy drew deep on the "reefer" and knew how good it was that he did not think. That no thought of Haile Selassie frowned on him. He couldn't think and that was well, for who wants time and space and physical fact—deed and thought contort distraught. Viva la Mussolini and cock-a-doodle-do—until time to sleep.

But water babies see many things, Algy knew, for as he swam beneath the carcass of a sea anemone, he thought, "how like Verlaine. How Gauguin the antennae." *Mouchoir* was the word—the strangely succinct word with which to wipe clean his muddied mood. So Algy blew his nose and slightly swam down the Nile, the Blue Nile, and the Nile, the White Nile, and joined the Italian army. But only to work black magic, for he conjured—

"Abrac-Adowa" and lo it fell, crashing mightily from 1896, and Algy entered Addis Ababa with forty thieves. They were looking for peace—pieces of eight— which were Africa and others through Africa. So Algy thought, "how simple," and Adigrat fell regained.

And it burned—the chains at his wrist were white hot now and Algy thought, "how needlessly painful, how annoying," and turned over to sleep through the lynching. But his lips were parched. Not that he liked it, but there he was—he'd no idea that being the fly in the ointment could be so sticky.

46 SILT
Richard Wright

FROM *NEW MASSES*, AUGUST 1937

At last the flood waters had receded. A black father, a black mother, and a black child tramped through muddy fields, leading a tired cow by a thin bit of rope. They stopped on a hilltop and shifted the bundles on their shoulders. As far as they could see the ground was covered with flood-silt. The little girl lifted a skinny finger and pointed to a mud-caked cabin.

"Look, Pa! Ain' that our home?"

The man, round-shouldered, clad in blue, ragged overalls, looked with bewildered eyes. Without moving a muscle, scarcely moving his lips, he said: "Yeah."

For five minutes they did not speak or move. The flood waters had been more than eight feet high here. Every tree, blade of grass, and stray stick had its flood-mark: caky, yellow mud. It clung to the ground, cracking thinly here and there in spider-web fashion. Over the stark fields came a gusty spring wind. The sky was high, blue, full of white clouds and sunshine. Over all hung a first-day strangeness.

"The hen house is gone," sighed the woman.

"N the pig pen," sighed the man.

They spoke without bitterness.

"Ah reckon them chickens is all done drowned."

"Yeah."

"Miz Flora's house is gone, too," said the little girl.

They looked at a clump of trees where their neighbor's house had stood.

"Lawd!"

"Yuh reckon anybody knows where they is?"

"Hard t' tell."

The man walked down the slope and stood uncertainly.

"There wuz a road erlong here somewheres," he said.

But there was no road now. Just a wide sweep of yellow, scalloped silt.

"Look, Tom!" called the woman. "Here's a piece of our gate!"

The gate-post was half buried in the ground. A rusty hinge stood stiff, like a lonely finger. Tom pried it loose and caught it firmly in his hand. There was nothing in particular he wanted to do with it; he just stood holding it firmly. Finally he dropped it, looked up, and said:

"C'mon. Le's go down n see whut we kin do."

Because it sat in a slight depression, the ground about the cabin was soft and slimy.

"Gimme tha' bag o' lime, May," he said.

With his shoes sucking in mud, he went slowly around the cabin, spreading the white lime with thick fingers. When he reached the front again he had a little left; he shook the bag out on the porch. The fine grains of floating lime flickered in the sunlight.

"Tha' oughta hep some," he said.

"Now, yuh be careful, Sal!" said May. "Don' yuh go n fall down in all this mud, yuh hear?"

"Yessum."

The steps were gone. Tom lifted May and Sally to the porch. They stood a moment looking at the half-opened door. He had shut it when he left, but somehow it seemed natural that he should find it open. The planks in the porch floor were swollen and warped. The cabin had two colors: near the bottom it was a solid yellow; at the top it was the familiar grey. It looked weird, as though its ghost were standing beside it.

The cow lowed.

"Tie Pat t' the pos' on the en' of the porch, May."

May tied the rope slowly, listlessly. When they attempted to open the front door, it would not budge. It was not until Tom had placed his shoulder against it and gave it a stout shove that it scraped back jerkily. The front room was dark and silent. The damp smell of flood-silt came fresh and sharp to their nostrils. Only one-half of the upper window was clear, and through it fell a rectangle of dingy light. The floors swam in ooze. Like a mute warning, a wavering flood-mark went high around the walls of the room. A dresser sat cater-cornered, its drawers and sides bulging like a bloated corpse. The bed, with the mattress still on it, was like a casket forged of mud. Two smashed chairs lay in a corner, as though huddled together for protection.

"Le's see the kitchen," said Tom.

The stove-pipe was gone. But the stove stood in the same place.

"The stove's still good. We kin clean it."

"Yeah."

"But where's the table?"

"Lawd knows."

"It must've washed erway wid the rest of the stuff, Ah reckon."

They opened the back door and looked out. They missed the barn, the hen house, and the pig pen.

"Tom, yuh bettah try tha ol' pump 'n see ef any watah's there."

The pump was stiff. Tom threw his weight on the handle and carried it up and down. No water came. He pumped on. There was a dry, hollow cough. Then yellow water trickled. He caught his breath and kept pumping. The water flowed white.

"Thank Gawd! We's got some watah."

"Yuh bettah boil it fo yuh use it," he said.

"Yeah. Ah know."

"Look, Pa! Here's yo ax," called Sally.

Tom took the ax from her. "Yeah. Ah'll need this."

"N here's somethin else," called Sally, digging spoons out of the mud.

"Waal, Ahma git a bucket n start cleanin," said May. "Ain no use in waitin, cause we's gotta sleep on them floors tonight."

When she was filling the bucket from the pump, Tom called from around the cabin. "May, look! Ah done foun mah plow!" Proudly he dragged the silt-caked plow to the pump. "Ah'll wash it n it'll be awright."

"Ah'm hongry," said Sally.

"Now, yuh jus wait! Yuh et this mawnin," said May. She turned to Tom. "Now, whutcha gonna do, Tom?"

He stood looking at the mud-filled fields.

"Yuh goin back t Burgess?"

"Ah reckon Ah have to."

"Whut else kin yuh do?"

"Nothin," he said. "Lawd, but Ah sho hate t start all over wid tha white man. Ah'd leave here ef Ah could. Ah owes im nigh eight hundred dollars. N we needs a hoss, grub, seed, n a lot mo other things. Ef we keeps on like this tha white man'll own us body n soul. . . ."

"But, Tom, there ain nothin else t do," she said.

"Ef we try t run erway they'll put us in jail."

"It coulda been worse," she said.

Sally came running from the kitchen. "Pa!"

"Hunh?"

"There's a shelf in the kitchen the flood didn't git!"

"Where?"

"Right up over the stove."

"But, chile, ain nothin up there," said May.

"But there's somethin on it," said Sally.

"C'mon. Le's see."

High and dry, untouched by the flood-water, was a box of matches. And beside it a half-full sack of Bull Durham tobacco. He took a match from the box and scratched it on his overalls. It burned to his fingers before he dropped it.

"May!"

"Hunh?"

"Look! Here's muh 'bacco n some matches!"

She stared unbelievingly. "Lawd!" she breathed.

Tom rolled a cigarette clumsily.

May washed the stove, gathered some sticks, and after some difficulty, made a fire. The kitchen stove smoked, and their eyes smarted. May put water on to heat and went into the front room. It was getting dark. From the bundles they took a kerosene lamp and lit it. Outside Pat lowed longingly into the thickening gloam and tinkled her cowbell.

"Tha old cow's hongry," said May.

"Ah reckon Ah'll have t be gitting erlong t Burgess."

They stood on the front porch.

"Yuh bettah git on, Tom, fo it gits too dark."

"Yeah."

The wind had stopped blowing. In the east a cluster of stars hung.

"Yuh goin, Tom?"

"Ah reckon Ah have t."

"Ma, Ah'm hongry," said Sally.

"Wait erwhile, honey. Ma knows yuh's hongry."

Tom threw his cigarette away and sighed.

"Look! Here comes somebody!"

"Tha's Mistah Burgess now!"

A mud-caked buggy rolled up. The shaggy horse was splattered all over. Burgess leaned his white face out of the buggy and spat.

"Well, I see you're back."

"Yessuh."

"How things look?"

"They don look so good, Mistah."

"What seems to be the trouble?"

"Waal, Ah ain got no hoss, no grub, nothing. . . . The only thing Ah is got is tha ol cow there. . . ."

"You owe eight hundred dollahs down at the store, Tom."

"Yessuh, Ah know. But, Mistah Burgess, can't yuh knock somethin off of tha, seein as how Ahm down n out now?"

"You ate that grub, and I got to pay for it, Tom."

"Yessuh, Ah know."

"It's going to be a little tough, Tom. But you got to go through with it. Two of the boys tried to run away this morning and dodge their debts, and I had to have the sheriff pick em up. I wasn't looking for no trouble out of you, Tom. . . . The rest of the families are going back."

Leaning out of the buggy, Burgess waited. In the surrounding stillness the cowbell tinkled again. Tom stood with his back against a post.

"Yuh got t go on, Tom. We ain't got nothin here," said May.

Tom looked at Burgess.

"Mistah Burgess, Ah don wanna make no trouble. But this is jus *too* hard. Ahm worse off now than befo. Ah got to start from scratch. . . ."

"Get in the buggy and come with me. I'll stake you with grub. We can talk over how you can pay it back." Tom said nothing. He rested his back against the post and looked at the mud-filled fields.

"Well," asked Burgess. "You coming?" Tom said nothing. He got slowly to the ground and pulled himself into the buggy. May watched them drive off.

"Hurry back, Tom!"

"Awright."

"Ma, tell Pa t bring me some 'lasses," begged Sally.

"Oh, Tom!"

Tom's head came out of the side of the buggy.

"Hunh?"

"Bring some 'lasses!"

"*Hunh?*"

"Bring some 'lasses fer Sal!"

"Awright!"

She watched the buggy disappear over the crest of the muddy hill. Then she sighed, caught Sally's hand, and turned back into the cabin.

47 THE RETURN OF A MODERN PRODIGAL

Octavia B. Wynbush

From *Crisis*, October 1937

The Illinois Central Flyer spun along the gleaming steel rails, farther and farther from the chill, blustery shores of Lake Michigan, deeper and deeper into the balmy warmth of the southland. Past Memphis, past rich fields of cotton, sugar cane and rice, deep, threatening swamp, and romantic vistas of old plantation mansions dating 'way before the days of the Civil War, rushed the train, while the wheels hummed and sang to the steel rails.

To Slim Sawyer, reared back in the Jim Crow smoker, his hat on the side of his head, a huge cigar in his mouth, and his feet planted comfortably on the cushion of the seat in front of him, the wheels spinning on the steel rails were singing, "Going home, Going home!"

There was a pleasurable exhilaration in listening to their steely song, an exhilaration mixed at the same time with a heaviness and an apprehension that was growing momentarily with the shortening of the miles between him and his destination. Slim was wondering. Would his folks know him after twenty-five years? He would know them, without a doubt.

His hand strayed to the side of his head uncovered by his hat, and felt the close-curled hair that covered it. He smiled as he had smiled a hundred times after performing the same act. A crop of hair felt good after a man had been forced to keep his head clean-shaven for nineteen years. Slim jerked himself out of his reverie and looked around with the air of one who fears he has whispered a secret too loudly. No one was paying him any attention. Evidently nobody had heard his thoughts.

Staring out the window at the fields, trees, mules and cabins that went spinning by, Slim saw back and beyond them all, the panorama of his own life unrolling. It had been boyish restlessness and dissatisfaction that had shaped his life into what it now was.

He saw himself as he must have looked at fifteen—like that youngster out there, leaning against the fence, watching the train rush by. He must have been like that—a tall, slim youngster out of whose face, blackened by the intimate acquaintance with the Louisiana sun, shone two eyes eager and alive with the dreams and longings of youth. Many a time when unobserved by his father, he had let the mules stand idle in the field at plowing time while he leaned against the fence and stared down the road that wound away into the distance. It always fascinated him, that road, yellow with powdery dust in the dry season, churned into black, sticky mud in the wet.

There, somewhere at the end of that road was a railway station where trains came puffing in three times a day and once at night. And these trains carried people away from the never-ending toil of the plantation. Somewhere in the great unknown these trains stopped at New Orleans, Memphis, Chicago and God only knew where else in that heaven called the North.

One day in plowing time the lure of the road had proved too strong for his boyish imagination. As he came opposite the fence on this particular day, he had dropped the reins of the mules, bolted over the fence, and taken to the road. His action was entirely unpremeditated, and was simply the result of dreams and the day which had beckoned him with teasing finger ever since he had risen at dawn.

Once in the road there was no turning back. Too many things lured him on. Every curve in the road, hidden by trees and clumps of bushes, hinted of something more alluring around the bend. That night he had slept in the station where he hid behind a pile of old boxes. At day-break he had started on his trek to New Orleans. Slim smiled as he pictured the dirty ragged black boy who had ventured from house to house begging food, and who had slept in field corners at night, and had stolen from those fields under the shadow of night what he needed to eat.

The man's smile was sadly reminiscent as his mind flew back over the many vicissitudes through which he had passed during the following years spent in New Orleans, in Memphis, in Chicago and Detroit. His mouth twisted wryly as he thought of Detroit. That city had been the scene of his undoing. A cloud of sadness and of shame descended upon him. Drink—a fight—fumes of poisonous whisky clearing away from his brain to reveal to him the still, dead form of a man they said he had killed—the trial—the cold pronouncement of the sentence by the judge—nineteen wasted years in the penitentiary; his time had been shortened to nineteen years because of his good behavior. He had spent the year following his release trying to lose the prison traces. His hand involuntarily went back to the hair on his head.

He wondered how the old folks would take his return. He did not wonder whether they were still alive. His first concern after leaving prison was to find that out by devious secret means. They were just as poor now as they were the day he had walked off. Certainly they were feebler. The years and the hard, back-breaking, spirit-grinding toil had taken care of that.

Slim smiled broadly. In an inside belt he was carrying enough money to put his parents on Easy Street the rest of their lives. Bootlegging had been the easiest and the most profitable business he had found open to him after his release. He had saved nearly every penny of his profits for the old folks.

The shadows cast by the coaches were gradually lengthening; the sky was growing less and less light. Evening was coming, quickly to be followed by the night. One more night in the uncomfortable coach, with his long body doubled "S" fashion on two seats in lieu of a berth, and he would be in New Orleans. From that point a local would carry him by slow, perspiring stages to the station in which he had slept the night he had run away.

The lights in the coach flared up. Night had fallen. Slim's preparations for retiring were simple. He removed his hat and placed it in the rack above him. Then he threw the remaining part of his cigar out of the window, removed his shoes and accommodating his long body to the two seats drew over him a light-weight overcoat to keep out the chill of the night.

It was six o'clock the next morning when the train pulled into the station in New Orleans. As he stepped from his coach Slim saw the local on the next track, getting up steam to pull out. Quickly he was aboard and settled in a seat. This train did not move with the speed of the Flyer he had just quitted. The wheels, however, sang, "Going home," but with a difference. It was like a funeral dirge now. "I feel more like a corpse than a livin' man," Slim muttered, wiping his face with a large fancy silk handkerchief.

The day was exceedingly warm and as the local crept from station to station, stopping often for a longer period than it was in motion, the oppressive heat weighed on Slim to such an extent that it gave him an oppressed feeling. Some-how, the nearer he was borne to his home, the farther away he felt from all that home represented. His mother, a saintly well-meaning woman; his father, a practical, hard-headed man who worshipped his God and measured mankind by the Ten Commandments.

The utter simplicity of their faith, the purity of their lives, the shining white-ness of them served only to make his misspent years stand out boldly black and ugly. His hand surreptitiously patted the money belt. How would these dollars be received? He had concocted a tale that to his ears had seemed plausible enough when he boarded the train in Chicago. But now at the thought of look-ing into his mother's calm, trusting eyes and telling the carefully planned lie, a feeling of nausea swept over him. Under the keen, shrewd, soul-scrutinizing eyes of his father, the best planned tale would seem weak and futile.

The tortuous hours crawled on. Noon had enveloped and smothered the passengers with its heat, and the slight breeze that had sprung up drove clouds of smoke and showers of cinders into the windows of the Jim Crow car. Slim noted with increasing irritation that his cuffs, collars and shirt front were growing momentarily dingier. Every now and then he removed his hat and carefully flicked the soot and cinders from its surface. He sighed with relief when the conductor shouted the name of the station.

Gathering his luggage, Slim made his way to the platform and sprang to the ground as soon as the train stopped. He looked around him. The dingy unpainted shed of a station that had once sheltered him was gone. In its place arose a trim bright yellow building bearing on one side the legend "Laurelville." There were two waiting rooms, also, one bearing the sign "White Waiting Room," the other, "Colored Waiting Room."

The next question was how to get to the plantation on which his father lived. Slim did not relish the long walk through the yellow dust. Surely there must be someone with a wagon and mule, who wouldn't mind earning a dollar by carrying him up that road.

He walked around the corner of the station, and there came upon a crowd of young men lolling and sprawling in all degrees of idleness and inertia. Looking at their dull, stagnant, yellow, brown and black faces, Slim reflected that here, but by the grace of chance, was Slim Sawyer. Singling out one of the group he walked up to him and spoke.

"Buddy, do you know where I can get a wagon to carry me out to Logan's plantation?"

The fellow questioned spat carefully into the dust beyond Slim, wiped his mouth on his ragged shirt cuff and answered, "Sho'. I'll take y' in my ole flivver. It's jes' aroun' the cornah behin' de station. Come, git in."

Slim followed his guide to the rear of the station, where stood the great, great grandfather of all flivvers. Battered, dented, with great gaping wounds in the top, and every shred of upholstery vanished from the interior, it looked entirely incapable of motion. Gingerly Slim deposited himself on the front scat through which a broken spring protruded. He made an effort to keep the spring between the owner and himself.

After much cranking, kicking, and coughing, the ancient chariot started off with the noise of a cannon shot. Its bounds and leaps at the starting made Slim think of a passage his father had once spelled out in the family Bible—something about horses pawing in the valley.

The light yellow dust rose in clouds from the dry road, sprinkling the vehicle and its occupants with a fine yellow film. It seeped between Slim's lips, making his mouth feel rough and gritty. He was thankful for the dust, though, for it kept his companion from asking the very personal questions that every native felt privileged to ask every newcomer.

The heat and the dust played havoc with Slim's freshly washed face and clean clothes. He cursed inwardly for not having kept on the clothes he had worn during his journey on the train. The handkerchief with which he swabbed his face came away streaked with dirt and perspiration. His silk shirt grew stickier and stickier. A longing to exchange his summer weight woolen suit for the airy tatters of his companion overcame him. The car engine seemed to add twenty degrees to the temperature of his feet.

At last the car turned a bend in the hot unshaded road and entered a narrow lane lined on either side with magnolias, live-oaks and a sprinkling of pecan trees. Slim sighed with relief for their shade. He knew that in a few minutes his ride would be over. The thought brought a flood of conflicting feelings.

"Well, hyah you is," drawled the owner of the car, bringing it to a standstill in front of a gate in a barbed wire fence.

Slim climbed out and took the luggage which the man handed him from the car.

"How much do I owe you?" he asked.

"O, 'bout two bits, I reckon."

Reaching into his pocket, Slim drew out a dollar and handed it to the fellow, saying with a smile, "Keep the change for lagniappe."

Ignoring the voluble thanks that followed his generosity, Slim turned and opened the gate. He stood just within it until the car had hiccoughed out of sight. He suddenly felt bewildered, frightened and very small-boyish. Strangely enough his mind flew back to a day in his childhood—a day when, often having disobeyed his father's injunction to stay out of the creek because the water wasn't warm enough yet, he had stood at that same gate, making up his mind to go to the house. He remembered wondering whether all signs of his disobedience were destroyed, and feeling then exactly as he felt now.

Slowly closing the gate behind him, he advanced up the path, merely a ribbon of trodden grass threading through a grove of trees similar to those lining the lane. A few moments of slow walking brought him to the end of the path and into an open grassy space. There, under the wide-flung branches of a live-oak whose Spanish moss dipped and touched the much-patched roof, stood the little cabin. It was black, now, with the wind and the sun and the rains. The same flower beds were flung out in front of it. The same little path led to the cabin steps. The railing around the porch supported wooden flower boxes similar to those Slim had seen there in his boyhood.

He halted again. Sudden panic overcame him. He wanted nothing so much as to run away. But any such intention was quickly put to an end by the appearance in the doorway of an old woman. The short, thin gray hair, the spectacles, the deep furrows on her brow and thin cheeks and the stoop that comes of old age and labor could not disguise her. It was his mother. His heart quaked into stillness. Would she know him? Did he want her to know him?

The old woman looked at him questioningly yet with a smile of unmistakable hospitality.

"Good evenin', sah," she said in a somewhat thin tremulous voice.

"Good evening, ma'am." Slim accompanied the words with a sweeping bow. His mind was made up as to the course he would pursue until she recognized him, or until he decided to drop his disguise.

At the beginning of his journey he had hoped for instant recognition. Now, somehow, he was glad it had not come. In a few words he established his assumed identity. His name was Adams, Lee Adams, and he was on a long journey from Chicago to a point still farther away. He wanted to break the trip by stopping somewhere tonight. On the train from New Orleans someone had told him of Mr. and Mrs. Sawyer as nice people to stop with, and here he was. Would she put him up overnight? He would pay her well for her trouble.

With true Louisiana hospitality Sarah Sawyer invited him into the house.

"Sho' you kin stay. We ain't much of a place, but ef you kin put up with it, why we'll be glad to have you. 'Tain't often strangers draps aroun' heah."

Slim followed her into the cabin. How familiar everything was! The oven of the big cook-stove in the center of the wall opposite the outside door, was sending forth fragrant whiffs of something baking. On the stove were a sauce pan, a kettle and a big black iron pot. In a corner of the room, near an open window was the table spread with a neatly patched blue checked table cloth, and laid for two people. Slim thrilled to think that soon another place would be there for him. The willow rocker that he had helped his father make sat turned toward the door, as if Sarah had been sitting in it looking out when the stranger came up the path.

She led him across the kitchen to a door on one side of the stove. Opening this door she stood aside with fine courtesy to let Slim enter.

"I'm sho' it ain't what you is used to, sah," she apologized, "but sech as it is, you is welcome to it. Jes' mak yo' se'f comfatible. I'll bring you some hot watah so you kin wash de dus' off yo'se'f. Dis Looziana dus' sho' sticks. My husban'll be in f'm de fiel' soon, an' we kin have suppah."

She walked out, closing the door behind her, and leaving Slim to look around him. He was in his own room once more. The rafters were darker now than they were when he used to lie in the white covered bed and look up at them at night. Vivid colored pictures from magazines, posters and newspapers were pasted on the walls. He fingered some of the prints tenderly, realizing the fact that he had often helped his mother paste such on the walls when he was a boy. White barred dimity curtains hung at the two windows. A rag carpet covered most of the floor. Near the door through which he had just come stood an old-fashioned wash stand with a large tin bowl and pitcher.

"Heah's yo' watah."

Stepping to the door Slim opened it and received a bucket of cold water and a kettle of hot water from Sarah.

When he reappeared in the kitchen, he was rewarded with a smile and an appreciative glance from Sarah.

"Son, yo' sho' looks a heap bettah sence gettin' shet of some of dat dus'. Dey ain't no dus' nowheres else in de whole worl' lak dis Looziana dus'. It sticks lak leeches. Set down an' res' yo' se'f. My husban' be comin' any time now. Set in de willow rocker."

"But won't I be robbing you?" Slim's whole being was throbbing with a strong ache at the sound of that word "son." But he realized that it was only a term of kindness and friendliness, nothing more.

"Shucks! A woman don' have time to set down near meal-time," he heard Sarah say, as she stooped to open the oven door.

Slim sat in the rocker, his eyes on his mother. She was so much thinner than he had ever known her. Already the trembling, uncertain movements of old age were creeping upon her. The spryness, while not altogether gone, was somehow less dynamic, less vital. A step on the porch—Slim looked up into the eyes of his father. Involuntarily he rose to his feet.

Sarah had heard the step, for she came forward.

"Andrew, dis is Mr. Lee Adams. He come f'um Chicago an' is on his way to Baker, an' he ast to stop heah ovah night. Mr. Adams, dis is my husban', Mr. Andrew Sawyer."

Feeling the shrewd, close scrutiny of the tall, straight old man's eyes, Slim felt a chill as he stretched out his hand to meet the other's. As their hands clasped, Slim's thumb doubled under his finger in a movement he had not made since leaving home. He felt a sudden fear. This little trick was one his father had taught him. It was their sign of sticking together in any plot conceived and carried out against the wishes of Sarah. Slim looked searchingly into Andrew's eyes, but they were the unfathomable, scrutinizing eyes of one meeting and appraising a stranger.

After a few words of formal greeting, Andrew withdrew to another room opening out of the kitchen. Slim remembered again. No matter how hungry or tired her men-folks, Sarah always made them "fresh up" before eating their evening meal.

By the time Andrew appeared once more, the supper was sending out tantalizing odors from the table. The three sat down and began to eat. Little was said, except by Sarah, full of womanly curiosity as to the ways of city folks. Andrew ate in silence, but Slim knew that the old man was mercilessly scrutinizing, analyzing and classifying him.

When the meal was over the two men repaired to the porch, Andrew to smoke, and Slim to watch the advancing night as it slowly conquered the west and spread up the heavens. Finally Sarah joined them, and began to speak.

"I put Mr. Adams into the little room, Andrew."

"Uh huh," grunted Andrew between puffs at his pipe.

Sarah leaned toward Slim.

"You know, Mr. Adams, it's our boy's room. He lef' us twenty-five years ago."

"Dead, you mean?"

"No. He runned off. Jes' lef' one day 'thout rhyme or reason."

Slim expressed his sympathy. Encouraged by his words Sarah poured out the whole story of her fears, her sorrow and her sleepless nights.

"Hain't a night passed since then what I don' pray for him. I ast God to let me see my baby boy once mo'. We ain' nevah knowed why he runned away. Lawd knows we was as kin' to him as we knowed how to be."

"Perhaps he'll come back some day, rich an' able to help you," suggested Slim.

"Dat's what I tells Andrew all time," answered Sarah, looking in the direction of the glowing pipe embers, "but he say de boy is daid, or good as daid."

"Good as dead?"

"Yes, he say ef his tuhned out to be a worthless no-'count rascal, his good as daid to him."

"An' I'm right!" exclaimed Andrew, and the glowing embers in his pipe came to rest with a slight thud on the railing. "A man what don' say nothin' in twenty-five years to his parents what done all they could fo' find him, is daid or a no-'count rascal."

"He may have been hindered in getting in touch with you. Maybe he couldn't send you anything. That is—something may have——"

"Ef he's lived de right kin' o' life, he'd write to his folks even ef he ain't got nothin' to send 'em."

"Andrew, go in an' light de lamp," Sarah's tone was peevish. She didn't want Andrew giving this stranger the wrong impression of her boy.

Slim leaped up. "Let me!" he exclaimed, "I know where it is."

In the darkness he walked across the porch into the kitchen. Unconsciously as he crossed the porch, there was a slight dragging sound as if one of his feet had gone suddenly lame, or was moved with difficulty because of a heavy weight.

As he placed the chimney on the lighted lamp, a cold sweat broke out on him. He realized what he had done. After a year of practicing and being on his guard, he had gone back to the habit burned into his blood by nineteen years of wearing the ball and chain. Cautiously, every nerve on guard, he walked back to his seat in the far corner of the porch. In passing, he cast a glance at Andrew's face, dimly visible in the faint reflection of the lamp in the kitchen. The old man was looking off into the darkness, smoking away. Slim fancied that the muscles of his mouth quivered an instant, and then set in a granite line.

Sarah took up the conversation. "My boy wouldn't do nothin' whut wuzn't right," she declared stoutly, "ez hard ez we tried to raise him right."

"But it might be easy for a young lad to get into trouble. Maybe he did go wrong, but if he was sorry an' wanted to come back——"

"He could come, bless God," cried Sarah, "but my baby wouldn't do no wrong. He's alive, too, somewhere an' he'll come back yet. I don' believe he's daid——"

"It would be too bad," murmured Slim.

Removing his pipe once more, Andrew remarked in low, tense tones. "I'd rather believe he's daid than come to some things I can think of. Some things is worse than death."

A slow tightening around Slim's throat and chest. "What, for instance?" he asked, after a thick silence.

"Servin' time in the pen," returned the old man.

"No mattah whah he is, or what he done, he's my own little baby whut I borned into dis worl'. He kin come to his mammy f'um any place he's at," sobbed Sarah.

With an effort Slim spoke again. "Suppose he had—served time—an' had got out—an' made money an' come back to take care o' you——"

Andrew bit in savagely, "Ef he done made his peace with God an' made his money clean, he be welcome. Ef he ain't, he could take hisse'f an' his money an' hit de highway. We kep' de family name clean an' clear fo' lo dese many yeahs, an' we done what was right in de sight of de Lawd. We ain't gwine be disgraced an' made ashame in ouah ol' age. Honest want is bettah dan dishonest plenty."

The yellow moon was now shining directly upon their faces. To hide whatever his countenance might betray, Slim leaned back in the shadow of the vines covering one side of the porch. He knew too well that old man. Arguing with him was about as effective as using one's fists to beat a way out of a tomb of solid granite. His mother, rocking softly, had covered her face with her apron and was sobbing softly.

At last Slim arose, said goodnight and went to his room. Locking the door he sat on the side of the bed. Dejectedly his head sank into his hands. For a long time he sat there. Finally he arose, walked to the chair upon which his bag rested, opened the bag, and took therefrom a writing case. After taking out an envelope and a piece of paper he closed the bag and seated himself beside the lamp stand. Slowly he began writing:—

"Dear Mrs. Sawyer,

I have decided to take the three o'clock morning train. So when you get up I'll be gone. I'm leaving a little gift in the letter. Think of me sometime.

Thank you,

Lee Adams"

From his money belt he counted out some of the currency—fifty ten dollar bills, twenty fives, and twenty twenties—$1,000 in all—placed it in the envelope with the letter, and stood the sealed letter against the bowl on the washstand.

The stars dimming in the early morning sky looked down upon a man trudging through the dusty road leading back to the railroad station. His well-tailored clothes and expensive luggage were covered with a film of yellow, clinging dust.

1938

- Mexico seizes $450 billion in U.S. and British oil company properties.
- Germany annexes Austria as well as the Sudetenland (western Czechoslovakia). The latter is permitted by the western powers per the Munich Agreement as a means for appeasing Germany's territorial ambitions.
- Italian dictator Benito Mussolini officially declares Libya to be part of metropolitan Italy.
- The first commercially successful ballpoint pen is patented.
- Comic book hero Superman debuts in print.
- Orson Welles's *War of the Worlds* radio broadcast about invading Martians induces nationwide panic.
- The Fair Labor Standards Act is passed, mandating a minimum wage and a 40-hour work week.
- Crystal Bird Fauset of Pennsylvania becomes the first African American woman elected to a state legislature.
- The Supreme Court rules in *Missouri ex rel Gaines v. Canada* that states must provide equal educational facilities for blacks and whites.
- German boxer Max Schmeling, a supposed symbol of Nazi supremacy, is defeated by Joe Louis after being knocked out in the first round.

U.S. unemployment: 19%

Lynchings in the United States: 6 blacks, 0 whites

Deaths:
King Oliver (8 Apr.)
James Weldon Johnson (26 June)

Spingarn Medal:
Marian Anderson (singer)

Books:

Frank Marshall Davis, *Through Sepia Eyes* (poetry)
Mercedes Gilbert, *Aunt Sara's Wooden God* (novel)
Langston Hughes, *A New Song* (poetry)
Zora Neale Hurston, *Tell My Horse: Voodoo and Life in Haiti and Jamaica* (nonfiction)
Richard Wright, *Uncle Tom's Children* (short stories)

48 HATE IS NOTHING
Marita Bonner

FROM *CRISIS*, DECEMBER 1938
(UNDER PSEUDONYM JOYCE N. REED)

The door would not open.

Lee's key hung in the lock. She pushed against the door with the fur coat that was slung over her left arm.

It would not yield.

She rattled the knob. And with the sudden perversity of old doors in old houses, the door swung wide.

Roger—Lee's husband—was coming down the stairs with the measured leisureliness that always marked his every move.

"Hey, ole Injun!" she started to greet him, but a door creaked open somewhere toward the back of the house.

That meant her mother-in-law was listening.

That meant her mother-in-law was standing somewhere between the kitchen and the inner hall.

In the shadow.

Listening.

Why didn't she walk out where they both could see her? Why did she have to stay out of sight—keep silent—and listen?

"Where were you all morning, Lee?" Roger asked and walked toward her.

Lee left the door and met him.

"I've been in jail!" Lee said distinctly so her voice would carry back in the shadow between the kitchen and the inner hall.

Roger moaned. "Anything left of the car?"

"The car? I wasn't in an accident. The car is all right. I was in a morals case— morals court or whatever you call it when you are taken out of a raided house!"

That banged the door shut.

That made the door bang shut in the shadow between the kitchen and the inner hall.

Roger said nothing. He took the coat gently from Lee's arm and stood aside so she could go upstairs. When he had laid the coat on the arm of the chair by the table, he came upstairs too. His steps were unhurried.

Lee was in her room, tossing off her hat, tearing off her gloves. She breathed in deeply and let her eyes rest on the color and loveliness that made the room.

"This is one place where Hell isn't! It has not brimstone in here yet!" Lee thought.

She touched a chair, a shade, fussed with her hair, then dropped back on the couch.

Roger closed the door carefully.

Lee turned her eyes up to the ceiling so that she would not see Roger.

There were times when she loved him for his calm immobility.

But when there was a tale to tell that carried her in quick rushes before everything—a speck of dust in the winds of Life—she never looked at him. He always made her impulses seem bad taste with his patience and aloofness.

Right now he sat silent.

There were no rays of disapproval pricking against her, but she could sense that he had gone deeper within himself. He was not reaching out to her.

"I ain't approved!" Lee commented racily to herself.

Then she began to talk.

"I couldn't sleep last night," she began then waited.

Her husband did not say anything.

She started again. "My mind was hurtling and racing and hurdling and hopping and skipping—so I got up at half past four—"

She stopped once more. He had told her where the keys to the car were before she went—so he knew all that.

He knew everything, too, that had kept her awake.

They had been reading—Lee had gone so far into what she was reading that she sensed rather than saw that Roger had dug a pencil out of a vest pocket and was scribbling—

He had spoken all at once. "Lee! Don't you think you spend too much money on the house?"

He had had to say it twice before she really heard him.

But she finally asked, "Why? I am spending no more than usual!"

Roger had tapped the pencil on the paper for a moment. "Well—," he seemed to be searching for words. "My mother said that she thought that we spent altogether too much!"

A geyser of angry words had roared inside of Lee's mind. "Tell your mother to end her visit that started six months ago and go home! Tell her that I did not spend nearly so much money until she decided to cook the meals alternate weeks!—And since she serves her Roger the fatted calf in every form from roast through salad and stew in her cooking weeks—my own menus have to be anemic assemblings of what I can afford! She blasts the hole in my household money—and I sweep up the dust! Tell her to go home!"

The geyser only roared inside. Lee only answered aloud soberly, "I'll look into it."

Then she had to grip her toes down in her slippers to keep from rushing out of the room at once to search out his mother—and tell her all the things that six months of pricking and prying had festered in her soul.

Lee did not go.

At thirty-three Lee was still struggling with impulse—for impulse had tangled her once in the barbed wires of an unhappiness that still—nine years after—was hard to heal.

With her eyes still on her book, Lee could see all of that unhappiness—her first marriage—spread out before her.

That first husband had drunk all of the time, yet Lee had never seen him reeling.

In the morning he would grab a cigarette in one hand, his bathrobe in the other and he would go and mix a drink.

That lit the devilish quirk in his eyes that some people called personality.

Lee had once thought that it was charm. Later she learned it was a tip of a flame from the hell-fire of the fastest living.

He drank in the morning, then he would go to see his patients and attend clinics.

Drunk—but not staggering. Only too gay, too cocky, too glib to be entirely sober.

Lee hated it. She had been afraid not for him but for the people he treated. A drunken doctor with needles and knives in his hands!

But nothing had ever happened. His touch was too devilishly sure. Still the fear had shadowed all her life with him.

That whole marriage had been uneasy from the start—stable as the shadow of a leaf. He had already lived three years for every year of his chronological age. But the keen edge of his excitement of living had cut new paths for her away from the conservative reserve of life as she had known it for twenty-two years—away from her Self—away from the sorrow that had given her no rest after both her parents had been swept away from her.

For a while her impulses outstripped his insatiable hunger for good times, until finally, so sawed by the teeth of his sensuality that her soul retched when she heard him leaping upstairs (for he could never seem to walk), Lee loosed herself suddenly from him.

"I am good to you, Lee! Why can't you stay?" he had pleaded at first.

(Good to you, Lee! Good because I never knocked you down! Never bruised or hurt you with my fists! But I say nothing of the blows I have hammered on YOU!)

"Why can't you stay, Lee?" (Stay and blot out more of your real SELF every time we quarrel and curse each other! Stay and blot out your Self! See if I can't make you and God lose each other!)

"I love you, Lee. There is something different about you! You are not stale-surfaced like most of these sisters! Stay with me!"

He had called Lee all the refreshing things like wildrose and seabreezes—and then he had gone off to stay with the stale-smooth-surfaces.

—Perhaps to test the surface tension of stale surfaces.

It was too much for Lee. You cannot live twenty odd years with the Ten Commandments then drown your Self in liquor and mad kissing in one year of unreal living.

Anyhow—who has ever been able to soak a wild rose in whiskey, flail it to straw on the threshing floors of fleshly lust, and then care for the rose—the straw—tenderly.

Lee cut herself away.

He fought to get her back. But by knowing the right persons here and there the marriage was annulled.

People called Lee odd.

Odd. The flavor of something foreign to You grafted on to your life.

You cannot lose both your parents at twenty-two—be married and divorced at twenty-four—anneal the surface of a second marriage so that your background, your pride, your prejudices, your likes and dislikes are fused to those of another so there will be no seams nor cracks that are loose enough to separate into chasms between you—and be a "placid pool of sweet content."

The tense aching spots left by the two edged sword of sorrow—the fearful doubt and shattering devastation of a disgusting love—stoke fires of unrest in you that will not cool to ashes no matter how many tears you pour over it all.

"It won't break me to lose you!" he had sneered at the last.

God did that breaking.

One night, following a lonely country road home from a gay carouse, his car turned over and pinned him underneath. Only ashes and charred metal were left next morning.

Some people say another man's wife was with him, but it was never known. It was all hushed up, erased by the sleight-of-hand coups of a society that whitewashes the crimson of Babylon with the blandest perfumes of deceitful sophistry.

It did not matter.

Lee had never loved him truly and intensely as she did Roger. But what woman who has been close enough to a man to have been his wife could hear that his funeral pyre had been lit one drunken midnight on a lonely road without a shudder? Who could have lain in the arms of a weak fool and not burned with remorse because she had left him as she had found him—a weak fool?

Lee shuddered and wondered what the Great One had said to a man who had lived for and by all the things He had told men to leave alone?

What had God said to a man who—drunk with all the excesses of living—had met Death on the run?

Just because a jumble of creeds have created a mist that blurs the simple boundaries of the Way, men who live as he had lived think Truth lies smothered under the dust of centuries of men's wilfulness—blotted out so that a God cannot even know the Way.

Cannot know the Way—or still see every man.

There could be, then, no mild ordinary wonder about painful things in a mind that had suffered as Lee's had.

If Roger's mother told him when Lee was not present that his wife spent too much of his money—and said nothing to Lee—she meant to cause trouble.

Trouble.

The first shadow of Hell once more across Lee's path of living.

Lee had thrown her book from her and left the room where she and Roger had been reading.

"Is she trying to turn him from me? It's a slow process—this turning a person away from someone else! A paw here! A claw there! A knife thrust there! Some wicked tonguing everywhere!"

Lee had run a warm bath to sooth herself. All the unspoken bitterness fretted her still, though.

—Was the snake curled up in the center of Eden from the very start—or did she just happen to come and visit one day? And when she had observed the love, the loveliness, the peace and plentitude, did she decide that all this was too good for a poor fool like Lee—and straightway begin her snakiness?

By three o'clock in the morning Lee had worked over a dozen-dozen unpleasant situations that had been set up during the past six months. They all chained together and led to what?

Now it happened that Lee's mother-in-law hated her. Mrs. Sands belonged to that generation of older Negroes most heavily cursed by the old inferiority hangover left from slave days.

She was one of those who believed that when an exceptional Negro is needed for an exceptional position—or when a colored man in an exceptional position marries—only the nearest approach to a pure Caucasian type is fit or suitable.

Mrs. Sands had never forgiven Roger, her only son.

He had raised her hopes to great heights when she saw him, an exceptional colored man in an exceptional position—and then he had dashed her sensibilities by bringing home a brown-skinned wife whose only claim to distinction was good breeding.

Not that Mrs. Sands conceded good breeding to Lee. To her the most necessary ingredient for anything that set a person apart was the earlier or later earmarks of bastardy.

Mrs. Sands hated Lee.

As long as the contacts between the two women had been limited to casual visits, there had been enough frosty smiles and felt-covered nippy remarks on the one hand and smothered annoyance on the other to pass for polite courtesy.

But when the frost and nippiness became a daily portion, the world inverted itself and what had been harmony and peace began to crack, and hell peeped through.

It was deep down. Only women know about claws sunk so deeply in an enemy's flesh that they are out of sight.

The surface skin—the civilized covering—is unbroken.

So small a thing as "my mother says we spend too much"—was like a fuse that might lead to one stick of dynamite—or it might lead to a whole mountain range of high explosives.

By four o'clock in the morning, hot-eyed and restless, Lee crawled out of bed. She lifted herself carefully so she would not waken Roger.

His breathing was even, steady and placid.

The very calmness of his sleep fretted her. She hurried into her slippers and crossed the hall to her own room.

Even here ugliness had stalked her.

"Why do you need satin chairs in a room that you use every day?" Mrs. Sands had asked her once.

"Because I love lovely things around me every day," Lee had retorted.

Had she been trying to make Roger think her extravagant even then?

What was she trying to do? Why was she always picking, twisting, prying, distorting the most ordinary things of their life together?

"I am going out! I can't stay in this place. I'll drive out on the river road," Lee decided suddenly.

She pulled on a black corduroy suit—yellow sweater—a yellow felt hat— caught up her fur coat.

She felt in her bag. Roger must have the keys to the garage. She opened the bedroom door again and went in.

Roger spoke suddenly through the darkness. "Lee?"

"Yes."

"The keys are in the gray tweed vest in the closet."

She turned on a small light, opened the closet door, inserted swift fingers and found the keys.

"Be careful!" Roger said and held out one arm.

That meant that he expected to be kissed.

Lee did not want to kiss anybody. She began a struggle to enter her coat drawing nearer to the door all the while.

"I am just going to take an early drive! Can't sleep!" she offered from the doorway.

Roger shifted his position in the bed.

"You live too intensely, Lee!" he replied and yawned.

"Some more of Mama's talk!" Lee's mind clicked. "We can't all take life in cow-like rhythmics!" she shot at him.

Then she raced down the stairs, crossed the kitchen and went out to the garage.

The city slid away behind her and the twists and turns of the broad road beside the water made her forget herself for a while.

It was not until she had run as far out as the little colored settlement—Tootsville—that she stopped. And then she had only stopped because the paved road ended where Tootsville began.

Deep yellow streaks were showing to the east where the sun was coming up out of the river mists. The tar-paper and tin houses of Tootsville looked so inadequate and barren of any beauty that Lee began to wish that she had driven in another direction.

But what was the need of trying to leave ugliness? It had to be seen through—and lived through—or fought through—like her own troubles.

Tears gathered swiftly in her eyes and she laid her head on her arms, crossed on the wheel, and cried for a long time.

Lee had raised her head to wipe her eyes when she saw, running toward her, a colored woman so stout that she might have been running off of a comic strip.

Though the fog of a wintry morning was just beginning to rise from the water, the woman was dressed only in a cotton housedress, a ragged sweater and a huge pair of felt bedroom slippers.

Stumbling and slipping grotesquely in the muddy road, she came abreast of Lee's car.

"It must be pretty terrible, whatever it is, to drive you out in those clothes on a morning like this," Lee thought to herself. She ran the glass down swiftly in the door beside her and called to the woman, "Need any help?"

For an answer the other woman wrenched at the back door of the car. Lee pivoted and unlocked the door.

She sat silent and waiting while the woman lay back against the cushions and puffed.

"Jesus sure sent you to help me!" the woman managed finally. "I got to go to the lockup! Annie Mae is in there!"

Lee turned her ignition key and put her gloves on. "I am sorry I don't know where the lockup is. Can you tell me?"

"O, shure, honey! You just go back down that away apiece and turn at Sis Joneses house and cross the railroad track and it's right nigh to the preacher's!"

"May God forgive us," Lee prayed to herself. "Suppose you tell me as I drive along. Get up front with me."

The woman began to outshout the motor. "Willie Shack, he come busting up to my door talking about my Annie Mae! She and Lee Andrew Miller both been put in the lockup! I keep telling that gal to let Lee Andrew alone! She ain't but eighteen and here now they gits into one of them raids last night and now she in jail this Sunday morning! I gonna stop at the preacher's if God helps me and see if he can't go up to the lockup with me!"

"Will he bail your daughter out?"

"Naw! I can do that myself!" She patted her bosom with the palm of her hand. "Got my rent money here! Landlord, he have to wait! The reverend he gonna marry them two right in the lockup so when some of these nosey niggers says to me long about next week— 'Seems like I heard somebody say your Annie Mae was in the lockup lass week!'—Then I can bust right back and say, 'You liable to hear 'bout anything, child! Meet Annie Mae's husband!' Then they'll heish! See?"

"I see," Lee told her.

"Here's de preacher's! Let me git out!" And she was out on the pavement and up the stairs before Lee had warped the car into where a curb should have been.

The Reverend must have been accustomed to being roused at dawn to minister to his flock. He came out surprisingly soon neatly dressed in a frock tail coat.

No one asked Lee her name, so she did not offer it. She merely drove off and pulled up before a two story tin shack that sat directly on the ground.

"Here's where that fool gal is!" the mother burst forth. "Git out, Reverend! Gawd have mercy! Much as I tried to do to raise that gal decent! That Lee Andrew Miller! Dirty dawg!" She muttered to herself as she waddled up the stairs.

Lee locked the car and walked in behind her.

A dirty slouch of a white man was sitting half asleep in a chair tilted against the wall.

The chair crashed down as the woman and her minister walked in.

"What you want?" the man in the chair growled.

The Reverend was the spokesman. "We want to see about the lady's daughter, Annie Mae Smith."

"When did she git in?"

"Last night, mister!"

"Hey, Jim," roared the man from his chair. "Second back!"

There was a sound of doors opening, of feet stumbling and an undersized black girl, shivering in a cheap velvet crumpled dress, came walking out.

"This must be Lee Andrew," Lee thought as a swaggerish black man followed the girl.

Annie Mae was blinking dazedly. "Morning, Reverend," she offered sheepishly. "Lo' ma!"

Ma sniffed and spoke not a word.

The man who had been asleep in the chair yawned to his feet and moved over to an old desk. "Couldn't you find no better place to take your girl, Willie?" he growled at the black man.

"Naw, sir." Lee Andrew accepted the "Willie" and all the rest of it with an apologetic grin.

"All right! That little visit will cost you fifteen bucks!"

Lee Andrew dug deep in a pocket and dragged forth a crumpled mass of dirty bills. He flung a ten and a five down on the desk with a more-where-that-came-from swagger.

"Why the hell didn't you make your boy friend take you somewhere else?" was the next demand—this time of Annie Mae.

She could only grin dazedly. She seemed to be wincing in fright, more from her mother than the officer.

"Fifteen bucks, too, sister!"

Lee Andrew dug deep again, swaggered a little more, but could only produce ten dollars in singles. Mama bustled forward and laid three dollars more on the desk. But there were still two dollars missing.

A panicky hiatus followed. No one seemed to know what to do.

"There are five dollars remaining for my table next week in my bag!" Lee calculated to herself. "If I risk two of them on this girl, I'll have to serve Roger tinted broths for dinner! And his mother—!"

Lee drew out the five dollar bill.

As he made the change, the man at the desk swept Lee with his eyes.

"Who are you? The dame that was running the joint?"

Before Lee could select the worst of the retorts that avalanched through her, the Reverend spoke. "She is just a lady what helps the community at times!" he supplied smoothly.

The other man made no reply. He made a great show of writing with a scratching pen.

From the place where she was still fastened with rage, Lee could see what he wrote.

"Willie Lee Miller—five dollars. Annie Mae Smith—five dollars." He wrote beside the two names.

"Dirty thief!" Lee had to choke the words deep in herself.

But already the mother and the minister, with much whispering and bustling, were pushing Lee Andrew and Annie Mae to the back of the room.

And standing right there in the ugliness and the dirt, the minister began: "Dearly beloved! We are gathered to unite this man and woman in the bonds of holy wedlock!"

Holy wedlock.—

Tears crowded into Lee's throat. She looked at the mother. She was grinning joyfully. Lee Andrew smirked. Annie Mae was still dazed and frightened.

Lee could feel that old tangle of barbed wire eating into her flesh. Her first marriage.—A runaway affair. A justice of the peace. Liquor on *his* breath.

Drunken fingers gripping tight—eating down into the flesh of her arms the way barbed wire does when it is settling for a grip.

Settling for a grip that always digs a scar too deep for eternity to ever fill again.

Lee told Roger all this.

Even as she talked there was a knocking at the door. A soft knocking, but a sharp insistent rupture of the peace in the room.

"It is time for dinner! Roger? Roger!! Your dinner will be cold!"

It was his mother, calling Roger for dinner. Calling Roger for dinner from his wife's room as if she were not there. All the prongs of ugly thoughts pricked Lee at once. "In my own home—she means to omit me!"

Roger stood up hastily. "Glad you could bail Annie Mae, Lee, but we'll talk about it all after dinner. It is time to go down, so we had better hurry." He left the room.

Lee did not follow him at once. She stood up and took off the jacket of her suit.

"I'd rather go out again. I can't sit to the table with her!" Lee stood alone with herself again.

But she had gone out hours before. She had driven fast and far and come back with still no peace in her.

"Oh there's no need to run and to think and talk to myself! I'll stay in! I'll eat dinner! Wrong things can't whip you around in Arabian cartwheels forever! There is a place where they have to stop! Things have to stop! Gouging into you! Something will turn it all aside and there'll be peace and no more whipping and gouging! I'll go down!"

She freshened her face.

She would have to step aside—let go of her own thoughts—push them aside and rest the case with herself and God.

It was the point where no human mind could unravel or untangle the snarls of her life. Only a greater mind could untangle—unravel—could go before her and straighten the crooked places.

Lee went downstairs.

———

Roger's mother was preening herself excitedly in the chair opposite her son. Lee sat at the side of the table.

As a guest should have sat—Lee sat at her own table.

The mother began to talk. "Lauretta Jones is having a little tea—a sort of wedding reception—for her son Henry and his bride this afternoon!"

"Oh did they finally work up to launching the bride?" Lee asked. "There was some talk the last time I heard as to whether she would be accepted."

An angry red crept over the older woman's face. "Any connection of the Jones family is most certainly the best this city can offer! Why Lauretta's husband, Atty. Henry Lyon Jones, represents the third generation of lawyers in that family! And Lauretta was a *Brewster* before she married! The Brewsters can trace their name back to the old aristocrat who owned their grandmother! The Jones family is certainly one colored family that can claim aristocracy, I can tell you! Acceptable? Any Jones is accepted!"

("The man who owned their grandmother." Lee's mind echoed. "Aristocratic!")

"Must is!" declared Roger. "If Miss Lauretta's darling Henry never went to jail for petty larceny—then they really must be exceptional! Why Lee, when we were all living in the frat house back at college, that guy would swipe anything hockable from anybody's room! Overcoat—watch—fountain pen—typewriter—anything! He even took my cuff links! Some that had belonged to mother's grandfather!"

Mrs. Sands' red glow deepened. "Roger, you must never tell that! It might get to poor Lauretta's ears and it would hurt her so! I just believe that you lost them yourself."

"I couldn't have lost them myself! I never wore them. I always kept them in my case!"

"Maybe the women who cleaned up stole them. Those ordinary Negroes are such petty thieves! I'll never believe Henry took them."

("The *man* who owned their grandmother! The Brewsters trace their *aristocratic* names to him. Now—! those *ordinary* Negroes"! Lee repeated this all to herself.)

"I wouldn't believe it either if Atty. Jones hadn't had to come up to school every year and pay off different guys for the stuff old Henry had swiped during the semester! I mean things they saw afterward in a pawn shop themselves! Everybody knew about Henry!"

Lee spoke suddenly. "Well, I don't understand why they are laying the red rug and elevating the canopy for Henry's Pearl—isn't that her name? They surely shut the door in Ann's face when she married six years ago! Mrs. Jones' daughter Ann certainly deserves as much as her son Henry!"

Mrs. Sands' voice took a higher note: "But look at what Ann married! Some *janitor's* son! And they say his mother was a perfect Aunt Jemima. Why poor

Lauretta nearly died! She was so afraid Ann would have a child that she didn't know what to do! Why there has never been anybody as colored as Ann's husband in any of the Jones family for generations!"

"Yet when Ann's husband bought up half the Negro district a little later, poor Lauretta began to ride everywhere everyday in one of her son-in-law's cars," finished Lee drily. "I won't be at the tea this afternoon! All of Ann's friends—her real friends—those who went to see her all the years when Miss Lauretta wouldn't—swore we'd never go to anything that the Jones tribe might give for Henry's wife. She and Henry lived together for two years before they finally decided to get married! Ann has really never forgiven her mother."

"Oh, you say the worst things, Lisa!" (Mrs. Sands never called Lee by her short name.) "Why shouldn't a girl forgive her mother—the one who gave her life?"

"And what a life! They tell that she always nagged Ann to death! Anyhow—why should a mother shut the doors of her home in the face of her daughter because she chose to marry a man blacker than her mother would have chosen for her son-by-marriage?"

Mrs. Sands drew her lips in with an I-won't-push-this-fool-argument sneer. "I shall want you to drive me to Lauretta's after dinner, Roger," she told him after a slight pause. "Lauretta expects you! She and I were girls together!"

"Roger," Lee asked, "do you care to meet a bride who spent two years as a wife before she was finally married?" Mrs. Sands' red paled to a gray. Roger laughed.

"Don't be so shocked, mother! That was town talk all the years Henry was supposed to be off on that tour for an intense study of business. Of course everybody who spent those years hashing over this situation is going to fall into Miss Lauretta's this afternoon! They'd be afraid to stay away for fear someone might think they didn't belong!"

"And they want to add a deceitful simper to the hee-haw chorus they'll all be pouring out to draw attention to the loveliness of their cliques—to see if they can perfume away the stench around the bride's past!" Lee laughed.

Mrs. Sands laid her fork down. "Really, Lisa, if you are going to carry on this objectionable talk at the table, I'll have to excuse myself. Lauretta Jones is my best friend"—with a cross between a snort and a sniffle—"and anyone dear to her is dear to me."

Roger's voice curved gently across to his mother: "But mother!" he laughed apologetically. "Lee is only stating plainly what every durn one of them there will *know* this afternoon! Lee is just separating the marrow from the bones for us."

("So! I am at the point that he needs to explain me to her! Upstairs will be better for me after all. At least there won't be any prejudiced ignorance in my own room! She can have the chair—the room—Roger—and everything!" Lee thought to herself.) "Sorry," she said aloud coolly to the mother, "the truth will always be the light, but light really blisters certain types of skin! I'll take a cup of tea upstairs in my own room."

Her chair went back in one swift push . . . —"If you'll excuse me!"

—So the cartwheels were still there.

—So this was not the time to straighten the crooked path.

Lee went out of the dining room to the small inner hall, where there was a cabinet of glass and dishes.

"I'll take my tea-pot and use my best small cloth upstairs. Maybe the touch of elegance will take my mind off of things."

She opened the drawer where the linens were and reached into a special corner where the cream damask lunch-cloth stayed.

It was not there.

Only two large table-cloths were left in the drawer.

"I know it isn't in the laundry! What on earth has happened to it!" Lee spoke aloud to herself.

She drew out an old stool and stood up to open the cabinet door.

Lee owned a tea set of cut glass with black inlay, a lovely Victorian ornate thing that had been her great grandmother's. That grandmother had been a seamstress for a wealthy group that had brought her gifts from every country they had visited.

Lee kept the tea set on a top shelf where nothing could possibly hurt its old-fashioned loveliness.

She climbed up on the stool.

The top shelf was bare.

Lee stared at the empty space.

Roger's voice reached her: "Lee! Telephone! It's Mrs. Jones! She's having some sort of hysteria on the wire! She says Henry's new wife just dropped two of your cups—Say! You ought not to jump off that chair like that! You will break your neck in those heels!"

Lee pushed Roger out of the way and threw the dining room door wide open.

Mrs. Sands was still in her seat. Something in Lee's face made her half rise.

"You gave Mrs. Jones my tea set!" Lee did not speak loudly at first. "You took grandmother's tea set—without asking me!"

The older woman dropped back. Her ready sneer rode her features. "Surely anything in my son's house is mine too!"

"There are some things in your son's house—(which happens to be my house too)—that do not belong to your son! That tea set was mine! You had no right to touch *one thing* in here without asking me!"

"Asking *you?* I am his *mother!*"

"And I am his *wife!*"

This was one of the spots where life left no words to fight with.

But *eyes* can carry a battle forward.

Roger spoke. "Answer the phone, Lee!"

"Throw the phone and everything else out of the window!" Lee told him. ("Any fool could have said something wiser!" Lee told herself.)

And she ran all the way upstairs to the couch in her room.

She heard Roger come up the stairs soon after.

He walked into his room. There was a sound of his closet door opening. He came out into the hall again and walked along the hall.

"Don't let him come in here!" Lee prayed to herself.

But the door opened. She kept her face buried on the couch. She could hear him cross two of the small spaces between the rugs. Then he stood still.

"I am going after your tea set, Lee," he said after a moment of silence.

There wasn't anything to say now. There was nothing to say unless you meant to use your words as a hatchet to hack out the roots of bitterness.

And Lee was too tired to hack. She'd spent too much strength trying to keep from blasting roots at the wrong time.

She kept her face turned to the pillow and waited.

Lee waited to hear Roger walk across the two small spaces between the rugs again. That would have meant that he was going out of the room.

But the sound did not come.

She twisted over suddenly.

Roger stood looking out of the window, his face in profile to her. Tense lines furrowed deep with a bitterness within, were drawn around his mouth. He stared far before him with the glaze of sadness you see in a person who has had to look a long time—alone—at some deep wound life has gashed in him.

"Why—*he* has seen how hatefully highhanded his mother can be—before this!" shot swiftly through Lee's mind. "He has seen her do things this way before! *Her own* way! And to hell with you—your sense—your sensibilities—your property—or even your own soul! He has seen this all his life."

She started to rush over to him and throw her arms around him. But if she did that, the glazed sadness and the tense bitterness might run together. Then things might be said that could never be unsaid.

She would have to put her mind—and not herself—between him and the thing that was hurting him.

That thought made her able to drop her feet to the floor.

"I'll go with you, Roger," she suggested. "There's a detour on the river road that I saw this morning. You might miss it in the dark. Better wear a heavy coat. It's damp over there near the water."

She began to talk lightly while she powdered her nose, touched her lips and her cheeks, put on her hat and coat.

Then she ran downstairs ahead of him.

Passed the dining room door.

Talking—talking—lightly—lightly—lightly—spinning a gossamer of light talk so that there would be no chance for even one weighted word.

There are some cancerous spots in people's lives that no one ever wants to touch.

She did not wait for Roger to answer. She did not want him to answer, until the lines in his face were softer.

There are some cancerous spots in people's lives that no one ever wants to touch. Never.

She shook the door of the car a dozen times before she realized it was locked and that Roger was digging in his pockets for the keys.

They were ten miles out on the river road before Roger spoke: "You take much better care of me than I do of you, I am afraid, Lee!" was all he said.

It was enough, though.

His face was not bitter, drawn, hard and old now. He was himself once more.

It was enough.

She had blurred, then, some of the saw-toothed edges of hatefulness that must have eaten into him before this.

"Why *she* meant to go! *She* wanted to go to the tea! And we forgot her!" Lee remembered suddenly.

"We forgot her!"

And the fear of the hate that had seemed so strong—so full of power?

"I even forgot to be afraid while I was trying to help Roger get back into himself!"

And if you can forget the fear of a hate—walk out even for one second from under the shadow of the fear—that means it is nothing.

Nothing.

No hate has ever unlocked the myriad interlacings—the *front* of love.

Hate is nothing.

1939

- World War II begins; U.S. maintains neutrality.
- The Soviet Union invades Poland and Finland; Italy invades Albania.
- Spain's civil war ends in victory for Gen. Francisco Franco's fascists.
- Major earthquakes in Chile and Turkey kill an estimated 80,000 people, while flooding in northern China kills an estimated 200,000.
- Pan-American Airways inaugurates the first regular commercial flights across the Atlantic.
- The New York World's Fair opens.
- A civil rights division is established as part of the U.S. Department of Justice.
- *Gone with the Wind* is released. Hattie McDaniel will be voted best actress in a supporting role, making her the first African American to receive an Oscar.
- Jane M. Bolin is appointed to New York City's Domestic Relations Court, becoming the first African American female judge.
- Marian Anderson sings at the Lincoln Memorial before an audience of 75,000 after the Daughters of the American Revolution bars her from performing at Constitution Hall.

U.S. unemployment: 17.2%

Lynchings in the United States: 2 blacks, 1 white

Deaths: Kelly Miller (29 Dec.)

Spingarn Medal: Louis T. Wright (physician)

Books:
>William Attaway, *Let Me Breathe Thunder* (novel)
>Arna Bontemps, *Drums at Dusk* (novel)
>Zora Neale Hurston, *Moses, Man of the Mountain* (novel)
>Anne Scott, *George Sampson Brite* (novel)
>Waters E. Turpin, *O Canaan!* (novel)

49 THE WHIPPING
Marita Bonner

FROM *CRISIS*, JUNE 1939

The matron picked up her coat. It was a good coat made of heavy men's wear wool and lined with fur. She always liked to let her hands trail fondly over it whenever she was going to put it on (the way women do who are used to nothing).

She shook it out and shrugged her shoulders into it.

"I'll be back home again in time for dinner!" She smiled at the warden as she talked. "Helga will have 'peasant-girl' for dessert, too!"

The hard lines that creased around the man's eyes softened a little. "Peasant-girl-with-a-veil! Ah, my mother could make that! Real home-made jam, yellow cream!—good! Nothing here ever tastes as good as it did back in the old country, I tell you!"

The woman balanced her weight on the balls of her feet and drew on one of her leather driving gloves. Through the window she saw her car, nicely trimmed and compactly modern, awaiting her. Beyond the car was a November sky, dismal, darkening, and melancholy as the walls that bounded the surrounding acres of land which belonged to the Women's Reformatory.

At the end of her drive of thirty-five miles back to the city again, she would go to her apartment that—through warmth of color and all the right uses of the best comforts—seemed to be full of sunshine on the darkest days. She looked down, now, as she stood near the warden and saw her right hand freshly manicured.

Her mother's hands back in the stone kitchen with the open hearth found in every peasant home in Denmark had always been grey and chapped with blackened nails this time of year. No woman who has to carry wood and coal from a frozen yard can have soft clean hands.

The thought made the matron shrug again. "I like things as they are here—but it would be good to go home some day to visit!"

She hurried a little toward the door now. Nobody lingers in the impersonal greyness of an institution whose very air is heavy with fierce anger and anguish and sorrow, buried and dulled under an angry restraint just as fierce and sorrowful.

She had nearly reached the door before she remembered the colored woman sitting alone on the edge of the bench beside the window. The matron had just driven up from the city to bring the woman on the bench to stay at the Reformatory as long as she should live.

She had killed her little boy.

The judge and the social worker said she had killed him.

But she had told the matron over and over again that she did not do it.

You could never tell, though. It is best to leave these things alone.

"Good-bye, Lizabeth!" the matron called in a loud voice. She meant to leave a cheerful note, but she only spoke overloud. "Be a good girl!"

"Yas'm!" Lizabeth answered softly. "Yas'm!"

And the women separated. One went out to the light. The other looked at the grey walls—dark—and growing darker in the winter sunset.

Everything had been grey around Lizabeth most all of her life. The two-room hut with a ragged lean-to down on Mr. Davey's place in Mississippi where she had lived before she came North had been grey.

She and Pa and Ma and Bella and John used to get up when the morning was still grey and work the cotton until the greyness of evening stopped them.

"God knows I'm sick of this!" Pa had cursed suddenly one day.

Ma did not say anything. She was glad that they had sugar once in a while from the commissary and not just molasses like they said you got over at McLaren's place.

Pa cursed a lot that day and kept muttering to himself. One morning when they got up to go to work the cotton, Pa was not there.

"He say he goin' North to work!" Ma explained when she could stop her crying.

Mr. Davey said Pa had left a big bill at the commissary and that Ma and the children would have to work twice as hard to pay it up.

There were not any more hours in any one day than those from sun-up to sun-down, no way you could figure it.

The Christmas after Pa left, Mr. Davey said Ma owed three times as much and that she could not have any flannel for John's chest to cover the place where the misery stayed each winter.

That was the day Ma decided to go North and see if she could find Pa.

They had to plan it all carefully. There was no money to go from Mississippi northward on the train.

John had to get an awful attack of the misery first. Then Bella had to stay home to take care of him.

The day Mr. Davey's man came to find out why Bella and John were not in the field, Bella had her hand tied up in a blood soaked rag and she was crying.

The axe had slipped and cut her hand, she told them.

That meant Ma would have to wait on Bella and John.

Lizabeth worked the cotton by herself and the Saturday after Ma laid off, Mr. Davey would not let them have any fat back.

"Y'all can make it on meal and molasses until you work off your debts!" he told Lizabeth.

Ma had said nothing when Lizabeth had told her about the fat back. She had sat still a long time. Then she got up and mixed up some meal.

"What you makin' so much bread to oncet?" Bella asked Ma.

"'Gainst our gittin' hungry!"

"Can't eat all that bread one time!" John blared forth. "Better save some 'cause you might not git no meal next time! We owe so much!"

"Heish, boy!!" Ma screamed so you could hear her half across the field. "I ain't owe nobody nuthin!"

Lizabeth's jaw dropped. "Mr. Davey, he say—!"

"Heish, gal!" Ma screamed again. "I ain't owe nuthin, I say! Been right here workin' nigh on forty years!"

She turned the last scrap of meal into a pan. Then she stood up and looked around the table at three pairs of wide-stretched eyes.

"I'm fixin' this 'gainst we git hungry! We goin' North to find Pa tonight!"

You would not believe that three women and a half-grown boy could get to Federal street, Chicago, from Mississippi without a cent of money to start with.

They walked—they begged rides—they stopped in towns, worked a little, and they rode as far as they could on the train for what they had earned. It took months, but they found Federal street.

But they never found Pa.

They found colored people who had worked the cotton just like they themselves had done, but these others were from Alabama and Georgia and parts of Mississippi that they had never seen.

They found the houses on Federal street were just as grey, just as bare of color and comfort as the hut they had left in Mississippi.

But you could get jobs and earn real money and buy all sorts of things for a little down and a little a week! You could eat what you could afford to buy—and if you could not pay cash, the grocer would put you on the book.

Ma was dazed.

John forgot the misery.

Bella and Lizabeth were looping wider and wider in new circles of joy.

Ma could forget Pa, who was lost, and the hard trip up from the South when she screamed and shouted and got happy in robust leather-lunged style in her store-front church run in the "down-home" tempo.

John spent every cent that he could lay a hand on on a swell outfit, thirty dollars from skin out and from shoes to hat!

Bella's circles of joy spread wider and wider until she took to hanging out with girls who lived "out South" in kitchenettes.

She straightened her hair at first.

Then she curled her hair. After that she "sassed" Ma. Said she was going to get a job in a tavern and stay "out South" too!

They heard she was married.

They heard she was not.

Anyway, she did not come back to 31st and Federal.

John's swell outfit wasn't thick enough to keep the lake winds from his misery. He began to have chills and night sweats. The Sunday he coughed blood, Lizabeth got a doctor from State street.

The doctor made Ma send John to the hospital.

"He be all right soon?" Ma asked after the ambulance had gone.

The doctor looked grim. "I doubt if they can arrest it!"

"Arrest it! Arrest what? John's a good boy! He ain't done nothing to git arrested!"

The doctor looked grimmer. "I mean that maybe they can't stop this blood from coming!"

Ma looked a little afraid. "Well, if they jes' gives him a tablespoon of salt that will stop any bleeding! My mother always—"

The doctor put his hat on and went out. He did not listen to hear any more.

The second fall that they were on Federal street, Lizabeth met Benny, a soft-voiced boy from Georgia.

Benny said he was lonely for a girl who did not want him to spend all his money on liquor and things for her every time he took her out. That is what these city girls all seemed to want.

They wanted men to buy things for them that no decent girl down home would accept from men.

Lizabeth was glad for just a ten-cent movie and a bottle of pop or a nickel bag of peanuts.

They were married at Christmas. The next year, in October, baby Benny came.

In November John died.

In February of the second year Benny—who had begun to go "out South" in the evening with the boys—suddenly stayed away all night.

Ma had hysterics in the police station and told the police to find him.

"He may be dead and run over somewhere!" she kept crying.

The policemen took their time. Ma went every day to find out if there were any news. Lizabeth went too!

She stopped going after she saw the policeman at the desk wink at another when he told her, "Sure! Sure! We are looking for him every day!"

Mrs. Rhone who kept the corner store asked Lizabeth one morning, "Where's your man? Left you?"

Lizabeth bridled: "He was none of these men! He was my husband!"

The other woman probed deeper: "Who married you? That feller 'round to the store front church? Say! Hee-hee! They tell me he ain't no reglar preacher! Any feller what'll slip him a couple of dollars can get 'married'—even if he's got a wife and ten kids 'out South,' they tell me—!"

Lizabeth shrank back. Benny had been truly married to her!!

This woman just did not have any shame!

But after that Lizabeth grew sensitive if she went on the street and saw the women standing together in gossiping groups.

"They talkin' about me! They saying I weren't married!" she would tell herself.

She and Ma moved away.

The place where they moved was worse than Federal street. Folks fought and cursed and cut and killed down in the Twenties in those days.

But rent was cheap.

Lizabeth only got twelve dollars a week scrubbing all night in a theater.

Ma kept little Benny and took care of the house.

There was not much money, but Lizabeth would go without enough to eat and to wear so that little Benny could have good clothes and toys that she really could not afford.

"Every time you pass the store you 'bout buy this boy somethin'!" the grandmother complained once.

"Aw I'd a liked pretty clothes and all that stuff when I was a kid!" Lizabeth answered.

"How she buy so much stuff and just *she* workin'!" the neighbors argued among themselves.

"She must be livin' wrong!" declared those who could understand all the fruits of wrong living in all its multiple forms.

Little Benny grew to expect all the best of things for himself. He learned to whine and cry for things and Lizabeth would manage them somehow.

He was six years old in 1929.

That was the year when Lizabeth could find no more theaters to scrub in and there were no more day's work jobs nor factory jobs. Folks said the rich people had tied up all the money so all the poor people had to go to the relief station.

Lizabeth walked fifteen blocks one winter day to a relief station. She told the worker that there was no coal, no food, the water was frozen, and the pipes had bursted.

"We'll send an investigator," the worker promised.

"When'll that come?" Lizbeth demanded vaguely.

"*She* will come shortly! In a few days, I hope!"

"I got nuthin for Ma and Benny to eat today!" Lizbeth began to explain all over again.

"I'm sorry! That is all we can do now!" The woman behind the desk began to get red as she spoke this time.

"But Benny ain't had no dinner and—"

"Next!" The woman was crimson as she called the next client.

The client—a stout colored woman—elbowed Lizbeth out of the way.

Already dazed with hunger and bone-weary from her freezing walk, Lizbeth stumbled.

"She's drunk!" the client muttered apologetically to the woman behind the desk.

Lizbeth had had enough. She brought her left hand up in a good old-fashioned back-hand wallop.

Everybody screamed. "They're fighting!"

"Look out for a knife!" yelled the woman behind the desk.

Her books had all told her that colored women carried knives.

A policeman came and took Lizbeth away.

They kept Lizbeth all night that night. The next day they said she could go home, but it was the third day that they finally set her on the sidewalk and told her to go home.

Home was thirty blocks away this time.

"Where you been, gal!" Ma screamed as soon as the door opened. "You the las' chile I got and now you start actin' like that Bella! Ain't no food in this house! Ain't a God's bit of fire 'cept one box I busted up—!"

"She busted up my boat! She busted up the box what I play boat in!" Benny added his scream to the confusion. "She make me stay in bed all the time! My stomach hurts me!"

Lizbeth was dizzy. "Ain't nobody been here?" She wanted to wait a little before she told Ma that she had been in the lock-up.

"Nobody been here? For what?"

"Get us some somepin' to eat! That's what the woman said!"

"No, ain't nobody been here!"

Lizbeth put on her hat again.

"Where you goin' now?" Ma shouted.

"I got to go back."

"You got to go back where?"

"See 'bout some somethin' to eat, Ma!"

Benny began to scream and jumped out of the bed. "You stay with me!" he cried as he ran to his mother. "I want my dinner! I—"

"Heish!" Lizbeth out-screamed everyone else in the room.

Frightened, Benny cowed away a little. Then he began again. "I want to eat! The lady downstairs, she say my mother ought to get me somethin' 'stead of stayin' out all night with men!"

Lizabeth stared wildly at her mother.

Hostile accusation bristled in her eyes, too.

"That's what the lady say. She say—," Benny repeated.

And Lizabeth, who had never struck Benny in her life, stood up and slapped him to the floor.

As he fell, the child's head struck the iron bedstead.

His grandmother picked him up, still whimpering.

Lizabeth went out without looking back.

Fifteen blocks put a stitch in her left side. Anger made her eyes red.

The woman behind the desk at the relief station paled when she saw Lizabeth this time. "You will have to wait!" she chattered nervously before Lizabeth had even spoken.

"Wait for what? Been waitin'! Nobody been there!"

"We are over-crowded now! It will take ten days to two weeks before our relief workers can get there!"

"What's Ma and little Benny going to do all that time! They gotta eat!"

The other woman grew eloquent. "There are hundreds and hundreds of people just like you waiting—!"

"Well, I stop waitin'! Benny got to eat!"

Fifteen blocks had put a stitch in her side. Worry and hunger made her head swim. Lizabeth put one hand to her side and wavered against the desk.

This time the woman behind the desk *knew* that Lizabeth had a knife—for her alone! Her chair turned over as she shot up from the desk. Her cries brought the policeman from the next corner.

"We better keep you for thirty days," the police court told Lizabeth when they saw her again.

"But little Benny—!" Lizabeth began crying aloud.

There was a bustle and commotion. A thin pale woman pushed her way up to the desk.

Lizabeth had to draw back. She stood panting, glaring at the judge.

He had been looking at her at first in tolerant amusement. But while this pale woman talked to him across his desk, cold, dreadful anger surged into his eyes.

"What's that you're saying about little Benny?" he demanded suddenly of Lizabeth. "He's dead!"

Lizabeth could not speak nor move at first. Then she cried out, "What happen to him? What happen to my baby?"

"You killed him." The judge was harsh.

A bailiff had to pick Lizabeth up off of the floor and stand her up again so the judge could finish. "You whipped him to death!"

"I ain't never whip him! I ain't never whip little Benny!" Lizabeth cried over and over.

They took her away and kept her.

They kept her all the time that they were burying Benny, even. Said she was not fit to see him again.

Later—in court—Ma said that Lizabeth had "whipped Benny's head" the last time she was at home.

"I ain't hit him but once!" Lizabeth tried to cry it to the judge's ears. "He didn't have nuthin to eat for a long time! That was the trouble."

"There was a deep gash on his head," testified the relief worker. "She was brutal!"

"She brought knives to the relief station and tried to start a fight every time she came there!"

"She's been arrested twice!"

"Bad character! Keep her!" the court decided.

That was why the matron had had to drive Lizabeth to the Women's Reformatory.

She had gone out now to her car. Lizabeth watched her climb into it and whirl around once before she drove away.

"Won't see her no more! She's kinder nice, too," Lizabeth thought.

"It is time for supper! Come this way!" the warden spoke suddenly.

Lizabeth stumbled to her feet and followed him down a long narrow hall lit with one small light.

That relief worker had said she would see that Ma got something to eat.

That seemed to settle itself as soon as they had decided they would send her to this place.

"You will work from dawn to sundown," the matron had said as they were driving up from the city.

She had always done that in Mississippi.

It did not matter here. But she asked one question. "They got a commissary there?"

"A commissary!" The matron was struck breathless when Lizabeth asked this. She had decided that Lizabeth was not normal. She had seemed too stupid to defend herself in court. "She must be interested in food!" the matron had decided to herself.

A slight sneer was on her face when she answered, "Of course they have a commissary! You get your food there!"

Lizabeth had drawn back into her corner and said nothing more.

A commissary. She understood a commissary. The same grey hopeless drudge—the same long unending row to hoe—lay before her.

The same debt, year in, year out.

How long had they said she had to stay?

As long as she lived. And she was only thirty now.

But she understood a commissary and a debt that grew and grew while you worked to pay it off. And she would never be able to pay for little Benny.

50 A MODERN FABLE
Chester Himes

FROM *CROSSROAD*, SUMMER 1939

I. THE GOVERNMENT.

Before all else Senator Harold A. McDull was an American citizen. He oozed Americanism. After that he was in turn a fine upstanding gentleman, the good husband of a gracious wife, the proud father of two children—a boy of fourteen and a girl of twelve—and owner of a comfortable estate consisting of two homes, two cars, and a half million dollars invested.

He was a portly, genial man with an easy laugh and a frank, open face which inspired confidence. To judge from his appearance he had never been hungry, ragged, nor scared, which indeed he had not; and that what little worrying he might have done had been of national, instead of personal, scope.

Although he was a staunch Presbyterian and regularly attended the Sunday services, his personal creed, the one by which he lived, would have read like this: I believe in the constitution of the United States, the American Way, and God; I believe in the freedom of speech, individual initiative, unhampered industry, reasonable taxes, and the . . . . party; I believe that communism is the bane and destruction of the human race and fascism the doctrine of the devil.

Practicing the democracy in which he so firmly believed, he made his children learn the constitution by rote, sent them to public school, and paid his servants living wages. He verbally lambasted Hitler at every opportunity for his treatment of minorities, joked about Mussolini, and deliberately ignored Stalin.

No worthy charity ever knocked and found him absent. In his limited way, having only a half million at his disposal instead of the customary millions, he was as much of a philanthropist as Rockefeller. He gave substantially to the Community Fund, aside from which he donated his time and services to many civic enterprises.

Nor was he a lone eagle of duckling descent. Behind him was a long line of illustrious forebears. On his maternal side there had been a captain who served under George Washington during the Revolutionary War, while his paternal grandparent had been a major under General Grant and died on the field of honor so that, as he was prone to remind his children, ". . . government of the people, by the people, for the people, shall not perish from the earth . . ." His father had been governor of the state, an uncle a member of cabinet and a cousin an ambassador. As for himself, during the World War he had served with distinction in the intelligence division in the capacity of a first lieutenant, and afterwards had gone into public life where he had served in turn as city alderman, state senator, and city mayor.

In view of this, it was only natural, when he was nominated by his party to run for senatorship, that the press speculated upon his presidential "possibilities." He refused to concede, however, that he had any presidential ambitions.

"At the present I am only looking forward to serving the people as their representative in the senate," he told the reporters, "and I shall devote my time and thought toward the preservation of those democratic principles which have made this country a great nation."

This noble purpose was further evidenced by his campaign speeches. When addressing groups composed chiefly of W. P. A. workers and their dependants, he was of the view that no W. P. A. wage should be lower than eighty dollars monthly.

"How can they possibly expect a man with a family to subsist for an entire month on sixty dollars?" he asked.

This brought loud and enthusiastic applause.

To older people, scatterings of Townsendites, he revived the old-age pension ballyhoo, stating emphatically and unequivocally that he thought it a good idea. To the small business men he preached the doctrine of individual initiative; at a banquet in a large hotel he spoke quietly but forcefully on balancing the budget; in rural neighborhoods he vigorously decried the tactics of labor; while at a union meeting he expressed this optimistic forecast: "With greater confidence in the Federal Government, private industry will re-employ the unemployed, wages will be higher, hours shorter."

He was indeed a most versatile man, oratorically.

Everywhere the people, laborers and farmers, butchers and bakers and candlestick makers, doddering oldtimers and disconsolate youngsters, were saying as if in unison,

"Why, that's the most sensible man I've ever heard."

To put it on ice, however, his addresses were sugar-coated with a hundred and fifty thousand dollars worth of tried and true campaigning. It was contended by the opposition that McDull himself put up the bulk of this; but knowing, as you must, how oppositions are, you can take this with a grain of salt.

Naturally, candidate McDull was elected.

II. THE PEOPLE.

W. P. A. laborer Henry Slaughter was no less an American than Senator McDull, although at the time McDull's maternal forebears were conducting themselves so gallantly upon the battlefields of liberty, his were scattered to hell and gone all over the European continent and the island of England. It wasn't until 1850 that the first Slaughter set foot upon this soil, and at that it was more from a lack of love for the British Man of War that he was bent upon deserting than from a love for this country.

But the bullet that caught up with him thirteen years later at the battle of Gettysburg, leaving a Polish-speaking widow and a fatherless lad of ten, was the same kind that killed Major McDull. The blood that flowed from him was just as red as the blood that has been shed by any other person who has fought and died for America, and he gave just as much.

"Hank" was unaware of this obscure heroism on the part of his grandfather. And had he been aware of it, he still would not have been impressed. Americanism did not ooze from Hank. He took it as a matter of course. When they drafted him for the World War he served his twelve months without complaint, three of them in France, but he was glad when it was over.

Never portly and seldom genial, Hank was a tall, lean man of fifty with a narrow, weather-cracked face, grim, tight-lipped mouth, and thinning, nondescript hair. His dull eyes squinted from too many years of watching hot sparks reamed from cold metal and his shoulders stooped from bending over a machine built for a man a good foot shorter.

Now, after seven years of poverty he appeared unutterably weary. Seeing him on the street car of an early winter evening, dirty and disheveled, slack and slow-motioned and shabby, dull and dispirited, one knew immediately that he was a W. P. A. laborer returning home from work.

Unlike Senator McDull, neither Hank nor any of his forebears had ever possessed any presidential qualifications, but for the twelve years following the war, notwithstanding, Hank had been one of the best mechanics in the Hamilton Tool Company.

When the shop had closed in 1930 he had been earning on the average of $73.50 a week. At that time he had owned a small home and a small car and had had a few thousands saved up. But having five children to support, the oldest of whom now at twenty-six never had a job, his savings dwindled very rapidly during his unemployment and by the end of 1932 he was broke. His home went next, and then his car. They moved into a cheaper neighborhood and began renting.

His wife, who had never been gracious, that superb virtue being restricted to the wealthy, began to lose what virtues she did possess. The serene agreeableness which had been her chief attraction soured into tartness. She became less neat as she became more disagreeable, and sagged and was tired and there was no longer any pleasure in her. Finally, as the pinch of poverty intensified and they moved into a neighborhood that was cheaper still, she deteriorated into a shrew.

As his wife became dowdier, Hank's mouth became grimmer and his eyes duller. So that when they had to move again, this time into three rooms in the squalid slums, and go on relief, he was unrecognizable as the same man who used to work at the Hamilton Tool Company.

It was then that he secured his job on the W. P. A. as a laborer earning sixty a month.

Now Hank had been a true believer. While no one had ever defined for him just the exact meaning of the term THE AMERICAN WAY, yet all his life he had believed in the substance of it. If he had been asked to explain just what it was that he believed in, he might have said something like this: "America for Americans, money for work; if you don't work you don't eat; capital's capital and labor's labor and as long as we're satisfied what the hell the 'reds' got to do with it." This belief, though not as loud as Senator McDull's, had been every bit as firm. But during his two years of poverty before getting on W. P. A. and his three years of poverty while on it, he had grown awful sick and goddamned tired of believing in anything.

And then he heard candidate McDull speak. He heard McDull promise, in his sincere, confidence-inspiring voice, to do all in his power to see that every American citizen with a family to support be given the opportunity to earn a living wage. There was more of the same thing that McDull said, there were glittering generalities and meaningless statistics, but all Hank heard was—"an opportunity to earn a living wage."

Against his better judgment he was swayed. A spark of hope burned brightly within his heart.

"Now you take this fellow McDull—," he said to his fellow workers on the job next day, startling them by his sudden emergence from three years of reticence.

"You take the son of a bitch yourself," a wild youngster replied. "You take him and beat him up for bread."

Ignoring the young man, Hank continued. "Now you take McDull, he's the one who's going to do more for this country than anyone. Now you watch and see if he don't. By '40 he'll be in the White House and I'll be back in the shop . . ."

On election day Hank was the first to cast a vote for senatorial candidate McDull.

III. THE DENOUEMENT.

One of the first duties which confronted the congress of which Senator McDull was a recently elected member was consideration of a bill for extended appropriation for the continuance of W. P. A.

Senator McDull contended that such an appropriation would increase the federal deficit to seventy billion dollars—or perhaps it was eighty billion, the numerous accounts that poured out at the time make the exact amount difficult to recall—and that the government could not carry such a debt and remain a democratic nation, so he campaigned tirelessly and zealously against it.

"It will destroy the very foundations of the government which we are fighting to preserve," he argued. "Like a Frankenstein monster it would turn upon us and destroy us."

No one could doubt his sincerity, for he staked his whole public career upon it.

After passing the house by the skin of its teeth, the bill was given to the senate, where, to a great extent due to Senator McDull's determined and unrelenting attack, it was defeated.

Slowly, like a mangled beast, W. P. A. closed up and died. During the following months local relief became clogged and broke down. The local governments could not care for all the cases so they cared for none.

Hank was among the first to be laid off. He and his family suffered greatly. Living, as they had been, from one pay to another, it did not take long for actual hunger to overtake them. Unable to obtain relief they were destitute within the month. Then came a day when they were evicted from their home. Their measly belongings were thrown into the street.

Hank went to a friend and borrowed a gun. Hollow-eyed and hungry, shabby and bearded, with the pistol burning in his pocket, he walked seven miles, out past the end of the car line and down miles of wide paved streets flanked by large houses set back from well kept lawns, until he came to Senator McDull's home.

Who knows what thoughts passed through his mind as he walked those long, weary miles on adamant concrete, hungry and hopeless, or, for that matter, all during the long hungry days when he had stood helplessly by while first his job had been taken, then his food, and now his shelter. Remember, he had heard Senator McDull speak once on the subject of every American citizen being given an opportunity to earn a living wage.

Maybe something wore away in his mind that left him a little crazy. Afterwards, that was what the papers said:

"CRAZY WORKER FIRES AT SENATOR."

"Senator Harold A. McDull, 47, was fired upon by a gunman late this morning as he left his home on Oakpark Drive. Henry Slaughter, a former W. P. A. laborer believed to have become deranged by the closing of W. P. A. and recent family troubles, was arrested at the scene, and confessed to the shooting, according to detectives. No motive for the crime has been established . . ."

Fortunately, Senator McDull was unharmed. But he was thoroughly, genuinely shocked.

"I can understand how a person might object to my political views, even strenuously," he confessed, a little incoherently, to the reporters. "But, my God, politics isn't fatal, it isn't a matter of life and death! Why, the poor man's insane! I've never seen him before in my life, he couldn't possibly have anything against me; why, I couldn't possibly have ever harmed him in any way!"

Hank, of course, was held for investigation. Later he was committed to an insane asylum for observation and from all reports he is still there.

Maybe by 1940 he will get out. Maybe by then the shops will be open and he will get his old job as a mechanic in the tool company back.

On the other hand, perhaps Senator McDull will run for and be elected to the presidency. Perhaps capitalism will have confidence in him and open up the country again and bring back prosperity. Who knows? As far as that goes, who can say what Hank shall be called, a martyr, a hero, or a fool; or whether, after all, the human thing would be just to ignore him.

1940

- Winston Churchill becomes prime minister of Great Britain.
- Exiled Soviet Communist leader Leon Trotsky is assassinated in Mexico City.
- After the fall of France, Britain stands alone as the sole unconquered allied power fighting against Germany.
- The Soviet Union annexes Latvia, Lithuania, and Estonia.
- Franklin D. Roosevelt reelected.
- Booker T. Washington is featured on a U.S. postage stamp, the first African American to be so honored.
- American Negro Theatre organized in Harlem.
- Harlem's Cotton Club goes out of business.
- Richard Wright's *Native Son* is first novel by a black writer chosen as a Book-of-the-Month Club selection.
- Benjamin O. Davis Sr. becomes first black general in U.S. armed forces.

Black population in the United States: 12,865,518 (9.77%)

U.S. unemployment: 14.6%

Lynchings in the United States: 4 blacks, 1 white

Deaths:
 Robert Sengstacke Abbott (29 Feb.)
 Marcus Garvey (10 June)

Spingarn Medal:
 Richard Wright (author)

Books:
 Countee Cullen, *The Lost Zoo* (juvenile poetry)
 W. E. B. Du Bois, *Dusk of Dawn* (autobiography)

Robert Hayden, *Heart-Shape in the Dust* (poetry)
Langston Hughes, *The Big Sea* (autobiography)
John M. Lee, *Counter-Clockwise* (novel)
Claude McKay, *Harlem: A Negro Metropolis* (nonfiction)
Effie Lee Newsome, *Gladiola Garden* (juvenile poetry)
Richard Wright, *Native Son* (novel)

Periodical:
Phylon (1940–current)

51 A MATTER OF RECORD
Ted Poston

FROM *NEW REPUBLIC*, FEBRUARY 1940

The sports editor had gone for the day when the thick-faced young Negro lumbered up the narrow stairway to the editorial offices of our Harlem weekly. He stood in the doorway twisting his greasy cap in his heavy hands and peering uncertainly around the room. Finally he shuffled over to my desk in the corner.

"I got to get a paper, Mister," he said.

I told him the circulation department was downstairs.

"They sont me up here," he said. "It ain't this week's I got to get. It's another'n. The one what's got in it about me fighting this Zivis. I beat him."

Well, when did he fight Zivis, I asked.

He didn't answer right away. One gnarled hand strayed absently to the top pocket of his ragged vest. His thick lower lip trembled slightly and he bit it nervously. It seemed for a moment he might cry.

"I disremember, Mister," he said finally. "I know it was just before Easter. Because I got thirty-five dollars and I bought me a blue suit and I sont five dollars home and—"

His voice trailed off and he stood looking at me beseechingly through eyes whose lids seemed permanently swollen.

Well, if it was sometime around last Easter, I said, we might be able to find it.

"No, sir. It wasn't *last* Easter," he said. "It was three-four Easters ago. It was down in Baltimore, and I beat him. You had it in your paper. My manager, he give me a clipping"—his hand strayed to the vest pocket again—"but I lose it. I leave it in my suit when I pawn it, and they sell the suit."

Was it 1935 or 1934? Did he know the year?

"I disremember what year, Mister." He was biting his lip again. "But I just got to get it. I just *got* to. They won't believe I beat this Zivis. If I can't show this paper, they won't give me this fight Saddidy. And I gets twenty dollars if I fights."

Well, what about his manager? Didn't he have the clipping?

He looked down at his seamed shoes and scuffed them on the floor.

"He ain't my manager no more. I don't know where he's at. He run out on me in Pittsburgh. I lose a fight to Eddie Nolan and he grab the money and scram. I rid the rods back."

I got out the bound volumes of our 1934–35 files and carried them to the copy desk. I told him to look through the sports pages and see if he could find the story. He hesitated a moment and then sat down. I went back to my desk.

In a few minutes he was standing over me again.

"Can you wait a little while, Mister?" he asked. "I'll be right back."

I nodded and he hurried down the steps. A half hour later he came back with a shabbily dressed Negro girl.

"This is my sister, Mister," he said proudly. "She can read. You mind if she reads them papers for me?"

They went to the copy desk and began searching studiously through the files. Two hours later I gave them the 1936–37 volumes. The girl went over each sports page carefully. Finally they closed the books and started whispering. I wasn't surprised when the boy started crying. The girl patted him on the shoulder and came over to my desk.

"We couldn't find it," she said dully.

I told her I was sorry, but she still stood there. She looked around at her brother and then leaned over my desk.

"Mister, would you help us?" she asked suddenly. "Buddy's just got to get this fight. Won't you please help us out?"

But what could I do, I asked. If she couldn't find the story, how could I?

"You could write a letter to the man, Mister. You could say you remember that fight. You could tell him that Buddy beat this Zivis. He'd believe it if he had a letter from a newspaper."

I frowned and glanced over at Buddy. He was sobbing quietly and methodically kicking his worn shoes against the desk. I turned back to his sister.

"That wouldn't be honest," I said lamely. "And besides, your brother shouldn't fight any more. Don't you know he's almost blind? He might get killed or something."

She nodded her head slowly and then burst out crying.

"I know it, Mister. I know it. But he's just *got* to fight this once. We're going to use that twenty dollars to get a bus to Richmond. We've got some cousins there and they can get Buddy a job. We just *got* to do it, Mister."

I felt like a fool, but I wrote the letter. Buddy had the promoter's name on a slip of paper. I wrote that I was in Baltimore in 1935 when Buddy (Killer) Smith outpointed Angelo Zivis in ten rounds. They took the letter and left.

I never saw either of them again, but for a long time I kept a clipping from the following Sunday's *New York Times*. It read:

"Buddy Smith, Negro, 147½, was knocked out by Willie Redmond, 142¼, in the first round of a scheduled four-round prelim."

52 GIRL, COLORED
Marian Minus

FROM *CRISIS*, SEPTEMBER 1940

> Girl, colored, to assist with house-
> work and baby; must be reliable;
> $20 per month. German girl con-
> sidered. Clark, 1112 Highdale Rd.,
> Long Island City.   Advt.

The subway wormed its way through the tunnel that lay below the frenzy and filth of urban streets into the dripping tube that arched its back beneath the river. The air that came in through the half-opened windows was moist and musty, and Carrie's wide brown nostrils flared in sullen offense. She watched the thoughtful contortions of her face reflected in the mirror of the train window, her timid eyes large and staring.

Carrie had come out of the South, the red clay clinging to her misshapen heels, made migrant by the disintegration of a crumbling age. She had been unconscious of the transmission of idea and attitude from age to age until its outworn mechanism and wild momentum had forced her outside the terminals of habit and sour acceptance.

German girl considered. Fear was filling a place which not even thought had filled before.

The train converged on light, and roared upward into high steel trestles. No longer able to see her face in the window, Carrie gave her attention to the neat brown paper bundle in her lap. Her thin fingers with their big knuckles smoothed out the wrinkles in the package. It held her stiffly starched white work dress, a pair of comfortable shoes, and a thick beef sandwich. Even if she got the job, she might not be provided with lunch. Her memory of fainting from hunger on the first day of her last job, six months before, was bitter-sharp.

As she left the train, Carrie hunched her shoulders in sudden fear that she would soon be retracing her steps. She hugged her parcel close to her breast.

"Number ten's over there," she said softly, gaining the street, "so number two must be down there a way."

She walked with a tread that was firmer than the resolution in her heart in the direction of her reasoning. For six months she had answered advertisements. She had related the necessary details of her life to prospective "madams," and she had returned beaten and cynical to her basement room.

She went through a gate and up a gravel path to a small brick house. Her nervous hands played with a dull knocker until sound was forced from the beat of brass on wood. A pale blonde woman opened the door. Wisps of inoffensive hair strayed from the leather thongs of a dozen curlers set at variance on her head.

"Yes?" The woman's voice was spuriously cheerful.

"I come about the job," said Carrie.

The woman opened the door wider. "Come in."

Carrie followed her into an untidy living room.

"We'll go into the kitchen," the woman said, pointing ahead.

Carrie's eyes flickered professionally about the room and her nose lifted on its wide base. They walked through to the kitchen, and she saw the table cluttered with unwashed dishes.

The woman waved her to a seat. "Sit down," she said briefly.

Carrie found a chair and settled on its edge, resting her package on her knees.

"My name is Clark," the woman said. "Mrs. Cado P. Clark."

"I'm Carrie Johnson," Carrie said quickly. She did not have the inclination or energy for a prolonged interview.

"Have you references?" Mrs. Clark asked.

"Yes." A flash of anger that started somewhere deep within her lighted Carrie's eyes. She resented being asked for information before being given any.

"I'll want to see them later," said Mrs. Clark.

Carrie gave her prospective employer an impatient glance. They measured each other in momentary silence. Carrie was the first to speak.

"You want somebody to help with the housework and the baby?" she asked. "At twenty a month?"

"Yes, I do," Mrs. Clark answered. "I want a reliable person. Someone I can put utter trust in."

Carrie did not speak. She smiled wryly and dropped her eyes.

"Have you had much experience?" Mrs. Clark asked. "Have you had to take much responsibility, I mean?"

Carrie shrugged weary shoulders. "I reckon so," she answered shortly. "I been on jobs where I had to do everything under the sun, and I did it. Guess that's being reliable."

Mrs. Clark gave her a sharp look. She murmured unintelligibly.

"Ain't that the right answer to your question?" Carrie parried maliciously.

"Right answer?" Mrs. Clark inquired. "You mean you're trying to give me the answers you think you ought to give, instead of just telling the truth?"

Carrie shrugged again. "I guess I didn't make myself clear," she said in simulated apology.

Mrs. Clark's face brightened. She took a deep breath.

"I want someone to clean, help with the cooking, look after the baby, and do general things about the house," she explained.

"'Bout how long would the hours be?" Carrie asked.

Mrs. Clark calculated quickly. "Well, my husband gets up at seven. He takes breakfast about seven-thirty then he goes to his office. I've been getting his breakfast, but if I get a girl, that'll be changed, of course."

"Oh, certainly," Carrie said with emphasis. "You'll get up 'bout nine then and have your breakfast, won't you, if you get a girl?"

"Yes," Mrs. Clark said eagerly. Then she looked hard at Carrie. She bit her lip and patted the curlers on her head. Carrie snorted audibly.

"Of course, if it'll be too much work for you," Mrs. Clark said waspishly, "I can get a German girl to do it."

The back of Carrie's resentful resistance was broken. She rolled her eyes about the kitchen, seeking some tangible evidence of the competitor whose spirit held nebulous hands at her throat.

"You say you can get a German girl?" she asked uneasily.

"Yes." Mrs. Clark pulled hard at her lip with her even teeth.

Carrie was silent. She did not think for a moment that Mrs. Clark had not already interviewed the omnipresent German girl.

"It's very simple," Mrs. Clark went on. "You see, there are quite a few impoverished refugees in this country now. They can't become public charges so they are very eager to work."

Carrie nodded dumbly. She did not trust herself to speak.

"I think it's wonderful the way they look for work right away after landing in the United States," Mrs. Clark continued, warming to her fantasy. "I've already talked to one of the refugees."

"What'd she say?" Carrie turned miserable eyes on her tormentor.

Mrs. Clark cleared her throat. "She said she'd let me know."

"She didn't think it was too much work for five dollars a week?" Carrie asked in a low voice.

Mrs. Clark looked taken aback. "Why," she stammered, "no."

"I was just wondering."

Carrie looked at the dishes on the table. She saw the smear of childish fingers around the woodwork. She remembered the mussed living-room.

"I don't see how her decision affects you," Mrs. Clark said slyly.

There was an unexpected hint of hardness in her voice that alarmed Carrie. For the first time she wondered if the German girl were not a bogey set up to frighten her by this wily woman. She shook her head and decided to take no chances.

"What about the baby?" she asked, her voice respectful.

"He's no trouble at all," Mrs. Clark said indulgently. "He's only four."

Carrie nodded wearily. "What would you expect me to do exactly?"

"After breakfast," Mrs. Clark elaborated, "there'd be the cleaning. I would expect you to do the marketing. I have a light lunch. In the afternoons you could rinse out a few pieces and do a bit of ironing. Dinner is usually about six-thirty. So you see you could have some free time between lunch and dinner if you got your other duties finished up. Of course, you'd have to take the baby out in the afternoons. After dinner your evenings would be free. Sometimes there is mending to be done. That would take one or two of your evenings a week."

Her recital finished, she waited for Carrie to speak. Carrie's throat was dry. She did not trust herself to do more than croak if she managed to get her mouth open.

"Would you give a day off a week?" she ventured finally.

"Oh, not a whole day," Mrs. Clark said quickly. "Just one afternoon a week. One day a month would be satisfactory."

"Oh." Carrie lifted her shoulders in a weary hunch. "There ain't much I could do with a day off every week nohow," she said philosophically, "if I ain't gonna be making but twenty a month."

There was a sighing silence into which Carrie's spent breath and Mrs. Clark's anxiety issued like desperate winds.

"Would I have a nice room?" Carrie asked after the pause.

Mrs. Clark rose, victorious, then sat down again. "Before we go that far," she said, "I'd like to see your references."

Carrie pulled a thin packet of letters from her purse. She passed them over silently.

"They're very flattering," Mrs. Clark said when she had finished reading.

"They ain't flattering," Carrie retorted. "They're the gospel truth. I worked hard for every word wrote on that paper."

Mrs. Clark rose hastily. "Your room's this way," she said.

They left the kitchen, and Carrie followed her upstairs to a little, box-like room. It was bare except for a bed and one chair.

"The last place I worked had a radio," Carrie said unreasonably.

"It did?" Mrs. Clark asked in surprise. She straightened her shoulders. "I don't approve of servants having too many advantages."

"I b'lieves you," Carrie said shortly. She walked around the room. "The floors ain't bad," she volunteered meaninglessly.

"It's a very nice room," Mrs. Clark said defensively. "It could be home."

Carrie looked at her searchingly. "Madam," she said with dignity, "one little room like this couldn't never be home 'less it was in the house of your loved ones."

"There's a table down in the basement," Mrs. Clark said, ignoring Carrie's remark, "that could be brought up here."

"What about a bureau to keep my clothes in?" Carrie asked. She walked to a closet in one corner of the room. "This ain't got no shelf space," she said, looking in, "for me to use."

"You'd have to use your suitcase."

Carrie sighed. The woman knew that she needed the job, and that she would like it. She was too weary to gamble on finding pleasure in upsetting all of Mrs. Clark's calculations by refusing to stay. She could not face the thought of taking the long, fruitless ride back to Harlem.

"You satisfied with my references?" she asked fearfully.

"Your references are satisfactory," Mrs. Clark said, enigmatically stressing the second word.

"You mean you got some doubts about me personally?" Carrie asked meekly.

"Well," Mrs. Clark informed her, "you understand that I must satisfy myself on every score. After all, you'll be coming into constant and close contact with my child."

"Did the German girl satisfy you?" Carrie asked, almost whispering.

Mrs. Clark nodded slowly. "They really work well," she said. "They don't ask for anything but the chance to make an honest living."

"I think I'd like it here," Carrie said quickly, hating her haste. "If it's all right with you, we could call it settled."

"All right," Mrs. Clark said indifferently. Carrie's released breath rushed through her trembling lips. "I think we can call it arranged. Can you begin working immediately?"

Carrie's face broke into a reluctant smile. She was working again.

"Right away," she said. "But I'll have to go up to Harlem tonight after dinner and pick up my belongings."

"You can't go tonight," Mrs. Clark said coldly. "My husband and I are going out after dinner and you'll have to stay with the baby."

"Oh."

Mrs. Clark read the disappointment on Carrie's face. She breathed deeply and smiled inscrutably.

"I know it's difficult for you to make quick adjustments," she said sweetly. "Perhaps I should hire the German girl after all. They don't have any ties in this country. They have fewer arrangements to make than you, for instance."

"That's all right, ma'am," Carrie said quickly. "I can 'tend to it tomorrow night just as easy."

SOURCES FOR ADDITIONAL SHORT STORIES BY THE AUTHORS

For those authors who have at least one published story collection and/or have had most or all of their short fiction gathered in a posthumous collection, only the collection is indicated below. For authors whose short fiction remains uncollected, individual stories are documented as well as information regarding in what anthologies those stories have been reprinted (where applicable). Marion Vera Cuthbert, Maude Irwin Owens, and Eloise Bibb Thompson do not appear below because they are not known to have published any short fiction other than that which appears in this book.

Gwendolyn B. Bennett
"Tokens," in *Ebony and Topaz* (1927); rpt. in *Double-Take* (2001)

Marita Bonner
Frye Street & Environs (1987)

Arna Bontemps
The Old South: "A Summer Tragedy" and Other Stories of the Thirties (1973)

Anita Scott Coleman
"Phoebe and Peter Up North," in *Half-Century Magazine* (Feb. 1919)
"Love's Power," in *Half-Century Magazine* (May 1919)
"Phoebe Goes to a Lecture," in *Half-Century Magazine* (June 1919)
"Billy Settles the Question," in *Half-Century Magazine* (Aug. 1919)
"The Nettleby's New Year," in *Half-Century Magazine* (Jan. 1920)
"Jack Arrives," in *Half-Century Magazine* (Feb. 1920)
"El Tisico," in *Crisis* (Mar. 1920); rpt. in *Short Fiction by Black Women, 1900–1920* (1991)
"Rich Man, Poor Man," in *Half-Century Magazine* (May 1920)
"Pot Luck," in *Competitor* (Aug.-Sept. 1920)
"The Hand That Fed," in *Competitor* (Dec. 1920)
"The Little Grey House," in *Half-Century Magazine* (July–Oct. 1922); rpt. in *The African American West* (2000)
"Three Dogs and a Rabbit," in *Crisis* (Jan. 1926); rpt. in *The Sleeper Wakes* (1993)
"The Brat," in *Messenger* (Apr. 1926)

"Silk Stockings," in *Messenger* (Aug. 1926); rpt. in *The* Messenger *Reader* (2000)

"G'Long, Old White Man's Gal," in *Messenger* (Apr. 1928)

"White Folks' Nigger," in *Messenger* (May-June 1928)

"The Eternal Quest," in *Opportunity* (Aug. 1931); rpt. in *Harlem's Glory* (1996) and *The* Opportunity *Reader* (1999)

"Two Old Women A-Shopping Go!" in *Crisis* (May 1933); rpt. in *Double-Take* (2001)

W. E. B. Du Bois

Darkwater: Voices from within the Veil (1920)
The Selected Writings of W. E. B. Du Bois (1970)
Creative Writings by W. E. B. Du Bois (1985)

Alice Dunbar-Nelson

Violets and Other Tales (1895)
The Goodness of St. Rocque and Other Stories (1899)
The Works of Alice Dunbar-Nelson (1988)

Jessie Redmon Fauset

"Emmy," in *Crisis* (Dec. 1912–Jan. 1913); rpt. in *Short Fiction by Black Women, 1900–1920* (1991), *Revolutionary Tales* (1995), *The Soul of a Woman* (1996), and *The* Crisis *Reader* (1999)

"My House and a Glimpse of My Life Therein," in *Crisis* (July 1914); rpt. in *Short Fiction by Black Women, 1900–1920* (1991), *Revolutionary Tales* (1995), and *The Soul of a Woman* (1996)

"There Was One Time!" in *Crisis* (Apr.-May 1917); rpt. in *Short Fiction by Black Women, 1900–1920* (1991)

"The Sleeper Wakes," in *Crisis* (Aug.-Oct. 1920); rpt. in *Short Fiction by Black Women, 1900–1920* (1991) and *The Sleeper Wakes* (1993)

"Double Trouble," in *Crisis* (Aug.-Sept. 1923); rpt. in *The Sleeper Wakes* (1993)

Rudolph Fisher

The City of Refuge: The Collected Stories of Rudolph Fisher (1987)
The Short Fiction of Rudolph Fisher (1987)
Joy and Pain (1996)

Mercedes Gilbert

Selected Gems of Poetry, Comedy and Drama (1931)

Eugene Gordon

"Rootbound," in *Opportunity* (Sept. 1926)
"Alien," in *Saturday Evening Quill* (June 1928)
"Cold-Blooded," in *Saturday Evening Quill* (June 1928)
"Buzzards," in *Opportunity* (Nov. 1928)
"Crazy Jesus," in *Saturday Evening Quill* (June 1930)
"The Agenda," in *Opportunity* (Dec. 1933–Jan. 1934)

Ottie B. Graham

"To a Wild Rose," in *Crisis* (June 1923); rpt. in *The Sleeper Wakes* (1993) and
Harlem's Glory (1996)

Angelina Weld Grimké

Selected Works of Angelina Weld Grimké (1991)

Chester Himes

Black on Black: Baby Sister and Selected Writings (1973)
The Collected Stories of Chester Himes (1990)

Langston Hughes

The Ways of White Folks (1934)
Simple Speaks His Mind (1950)
Laughing to Keep from Crying (1952)
Simple Takes a Wife (1953)
Simple Stakes a Claim (1957)
The Langston Hughes Reader (1958)
The Best of Simple (1961)
Something in Common and Other Stories (1963)
Simple's Uncle Sam (1965)
The Return of Simple (1994)
Short Stories (1996)
The Early Simple Stories (2002)
The Later Simple Stories (2002)

Zora Neale Hurston

Spunk: The Selected Stories of Zora Neale Hurston (1985)
The Complete Stories (1995)
Novels and Stories (1995)

Georgia Douglas Johnson

The Selected Works of Georgia Douglas Johnson (1997)

Nella Larsen

An Intimation of Things Distant: The Collected Fiction of Nella Larsen (1992)
The Complete Fiction of Nella Larsen (2001)

John F. Matheus

"Fog," in *Opportunity* (May 1925); rpt. in *The New Negro* (1925), *The Negro Caravan* (1941), *The* Opportunity *Reader* (1999), and *Double-Take* (2001)

"Mr. Bradford Teaches Sunday School," in *Opportunity* (Apr. 1926)

"Clay," in *Opportunity* (Oct. 1926); rpt. in *The* Opportunity *Reader* (1999)

"Swamp Moccasin," in *Crisis* (Dec. 1926); rpt. in *Readings from Negro Authors* (1931)

"General Drums," in *Ebony and Topaz* (1927)

"Coulév' Endormi," in *Opportunity* (Dec. 1929); rpt. in *The* Opportunity *Reader* (1999)

"Nomah," in *Opportunity* (July 1931); rpt. in *The* Opportunity *Reader* (1999)

"The Citadel," in *Crisis* (Nov. 1931)

"La Brutta," in *Opportunity* (Feb. 1936)

"Sallicoco," in *Opportunity* (Aug. 1937)

Claude McKay

Gingertown (1932)
Trial by Lynching: Stories about Negro Life in America (1977)
My Green Hills of Jamaica and Five Jamaican Short Stories (1979)

May Miller

"One Blue Star," in *Opportunity* (July–Sept. 1945); rpt. in *Bitter Fruit* (1999)

Marian Minus

"The Fine Line," in *Opportunity* (Nov. 1939)

"Half-Bright," in *Opportunity* (Sept. 1940)

"If Tom Were Only Here," in *Woman's Day* (June 1945)

"Another Winter," in *Woman's Day* (May 1946)

"The Threat to Mr. David," in *Woman's Day* (June 1947)

"Mr. Oscar Goes to the Market," in *Woman's Day* (July 1947)

"Ambitious Mr. Trueworthy," in *Woman's Day* (June 1948)

"Twice in His Lifetime," in *Woman's Day* (Dec. 1949)

"Women and Mr. Oscar," in *Woman's Day* (Feb. 1951)

"Lucky Man," in *Woman's Day* (June 1951)

Richard Bruce Nugent
 Gay Rebel of the Harlem Renaissance: Selections from the Work of Richard Bruce Nugent (2002)

Leila Amos Pendleton
 "Aunt Calline's Sheaves," in *Crisis* (June 1917); rpt. in *Short Fiction by Black Women, 1900–1920* (1991)

Ted Poston
 The Dark Side of Hopkinsville (1991)

J. Saunders Redding
 "Delaware Coon," in *transition* (June 1930)
 "A Battle behind the Lines," in *Reporter* (9 Jan. 1958)

Florida Ruffin Ridley
 "Two Gentlemen of Boston," in *Opportunity* (Jan. 1926); rpt. in *Harlem's Glory* (1996)
 "Two Pairs of Gloves," in *Saturday Evening Quill* (June 1930)

George S. Schuyler
 "Seldom Seen," in *Messenger* (Nov. 1926)
 "The Shoemaker Murder," in *Pittsburgh Courier* (3 June 1933); rpt. in *Spooks, Spies, and Private Eyes* (1995)

Wallace Thurman
 The Collected Writings of Wallace Thurman (2003)

Jean Toomer
 Cane (1923)
 The Wayward and the Seeking: A Collection of Writings by Jean Toomer (1980)
 A Jean Toomer Reader: Selected Unpublished Writings (1993)

Eric Walrond
 Tropic Death (1926)
 "Winds Can Wake Up the Dead": An Eric Walrond Reader (1998)

Dorothy West
 The Richer, the Poorer: Stories, Sketches, and Reminiscences (1995)

Richard Wright
Uncle Tom's Children (1938)
Eight Men (1961)
Richard Wright Reader (1978)

Octavia B. Wynbush
"The Noose," in *Opportunity* (Dec. 1931); rpt. in *Harlem's Glory* (1996)
"Serena Sings," in *Crisis* (Oct. 1935)
"The Conversion of Harvey," in *Crisis* (Mar. 1936)
"Lady Blanche and the Christ," in *Crisis* (Jan. 1937)
"The Christmas Candle," in *Crisis* (Dec. 1937)
"Conjure Man," in *Crisis* (Mar. 1938); rpt. in *Revolutionary Tales* (1995)
"Bride of God," in *Crisis* (Oct. 1938)
"Ticket Home," in *Crisis* (Jan. 1939)
"The Black Streak," in *Crisis* (Oct. 1945); rpt. in *Bitter Fruit* (1999)

AWARD-WINNING SHORT FICTION FROM *OPPORTUNITY* AND *CRISIS*

The following list denotes short stories that earned prizes in literary contests sponsored by the National Urban League's *Opportunity* and the NAACP's *Crisis*, the two most respected and influential African American magazines in the United States during the 1920s and 1930s. While only short fiction is represented below, the *Opportunity* and *Crisis* contests regularly awarded prizes in separate genre categories (e.g., drama, poetry, essays). However, in a few cases such categorization did not occur, leaving contestants to compete against each other regardless of genre. For this reason, there sometimes was no award-winning short story for a given year or month. Some of the stories identified below are reprinted in this book and as well as in other anthologies and story collections. Regrettably, a few stories were never published and are likely permanently lost to posterity.

Contests Sponsored by Opportunity

OPPORTUNITY LITERARY CONTEST, 1924–25

1st Prize: John Matheus, "Fog"
2nd Prize: Zora Neale Hurston, "Spunk"
3rd Prize: Eric Walrond, "The Voodoo's Revenge"

Honorable Mention: Marita Bonner, "The Hands"—John P. Davis, "Ante Bellum"—Eugene Gordon, "The Examination"—Frank Horne, "A Soul Goes West on the B. & O."—Zora Neale Hurston, "Black Death"— Louis L. Redding, "A Christmas Journey"—Benjamin Young, "All God's Chillun Got Shoes"—Benjamin Young, "The Boll Weevil Starts North"

Judges: Robert Hobart Davis, Dorothy Canfield Fisher, Zona Gale, Fannie Hurst, Alain Locke, Dorothy Scarborough, Edna Worthley Underwood, Carl Van Doren, and Blanche Colton Williams

OPPORTUNITY LITERARY CONTEST, 1925–26

1st Prize: Arthur Huff Fauset, "Symphonesque"
2nd Prize: (tie) Zora Neale Hurston, "Muttsy"—Dorothy West, "The Typewriter"
3rd Prize: Lee Wallace, "The Heritage of the Heathen"
4th Prize: Eugene Gordon, "Rootbound"

Honorable Mention: Carol Carson, "Polly"—John P. Davis, "Waters of Megara"—Pearl Fisher, "High Falutin'"—William V. Kelley, "Black Gum"—John Matheus, "Clay" and "General Drums"—Warren A. McDonald, "A Matter of Inches"—Claude McKay, "High-Ball"

Judges: Zona Gale, Fannie Hurst, Stuart Sherman, Jean Toomer, Carl Van Doren, and Blanche Colton Williams

OPPORTUNITY LITERARY CONTEST, 1926–27

1st & 2nd Prize: (tie) Eugene Gordon, "Game" and Cecil Blue, "The 'Flyer'"

3rd Prize: (tie) Eugene Gordon, "Buzzards" and John P. Davis, "The Overcoat"

Judges: Theodore Dreiser, Zona Gale, Harry Hansen, Wilbur Daniel Steele, Irita Van Doren, and Eric Walrond

Special Buckner Award (for conspicuous promise): Dorothy West, "An Unimportant Man"—Emily May Harper, "Ma Kilpatrick, Boss"

THE VAN VECHTEN AWARD FOR 1927
[AWARDED IN 1928]

Honorable Mention: Claude McKay, "High Ball"—Eloise Bibb Thompson, "Masks"

Judges: Charles S. Johnson, James Weldon Johnson, and Robert Morss Lovett

OPPORTUNITY LITERARY CONTEST, 1931
[AWARDED IN 1932]

Winner: Charles W. Cranford, "A Plantation Episode"

Honorable Mention: Ephraim A. Berry, "Don't Sweep under the Bed!"—Roy De Coverley, "Theme, with Variations"

Judges: Rudolph Fisher, Edward J. O'Brien, and Carl W. Ackerman

OPPORTUNITY LITERARY CONTEST, 1932
[AWARDED IN 1933]

Winner: Arna Bontemps, "A Summer Tragedy"

Honorable Mention: Marita Bonner, "A Possible Triad on Black Notes"
Henry B. Jones, "Gin and Moonlight"—Eugene Gordon, "The Agenda"

Judges: Sterling A. Brown, Fannie Hurst, and Richard Walsh

OPPORTUNITY LITERARY CONTEST, 1933
[AWARDED IN 1934]

Winner: Marita Bonner, "Tin Can"

Honorable Mention: Henry B. Jones, "Cletus"

Judges: Royal Davis, John Farrar, and James Weldon Johnson

Contests Sponsored by Crisis

CRISIS PRIZES IN LITERATURE AND ART, 1925

1st Prize: Rudolph Fisher, "High Yaller"
2nd Prize: Marie French, "There Never Fell a Night So Dark"
3rd Prize: Anita Scott Coleman, "Three Dogs and a Rabbit"

Judges: Charles W. Chesnutt, Sinclair Lewis, Mary White Ovington, and H. G. Wells

CRISIS PRIZES IN LITERATURE AND ART, 1926

1st Prize: John Matheus, "Swamp Moccasin"
2nd Prize: Edmund Drummond Shean, "Death Game"

Honorable Mention: Ethel R. Clark, "In Houses of Glass"—Anita Scott Coleman, "Flaming Flame"

Judges: Charles W. Chesnutt, Otelia Cromwell, and Ernest Poole

CRISIS PRIZES IN LITERARY ART
AND EXPRESSION, 1927

1st Prize: Marita Bonner, "Drab Rambles"
2nd Prize: Brenda Ray Moryck, "Old Days and New," "Days," and "Her Little Brother"

CHARLES WADDELL CHESNUTT,
HONORARIA, 1928

April—1st Prize: Maude Irwin Owens, "Bathesda of Sinners Run"
July—2nd Prize: Frank Horne, "The Man Who Wanted to Be Red"
Sept.–Oct.—2nd Prize: A. L. Shands, "No White Woman"

SELECTED RESOURCES FOR
THE HARLEM RENAISSANCE

Topical Commentary (1919–1940)

Brawley, Benjamin. "The Negro Literary Renaissance." *Southern Workman* Apr. 1927:
177–84.

———. "The Promise of Negro Literature." *Journal of Negro History* 19 (1934):
53–59.

Brown, Sterling A. "Contemporary Negro Poetry (1914–1936)." *Negro Poetry and
Drama*. By Brown. Washington, D.C.: Associates in Negro Folk Education, 1937.
60–81.

———. "Our Literary Audience." *Opportunity* Feb. 1930: 42–46, 61.

———. "The Urban Scene." *The Negro in American Fiction*. By Brown. Washington,
D.C.: Associates in Negro Folk Education, 1937. 131–50.

Davis, Allison. "Our Negro 'Intellectuals.'" *Crisis* Aug. 1928: 268–69, 284–86.

"The Debut of the Younger School of Negro Writers." *Opportunity* May 1924: 143–44.

Du Bois, W. E. B. "Criteria of Negro Art." *Crisis* Oct. 1926: 290–97.

Edmonds, Randolph. "Some Reflections on the Negro in American Drama." *Opportunity* Oct. 1930: 303–05.

Harrison, Hubert. "On a Certain Condescension in White Publishers." *Negro World* 4
Mar. 1922: 7; 11 Mar. 1922: 7.

Holmes, Eugene C. "Problems Facing the Negro Writer Today." *New Challenge* Fall
1937: 69–75.

Hughes, Langston. "Harlem Literati of the Twenties." *Saturday Review of Literature* 22
June 1940: 13–14.

———. "The Negro Artist and the Racial Mountain." *Nation* 23 June 1926: 692–94.

———. "These Bad Negroes: A Critique on Critics." *Pittsburgh Courier* 9 Apr. 1927,
sec. 2: 1; 16 Apr. 1927: 8.

Johnson, Charles S. "The Negro Enters Literature." *Carolina Magazine* May 1927: 3–9,
44–48.

Johnson, James Weldon. "The Dilemma of the Negro Author." *American Mercury*
Dec. 1928: 477–81.

———. "Foreword." *Challenge* Mar. 1934: 2.

———. "Negro Authors and White Publishers." *Crisis* July 1929: 228–29.

———. "Race Prejudice and the Negro Artist." *Harper's Magazine* Nov. 1928: 769–76.

Locke, Alain. "Art or Propaganda?" *Harlem* Nov. 1928: 12.

———. "Beauty Instead of Ashes." *Nation* 18 Apr. 1928: 432–34.

———. "The Negro's Contribution to American Art and Literature." *Annals* [of the
American Academy of Political and Social Science] 140 (1928): 234–47.

———. "The New Negro." *The New Negro: An Interpretation*. Ed. Locke. New York:
Boni, 1925. 3–16.

———. "Our Little Renaissance." *Ebony and Topaz: A Collectanea.* Ed. Charles S. Johnson. New York: Opportunity, 1927. 117–18.

Minus, Marian. "Present Trends of Negro Literature." *Challenge* Apr. 1937: 9–11.

Moryck, Brenda Ray. "A Point of View: An *Opportunity* Dinner Reaction." *Opportunity* Aug. 1925: 246–49, 251–52.

"The Negro in Art: How Shall He Be Portrayed? A Symposium." *Crisis* Mar. 1926: 219–20; Apr. 1926: 278–80; May 1926: 35–36; June 1926: 71–73; Aug. 1926: 193–94; Sept. 1926: 238–39; Nov. 1926: 28–29.

Pickens, William. "Art and Propaganda." *Messenger* Apr. 1924: 111.

Randolph, A. Philip, and Chandler Owen. "The New Negro—What Is He?" *Messenger* Aug. 1920: 73–74.

Redding, J. Saunders. "Emergence of the New Negro." *To Make a Poet Black.* By Redding. Chapel Hill: University of North Carolina Press, 1939. 93–125.

Richardson, Willis. "The Hope of a Negro Drama." *Crisis* Nov. 1919: 338–39.

———. "Propaganda in the Theatre." *Messenger* Nov. 1924: 353–54.

Rogers, J. A. "Who Is the New Negro, and Why?" *Messenger* Mar. 1927: 68, 93–94.

Schuyler, George S. "Advice to Budding Literati." *Messenger* Jan. 1926: 9.

———. "Ballad of Negro Artists." *Messenger* Aug. 1926: 239.

———. "The Negro-Art Hokum." *Nation* 16 June 1926: 662–63.

Thurman, Wallace. "Negro Artists and the Negro." *New Republic* 31 Aug. 1927: 37–39.

———. "Negro Poets and Their Poetry." *Bookman* July 1928: 555–61.

———. "Nephews of Uncle Remus." *Independent* 24 Sept. 1927: 296–98.

Tolson, Melvin B. *The Harlem Group of Negro Writers.* 1940. Westport: Greenwood, 2001.

Walrond, Eric. "Junk." *Negro World* 30 Dec. 1922: 4.

———. "The Negro Literati." *Bretano's Book Chat* Mar.–Apr. 1925: 31–33.

"Welcoming the New Negro." *Opportunity* Apr. 1926: 113.

White, Walter. "The Negro Renaissance." *Palms* Oct. 1926: 3–7.

Wright, Richard. "Blueprint for Negro Writing." *New Challenge* Fall 1937: 53–65.

Periodical Articles

Abramson, Doris E. "Angelina Weld Grimké, Mary T. Burrill, Georgia Douglas Johnson, and Marita O. Bonner: An Analysis of Their Plays." *SAGE* 2.1 (1985): 9–13.

Akam, Everett H. "Community and Cultural Crisis: The 'Transfiguring Imagination' of Alain Locke." *American Literary History* 3 (1991): 255–76.

Ako, Edward O. "Leslie Pinckney Hill's *Toussaint L'Ouverture.*" *Phylon* 48 (1987): 190–95.

Anderson, David. "Sterling Brown's Southern Strategy: Poetry as Cultural Evolution in *Southern Road.*" *Callaloo* 21 (1998): 1023–37.

Avi-Ram, Amitai F. "The Unreadable Black Body: 'Conventional' Poetic Form in the Harlem Renaissance." *Genders* 7 (1990): 32–46.

Bernard, Emily. "What He Did for the Race: Carl Van Vechten and the Harlem Renaissance." *Soundings* 80 (1997): 531–42.

Carroll, Richard A. "Black Racial Spirit: James Weldon Johnson's Critical Perspective." *Phylon* 32 (1971): 344–64.

Cobb, Michael L. "Insolent Racing, Rough Narrative: The Harlem Renaissance's Impolite Queers." *Callaloo* 23 (2000): 328–51.

Condé, Mary. "Passing in the Fiction of Jessie Redmon Fauset and Nella Larsen." *Yearbook of English Studies* 24 (1994): 94–104.

Cooney, Charles F. "Walter White and the Harlem Renaissance." *Journal of Negro History* 57 (1972): 231–40.

Dalsgård, Katrine. "Alive and Well and Living on the Island of Martha's Vineyard: An Interview with Dorothy West, October 29, 1988." *Langston Hughes Review* 12.2 (1993): 28–44.

Daniel, Walter C. "*Challenge Magazine:* An Experiment That Failed." *CLA Journal* 19 (1976): 494–503.

Dean, Sharon, and Erlene Stetson. "Flower-Dust and Springtime: Harlem Renaissance Women." *Radical Teacher* 18 (1980): 1–8.

Deutsch, Leonard J. "'The Streets of Harlem': The Short Stories of Rudolph Fisher." *Phylon* 40 (1979): 159–71.

Elimimian, Isaac I. "Theme and Technique in Claude McKay's Poetry." *CLA Journal* 25 (1981): 203–11.

Emanuel, James A. "Renaissance Sonneteers." *Black World* Sept. 1975: 32–45, 92–97.

English, Daylanne K. "Selecting the Harlem Renaissance." *Critical Inquiry* 25 (1999): 807–21.

Ford, Charita M. "Flowering a Feminist Garden: The Writings and Poetry of Anne Spencer." *SAGE* 5.1 (1988): 7–14.

Gaither, Renoir W. "The Moment of Revision: A Reappraisal of Wallace Thurman's Aesthetics in *The Blacker the Berry* and *Infants of the Spring.*" *CLA Journal* 37 (1993): 81–93.

Gibson, Lovie N. "W. E. B. Du Bois as a Propaganda Novelist." *Negro American Literature Forum* 10 (1976): 75–77, 79–83.

Giles, Freda Scott. "Willis Richardson and Eulalie Spence: Dramatic Voices of the Harlem Renaissance." *American Drama* 5.2 (1996): 1–22.

Goldstein, Philip. "Critical Realism or Black Modernism? The Reception of *Their Eyes Were Watching God.*" *Reader* 41 (1999): 54–73.

Greenberg, Robert M. "Idealism and Realism in the Fiction of Claude McKay." *CLA Journal* 24 (1981): 237–61.

Greene, J. Lee. "Anne Spencer of Lynchburg." *Virginia Cavalcade* Spring 1978: 178–85.

Griffin, Barbara J. "Claude McKay: The Evolution of a Conservative." *CLA Journal* 36 (1992): 157–70.

Harris, Violet J. "Race Consciousness, Refinement, Radicalism: Socialization in *The Brownies' Book.*" *Children's Literature Association Quarterly* 14 (1989): 192–96.

Hart, Robert C. "Black-White Literary Relations in the Harlem Renaissance." *American Literature* 44 (1973): 612–28.

Haslam, Gerald. "Wallace Thurman: A Western Renaissance Man." *Western American Literature* 6 (1971): 53–59.

Helbling, Mark. "Carl Van Vechten and the Harlem Renaissance." *Negro American Literature Forum* 10 (1976): 39–47.

Hughes, Langston. "The Twenties: Harlem and Its Negritude." *African Forum* 1.4 (1966): 11–20.

Hull, Gloria T. "Shaping Contradictions: Alice Dunbar-Nelson and the Black Creole Experience." *New Orleans Review* 15.1 (1988): 34–37.

Hutchinson, George B. "Jean Toomer and the 'New Negroes' of Washington." *American Literature* 63 (1991): 683–92.

———. "Nella Larsen and the Veil of Race." *American Literary History* 9 (1997): 329–49.

Ijeoma, Charmaine N. "Alice Dunbar-Nelson: A Biography." *Collections* 10 (2000): 25–54.

Ikonné, Chidi. "*Opportunity* and Black Literature, 1923–1933." *Phylon* 40 (1979): 86–93.

Jablon, Madelyn. "The Zora Aesthetic." *Zora Neale Hurston Forum* 6.1 (1991): 1–15.

James, Charles L. "On the Legacy of the Harlem Renaissance: A Conversation with Arna Bontemps and Aaron Douglas." *Obsidian* 4.1 (1978): 32–53.

Jenkins, Wilbert. "Jessie Fauset: A Modern Apostle of Black Racial Pride." *Zora Neale Hurston Forum* 1.1 (1986): 14–24.

Johnson, Abby Arthur. "Literary Midwife: Jessie Redmon Fauset and the Harlem Renaissance." *Phylon* 39 (1978): 143–53.

Johnson, Ronald M. "Those Who Stayed: Washington Black Writers of the 1920's." *Records of the Columbia Historical Society* 50 (1980): 484–99.

Jones, Robert. "Jean Toomer as Poet: A Phenomenology of the Spirit." *Black American Literature Forum* 21 (1987): 253–73.

Kelley, James. "Blossoming in Strange New Forms: Male Homosexuality and the Harlem Renaissance." *Soundings* 80 (1997): 499–517.

Kent, George E. "The Soulful Way of Claude McKay." *Black World* Nov. 1970: 37–51.

Lemke, Sieglinde. "Blurring Generic Boundaries: Zora Neale Hurston: A Writer of Fiction and Anthropologist." *REAL* 12 (1996): 163–77.

Levy, Eugene. "Ragtime and Race Pride: The Career of James Weldon Johnson." *Journal of Popular Culture* 1 (1968): 357–70.

Lewis, Vashti Crutcher. "Mulatto Hegemony in the Novels of Jessie Redmon Fauset." *CLA Journal* 35 (1992): 375–86.

Lomax, Michael L. "Fantasies of Affirmation: The 1920's Novel of Negro Life." *CLA Journal* 16 (1972): 232–46.

Long, Richard A. "The Genesis of Locke's *The New Negro*." *Black World* Feb. 1976: 14–20.

———. "A Weapon of My Song: The Poetry of James Weldon Johnson." *Phylon* 32 (1971): 374–82.

Lowe, John. "From Mule Bones to Funny Bones: The Plays of Zora Neale Hurston." *Southern Quarterly* 33.2–3 (1995): 65–78.

Lucky, Crystal J. "The Harlem Renaissance: A Revisionist Approach." *Focus on Robert Graves and His Contemporaries* 1.12 (1991): 25–29.

McCabe, Tracy. "The Multifaceted Politics of Primitivism in Harlem Renaissance Writing." *Soundings* 80 (1997): 475–97.

MacCann, Donnarae. "Effie Lee Newsome: African American Poet of the 1920s." *Children's Literature Association Quarterly* 13 (1988): 60–65.

Manuel, Carme. "*Mule Bone*: Langston Hughes and Zora Neale Hurston's Dream Deferred of an African-American Theatre of the Black Word." *African American Review* 35 (2001): 77–92.

Mason, Julian. "James Weldon Johnson: A Southern Writer Resists the South." *CLA Journal* 31 (1987): 154–69.

Miller, Jeanne-Marie A. "Angelina Weld Grimké: Playwright and Poet." *CLA Journal* 21 (1978): 513–24.

———. "Georgia Douglas Johnson and May Miller: Forgotten Playwrights of the New Negro Renaissance." *CLA Journal* 33 (1990): 349–66.

Miller, R. Baxter. "Café de la Paix: Mapping the Harlem Renaissance." *South Atlantic Review* 65.2 (2000): 73–94.

Moses, Wilson Jeremiah. "More Stately Mansions: New Negro Movements and Langston Hughes' Literary Theory." *Langston Hughes Review* 4.1 (1985): 40–46.

———. "The Poetics of Ethiopianism: W. E .B. Du Bois and Literary Black Nationalism." *American Literature* 47 (1975): 411–26.

Musser, Judith. "African American Women's Short Stories in the Harlem Renaissance: Bridging a Tradition." *MELUS* 23.2 (1998): 27–47.

Patterson, Anita. "Jazz, Realism, and the Modernist Lyric: The Poetry of Langston Hughes." *Modern Language Quarterly* 61 (2000): 651–82.

Perkins, Huel D. "Renaissance 'Renegade'? Wallace Thurman." *Black World* Feb. 1976: 29–35.

Peterson, Bernard L., Jr. "Willis Richardson: Pioneer Playwright." *Black World* Apr. 1975: 40–48, 86–88.

Potter, Vilma. "Counteé Cullen: The Making of a Poet-Editor." *Pacific Coast Philology* 15.2 (1980): 19–27.

Priebe, Richard. "The Search for Community in the Novels of Claude McKay." *Studies in Black Literature* 3.2 (1972): 22–30.

Rampersad, Arnold. "W. E. B. Du Bois as a Man of Literature." *American Literature* 51 (1979): 50–68.

Rayson, Ann. "George Schuyler: Paradox among 'Assimilationist' Writers." *Black American Literature Forum* 12 (1978): 102–06.

Roses, Lorraine Elena, and Ruth Elizabeth Randolph. "Marita Bonner: In Search of Other Mothers' Gardens." *Black American Literature Forum* 21 (1987): 165–83.

Runcie, John. "Marcus Garvey and the Harlem Renaissance." *Afro-Americans in New York Life and History* 10.2 (1986): 7–28.

Scott, Freda L. "Black Drama and the Harlem Renaissance." *Theatre Journal* 37 (1985): 426–39.

Scruggs, Charles W. "Alain Locke and Walter White: Their Struggle for Control of the Harlem Renaissance." *Black American Literature Forum* 14 (1980): 91–99.

———. "'All Dressed Up but No Place to Go': The Black Writer and His Audience during the Harlem Renaissance." *American Literature* 48 (1977): 543–63.

Silberman, Seth Clark. "Looking for Richard Bruce Nugent and Wallace Henry Thurman: Reclaiming Black Male Same-Sexualities in the New Negro Movement." *In Process* 1 (1996): 53–73.

Simmons, Hortense E. "Sterling A. Brown's 'Literary Chronicles.'" *African American Review* 31 (1997): 443–47.

Stepto, Robert. "'When De Saint Go Ma'chin' Home': Sterling Brown's Blueprint for a New Negro Poetry." *Callaloo* 21 (1998): 940–49.

Stetson, Erlene. "Anne Spencer." *CLA Journal* 21 (1978): 400–409.

Stewart, Jeffrey C. "Alain Locke and Georgia Douglas Johnson, Washington Patrons of Afro-American Modernism." *GW Washington Studies* 12 (1986): 37–44.

Story, Ralph D. "Patronage and the Harlem Renaissance: You Get What You Pay For." *CLA Journal* 32 (1989): 284–95.

Sullivan, Megan. "Folk Plays, Home Girls, and Back Talk: Georgia Douglas Johnson and Women of the Harlem Renaissance." *CLA Journal* 38 (1995): 404–19.

Tignor, Eleanor Q. "Rudolph Fisher: Harlem Novelist." *Langston Hughes Review* 1.2 (1982): 13–22.

———. "The Short Fiction of Rudolph Fisher." *Langston Hughes Review* 1.1 (1982): 18–24.

Turner, Darwin T. "Jean Toomer's *Cane.*" *Negro Digest* Jan. 1969: 54–61.

Wade, Carl A. "African-American Aesthetics and the Short Fiction of Eric Walrond: *Tropic Death* and the Harlem Renaissance." *CLA Journal* 42 (1999): 403–29.

Walden, Daniel. "W. E. B. Du Bois: A Renaissance Man in the Harlem Renaissance." *Minority Voices* 2.1 (1978): 11–20.

Waldron, Edward E. "The Blues Poetry of Langston Hughes." *Negro American Literature Forum* 5 (1971): 140–49.

Walker, Alice. "In Search of Zora Neale Hurston." *Ms.* Mar. 1975: 74–79, 85–89.

Walker, Daniel E. "Exploding the Canon: A Re-Examination of Wallace Thurman's Assault on the Harlem Renaissance." *Western Journal of Black Studies* 22 (1998): 153–58.

Washington, Mary Helen. "The Black Woman's Search for Identity: Zora Neale Hurston's Work." *Black World* Aug. 1972: 68–75.

West, Dorothy. "Elephant's Dance: A Memoir of Wallace Thurman." *Black World* Nov. 1970: 77–85.

Williams, Bettye J. "Nella Larsen: Early Twentieth-Century Novelist of Afrocentric Feminist Thought." *CLA Journal* 39 (1995): 165–78.

Wintz, Cary D. "Langston Hughes: A Kansas Poet in the Harlem Renaissance." *Kansas Quarterly* 7.3 (1975): 58–71.

Young, Mary E. "Anita Scott Coleman: A Neglected Harlem Renaissance Writer." *CLA Journal* 40 (1997): 271–87.

Portions of Books
(Essays, Chapters, Introductions)

Berghahn, Marion. "The 'Harlem Renaissance.'" *Images of Africa in Black American Literature.* By Berghahn. Totowa: Rowman, 1977. 118–51.

Bontemps, Arna. "The Negro Renaissance: Jean Toomer and the Harlem Writers of the 1920's." *Anger and Beyond: The Negro Writer in the United States.* Ed. Herbert Hill. New York: Harper, 1966. 20–36.

Brown-Guillory, Elizabeth. "Black Theater Tradition and Women Playwrights of the Harlem Renaissance." *Their Place on the Stage: Black Women Playwrights in America.* By Brown-Guillory. New York: Greenwood, 1988. 1–23.

Byerman, Keith E. "The Propaganda of Art: Ideology and Literary Practice." *Seizing the Word: History, Art, and Self in the Work of W. E. B. Du Bois.* By Byerman. Athens: University of Georgia Press, 1994. 100–14.

Coles, Robert. "Expatriates and the New Negro." *Black Writers Abroad: A Study of Black American Writers in Europe and Africa.* By Coles. New York: Garland, 1999. 71–99.

Davis, Arthur P. "Growing up in the New Negro Renaissance." *Cavalcade: Negro American Writing from 1760 to the Present.* Ed. Arthur P. Davis and Saunders Redding. New York: Houghton, 1971. 428–37.

Flynn, Joyce. Introduction. *Frye Street and Environs: The Collected Works of Marita Bonner.* Ed. Joyce Flynn and Joyce Occomy Stricklin. Boston: Beacon, 1987. xi–xxvii.

Garber, Eric. "A Spectacle in Color: The Lesbian and Gay Subculture of Jazz Age Harlem." *Hidden from History: Reclaiming the Gay and Lesbian Past.* Ed. Martin B. Duberman, Martha Vicinus, and George Chauncey, Jr. New York: New American Library, 1989. 318–31.

Grandel, Hartmut. "The Role of Music in the Self-Reflexive Poetry of the Harlem Renaissance." *Poetics in the Poem: Critical Essays on American Self-Reflexive Poetry.* Ed. Dorothy Z. Baker. New York: Lang, 1997. 119–31.

Gruesser, John Cullen. "The New Negro and Africa." *Black on Black: Twentieth-Century African American Writing about Africa.* By Gruesser. Lexington: University Press of Kentucky, 2000. 50–93.

Gysin, Fritz. "Black Pulp Fiction: George Schuyler's Caustic Vision of a Panafrican Empire." *Empire: American Studies.* Ed. John G. Blair and Reinhold Wagnleitner. Tübingen: Narr, 1997. 167–79.

Hill, Robert A. Introduction. *Ethiopian Stories.* By George S. Schuyler. Boston: Northeastern University Press, 1994. 1–50.

Hull, Gloria T. "'Under the Days': The Buried Life and Poetry of Angelina Weld Grimké." *Home Girls: A Black Feminist Anthology.* Ed. Barbara Smith. New York: Kitchen Table, 1983. 73–82.

Hutchinson, George B. "The Whitman Legacy and the Harlem Renaissance." *Walt Whitman: The Centennial Essays.* Ed. Ed Folsom. Iowa City: University of Iowa Press, 1994. 201–16.

Jackson, Blyden. "Harlem Renaissance in the Twenties." *The Waiting Years: Essays on American Negro Literature.* By Jackson. Baton Rouge: Louisiana State University Press, 1976. 165–78.

Jackson, Blyden, and Warren French. "Jean Toomer's *Cane:* An Issue of Genre." *The Twenties: Fiction, Poetry, Drama.* Ed. French. Deland: Everett/Edwards, 1975. 317–33.

Klotman, Phyllis. "The Black Writer in Hollywood, circa 1930: The Case of Wallace Thurman." *Black American Cinema.* Ed. Manthia Diawara. New York: Routledge, 1993. 80–92.

Lawson, Benjamin S. "George S. Schuyler and the Fate of Early African-American Science Fiction." *Impossibility Fiction: Alternativity—Extrapolation—Speculation.* Ed. Derek Littlewood and Peter Stockwell. Amsterdam: Rodopi, 1996. 87–105.

Lewis, David Levering. "Harlem Renaissance." *Africana: The Encyclopedia of the African and African American Experience.* Ed. Kwame Anthony Appiah and Henry Louis Gates Jr. New York: Basic Civitas, 1999.

———. "Harlem Renaissance." *Encyclopedia of African-American Culture and History.* Vol. 3. Ed. Jack Salzman, David Lionel Smith, and Cornel West. New York: Simon, 1996.

Long, Richard A. "Alain Locke and Afro-American Fiction." *Swords upon This Hill: Preserving the Literary Tradition of Black Colleges and Universities.* Ed. Burney J. Hollis. Baltimore: Morgan State University Press, 1984. 44–57.

Lucky, Crystal J. "Black Women Writers of the Harlem Renaissance." *Challenging Boundaries: Gender and Periodization.* Ed. Joyce W. Warren and Margaret Dickie. Athens: University of Georgia Press, 2000. 91–106.

McCluskey, John, Jr. Introduction. *The City of Refuge: The Collected Stories of Rudolph Fisher.* Ed. McCluskey. Columbia: University of Missouri Press, 1987. xi–xxxix.

McDowell, Deborah E. "The Neglected Dimension of Jessie Redmon Fauset." *Conjuring: Black Women, Fiction, and Literary Tradition.* Ed. Marjorie Pryse and Hortense J. Spillers. Bloomington: Indiana University Press, 1985. 86–104.

Miller, James A. "African-American Writing of the 1930s: A Prologue." *Radical Revisions: Rereading 1930s Culture.* Ed. Bill Mullen and Sherry Lee Linkon. Urbana: University of Illinois Press, 1996. 78–90.

Miller, Ruth, and Peter J. Katopes. "The Harlem Renaissance: Arna W. Bontemps, Countee Cullen, James Weldon Johnson, Claude McKay, and Jean Toomer." *Black American Writers: Bibliographical Essays.* Vol. 1. Ed. M. Thomas Inge, Maurice Duke, and Jackson R. Bryer. New York: St. Martin's, 1978. 161–86.

Mitchell, Verner D. Introduction. *This Waiting for Love: Helene Johnson, Poet of the Harlem Renaissance.* Ed. Mitchell. Amherst: University of Massachusetts Press, 2000. 3–20.

Neal, Larry. "Langston Hughes: Black America's Poet Laureate." *American Writing Today.* Ed. Richard Kostelanetz. Troy: Whitston, 1991. 61–72.

Parascandola, Louis J. Introduction. *"Winds Can Wake Up the Dead": An Eric Walrond Reader.* Ed. Parascandola. Detroit: Wayne State University Press, 1998. 11–42.

Russell, Sandi. "Words to a White World." *Render Me My Song: African-American Women Writers from Slavery to the Present.* By Russell. London: Pandora, 1990. 20–34.

Sanders, Leslie Catherine. "'How Shall the Negro Be Portrayed?' Willis Richardson and Randolph Edmonds, the Pioneers." *The Development of Black Theater in America: From Shadows to Selves.* By Sanders. Baton Rouge: Louisiana State University Press, 1988. 19–61.

Schroeder, Patricia R. "Remembering the Disremembered: Feminist Realists of the Harlem Renaissance." *Realism and the American Dramatic Tradition.* Ed. William W. Demastes. Tuscaloosa: University of Alabama Press, 1996. 91–106.

Shockley, Ann Allen. "Afro-American Women Writers: The New Negro Movement, 1924–1933." *Rereading Modernism: New Directions in Feminist Criticism.* Ed. Lisa Rado. New York: Garland, 1994. 123–35.

Smith, Charles Michael. "Bruce Nugent: Bohemian of the Harlem Renaissance." *In the Life: A Black Gay Anthology.* Ed. Joseph Beam. Boston: Alyson, 1986. 209–20.

Tate, Claudia. Introduction. *The Selected Works of Georgia Douglas Johnson.* New York: Hall, 1997. xvii–lxxx.

Tyler, Bruce M. "The Art Ideology of the Harlem Renaissance." *From Harlem to Hollywood: The Struggle for Racial and Cultural Democracy, 1920–1943.* By Tyler. New York: Garland, 1992. 3–33.

Washington, Robert E. "The Era of the Primitivist School: The Beginning of Black American Literature's Public Role." *The Ideologies of African American Literature: From the Harlem Renaissance to the Black Nationalist Revolt.* By Washington. Lanham: Rowman, 2001. 13–117.

Whitlow, Roger. "1920–1940: The Harlem Renaissance and Its Influence." *Black American Literature: A Critical History.* By Whitlow. Chicago: Hall, 1973. 71–106.

———. "Alice Dunbar-Nelson: New Orleans Writer." *Regionalism and the Female Imagination: A Collection of Essays.* Ed. Emily Toth. New York: Human Sciences, 1985. 109–25.

Wirth, Thomas H. Introduction. *Gay Rebel of the Harlem Renaissance: Selections from the Work of Richard Bruce Nugent.* Ed. Wirth. Durham: Duke University Press, 2002. 1–61.

Books about Specific Authors

Allen, Carol. *Black Women Intellectuals: Strategies of Nation, Family, and Neighborhood in the Works of Pauline Hopkins, Jessie Fauset, and Marita Bonner.* New York: Garland, 1998.

Aptheker, Herbert. *The Literary Legacy of W. E. B. Du Bois.* White Plains: Kraus, 1989.

Baker, Houston A., Jr. *A Many-Colored Coat of Dreams: The Poetry of Countee Cullen.* Detroit: Broadside, 1974.

Benson, Brian Joseph, and Mabel Mayle Dillard. *Jean Toomer.* Boston: Twayne, 1980.

Bloom, Harold, ed. *Zora Neale Hurston.* New York: Chelsea, 1986.

Boyd, Valerie. *Wrapped in Rainbows: The Life of Zora Neale Hurston.* New York: Scribner, 2003.

Bronz, Stephen H. *Roots of Negro Racial Consciousness: The 1920's: Three Harlem Renaissance Authors.* New York: Libra, 1964. [James Weldon Johnson, Countee Cullen, and Claude McKay]

Byrd, Rudolph P. *Jean Toomer's Years with Gurdjieff: Portrait of an Artist, 1923–1936.* Athens: University of Georgia Press, 1990.

Cooper, Wayne F. *Claude McKay: Rebel Sojourner in the Harlem Renaissance: A Biography.* Baton Rouge: Louisiana State University Press, 1987.

Cronin, Gloria L., ed. *Critical Essays on Zora Neale Hurston.* New York: Hall, 1998.

Davis, Thadious M. *Nella Larsen, Novelist of the Harlem Renaissance: A Woman's Life Unveiled.* Baton Rouge: Louisiana State University Press, 1994.

Durham, Frank, comp. *The Merrill Studies in* Cane. Columbus: Merrill, 1971.

Emanuel, James A. *Langston Hughes.* Boston: Twayne, 1967.

Fabre, Geneviève, and Michel Feith, eds. *Jean Toomer and the Harlem Renaissance.* New Brunswick: Rutgers University Press, 2001.

Ferguson, Blanche E. *Countee Cullen and the Negro Renaissance.* New York: Dodd, 1966.

Fleming, Robert E. *James Weldon Johnson.* Boston: Twayne, 1987.

Gabbin, Joanne V. *Sterling A. Brown: Building the Black Aesthetic Tradition.* Westport: Greenwood, 1985.

Gates, Henry Louis, Jr., and K. A. Appiah, eds. *Langston Hughes: Critical Perspectives Past and Present.* New York: Amistad, 1993.

———. *Zora Neale Hurston: Critical Perspectives Past and Present.* New York: Amistad, 1993.

Gayle, Addison, Jr. *Claude McKay: The Black Poet at War.* Detroit: Broadside, 1972.

Giles, James R. *Claude McKay.* Boston: Twayne, 1976.

Gray, Christine Rauchfuss. *Willis Richardson, Forgotten Pioneer of African-American Drama.* Westport: Greenwood, 1999.

Greene, J. Lee. *Time's Unfading Garden: Anne Spencer's Life and Poetry.* Baton Rouge: Louisiana State University Press, 1977.

Harris, Leonard, ed. *The Critical Pragmatism of Alain Locke: A Reader on Value Theory, Aesthetics, Community, Culture, Race, and Education.* Lanham: Rowman, 1999.

Hemenway, Robert E. *Zora Neale Hurston: A Literary Biography.* Urbana: University of Illinois Press, 1977.

Horne, Gerald, and Mary Young, eds. *W. E. B. Du Bois: An Encyclopedia.* Westport: Greenwood, 2001.

Howard, Lillie P. *Zora Neale Hurston.* Boston: Twayne, 1980.

Hull, Gloria T. *Color, Sex, and Poetry: Three Women Writers of the Harlem Renaissance.* Bloomington: Indiana University Press, 1987. [Alice Dunbar-Nelson, Angelina Weld Grimké, and Georgia Douglas Johnson]

James, Winston. *A Fierce Hatred of Injustice: Claude McKay's Jamaica and His Poetry of Rebellion.* London: Verso, 2000.

Janken, Kenneth Robert. *White: The Biography of Walter White, Mr. NAACP.* New York: New, 2003.

Jemie, Onwuchekwa. *Langston Hughes: An Introduction to the Poetry.* New York: Columbia University Press, 1976.

Jones, Kirkland C. *Renaissance Man from Louisiana: A Biography of Arna Wendell Bontemps.* Westport: Greenwood, 1992.

Jones, Sharon L. *Rereading the Harlem Renaissance: Race, Class, and Gender in the Fiction of Jessie Fauset, Zora Neale Hurston, and Dorothy West.* Westport: Greenwood, 2002.

Kellner, Bruce. *Carl Van Vechten and the Irreverent Decades.* Norman: University of Oklahoma Press, 1968.

Kerman, Cynthia Earl, and Richard Eldridge. *The Lives of Jean Toomer: A Hunger for Wholeness.* Baton Rouge: Louisiana State University Press, 1987.

Larson, Charles R. *Invisible Darkness: Jean Toomer and Nella Larsen.* Iowa City: University of Iowa Press, 1993.

Leuders, Edward. *Carl Van Vechten and the Twenties.* Albuquerque: University of New Mexico Press, 1955.

Levy, Eugene. *James Weldon Johnson: Black Leader, Black Voice.* Chicago: University of Chicago Press, 1973.

Lewis, David Levering. *W. E. B. Du Bois: The Fight for Equality and the American Century, 1919–1963.* New York: Holt, 2000.

Linnemann, Russell J., ed. *Alain Locke: Reflections on a Modern Renaissance Man.* Baton Rouge: Louisiana State University Press, 1982.

McKay, Nellie Y. *Jean Toomer, Artist: A Study of His Literary Life and Work, 1894–1936.* Chapel Hill: University of North Carolina Press, 1984.

McLaren, Joseph. *Langston Hughes: Folk Dramatist in the Protest Tradition, 1921–1943.* Westport: Greenwood, 1997.

McLendon, Jacquelyn Y. *The Politics of Color in the Fiction of Jessie Fauset and Nella Larsen.* Charlottesville: University Press of Virginia, 1995.

McLeod, A. L., ed. *Claude McKay: Centennial Studies.* New Delhi: Sterling, 1992.

Martin, Tony. *Literary Garveyism: Garvey, Black Arts, and the Harlem Renaissance.* Dover: Majority, 1983.

Miller, Ericka M. *The Other Reconstruction: Where Violence and Womanhood Meet in the Writings of Wells-Barnett, Grimké, and Larsen.* New York: Garland, 2000.

Miller, R. Baxter. *The Art and Imagination of Langston Hughes.* Lexington: University Press of Kentucky, 1989.

Moore, Jack B. *W. E. B. Du Bois.* Boston: Twayne, 1981.

Mullen, Edward J., ed. *Critical Essays on Langston Hughes.* Boston: Hall, 1986.

Notten, Eleonore van. *Wallace Thurman's Harlem Renaissance.* Amsterdam: Rodopi, 1994.

O'Daniel, Therman B., ed. *Jean Toomer: A Critical Evaluation.* Washington, D.C.: Howard University Press, 1988.

Ostrom, Hans. *Langston Hughes: A Study of the Short Fiction.* New York: Twayne, 1993.

———. *A Langston Hughes Encyclopedia.* Westport: Greenwood, 2002.

Peplow, Michael W. *George S. Schuyler.* Boston: Twayne, 1980.

Plant, Deborah G. *Every Tub Must Sit on Its Own Bottom: The Philosophy and Politics of Zora Neale Hurston.* Urbana: University of Illinois Press, 1995.

Price, Kenneth M., and Lawrence J. Oliver, eds. *Critical Essays on James Weldon Johnson.* New York: Hall, 1997.

Rampersad, Arnold. *The Art and Imagination of W. E. B. Du Bois.* Cambridge: Harvard University Press, 1976.

———. *The Life of Langston Hughes.* 2nd ed. 2 vols. Oxford: Oxford University Press, 2002.

Sanders, Mark A. *Afro-Modernist Aesthetics and the Poetry of Sterling A. Brown.* Athens: University of Georgia Press, 1999.

Scruggs, Charles. *The Sage in Harlem: H. L. Mencken and the Black Writers of the 1920s.* Baltimore: Johns Hopkins University Press, 1984.

Shucard, Alan R. *Countee Cullen.* Boston: Twayne, 1984.

Sylvander, Carolyn Wedin. *Jessie Redmon Fauset, Black American Writer.* Troy: Whitston, 1981.

Tillery, Tyrone. *Claude McKay: A Black Poet's Struggle for Identity.* Amherst: University of Massachusetts Press, 1992.

Trotman, C. James, ed. *Langston Hughes: The Man, His Art, and His Continuing Influence.* New York: Garland, 1995.

Turner, Darwin T. *In a Minor Chord: Three Afro-American Writers and Their Search for Identity.* Carbondale: Southern Illinois University Press, 1971. [Jean Toomer, Countee Cullen, and Zora Neale Hurston]

Waldron, Edward E. *Walter White and the Harlem Renaissance.* Port Washington: Kennikat, 1978.

Wall, Cheryl A., ed. *Zora Neale Hurston's* Their Eyes Were Watching God: *A Casebook.* Oxford: Oxford University Press, 2000.

Washington, Johnny. *A Journey into the Philosophy of Alain Locke.* Westport: Greenwood, 1994.

Books of General Criticism

Aberjhani, and Sandra L. West. *Encyclopedia of the Harlem Renaissance.* New York: Facts on File, 2003.

Abramson, Doris E. *Negro Playwrights in the American Theatre, 1925–1959.* New York: Columbia University Press, 1969. [chaps. 2 and 3]

Baker, Houston A., Jr. *Modernism and the Harlem Renaissance.* Chicago: University of Chicago Press, 1987.

Balshaw, Maria. *Looking for Harlem: Urban Aesthetics in African American Literature.* London: Pluto, 2000.

Bassett, John E. *Harlem in Review: Critical Reactions to Black American Writers, 1917–1939.* Selinsgrove: Susquehanna University Press, 1992.

Bone, Robert. *Down Home: Origins of the Afro-American Short Story.* New York: Columbia University Press, 1988.

Bontemps, Arna, ed. *The Harlem Renaissance Remembered.* New York: Dodd, 1972.

Davis, Arthur P. *From the Dark Tower: Afro-American Writers, 1900 to 1960.* Washington, D.C.: Howard University Press, 1974.

de Jongh, James. *Vicious Modernism: Black Harlem and the Literary Imagination.* Cambridge: Cambridge University Press, 1990. [chaps. 1–4]

Fabre, Geneviève, and Michel Feith, eds. *Temples for Tomorrow: Looking Back at the Harlem Renaissance.* Bloomington: Indiana University Press, 2001.

Harris, Trudier, ed. *Afro-American Writers from the Harlem Renaissance to 1940.* Dictionary of Literary Biography. Vol. 51. Detroit: Gale, 1987.

Helbling, Mark. *The Harlem Renaissance: The One and the Many.* Westport: Greenwood, 1999.

Huggins, Nathan Irvin. *Harlem Renaissance.* New York: Oxford University Press, 1971.

Hutchinson, George. *The Harlem Renaissance in Black and White.* Cambridge: Harvard University Press, 1995.

Ikonné, Chidi. *From Du Bois to Van Vechten: The Early New Negro Literature, 1903–1926.* Westport: Greenwood, 1981.

Johnson, Abby Arthur, and Ronald Maberry Johnson. *Propaganda and Aesthetics: The Literary Politics of Afro-American Magazines in the Twentieth Century.* Amherst: University of Massachusetts Press, 1979.

Kellner, Bruce, ed. *The Harlem Renaissance: A Historical Dictionary for the Era.* Westport: Greenwood, 1984.

Kramer, Victor A., ed. *The Harlem Renaissance Re-Examined.* New York: AMS, 1987.

Kramer, Victor A., and Robert A. Russ, eds. *Harlem Renaissance Re-Examined: A Revised and Expanded Edition.* Troy: Whitston, 1997.

Lewis, David Levering. *When Harlem Was in Vogue.* New York: Knopf, 1981.

Logan, Rayford W., Eugene C. Holmes, and G. Franklin Edwards, eds. *The New Negro Thirty Years Afterward: Papers Contributed to the Sixteenth Annual Spring Conference of the Division of the Social Sciences, April 20, 21, and 22, 1955.* Washington, D.C.: Howard University Press, 1955.

McConnell, William S., ed. *Harlem Renaissance.* San Diego: Greenhaven, 2003.

Maxwell, William J. *New Negro, Old Left: African-American Writing and Communism between the Wars.* New York: Columbia University Press, 1999.

Mishkin, Tracy. *The Harlem and Irish Renaissances: Language, Identity, and Represen-tation.* Gainesville: University Press of Florida, 1998.

Nelson, Emmanuel S., ed. *African American Authors, 1745–1945: A Bio-Bibliographi-cal Critical Sourcebook.* Westport: Greenwood, 2000.

Perry, Margaret. *The Harlem Renaissance: An Annotated Bibliography and Commen-tary.* New York: Garland, 1982.

———. *Silence to the Drums: A Survey of the Literature of the Harlem Renaissance.* Westport: Greenwood, 1976.

Peterson, Bernard L., Jr. *Early Black American Playwrights and Dramatic Writers: A Biographical Directory and Catalog of Plays, Films, and Broadcasting Scripts.* New York: Greenwood, 1990.

Rodgers, Marie E. *The Harlem Renaissance: An Annotated Reference Guide for Student Research.* Englewood: Libraries Unlimited, 1998.

Roses, Lorraine Elena, and Ruth Elizabeth Randolph. *Harlem Renaissance and Be-yond: Literary Biographies of 100 Black Women Writers, 1900–1945.* Boston: Hall, 1990.

Schwarz, A. B. Christa. *Gay Voices of the Harlem Renaissance.* Bloomington: Indiana University Press, 2003.

Shafer, Yvonne. *American Women Playwrights, 1900–1950.* New York: Lang, 1995.

Singh, Amritjit. *The Novels of the Harlem Renaissance: Twelve Black Writers, 1923–1933.* University Park: Pennsylvania State University Press, 1976.

Singh, Amritjit, William S. Shiver, and Stanley Brodwin, eds. *The Harlem Renaissance: Revaluations.* New York: Garland, 1989.

Smith, Valerie, ed. *African American Writers.* 2nd ed. New York: Scribner's, 2001.

Vincent, Theodore G., ed. *Voices of a Black Nation: Political Journalism in the Harlem Renaissance.* San Francisco: Ramparts, 1973.

Wagner, Jean. *Black Poets of the United States: From Paul Laurence Dunbar to Langston Hughes.* Urbana: University of Illinois Press, 1973.

Wall, Cheryl A. *Women of the Harlem Renaissance.* Bloomington: Indiana University Press, 1995.

Watson, Steven. *The Harlem Renaissance: Hub of African-American Culture, 1920–1930.* New York: Pantheon, 1995.

Wintz, Cary D. *Black Culture and the Harlem Renaissance.* Houston: Rice University Press, 1988.

———, ed. *The Harlem Renaissance, 1920–1940.* 7 vols. New York: Garland, 1996.

Witalec, Janet, ed. *The Harlem Renaissance: A Gale Critical Companion.* 3 vols. De-troit: Gale, 2003.

Young, James O. *Black Writers of the Thirties.* Baton Rouge: Louisiana State University Press, 1973.

Autobiographies by Harlem Renaissance Authors

Du Bois, W. E. B. *The Autobiography of W. E. B. Du Bois.* New York: International, 1968.

———. *Dusk of Dawn: An Essay toward an Autobiography of a Race Concept.* New York: Harcourt, 1940.

Hughes, Langston. *The Big Sea: An Autobiography.* New York: Knopf, 1940.

———. *I Wonder as I Wander: An Autobiographical Journey.* New York: Rinehart, 1956.

Hurston, Zora Neale. *Dust Tracks on a Road: An Autobiography.* Philadelphia: Lippincott, 1942.

———. *Dust Tracks on a Road: An Autobiography.* 2nd ed. Urbana: University of Illinois Press, 1984.

Johnson, James Weldon. *Along This Way: The Autobiography of James Weldon Johnson.* New York: Viking, 1933.

McKay, Claude. *A Long Way from Home.* New York: Furman, 1937.

———. *My Green Hills of Jamaica and Five Jamaican Short Stories.* Kingston: Heinemann, 1979.

Schuyler, George S. *Black and Conservative: The Autobiography of George S. Schuyler.* New Rochelle: Arlington, 1966.

White, Walter. *A Man Called White: The Autobiography of Walter White.* New York: Viking, 1948.

A Selected Checklist of Common Issues, Topics, and Plot Components

	marriage, family	parenthood, pregnancy	male-female relations	intra-/interracial relations	interracial male-female relations	prejudice, racism, racial violence	law, crime, imprisonment, war	business, economics, income	(un)employment, profession	religion, superstition, supernatural	science, technology, arts	education, literacy, storytelling	health (physical and/or mental), drugs	death, murder	immigration, migration	foreign culture/location
Anthropoi (John F. Matheus)	•	•	•		•	•	•	•	•						•	•
Barrel Staves (Arna Bontemps)	•		•				•	•	•							
Bathesda of Sinners Run (Maude Irwin Owens)	•	•	•	•	•	•		•		•			•			
Becky (Jean Toomer)	•	•	•	•	•	•				•			•			
Blue Aloes (Ottie B. Graham)	•		•	•	•					•				•	•	•
City Love (Eric Walrond)	•	•	•												•	•
The City of Refuge (Rudolph Fisher)			•			•	•	•	•				•	•	•	•
The Closing Door (Angelina Weld Grimké)	•	•	•	•		•	•							•	•	
The Comet (W. E. B. Du Bois)	•	•	•	•	•	•					•		•	•		
Cordelia the Crude (Wallace Thurman)	•		•				•	•						•		
Crazy Mary (Claude McKay)	•	•	•							•	•	•	•	•		•
Cross Crossings Cautiously (Anita Scott Coleman)	•	•		•	•	•		•	•							
Door-Stops (May Miller)	•	•	•				•							•	•	
The Eatonville Anthology (Zora Neale Hurston)	•	•	•				•					•		•		
Esther (Jean Toomer)		•								•	•					
The Foolish and the Wise: Sallie Runner ... (Leila Amos Pendleton)	•		•	•	•		•			•	•		•		•	•
The Foolish and the Wise: Sanctum 777 ... (Leila Amos Pendleton)	•		•		•		•						•		•	•

525

	marriage, family	parenthood, pregnancy	male-female relations	intra-/interracial relations	interracial male-female relations	prejudice, racism, racial violence	law, crime, imprisonment, war	business, economics, income	(un)employment, profession	religion, superstition, supernatural	science, technology, arts	education, literacy, storytelling	health (physical and/or mental), drugs	death, murder	immigration, migration	foreign culture/location
Game (Eugene Gordon)	•		•					•	•					•		
Gesture (Georgia Douglas Johnson)			•								•					
Girl, Colored (Marian Minus)				•		•		•	•						•	
The Golden Penknife (S. Miller Johnson)	•	•	•	•	•	•	•	•	•	•			•	•	•	•
Grist in the Mill (Wallace Thurman)			•			•	•	•			•			•	•	
Hannah Byde (Dorothy West)	•	•	•											•		
Hate Is Nothing (Marita Bonner)	•	•	•	•		•	•	•						•	•	
He Must Think It Out (Florida Ruffin Ridley)	•	•		•	•	•	•	•	•							
Highball (Claude McKay)	•		•	•	•	•				•		•				
His Last Day (Chester Himes)			•				•	•	•					•		
Hope Deferred (Alice Dunbar-Nelson)	•		•	•		•	•	•	•		•	•				
John Archer's Nose (Rudolph Fisher)	•	•	•			•				•	•	•		•	•	
Lynching for Profit (George S. Schuyler)				•		•	•	•						•		
Mademoiselle 'Tasie (Eloise Bibb Thompson)	•		•	•		•		•	•					•		
Mary Elizabeth (Jessie Redmon Fauset)	•	•	•					•				•				
Masks (Eloise Bibb Thompson)	•	•	•	•	•	•	•			•	•	•			•	•
A Matter of Record (Ted Poston)	•						•	•					•	•		
Mob Madness (Marion Vera Cuthbert)	•	•	•	•		•	•							•	•	
A Modern Fable (Chester Himes)	•					•	•	•						•		

	marriage, family	parenthood, pregnancy	male-female relations	intra-/interracial relations	interracial male-female relations	prejudice, racism, racial violence	law, crime, imprisonment, war	business, economics, income	(un)employment, profession	religion, superstition, supernatural	science, technology, arts	education, literacy, storytelling	health (physical and/or mental), drugs	death, murder	immigration, migration	foreign culture/location
Muttsy (Zora Neale Hurston)	•		•					•	•						•	
The Needle's Point (J. Saunders Redding)			•			•							•			
Pope Pius the Only (Richard Bruce Nugent)				•		•							•			•
Prologue to a Life (Dorothy West)	•	•	•					•	•	•		•	•	•		
The Return of a Modern Prodigal (Octavia B. Wynbush)	•	•					•	•	•						•	
Sanctuary (Nella Larsen)	•	•					•								•	
Silt (Richard Wright)	•	•	•	•				•	•							
Slackened Caprice (Ottie B. Graham)	•	•		•		•	•					•		•	•	
Smoke, Lilies and Jade (Richard Bruce Nugent)	•		•								•		•	•		
Spanish Blood (Langston Hughes)	•	•	•	•	•			•	•	•		•			•	•
A Summer Tragedy (Arna Bontemps)	•	•	•					•	•			•	•	•		
Vignettes of the Dusk (Eric Walrond)			•	•		•									•	•
Wedding Day (Gwendolyn B. Bennett)	•		•	•	•	•	•			•		•			•	•
The Whipping (Marita Bonner)	•	•	•	•		•	•	•	•				•	•	•	
Why Adam Ate the Apple (Mercedes Gilbert)	•		•							•	•					
Why, You Reckon (Langston Hughes)				•		•	•	•	•							

ABOUT THE AUTHORS

GWENDOLYN B. BENNETT (1902–81) *poetry, short stories, nonfiction, journalism.* Bennett was born in Texas and lived at various times in Nevada, Washington, D.C., New York, Florida, and Pennsylvania. She attended Columbia University and Pratt Institute, earning a degree from the latter. She also studied art at the Barnes Foundation and separately for a year in Paris. Her background in literature and the visual arts gained her faculty positions at Howard University and Tennessee State College. Bennett also served in administrative positions at the Harlem Community Art Center, Jefferson School for Democracy, and George Washington Carver School. Her writing and artwork appeared in various periodicals, and her poetry and fiction were reprinted in such important collections from the period as Cullen's *Caroling Dusk,* C. S. Johnson's *Ebony and Topaz,* and J. W. Johnson's *The Book of American Negro Poetry.* Notably, her poem "To Usward" was selected as the commemorative verse for the now famous 1924 Civic Club dinner. She served as a founding editorial member of the short-lived radical black arts magazine *Fire!!* and also as an editorial assistant and columnist for *Opportunity.* Her "Ebony Flute" literary gossip column in *Opportunity* is now regarded as a significant record of African American cultural history in the late 1920s.

MARITA BONNER (1899–1971) *short stories, drama, nonfiction.* Bonner was born and raised in Massachusetts and graduated from Radcliffe College. She worked as a teacher in Massachusetts while still in college then afterwards in Virginia, Washington, D.C., and, finally, Illinois, where she settled for the remainder of her life. While living in Washington, D.C., she was a regular attendee at Georgia Douglas Johnson's "S" Street literary salon. She produced numerous essays, short stories, and plays, most of which appeared in *Crisis* and *Opportunity.* Curiously, though, her writing was conspicuously absent from anthologies of the 1920s and 1930s save for her appearance (pseud. Joseph Maree Andrew) in C. S. Johnson's *Ebony and Topaz.* Bonner won prizes in literary competitions in each of the three genres. Though she continued to write, she ceased publishing in 1941. Most of her writings are collected in *Frye Street & Environs* (1987), including a few previously unpublished stories.

ARNA BONTEMPS (1902–73) *poetry, novels, short stories, drama, nonfiction, children's literature.* Bontemps was born in Louisiana and raised primarily in California. He graduated from Pacific Union College and, after relocating to New York, embarked on a career as a teacher and educational administrator while continuing his studies at Columbia University and City College of New York. He later worked in various academic positions at Oakwood Junior College (Alabama) and Shiloh Academy (Illinois) and also worked as a technical assistant for the Federal Writers' Project. Bontemps soon thereafter completed a master's degree in library science at the University of Chicago in preparation for a twenty-year career at Fisk University in Tennessee. He was also employed briefly by the University of Illinois and Yale University after his retirement from Fisk. During the 1920s and 1930s, Bontemps gained notoriety chiefly as a poet and novelist. His poems, two of which won literary competitions, appeared in such periodicals as *Opportunity, Crisis,* and *Messenger* as well as in Cullen's *Caroling Dusk* and C. S. Johnson's *Ebony and Topaz.* He authored three novels, each of which was published in the 1930s: *God Sends Sunday* (1931), *Black Thunder* (1936), and *Drums at Dusk* (1939). Bontemps published a few short stories, too, in the 1930s, including his prize-winning "A Summer Tragedy." Book-length collections of his poems (*Personals*) and stories (*The Old South*) appeared in print in 1963 and 1973, respectively. A well-received collaboration with Langston Hughes on *Popo and Fifina* (1932) launched him on a long career as a children's literature author. After the Harlem Renaissance, Bontemps took up nonfiction and editing. His articles appeared in *American Scholar, Negro Digest, Saturday Review, Phylon,* and other periodicals. Of the several books he edited or coedited, some of the more important include *Golden Slippers: An Anthology of Negro Poetry for Young Readers* (1941), *The Poetry of the Negro, 1746–1949* (1949, rev. 1970), *The Book of Negro Folklore* (1951), and *The Harlem Renaissance Remembered* (1972).

ANITA SCOTT COLEMAN (1890–1960) *poetry, short stories, screenplays, nonfiction.* Born in Mexico, Coleman lived in New Mexico and southern California. After earning a degree from New Mexico Teachers College, she worked briefly as a teacher and then, once married, operated a children's boarding home while raising her own four children. Coleman's writing, largely short stories and poetry, initially appeared in *Crisis, Opportunity, Messenger, Half-Century Magazine,* and *Competitor.* Her essays twice earned her awards in literary competitions, and her short story "Three Dogs and a Rabbit" placed third in a 1925 *Crisis*-sponsored contest. By the mid-1930s, Coleman gave up short fiction and devoted herself to poetry, the result of which was three published collections: *Small Wisdom* (1937, pseud. Elizabeth Stapleton Stokes), *Reason for Singing* (1948), and *The Singing Bells* (1961).

MARION VERA CUTHBERT (1896–?) *poetry, short stories, nonfiction.* Cuthbert was born in Minnesota and earned degrees from Boston University and Columbia University. Aside from her career as a writer, she served as dean of Talladega College (1927–30) and was employed as an instructor at Brooklyn College (1945–60). Most of her writings appeared in the 1920s and 1930s, including *April Grasses* (1936), the first of two poetry collections. Her shorter works appeared in *Crisis, Opportunity, Journal of Negro Education, Social Action,* and *World Tomorrow.* Cuthbert published books and essays on sociopolitical topics, placing special emphasis on the unique plight of black women in the United States. *Songs of Creation,* her second book of poetry, was published in 1949. "Mob Madness," reprinted in this anthology, is her only short story.

W. E. B. DU BOIS (1868–1963) *poetry, novels, short stories, drama, nonfiction, children's literature, autobiography, journalism.* Du Bois was born and raised in Massachusetts. He earned degrees from Fisk University and Harvard University, including a Ph.D. from the latter, and studied at the University of Berlin for two years. After completing his education, he embarked on a prestigious and sometimes controversial career as an educator, diplomat, politician, sociologist, scholar, author, editor, and activist. Du Bois was a founding member of the Niagara Movement, a black protest organization intended to counter Booker T. Washington's accommodationist philosophy. In its wake came the formation of the NAACP, an organization through which Du Bois gained international prominence and exerted enormous influence, particularly so as the editor for over two decades of the NAACP's flagship publication, *Crisis,* an indispensable centerpiece of the Harlem Renaissance. His employment also included teaching positions at Wilberforce College and Atlanta University. He founded the journal *Phylon* and previously edited two short-lived magazines, *Moon* and *Horizon.* Du Bois expatriated to Ghana late in life and remained there until his death. Honors include the Spingarn Medal and the Lenin International Peace Prize. While a large portion of Du Bois's writing is scholarly, he also produced a fair amount of creative literature. Such works include two early novels, *The Quest of the Silver Fleece* (1911) and *Dark Princess* (1928), plus three later novels comprising his *Black Flame* trilogy (*The Ordeal of Mansart,* 1957; *Mansart Builds a School,* 1959; *Worlds of Color,* 1961). He produced two autobiographies, *Dusk of Dawn* (1940) and *The Autobiography of W. E. B. Du Bois* (1968). Furthermore, among his most important books are two collections: *The Souls of Black Folks* (1903) and *Darkwater* (1920). The latter is a selection of essays, autobiography, poetry, and short stories while the former, primarily essays, is arguably the single most important twentieth-century work by an African American. A sampling of Du Bois's shorter writings can be found in *Creative Writings by W.E.B. Du Bois* (1985). More generic samplings are available in *W. E. B. Du Bois: The Crisis Writings* (1973), *W. E. B. Du Bois: A Reader* (1995), and *The Oxford W. E. B.*

Du Bois Reader (1996). Despite his own limitations as a creative writer, Du Bois's role in promoting African American literature and, more generally, his larger impact on African American culture and status as one of the preeminent black figures of the twentieth century testify to his inestimable importance in the growth and development of African American literature.

ALICE DUNBAR-NELSON (1875–1935) *poetry, short stories, drama, nonfiction, journalism.* Dunbar-Nelson was born and raised in Louisiana and lived at various times in Massachusetts, New York, Washington, D.C., Delaware, and Pennsylvania. She graduated from Straight College and later studied at the University of Pennsylvania, Cornell University, and the School of Industrial Arts, Philadelphia. She was employed much of her life as a public school teacher and also helped to found the White Rose Mission and the Delaware Industrial School for Colored Girls. Other work included being a columnist for the *Washington Eagle* and *Pittsburgh Courier* and an associate editor for the *Wilmington Advocate* and *A.M.E. Church Review.* She also lectured and was a political activist. Dunbar-Nelson's writing career began in earnest with the release of *Violets and Other Tales* (1895), a collection of short stories, poetry, and essays. Other books include *The Goodness of St. Roque and Other Stories* (1899) as well as two edited collections, *Masterpieces of Negro Eloquence* (1914) and *The Dunbar Speaker and Entertainer* (1920). In 1927 she was awarded an honorable mention in *Opportunity*'s literary contest for her poem "April Is on the Way." Her poems, essays, reviews, plays, and stories appeared in numerous periodicals, including *Smart Set, Crisis, Opportunity, Modern Language Notes, Saturday Evening Mail, Southern Workman, Harlem, Leslie's Weekly,* and *Messenger.* Likewise, her work was frequently anthologized, appearing in such collections as C. S. Johnson's *Ebony and Topaz,* Eleazer's *Singers in the Dawn,* Kerlin's *Negro Poets and Their Poems,* White and Jackson's *Anthology of Verse by American Negroes,* Cullen's *Caroling Dusk,* and Cromwell, Turner, and Dykes's *Readings from Negro Authors.* Four posthumous works by Dunbar-Nelson have been published: *An Alice Dunbar-Nelson Reader* (1978), *Give Us Each Day: The Diary of Alice Dunbar-Nelson* (1984), *The Works of Alice Dunbar-Nelson* (1988), and *Laughing to Stop Myself Crying* (2000).

JESSIE REDMON FAUSET (1882–1961) *poetry, novels, short stories, nonfiction, children's literature.* Fauset was born in New Jersey. She earned degrees from Cornell University and the University of Pennsylvania and studied for half a year at the Sorbonne in France. She taught briefly at Fisk University and Hampton Institute; however, her main employment as a teacher was in public schools in Baltimore, Washington, D.C., and New York. In her later years she lived again in New Jersey and Pennsylvania. Fauset's role in the Harlem Renaissance is twofold, being both a writer and literary editor. As a writer she is probably most famous as the author of four novels: *There Is Confusion* (1924), *Plum*

Bun (1929), *The Chinaberry Tree* (1931), and *Comedy: American Style* (1933). But she also produced poetry, short fiction, essays, numerous book reviews, juvenile literature, and translations. Although most of her work appeared in the two magazines she worked for (*Crisis* and *Brownies' Book*), her writing also emerged in *Carolina Magazine, Palms, Black Opals, Metropolitan, Opportunity, World Tomorrow,* and *Independent* and was included in Locke's *New Negro,* J. W. Johnson's *Book of American Negro Poetry,* Braithwaite's *Anthology of Magazine Verse,* Porter's *Double Blossoms,* Kerlin's *Negro Poets and Their Poems,* Wormley and Carter's *Anthology of Negro Poetry by Negroes and Others,* C. S. Johnson's *Ebony and Topaz,* Bontemps's *Golden Slippers,* Cullen's *Caroling Dusk,* White and Jackson's *Anthology of Verse by American Negroes,* and Cromwell, Turner, and Dykes's *Readings from Negro Authors.* Fauset's 1919–26 tenure as the literary editor of *Crisis* placed her alongside Charles S. Johnson and Alain Locke as a "literary midwife" for the Harlem Renaissance. Accordingly, her importance to the movement and its many younger, aspiring artists cannot be overstated. Her editorial involvement with (and contributions to) the short-lived children's magazine *Brownies' Book* (1920–21) is likewise significant in that the publication marks the advent in the twentieth century of serious and authentic African American children's literature.

RUDOLPH FISHER (1897–1934) *novels, short stories, nonfiction, children's literature.* Fisher was born in Washington, D.C., and raised in Rhode Island. He earned degrees from Brown University and Howard University, becoming a practicing physician specializing in roentgenology. While in medical school he published his first short story ("The City of Refuge") in *Atlantic Monthly,* with other stories later appearing in *Crisis, Opportunity, Story, Metropolitan, McClure's, American Junior Red Cross News,* and *Survey Graphic.* His work was reprinted in Locke's *New Negro,* Calverton's *Anthology of American Negro Literature,* O'Brien's *Best Short Stories of 1925,* Dykes's *Readings from Negro Authors,* and O'Brien's *Best Short Stories: 1934.* He won first prize for "High Yaller" in the 1925 *Crisis* literary competition and was himself a judge for *Opportunity's* 1931–32 competition. Fisher authored two novels, *The Walls of Jericho* (1928) and *The Conjure-Man Dies* (1932), as well as "The Caucasian Storms Harlem," a seminal essay examining mainstream America's growing fascination with black culture. Fisher, who later relocated to Harlem, was unique among his contemporaries in that nearly all of his creative writing featured Harlem as both locale and subject matter. He also distinguished himself as one of the first African American detective fiction authors. Fisher's untimely demise at age 37 cut short what appeared to be promising and productive careers in medicine and literature. His short fiction has been posthumously collected in *The City of Refuge* (1987), *The Short Fiction of Rudolph Fisher* (1987), and *Joy and Pain* (1996).

MERCEDES GILBERT (1889–1952) *poetry, novels, short stories, drama, journalism.* Gilbert was born in Florida and graduated from Edward Waters College and Brewster Hospital Nurses' Training School, afterwards moving to New York. After brief careers in teaching and nursing, she found a lasting success in the arts first as a songwriter then, most notably, as a stage and film actress. She starred alongside Paul Robeson in Oscar Micheaux's silent film *Body and Soul* (1924) and performed on and off Broadway in several productions, including *The Green Pastures* and Langston Hughes's *Mulatto*. As a published author Gilbert found considerably less success. Both her novel, *Aunt Sara's Wooden God* (1938), and her self-edited compilation, *Selected Gems of Poetry, Comedy and Drama* (1931), were all but ignored in her own time and have until only recently languished in obscurity. Moreover, although she contributed poetry to *Abbott's Monthly* and *Negro Needs Education* in the 1930s, her work did not normally appear in periodicals. Of the plays she authored, only one (*Environment*, 1931) is extant.

EUGENE GORDON (1890–?) *poetry, short stories, nonfiction, journalism.* Gordon was born in Florida and lived in Massachusetts. He attended Howard University and Boston University. Aside from a brief stint in the military, he spent most of his career working as a journalist. His primary affiliation is with the *Boston Post,* where he worked for over fifteen years as a reporter, editor, and editorialist. Gordon's communist leanings led him to work in Russia for three years for the *Moscow Daily News* and then briefly, back in the United States, for the *Daily Worker.* As a writer his chief output consisted of short stories and essays appearing in such periodicals as *Fourth Estate, American Mercury, Opportunity, Scribner's, Nation, New Masses, Labor Defender,* and the American Academy of Political and Social Science's *Annals.* Notably, from 1925 to 1927 his short fiction and essays earned him prizes in *Opportunity*'s literary competition. ("Game," reprinted here, tied for first place in 1927.) Gordon was instrumental, too, in providing an outlet for African American writers based in New England through his editing of *Saturday Evening Quill* (1928–30), a literary magazine whose contributors included Florida Ruffin Ridley, Dorothy West, and Gordon himself, who contributed twelve stories, poems, and essays.

OTTIE B. GRAHAM (1900–?) *poetry, short stories, drama.* Graham was born in Virginia and later resided in Pennsylvania. She studied at Howard University and Columbia University. From all indications, her literary output was limited to the years 1923–24, during which she appeared in *Crisis, Opportunity,* and *Messenger.*

ANGELINA WELD GRIMKÉ (1880–1958) *poetry, short stories, drama, nonfiction.* Grimké was a Massachusetts native who took courses at Harvard University. She worked as a teacher in Washington, D.C., and later resided in New

York. Her *Rachel* (1920) bears the honor of being the first play in the twentieth century by an African American woman to be produced and enacted by African Americans. She published only a few short stories during her lifetime, those appearing in *Colored American Magazine* and *Birth Control Review*. Grimké was more prolific as a poet, though, publishing in such periodicals as *Opportunity, Pilot, Survey Graphic, Boston Evening Transcript, Crisis, Carolina Magazine,* and *Messenger*. Her verse was well represented in anthologies, too, including Wormley and Carter's *Anthology of Negro Poetry by Negroes and Others,* Byars's *Black and White,* Kerlin's *Negro Poets and Their Poems,* Locke's *New Negro,* Cullen's *Caroling Dusk,* C. S. Johnson's *Ebony and Topaz,* and Cromwell, Turner, and Dykes's *Readings from Negro Authors*. Much of her work, including previously unpublished items, can be found in the posthumous *Selected Works of Angelina Weld Grimké* (1991).

CHESTER HIMES (1909–84) *novels, short stories, screenplays, nonfiction, autobiography, journalism.* Born in Missouri, Himes later lived in Ohio, Mississippi, Georgia, and Arkansas. In 1928 he was sentenced to prison for armed robbery and served seven years in the Ohio State Penitentiary. Following prison he held mostly unskilled positions in Ohio, California, and New York, including a brief stint with the Ohio branch of the Federal Writers' Project. In 1944 he received a Julius Rosenwald fellowship to aid him in completing his first novel. In the 1950s Himes expatriated to Europe, where he lived out the remainder of his life in France and Spain. Though best known as a novelist, he was also a prolific short story writer whose first publications appeared while he was still incarcerated. From 1928 to the late 1970s he published over fifty short stories, some of which appeared in *Abbott's Monthly, Esquire, Coronet, Crisis, Negro Story,* and *Opportunity*. His first novel, *If He Hollers Let Him Go,* appeared in 1945 and would be followed by sixteen more, many of which were first published in France. His *For Love of Imabelle* (1957), *Cotton Comes to Harlem* (1965), and *The Heat's On* (1966) were each adapted as films, and the former received the Grand Prix du Roman Policier award in 1957. As a novelist Himes is perhaps best remembered for his detective fiction authored in the 1950s and 1960s, most of which features the detective duo of Grave Digger Jones and Coffin Ed Johnson. In addition to the three aforementioned titles, his other detective novels from this period include *The Real Cool Killers* (1959), *The Crazy Kill* (1959), *The Big Gold Dream* (1960), *All Shot Up* (1960), *Run Man Run* (1966), and *Blind Man with a Pistol* (1969). He also published two autobiographies, *The Quality of Hurt* (1972) and *My Life of Absurdity* (1976). His *Black on Black* (1973) includes a selection of his shorter works while the posthumous *Collected Stories of Chester Himes* (1990) brings together Himes's short fiction.

Langston Hughes (1902–67) *poetry, novels, short stories, drama, screenplays, nonfiction, children's literature, autobiography, journalism.* Hughes was born in Missouri and reared in Ohio, Illinois, and Kansas. He attended Columbia University and graduated from Lincoln University. Aside from living in New York, he traveled extensively, living at times in Mexico, France, Spain, and the Soviet Union. Early in life Hughes labored as a cook, launderer, janitor, cabin boy, and busboy; however, his popularity, productivity, and range of talent as a writer enabled him to become one of the first African Americans to establish a self-supporting career as a writer. His works won prizes in contests sponsored by *Opportunity, Crisis,* and *Palms* magazines and earned him a Harmon Gold Medal for Literature, Spingarn Medal, Anisfield-Wolf Award, Guggenheim and Rosenwald fellowships, and honorary degrees from Lincoln University, Howard University, and Western Reserve University. Though active in several genres, Hughes is most commonly remembered as a poet. His several collections include *The Weary Blues* (1926), *Fine Clothes to the Jew* (1927), *Dear Lovely Death* (1931), *The Dream Keeper and Other Poems* (1932), *A New Song* (1938), *Shakespeare in Harlem* (1942), *Fields of Wonder* (1947), *Montage of a Dream Deferred* (1951), *Ask Your Mama* (1961), and *The Panther and the Lash* (1967). His poems are gathered in *The Collected Poems of Langston Hughes* (1994). He was also a prolific writer of fiction, issuing two novels (*Not without Laughter,* 1930; *Tambourines to Glory,* 1958), three general short story collections (*The Ways of White Folks,* 1934; *Laughing to Keep from Crying,* 1952; *Something in Common and Other Stories,* 1963), and several collections of Jesse B. Semple (a.k.a. Simple) stories (including *Simple Speaks His Mind,* 1950; *Simple Takes a Wife,* 1953; *Simple Stakes a Claim,* 1957; *Simple's Uncle Sam,* 1965). Hughes was an active dramatist as well, and many of his plays are included in two posthumous collections: *The Political Plays of Langston Hughes* (2000) and *The Plays to 1942* (2002). His stage comedy *Mule Bone,* an ill-fated collaboration with Zora Neale Hurston, was first published in 1991. He authored two critically acclaimed autobiographies, *The Big Sea* (1940) and *I Wonder as I Wander* (1956). Additionally, a sampling of his nonfiction is available in *Langston Hughes and the* Chicago Defender: *Essays on Race, Politics, and Culture, 1942–62* (1995), Fight for Freedom *and Other Writings on Civil Rights* (2001), and *Essays on Art, Race, Politics, and World Affairs* (2002). He collaborated with Arna Bontemps on two anthologies (*The Poetry of the Negro, 1746–1949,* 1949, rev. 1970; *The Book of Negro Folklore,* 1958) plus the groundbreaking children's story *Popo and Fifina* (1932). Both during the Harlem Renaissance and afterwards, Hughes was widely published in periodicals and a mainstay of black literature anthologies, ultimately attaining an unprecedented level of recognition and celebrity in mainstream America and the international community. His legacy looms large in African American literature and twentieth-century American letters.

Zora Neale Hurston (1891–1960) *poetry, novels, short stories, drama, nonfiction, autobiography, journalism.* Hurston was born in Alabama and raised in Florida. She earned degrees from Howard University and Barnard College and continued her studies at Columbia University. She lived at times in New York, California, and Florida, although much of her adult life was spent traveling in the United States and the Caribbean while collecting folklore, conducting anthropological research, and touring with stage productions. Aside from being an anthropologist, Hurston worked at various times as a librarian, substitute teacher, college instructor, lecturer, waitress, maid, manicurist, reporter for the *Pittsburgh Courier* and *Fort Pierce Chronicle,* dramatic coach for the Federal Theatre Project, supervisor of the Florida unit of the Federal Writers' Project, story consultant for Paramount Pictures, and personal secretary to novelist Fannie Hurst. During her career as an author she received Carter G. Woodson Foundation and Guggenheim fellowships, a Book-of-the-Month Club recommendation (*Jonah's Gourd Vine*), the Anisfield-Wolf Award (*Dust Tracks on a Road*), and an honorary doctor of letters degree from Morgan State College. She first gained notoriety as a writer in the mid-1920s for her prize-winning stories and plays. Her shorter works (stories, reviews, essays, and articles) appeared in a wide range of periodicals, including *Opportunity, World Tomorrow, American Mercury, Saturday Evening Post, Story, Journal of American Folklore,* and *Negro Digest,* as well as in Locke's *New Negro* and Cunard's *Negro.* During her lifetime she published four novels (*Jonah's Gourd Vine,* 1934; *Their Eyes Were Watching God,* 1937; *Moses, Man of the Mountain,* 1939; *Seraph on the Suwanee,* 1948), an autobiography (*Dust Tracks on a Road,* 1942), and two nonfiction works (*Mules and Men,* 1935; *Tell My Horse: Voodoo and Life in Haiti and Jamaica,* 1938). Hurston was also an active dramatist, publishing plays in *X-Ray, Fire!!,* and C. S. Johnson's *Ebony and Topaz.* A play she coauthored with Langston Hughes, *Mule-Bone,* was posthumously published in 1991. Her "rediscovery" in the 1970s by African American and feminist scholars catapulted Hurston to a prominence once only reserved for Langston Hughes among Harlem Renaissance writers. Nowadays she is generally acknowledged to be one of the most important African American authors of the twentieth century. Several posthumous collections of her writing have been issued, including the following: *I Love Myself When I Am Laughing . . . & Then Again When I Am Looking Mean & Impressive* (1979); *The Sanctified Church* (1981); *Spunk: The Selected Stories of Zora Neale Hurston* (1985); *The Complete Stories* (1995); *Folklore, Memoirs, and Other Writings* (1995); *Go Gator and Muddy the Water* (1999); *Every Tongue Got to Confess: Negro Folktales from the Gulf States* (2001); and *Zora Neale Hurston: A Life in Letters* (2001).

GEORGIA DOUGLAS JOHNSON (1877–1966) *poetry, short stories, drama, nonfiction, journalism.* Johnson was born in Georgia and studied at Atlanta University, Oberlin Conservatory of Music, Cleveland College of Music, and Howard University. Most of her adult life was lived in Washington, D.C., where she worked at various jobs to support herself and raise and educate her two sons in the wake of her husband's death in 1925. She was most prolific as a poet, publishing four collections: *The Heart of a Woman and Other Poems* (1918), *Bronze* (1922), *An Autumn Love Cycle* (1928), and *Share My World* (1962). Her poetry appeared in various periodicals, including *Messenger, Crisis, Voice of the Negro, Opportunity,* and *A.M.E. Church Review.* Her poems were reprinted in collections, too, such as Braithwaite's *Anthology of Magazine Verse,* Cunard's *Negro,* Cullen's *Caroling Dusk,* and Kerlin's *Negro Poets and Their Poems.* Her "Song of Many Loves" earned an honorable mention in 1926 in *Opportunity's* literary contest. Johnson established herself as a respected dramatist with such works as *Blue Blood* (1928) and the award-winning *Plumes* (1927) and had her plays included in Shay's *Fifty More Contemporary One-Act Plays,* Richardson and Miller's *Negro History in Thirteen Plays,* Locke and Gregory's *Plays of Negro Life,* and Calverton's *Anthology of American Negro Literature.* Other published writings include short stories published in *Challenge* (pseud. Paul Tremaine) and syndicated newspaper columns. A sampling of her writings can be found in *The Selected Works of Georgia Douglas Johnson* (1997). Aside from her writing, her most enduring contribution to Harlem Renaissance is her role as hostess of the literary salon she conducted in her home on "S" Street at which the aspiring generation of writers would meet, mingle, network, and encourage one another.

S. MILLER JOHNSON (CA. 1900–?) *poetry, short stories.* Johnson was born in Arkansas. He graduated from Hampton Institute and also attended City College in Detroit. His only known employment was as a post office employee. "The Golden Penknife," included in this anthology, is thought to be his only published short story. From 1927 to 1931 he contributed poetry to *Messenger* and *Abbott's Monthly.*

NELLA LARSEN (1891–1964) *novels, short stories, nonfiction.* Larsen was born in Illinois. After attending the University of Copenhagen she studied nursing at Lincoln Hospital in New York. She worked briefly in nursing at the Tuskegee Institute in Alabama and also for the New York City Department of Health before switching to librarianship and working at the 135th Street branch of the New York Public Library in Harlem for a short time. Larsen published a few stories, reviews, and articles in *Brownies' Book, Opportunity, Messenger, Young's Realistic Stories Magazine,* and *Forum;* however, it is for her two deftly crafted novels, *Quicksand* (1928) and *Passing* (1929), that she gained notoriety and acclaim. In 1929 she received the Harmon Foundation's bronze medal for achievement in literature, and in 1930 she became the first African American woman to receive a Guggenheim fellowship. A plagiarism scandal in 1930 over her short story "Sanctuary" combined with marital and financial difficulties and a loss of confidence led Larsen to give up writing, withdraw from public life, and return to nursing for the last two decades of her life. All of her fiction, short and long, can be found in *An Intimation of Things Distant* (1992) and *The Complete Fiction of Nella Larsen* (2001).

JOHN F. MATHEUS (1887–1983) *poetry, short stories, drama, nonfiction, journalism.* Matheus was born in West Virginia and grew up partly in Ohio. He earned degrees from Western Reserve University and Columbia University. For twelve years he taught languages at Florida A&M College, Tallahassee, and for over three decades he was a professor of foreign languages at West Virginia State College. His legacy as a writer lies primarily with his short fiction and drama. In four successive years he earned prizes in literary competitions for his short stories, plays, poems, and essays, and his works were included in various collections from the 1920s and 1930s, including Locke's *New Negro,* Calverton's *Anthology of American Negro Literature,* and Richardson's *Plays and Pageants from the Life of the Negro.* His work appeared in such periodicals as *Crisis, Carolina Magazine,* and *Opportunity.* Following the 1930s Matheus effectively ceased publishing creative writing. His drama remains uncollected, but his short fiction was gathered in the privately printed *A Collection of Short Stories* (1974).

CLAUDE MCKAY (1890–1948) *poetry, novels, short stories, nonfiction, autobiography, journalism.* McKay was born and raised in Jamaica. He relocated to the United States and studied at the Tuskegee Institute and Kansas City College, later living in New York and Illinois. He also spent several years living in Russia, England, France, Spain, Germany, and Morocco. Over the years he worked as a constable, longshoreman, film studio worker, porter, bartender, waiter, artist's model, shipyard worker, and teacher as well as a writer for *Workers' Dreadnought* and an associate editor for *Liberator.* McKay, like Jean Toomer, made a name for himself early in the Harlem Renaissance. He published two collections of primarily dialect poetry in 1912 (*Constab Ballads* and *Songs of Jamaica*), but his real breakthrough came with the release of *Spring in New Hampshire* (1920) and *Harlem Shadows* (1922). The latter includes his "If We Must Die," one of the most famous and most frequently anthologized black-authored poems from the first half of the twentieth century. McKay's verse was reprinted in numerous anthologies, and his verse and prose appeared in periodicals, including *Negro World, Challenge, Pearson's Magazine, Seven Arts, Crusader, Crisis, Jewish Frontier, Interracial Review, Opportunity, Catholic Worker, Messenger,* and *Ebony.* His fame as a poet would later give way to even greater success as the author of the somewhat controversial novel *Home to Harlem* (1928), the first commercial best-seller by a black author in the United States. Two more novels followed, *Banjo* (1929) and *Banana Bottom* (1933), plus *Gingertown* (1932), a collection of short stories. McKay then turned to nonfiction, authoring an autobiography (*A Long Way from Home*, 1937) and a work on Harlem (*Harlem: A Negro Metropolis*, 1940). Furthermore, though not appearing in English until the 1970s, *Trial by Lynching*, a collection of short stories, and the nonfiction work *The Negroes in America* were both originally translated into Russian and published in the Soviet Union in the 1920s. McKay's posthumous works include *Selected Poems* (1953), *Selected Poems of Claude McKay* (1971), *The Dialect Poetry of Claude McKay* (1972), *The Passion of Claude McKay: Selected Poetry and Prose, 1912–1948* (1973), *My Green Hills of Jamaica and Five Jamaican Short Stories* (1979), and *Harlem Glory: A Fragment of Aframerican Life* (1990), an unfinished novel. Honors include awards from the Jamaican Institute of Arts and Sciences, Harmon Foundation, and James Weldon Johnson Literary Guild. He was also awarded the Order of Jamaica and declared that country's national poet in 1977.

MAY MILLER (1899–1995) *poetry, short stories, drama*. Miller was born and raised in Washington, D.C., a daughter of distinguished Howard University professor and dean Kelly Miller. Her high school instructors included fellow writers Mary P. Burrill and Angelina Weld Grimké. Miller graduated from Howard University, taught at public schools and colleges, and served as poet-in-residence at several institutions. During the Harlem Renaissance she was a frequenter of Georgia Douglas Johnson's "S" Street literary salon in Washington, D.C., and she became one of the most prolific African American dramatists, publishing plays in *Carolina Magazine*, Richardson's *Plays and Pageants from the Life of the Negro* (1930), and *Negro History in Thirteen Plays* (1935), which she coedited with Richardson. She placed third and earned an honorable mention in literary competitions for two of her plays. Miller penned a few short stories as well and then, beginning in the mid-1940s, turned exclusively to poetry. Between 1959 and 1983, she published seven books of poetry and one book of children's poems. Her *Collected Poems* was issued in 1989.

MARIAN MINUS (1913–73) *short stories, nonfiction, journalism*. Minus graduated from Fisk University and also attended the University of Chicago. She resided in New York and is known to have worked for the Consumers Union. Her short stories, the first of which appeared in 1939, were published in *Opportunity*, *Crisis*, and *Woman's Day*. In 1937 she and Dorothy West coedited *New Challenge*, a literary magazine that ceased publication after its debut issue.

RICHARD BRUCE NUGENT (1906–87) *poetry, short stories, drama, nonfiction.* Nugent was born and raised in Washington, D.C. As a teenager he relocated to New York, where he ultimately fell in with his fellow artists, writers, and intellectuals. He was a cast member of Broadway's *Porgy* and *Run, Little Chillun,* touring with both productions, and he danced with the Negro Ballet Company. He was also employed by the Federal Writers' Project and worked as a freelance artist for the last half of his life. Nugent sporadically published poetry, short stories, drama, nonfiction, and artwork. During the 1920s and 1930s, his writing (oftentimes pseudonymous) and artwork appeared in *Messenger, Opportunity, Trend, Palms, American Monthly, Challenge,* and *Dance Magazine* as well as in Cullen's *Caroling Dusk,* Locke's *New Negro,* Locke and Gregory's *Plays of Negro Life,* and C. S. Johnson's *Ebony and Topaz.* He also contributed to and served in editorial capacities on the short-lived African American arts magazines *Fire!!* and *Harlem.* Nugent's "Smoke, Lilies and Jade" is acclaimed as the first explicitly homosexual African American short story. A ballet based on his story "Sahdji" was performed in 1931 at the Eastman School of Music. His literary legacy, too, lies in part as a onetime resident of Wallace Thurman's infamous bohemian "Niggeratti Manor," ultimately serving as the model for the character Paul Arbian in Thurman's satirical *Infants of the Spring* (1932). Much of Nugent's writing, including previously unpublished works, has been collected in *Gay Rebel of the Harlem Renaissance* (2002).

MAUDE IRWIN OWENS (1899–1992) *poetry, short stories, drama.* Owens was born in Connecticut and reared in Massachusetts and Pennsylvania. She resided most of her life in Pennsylvania, but she also spent time in New York. She was a painter and illustrator, studying at the Philadelphia Graphic Sketch Club, but she also worked at various times as an art therapist's assistant and a private instructor in music and painting. The original appearance of "Bathesda of Sinners Run" in *Crisis,* which earned Owens a Charles Waddell Chesnutt Honorarium, was accompanied by two illustrations drawn by the author herself. She also wrote plays, some of which were produced but never published, and contributed a poem to *Messenger.*

LEILA AMOS PENDLETON (1860–?) *poetry, short stories, nonfiction.* Pendleton resided in Washington, D.C. She worked as a public school teacher for four years and was highly active as a founder, officer, and/or member of various social organizations. She contributed articles to *Alexander's Magazine* and *Journal of Negro History* as well as short stories to *Crisis.* In 1912 she published *A Narrative of the Negro,* a book for children profiling the lives of famous African Americans.

TED POSTON (1906–74) *poetry, short stories, nonfiction, journalism.* Poston was born and reared in Kentucky and graduated from Tennessee Agricultural and Industrial College (now Tennessee State University). He relocated to New York and would later take classes at New York University. For nearly fifty years he worked as a journalist, beginning in earnest as a columnist for the *Pittsburgh Courier* and shortly afterwards as a reporter and city editor for the *Amsterdam News.* In 1932 he traveled to Russia with an all-black cast (including Langston Hughes and Dorothy West) to film *Black and White,* an exposé on American racism that was never completed. Like Richard Wright, Zora Neale Hurston, and many others, he worked for the Federal Writers' Project for a short time during the Depression. Poston's addition to the *New York Post* in 1937 made him the first African American writer on staff and only the third African American reporter hired by a major New York City daily newspaper. During World War II he left the *Post* for five years to join Roosevelt's "Black Cabinet," ultimately heading the Negro News Desk of the Office of War Information in Washington, D.C. Aside from his work appearing in the three aforementioned newspapers, he contributed articles, reviews, and stories to *Negro Digest, Reporter, New Republic, Editor and Publisher, Crisis,* and *New Leader* and collaborated on articles appearing in *Life* and *Ebony.* Two posthumous collections of Poston's work have been issued: *The Dark Side of Hopkinsville* (1991), a collection of short fiction, and *A First Draft of History* (2000), a selection of poems, stories, and articles.

J. SAUNDERS REDDING (1906–88) *novels, short stories, nonfiction.* Redding was born and reared in Delaware. He attended Lincoln University and earned degrees from Brown University. Over the years he served as a college professor at several institutions, including Morehouse College, Louisville Municipal College, Southern University, Elizabeth City State Teachers College, Hampton Institute, and Cornell University. His stint as a visiting professor at Brown University made him the first African American faculty member at an Ivy League school. Redding's career as a writer began at Brown University where he wrote for campus publications. Despite early forays into short fiction, Redding's distinguished career as a writer was devoted almost exclusively to literary and cultural criticism. His articles and reviews appeared in periodicals such as *Atlantic Monthly, American Scholar, Afro, Nation, Negro Digest, Presence Africaine,* and *North American Review.* He wrote and edited several books, some of which include *To Make a Poet Black* (1939), *No Day of Triumph* (1942), *On Being a Negro in America* (1951), *The Lonesome Road* (1958), and *Cavalcade: Negro American Writing from 1760 to the Present* (1971, coedited with Arthur P. Davis). He also published one novel, *Stranger and Alone* (1950). Redding received Rockefeller, Guggenheim, and Ford Foundation fellowships as well as other awards and honors.

FLORIDA RUFFIN RIDLEY (1861–1943) *short stories, nonfiction, journalism.* Ridley was born and raised in Massachusetts and studied at Boston Teachers' College. She worked as a teacher but was mainly busied during her life with activism and her involvement with organizations like the National Federation of Afro-American Women, League of Women for Community Service, and the Society of Descendants, Early New England Negroes. From 1894 to 1910 she was the assistant editor of *Woman's Era* and later edited the *Social Service News,* organ of the Cooperative Social Agencies. She contributed to *Our Boston, Opportunity,* and *Saturday Evening Quill* and was a member of the Cambridge-based literary club that produced the *Quill.* Ridley won an honorable mention in *Opportunity*'s 1925–26 literary contest for her personal essay "Lucille Speaks."

GEORGE S. SCHUYLER (1895–1977) *poetry, novels, short stories, drama, nonfiction, autobiography, journalism.* Schuyler was born in Rhode Island and reared in New York. He enlisted in the army at age seventeen and served for six years, attaining the rank of first lieutenant. After a few years of uncertainty, Schuyler settled into journalism as a career, working in editorial capacities for *Messenger, National News, Plain Talk, American Opinion, Manchester Union Leader, African, Review of the News,* and the syndicated *Illustrated Features Section.* He was briefly employed as a foreign correspondent for the *New York Evening Post,* making him the first African American journalist to be employed in such a position by a major metropolitan newspaper, and also as a syndicated writer for Spadeau Columns. For seven years he was the business manager for *Crisis.* His main employer, however, was the *Pittsburgh Courier,* for whom Schuyler worked as an editor, writer, columnist, and special correspondent for four decades beginning in the mid-1920s. During the Harlem Renaissance he established himself as a satirist and iconoclast through his "Shafts and Darts" (*Messenger*) and "Views and Reviews" (*Courier*) columns as well as through his fiction, essays, and reviews. One of his most enduring (and controversial) contributions to African American literature is his essay "The Negro-Art Hokum," a piece which provoked Langston Hughes's now famous rebuttal, "The Negro Artist and the Racial Mountain." Like Hughes, Schuyler was prolific and widely published in periodicals, some of which include *New Masses, Opportunity, Crisis, Nation, Negro Digest, Common Ground, American Mercury, Modern Quarterly, World Tomorrow,* and *Phylon.* In 1931 he published two novels, *Black No More,* one of the first black science fiction novels, and *Slaves Today.* He also wrote seventy-five pulp fiction stories, including serialized and detective stories, for the *Courier* from 1933 to 1939 (only nine of which were under his own name). Following the Harlem Renaissance Schuyler devoted himself to journalism and nonfiction. His autobiography, *Black and Conservative,* appeared in 1966. Since Schuyler's death, three collections of his work have been issued:

Black Internationale (1991), *Ethiopian Stories* (1994), and *Rac(e)ing to the Right: Selected Essays of George S. Schuyler* (2001).

ELOISE BIBB THOMPSON (1878–1928) *poetry, short stories, drama, nonfiction, journalism.* Born in Louisiana, Thompson later lived in Washington, D.C., California, and New York. She graduated from Howard University and worked first as a teacher and then as head resident in a settlement house. As a writer and journalist she contributed to Los Angeles newspapers as well as *Out West, Tidings,* and *Opportunity.* Thompson is believed to have published only two short stories, both of which appeared in *Opportunity.* Her last story, "Masks," received honorable mention in the 1927 Van Vechten Award competition. She is known to have written three plays, two of which were produced during her lifetime though none of them was published. "Cooped Up" earned her an honorable mention in the drama category in *Opportunity*'s 1924 literary contest. Thompson also issued a single collection of poetry, *Poems* (1895).

WALLACE THURMAN (1902–34) *poetry, novels, short stories, drama, screenplays, nonfiction, journalism.* Thurman was born and raised in Utah and studied at the University of Utah and University of Southern California. While in California he produced a column for a local African American newspaper and also edited a short-lived literary magazine, *Outlet.* Once relocated to New York he worked as a reporter for *Looking Glass,* managing editor for *Messenger,* circulation manager for *World Tomorrow,* ghost writer for *True Story,* and editor at Macaulay. Thurman edited two literary magazines, both of which, though important achievements, failed to get beyond the first issue for financial reasons: *Fire!!* (1926) and *Harlem* (1928). He wrote two novels, *The Blacker the Berry* (1929) and *Infants of the Spring* (1932), and collaborated with white writer A. L. Furman on a third, *The Interne* (1932). He also cowrote two screenplays and two dramas, the first of which, *Harlem,* had a successful Broadway run and was based in part on Thurman's "Cordelia the Crude" short story. His poems, stories, reviews, and essays appeared in such periodicals as *Opportunity, Greenwich Village Quill, New Republic, Independent, Bookman,* and *Dance Magazine.* Notably, his essay "This American Negro Renaissance" earned him an honorable mention in 1926 in *Opportunity*'s literary contest. Sadly, Thurman's decadent lifestyle, unending financial problems, and dissatisfaction with his own artistic shortcomings exacerbated his physical and mental deterioration, leading to his early death at age thirty-two. Much of his work can be found in *The Collected Writings of Wallace Thurman* (2003).

JEAN TOOMER (1894–1967) *poetry, short stories, drama, nonfiction.* Toomer was born in Washington, D.C., and reared there and in New York. Though never earning a degree, he attended the University of Wisconsin, Massachusetts College of Agriculture, American College of Physical Training, University of Chicago, New York University, and City College of New York. He resided in New York, Washington, D.C., and Pennsylvania. Aside from his writing, Toomer worked as a car salesman, physical education instructor, college lecturer, shipyard worker, and grocery clerk. His legacy as a writer rests largely upon *Cane* (1923), a collection of poetry, short stories, prose poems, and experimental drama that is now widely regarded as one of the greatest achievements in twentieth-century African American literature. His writing appeared in numerous periodicals, including *Crisis, Survey Graphic, S4N, Double Dealer, Little Review, Dial, Pagany, Modern Review,* and *Prairie.* Likewise, his work was often reprinted in collections, some of which include O'Brien's *Best Short Stories,* Locke's *New Negro,* Untermeyer's *Modern American Poetry,* Cullen's *Caroling Dusk,* Locke and Gregory's *Plays of Negro Life,* Brownell's *Problems of Civilization,* and Kreymborg, Mumford, and Rosenfeld's *New American Caravan.* Shortly after the publication of *Cane,* Toomer declined to be further identified as African American and, instead, began producing increasingly philosophical and didactic works which reflected the teachings of European mystic-philosopher G. I. Gurdjieff and, on that account, proved largely unmarketable. After the 1930s Toomer continued writing but published infrequently. Four posthumous collections have been issued, bringing together much of his published and previously unpublished work: *The Wayward and the Seeking* (1980), *The Collected Poems of Jean Toomer* (1988), *A Jean Toomer Reader: Selected Unpublished Writings* (1993), and *Jean Toomer: Selected Essays and Literary Criticism* (1996).

ERIC WALROND (1898–1966) *short stories, nonfiction, journalism.* Walrond was born in British Guiana (now Guyana) and was raised there as well as in Barbados and Panama. He worked initially as a clerk and, later, as a reporter for a Panamanian newspaper. Once he migrated to New York, he held editorial positions on the *Negro World* and *Brooklyn and Long Island Informer* and served as *Opportunity*'s business manager for two years. Walrond studied at City University of New York, Columbia University, and the University of Wisconsin. In the early 1930s he expatriated to England and spent the remainder of his life there. Unlike many of his Harlem Renaissance peers, Walrond published extensively in mainstream (white) periodicals such as *New Republic, Current History, Vanity Fair, Independent, World Tomorrow,* and many others (including in Spanish and French). Though best remembered as a short story writer, he actually authored more nonfiction than fiction, ultimately publishing over one hundred essays and reviews, most of which appeared in print during the 1920s and 1930s. Twice his short stories earned him prizes in literary competitions, and by 1927 he was serving as a judge for *Opportunity*'s annual literature contest. He also was a recipient of the Harmon Award for Literature and a Guggenheim fellowship. Walrond published only one short story collection, *Tropic Death* (1926), yet he produced numerous other stories and sketches which appeared in such periodicals as *Carolina Magazine, Black Man, West Indian Review, Smart Set,* and *Argosy All Story Weekly.* His work appeared, too, in Locke's *New Negro,* Calverton's *Anthology of American Negro Literature,* and Kreymborg's *American Caravan.* "Winds Can Wake Up the Dead" (1998) is a posthumous selection of Walrond's articles and stories.

DOROTHY WEST (1907–98) *novels, short stories, nonfiction, journalism.* West was born and reared in Massachusetts and studied at Boston University and Columbia University. She lived briefly in New York, where she worked during the Depression as a member of Broadway's *Porgy* cast, as a welfare investigator, and as a writer for the Federal Writers' Project. In 1932 she traveled to Russia with an all-black cast (including Langston Hughes and Ted Poston) to film *Black and White,* an ill-fated Russian film project that was never completed. West began publishing short fiction in the *Boston Post* as a teenager and first garnered widespread attention at age nineteen for her story "The Typewriter," which tied for second with Zora Neale Hurston in *Opportunity*'s 1926 literary competition. The following year she earned a Buckner Award for demonstrating "conspicuous promise" with her story "An Unimportant Man." West published short fiction initially in periodicals such as *Messenger, Opportunity,* and *Saturday Evening Quill,* but her work was not anthologized during the Harlem Renaissance. From 1940 to 1961 she published more than twenty stories in the *New York Daily News.* She also founded and edited two literary magazines, *Challenge* (1934–37) and *New Challenge* (1937), both of which failed due to financial problems. She wrote two novels, *The Living Is Easy* (1948) and *The Wedding* (1995), and issued a collection of stories and essays, *The Richer, the Poorer* (1995). West spent the last fifty years of her life living in Massachusetts, where she was a writer and columnist for the *Vineyard Gazette* for nearly three decades, a selection of which can be found in the posthumous *Dorothy West Martha's Vineyard* (2001).

RICHARD WRIGHT (1908–60) *poetry, novels, short stories, drama, screenplays, nonfiction, children's literature, autobiography, journalism.* Wright was born in Mississippi and grew up there as well as in Tennessee and Arkansas. After leaving the South he lived in Illinois and New York and, in the mid-1940s, expatriated to France, where he remained until his death. He was employed as a postal clerk, publicity agent for the Federal Negro Theater, writer for the Federal Writers' Project, editor for *Daily Worker,* and associate editor for *New Challenge.* Wright first gained national acclaim as an author in 1938, but he had been publishing since the early 1930s. Such early works included propagandistic poetry appearing in left-wing periodicals and "Superstition" (1931), his first short story to appear in a nationally distributed magazine (*Abbott's Monthly*).

Before the end of the decade he completed his first novel, but it was rejected by publishers and remained unpublished until after his death (*Lawd Today*, 1963). His winning of *Story* magazine's contest for best book-length manuscript set the stage for the publication of his short story collection, *Uncle Tom's Children* (1938), while his militant 1937 essay "Blueprint for Negro Writing" in *New Challenge* signaled the onset of the new school of African American social protest writing. Wright rocketed to international fame with his 1940 novel *Native Son*, for which he received a Guggenheim fellowship and a Spingarn Medal. The novel sold over 200,000 copies in under three weeks and was a Book-of-the-Month Club selection, making it the first African American novel so chosen. It was later adapted for stage and screen, appearing on Broadway and as a motion picture starring the author. Wright's 1945 autobiography, *Black Boy*, was also a best-seller. Other books include novels (*The Outsider*, 1953; *Savage Holiday*, 1954; *The Long Dream*, 1958), autobiography (*American Hunger*, 1977), nonfiction (*Twelve Million Black Voices*, 1941; *Black Power*, 1954; *The Color Curtain*, 1956; *Pagan Spain*, 1957; *White Man, Listen!*, 1957), short fiction (*Eight Men*, 1961), juvenile fiction (*Rite of Passage*, 1994), and poetry (*Haiku*, 1998). He also contributed to numerous periodicals, including *Atlantic Monthly, New York Post, Free World, Saturday Review, Ebony, New Republic, New Masses, Negro Digest, Crisis, Twice a Year*, and *New York World Telegram*. Wright is universally regarded as one of the most important American writers of the twentieth century.

OCTAVIA B. WYNBUSH (1894 OR 1897–?) *poetry, short stories, children's literature.* Wynbush was born in Pennsylvania and earned degrees from Oberlin College and Columbia University. She lived in Louisiana, Arkansas, Indiana, and Missouri while working as a teacher at colleges and public schools. Wynbush published a few poems in *Half-Century Magazine* and *Opportunity*, but the bulk of her writing consists of short stories appearing in *Crisis* in the 1930s and 1940s. She also authored a children's book, *The Wheel That Made Wishes Come True* (1941).

AUTHOR INDEX

CREDITS

"His Last Day" and "A Modern Fable" from *The Collected Stories of Chester Himes* by Chester Himes. Copyright © 1990 by Lesley Himes. Appears by permission of the publisher, Thunder's Mouth Press.

"Spanish Blood" and "Why, You Reckon?" from *Short Stories* by Langston Hughes. Copyright © 1996 by Ramona Bass and Arnold Rampersad. Reprinted by permission of Hill and Wang, a division of Farrar, Straus and Giroux, LLC. Reprinted by permission of Harold Ober Associates Incorporated. Copyright as given by Farrar Straus/Hill & Wang.

"Muttsy" and "The Eatonville Anthology" as taken from *The Complete Stories* by Zora Neale Hurston. Introduction copyright © 1995 by Henry Louis Gates Jr. and Sieglinde Lemke. Compilation copyright © 1995 by Vivian Bowden, Lois J. Hurston Gaston, Clifford Hurston, Lucy Ann Hurston, Winifred Hurston Clark, Zora Mack Goins, Edgar Hurston Sr., and Barbara Hurston Lewis. Afterword and bibliography copyright © 1995 by Henry Louis Gates. Reprinted by permission of HarperCollins Publishers Inc.

"Crazy Mary" and "Highball" by Claude McKay courtesy of the Literary Representative for the Works of Claude McKay, Schomburg Center for Research in Black Culture, New York Public Library, Astor, Lenox and Tilden Foundations.

"Esther," from *Cane* by Jean Toomer. Copyright 1923 by Boni & Liveright, renewed 1951 by Jean Toomer. Used by permission of Liveright Publishing Corporation.

"The Man Who Saw the Flood," herein reprinted as "Silt," from *Eight Men* by Richard Wright. Copyright 1940 © 1961 by Richard Wright; renewed © 1989 by Ellen Wright. Introduction by Paul Gilmore. Reprinted by permission of HarperCollins Publishers Inc.

For all material from *Crisis*, the author and publisher wish to thank the Crisis Publishing Co., Inc., the publisher of the magazine of the National Association for the Advancement of Colored People, for the use of these works. They include Marita Bonner, "Hate Is Nothing" and "The Whipping"; Marion Vera

Cuthbert, "Mob Madness"; Ottie B. Graham, "Blue Aloes"; Marian Minus, "Girl, Colored"; Maude Irwin Owens, "Bathesda of Sinners Run"; Octavia B. Wynbush, "The Return of a Modern Prodigal."

All of the following material from *Opportunity* is reprinted by permission of the National Urban League: Arna Bontemps, "A Summer Tragedy"; Anita Scott Coleman, "Cross Crossings Cautiously"; Eugene Gordon, "Game"; Ottie B. Graham, "Slackened Caprice"; John F. Matheus, "Anthropoi"; Eloise Bibb Thompson, "Mademoiselle 'Tasie" and "Masks"; Eric Walrond, "Vignettes of the Dusk."

All material not appearing above is in the public domain.

Lynching statistics courtesy of Jessie Parkhurst Guzman's *Negro Year Book: A Review of Events Affecting Negro Life, 1941–1946* (Tuskegee Institute, 1947). Unemployment statistics courtesy of Lois and Alan Gordon's *American Chronicle: Year by Year through the Twentieth Century* (Yale University Press, 1999).

Craig Gable is an independent scholar and professional librarian. He is a Harlem Renaissance bibliographer and editor of the *Rudolph Fisher Newsletter* (www.fishernews.edu), an online newsletter and general research resource web site devoted to Rudolph Fisher and the Harlem Renaissance at large.

Darryl Dickson-Carr is Associate Professor of English at Florida State University, Tallahassee, and author of *African American Satire: The Sacredly Profane Novel* (University of Missouri Press, 2001) and *The Columbia Guide to African American Fiction, 1970–2000* (Columbia University Press, forthcoming).